U0740766

2019 中非纺织服装国际论坛论文集

Proceedings of 2019 Sino-Africa International Symposium on Textiles and Apparel

邱夷平　主编

Edited by Qiu Yiping

中国纺织出版社有限公司·北京

China Textile & Apparel Press · Beijing

图书在版编目(CIP)数据

2019 中非纺织服装国际论坛论文集 = Proceedings of 2019 Sino-Africa International Symposium on Textiles and Apparel:英文/邱夷平主编.--北京:中国纺织出版社有限公司,2019.11

ISBN 978-7-5180-6625-4

Ⅰ.① 2… Ⅱ.①邱… Ⅲ.①纺织工业—中国、非洲—国际学术会议—文集—英文 ②服装工业—中国、非洲—国际学术会议—文集—英文 Ⅵ.①F426.81-53 ②F440.68-53

中国版本图书馆 CIP 数据核字(2019)第 186599 号

策划编辑:符 芬 特约编辑:刘凡茜子 责任印制:何 建

中国纺织出版社有限公司出版发行
地址:北京市朝阳区百子湾东里 A407 号楼 邮政编码:100124
销售电话:010—67004422 传真:010—87155801
http://www.c-textilep.com
E-mail:faxing@ c-textilep.com
中国纺织出版社天猫旗舰店
官方微博 http://weibo.com/2119887771
北京虎彩文化传播有限公司印刷 各地新华书店经销
2019 年 11 月第 1 版第 1 次印刷
开本:889×1194 1/16 印张:29
字数:1000 千字 定价:368.00 元

凡购本书,如有缺页、倒页、脱页,由本社图书营销中心调换

Organizing Committee of 2019 SAISTA

Chairman：

QIU Yiping   PAUL Wambua

Committee Members：

GU Bohong   LI Jun   LI Min
QIN Xiaohong   ZHAO Mingwei

Academic Committee of 2019 SAISTA

Chairman：

YU Jianyong   Donghua University, China

Committee Members：

PAUL Wambua   Moi University, Kenya
CHEN Nanliang   Donghua University, China
GU Bohong   Donghua University, China

Preface

Since the first Sino-Africa International Symposium on Textiles and Apparel five years ago, the Belt and Road Initiative has attracted more and more attention around the world under the strong leadership of President Xi Jinping. Significant progress has been made in our collaboration with the countries along the ancient maritime and inland silk roads in terms of textile and apparel research, cultural and student exchanges as well as education collaboration. In this symposium, we intend to present more recent outcomes of relevant research in the field. A total of more than 100 research papers have been submitted and most of them have been accepted for the proceeding . The quality and diversity of the papers have also been steadily improved. These papers cover a wide range of topics such as textile engineering, nano-technology, textile materials, wearable technologies, apparel design and technology, textile management and marketing, textile history, culture exchange, and economics. The authors come from more than 18 countries including many African and Asian countries. SAISTA 2019 has attracted attentions from China, Africa, and Asia as well as around the world. The symposium is attended by educators and professionals from Ethiopia, Kenya, Sudan, Zimbabwe, Tanzania, Uganda, and South Africa, Pakistan, Bangladesh, Iran, Syria, Uzbekistan, Serbia as well as China. About 20 presentations will be given in the symposium. I believe that this symposium provides a platform to review the latest progress of the collaboration and exchange in the textiles and apparel education and research among China, Africa and many other countries in the Belt and Road regions.

This year, in collaboration with the Institute of African Studies at Zhejiang Normal University, SAISTA 2019 has greatly increased its depth and width in research in Sino-Africa cultural exchanges. I hope the diverse cultural treasures in both China and African countries will be better appreciated and respected through in-depth research from both sides.

Professor YU Jianyong
Academician of Chinese Academy of Engineering

Contents

Surface Modification of Weft-Knitted Spacer Fabrics for Hydrophobic Behavior Using Silica Aerogels Dip-Coating

SYED Rashedul Islam[1,2], YU Weidong[1,2]*, ABDUL Wahid[1,2], RAJNESH Kumar[3], ABEER Alassod[1,2], MUHAMMAD Usman Ghani[1,2], MD. Sohag Miah[1,2]

[1] *Department of Textile Engineering, College of Textiles, Donghua University, Shanghai, 201620, China*

[2] *Key Laboratory of Textile Science & Technology, Ministry of Education, College of Textiles, Donghua University, Shanghai, 201620, China*

[3] *State Key Laboratory for Modification of Chemical Fibers and Polymer Materials, College of Material Science & Engineering, Donghua University, Shanghai, 201620, China*

* *Corresponding author's email: wdyu@ dhu.edu.cn*

Abstract: In order to enhance the hydrophobicity of weft-knitted spacer fabrics with optimum performance silica aerogels (SAs) coating demands exceptional attention. The silica aerogels were prepared by sol-gel method and were applied on the spacer fabric samples to modify them. Scanning electron microscope (SEM) images of untreated and treated spacer fabrics were analyzed to demonstrate the influence of silica aerogels on the fabrics. The basic properties of uncoated and coated weft-knitted spacer fabrics such as water contact angle and bending properties were studied. Contact angles were studied by using an optical video contact angle instrument (OCA 40). Bending properties of spacer fabrics were also tested by using KES. Spacer fabrics are characteristically hydrophilic. However, It was found that coating of silica aerogels has a significant impact on hydrophobic behavior of weft-knitted spacer fabrics and showed higher water contact angle (CA) of $141° \pm 1°$ (sample 2) as well as better bending properties.

Keywords: Weft-knitted 3D spacer fabrics; Silica aerogels coating; Sol-gel method; Hydrophobic behavior; Contact angle; Bending properties.

1 Introduction

Recently, the attention for high-performance textiles has been expanded because of the growing utilization of new advancements and the requirement for the improvement in comfort, medical services and safety of living beings[1]. As the business sectors for easygoing wear, rainwear and sportswear were increasing as a pattern in recent years; the needs for superhydrophobic textiles additionally have been persistently expanded. Spacer fabric is a terrific alternative once strength, thermal insulator, comfort and cheap are main alarms[2]. Spacer fabrics are characteristically hydrophilic but to make them hydrophobic two key factors such as surface energy and surface roughness are to be considered. Surface roughness is very essential if higher superhydro-phobicity is to be attained[3]. Moreover, they are considered as eco-friendly textile materials since can be reused as well[4]. SAs are superhydrophobic nano-porous materials[5]. The addition of these types of additives increases the dilution of textile fabrics. Silica aerogels have a lower density, smaller pore size, larger internal surface area, and larger pore volume[6]. They retain higher thermal insulation properties, lower thermal conductivity, and superior stability due to the lessening in the conduction, convection, and radiation[7]. Hence, it has turned out to be prominent in setting up desired modifications in industrial textiles i. e. weft knitted spacer fabric used in winter clothing, aerospace suits, sea, and biological uses and so on[8]. The lack of comprehensive studies on hydrophobic properties of weft-knitted 3D spacer fabrics are a sound basis for this research. In the present study, the effect of silica aerogels on hydrophobic behavior of weft-knitted spacer fabrics, particularly contact angle and bending properties were investigated.

2 Experimental Works

2.1 Materials

Three types of weft-knitted spacer fabrics (92% polyester/8% spandex) were collected from Tianbin Textile Co. Ltd., Changshu, China. These weft knitted tuck spacer fabrics were prepared on a circular knitting machine of gauge 28. The thickness of the three samples was typical such as 2mm, 3mm, and 4mm respectively. The first and second samples were delivered with similar yarn count (75D) while the third sample with 100D. The yarn count of the middle layers of the three spacer fabrics was the same (40D). Tetraethyl Orthosilicate (TEOS), Ethyl alcohol (99%, EtOH) and HMDS (hexamethyldisilazane) were bought from National Drug Group Chemical Reagent Co. Ltd., Shanghai Union Chemical Industry Co. Ltd. and Shanghai Code Group Chemical Brake Co. Ltd. N-hexane (> 99%), Hydrochloric acid (37%, HCl), N, N-dimethyl-formamide (>98%, DMF), and Ammonia (25%, NH_4OH) were procured from Yangyuan Chemical Texnology Co. Ltd., Algae Group Chemical Reagent Co. Ltd., Shanghai Lingfeng Chemical Reagent Co. Ltd. and Shanghai Macklin Biochemical Co. Ltd. All chemicals and reagents were of logical assessment and employed without any purification.

2.2 Silica Sol Preparation

The silica sol-gel process was completed in two stages i. e. firstly acid-catalyzed TEOS hydrolysis and lastly base-catalyzed gelation (Fig. 1). The entire silica sol preparation process was explained clearly and deeply in our first research paper (JEFF)[9].

2.3 Spacer Fabric Samples Coated with Silica Gels

Weft knitted spacer fabric samples were cut into $35cm^2$ pieces and dipped into the silica sol for 15min. Subsequently, the samples were solidified into a tightly sealed container. After the formation of the gelled layer on fabric samples (20min), the wet-gelled samples were

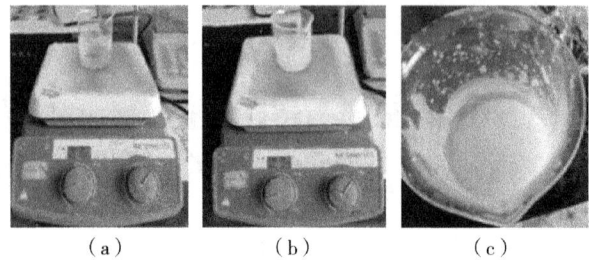

Fig.1　The preparation of the silica sol-gel process (a) Acid-catalyzed TEOS hydrolysis; (b) Base-catalyzed gelation structure; (c) Presented the prepared silica gels

additionally kept for 24 hours at 25℃ to secure the gel network structures (shown in Fig. 2). The wet-gelled samples were washed with ethanol for 8 hours. The washing was repeated 3 times with the exchanging into N-hexane. The wet-gelled films were washed with N-hexane for 8 hours to remove the ethanol-containing fluid. It was then dried in an oven at 40℃ and 60℃ methodically for 5 hours, followed by further drying at 100℃ for 5 hours.

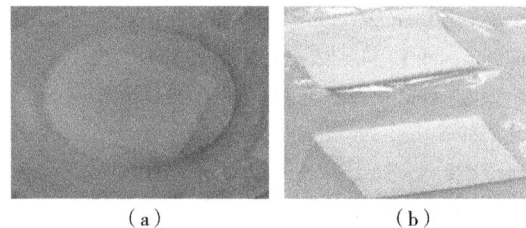

Fig. 2　Spacer fabrics treated with silica aerogels during (a) dip-coating and (b) forming gel network structure

2.4 SEM Analysis

The scanning electron microscopy (SEM) was performed with a Flex-SEM 1000, (SU1000, Hitachi Ltd. Japan). Before analysis, all weft-knitted spacer fabric samples were coated with a gold layer using a vacuum sputter coater. The surface morphology of fabric samples was observed by SEM.

2.5 Water Contact Angle Test

The water contact angle was estimated by an optical video contact angle instrument (Model OCA 40, Germany). The water contact angle was assessed 60s after a water droplet of 5μL was put on fabric samples. All the contact angles exhibited were the average of estimation at five separate areas for each sample.

2.6 Bending Test

The test was done using a self-fabricated test stage since spacer fabrics are too thick to even consider being tested by Fabric Assurance by Simple Testing (FAST) or KES. In any case, the test rule was equivalent to FAST. The samples were cut into 10cm × 10cm. The applied force to bend the samples in Newtons and output in mm. Bend tests for ductility provided a modest way to evaluate the quality of materials by their ability to resist other surface irregularities during one continuous bend. The typical test condition for this test was 20℃ and relative humidity was 65%. Bending lengths were attained in two individual directions of the spacer fabrics.

3　Results and Discussion

3.1　Morphological Properties of the Uncoated and Coated Weft-Knitted Spacer Fabrics

The surface particle morphology and microstructure of the untreated and treated samples with silica gels were observed by the SEM test as shown in Fig. 3. Fig. 3 (a) has not shown any effect of the silica gels on the fabric surface while Fig. 3 (b) has displayed a dense surface morphology and incessant structure. The silica gels have a nanoporous, tantamount and well-structured network on the surface of treated fabric samples. After treated with silica gels, the morphology and uniformity coating of all treated fabrics were exaggerated by the substrate surface. Furthermore, the surfaces of fabrics coated by silica particles were found denser than uncoated fabrics. Thus the treated fabrics have the existence of the SiO_2 network in their structures. Additionally, several large bridges and crusts of interphase substantial were noted in the spaces of the fibers. The treated samples with silica aerogels were totally covered with silica sol nano-particles which make the surface harsh. The surface morphologies of all the treated samples were almost similar except sample 2. It was noticed that sample 2 has a higher contact angle (CA) 141°±1° as compared to sample 1 and sample 3 due to having a rough surface.

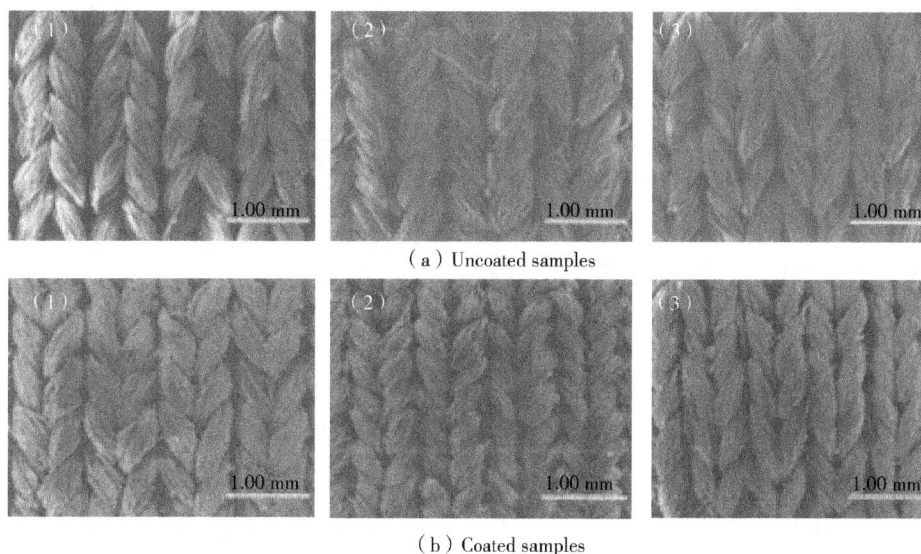

(a) Uncoated samples

(b) Coated samples

Fig.3　SEM images of (a) uncoated and (b) coated samples with silica gels (scale bars 1mm)

3.2　Water Contact Angle Test

The water contact angle of treated weft-knitted spacer fabrics was discovered higher than that of their concerning untreated weft-knitted spacer fabrics. The water contact angles of untreated and treated samples were represented in Fig. 4. The water contact angle improved from 88°±1° to 136°±1°, 90°±1° to 141°±1° and 86°±1° to 133°±1° after silica aerogels coating for sample 1, sample 2 and sample 3 respectively. That might be caused by the harsh and rough surface of treated samples.

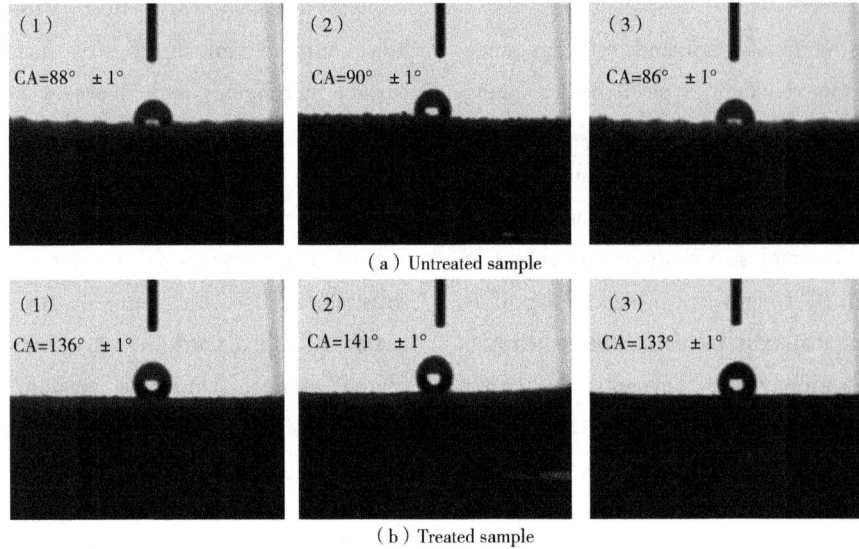

| (1) CA=88° ±1° | (2) CA=90° ±1° | (3) CA=86° ±1° |

(a) Untreated sample

| (1) CA=136° ±1° | (2) CA=141° ±1° | (3) CA=133° ±1° |

(b) Treated sample

Fig.4　The water contact angle of (a) untreated and (b) treated weft-knitted spacer fabrics

The higher hydrophobicity of the silica aerogels coated samples demonstrated the successful surface modification of weft-knitted spacer fabrics.

3.3　Bending Properties of Weft-Knitted Spacer Fabrics

Bending properties of untreated and treated weft-knitted spacer fabrics were led along with the transverse and longitudinal directions separately, and the outcomes appeared in Tab.1. The bending rigidity of treated weft-knitted spacer fabrics was revealed higher than that of their relating untreated weft-knitted spacer fabrics. This might be clarified by the way that the impact of silica aerogels on fabrics structures. The bending rigidity increased from 3.87cN · cm to 4.75cN · cm, 4.25cN · cm to 5.03cN · cm and 4.50cN · cm to 5.40cN · cm for sample 1, sample 2 and sample 3 respectively in the transverse direction after silica aerogels treatment. Similarly, the bending rigidity of spacer fabrics increased from 3.98cN · cm to 4.88cN · cm, 4.30cN · cm to 5.10cN · cm and 4.45cN · cm to 5.38cN · cm for sample 1, sample 2 and sample 3 gradually. From both transverse and longitudinal directions, it was observable that sample 3 gained the highest rigidity and sample 2 possessed the lowest rigidity among the three samples. That showed sample 3 has the most noteworthy bending rigidity results pursued by sample 1 and sample 2. That was due to the impact of the fabric structures on

bending properties. Moreover, the fact of the SAs on bending properties was also additionally huge. The bending properties of weft-knitted spacer fabrics can be changed by planning exceptional structure and changing the chemical composition of SAs, in order to meet firmness necessities of various attires.

Tab.1　The bending properties of weft knitted spacer fabrics

Samples	Transverse direction bending rigidity (cN · cm)	Longitudinal direction bending rigidity (cN · cm)
UTS 1	3.87	3.98
TS 1	4.75	4.88
UTS 2	4.25	4.30
TS 2	5.03	5.10
UTS 3	4.50	4.45
TS 3	5.40	5.38

Note UTS = Untreated sample and TS = Treated sample

4　Conclusions

The treatment of the weft-knitted spacer fabrics using silica aerogels formed of sol nanoparticles on the fabrics, thus enhancing the fabric surface roughness and presenting the higher hydrophobicity to the surfaces. Although weft-knitted spacer fabrics are characteristically hydrophilic, however, this silica aerogels treatment produced super hydrophobic weft-knitted spacer fabrics with a higher water contact angle of 141°±1°. Consequently, such kind of treatment thus also demonstrated the higher bending properties to the fabrics.

Acknowledgements

This research work was financially supported by Donghua University.

References

[1] VARNAITĖ-ŽURAVLIOVA S. et al. The investigation of barrier and comfort properties of multifunctional coated conductive knitted fabrics[J]. Journal of Industrial Textiles, 2016, 45(4):585-610.

[2] CHEN C., et al. Analysis of physical properties and structure design of weft-knitted spacer fabric with high porosity[J]. Textile Research Journal, 2018, 88(1):59-68.

[3] ZHU Q., et al. Modified silica sol coatings for highly hydrophobic cotton and polyester fabrics using a one-step procedure [J]. Industrial & Engineering Chemistry Research, 2011, 50 (10):5881-5888.

[4] YIP J, NG S P. Study of three-dimensional spacer fabrics: Physical and mechanical properties[J]. Journal of Materials Processing Technology, 2008, 206(1-3):359-364.

[5] YOKOGAWA H, YOKOYAMA M. Hydrophobic silica aerogels[J]. Journal of Non-Crystalline Solids, 1995, 186: 23-29.

[6] STARK C, FRICKE J. Improved heat-transfer models for fibrous insulations[J]. International Journal of Heat and Mass Transfer, 1993, 36(3):617-625.

[7] DARYABEIGI K. Heat transfer in high-temperature fibrous insulation[J]. Journal of Thermophysics and Heat Transfer, 2003, 17(1):10-20.

[8] PAN N, SUN G. Functional textiles for improved performance[J]. Protection and Health, 2011.

[9] SYED R I. Influence of silica aerogels on fabric structural feature for thermal isolation properties of weft-knitted spacer fabrics[J]. Journal of Engineered Fibers and Fabrics, 2019, 14:1-11.

Study of Hydrophobic and Oleophilic Nanocoated PMMA Based Cotton Fabrics

KUMAR Rajnesh[1], ZHANG Youwei[1]*, MEMON Hafeezullah[2,3],
RASHEDUL Islam Syed[3], QIN Zongyi[1]*

[1] *State Key Laboratory for Modification of Chemical Fibers and Polymer Materials, College of Material Science and Engineering, Donghua University, Shanghai, 201620, China*

[2] *Donghua University Center for Civil Aviation Composites, Donghua University, Shanghai, 201620, China*

[3] *Key Laboratory of Textile Science & Technology, Ministry of Education, College of Textiles, Donghua University, Shanghai, 201620, China*

* *Corresponding author's email:* zhyw@dhu.edu.cn, rajnesh_kumar@mail.dhu.edu.cn

Abstract: The oil-water separation is one of the critical issues worldwide due to massive oil spills recently. Moreover, domestic and industrial water pollution due to oil discharge affects marine and aquatic life. Cotton is the most predominant fiber in the world because of its use as a principal and popular clothing material. Cotton is also leading raw material for technical and functional textile application. In this study, the fabric was cured with poly (methyl methacrylate) (PMMA) nanoparticles to develop the hydrophobic and oleophilic cotton fabrics. N,N'-dicyclohexylcarbodiimide (DCC) and dimethylaminopyridine (DMAP) were used to catalyze the esterification. The results proved that the excellent hydrophobicity of treated cotton fabric provides with a water contact angle higher than 140°. Besides, Fourier transform infrared (FTIR) spectroscopy analysis, confirmed the fabric surface modification. Surface morphological analysis by field emission scanning electron microscope (FESEM) revealed the uniform rough surface structure of the modified fabric with nano coating. The modified fabric resulted in the high separation efficiency of oil and water without affecting the mechanical properties of the fabric, suggesting this strategy to be suitable for advanced oil-water separation.

Keywords: Cotton fabrics; PMMA nanoparticles; Oil-water separation; Hydrophobicity

1 Introduction

The fantastic water repellence of many biological surfaces, inparticular, plant leaves, has recently aroused great interest. Nowadays, owing to the increasing amount of oil-containing wastewater from our daily life, oil spills, chemical leaks and industries discharges, which have caused severe threat to the environmental and ecological system, oil/water separation has become an urgent world challenge[1-2]. Recently, as markets in leisure and outdoor sporting textiles have been expanded, the needs for superhydrophobic fabrics have increased. Cotton fabric, as a principal and popular clothing material, has excellent comfort, softness, sustainable, enough tensile strength, and biodegradability. Many novel methods have been designed to prepare superhydrophobic cotton fabrics, such as sol-gel coating, chemical vapor deposition, dip-coating and layer-by-layer assembly technique. Although surfaces with the superhydrophobic and super-oleophilic property have been successfully fabricated on cotton fabrics, challenges still exist. For instance, high cost of reagents like dopamine, graphene or precious metals are used in modifying the surface to achieve rough structure, fluorine-containing compounds and fluorinated polymers are of particular interest due to their shallow surface free energies, roughening these polymers in specific ways leads to super-hydrophobicity directly, furthermore, in the process of conventional polymerization of fluorinated polymers, amounts of toxic and volatile organic compounds were used as solvents, such as THF, isopropyl alcohol and DMF. Therefore, the superhydrophobic materials which could selectively absorb oil and oil-based organic contaminants but repel water draw much attention for their high efficiency and selectivity for removal and separation of oil from water. Therefore, the development of oil-water separation materials is of great significance.

In this work, a simple and cost-effective method to developed hydrophobic cotton fabric by using PMMA nanoparticles is reported. More prominently, even after washing for several times with water as well as with solvent, the modified cotton fabrics can still keep excellent hydrophobicity without losing its tensile strength. Furthermore, the possibility of using hydrophobic fabric as a filter for the separations of oil from the water was explored with high efficiency.

2 Materials and Methods

2.1 Materials

Woven cotton fabric with warp and weft both count the 60s, warp/inch 140 and weft/inch 110 was purchased from the local market and used as a substrate. Methyl methacrylate (MMA) and Methacrylic acid (MAA) were distilled at reduced pressure before use. Hydrophobic initiator 2, 2'-azodiisobutyronitrile (AIBN, Adamas) and cross-linker N, N'-methylenebisacrylamide (MBA, Adamas) were purified by recrystallization in methanol. Polyoxyethylene (20) sorbitan monolaurate (tween 20), sodium dodecyl sulfate (SDS) were used as received. N, N'-dicyclohexylcarbodiimide (DCC, 99%) was purchased by Shanghai Macklin Biochemical Company Limited. Triethylamine (TEA), ethanol, acetonitrile toluene, and N-hexane were bought from Shanghai Reagent. Methylene blue, Oil Red O purchased from Damas-Beta. Nitric acid (HNO$_3$), H$_2$O$_2$ and dichloromethane (DCM) were bought from Shanghai Titan Technology Company Ltd.. Vegetable oil and vacuum oil were purchased from the local market. Deionized distilled water was used in all experiments.

2.2 Synthesis of PMMA Nanoparticles

The typical synthesis process was as follows: 55mL of HNO$_3$ aqueous solution (pH = 1.8) were first placed in a three-necked round-bottomed flask (100mL) equipped with a magnetic stirrer, a reflux condenser and a nitrogen inlet for 30min, later 90mg of SDS diluted in water, 80mg of AIBN diluted in DMF and the solution was stirred at a constant rate (300r/min) after that, temperature was increased to 70℃. 1mL of MMA was then injected continuously within 20min via an ALC-IP 800 syringe pump. One hour later, 0.22mL of Tween 20, 2mL of MAA and 120g of MBA were injected successively, with 10min between each injection. 5min later, 300g of SDS was continuously fed over 1 hour. The reaction was allowed to proceed for another 3 hours.

2.3 Pre-Treatment of Cotton Fabric

The desired, scoured and bleached fabric was washed and rinsed with detergent and deionized water to remove the surface impurities. Then the washed fabric was soaked into acetone for 10min and gently rinsed with deionized water, followed by drying at 80℃ for 20min. The pre-treated cotton fabric was cut into 5cm × 5cm small squares.

2.4 Fabrication of Hydrophobic Cotton Fabric

The preparation process of hydrophobic cotton fabric is shown in Fig 1. The dried fabric was soaked into a dispersion of synthesized PMMA nanoparticles at room temperature for 5 minutes and dried for 1 hour at 50℃ in a laboratory oven. After that, the fabric was put into a closed vessel containing DCC/DMAP in ethanol solution at 50℃ for 2 hours later on dried for 1 hour and then rinsed successively with ethanol and water to remove an excessive amount of DCC and physically-absorbed nanoparticles. Finally, the fabric was dried at 50℃ for another 1 hour.

2.5 Characterization

The size and distribution of PMMA nanoparticles were measured by a Zeta Potential and Particle Size Analyzer (DTS1060, Malvern, UK). Surface morphologies of cotton fabric before and after applying the PMMA nanoparticles on the cotton fabric were analyzed by field emission scanning electron microscopy (FESEM SU8010 Hitachi). The wettability of the cotton surface was de-

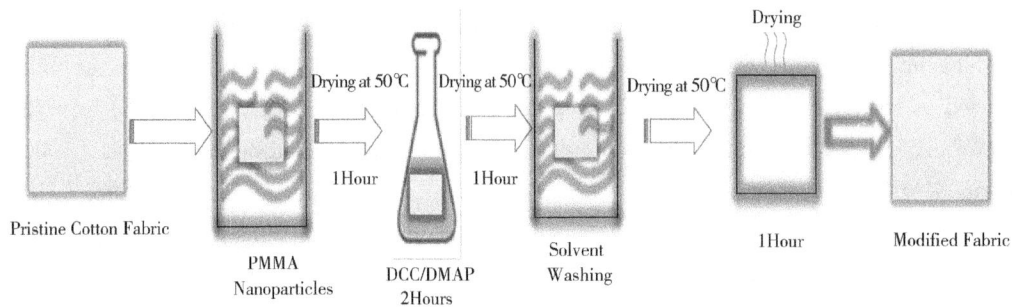

Fig.1 Flow diagram of the fabrication process of hydrophobic cotton fabric

termined by the water contact angle using a fully automatic instrument (OCA40 Micro), the water contact angle was measured at different positions and then the average value was taken. The infrared absorption spectra from $4000cm^{-1}$ to $650cm^{-1}$ of the pristine and modified cotton fabric were measured by a Fourier infrared microscopic imaging spectrometer (Nicolet 6700) using an attenuated total reflection (ATR) mode. The tensile properties of both fabrics were tested on Materials Testing, Machine Tinius Olsen according to ASTM Standard test method (ASTM D – 5034 – 95), where the specimens with the width of 100mm and length of 150mm were mounted in clamps jaws with speed for the measurement of tensile strength was 300mm/min and the distance between clamps was 75mm. Oil absorption capacity, the test process of the total oil absorption by using ASTM Standard test methods

(ASTM D281 – 12, 2016) that can be calculated by formula $N = W - W_0$ where, N is final weight, W is weight absorbed by fabric and W_0 is initial weight of the fabric.

3   Results and Discussions

3.1   Surface Morphology

The surface morphologies of pristine and modified fabrics at different magnifications were observed using field emission scanning electron microscope (refer, Fig. 2). Before the surface modification, the surface of the fabric was relatively smoother; however, after modification, the nano-sized roughness could be observed on the fabric surface. On further magnifying, the PMMA nanoparticles were seen on the surface of the fibers that resulted in nano-sized roughness, which is responsible for the hydrophobicity of the fabric.

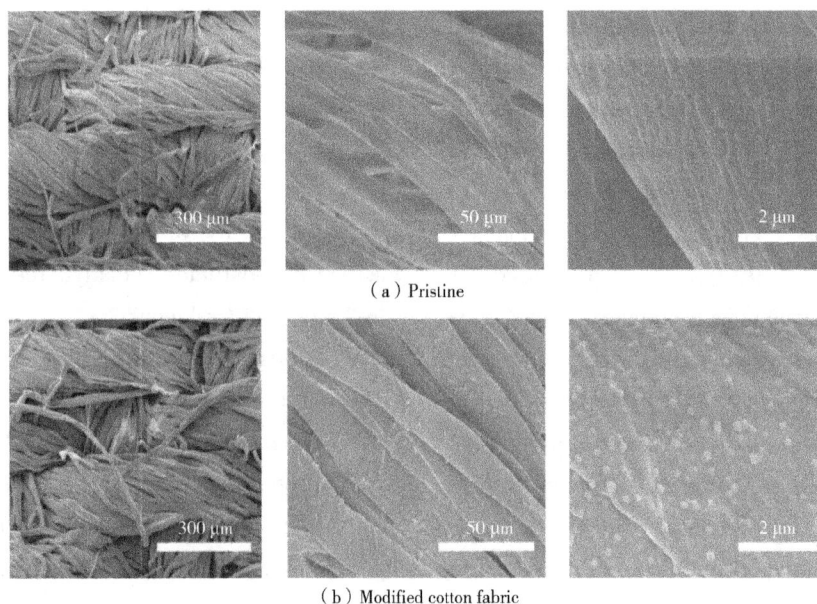

(a) Pristine

(b) Modified cotton fabric

Fig.2   FESEM images of pristine and modified cotton fabric

3.2 FTIR Spectra

The FTIR spectra of pristine and modified cotton fabric (Fig.3). In the spectrum of pristine cotton fabric, the stretching vibrations of —OH,—CH$_2$—, and C—O—C appeared at 3337cm^{-1}, 2998cm^{-1}, 1162cm^{-1}, 1110cm^{-1} and 1054cm^{-1}, respectively. In the spectrum of modified cotton fabric, new peaks appeared at 1786cm^{-1}, 1803cm^{-1}, 1858cm^{-1}, and 2949cm^{-1}. They are the stretching vibrations of anhydride carbonyl, ester carbonyl, carboxy carbonyl and methyl, respectively. This indicated the presence of carboxylic groups, and the formation of ester and anhydride linkages on the surface of the modified cotton fabric. Further, it can be seen that hydroxyl peak in the modified FTIR has become shallower for the modified fabric showing the relative less hydroxyl groups available on the treated surface.

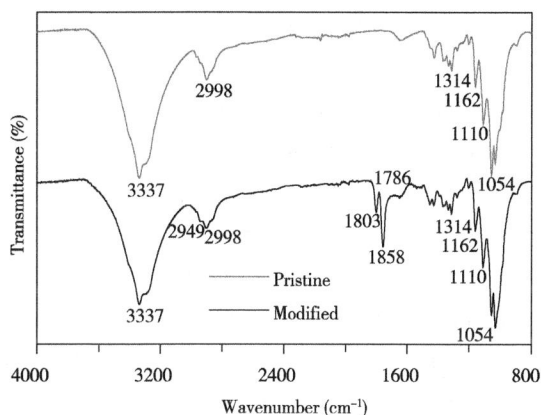

Fig.3　FTIR spectra of the pristine and modified cotton fabric

3.3 Tensile Strength

The force—elongation curve of pristine and treated fabric, and the breaking force and elongation data were assembled in Tab.1 It can be seen that after modification, the breaking force of the fabric decreased slightly, while the breaking elongation of the fabric increased slightly, indicating that the treatment made little influence on the mechanical property of the cotton fabric.

Tab.1　Breaking force and elongation of pristine fabric and modified fabric

Sample	Breaking force (N)	Breaking elongation (%)
Pristine fabric	562.5	16.8
Modified fabric	546.7	19.5

3.4 Hydrophobicity

When the pristine and modified cotton fabrics were placed onto the water surface, from Fig.4 it was seen that the pristine one quickly drowned to the bottom, while the modified one floated on the water surface. The static water contact angles of the pristine and modified cotton fabrics were determined by dropping 5μL water droplets on the surface of the fabrics at a different position. The droplet readily permeates into the pristine fabric to a full extent, indicating the excellent hydrophilicity of the pristine cotton fabric, whereas, the water droplet could stay on the surface of the modified fabric for a long time with the contact angle more than 140°, indicating the excellent hydrophobicity of the modified cotton fabric. The modified cotton fabric can float on the surface of the water for a long time while pristine settles down in the water.

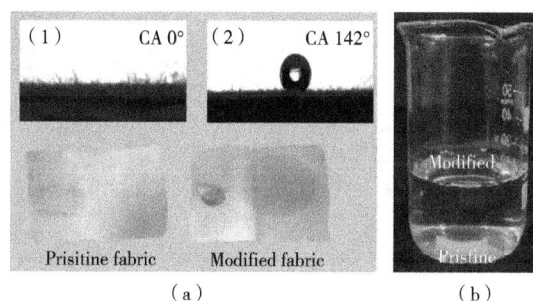

Fig.4　(a) Water droplet (dyed with methylene blue) and oil droplet (dyed with Oil Red O) on the (1) pristine and (2) modified cotton fabric; (b) The modified fabric floating on the surface whereas pristine sunk down

3.5 Oil/Water Separation and Absorption Property

The properties of hydrophobicity and underwater oleophilicity are essential for oil/water separation. The modified cotton fabric with exclusive wetting property can be used for selectively absorption oil from oil/water mixtures efficiently under various conditions (e. g., floating oil layer or underwater oil droplet or even oil/water mixtures).

The modified cotton fabric was used for the selective absorption of the N-hexane layer floating on the water (see, Fig. 5, the results showed that the N-hexane floating layer on the water could be completed removed by contacting with a small piece of modified cotton fabric.

Fig.5 Modified cotton fabric absorbing floating oil layer (a) N-hexane in the water; (b) Placing and immersing; (c) Absorbing the N-hexane from water and (d) N-hexane absorbed by the modified cotton fabric

The modified cotton fabric was also used for the selective absorption of underwater (DCM) droplets, presented in Fig.6, the modified cotton fabric completely absorbed dichloromethane leaving behind the clean water.

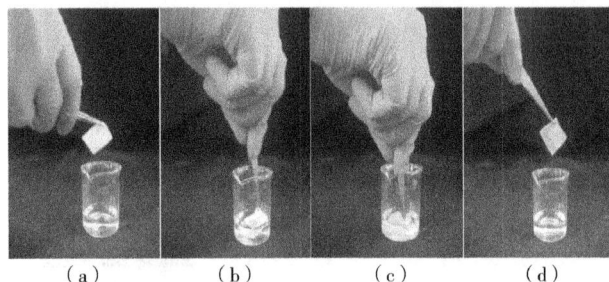

Fig.6 The modified cotton fabric absorbed underwater dichloromethane (DCM) droplets (a) DCM drops in the water; (b) Modified fabric dipped; (c) Absorbing the DCM from the water; (d) DCM absorbed by the modified fabric

The modified cotton fabric was further used for the separation of DCM/water mixture. After dyeing the DCM with Oil Red O, it was mixed with methylene blue-stained water in an equal volume. Then, the oil-water mixture was poured into a water-oil separation device, shown in Fig.7, using modified cotton fabric as a separation material and subjected to oil-water separation test. It was observed that the red DCM was passed through the modified cotton fabric to the lower side of the separation device, and the blue water remained on the cotton fabric. Thus, the modified cotton fabric can be successfully applied to an oil-water separation.

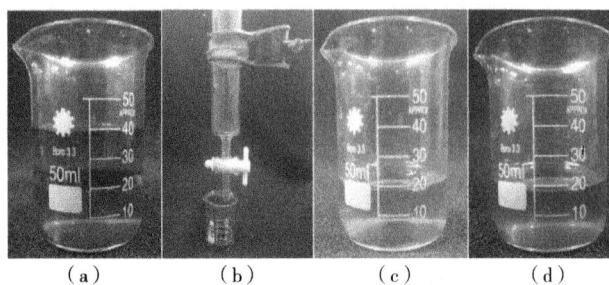

Fig.7 The separation of oil from oil/water mixture by the modified fabric (a) Mixture of DCM red oil and blue water; (b) Pour into the oil/water separation device; (c) Amount of water and (d) Amount of purifying DCM

3.6 THe Oil Sorption Capacity of Pristine and Modified Cotton Fabric for Various Oils

The hydrophobic modification of cotton fabric enables it to repel water and absorb oil. The sorption trial was taken out in pure oil without water to study and relate the maximum oil sorption capacity of pristine and modified cotton fabric for different oils. As shown in Fig.8, the oil sorption capacity of pristine cotton fabric for N-hexane, toluene, dichloromethane, vegetable oil and vacuum oil is 7.14g/g, 12.79g/g, 13.04g/g, 17.89g/g and 23.93g/g respectively, while the corresponding oil sorption capacity of modified cotton fabric for mentioned oil reaches about 12.59g/g, 15.83g/g, 18.26g/g, 22.75g/g and 25.24g/g respectively. Thus, there is a significant improvement in the absorbency of oil of modified fabric, and this strategy is beneficial for preparing oil sorbent with better oil sorption performance.

3.7 The Separation Efficiency of Modified Cotton Fabric

The result specifies that the modified cotton fabric showed admirable oil/water separation efficiency from 95.5% to 99.0% for a selection of oil/water mixtures with different density andviscosity, as shown in Fig.9 the relative low separation efficiency of vegetable oil was due to its high viscosity. Overall the modified cotton fabric showed high selectivity for water and oil; hence, it can be used as a separation substrate for various water/oil separations.

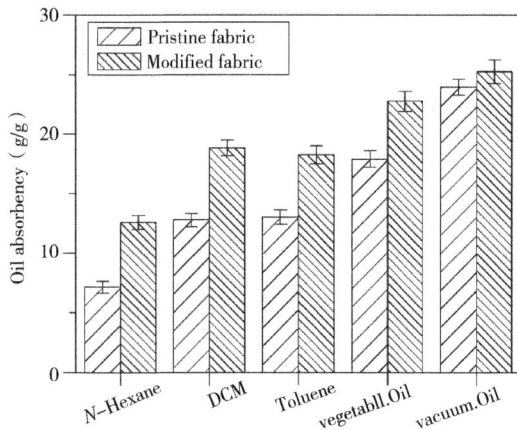

Fig.8　Sorption capacities of pristine and modified cotton fabric for different oils

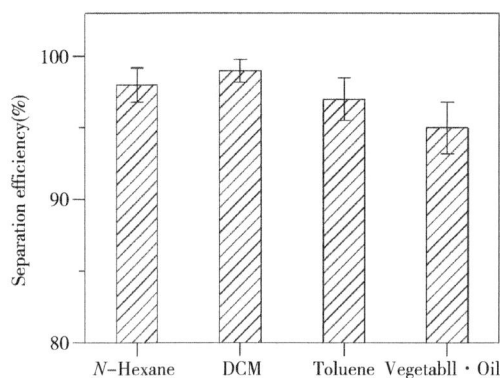

Fig.9　The separation efficiency of modified cotton fabric

4　Conclusions

In summary, a practical top-down approach to fabricate cotton fabric with PMMA nanoparticles by using simply coating method is demonstrated. Through oil absorption and oil-water separation experiment, DCC/DMAP catalytically modified cotton fabric can be successfully applied to oil-water separation when ethanol is used as solvent, which provides a new choice for oil-water separation materials. This modified fabric can be used to remove floating oil layers, underwater oil droplets as well as for the water/oil separation without affecting the mechanical properties. As a result, the modified fabric shows excellent hydrophobicity even after numerous water and solvent washing. This worthwhile, along with eco-friendly technique to prepare functional cotton fabrics show excellent separation efficiency.

Acknowledgements

The authors gratefully acknowledge the financial support of the Shanghai Natural Science Foundation (15ZR1401300).

References

[1] HUSSENEDER C, DONALDSON J R, FOIL L D. Impact of the 2010[J]. Deepwater Horizon Oil Spill on Population Size and Genetic Structure of Horse Flies in Louisiana Marshes, Scientific Reports, 2016(6): 18968.

[2] KERR R A, A lot of oil on the loose, not so much to be found[J]. American Association for the Advancement of Science, 2010.

[3] HOU A, ZHANG C, WANG Y, Preparation and UV-protective properties of functional cellulose fabrics based on reactive azobenzene Schiff base derivative[J]. Carbohydrate Polymers, 2012,87(1): 284-288.

[4] KIM Y, MCCOY L T, LEE E, et al. Environmentally sound textile dyeing technology with nanofibrillated cellulose[J]. Green Chemistry, 2017, 19(17): 4031-4035.

[5] MAJUMDAR A, MUKHOPADHYAY S, YADAV R, Thermal properties of knitted fabrics made from cotton and regenerated bamboo cellulosicfibers[J], International Journal of Thermal Sciences, 2010, 49(10): 2042-2048.

[6] ZHANG X, SHI F, NIU J, et al. Superhydrophobic surfaces: from structural control to functional application[J]. Journal of Materials Chemistry, 2008, 18(6): 621-633.

[7] XUE C H, JIA S T, CHEN H Z, et al. Superhydrophobic cotton fabrics prepared by sol-gel coating of TiO_2 and surface hydrophobization[J]. Science and Technology of Advanced Materials, 2008, 9(3): 035001.

[8] GURAV A B, XU Q, LATTHE S S, et al. Superhydrophobic coatings prepared from methyl-modified silica particlesusing simple dip-coating method[J]. Ceramics International, 2015, 41(2): 3017-3023.

[9] SHIU J Y, KUO C W, CHEN P, Fabrication of tunable superhydrophobic surfaces[J]. Smart Materials III, International Society for Optics and Photonics, 2004: 325-333.

[10] TISSERA N D, WIJESENA R N, PERERA J R, et al. Hydrophobic cotton textile surfaces using an amphiphilic graphene oxide (GO) coating[J]. Applied Surface Science, 2015, 324: 455-463.

[11] YANG J, XU H, ZHANG L, et al. Lasting superhydrophobicity and antibacterial activity of Cu nanoparticles immobilized on the surface of dopamine modified cotton fabrics[J]. Surface and Coatings Technology, 2017, 309: 149-154.

[12] WANG B, LI J, WANG G, et al. Methodology for robust superhydrophobic fabrics and sponges from in situ growth of transition metal/metal oxide nanocrystals with thiol modification and their applications in oil/water separation [J]. ACS Applied Materials & Interfaces, 2013, 5(5): 1827－1839.

Locating the Center of Three-Dimensional Triangular Mesh of Draped Fabric and Studying Its Application on Fabric Hand

YU Zhicai[1], ZHONG Yueqi[1,2]*, GONG Rong[3], XIE Haoyang[1], HUSSAIN Azmat[1]

[1] *College of Textiles, Donghua University, Shanghai 201620, China*

[2] *Key Laboratory of Textile Science & Technology, Ministry of Education, College of Textiles, Donghua University, Shanghai, 201620, China*

[3] *The School of Material, University of Manchester, Manchester, UK*

* *Corresponding Author: zhyq@ dhu.edu.cn*

Abstract: Two methods of computing the center of three dimensional (3D) fabric drape model were proposed based on Locally Linear Embedding (LLE) and Maximum Geodesics Matrix (MGM) separately. With the former method, the three-dimensional mesh model of draped fabric was projected onto the two-dimensional mesh with Locally Linear Embedding. The center of the two-dimensional mesh was mapped to the center of the three-dimensional mesh according to the shared weights. In the latter method, the Geodesics Matrix of vertices in a three-dimensional mesh model was solved. The center of the three-dimensional mesh model was located according to the principle that the maximum Geodesics distance between the original point and other points is the smallest. The distances between the original center and three-dimensional boundary of draped fabric were calculated. The Fourier Descriptor (FD) of distance were extracted and used to train a neural network to predict the total hand value (THV) of draped fabric. The result shows that the center located based on LLE was more accurate than the center located based on MGM. The accuracy of predicted total hand value with Fourier Descriptor of distance could reach 71.43%.

Keywords: Draped fabric; Triangular mesh; Locally linear embedding; Geodesics distance; THV

1 Introduction

Fabric Hand Evaluation (FHE) is widely applied in selecting fabric materials for fashion design and garment production. The subjective FHE is performed by experienced and trained textile experts. They use their instinct to assess fabric quality and suitability for a specific end-use[1]. However, there are several issues involved in subjective evaluation. The first one is the determination of evaluation criteria and their degrees of importance. In addition, fabric hand evaluation requires multiple perspectives of different people as one evaluator may not have enough knowledge to assess well on their own. Therefore, FHE activities are often undertaken in groups[2]. However, evaluators may have different weights in the ranking process. Therefore, the third issue is how to present, and fuse linguistic values given by evaluators to each material under each criterion. Based on this, a lot of efforts have been made in the objective evaluation of fabric hand. Peirce et al first proposed the evaluation of fabric handle using a series of measurable low-stress physical and mechanical properties of fabrics. Subsequently, many investigations have been reported in relation to the development of instrumental systems for objective evaluation of fabric hand[3]. Especially, the emerging of the Kawabata Evaluation System for Fabrics (KES-FB), Fabric Assurance by Simple Testing (FAST) and the Phabr Ometer promote the development of objective fabric hand evaluation significantly[4]. However, both the KES-FB and FAST systems consist of multiple instruments which are used for testing individual mechanical and physical properties. In practice, the operational time and costs in performing the measurements represented major impediments to the widespread use of these instrumental systems[5]. Therefore, researchers attempt to predict fabric hand with some vision features of the fabric. For example, XUE et al[6] proposed a novel algorithm based on rough set theory and fuzzy set theory to measure relations between fabric hand and the visual perception of flared skirt fabric. CAPDEVILA et al[7] proposed a linearity model based on seven variables to discriminate the fabric drapery or lining. KUIJPERS et al[8] recruited a panel to predict the rigid of woven fabric by some images of the draped fabric. WU et al[9] conducted similar research either. In their study, several planes were used to cut the 3D draped fabric in a virtual environment. However, it is observed that different fabrics may have different drape height. Besides, the most obvious part is the 3D boundary of draped fabric. Other parts have a high relationship with the 3D boundary. It is not necessary to infer the fabric hand with the whole 3D drape model. Therefore, we proposed to evaluate the THV of fabric with the 3D boundary in this study.

Based on this, the 3D point cloud of draped fabric was scanned first in this study. The position where the center of fabric sample located, which was marked manually before scanning, was moved to the original point manually. Two methods based on LLE and MGM separately were used to compute the center of 3D draped fabric automatically. Then, the distances between the points on the 3D boundary and the original point were evaluated. The FD of the curve composed of distances was extracted. Meanwhile, the THV of fabric samples were evaluated by a panel. At last, a neural network was constructed to draw the connection between FD and THV.

2 Materials and Methods

2.1 Preparing Fabric Samples and Scanning the 3D Mesh Model

Fifty-one fabrics which have a wide range in fabric hand were purchased from the market in China. All samples were ironed to remove wrinkles before conditioned under constant temperature and humidity (Temperature: $23^{\circ}\text{C} \pm 2^{\circ}\text{C}$, Humidity: $65\% \pm 2\%$) for 48 hours. Each

fabric was cut into a circular specimen with a radius of 120mm. The fabric was centered on a supporting disk with a radius of 60mm surrounding by four RGB-Depth cameras, as shown in Fig.1(a). The angle between two adjacent cameras is 90°. To reach an accurate scanning result, a T-shaped checkerboard [as shown in Fig.1 (b)] was used to calibrate the extrinsic parameters for the four cameras based on the algorithm proposed by ZHANG[10] and WU et al[11].

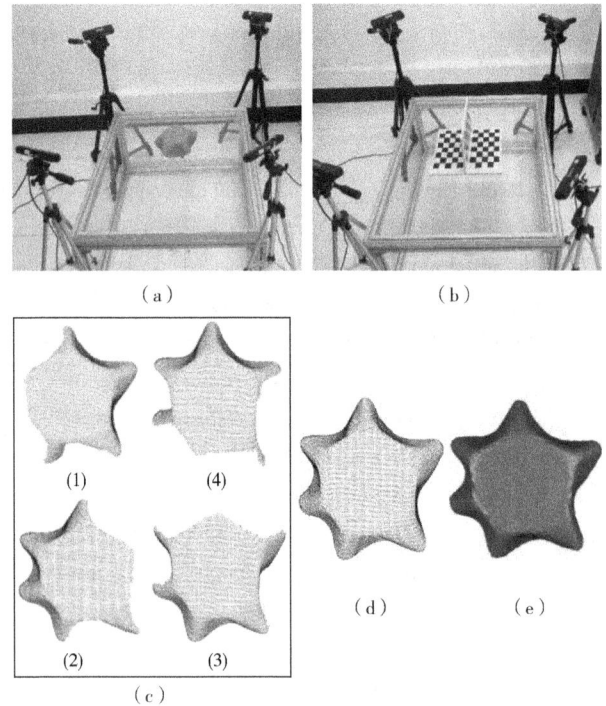

Fig.1   The workflow of scanning fabric drape (a) Calibration;
(b) Scanning; (c) Four patches; (d) Completed
3D points cloud; (e) 3D triangulated mesh

Fig.1(c) demonstrates four point-cloud patches of the draped fabric captured by each camera. They were fused to generate a complete point cloud, as shown in Fig.1 (d). The corresponding triangulated mesh was generated after surface reconstruction, as shown in Fig.1(e). The center of the 3D triangular mesh was marked manually and was moved to the original point. The original point was used as ground-truth of mesh center. Then two methods to compute the center of draped fabric based on LLE and GSM were proposed separately.

2.2 Computing the Center of Draped Fabric Based on LLE

The 3D triangular mesh, as shown in Fig.2(a), was marked as Mesh. The number of vertices of Mesh is N. The set of vertices on the boundary of Mesh was supposed to be B_{3D}. B_{3D} was projected onto B_{2D}. The perimeter of B_{2D} is equal to the total length of B_{3D}. With B_{2D} as the constraint, LLE algorithm is applied to map the 3D triangular mesh [as shown in Fig.2(a)] into a 2D triangular mesh [as shown in Fig.2(b)].

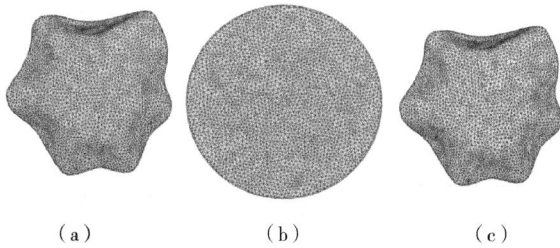

(a)   (b)   (c)

Fig.2   The schematic diagram of locating the center of Mesh based on LLE

As shown in Fig.2(b), the center of Fig 2(b) was located first. Because the topology of Fig.2(a) was the same as the topology of Fig.2(b), the center of Fig.2(a) could be located as the following principle.

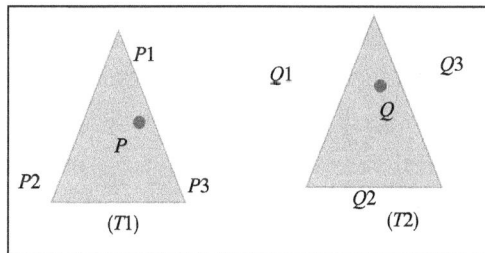

Fig.3   The schematic diagram of the 3D triangle and the corresponding mapped triangle

As shown in Fig.3, P is the center of Fig.2b. P_1, P_2, P_3 are three vertices of triangle $T1$.

$$P = m \times P_1 + n \times P_2 + (1 - m - n) \times P_3 \quad (1)$$

where m and n are the weights of point P_1 and P_2, $0 \leqslant m \leqslant 1$, $0 \leqslant n \leqslant 1$, $0 \leqslant m+n \leqslant 1$. Because, Fig.2(b) has the same triangular topology with Fig.2(a), the center of Mesh could be located with equation (2),

$$Q = m \times Q_1 + n \times Q_2 + (1 - m - n) \times Q_3 \quad (2)$$

2.3 Computing the Center of Draped Fabric Based on MGM

Because the fabric specimens were continuous block objects and there is little stretch deformation[12] after draping. Therefore, the Geodesics distances between vertices in the draped fabric would stay the same during deformation. Before draping, the maximum of Geodesics distances between the center and other points was the radius of the fabric specimen. The maximum of Geodesics distances between another random point and other points was more than the radius of fabric specimen. Therefore, the center of the 3D mesh model could be located according to this principle. The Geodesics Matrix of vertices in Mesh was solved first. It was marked as M:

$$M = \begin{bmatrix} d_{11} & d_{12} & \cdots & d_{1r} & \cdots & d_{1n} \\ d_{21} & d_{22} & \cdots & d_{2r} & \cdots & d_{2n} \\ \vdots & \vdots & \ddots & \vdots & \vdots & \vdots \\ d_{r1} & d_{r2} & \cdots & d_{rr} & \cdots & d_{rn} \\ \vdots & \vdots & \vdots & \vdots & \ddots & \vdots \\ d_{n1} & d_{n2} & \cdots & d_{nr} & \cdots & d_{nn} \end{bmatrix} \quad (3)$$

where, M is a Symmetric Matrix, where, d_{rn} was the Geodesics distance between vertex r and vertex n in Mesh. The column r was the Geodesics distance between vertex r and other vertices in Mesh. The maximum value of column r was the biggest Geodesics distances between vertex r and other vertices. Then the maximum value of each column of M were marked. The result was marked as R_{max}. It was a vector. The element e in R_{max} was the maximum Geodesics distance between vertex e and all other vertices in Mesh. The minimum value of R_{max} was the radius of fabric specimen. Therefore, the vertex which was close to the center of Mesh the most could be inferred.

2.4 Evaluating the THV of Fabric Samples

A panel with 6 graduate students with the background of textile was recruited in the College of Textile, Donghua University, China. There are 3 females and 3 males in the panel. A training session was organized to help the panel familiar with the evaluation method. The THV of fabric samples were evaluated under constant temperature and humidity (Temperature: 23℃±2℃, Humidity: 65%±2%). The final result of THV is an integer between 0 and 6.

2.5 Training A Neural Network to Rating the Fabric Hand

The located center was translated to the original point. The 3D boundary of draped fabric was resampled into 240 discrete points evenly. The distance vector between the original center and 3D discrete points was obtained (Fig.4). The FD of the curve composed of the distances was extracted. The length of FD was determined experimentally as 32. A neural network with the FD as input and the THV as output was constructed. There is a hidden layer with 6 nodes in the neural network. Thirty-seven fabrics were used as training samples and other fourteen fabrics were used as testing samples.

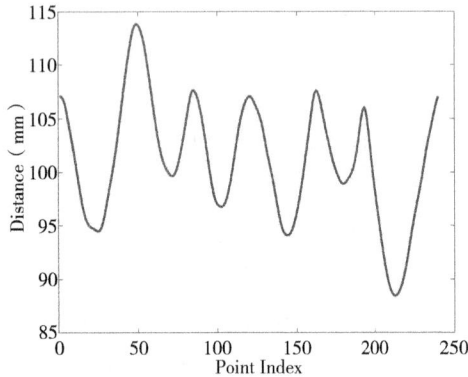

Fig.4   The curve composed of the distances between the original point and 3D boundary

3   Results and Discussions

The histogram of errors between the original point and the centers located with the two methods were shown in Fig.5.

The result revealed that the centers located based on the method of LLE are more close to the real centers than the centers located based on MGM. The reason lies that there was an obvious difference between the two methods. The first step of the method based on LLE was to identify the index of the triangle where the center lies. Then the center of Mesh1 was mapped to the center of Mesh based on shared weights. The method based on MGM was aimed to identify which vertices in Mesh was close to the center of Mesh most. Therefore, the more the density of vertices in Mesh is, the more accurate the

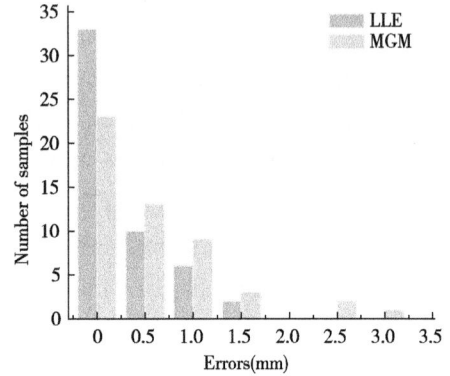

Fig.5   The histogram of errors between the original point and centers located based on LLE and Geodesic Matrix

center located is.

The 3D boundary of draped fabric was shown in Fig.6 (a). If the 3D boundary is divided uniformly, the statistical information based on the boundary is able to reflect the whole drape performance. When the boundary is projected on the X—Y plane [Fig.6(b)], the statistical information based on the contour would be not completed. The fabric part between drape valley and drape peak would be effected in the most degree. The reason lies that these parts are transition part between drape valley and drape peak. If we view the draped fabric from the top view direction, these parts would show obvious distortion (shearing deformation). That is to say, with dimension-reduction, the 2D contour of the draped image is unable to represent the whole 3D boundary of draped fabric uniformly. Therefore, the statistical information based on the top view images of draped fabric would be incomplete. However, if the whole 3D boundary of draped fabric is used to infer the fabric, the problem would be solved. Therefore, more and more researches about obtaining the 3D model of draped fabric with novel methods were conducted.

The advantage of the 3D boundary can be demonstrated with Fig. 7 either. As shown in Fig. 7, the real 3D boundary of draped fabric was overlapped by the supporting disk partly, i.e. we cannot see the entire 3D boundary of draped fabric from the top view. Because parts of the 3D boundary are covered by the fabric itself. Therefore, the 2D contours [Fig. 7 (a)] of

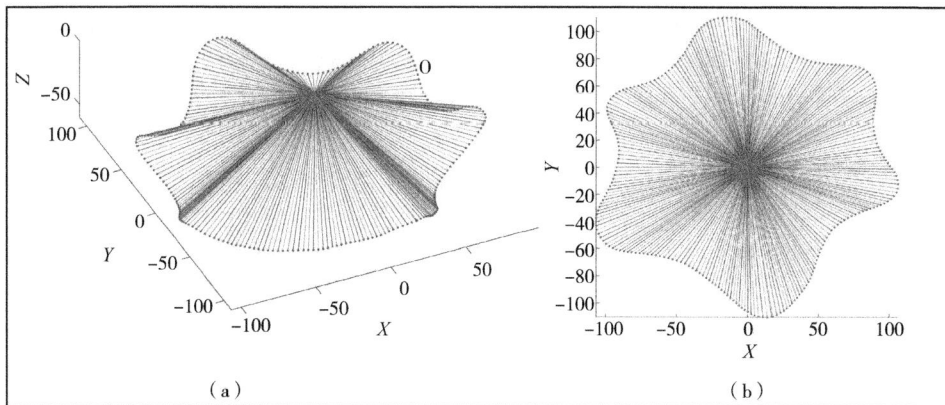

Fig.6　The 3D boundary and the original point (a) Normal view; (b) Top view

draped fabrics captured with traditional fabric testing methods are not the completely true boundaries of fabric sample [Fig.7(b)].

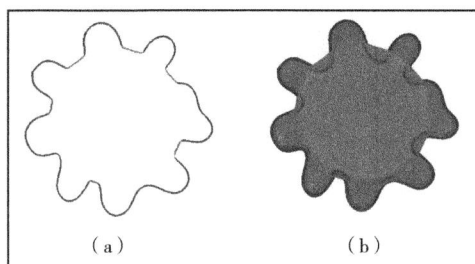

Fig.7　The the 2D contour and top view image of draped fabric (a) The top view image; (b) The 2D contour

In the aspect of predicting fabric THV, the accuracy of fabric hand evaluation for fourteen testing samples could reach 71.43%. The low accuracy may lie that fabric drape performance is affected by mechanical properties, structure parameters and the environment where the fabric is located. When one of the factors changes, different fabrics may have similar drape shapes. In another aspect, the same fabric may have discrete drape results under different experiments despite the same experiment condition. This character limits the prediction of fabric hand under only drape performance as a constraint. This problem may be solved by adding fabric weight or fabric thickness. Despite this, the method proposed in this study could provide a meaningful reference for fabric hand evaluation under only drape performance as a constraint.

4　Conclusions

In this study, two methods of computing the center of 3D draped fabric were proposed. The distances between the original point and 3D boundary points were computed. FD of the curve composed of the distances was extracted and used to infer the THV of fabric samples. Three conclusions were drawn: (1) The method of computing the center of draped fabric based on LLE is more accurate than that based on MGM. (2) The 3D boundary of draped fabric contains more information than the 2D contour of fabric projection. (3) The FD of the curve composed of the distances between the original point and the 3D boundary point was suitable in inferring the THV of fabric samples. To infer fabric hand more accurately, the weight or thickness of fabric would be considered in further study.

Acknowledgements

This work was supported by the National Natural Science Foundation of China (Grant No. 61572124) and the Special Excellent Ph.D. International Visit Program by Donghua University (DHU).

References

[1] VROMAN P, PERWUELZ A, SIMON P. Nonwoven-based super absorbent structures[C]. 5th World Textile Conference AUTEX, 2005.

[2] HERRERA-VIEDMA E, ALONSO S, CHICLANA F et al. A consensus model for group decision making with incomplete fuzzy preference relations[J]. IEEE Transactions on Fuzzy

Systems. 2007, 15:863-77.

[3] KAWABATA S; NIWA M. Objective measurement of fabric mechanical property and quality[J]. International Journal of Clothing Science and Technology. 1991, 3(1):7-18.

[4] DHINGRA R C, LIU D, POSTLE R. Measuring and interpreting low-stress fabric mechanical and surface properties. II. Application of finishing, drycleaning, and photodegradation of wool fabrics [J]. Textile Research Journal. 1989, 60: 7-17.

[5] BISHOP D P. Fabrics: sensory and mechanical properties [J]. Textile Progress. 1996, 26(3):1-62.

[6] XUE Z, ZENG X, KOEHL L. Extracting fabric hand information from visual representations of flared skirts[J]. Textile Research Journal. 2014, 84:246-66.

[7] CAPDEVILA X, CARRERA-GALLISSÃ E. Application of discriminant analysis to parameters describing the drape for two types of woven fabrics[J]. Journal of the Textile Institute Proceedings & Abstracts. 2016, 107:784-790.

[8] KUIJPERS A. Evaluation of physical and virtual fabric draped from objective fabric properties[D]. UK: The University of Manchester, 2017.

[9] WU G, YU ZC, HUSSAIN A, et al. 3D drape reconstruction and parameterization based on smartphone video and elliptical fourier analysis [C]. International Conference on Computational Science. Zurich, Switzerland, 2017:12-14.

[10] ZHANG Z Y. A flexible, new technique for camera calibration[J]. IEEE Computer Society. 2000, 22:1330-1334.

[11] WU G. Three-dimensional reconstruction and shape analysis based on multiple depth cameras[D]. Shanghai: Donghua University, 2017.

[12] SZE K Y, LIU X H. A co-rotational grid-based model for fabric drapes[J]. International Journal for Numerical Methods in Engineering. 2003, 57:1503-1521.

Poly (Vinylidene Fluoride) Modification via Electrostatic Spray of Copper-Nickel Plated PET Woven Filters with Low Pressure Drop for Effective PM 2.5 Removal

HAN Shijiao[3], ZHAI Wen[3], TANG Ge[3], WANG Yichao[3], FAN Weisi[3], WEI Yi[4],
LIU Wanshuang[4], QIU Yiping[1,2,3,5], JIANG Qiuran[1,2,3] *

[1] *Key Laboratory of Textile Science & Technology, Ministry of Education, College of Textiles, Donghua University, Shanghai, 201620, China*

[2] *Engineering Research Center of Technical Textiles, College of Textiles, Donghua University, Shanghai, 201620, China*

[3] *Department of Technical Textiles, College of Textiles, Donghua University, Shanghai, 201620, China*

[4] *Donghua University Center for Civil Aviation Composites, Donghua University, Shanghai, 201620, China*

[5] *College of Textiles and Apparel, Quanzhou Normal University, Fujian, 362000, China*

* *Corresponding author's email*: jj@ dhu.edu.cn

Abstract: Polyester plain fabrics plated with copper-nickel were modified by electrospraying of poly (vinylidene fluoride) and served as the high electrostatic charge loaded filter for the removal of PM 2.5. It was proven that the filtration efficiency of the unmodified filter could be raised for 3.1 folds by elevating the supplied high voltage from 0 to 40kV, while the addition of the PVDF charge storage layer was able to enhance the influence of the supplied high voltage and elevate the filtration efficiency to 3.6 folds. With a loose and thin woven structure, the pressure drops of filters were extremely low and maintained around 6.5Pa. The quality factors of all the filters were of similar trend with the results of filtration efficiency. This work provided a new filter model with both conductive layer and charge storage layer for charge loading and electrostatic field establishment and proved the excellent filtration performance of this new system for PM 2.5 removal.

Keywords: Electrospray, Poly (vinylidene fluoride); Filtration efficiency; Pressure drop; Charge storage

1 Introduction

Due to the rapid economic growth and a surge in car usage, China is suffering from severe atmospheric pollution of particulate matters (PM)[1-2]. Fine particulate matters small than 2.5μm (PM 2.5) are severe pollutants characterized by their small size, large specific area and high affinities to poisonous substances, bacteria and virus[1,3-4]. A high concentration of fine particle matters can induce lethal diseases, such as cardiovascular, respiratory and cancer disease[5].

Besides, PM 2.5 also leads to adverse impact on the living conditions, such as reduced visibility, climate degradation and ecosystem damage[5]. Therefore, the removal of PM 2.5 is of vital importance for public health and safety.

Conventional approaches to remove PM 2.5 usually employ filters with micro-or nanofibrous nonwoven fabrics. These filters suffer from low mechanical properties, poor morphological stability, difficulty in cleaning and refreshing and short working life. In our previous work, a new filter model was presented with a conductive carbon woven fabric as the filter which was supplied with electrostatic high voltage. Particles were removed by the generated electrostatic field[6-7]. However, the conductivity and electric storage ability of the carbon-based filter were not sufficient, and a relative high voltage was required to produce a substantial enhancement in particle removal.

In this research, polyester plain fabrics plated with copper-nickel (PET-f) served as the base filter. Besides, these fabrics also had a high surface conductivity to transfer and distribute electrostatic charges on the filter. Nevertheless, the insufficient charge storage ability is still the key factor to limit the filtration performance. Poly (vinylidene fluoride) (PVDF) with a high dielectricity displays excellent charge storage property, and thus has been employed to develop photovoltaic energy storage materials[8]. In this current work, aimed to enhance the charge storage ability of filter and generate a stronger electrostatic field for filtration, PVDF was coated on the PET-f via electrostatic spray to provide the filter with a charge storage layer. The effects of the loaded PVDF amount and the supplied high voltage of the filtration system on the filtration performance were investigated.

2 Experiments

2.1 Materials

Polyester plain fabrics (60g/m²) plated with copper-nickel (PET-f) were custom developed and supplied by Jiaxing Haorui Intelligent Technology Co., Ltd.. Polyvinylidene fluoride (PVDF, $Mw = 680,000$) was purchased from Shanghai Sanaifu New Material Technology Co., Ltd.. N,N-dimethylformamide (DMF) (certified ACS grade, >99.9%) and acetone (certified ACS grade, >99.7%) were bought from Shanghai Lingfeng Chemical Reagent Co., Ltd..

2.2 PVDF Modification by Electrostatic Spray

PVDF powders were dissolved at 3% in amixed solvent with DMF to acetone weight ratio of 4∶1, and stirred overnight at 70℃. The PVDF solution was loaded in a spinning syringe and kept a distance of 9cm from the needle tip to the grounded collector mounted with the PET-f. During the electrospray process, the spray speed was set at 1.0mL/h and the applied voltage was 15kV. The amount of PVDF sprayed on the PET-f was controlled by the spraying duration from 60s to 180s. The loaded amount was calculated from the weight change of each filter before and after PVDF modification.

2.3 Evaluation of Filtration Performance

The filtration process was tested according to European EN779—2002 standards. The filtration performance of the modified fabric filters was tested on a self-designed filtration system as shown in Fig. 1. The filter was mounted in the sample chamber which was connected to a high voltage supplier (GAMMA ES50P - 10W/DDPM). The supplier provided high voltages ranging from 10kV to 40kV to the filters. The dusts were fed into the filtration channel by a dust generator (PALAS, RGB1000) loaded with the standard dusts (PTI's ISO 11023). The dust concentrations before and after filtration were tested at the spots 35cm away from the filter by a particle spectrometer (PALAS, Fidas Frog). The filtration efficiency was calculated according to the following equation:

$$E = 1 - \frac{C_{\mathrm{down}}}{C_{\mathrm{up}}} \qquad (1)$$

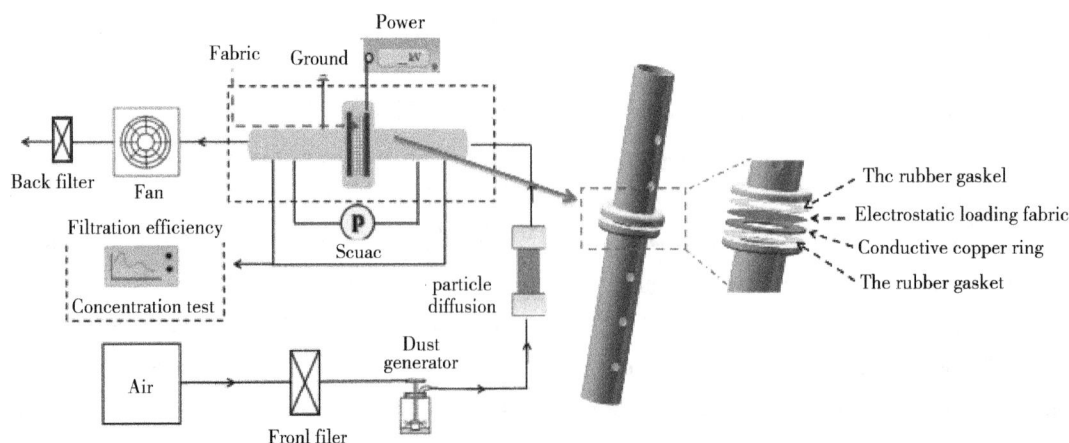

Fig.1　Schematic diagram of filtration system

where E is the filtration efficiency; C_{up} and C_{down} are the particulate concentrations before and after filtration (particles/cm^3) . The air pressures at 5cm in front and behind the filter were measured by a multi-function ventilation meter (TSI, 9565 − P VeloclCalc) , and pressure drop was calculated. The quality factor of each filter was calculated based on the following equation:

$$QF = -\frac{\ln(1-E)}{\Delta P} \qquad (2)$$

where QF is the filter quality factor; E is the filtration efficiency; ΔP is the pressure drop.

2.5 Statistical Analysis

One-way ANOVA was used to analyze the experimental data. The confidence interval was set at 95%. When p-value was greater than 0.05, it indicated that there was no significant difference between the compared data which were labeled with the same characters in each figure. The standard deviations were shown as error bars.

3 Results and Discussions

3.1 The Relationship Between the Electrospray Duration and the PVDF Deposition Amount

Tab.1 presents the PVDF deposition amounts on filters modified for different durations. It could be seen that as the electrospray duration from 60s to 180s, the PVDF deposition amounts on filters were elevated linearly at the rate of 0.002g/min. However, a longer duration than 180s was not applied, because there was obvious polymer agglomeration on the surface of the yarns. At the same time, microfibers would gradually spread from the interlacing point to the pores of the fabrics to form a network, which would block the porous structure of the fabric.

Tab.1 PVDF deposition amount applied by electrospray for different durations

Electrospray duration (s)	PVDF deposition amount (g)
60	0.002
120	0.004
180	0.006

3.2 Effect of PVDF Modification and High Voltage on Filtration Efficiency

Fig.2 shows the filtration efficiency of filters deposited with different amounts of PVDF and supplied with different high voltage. With no high voltage, the filtration efficiency of the filter without PVDF was only 21.47%. Once PVDF was deposited, the filtration efficiency increased slightly to around 25.00%. It indicated that the deposition of PVDF by electrospray did not block the fabric porous structure. The enhanced filtration effect might be contributed by the roughened surface of yarns in the filter. When 10kV was applied on the filters, the original filter and the filter deposited with 0.002g PVDF displayed 20.03% elevation in filtration efficiency, while the filters modified with 0.004g and 0.006g PVDF could achieve 30.32% and 41.53% enhancement in filtration efficiency. The highest filtration efficiency of the original filter could achieve 67.02%, which was enhanced about 2 folds compared to the value with no supplement of high voltage. It indicated that there were limitations in the elevation of filtration efficiency by the supplement of high voltage for these two samples, and a 30kV might be the higher effective voltage. On the contrary, the filters loaded with 0.004g and 0.006g PVDF at 40kV displayed substantial increments in filtration efficiency compared to the values at 30kV. The maximum filtration efficiencies could achieve 88.00% and 94.29%, about 3.6 folds of the values with no high voltage. To further raise the supplied voltage might provide better performance, but the filtration system was not stable at higher voltage and electric sparks were observed. These results indicated that application of high voltage to the special conductive PET fabric filters could generate filtration effect, and the filtration efficacy could be enhanced by applying a charge storage layer of PVDF.

3.3 Effect of PVDF Adhesion on Pressure Drop

Fig.3 describes the filtration resistance of the original and modified filters with PVDF. With no high voltage, the pressure drops of all the filters were around 6.5Pa and no significant differences among samples. Besides, the applied high voltage showed no effect on the pressure drops (data not shown) . These filters had a plain-woven structure with large pore sizes and thin

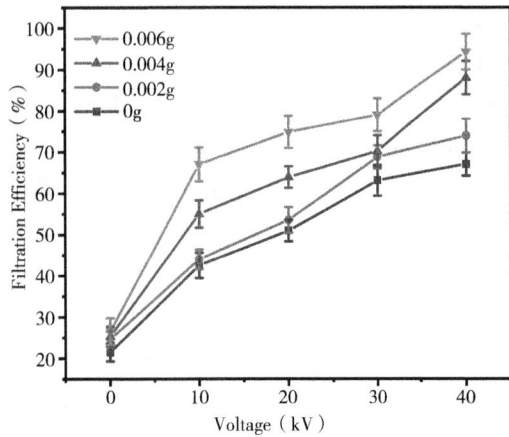

Fig.2　Effect of PVDF modification and high voltage on filtration efficiency

thicknesses when compared to conventional filters. Therefore, the filtration at 0.1m/s displayed a very low pressure drop, while the pressure drops of conventional filters were in the range of 150Pa to 200Pa. Since the loaded PVDF was only distributed on the yarns rather than the pores, the pressure drop was not affected by the modification. Usually, with an elevated filtration efficiency, the pressure drop of a filter will be increased due to the fast blocking of pores by the accumulated dust and the formation of the dust cake layer. However, although the applied voltage could efficiently enhance the filtration efficiency, the pressure drop did not vary much, probably because the removed dusts did not accumulate on the filters and induced limited change on the filter structure.

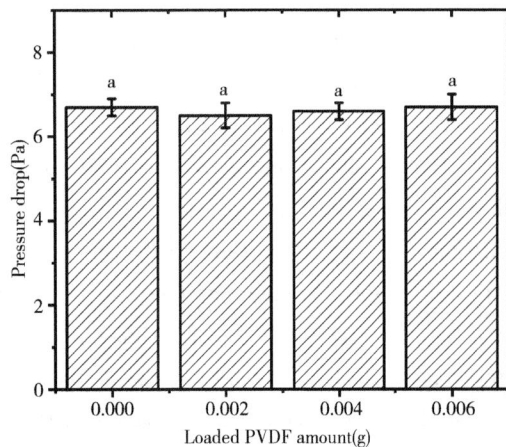

Fig.3　Pressure drop of the filters along with loaded PVDF amount

3.4　Effect of PVDF Adhesion on Quality Factor

The changes in quality factor of the original and modified filters under different voltages are shown in Fig.4. Since the pressure drops of all samples were similar, the quality factors of all the samples were with the same trend as the results of filtration efficiency. By applying the high voltage, the quality factors of all filters were raised, and the loading of PVDF could substantially enhance the efficacy. The original fabric showed only 78.21% elevation, while the filter loaded with 0.006g PVDF presented a 89.23% enhancement in the quality factor.

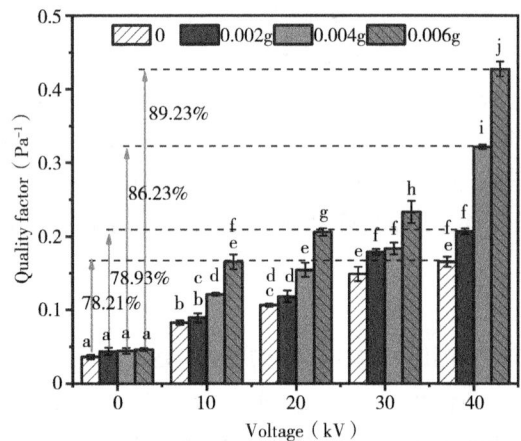

Fig.4　Effect of PVDF modification and high voltage on quality factor

4　Conclusions

In order to reduce indoor fine particulate pollution, PVDF loaded on the PET-f by electrostatically spraying was used to improve filtration performances of filters. As the amount of loaded PVDF increased, the filtration effects of the filters continued to increase. When the amount of loaded PVDF was 0.006g, the filtration efficiency can reach 94.29%, and the pressure drop was only 6.7Pa while the quality factor was 6.7Pa^{-1}, and the filtration performance was greatly improved. Therefore, loading PVDF on the surface of the filters had great application potential in reducing indoor particulate matter pollution.

Acknowledgements

This research was financially supported by the National Natural Science Foundation of China (51503031) and the Scientific Research Foundation for the Returned Overseas Scholars from the Ministry of Education (15B10127).

References

[1] LIU C, HSU P C, LEE H W, et al. Transparent air filter for high-efficiency PM2.5 capture[J]. Nature Communications, 2015, 6:1-9.

[2] LIU B, ZHANG S, WANG X, et al. Efficient and reusable polyamide-56 nanofiber/nets membrane with bimodal structures for air filtration[J]. Journal of Colloid and Interface Science, 2015, 457:203-211.

[3] LEE E S, FUNG C C, ZHU Y. Evaluation of a high efficiency cabin air (HECA) filtration system for reducing particulate pollutants inside school buses[J]. Environmental Science & Technology, 2015, 49(6): 3358-3365.

[4] PENG R D, BELL M L, GEYH A S, et al. Emergency admissions for cardiovascular and respiratory diseases and the chemical composition of fine particle air pollution[J]. Environmental Health Perspectives, 2009, 117(6): 957-963.

[5] HE M, ICHINOSE T, KOBAYASHI M, et al. Differences in allergic inflammatory responses between urban PM2.5 and fine particle derived from desert-dust in murine lungs[J]. Toxicology and Applied Pharmacology, 2016, 297:41-55.

[6] WANG Q, BAI Y, XIE J, et al. Synthesis and filtration properties of polyimide nanofiber membrane/carbon woven fabric sandwiched hot gas filters for removal of PM 2.5 particles[J]. Powder Technology, 2016, 292:54-63.

[7] WANG Q, KHAN F, WEI L, et al. Filtration properties of carbon woven fabric filters supplied with high voltage for removal of PM 1.0 particles[J]. Separation and Purification Technology, 2017, 177:40-48.

[8] LIU G, XIAO M, ZHANG X, et al. A review of air filtration technologies for sustainable and healthy building ventilation[J]. Sustainable Cities and Society, 2017, 32:375-96.

Conductive Fabric-Based Alternating-Current Electroluminescence Textile with Excellent Luminescence Properties

LI Jingyi[1], BAI Zhiqing[1], YANG Jiahua[1], GUO Jiansheng[1]*

[1] College of Textiles, Donghua University, Shanghai, 201620, China

* Corresponding author's email: jsguo@ dhu.edu.cn

Abstract: The flexible textile with high light electroluminescence is beneficial for protective garment to improve safety performance by increasing the visibility and interactive design for non-verbal communication. Meanwhile, both the additional application value and the satisfaction of smart textiles can be achieved by giving illuminating functions to fabrics. In this work, the flexible alternating-current electroluminescence (ACEL) textile was fabricated via a simple blade-coating method. Specially, the conductive woven fabric, $BaTiO_3$/WPU (water polyurethane) dielectric layer, ZnS:Cu/WPU electroluminescence layer, and the transparent poly (3,4-ethylenedioxythiophene) (PEDOT) electrode layer were assembled to form the ACEL textile with sandwiched structure. The FE-SEM image showed that each layer was bonded tightly without clear interface. Moreover, the optical performance of the ACEL textile was measured by spectrophotometer. The illuminance of the ACEL device can be up to 203.1 lux at the condition of 150V at 2000Hz frequency, exhibiting the excellent optical performance of the ACEL textile. Furthermore, the luminescence intensity increased with the increase of the driven voltage and frequency, and the color of the ACEL device mainly depended on the frequency of the power.

Keywords: Alternating-Current electroluminescence; ACEL textile; Blade coating; PEDOT

1 Introduction

With the development of the electronics technology recently, wearable smart textiles have attracted extensive attention. As one of the smart textiles, light-emitting textiles have aroused public concern widely[1]. The smart luminous textile is attractive to public because of its wide range of applications, such as clothing, interior design and visual merchandizing[2].

Light emitting phenomenon at the condition of direct current or alternating current, and the different emitting modes depend on the kinds of phosphor materials[3]. The discovery of electroluminescence can be dated back to 1936 by George Destriau[4]. The alternating electroluminescence of ZnS powder was discovered and applied to ACEL foils for light emitting applications[5]. While the low light output and poor durability limited its application. Afterwards, it took some time for others to develop the basic understanding of the new effect until the 1950s[6-7], and Piper and Williams started to establish first theoretical concepts during that time[8]. Since then, the electroluminescence devices have been developed inorganic-film based alternating-current EL[9], inorganic semiconductor based EL[10], and organic semiconductor EL[11]. In recent decades, the development of electroluminescence device is processing in a rapid way. In 2016, Marc de Vos and Russel Torah have fabricated the flexible EL lamps onto woven fabrics using a novel dispenser printing process[12], and HU Bin and CALVERT Paul formed an alternating current electroluminescent device with extrusion printing process[13].

Owing to the advantages of flexibility, wearability and tailorability, fabric is expected as an attractive substrate for electroluminescent elements[14]. If the electronic functions can be endowed to fabric, it offers the opportunity to transform the traditional textiles into high-end textiles, and add a second-high value function to the

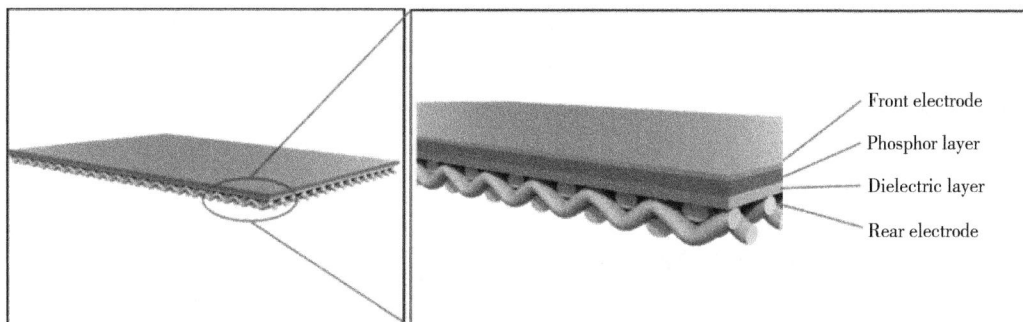

Fig.1 Structural schematics of the ACEL textile

fabric primary function. In this paper, the conductive fabric based alternating current electroluminescence device (ACEL textile) was mainly explored by a simple route. The optical performance and surface morphology of the ACEL textile were studied in detail. The paper is to provide a new thought for light emitting E-textiles and a better understanding of the effects of different voltages and frequency of the power on optical properties of ACEL textile.

2　Experiments

2.1　Materials Preparation

The conductive woven fabric (thickness of 0.02mm, gram weight of $25g/m^2$) was selected as primary substrate and electrode. The phosphor powder (ZnS : Cu) and the WPU (ERW-T2818) were used for the preparation of light-emitting layer. The dielectric powder (BaTiO$_3$) and conductive polymer (PEDOT) were utilized as the dielectric layer and transparent conductive layer respectively.

2.2　Design of ACEL Textile

The proposed ACEL textile is a typical multilayered composite with an emitting phosphor layer sandwiched between the two electrodes. The conductive woven fabric acts both as the substrate and the bottom electrode forming a capacitor structure with the top PEDOT electrode as show in Fig.1. Between these two electrodes, the BaTiO$_3$/WPU dielectric layer and the Zns : Cu/WPU light-emitting layer were subsequently coated and dried. When the strong electric field was applied, the light will be emitted from the phosphor layer and pass through the transparent PEDOT electrode layer without losing too much light intensity. Note that the BaTiO$_3$/WPU dielectric layer can prevent a short circuit causing by the breakage of phosphor layer under the high field strength.

2.3　Fabrication Process and Characterization

In this work, the ACEL textile was prepared by the blade-coating method. First of all, the conductive woven fabric was cut into square with the same size of 8cm×8cm. Secondly, the dielectric paste was prepared by mixing the BaTiO$_3$ particles with the WPU at a weight ratio of 2 : 1, and then it was dispensed by ultrasonic method for 15min. After that the dielectric layer was formed through blade-coating. Subsequently, the phosphor paste was prepared by mixing ZnS : Cu and the WPU at a weight ratio of 2 : 1 and was dispensed by ultrasonic method for 15min, and then was coated onto the dielectric layer forming the phosphor layer. After that, the PEDOT was sprayed onto the phosphor layer forming the transparent conductive layer, and the flexible ACEL textile was obtained. After that, a bus electrode was prepared with conductive silver paste, and the flexible ACEL textile was obtained. At last, the morphology of the prepared ACEL textile was characterized by FE-SEM, and the optical performance was tested by the spectrophotometer.

3　Results and Discussions

3.1　Morphology of ACEL Textile

In the ACEL textile, the rear electrode acts as both the substrate and rear electrode. Compared with the traditional silver paste coated fabric, the conductive fabric is not only more cost-effective and flexible, but also with better cohesive force owing to their different processing styles. The SEM image of the conductive woven fabric in Fig.2(a) shows that the warp and weft yarns are well interwoven, leading to a smooth surface which is beneficial for subsequent coating.

The cross-section FE-SEM image of the ACEL textile shown in Fig.2(b) exhibites the multilayered structure.

Note that the structure of each layer of the ACEL textile could be observed clearly and the interface between each layer were bonded tightly with each other, indicating the good adhesion of each layers.

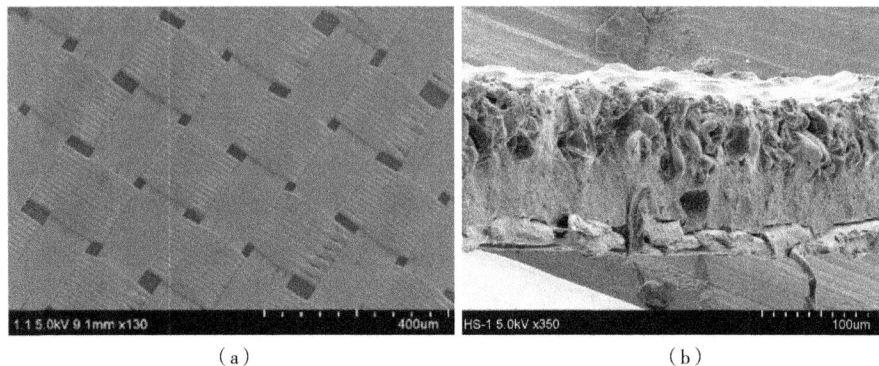

(a)　　　　　　　　　　　　　　(b)

Fig.2　The FE-SEM image of the (a) conductive woven fabric; (b) cross-section of the ACEL textile

3.2　Transmittance of the Polymer and Front Electrode

Choosing the polymer and front electrode with good transparency is quite essential for ACEL textile fabrication. Therefore, the transmittance of the WPU and PEDOT were measured, and the results are shown in Fig. 3. It can be seen that the transmittances of the WPU and PEDOT are more than 86.5% and 83.1% respectively in the range of visible light wavelength, indicating the right choice of materials for the ACEL textile, which is conducive to promoting the luminescence properties of the ACEL textile.

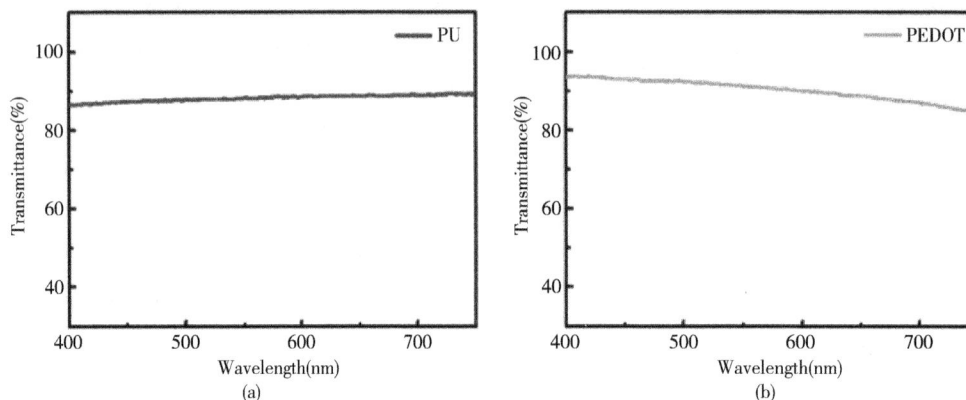

(a)　　　　　　　　　　　　　　(b)

Fig.3　The transmittance of (a) WPU film and (b) PEDOT electrode

3.3　Optical Performance of the ACEL Textile

The durability of ACEL textile is of importance for real application. As shown in Fig.4(a), the ACEL textile emitted uniform and bright blue light. It is worth mentioning that the luminescence of ACEL textile still remained the same even if it was bent for many times, which indicates the excellent light-output and flexibility performance of the ACEL textile. Additionally, the optical performance of the prepared ACEL textile was performed under various alternative voltages (30 – 150V), and different frequencies (500Hz, 1000Hz and 2000Hz). As shown in Fig.4(b) and Fig.4(c), the peak wavelength of the device was at 450–500nm under various frequencies and slightly turned from light color to dark color with the increase of the voltage.

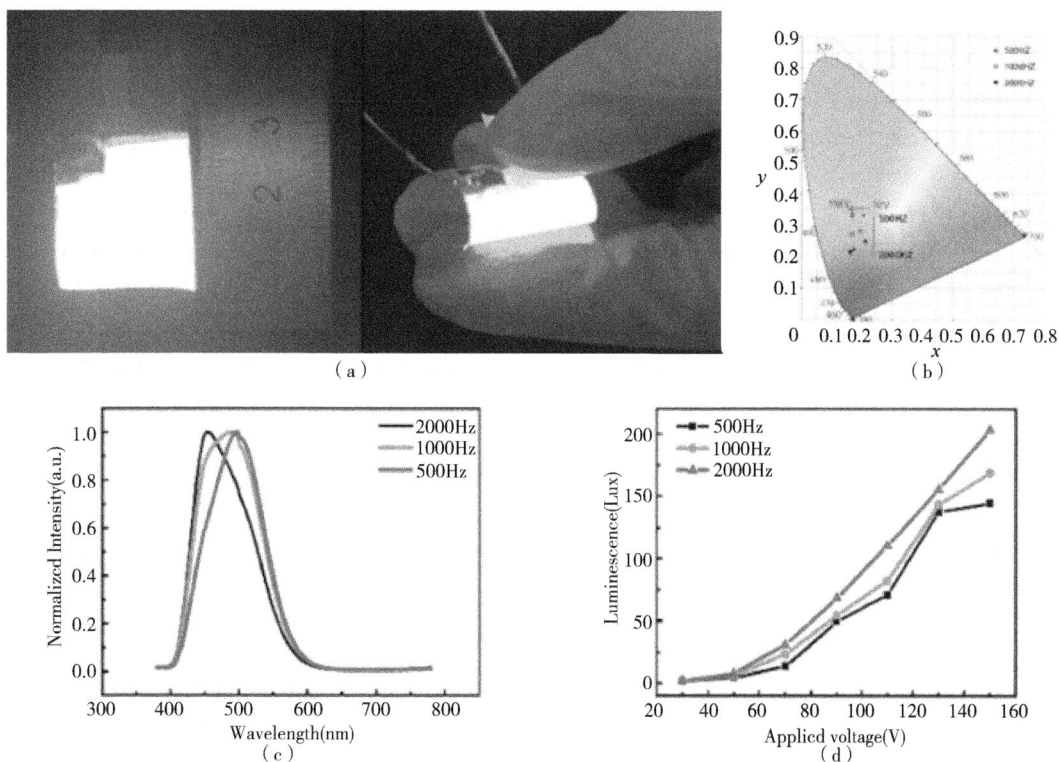

Fig.4 (a) Optical performance of ACEL textile; (b) CIE 1931 color space chromacity diagram at various voltages and frequencies; (c) Luminescence of the ACEL textile under different voltages and frequencies; (d) Electroluminescent spectrum of the ACEL textile at various frequencies

Furthermore, with the decrease of the frequency, the color and the wavelength of the ACEL device turned from blue light to green light, shifted from 450nm to 500nm. The luminescence of the ACEL textile under various voltages and frequencies was shown in Fig.4(d). It can be seen that the luminescence of the device can be up to 203.1 lux.

under the condition of 150V at 2000Hz frequency. In addition, the luminescence of the device increased with higher driving voltages and frequencies.

4 Conclusions

In this study, the highly flexible ACEL textile with excellent light output performance was fabricated by blade coating method. The surface and cross-section morphology of ACEL textile were obtained, exhibiting the good interface between the adjacent layers. The optical performance of the device was measured, and it concluded that the color of the device was mainly related to the frequency of the power, and the lumines-

cence of the device increased with the increase of the driven voltage and frequency. The proposed flexible ACEL textile exhibited good luminescence properties, which lead a promising future in clothing, interior design and visual merchandizing.

References

[1] LANGENHOVE L V, HERTLEER C. Smart clothing: a new life[J]. International Journal of Clothing Science & Technology, 2004, 16(1/2):63-72.

[2] INGE V, JEROEN S, VIKTORJIA M, et al. Printing smart designs of light emitting devices with maintained textile properties[J]. Materials, 2018, 11(2):290.

[3] TADESSE M G, DUMITRESCU D, LOGHIN C, et al. 3D printing of ninja flex filament onto pedot:pss-coated textile fabrics for electroluminescence applications[J]. Journal of Electronic Materials, 2017.

[4] DESTRIAU G. AC electroluminescence in ZnS[J]. Chim. Phys. 1936, 33, 587.

[5] MICHAEL B, HUBERT S D. Materials for powder-based AC-electroluminescence[J]. Materials, 2010, 3(2):1353-1374.

[6]HOWARD B T, IVEY H F, LEHMANN W. Voltage dependence of electroluminescent brightness[J]. Physical Review, 1954, 96(3):799-800.

[7]LEHMANN W. Frequency dependence of electroluminescent brightness of impurity-quenched phosphors[J]. Physical Review, 1956, 101(1):489-490.

[8]PIPER, W W, WILLIAMS F E. Theory of electroluminecence [J]. Phys. Rev. 1955, 98, 1809-1813.

[9]RACK P D, HOLLOWAY P H. The structure, device physics, and material properties of thin film electroluminescent displays[J]. Materials Science & Engineering R Reports, 1998, 21(4):171-219.

[10]BURROUGHES J H, BRADLEY D D C, BROWN A R, et al. Erratum: light-emitting diodes based on conjugated polymers[J]. Nature, 1990, 348(6299):352-352.

[11]TANG C W, VANSLYKE S A. Organic electroluminescent diodes[J]. Applied Physics Letters, 1998, 51 (12): 913-915.

[12]DE V M, TORAH R, TUDOR J. Dispenser printed electroluminescent lamps on textiles for smart fabric applications[J]. Smart Materials and Structures, 2016, 25(4):045016.

[13]HU B, CALVERT P. Printed electro-luminescent fabrics [J]. Advances in Science & Technology, 2017, 100: 27-30.

[14]WANG J, YAN C, CHEE K J, et al. Highly stretchable and self-deformable alternating current electroluminescent devices[J]. Advanced Materials, 2015, 27(18):2876-2882.

[15]WANG X, SUN J, DONG L, et al. Stretchable and transparent electroluminescent device driven by triboelectric nanogenerator[J]. Nano Energy, 2019, 58:410-418.

Design and Development of Manual Hank Reeling Machine

FITSUM Etefa Ahmed[1] [*]

[1] *Ethiopian Institute of Textile and Fashion Technology (EiTEX), Bahir Dar University, Ethiopia*

[*] *Corresponding author's email*: Oneday790@ gmail.com

Abstract: In today's Textile product processing, customers are demanding lower prices, the best quality product and service. An effective cost reduction and higher productivity with short processing time is the main objective for textile manufacturer to be a strong competitor by having high market share with profitability and to compete successfully in the world market by keeping benefits of stoke holders including customers. In textile manufacturing, the main input fiber material can be converted in to yarn by using different spinning machinery. There are different types of yarn winding or reeling. Hank yarn is a type of yarn which used for woven and knitted fabric manufacturing. Hank reeling machine is used to convert cone package yarn into a hank form yarn.

In Ethiopia, there are more than 3000 small and medium scale enterprises (SME) who engaged in manufacturing of woven and knitted fabric. Most SME are using manual or hand driven hank reeling machine in order to convert cone or cop package yarn into hank form yarn. However, the amount of hank produced by manual reeling machine does not satisfy the need of SME and it leads to very high hank yarn cost.

Based on primary and secondary data analysis, the researcher designed and fabricated manual hank reeling machine which can be driven easily by using fabric sewing machine treadle or pedal system. Fabricated hank reeling machine can wind up to 11 perreeling cycle. The study will have a positive impact for small and medium enterprises engaged in the sector. The Researcher planned to fabricate more machines for SME found in Ethiopia who engaged in the sector.

Keywords: Yarn; Hank yarn; Cone yarn; Hank reeling; Weaving; Knitting

1 Introduction

The interest of producing textile and related products are increasing in the world. The abundance in nature combined with the ease of textile manufacturing is an attractive feature, which makes it an important income for the development of a given country. Nowadays different latest textile machineries are developed by different manufacturers. In production of yarn, the main input fiber material can be converted into a yarn by passing through different yarn production sequence. Yarn winding and reeling are the most important operations, which are mainly occurred in spinning section.

In textile industry, a hank is a coiled or wrapped unit of yarn. This is often the best form for use with handlooms, compared to the cone form needed for power looms. Hanks come in varying lengths depending on the type of material and the manufacturer. For instance, a hank of linen is often 300 yards (270m), and a hank of cotton or silk is 840 yards (770m). While hanks may differ by manufacturer and by product, a skein is usually considered 1/6 of a hank (either by weight or by length).

In Ethiopia, most small-and medium-sized enterprises engaged in knitted and woven fabric manufacturing use hank yarn as a main input material. Hank yarn is not fixed in length but is sold in units by weight, most commonly 50 grams. Depending on the thickness of the strand as well as the inherent density of the material, hanks can range widely in yardage per 50 gram unit. Knitters and weavers rewind the hanks into balls or centre-pull skeins prior to use, in order to prevent the yarn from becoming tangled. Hank reeling machine is used to change cone or cop packed yarn into a hank form by reeling the yarns into a circular or round shaped reel. Automatic hank reeling machine works by use of electric power system and has motor for hank reeling. This machine can reel more than 12 hanks per reeling cycle of machine. It's less time consuming, but expensive.

In Ethiopia, textile product manufacturing is one of a key sector that identified by the government since 2010. The country industrialization strategy has given top priority for textile manufacturing. Daeto the several opportunity and suitability of the general atmosphere for the growth of textile industries in the country, some local and foreign investors are investing their knowledge and capital in the sector.

Local knitted and woven fabric producers can purchase a cone or cop packed yarn from market and they can change the yarns into hank form by using small manual hand driven hank reeling machine. This machine can be used to reel single hank per reeling cycle. The amount of hank produced by manual reeling machine does not satisfy the need of small scale knitted and woven fabric producers and it leads very high hank cost. Therefore, this problem was a notable hindrance limiting the productivity of small and medium-sized enterprises. The present work aims at fabricating a manual hank reeling machine that can be operated easily by pedal system and capable of reeling 11 hanks per reeling cycle with less manufacturing cost.

2 Methodology

2.1 Materials

Hollow structural sections of circular (CHS) pipe, rectangular (RHS), tubular steel, sheet metal, bearing, pulley, belt, sewing machine treadle, worm gear were used in fabrication hank reeling machine.

2.2 Methods

Currently there are various types of hank reeling machine available in the market. Different research activities have been conducted in order to increase hank reeling machine productivity.

Based on primary and secondary data analysis, the researcher designed hank reeling machine which shown in Fig.1. The machine has a reeling part which used to wind hank yarn and has a worm gear which used to traverse or distribute the yarn uniformly throughout the width of the hank yarn.

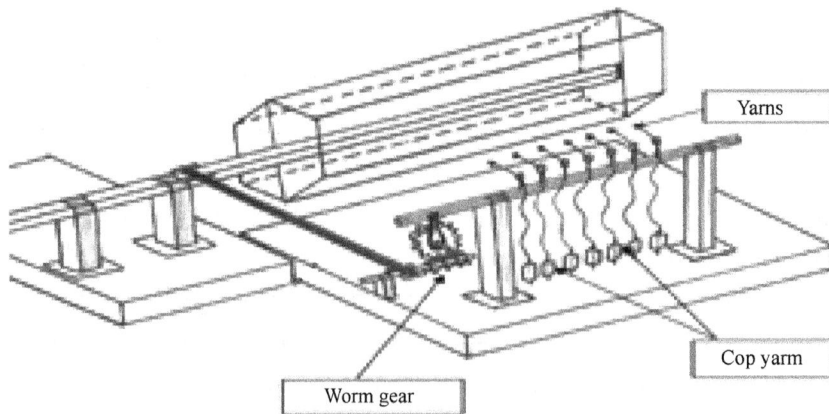

Fig.1　Manual hank reeling machine design

As shown in Tab.1, the machine has a 160cm long 25× 1. 25 hollow structural sections of circular (CHS) pipe main shaft, on which 20cm length 6 round bars are welded at one end of the shaft and 20cm length 6 round bars are welded at 90cm end of the shaft in opposite direction. A 90cm Length 6 round bar reeling parts are welded with 20cm Length round bars in both edge of reel parts.

Tab.1 Manual hank reeling machine specification

No	Machine parts	Dimension	Material type
1	Reel length	Reel length 90cm, reel Circumference 80cm	10mm Round bar
2	Reel support	Length 50cm	CHS pipe 50×2
3	Yarn traverse support	Length 65cm	CHS Pipe 25×1.25
4	Yarn traverse	Length 110cm	10mm Round bar
5	Reel frame	60cm×40cm	RHS Tubular steel
6	Feeding frame	110cm×60cm	RHS Tubular steel
7	Shaft	Length 160cm	CHS pipe 25×1.25
8	Ball Bearing	25×52	—
9	Worm gear	100 Teeth number	—
10	Sheet metal	1.25mm Thickness	—

The main shaft is supported by two 50cm long 50×2 hollow structural sections of circular (CHS) pipe vertically welded on machine frame with having two 25×52 ball bearing and bearing house at the edge of shaft support. The one edge of main shaft is welded with the driving unit pit man rod and sewing machine treadle part. The machine has a feeding unit to feed cone or cop packed yarn to the machine reeling unit. A 1.25mm thickness sheet metal is welded on machine frame in order to hold yarn cones and cops. There is 110cm long yarn traverse round bar used to distribute the yarn throughout the hank width. The machine has worm gear with 100 teeth number. The worm gear is connected with main shaft by belt. A small length rod is welded on the worm gear there is a small length rod. In yarn traverse rod a small key like tongue is connected. During reeling, when the shaft rotates one cycle, one of the worm gear teeth forward one tooth and a small rod on the worm gear pushes the key like tongue welded on yarn traverse rod. Yarn traverse distribute the hank yarn uniformly throughout the width of hank. As shown in Fig.2, when the foot treadle driving unit pushed up and down, the reel which is fixed on the shaft starts reeling the cone or cop yarn into the reeling part and it forms a hank yarn.

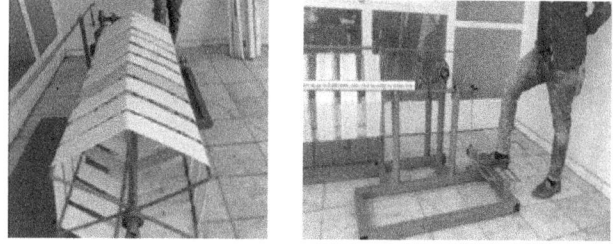

Fig.2　Hank reeling driving unit

3　Results and Discussions

Tab.2 shows, fabricated manual hank reeling machine description. The machine has a dimension of $1.8\text{m} \times 1.1\text{m} \times 1\text{m}$ ($l \times w \times h$). The machine requires one operator and simple maintenance system. It can wind up to 11 hanks per reeling cycle.

Tab.2　Fabricated manual hank reeling machine description

No	Description	Description
1	Type of machine	Manual hank reeling machine
2	Number of hank produced per cycle	11
3	Working condition	Manual
4	Required operator	Single
5	Spinning method	Winding
6	Material input	Cone or cop yarn
7	Material output	Hank yarn
8	Maintenance system used	Oiling and cleaning
9	Swift circumference	1.2meter
10	Length of machine	1.8 meter
11	Width of machine	1.1meter
12	Height of machine	1meter

The main aim of designing and fabricating a manual hank reeling machine which winds more hank per reeling cycle, was achieved by changing some mechanism of single hank reeling machine. In single hank reeling machine, the operator uses his hand to wind hank yarn which is time consuming and tiresome. The present work changes single hank reeling machine design by changing the driving unit from hand driven to foot driven and extends the width of the reel in order to wind up to 11 hanks per reeling cycle. This allows comfort for the operator, because the operator get a possibility to drive the machine by his foot like fabric sewing machine easily by sitting on a chair.

As shown in Fig.3, fabricated manual hank reeling machine can be driven easily by foot like sewing machine treadle. The machine has 80 circumference reels. In one rotation, the reel can wind 80cm hank. The author recorded reel rotation of 5 people in minutes. Each person rotated 10 times and the average reel rotation was 120r/min. Machine could wind 96 meters in a minutes. The length of one hank of cotton is 760m and machine winds full hank within 7.91 minutes per reeling cycle. The new fabricated Manual hank reeling machine can reel 11 hanks within one reeling cycle or within 7.91 minutes. The produced hank yarn is distributed uniformly throughout the width of hank. The cost to fabricate this machine is very cheap compared to automatic electrical hank reeling machine. To fabricate this machine, it costs only around $ 530 as compared to $ 4000 in case of an automatic electrical hank reeling machine.

Fig.3　Front and side view of fabricated hank reeling machine

4　Conclusions

In Ethiopia, textile sectoris playing a very important role in the economic growth of the country, but, most of small－and medium－sized enterprises participated in the sector using traditional methods of knitted and woven fabric manufacturing system. In the country, there is lack of research work have been done before and further studies are required to increase SME productivity. The fabricated hank reeling machine will have a positive impact on the development of the sector and it is proposed to fabricate the hank reeling machine to distribute for the community in the country.

References

[1] MARIE C. Ultimate A to Z companion to 1,001 needle craft terms: applique, crochet, embroidery, knitting, quilting, sewing and more[J]. St. Martin's, 2007.

[2] HUNTER A R. Manufacture of textile yarn[P]. U.S. Patent, 1943, No.2,328,074. 31.

[3] TABATA M A. Spinning method and apparatus for manufacturing yarn from textile fibers[P]. U. S. Patent, 1970, No.3523300.

[4] TAVANAI H, DENTON M, TOMKA J. Direct objective measurement of yarn-torque level[J]. Journal of the Textile Institute, 1996, 87(1):50-58.

[5] HEINRICH B U. Method and means for reeling of yarn[P]. U.S. Patent, 1959, No.2889610. 9.

[6] DOROTHY T. Knitting know-how[M]. Krause Publications, 2012:11.

[7] CHIYUKI S A. Small step by-consideration on the small steps in learning the weaving process and the process of creating teaching materials-with CD-ROM[J]. Kashimura Printing Co. Ltd., 2004:14.

[8] MILIND K. Fundamentals of yarn winding[M]. Cambridge: Woodhead Publishing, 2016.

[9] FABTEX E. Fabtex auto reeling machine[EB/OL]. Irugur Rd, 2019, available at www.fabtexbaler.com, 240/7.

[10] AKASH S, PRAMOD G, SAGAR P, et al. Design and manufacturing of silk winding machine[J]. International Research Journal of Engineering and Technology (IRJET), 2017, 04.

[11] CHELLAMANI K, CHATTOPADHYAY D. Yarn quality improvement with an air jet attachment in cone winding[J]. Indian Journal of Fiber & Textile Research, 2000, 25: 289-294.

[12] ALHAYAT G E, ÖMER F. The art of hand weaving textiles and crafting on socio-cultural values in ethiopian (review)[J]. International Journal of Advanced Multidisciplinary Research, 2018, 5(12).

[13] ITAGAKI J. Gender-based textile-weaving techniques of the amhara in northern Ethiopia[D]. Kyoto: Center for African Area Studies, Kyoto University, 2013.

[14] HENZE M. Tablet-woven curtains from Ethiopia[J]. The Textile Museum Journal, 2000:85-100.

[15]GERVERS M. Cotton and cotton weaving in Meroitic Nubia and medieval Ethiopia [J]. Textile History, 1990, 21: 13-30.

[16]ABDELLA A. Assessment of challenges, opportunities and prospects of textile industry in Ethiopia [J]. The Case of Yirgalem Addis Textile Factory PLC, 2016.

[17]TANNO N A. Automatic reeling machine[P]. U.S. Patent, 1972, No.3656215. 18.

[18]DOMINIQUE M. Reeling machine for forming a hank[P]. U.S. Patent, 1980, No.4185790.

Stress and Strain of Polymer Components During the Bicomponent Electrospining Process

CHEN Jiawei[1,2], ZENG yongchun[1,2]*

[1] Key Laboratory of Textile Science & Technology, Ministry of Education, College of Textiles, Donghua University, Shanghai, 201620, China

[2] Department of Technical Textiles, College of Textiles, Donghua University, Shanghai, 201620, China

* Corresponding author's email: yongchun@ dhu.edu.cn

Abstract: Increasing attention has been paid to the bicomponent electrospining, one of the methods to fabricate bicomponent nanofibers. Different process conditions cause different structures of bicomponent nanofibers and the helical structure was stduied in this study. The thermoplastic polyurethane (TPU) and cellulose acetate (CA) were chosen for spinning and the helical structure was observed by scanning electron microscopy (SEM). The behaviour of the polymer components during electrospinning process was simulated by the bead-chain model. And then the stress and stain along the jet of different components was calculated individually to explain the generation of helical structure. The intrinsic polymer properties and process conditions which have effects on the generation of helical structure were also studied in this research.

Keywords: Electrospining; Bicomponent; Numerical simulation; Stress and strain

1 Introduction

Electrospining is the main method to produce fibers at nanoscales. Recently, the electrospun nanofibers obtained by conventional single polymer gradually fail to meet the versatility requirements and replaced by bicomponent fibers. According to the production process, the bicomponent fibers could mainly be divided to islands-in-sea, sheath-core and side-by-side which play important roles in bioengineering, energy, filtration and so on[1].

Spinning methods, combination of polymer components and mixing ratio have great effects on the final structure of bicomponent fibers. Researchers[2-6] declared the helical structures generated by side by side and offcentered technology. The helical structure of electrospun nanofibers leads to high elastic deformation, porosity and surface area[7] which means endless possibilities. The formation mechanism of helical structures is quite complicated and attracts our interests.

Based on mechanical properties of the components and simulated electric filed, longitudinal stress and strain difference between the components was calculated, which is the most important to explain the formation of helical structures theoretically.

Moreover, other parameters which influence the helical structure, such as applied voltage and elastic modulus of polymers, which make great contributions to the helical structures, are also included in this study.

2 Model for Electrospining Process

The polymer jet could be thought as a viscoelastic non-Newton fluid during the electrospinning process. RENEKER D H[8] and SUN Y F[9] used the bead-chain model, seen in Fig.1, to simulate the fiber motion and predict the path and final diameter. In this study, the model has been modified to calculate the stress and strain of different components individually so that the difference in the interface of polymer components during the bicomponent electrospinning process (only the type of side by side is discussed in this study) could be predicted.

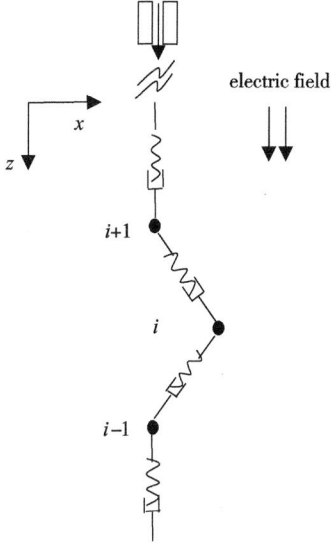

Fig.1　The bead-chain model for electrospining process

2.1　Introduction of Parameters

The electric field is directly introduced to the model for calculation because it has been simulated by Comsol software in our previous work[10]. For the same reason, the polymer combination is set as thermoplastic polyurethane (TPU) and cellulose acetate (CA) to correspond with our previous work. The polymer properties and processing conditions used for calculation are shown in Tab.1.

Tab.1　Specification of property parameters

Electrospinning	CA	TPU
Density(kg/m^3)	1.3×10^3	1.2×10^3
Viscosity(Pa · s)	0.741	0.621
Elastic modulus(Pa)	2×10^5	1×10^5
Surface tension(N/m)	0.035	0.037
Charge(C)	2.83×10^{-9}	2.83×10^{-9}
Voltage(V)	2.2×10^4	2.2×10^4
Collect distance(m)	0.15	0.15

2.2　Stress and Force Equation System

The motion of the bead i could be described by Newton's second law and the definitions of symbols are shown in Tab.2 and the international systems of units are adopted. The explains of the subscript i are ignored.

Tab.2　Definitions of empoled symbols

Symbol	Definition
a_i	Acceleration of the bead i
F_{ei}	Electric field force
F_{ci}	Coulomb force
F_{gi}	Gravity
F_{vi}	viscoelastic force
F_{bi}	Bending restoring force
m_i	Mass
r_i	Vector coordinate
e_i	Charge
E_i	Electric field intensity
g	Gravity acceleration
$\sigma_{i-1,i}$	Stress of the element $(i-1,i)$
G	Elastic modulus
μ	Viscosity
R_{ij}	Distance of the bead i and j
η	Surface tension coefficient
k_i	The fiber part curvature

$$a_i = \frac{d^2 r_i}{dt^2} = (F_{ei} + F_{ci} + F_{gi} + F_{vi} + F_{bi})/m_i \quad (1)$$

$$r_i = ix_i + jy_i + kz_i \quad (2)$$

Where i, j, and k are unit vectors in the Cartesian coordinate system and the x_i, y_i, z_i are the coordinate of the bead i.

The whole equations system which control the behavior of fibers in the electric field are shown as follows:

$$F_{ei} = e_i E_i \quad (3)$$

$$E_i = E_{xi} i + E_{yi} j + E_{zi} k \quad (4)$$

$$F_{gi} = m_i g k \quad (5)$$

$$\frac{d\sigma_{i-1,i}}{dt} = G \frac{1}{l_{i-1,i}} \frac{dl_{i-1,i}}{dt} - \frac{G}{\mu} \sigma_{i-1,i} \quad (6)$$

$$F_{ci} = \sum_{\substack{j=1,N \\ j \neq i}} \frac{e_i^2}{R_{ij}^2} \left(i \frac{x_i - x_j}{R_{ij}} + j \frac{y_i - y_j}{R_{ij}} + k \frac{z_i - z_j}{R_{ij}} \right) \quad (7)$$

$$F_{bri} = \frac{\eta \pi \left(\dfrac{d_{i-1,i} + d_{i,i+1}}{2} \right)^2 k_i}{4 (x_i^2 + y_i^2)^{1/2}} [i |x_i| \text{sign}(x_i) + j |y_i| \text{sign}(y_i)] \quad (8)$$

Where $d_{i-1,i}$ is the diameter of the element $(i-1,i)$, similarly the $d_{i,i+1}$.

The charge possessed by each bead is set as the same

and given out according to the work of Hohman et al.[11] and Feng[12-13].

$$e_i = \pi d_0^2 K E_0 + \pi d_0 l_0 \tau_0 \qquad (9)$$

Where K is the conductivity of the liquid, d_0, l_0, E_0, and τ_0 are the initial diameter, fiber element length, electric strength, and surface charge density at initial state.

Each bead must meet the conservation of mass which means:

$$\rho l_{i,i+1} \frac{\pi d_{i,i+1}^2}{4} = m_0 \qquad (10)$$

Where ρ is the polymer density, m_0 is the initial fiber mass, which is determined by the polymer flow rate.

3 Results and Discussions

With the numerical model described above, we figure out the stress and strain of different components in the same electric field. The final diameter we got was 1.23 μm for TPU and 1.21 μm for CA, which is consistent with the experiments.

The stress and strain of polymer components CA and TPU are calculated and the maximum are chosen for more clear comparison. During the actual spinning process, the only processing condition which is convenient for adjustment is the collecting distance, so we take it as the independent variable of stress and strain. For the two components, seen in Fig.2(a), the stress first keeps increasing rapidly, reaching the peak, and then decreases until the end, which is due to the relaxation effects[8]. Larger stress exists in the CA jet than TPU because of the property differences, such as viscosity and elastic modulus. Fig.2(b) shows obviously that the strain in the TPU jet is much higher than CA jet. The difference could almost be ignored in the first 0.01m because the fiber still keeps straight. The strain difference begins at the point where the stress reaches the maximum and becomes more and more apparent. These stress and strain differences of two polymers in the interface contribute to the helical morphology, seen in Fig.3. The inward contraction of porous part (CA) confirms that the stress and strain difference exists between the two polymer components.

The electric field provides the force to stretch the poly-

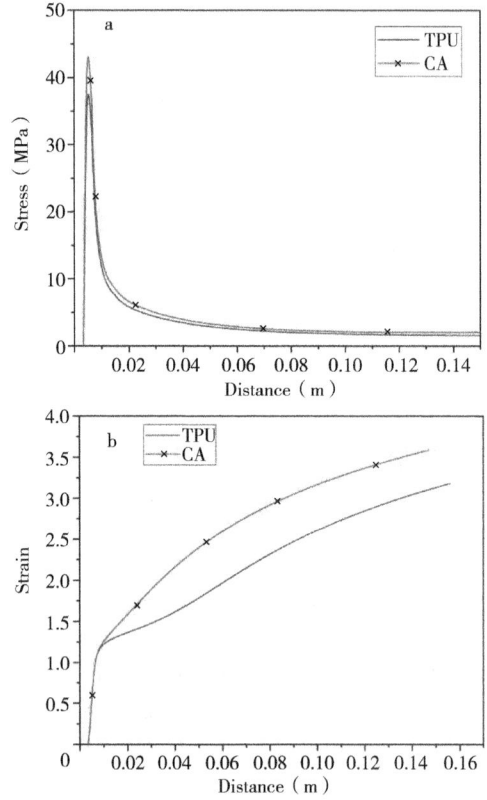

Fig.2 Stress and strain for polymer components (CA and TPU)

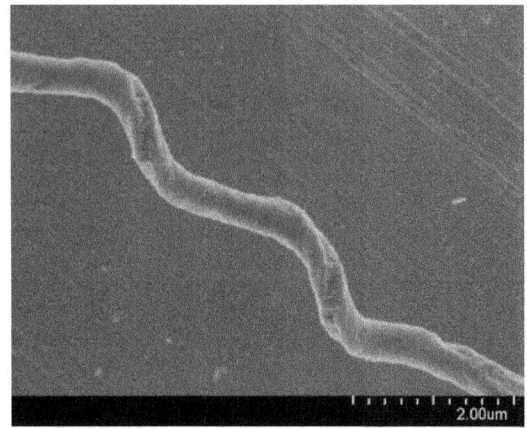

Fig.3 The helical morphology image of CA/TPU bicomponent electrospun fiber

mer jet to produce nanofibers we need. Different voltage applied for spinning process influences the helical structure a lot. The strains in the voltage of 18kV, 22kV and 25kV were calculated and the result is presented in the form of $\varepsilon_{TPU} - \varepsilon_{CA}$ for a clear comparison, seen in Fig.4. It is easy to find that the strain difference becomes higher and higher with the increase of voltage, which means the helical structure becomes more and more obvious. The maximal strain difference occurs later and later with the increase of the applied voltage, which means the collecting distance need to be set higher to provide enough time to generate the helical structure in high voltage. After the maximum, the strain difference decreases because the helix structure needs to increase the number of its turns.

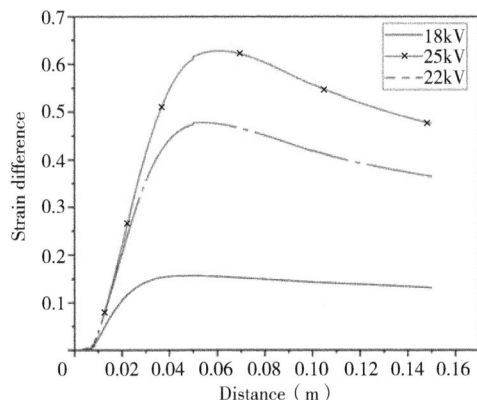

Fig.4   The strain difference in different voltages

The viscosity and elastic modulus of the polymer cannot be separated for analysis by experiment methods but this could be done in the theoretical model. We kept the viscosity same and only changed the elastic modulus to calculate the strain difference, seen in Fig. 5. Higher elastic modulus difference leads to higher strain difference, which means better helical structure. However, compared to the voltage, the influence of elastic modulus is relatively small.

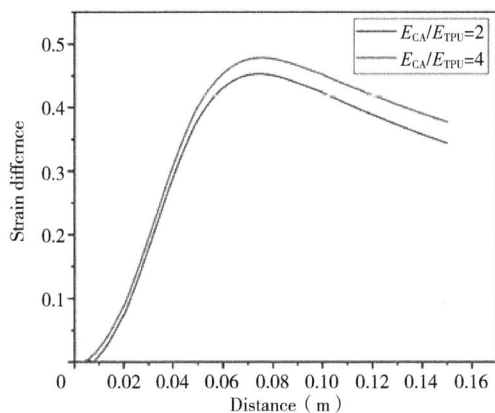

Fig.5   The strain difference of different elastic modulus

4   Conclusions

The intrinsic reason of the helical structure observed in the bicomponent electrospinning fibers is property differences of the components. The stress and strain of the polymer components (CA and TPU) we calculated during the spinning process confirm this conclusion. Also, appropriate processing conditions could enlarge mechanical differences and make the helical structure much more apparent. The results in the voltage of 18kV, 22kV and 25kV show that high voltage has good effects on the generation of helical structure. According to our theoretical calculation, high difference of elastic modulus between the two components also works. Other important parameters, such as mixing ratio, also need to be done for further study. This study of the helical structure is only the beginning of hard work and more will be done in future.

References

[1]CAI M, HE H W, ZHANG X, et al. Efficient synthesis of PVDF/PI side-by-side bicomponent nanofiber membrane with enhanced mechanical strength and good thermal stability [J]. Nanomaterials (Basel, Switzerland), 2018,9 (1).

[2]CHEN S, HOU H, HU P, et al. Polymeric nanosprings by bicomponent electrospinning [J]. Macromolecular Materials & Engineering, 2009, 294(4):265-271.

[3] LIN T, WANG H, WANG X. Self-crimping bicomponent nanofibres electrospun from polyacrylonitrile and elastomeric polyurethane[J]. Advanced Materials, 2010, 17(22):2699-2703.

[4]WU H, BIAN F, GONG R H, et al. Effects of electric field and polymer structure on the formation of helicalnanofibers via coelectrospinning [J]. Industrial & Engineer-ing Chemistry Research, 2015, 54(39):9585-9590.

[5] WU H, ZHENG Y, ZENG Y. Fabrication of helical nanofibers via co-electrospinning[J]. Industrial & Engineering Chemistry Research, 2015, 54(3):987-993.

[6]WU H, ZHAO S, HAN L. Fabrication of CA/TPU helicalnanofibers and its mechanism analysis[J]. Nanoscale Research Letters, 2018, 13(1):104.

[7]LI H, HUANG H, MENG X, et al. Fabrication of helical microfibers from melt blown polymer blends[J]. Journal of Polymer Science Part B: Polymer Physics, 2018, 56(13).

[8]RENEKER D H, YARIN A L, FONG H, et al. Bending instability of electrically charged liquid jets of polymer

solutions in electrospinning[J]. Journal of Applied Physics, 2000, 87(9):4531.

[9]SUN Y, ZENG Y,WANG X. Three-Dimensional model of whipping motion in the processing of microfibers[J]. Industrial & Engineering Chemistry Research, 2011, 50(2):1099-1109.

[10]LI X, BIAN F, LIN J, et al. Effect of electric field on the morphology and mechanical properties of electrospun fibers [J]. 2016.

[11]HOHMAN M M, SHIN M, RUTLEDGE G, et al. Electro-spinning and electrically forced jets. I. stability theory[J]. Physics of Fluids, 2001, 13(8):2201.

[12]FENG J J. The stretching of an electrified non-Newtonian jet: a model for electrospinning [J]. Physics of Fluids, 2002, 14(11):3912-3920.

[13]FENG J J. Stretching of a straight electrically charged visco-elastic jet[J]. Journal of Non-Newtonian Fluid Mechanics, 2003, 116(1):55-70.

Preparation and Properties of Pyrrole-Reduced Graphene Oxide Based Fabric Electrode Materials

ZHANG Suyi[1,2], NIE Wenqi[1,2], DING Xin[1,2]*

[1] *Key Laboratory of Textile Science & Technology, Ministry of Education, College of Textiles, Donghua University, Shanghai, 201620, China*

[2] *Department of Technical Textiles, College of Textiles, Donghua University, Shanghai, 201620, China*

* *Corresponding author's email*: xding@ dhu.edu.cn

Abstract: In order to solve the low electrochemical performance of the graphene oxide (GO) fabric electrode. And the problem of the acid and alkali reducing agent of graphene oxides that damages the fabric substrate. The GO solution prepared by the modified Hummer method was ultrasonically uniformly dispersed, and loaded on the PET fabric by an immersion-drying method. The pyrrole was used as a reducing agent to reduce the GO coated on the fabric to attain N-doped reduced graphene oxide (rGO) fabric electrode. The results show that the resistance of rGO@ PY/PET fabric decreases with the increase of reduction reaction time and temperature at first, then the decreases tend to be gentle. The minimum resistivity that can be achieved by rGO@ PY/PET fabric is $2.11 \cdot 104\Omega/cm^2$. Before and after reduction, the carbon-oxygen ratio (C/O) of rGO@ PY/PET fabric increased from 2.61 to 5.72. Under the condition of reaction temperature of 90℃ and reaction time of 6 hours, the optimal capacitance performance can be obtained, which can reach $26.35mF/cm^2$.

Keywords: Pyrrole reducing agent; N-doped reduced graphene oxide; GO reaction site; Fabric electrode; Supercapacitor

1 Introduction

Flexible supercapacitors (SCs) have many potential applications in various portable electronic devices[1-2]. Fabric electrode has gained much attention and interest due to the growing need for flexible and wearable electronics. The use of flexible material as a base material to load graphene could impart excellent properties to flexible composite electrodes. Such as porous graphene (PG) on carbon cloth via an electrophoretic deposition process was used as electrodes for flexible all-solid-state SCs[3]. The resultant flexible SCs showed high specific capacitance, good cycling stability, and enhanced energy density and power density (1. 64Wh/kg and 0. 67kW/kg). ZHENG[4] et al, have further extended this idea to graphene-paper. Multilayer graphene was directly painted onto a cellulose paper. The areal capacitance of the flexible SCs based on the graphene-paper reached $2.3mF/cm^2$. Furthermore, porous cotton textiles and synthetic fabricated from various polymers were also used as alternative supporting substrates.

Graphene can be prepared by several kinds of methods. For example, chemical synthesis of graphene using graphite, graphite oxide (GO) or other graphite derivatives. The reduction of GO to manufacture graphene can not only be scalable but also provide graphene with machinability and new functions[5]. Various attempts have been made by using reduced graphene oxide materials, specific capacitance of GO increases after reduction and the value has been reported to be 100 – 300F/g. GO sheets consists many oxygen functional groups (e.g. hydroxyl, epoxide, carbonyl, and carboxyl groups) on it. These functional groups significantly alter van der Waals interactions between the layers and endow GO with strong hydrophilicity[6-7] which can help GO coated with fabric easily in aqueous solution by dipping and drying. About effective reduction methods of GO, CUI[8] et al using hydriodic acid as a reducing agent to reduce GO, the atomic ratio of C/O attained 12.5. STANKOVICH[9] et al, using ruthenium as a chemical reducing agent to obtain a single layer graphene through GO, the atomic ratio of C/O was increased from 2.7 to 10.3. The reduction process must involve the removal of oxygen functional groups. The common for graphite oxide to retain a C/O ratio of approximately 1.5 to 2.5[10]. Therefore, reduced materials of significantly higher carbon-oxygen ratio than 2.5 can be considered to have made a reduction effect. However, there are still some problems existence. Acid and alkali are used as the reducing agent which could damage the fabric substrate.

AMARNATH[11] et al heated GO and pyrrole at 95℃ for 15h to prepare rGO composite with C/O atomic ratio of 7.7. When pyrrole used as a reducing agent which can react with GO, embed its own monomer into GO to provide N-doping without damage for fabric-based electrode. Therefore, the method to made reduced graphene fabric electrode was feasible for graphene and pyrrole, but it still need demonstration.

Herein, a strong interfacial adhesion is achieved between GO/PET fabric and pyrrole monomer. Heating treatment with pyrrole monomer could create hydrogen bonds, π bonds and covalent bonds which can react with GO and grant new functional groups on the surface. The process results in a good bonding and avoids self-stacking of GO. In this way, a fabric electrode could be manufactured.

2 Experiments

2.1 Materials

Commercial polyester fabric (PET) with a surface density of 50g/m² was purchased from Jialianda Textile Co., Ltd. Hydroiodic acid reagent (HI), pyrrole monomer, anthraquinone-2-sulfonic acid (AQSA) as a dopant, $FeCl_3 \cdot 6H_2O$, were purchased from Sinopharm Chemical Reagent Co., Ltd.

2.2 Preparation of rGO/PET Fabric Electrode Reduced by Pyrrole

PET fabric was washed sequentially with acetone and deionized water to remove impurities. GO was prepared by chemical oxidation of natural graphite powder according to the modified Hummer's method[12]. Afterwards PET was immersed into an aqueous solution of GO (2mg/mL) with 60 min (labeled as GO/PET), promoting adsorption of GO in aqueous solution on PET by ultrasonic and heating. Then GO/PET was washed with deionized water until pH value reached neutral. Later the GO/PET fabric was immersed into pyrrole monomer and heated by oil bath heating pot. Then rGO @ Py/PET fabric was obtained.

In order to classify the reduction degree of rGO@ Py/PET fabric, HI was selected as the compared reducing agent which could remove oxygen-containing groups in GO to a large extent. The preparation of HI reduced GO/PET composite fabrics is briefly described: The GO/PET fabric was immersed into 40mL (98%) acid reagent (HI), and heated by an oil bath heating pot. After a chemical reduce process in the heating pot rGO @ HI/PET fabric was obtained.

2.3 Characterization

To characterize the electrochemical properties of the rGO/PET fabric electrodes which were manufactured in different reducing agents, temperature and time, and to clarify the effect of reducing GO of the fabric electrode. The degree of reduction of oxygen-containing groups between the GO upper surface and the interlayer was tested by X-ray photoelectron spectrometer (XPS). The fabric was characterized by scanning electron microscopy (SEM, Zeiss, Gemini SEM G500), electrical performance was measured directly using an agilent resistance tester. Electrochemical measurements were carried out using a three-electrode test cell on a CHI 660 D electrochemical workstation (Shanghai Chenghua Co., China) at room temperature. Cyclic voltammetry (CV) was conducted in the range of 0−0.8V with incremental sweep rates (5mv, 10mv, 20mv, 50mv, 100mv). Electrochemical impedance spectroscopy (EIS) was measured under low frequency of 0.01Hz and high frequency of 100000Hz. Galvanostatic charge-discharge (GCD) properties were measured at different current densities with a cutoff voltage of 0−0.8V.

3 Results and Discussions

3.1 Effect of Temperature and Time on the Reduction of GO by Pyrrole

According to the principle of pyrrole to reduce GO,

pyrrole monomer excites electrons at a certain temperature which could not only attack the reaction site on GO to remove the oxygen-containing group, but also react with GO in covalent bond. Manufacture reduction fabric electrode in different temperature in order to evaluate the reduction performance and to direct the following process. Fig. 1 illustrates the preparation of rGO/PET fabric electrode. Fig. 2 (a) shows the change of the resistance value of rGO@Py/PET at different temperatures. Temperature increased from 80℃ to 120℃, the resistivity was decreased significantly under the temperature of 80℃ to 90℃, and as the temperature rising to 100℃ or even higher the resistivity tends to be flat or rising again. It indicated that the low temperature is insufficient to stimulate pyrrole monomer to reduce GO which leads poor performance directly. When the temperature rises to 90℃, the pyrrole monomer can be used as a reducing agent.

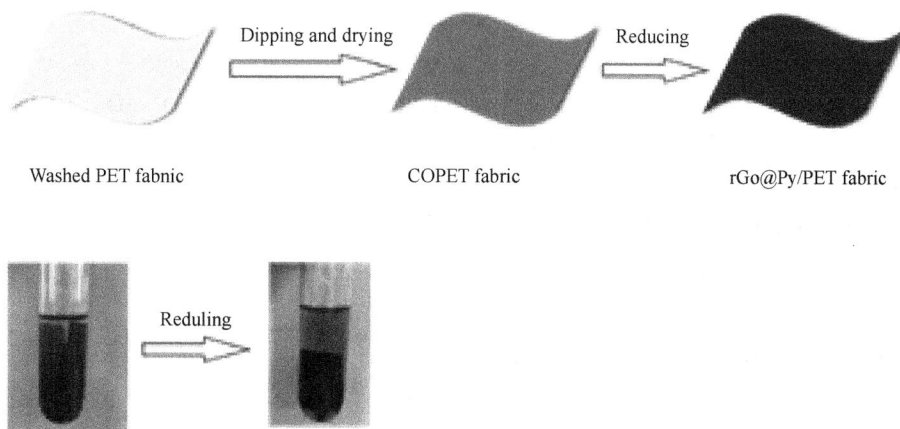

Fig.1　Scheme to the preparation of rGO@Py/PET fabric

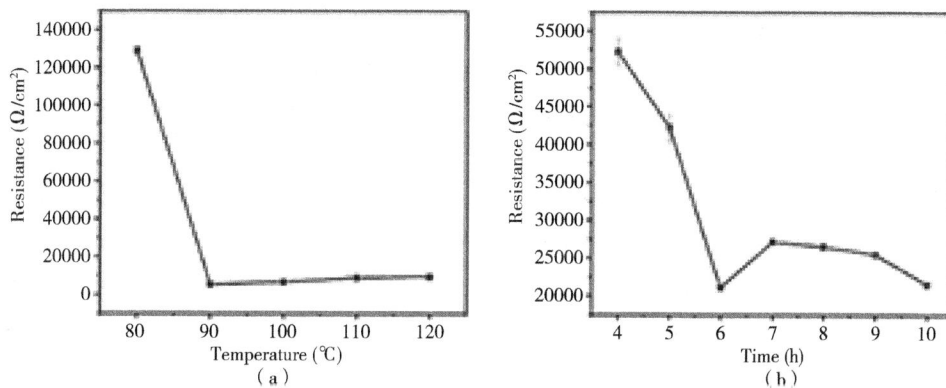

Fig.2　(a) Resistance of rGO@Py/PET at different reduction temperatures; (b) Resistance of rGO@Py/PET at different reaction time

In order to determine the optimum reduction time, keeping temperature at 90℃, the reaction time are from 4-10h. The resistivity of pyrrole reduced fabric is shown at Fig.2 (b). From the result, the resistivity of the rGO@Py/PET is reached $2.11 \times 10^4 \Omega/cm^2$ when the reaction time is 6h. Meanwhile, the resistivity is increased when the reaction time exceeds 6h. The capacitance of fabric electrode in different reaction time is shown in Fig.3. It can be seen that when reaction time is 6h the capacitance reaches the maximum value $26.35 mF/cm^2$. As the extension of reaction time, the capacitance decreases. Its capacitance performance is poor due to the nonporous structure which could block ion movement. Considering the degree of reduction and capacitance, the

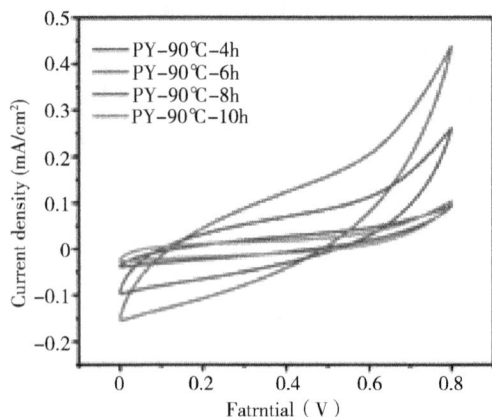

Fig.3　Capacitance performance of rGO @ Py/ PET at different reduction temperatures

Fig.4　(a) SEM image of rGO@ Py/PET fabric the magnification is of 800 times; (b) SEM image of rGO @ Py/PET fabric the magnification is of 3000 times

optimal reduction condition of rGO@ PY/PET is determined as temperature of 90℃ and reaction time of 6h.

3.2　The Reduction Degree of rGO@Py/PET

After manufacturing the reduced fabric in the optimal conduction, the degree of reduction which can reveal the electrode mechanism and oxygen-containing groups between the surface and interlayer of GO was tested by X-ray photoelectron spectrometer (XPS) that shows the analysis of C, O, N elements contained of rGO@ HI/ PET fabric and rGO@ Py/PET fabric. The rGO@ HI/ PET fabric was prepared in the optimal conduction (100℃, 4h) which has low resistance of $1097\Omega/cm^2$. The C/O ratio of rGO@ HI/PET fabric electrode which was calculated to be 5.40 and has an extremely high C contains. The C/O ratio of rGO@ Py/PET fabric electrode which was calculated to be 5.72 and a new N peak appeared in it. Compared with the low C/O ratio of GO/PET fabric is 2.61. Both of the reduced fabrics have increased their C/O ratio by reduction of GO to a certain extent. The loaded polypyrrole on the fabric electrode which could be clearly observed by scanning electron microscopy (SEM) of rGO@ Py/PET fabric that shown in Fig.4. The small amount of layered polypyrrole is deposited on the surface of the fiber which means the C/O ratio of the rGO@ Py/PET fabric is introduced by the five-membered heterocyclic rings of C and N in the pyrrole oligomer, and the corrected C/O ratio is 4.7. Different from rGO@ HI/PET fabric, the covalent bond of rGO@ Py/PET fabric electrode could offer high pseu-

do-capacitance and provide the reaction site which could easily react with active substance in the following process. Compared with the GO/PET fabric which has an obviously C =O peak shows in Fig.5 (a), the C = O band of rGO@ HI/PET fabric shown in Fig.5 (b) shifted from 286.8eV to 285.5eV, which means the GO/PET fabric remained oxygen-containing bonds of graphene and rGO @ HI/PET fabric have already removed C =O by reduction. This also happened on reduction of rGO @ Py/PET, the C = O bond was vanished by the reaction between pyrrole and GO, new peak was shown in Fig.5 (c) at 398.9eV and 401.2eV, which attributes to the new-born bond C—N and C =N respectively.

3.3　Electrochemical Performance of the rGO @ Py/PET Fabric Electrode

The electrochemical properties of the reduced fabric directly determine the internal resistance loss of the capacitor. The conductivity of rGO @ HI/PET fabric reached $1097\Omega/cm^2$. According to Nyquist plots in Fig.6 (a), it can indicate the equivalent series resistance (ESR) of rGO @ Py/PET fabric electrode, the intercept of the high-frequency region with the real axis, is rather low, and the small semi-circle region indicats a rapid charge transport. The high slope of the curve indicates easy ion diffusion at the low frequency region. Fig.6 (b) shows the capacitance of rGO@ Py/ PET and rGO @ HI/PET, although rGO @ HI/PET fabric electrode has a relatively high capacitance, the accompanying polarization phenomenon is relatively serious. After reduction the capacitance of rGO@ Py/PET reached $26.35mF/cm^2$. The capacitance of rGO@ Py/

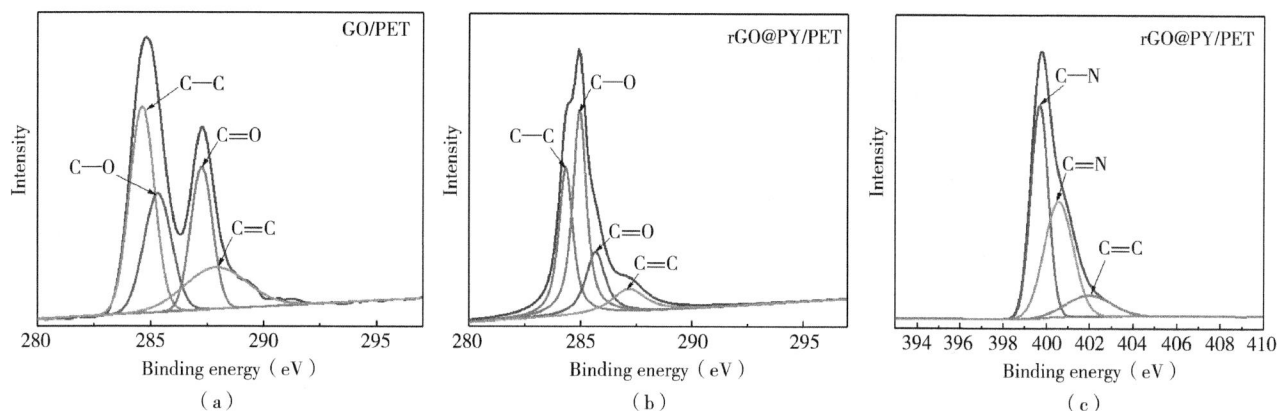

Fig.5 （a）The C1s core-level XPS spectra of GO/PET fabric；（b）The C1s core-level XPS spectra of rGO@HI/PET fabric；（c）The C1s core-level XPS spectra of rGO@Py/PET fabric

PET fabric was measured at different sweep speeds exhibited in Fig.6（c）which tends to increase steadily when the sweep speed increases from 5mv/s to 100mv/s. Simultaneously, the high capacitance is due to the fast ion-to-electron transfer between the electrode and the electrolyte, which can also be verified by Fig.6（a）. Fig.6（d）shows the Galvanostatic charge-discharge （GCD）properties of rGO@Py/PET and rGO@HI/PET, the former has a longer discharge time and a smaller voltage drop which means the former is much better as a capacitor electrode material. The GCD curve of rGO@Py/PET fabric at different current densities maintains an approximately symmetrical triangle with a high coulombic efficiency of 78.6%.

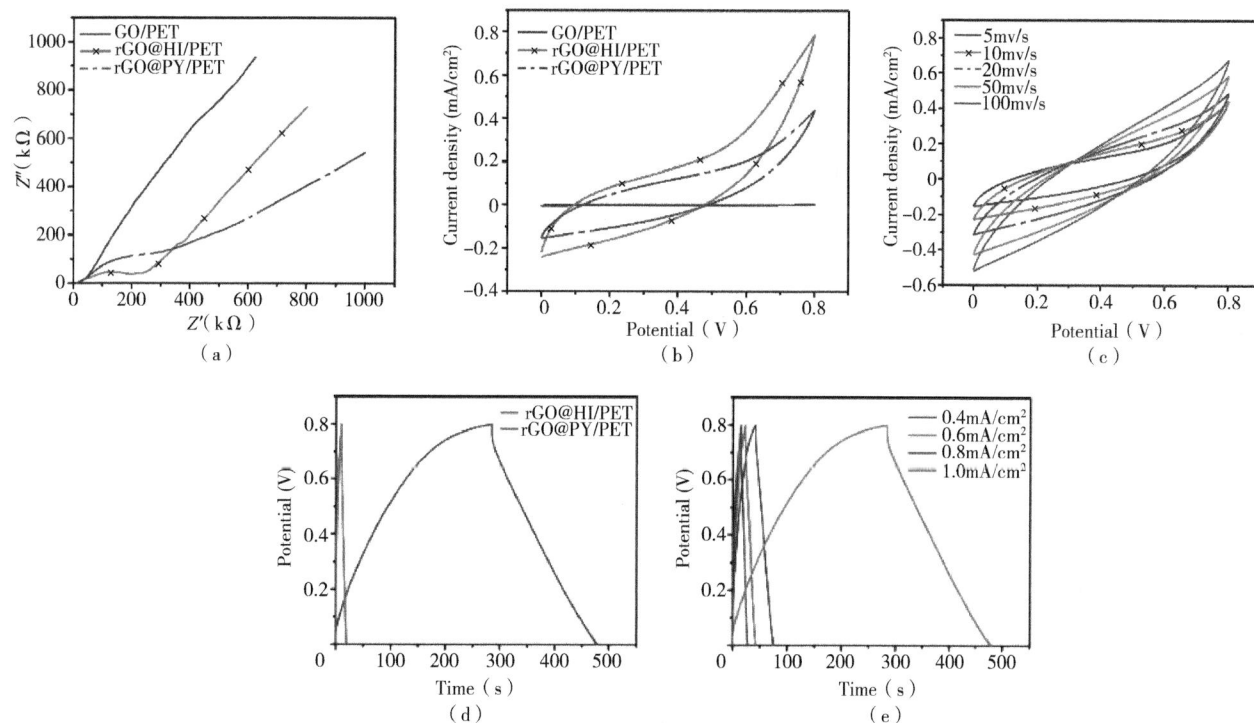

Fig.6 （a）EIS of GO/PET, rGO@HI/PET and rGO@Py/PET；（b）CV of GO/PET, rGO@HI/PET and rGO@Py/PET；（c）CV of rGO@Py/PET at different sweep speed；（d）GCD of rGO@HI/PET and rGO@Py/PET at current density of 1mA/cm²；（e）GCD of rGO@PY/PET at different current density from 0.4mA/cm²to 1.0mA/cm²

4　Conclusions

In this study, we demonstrate the feasibility and superiority of preparing pyrrole as a reducing agent for electrodes. During the reduction new peak of C—N and C=N were generated on the rGO@Py/PET fabric electrode. The C/O ratio of rGO@Py/PET fabric was increased from 2.61 to 5.72 after reduction, which could inject high pseudo-capacitance in fabric electrode. The prepared rGO@Py/PET fabric electrode exhibits good capacitance at 26.35mF/cm^2. Compared with the use of HI as a reducing agent, the obtained rGO@HI/PET electrode has obvious polarization phenomenon and short cycle charge and discharge time. rGO@Py/PET has good cycle charge and discharge performance with a high coulombic efficiency of 78.6%. There is no such significant damage to the fabric substrate indicats that pyrrole has demonstrating potential and availability as a fabric electrode material. The application value of using pyrrole as a reducing agent for preparing an electric double layer and a pseudo-capacitance mixed electrode is proved.

References

[1]SUGIMOTO W,YOKOSHIMA K,OHUCHI K,et al. Fabrication of thin-film, flexible, and transparent electrodes composed of ruthenic acid nanosheets by electrophoretic deposition and application to electrochemical capacitors[J]. Electrochemical Society,2006,153, A255.

[2] NAM K T, KIM D W, YOO P J, et al. Virus-enabled synthesis and assembly of nanowires for lithium ion battery electrodes[J]. Science, 2006,312,885.

[3]WANG S,PEI B,ZHAO X,et al. Highly porous graphene on carbon cloth as advanced electrodes for flexible all-solid-state supercapacitors[J]. Nano Energy,2013,2, 530-536.

[4]ZHENG G Y,HU L B,WU H,et al. Paper supercapacitors by a solvent-free drawing method[J]. Energy Environ, 2011, 4,3368.

[5]PARK S,RUOFF S R. Chemical methods for the production of graphenes[J]. Nanotechnology, 2009,4,217.

[6]PAREDES J I,VILLAR-RODIL S,MARTÍNEZ-ALONSO A, et al. Graphene oxide dispersions in organic solvents[J]. Langmuir,2008,24,10560-10564.

[7].DREYER R D, PARK S, BIELAWSKI C W, et al. The chemistry of graphene oxide[J]. Chemical Society Reviews, 2010,39,228-240.

[8]MAO S,YU K,CUI S,et al. A new reducing agent to prepare single-layer, high-quality reduced graphene oxide for device applications[J]. Nanoscale,2011,3 (7):2849-2853.

[9]STANKOVICH S,DIKIN D A,PINER R D,et al. Synthesis of graphene-based nanosheets via chemical reduction of exfoliated graphite oxide[J]. Carbon, 2007, 45 (7):1558-1565.

[10] AKBAR B, CECILIA M, MUGE A, et al. Structural evolution during the reduction of chemically derived graphene oxide[J]. Nature Chemistry,2010,2,581-587

[11]AMARNATH C A,HONG C E,KIM N H,et al. Efficient synthesis of graphene sheets using Pyrrole as a reducing agent[J]. Carbon,2011,49 (11):3497-3502.

[12]REN W, CHENG H M.The global growth of graphene[J]. Nanotechnology,2014,9,726.

Evaluation of Polypropylene Melt-Blown
Nonwoven as Oil Sorbents

ABEER Alassod[1,2], XU Yanfang[1], XU Guangbiao[1*]

[1] *Key Laboratory of Textile Science & Technology, Ministry of Education, College of Textiles, Donghua University, Shanghai, 201620, China*

[2] *Department of Textile Engineering, Mechanical and Electrical Engineering University, Damascus, Syria*

* *Corresponding author's email*: guangbiao_xu@ dhu.edu.cn

Abstract: This article reports oil sorption behavior of polypropylene (PP) melt-blown nonwoven (sorbents) using oils. The experimental results showed that oil sorption capacity of the motor oil and soybean oil were in the range (11.3–17.2) g/g and (10.99–13.6) g/g, respectively. Oil retention capacity of both oils after 24 hours was over 65%; it was observed the main role of voids among fibers to determine oil sorption capacity. Sorbent 3 exhibited the highest sorption capacity (g/g) at porosity (85.78%) for both oils followed by Sorbent 2 and Sorbent 1, respectively. Besides, the analysis adsorption mechanism of PP melt-blown nonwoven was systematically studied based on wettability properties and structure, which revealed to have high oleophilic and hydrophobic properties. The water contact angle values were above 130° for all sorbents, while oil droplet disappeared quickly from the surface.

Keywords: Polypropylene; Nonwoven; Oil sorption; Retention; Surface energy

1 Introduction

Recently, among these polluted phenomena, oil spillage has received increasing attention due to a significant environmental problem and economic losses. Generally, oil spill occurs during production and transporting, exploring, storage, using, operation failures, equipment breakdown, and natural disasters[1-2]. In this case, to clean and recover the spilled oil, many advanced methods are developed and applied in oily water remediation including mechanical separation, chemical separation, in situ burning of oil, and biological remediation[3-5]. Among these existing methods, sorbents are considered one of the essential countermeasures in marine oil-spill response. The characteristics of ideal sorbent material for oil spill clean-up should have the following properties: oleophilic, high absorption capacity, good absorption selectivity, and reuse, lower density than water[6-7].

PP melt-blown nonwoven is widely used for oil spillage clean up due to low density, hydrophobicity, high oil sorption capacity[6, 8]. This characteristic has received extensive attention as proper candidate sorbents and ideal solution of many problems due to melting blown advantages such as cost-effective, simple methods of production, low energy consumption, the large scale of fabric and eco-friendly[8-9]. Although most of the published studies indicated that the PP melt-blown nonwoven had massive oil sorption capacity. However, less of them mention porosity, mean pore size, and the contact angle in order to understand the oil sorption mechanism fully[8]. In this work, a comparative study on terms of oil sorption capacity, retention of three different thickness made by PP melt-blown nonwoven. Additionally, the analysis of the oil sorption mechanism was studied by way of investigating the morphological structure, porosity, and the contact angles of the sorbent.

2 Experiments

2.1 Materials

Polypropylene melt-blown nonwoven assorbents were obtained from Shanghai Xin Lou Filter Materials Co, Ltd. (Shanghai, China). The morphology of sorbents was SEM-TM3000 (Hitachi, Japan). The thickness of sorbents was measured according to the ISO 9073-2 standard method, the tests were repeated for ten times. Mean pore diameter was recorded from capillary flow porometry. The following equation calculated the porosity of all polypropylene melt-blown nonwoven:

$$\eta = \left(1 - \frac{m}{Z \times A \times \rho}\right) \times 100\% \qquad (1)$$

Where η is the porosity of PP melt-blown nonwoven, and m, Z and A are the mass, thickness, and area of per unit measured pp melt-blown nonwoven, respectively. ρ is the density of polypropylene fiber which is $0.91\,g/cm^3$. Properties of the sorbent is listed in Tab. 1. Two types of oils, namely motor oil and soybean oil, were used. The densities and surface tensions of those oils were examined using dynamic contact angle tester (DCAT1), and ASNB2 Digital Rotary Viscometer tested the viscosities. Every test was repeated three times to obtain an average value. The test temperature was maintained at $22-24\,°C$. The properties of the studied oils are listed in Tab. 2.

Tab.1 Properties of PP melt-blown nonwoven

	Thickness (mm)	Calculated porosity (%)	Mean pore diameter (μm)
1	5.6	89.6	9.51
2	2.4	88.1	15.61
3	0.85	85.78	19.96

Tab.2 Physical properties of studied oils

Oil	Soybean oil	Motor oil
Viscosity (mPa · s)	63.0	250
Density (g/cm³)	0.90	0.86
Surface tension (mN/m)	31.0	28.8

2.2 The Experimental Procedure of Determination Sorption Capacity

400mL of oil was poured into 1000mL beaker. A known mass of sorbents was placed above the surface of the oil and allowed to absorb oil for 15 minutes to reach equilibrium oil sorption level, after that the sorbent was lifted and put over a wire mesh to drain for 60 seconds, the wet sorbent was weighed. The oil sorption and retention capacity of sorbents were calculated according to equation as follows:

$$\text{Oil sorption capacity} = \frac{m_{f15} - m_f}{m_f} \qquad (2)$$

$$\text{Oil retention capacity} = \frac{m_{f24} - m_f}{m_{f15} - m_f} \times 100\% \qquad (3)$$

Where m_f is the dry sorbent mass (g), m_{f15} is the wetted sorbent mass at 15 min dipping (g), m_{f24} is the mass of wetted sorbent (g) at 24h dripping.

2.3 Adsorption Mechanism of Polypropylene Melt-blown Nonwoven

Oil sorption by nonwoven occurs via two mechanisms: adsorption by the interaction of oil molecules on the fiber surface through Van Der Waals forces and oil molecular besides capillary action through capillary bridges between fibers due to pore structure[8, 10]. So, it is entirely based on the structure of the sorbent and wettability properties. For better understanding the oil sorption capacity behavior, the sorbents were investigated by using the scanning electron microscopy and the contact-angles with oil and water as it is explaining as follows.

2.3.1 Determination Surface Energy

Wettability properties of sorbents were described by contact angle values of liquids. The contact angle was taken from optical contact angle meter (OCA15EC, Data physics, Germany). Static sessile drop method and captive bubble method were adopted in this test the process was repeated for 5 times and took the average. Surface free energy of sorbents was calculated based on OWRK method[11]. Three different liquids are used: water, ethanol, and ethylene glycol, the surface tension of liquids and contact angle are given in Tab. 3.

Tab.3 Properties of liquids solution for surface energy measurement of sorbents

Liquid type	Surface tension (mN/m)	Polar component (mN/m)	Dispersion component (mN/m)
Water	72.10	52.20	19.90
Ethylene glycol	48.00	29.00	19.00
Ethanol	22.10	4.60	17.50

3 Results and Discussions

3.1 Sorption Capacity and Retention

As is seen from Fig.1, sorbents with the motor oil register the higher sorption capacity. Besides, it was interesting to note the highest sorption capacities of sorbents registered by sorbent 3 for motor oil and soybean oil are 17.2g/g and 13.6g/g, respectively followed by sorbent 2 and sorbent 1. This can be explained as the following: more pores (voids) were available to provide large space for oil to be stored in the room as the oil reservoir with porosity (85.78%) and pore diameter (19.96μm) for sorbent 3, however, when the web of melt-blown nonwoven porosity was increased from range (88.1% ~ 89.6%) and decreased pore diameter (15.61 − 9.51μm) oil sorption capacities decreased for sorbent 1 and sorbent 2, respectively. Indicating that suitable porosity and pore diameter were significant parameters in determining high oil sorption capacity. This difference is due to different viscosity (η) and surface tension (γ) of liquids. It was observed that the motor oil has a high viscosity (250MPa · s) and lower surface energy (28.8mN/m) compared with soybean oil (63MPa · s, 31mN/m), respectively.

The high viscosity of oil gives two opposite effects: Increasing sorption by improving adherence of oil on sorbents surface or decreasing sorption by making oil penetration to voids (pores) difficult. For melt-blown nonwoven, sorbent plays a significant role in sorption capacity, the observation is in agreement with the literature[7-8]. As shown in Fig.2. Among all sorbents, it is clear that sorbent 1 which had the highest porosity (89.6%) and small pore diameter (9.51μm) had the highest retention ratio of the motor oil and soybean oil

were 82% and 76% respectively as compared to sorbent 2 and sorbent 3. This explanation, according to apart of oils flees from some large voids.

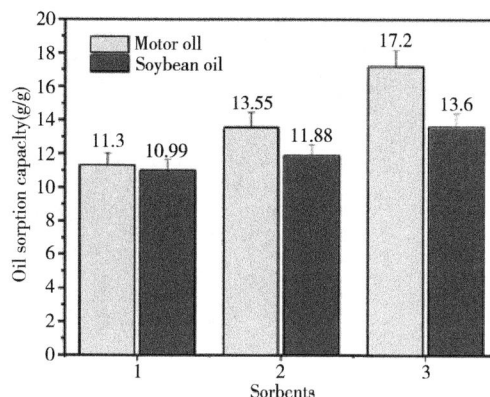

Fig.1 Oil sorption capacities of PP melt-blown nonwoven

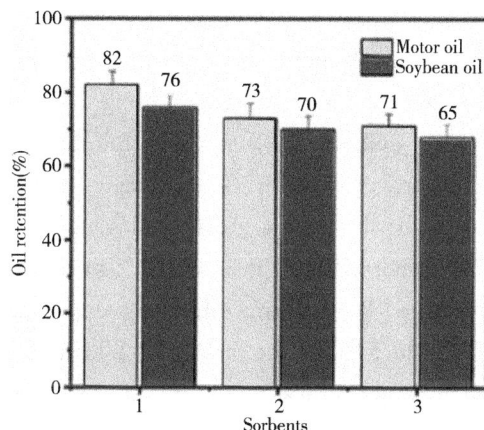

Fig.2 Oil retention capacity of PP melt-blown nonwoven

3.2 Analysis of Oil Sorption Mechanism

3.2.1 Surface Morphology of the Sorbents

The surface appearance of sorbents was examined by SEM as seen in Fig.3; many various voids appeared on the surface; this porous structure provided sufficient storage space for absorbed oil. It can be seen a wide range of pore size distribution of PP melt blown nonwoven range from 9.51 − 19.96μm. This kind of porous structure supplies physical barrier and high sorption capacity due to the large porous surface, which enables hold a high amount of oil. In this case, as presented in Fig.3 (c). Sorbent 3 has a large and accessible void space to provide the good performance of adsorption according to Darcy's law[8, 12], with porosity about 85.78%, mean pore diameter 19.96μm followed by sorbent 2 with porosity about 88. 1%, mean pore diameter 15. 61μm and sorbent 1 with porosity about 89.6%, and mean pore diameter 9.51μm, respectively.

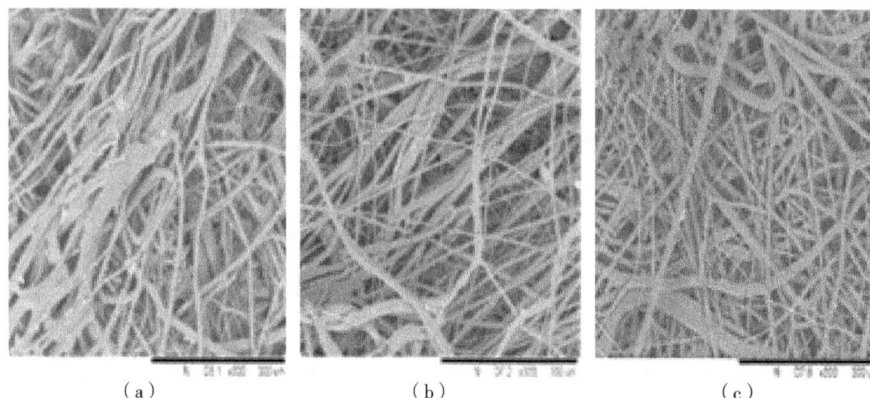

Fig.3　SEM images of the structure of PP melt-blown nonwoven sorbents: (a) Sorbents 1; (b) Sorbents 2; (c) Sorbents 3

3.2.2　Contact Angle and Wettability

Hydrophobic and oleophilic properties of PP melt-blown nonwoven sorbents were examined using the contact angle of water and tested oils as listed in Tab.4. It was observed clearly that water contact angle values are above 130°, for all sorbents. As for static contact angles between oils and sorbents, it was noted that oil contact angles measured by the captive bubble method ranging from 43.22° to 54,56° for both oils. Which indicate high wettability properties.

Tab.4　Contact angle of water and experimental oils on PP melt-blown nonwoven[a]

Sorbent	Contact angle (°)		
	Water	Soybean oil	Motor oil
1	137.82 (2.12)	54.56 (2.65)	47.16 (2.38)
2	136.28 (1.43)	51.66 (1.88)	43.80 (1.72)
3	137.72 (1.94)	48.72 (1.52)	43.22 (1.55)

[a] Values within parentheses refer to the standard deviations for five repeats.

3.2.3　Surface Energy

Tab.5 gives the surface free energy of sorbents with their (water, ethylene glycol, and ethanol) contact angle. As evident in Tab.6, there is no significant dif ference in surface energies observed among the sorbents. All of them close quite to surface energy of selected oils (20－30mN/m) and far below that of water (72mN/m), indicating to excellent hydrophobicity with the static contact angles of water droplet up 130°. However, when comparing the surface energies between sorbents, the lowest surface energy was found with sorbent 3 followed by sorbent 2 and sorbent 3, respectively.

Tab.5　Surface free energy of PP melt-blown nonwoven sorbents

Sorbent	Contact angle (°)			Surface energy (mN/m)
	Water	Ethylene glycol	Ethanol	
1	139.5	102	26.3	43.35
2	138	99.50	36.10	39.90
3	138	108.9	27	37.22

Surface energy plays anessential feature of a sorbent to separate oil from polluted water. At low surface energy sorbent where the adhesive forces between oil molecules and sorbent surface are much higher than that between water molecules and sorbent surface oils absorbed quickly into the porous structure of sorbent in water by capillary force. While water is hard to displace oil droplets due to large contact angle value and a high energy barrier.

4　Conclusions

Findings reveal that sorbents had good oil sorption capacity. Sorption capacity for motor oil and soybean oil in the range (11.3－17.2) g/g, and (10.99－13.6) g/g, respectively. Oil retention capacity for both oil after 24 hours was over 65%. The results indicate the importance of porosity and oil properties to have a significant effect in determining oil sorption behavior and oil retention. All sorbents showed higher oil sorption capacity and retention with motor oil as compared to soybean oil. The low surface energy and high-water contact angles indicate the excellent oleophilic and hydrophobic properties of PP melt-blown nonwoven sorbents. Beside the combination between porosity and wettability properties is the primary mechanism to oil adsorption.

References

[1] PANG Y, WANG S, WU M, et al. Kinetics study of oil sorption with open-cell polypropylene/polyolefin elastomer blend foams prepared via continuous extrusion foaming[J]. Journal of Polymers for Advanced Technologies, 2018, 29: 1313-1321.

[2] THILAGAVATHI G, KARAN C P, DAS D. Oil sorption and retention capacities of thermally-bonded hybrid nonwovens prepared from cotton, kapok, milkweed and polypropylene fibers[J]. Journal of Environmental Management, 2018, 219:340-349.

[3] CUI Y, XU G, LIU Y. Oil sorption mechanism and capability of cattail fiber assembly[J]. Journal of Industrial Textiles, 2014, 43:330-337.

[4] DEMIREL Y T, YATI I, DONMEZ R, et al. Clean-up of oily liquids, fuels and organic solvents from the contaminated water fields using poly (propylene glycol) based organogels [J]. Journal of Chemical Engineering, 2017, 312:126-135.

[5] DURGADEVI N, SWARNALATHA V. Polythiophene functionalized hydrophobic cellulose kitchen wipe sponge and cellulose fabric for effective oil-water separation[J]. J RSC Advances, 2017, 7: 34866-34874.

[6] WEI Q, MATHER R, FOTHERINGHAM A, et al. Evaluation of nonwoven polypropylene oil sorbents in marine oil-spill recovery[J]. Journal of Marine Pollution Bulletin, 2003, 46:780-783.

[7] ZHU H, QIU S, JIANG W, et al. Evaluation of electro spun polyvinyl chloride/polystyrene fibers as sorbent materials for oil spill cleanup[J]. Journal of Environmental Science & Technology, 2011, 45:4527-4531.

[8] GUO M, LIANG H, LUO Z, et al. Study on melt-blown processing, web structure of polypropylene nonwovens and its BTX adsorption[J]. Journal of Fibers and Polymers, 2016, 17:257.

[9] LIU L, XU Z, SONG C, et al. Adsorption-filtration characteristics of melt-blown polypropylene fiber in purification of reclaimed water [J]. Journal of Desalination, 2006, 201: 198-206.

[10] CHOI H M, KWON H J, MOREAU J P. Cotton nonwovens as oil spill cleanup sorbents[J]. Journal of Textile Research, 1993, 63:211-218.

[11] DONG T, XU G, WANG F. Adsorption and adhesiveness of kapok fiber to different oils[J]. Journal of Hazardous Materials, 2015, 296:101-111.

[12] RENGASAMY R, DAS D, KARAN C P. Study of oil sorption behavior of filled and structured fiber assemblies made from polypropylene, kapok and milkweed fibers [J]. Journal of Hazardous Materials, 2011, 186:526-532.

Experimental Study on the Wicking Effect of Fiber Slivers Applied to Irrigation Based on the Principle of Plant Nutrient Transportation

ZHONG Chaoqun[1], BAI Zhiqing[1], ZHANG Yao[1],
QIU Zhizhe[1], DAI Tianjiao[1], GUO Jiansheng[1]*

[1] *College of Textiles, Donghua University, Shanghai, 201620, China*

* *Corresponding author's email: jsguo@dhu.edu.cn*

Abstract: As a large agricultural country, the utilization rate of agricultural irrigation water in China is less than 50%, which causes great waste of water resources. Therefore, the improvement of water-saving irrigation technology has become the focus of domestic research. Based on the principle of plant nutrient transportion, this paper explored the wicking performance of fiber slivers and proposed an adaptive capillary-irrigation technique for agroforestry, especially suitable for arid regions. The effects of fiber type, bundle density on the wicking properties of fiber slivers were investigated. By selecting fiber materials with better wicking performance, the water delivery length test and water delivery volume test were carried out at suitable bundle density. The experimental results show the ramie fiber slivers performed well in wicking height, water delivery length and water delivery volume when the bundle density was 0.424g/cm^3. Specially, the water delivery length could reach 3 meters in 40 hours, and the amount of water transfer to soil could reach 25mL in 6 hours. The ramie slivers as acrylic tube fillers can achieve adaptive capillary irrigation without a pump, demonstrating that the fiber slivers are viable and potential option for irrigation of common dry crop plants.

Keywords: Bionics; Agricultural irrigation; Fiber slivers; Wicking height; Delivery length

1 Introduction

According to insights, the utilization rate of rural irrigation water in China is less than 50%, which in Israel is as high as 95%[1-2]. The gap with developed countries is partly reflected in the backwardness of water-saving irrigation technology. Therefore, in the case of shortage of agricultural water, it is urgent to develop various efficient irrigation and water supply technologies[2-3], compared to traditional water-saving irrigation techniques such as drip irrigation, sprinkler irrigation, channel anti-seepage, etc. The capillary micro-irrigation method is a new technology that can save up to 60% of water[4-5]. For capillary micro-irrigation technology, the materials and geometric parameters used to transfer water to the rooting zone are very important[5], directly affecting the efficiency of water-saving irrigation. Capillary irrigation is based on the capillary principle of liquid flowing in porous media[6]. The accumulation of fibers in the fiber aggregate can form enough capillaries to spontaneously transport liquid into the porous system through capillary force[7], fiber slivers with excellent wicking properties are very suitable for transferring water to rooting zone by capillary irrigation. In this paper, the principle of plant nutrient transportion was carried out to explore the fiber-sliver water-saving irrigation system. The effects of fiber type, bundle density on the wicking performance of fiber slivers were discussed in detail. The feasibility of using fiber slivers as a capillary irrigation system to transfer water to the rooting zone of plants was verified.

2 Experiments

2.1 Materials

A series of fiber slivers (cotton fiber slivers, ramie fiber slivers, viscose fiber slivers, Tencel fiber slivers, Modal fiber slivers, polylactic acid (PLA) fiber slivers, and polyester fiber slivers) with a mass basis weight of $3g/cm^3$ were prepared by spinning technology. Water repellent finishing agent was provided by Xibao Textile Co., Ltd. (Suzhou). Potassium dichromate was supplied by Xinkang Pharmaceutical Chemical Co., Ltd. (Tianmen). The Acrylic tubes were obtained from Ruicheng Plastic Materials Co., Ltd. (Dongguang).

2.2 Water Contact Angle Test

The wicking performance of the fiber slivers is mostly related to the contact angle between the fibers and the water. The contact angle test of various fibers is carried out using the OCA40 Micro automatic video micro contact angle measuring instrument for studying the hydrophilic property of each fiber. Specifically, the combed fiber slivers were placed on the glass slide in parallel and evenly. The test schematic appears in Fig.1.

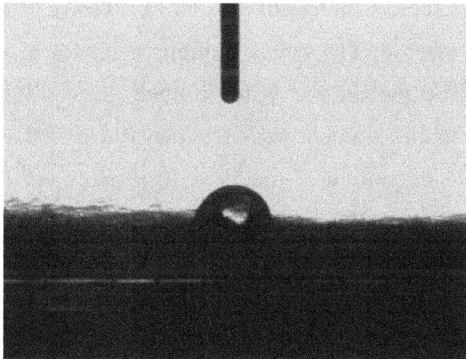

Fig.1　Optical contact angle measurement process

2.3 Vertical Wicking Height Test

The vertical wicking test was designed to explore the wicking properties of various fibers intuitively for selecting the most suitable irrigation fill material. Different types of fiber slivers have been placed into the acrylic tube to investigate the effect of fiber type and bundle density on the wicking properties of the fiber slivers. The schematic of the capillary performance test device is shown in Fig.2, Using potassium dichromate solution as a color developer, the wicking heights of the fiber slivers were observed within 30 minutes, and the amount of wicking liquid of the fiber sliver was measured using an analytical balance.

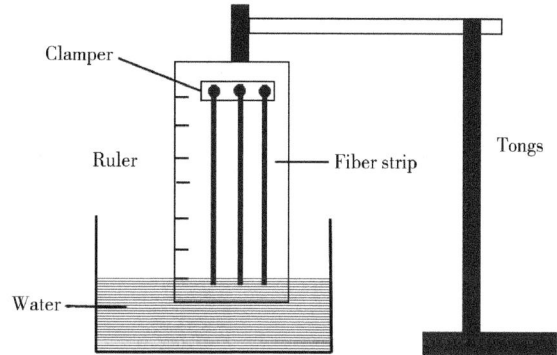

Fig.2　Schematic of the capillary performance test device

2.4 Water Delivery Length Test

The water delivery length experimentwas performed to explore whether the fiber-based irrigation system can achieve the required water delivery length in actual farmland. The fiber slivers with relatively good wicking performance were selected for the water delivery length test. One end of the fiber slivers was placed in a container filled with water (the water was dyed by potassium dichromate), and the fiber slivers wrapped with an acrylic tube (bundle density of $0.424g/cm^3$) were supported by a support frame. In the horizontal state, the delivery length of water in the fiber slivers was measured every 20 minutes, and the relationship between the delivery water distance and the delivery water time was recorded.

2.5 Water Delivery Volume Test

The water delivery volume test was performed to explore whether the adaptive irrigation system based on fiber slivers can provide the amount of water needed for plant growth, and to confirm its ability of automatically regulation and control water delivery. Notably, one end of the fiber sliver was immersed into the liquid. When the water over flowed at the other side of sliver, this side was inserted into the beaker full of soil. And the weight of the cup was recorded in every 20 minutes.

3　Results and Discussions

3.1　Principle of Wicking Effect

Plants can transport nutrients to the leaves lying on the height of more than a dozen meters without extra mechanical pumps. Plant nutrient transport phenomena provided the inspiration for designing and developing adaptive capillary irrigation system. There are many conduits in the xylem of plants. The inner wall of the duct has strong hydrophilic property. The surface tension of the inner wall and the liquid can overcome the liquid gravity and adhesion work, thereby enabling the liquid to be transported.

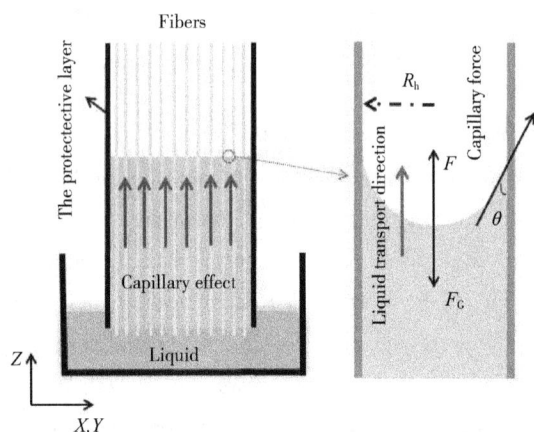

Fig.3　Schematic diagram of active transport of textile-based materials

Based on the principle of plant nutrient transportation, the application of textile fiber aggregates in water-saving irrigation was demonstrated. In Fig. 3, a sufficient number of elongated capillary tubes were formed between the fibers in the textile fiber assembly, and the liquid moved up to a certain height in virtue of the capillary action, until the capillary force and the liquid gravity formed an equilibrium.

According to the Washburn-Lucas equation, the wicking rate of liquid flow in porous media can be derived from Equation (1).

$$\frac{\mathrm{d}l}{\mathrm{d}t} = \frac{r\gamma_{\mathrm{LA}}}{4\eta l}\cos\theta_{\mathrm{d}} \qquad (1)$$

Where r is the capillary radius, θ_{d} is the dynamic contact angle, η is the liquid viscosity, and l is the distance of the capillary covered by the liquid front in

time t.

When the capillary force is balanced with the weight of the liquid, the wicking length can be calculated from Equation (2).

$$l = \frac{2\gamma_{\mathrm{LA}}\cos\theta}{r\rho g} \qquad (2)$$

Where ρ is the liquid density and g is the gravity acceleration.

3.2　The Characterization of Fiber Hydrophilic Properties

The water contact angle test of various fiber aggregates is shown in Tab.1.

Tab.1　Water contact angle of various fibers

Fiber type	LA(°)	RA(°)	Average value(°)
Viscose	64.9	73	68.95
Tencel	83.3	83.3	83.3
Modal	84.2	81.2	82.7
PLA	109.3	107.5	108.4
Cotton	57.6	59.3	58.45
Polyester	115.4	116.6	116
Ramie	74.9	75	74.95

The Tab. 1 shows that polyester has the largest water contact angle, followed by PLA, Tencel, Modal, ramie, viscose. The cotton exhibits a minimum contact angle. The greater the water contact angle, the worse the hydrophilic properties. It is concluded that the hydrophilic properties of the fiber aggregates are cotton, viscose, ramie, Modal, Tencel, PLA, polyester, from strong to weak.

3.3　Effect of Fiber Type and Structure on Wicking Height

3.3.1　Effect Offiber Material Type

The bundle density of the fiber aggregate was controlled to be 0.424g/cm³, and the wicking properties of various materials were investigated.

As shown in Fig. 4, the slope of the relationship between the wicking height and the wicking time of various types of fiber slivers was high at the beginning, and then the slope gradually became smaller. The reason is that the weight of the liquid inside the fiber slivers increased under the wicking effect, causing the increased resistance of the capillary inside the fiber slivers, which thus reduced the speed of wicking.

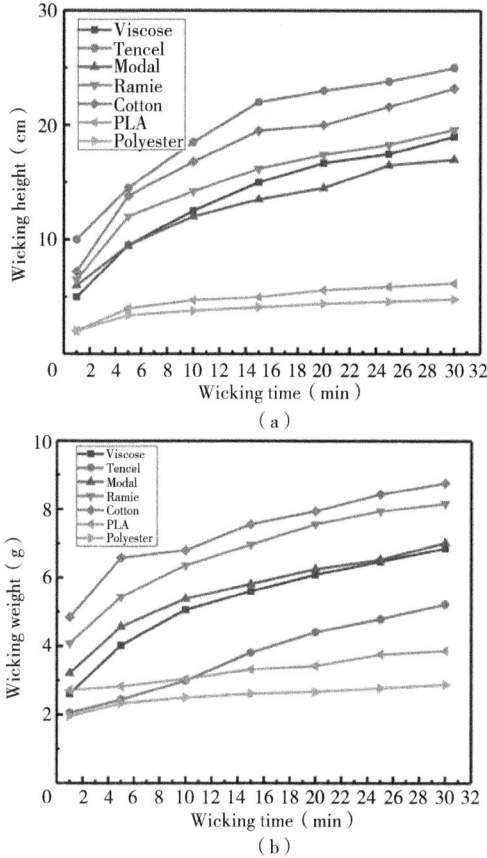

Fig.4　Wicking performance of different materials（a）
Wicking height;（b）Wicking weight

Different fiber materials have different hydrophilic properties and cross-sectional morphologies, so the wicking properties are different. In order to meet the demand for irrigation water supply, it is necessary to be able to achieve a certain wicking length while achieving a larger wicking liquid weight. Under the comprehensive consideration, the cotton fiber slivers, ramie fiber slivers and viscose fiber slivers are more suitable as the candidate material of the adaptive capillary effect system of textile fiber aggregate.

3.3.2　Effect of Fiber Bundle Density

It can be seen from the Fig.5 that the wicking height of the fiber aggregate and the weight of the wicking liquid increased with the increase of the bundle density. The increase of the bundle density leads to a decrease in the capillary radius. The smaller capillary radius facilitates the wicking process, increasing the wicking height.

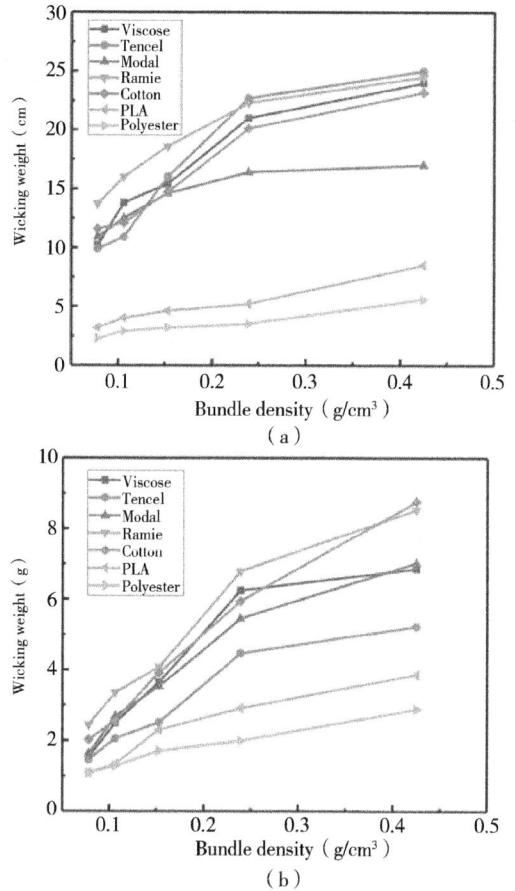

Fig.5　Influence of bundle density on wicking performance;
（a）Wicking height;（b）Wicking weight

The wicking weight and the bundle density of the seven kinds of fibers had an excellent linear relationship within a certain range. The bundle density is m, and the wicking amount is G_m. The specific regression equation and correlation coefficient were shown in Tab.2.

Tab.2　Regression equations for seven fiber wicking weights and bundle densities

Fiber type	Regression equation	R2
Viscose	$Gm = 15.2715m + 1.09471$	0.8399
Tencel	$Gm = 10.9916m + 0.94328$	0.8960
Modal	$Gm = 15.0312m + 1.05088$	0.9351
Ramie	$Gm = 17.6382m + 1.50726$	0.9394
Cotton	$Gm = 19.5769m + 0.72137$	0.9829
Polyester	$Gm = 7.56625m + 0.88514$	0.8236
PLA	$Gm = 5.03284m + 0.78019$	0.9824

3.4 Water Delivery Length Test

The bundle densities of cotton fiber slivers, ramie fiber slivers and viscose fiber slivers were controlled to be 0.424g/cm^3, and the water delivery length test was carried out. The test results appear in Tab.3. After testing for 6 hours, the water delivery length of the three types of fiber slivers reached more than 1.2m. And it could reach more than 2.4m after 40 hours, of which the ramie fiber sliver was close to more than 3m. It showed that the cotton slivers, ramie fiber slivers and viscose fiber slivers in water delivery length and water delivery speed had a high application value in real irrigation owing to their good performance.

Tab.3 Water delivery length test (cm)

Time(h)	2	6	10	20	30	40
Cotton	63	99	112	189	221	245
Ramie	71	120	153	221	268	313
Viscose	61	113	137	203	222	286

3.5 Water Delivery Volume Test

The bundle densities of cotton slivers, ramie fiber slivers and viscose fiber slivers were controlled to be 0.424g/cm^3. The test results are shown in Fig.6.

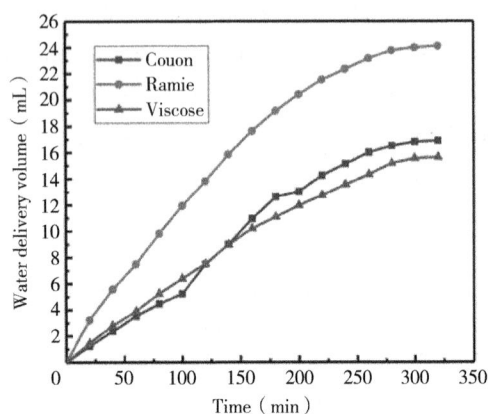

Fig.6 Water delivery volume test

The amount of liquid transferred from the ramie fiber slivers to the soil was greater than that of the cotton fiber slivers and the viscose fiber slivers, as shown in Fig.6. This is because the longer length of the ramie fiber is beneficial to the formation of a smooth capillary channel, which is advantageous for long-distance wicking get on. In Fig.6, the curve gradually became flat with the soil water content increased and the soil matrix suction decreased. When the soil matrix suction does not reach the capillary holding capacity of the filling material, the water pipe will continue to transport water, and then achieve the balance. It can maintain the proper moisture of soil water, which shows that the capillary water-saving irrigation system has the ability to automatically regulate soil moisture.

4 Conclusions

Based on the principle of plant nutrient transportion the fiber-sliver water-saving adaptive capillary irrigation system was designed and discussed, and the experiment results showed that the system is feasible in agricultural irrigation. The ramie fiber slivers having a bundle density of 0.424g/cm^3 were selected as the water delivery material of the capillary irrigation system. It had strong superiority in water delivery height, water delivery length and water delivery volume, which is beneficial to irrigation applications. The fiber sliver irrigation system could ensure sufficient water volume while ensuring the transportation distance. The fiber slivers adaptive capillary irrigation system can actively irrigate water when the plant needs water. When the soil around the root of the plant was saturated, it could actively suppress water, automatically adjusted the water and used water efficiently, and has the advantages of low energy consumption and environmental protection.

References

[1] RUI J L, ZHI X C. Experimental study on water-saving irrigation system in arid areas on the basis of the principle of capillary water conveyance system[J]. Science & Technology of Qinghai Agriculture & Forestry, 2016.

[2] WEN J X, XIANG X W, LIU L S, et al. Current condition and developing tendency of water-saving irrigation technology in China[J]. Chinese Agricultural Science Bulletin, 2016.

[3] KRATKY B A. Design of a capillary, sub-irrigation hydroponic lettuce cultivation system for a remote area[C]. National Agricultural Plastics Congress, 1990.

[4] JIQ N, JUNFU X, YIFU S, et al. Optimization and application of filler for capillary water feeder[J]. Journal of Irrigation and Drainage, 2012.

[5] ABIDIN M S B Z, SHIBUSAWA S, BUYAMIN S, et al. Intelligent control of capillary irrigation system for water-saving cultivation[C].Control Conference, IEEE, 2015.

[6] STAPLES T L, SHAFFER D G. Wicking flow in irregular capillaries[J]. Colloids & Surfaces A, 2002, 204(1): 239-250.

[7] PATNAIK A, RENGASAMY R S, KOTHARI V K, et al. Wetting and wicking in fibrous materials[J]. Textile Progress, 2006, 38(1):1-105.

A Flexible Yarn-Like Lithium Ion Battery

QIAN Xiangyu[1], QIU Ruoyu[2], QIU Yiping[1],
WU Zhuangchun[2]*, ZHANG Kun[1]*

[1] *College of Textiles, Donghua University, Shanghai, 201620, China*

[2] *College of Science, Donghua University, Shanghai, 201620, China*

* *Corresponding author's email*: kun.zhang@ dhu.edu.cn

Abstract: At present, the design and fabrication of conventional energy storage devices are heavily hindered in terms of deformation scenarios. To solve this problem, a new generation of energy storage devices should possess flexibility, convenience, compactness and weaving. Therefore, the best way to solve that is the yarn-like lithium ion battery (LIB). Here, the anode and cathode materials were sequentially deposited onto the stainless steel conductive yarns by a dip-dry method. A layer of gel electrolyte was coated on each electrode material. The prepared positive and negative yarns with gel electrolyte were wound together and assembled into a one-dimensional linear battery core. The 7cm long yarn-like lithium ion battery assembled by natural graphite, lithium iron phosphate and gel electrolyte can output a capacity of 0.45mAh. Even in the performance test of 50 cycles, the capacity retention rate was 54.2%. The as-prepared flexible battery can provide a broad prospect for smart wearable devices.

Keywords: Flexible lithium ion batteries; Gel electrolyte; Yarn-Like; Wearable devices; Safety; Low cost

1 Introduction

With the development of wearable devices, such as smart watch, wearable tiny healthcare devices and the smart clothes, the demand for flexible and wearable energy powering system is more and more urgent[1-2]. The traditional lithium ion batteries are rigid and thus not suitable for varies of wearable electronics. Recently, many attempts have been made to design and fabricate flexible energy storage devices using materials and products of the existing technology. Among these strategies, the prepared yarn-like lithium ion battery not only can widely adapt to daily deformations such as bending and folding, but also can adapt to complex and extreme shape changes such as rolling and twisting[3-8]. WANG et al. reported a fibrous lithium ion battery made of intrinsically conductive polymer should be immersed in liquid electrolyte, which is not suitable for wearable applications[9]. HU et al. have prepared a yarn-shaped lithium ion battery by twisting the fibrous positive and negative electrodes and sealing them in a heat-shrinkable tube. However, the battery needs to be injected with electrolyte at the end, so there are also existing safety issues[10]. HANG Qu et al. deposited the active material onto the flexible substrate one by one by dipping-drying, and then wound the electrode material by a self-made mold. The entire process is completed in a glovebox[11]. Prof. PENG and colleagues successfully developed various flexible 1D yarn-shaped LIBs by combining aligned multi-walled carbon nanotube fibers with electrode materials including MnO_2[12], silicon[13], and $LiMn_2O_4$[14]. But the price of materials is relatively expensive. In general, the current preparation of yarn-like lithium ion batteries is still in the research and development stage. Therefore, it is critical to find materials with good safety performance, flexible, low cost, and stable output performance after assembly into a 1D structure battery, especially for high-yield wearable electronic applications.

In this work, we adopted the method of dipping-drying, which has simple process and high safety. The stainless steel yarns were used as flexible substrates to which the positive and negative electrode active materials were attached. The positive and negative active materials were selected from cheap and non-toxic lithium iron phosphate and natural graphite which are commonly used in the market. The electrolyte was a gel electrolyte in which PVDF-HFP was a polymer substrate. The prepared yarn-like lithium ion battery could provide a amount of specific capacity and stable performance.

2 Experiments

2.1 Reagents

Lithium iron phosphate (LFP, Shenzhen Tianchenghe Technology Co., Ltd.), propylene carbonate and ethylene carbonate (Shanghai Aladdin Biochemical Technology Co., Ltd.), lithium tetrafluoroborate (Shanghai Binlian Industrial Co., Ltd.), acetone (Shanghai Lingfeng Chemical Reagent Co., Ltd.), N-methyl-2-pyrrolidone (NMP, Shanghai Aladdin Biochemical Technology Co., Ltd.), natural graphite, poly vinylidenefluoride—hexafluoropropylene (PVDF—HFP, $M_w = 400000$, Sigma-Aldrich), polyvinylidene fluoride (PVDF Arkema HSV900), carbon nanotube.

2.2 Preparation of Yarn-Shaped Negative Electrode and Positive Electrode

Three stainless steel conductive yarns (SSCY) were woven as a flexible substrate. 960mg of natural graphite, 120mg PVDF, 120mg CNT were dissolved in 4mL of NMP by a magnetic stirrer for 10 hours. Stainless steel conductive yarn coated with graphite referred as SSCY@G. 1120mg of lithium iron phosphate, 140mg PVDF, 140mg CNT were dissolved in 4mL of NMP. Stainless steel conductive yarn coated with LFP referred as SSCY@LFP.

2.3 Preparation of Gel Electrolyte

The dip-dry method was also applied to the preparation of the gel electrolyte. 0.125g $LiBF_4$ was dissolved in 12.5mL of acetone solvent. The mixture was stirred at 48℃ for 2 hours by a thermostatic magnetic stirrer. Then added 0.47mL ethylene carbonate, 0.53mL propylene carbonate and 0.708g of PVDF—HFP to the beaker. The entire process is completed in a glovebox with water and oxygen less than 5mg/kg.

2.4 Preparation of Yarn-Like Full Battery

The experimental flow chart is shown in Fig.1. Yarn-like electrodes were both prepared by dipping and coating method in the glovebox.

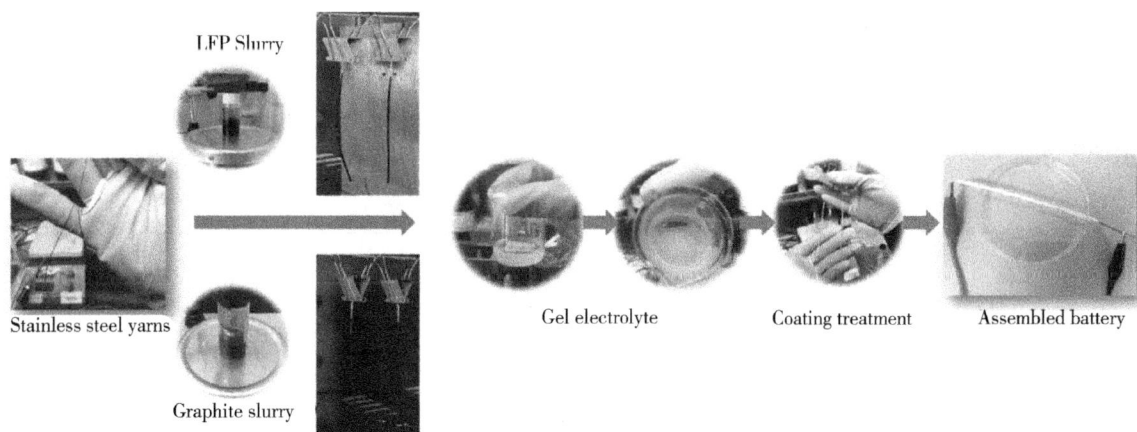

Fig.1 Schematic of the procedure for preparing electrodes and fabricating a yarn-like battery with stainless steel conductive yarns acting as a flexible substrate and current collector

2.5 Characterization of Materials

Scanning Electron Microscope (SEM) was used to examine the morphologies of anode, cathode and electrolyte. The galvanostatic charge/discharge measurements, rate performance and constant-capacity cycling tests were conducted using a LAND battery testing system at room temperature. The electrochemical impedance spectroscopy (EIS) was measured by an electrochemical workstation (CHI660E, Shanghai Chenhua Instrument Co., Ltd.).

3 Results and Discussions

3.1 Morphological Properties of Electrodes and Electrolyte

Fig.2 (a) is the microscopic appearance of the yarn under SEM. It can be clearly seen that after cleaning, the surfaces of the entangled in parallel stainless steel conductive yarns are very smooth. From Fig.2 (b), the CNTs are quite uniformly dispersed in the positive electrode slurry, which is sufficiently mixed with the LFP. Here, the CNT as a conductive material of the electrode material can improve the electron migration ability. From the Fig.2 (c), the surface of the graphite having a sheet structure is dispersed with carbon nanotubes. Fig.2 (d) is the morphology after coating of the electrolyte. According to the SEM images, we can clearly see that there are a large number of pores in the internal structure of the prepared gel electrolyte. The increase in the number of micropores enhances the specific surface area inside the gel-state polymer electrolyte, providing more channels for the transport of ions, which improves the ionic conductivity of the gel-state polymer electrolyte. In addition, the interpenetrating microporous structure can reduce the resistance of ion transport and polymer chain scission migration, and also increase its ionic conductivity[15].

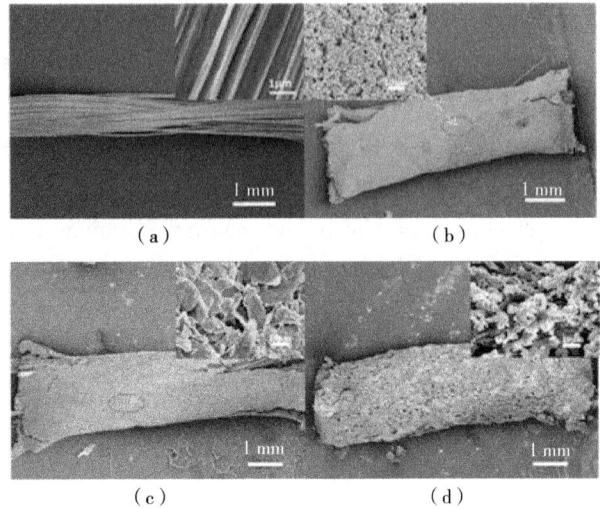

(a)   (b)

(c)   (d)

Fig.2   SEM images of (a) Pure stainless steel conductive yarn; (b) SSCY @ LFP; (c) SSCY @ G; (d) Gel electrolyte coated on the electrode

3.2 Electrochemical Properties of the Yarn-Like LIB

From Fig.3 (a) and Fig.3 (b), it shows that the performance of gel electrolyte is gradually deteriorated during the standing process. Because plasticizers play a multitude of roles in the gel electrolyte: reducing the crystallinity of the polymer, increasing the mobility of the polymer segment, reducing the activation energy of ion transport, promoting the dissociation of lithium salts and increasing the concentration of free ions and so on[16]. Therefore, it is not difficult to conclude that when the solvent (acetone) in the electrolyte mixed solution is completely volatilized, the battery performance prepared at this time should be the best.

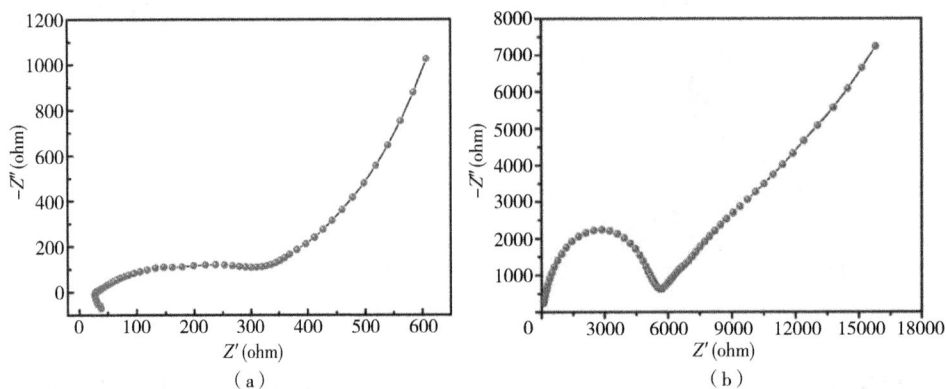

(a)

(b)

Fig.3   (a) Nyquist plots of the assembled battery after standing for 1 hour; (b) Nyquist plots of the assembled battery after standing for 24 hours

Fig.4(a) and Fig.4(c) show the charge/discharge test of an assembled yarn-like lithium ion battery (N/P ratio is 1.1). With discharge platform between 3.0V and 3.2V, the battery has a voltage curve similar to a coin-type full battery, which rationalizes the design principle of the yarn-like lithium ion battery. As can be seen from Fig.4(b), the battery can output a specific capacity of 67.2mAh/g. The yarn-like LIB [Fig.4(d)] having an effective length of 7cm and a diameter of 1.76mm is much smaller than the diameter of the charging line of the Apple mobile phone. This 7cm long yarn-like LIB is capable of storing a capacity of 0.45mAh at 0.1 C. From the first cycle to the end of the 50th cycle, the capacity retention of the battery was 42.78% and the coulomb efficiency was 54.2%.

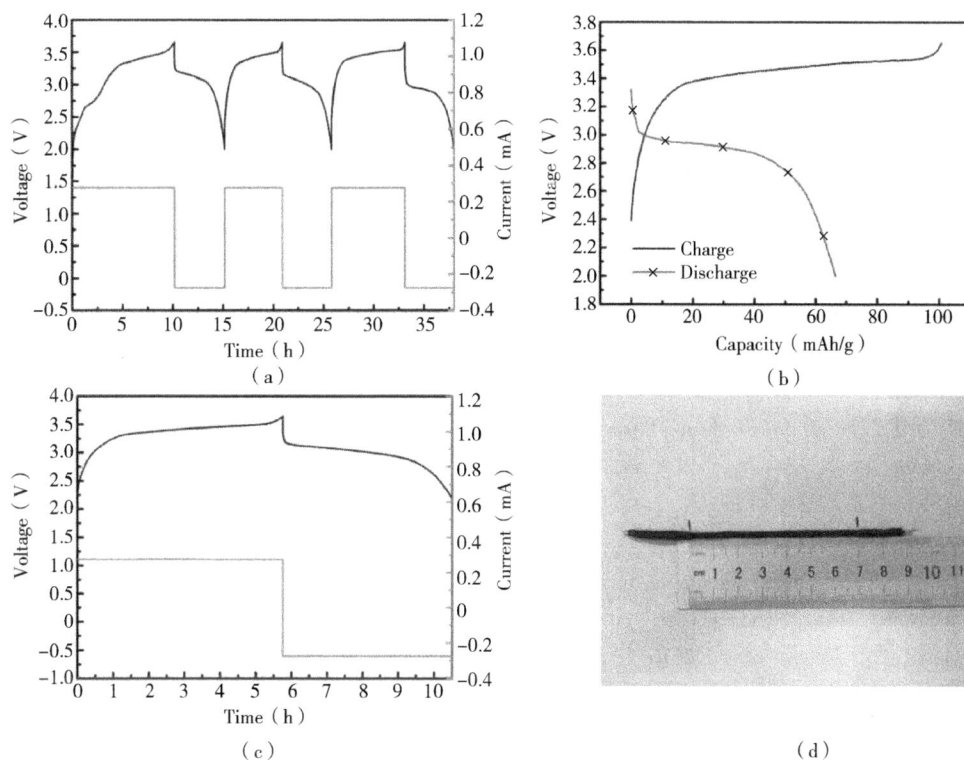

Fig.4 (a) Yarn-like LIB voltages and currents in the first 3 cyclic charge-discharge tests at 0.08C; (b) Voltage profiles of the assembled yarn-like LIB at the 2nd cycle at 0.08C; (c) Voltages and currents curve at the 2nd cycle; (d) Photograph of the yarn-like LIB with length of 7cm

4 Conclusions

In summary, we assemble a fiber-like lithium ion battery with high flexibility by using a stainless steel yarn as a base material of the electrode. Different from the traditional lithium ion battery, the assembled battery can maintain good electrochemical performance under high deformation conditions such as bending and knotting. At the same time, the electrolyte of the battery is a gel electrolyte rather than a liquid, thus avoiding the disadvantages of the lithium ion battery being flammable, explosive and leaking during use. Therefore, this is a simple preparation process, material safety, low cost and practical preparation method. The diameter of the finished product can be made thinner than the ordinary data line, and can reach less than 2mm. As a result, a yarn-like lithium ion battery of about 7cm in length can output a capacity of 0.45mAh. Under the charge and discharge conditions of 0.2C, the assembled battery can maintain a capacity retention rate of 54.2% after 50 cycles. Therefore, the as-prepared simple, safe and low cost yarn-shaped lithium ion battery has a great potential in the powering system of smart wearable electronics.

References

[1] HAN Y, ZOU M, LV W, et al. Three-dimensional ionic conduction in the strained electrolytes of solid oxide fuel cells[J]. Journal of Applied Physics, 2016, 119(17):1307-1338.

[2] LU X, YU M, WANG G, et al. Flexible solid-state supercapacitors: design, fabrication and applications[J]. Energy & Environmental Science, 2014, 7(7):2160-2181.

[3] ZHAI S, KARAHAN H E, LI W, et al. Textile energy storage: structural design concepts, material selection and future perspectives[J]. Energy Storage Materials, 2016, 3: 123-139.

[4] KYEREMATENG N A, BROUSSE T, PECH D. Microsupercapacitors as miniaturized energy-storage components for on-chip electronics[J]. Nature Nanotechnology, 2016, 12 (1):7.

[5] LIU Z, LI H, ZHU M, et al. Towards wearable electronic devices: a quasi-solid-state aqueous lithium-ion battery with outstanding stability, flexibility, safety and breathability[J]. Nano Energy, 2017, 44.

[6] LIU W, LIU N, SHI Y, et al. A wire-shaped flexible asymmetric supercapacitor based on carbon fiber coated with metal oxide & polymer[J]. J Mater Chem A, 2015, 3(25): 13461-13467.

[7] TIAN L, YAO Y, NING L, et al. Wearable fiber-shaped energy conversion and storage devices based on aligned carbon nanotubes [J]. Nano Today, 2016, 11 (5): S1748013216301803.

[8] XIN C, ZHANG C, ZHANG S, et al. Application of carbon fibers to flexible, miniaturized wire/fiber-shaped energy conversion and storage devices[J]. Journal of Materials Chemistry A, 2016, 5(6).

[9] WANG J, TOO C O, WALLACE G G. A highly flexible polymer fibre battery[J]. Journal of Power Sources, 2005, 150 (150):223-228.

[10] WANG Y, CHEN C, XIE H, et al. 3D-printed all-fiber li-ion battery toward wearable energy storage[J]. Advanced Functional Materials.

[11] HANG Q, XIN L, SKOROBOGATIY M. All-solid flexible fiber-shaped lithium ion batteries[J]. J Electrochem Soc, 2018, 165(3):A688-A695.

[12] JING R, LI L, CHEN C, et al. Twisting carbon nanotube fibers for both wire-shaped micro-supercapacitor and micro-battery[J]. Advanced Materials, 2013, 25 (8): 1155-1159.

[13] WENG W, SUN Q, ZHANG Y, et al. Winding aligned carbon nanotube composite yarns into coaxial fiber full batteries with high performances[J]. Nano Letters, 2014, 14(6): 3432.

[14] YE Z, WENYU B, XUNLIANG C, et al. Flexible and stretchable lithium-ion batteries and supercapacitors based on electrically conducting carbon nanotube fiber springs[J]. Angewandte Chemie, 2015, 53(52):14564-14568.

[15] KREBS H, LE Y, SHIRSHOVA N, et al. A new series of cross-linked (meth)acrylate polymer electrolytes for energy storage[J]. Reactive & Functional Polymers, 2012, 72 (12):931-938.

[16] STALLWORTH P E, FONTANELLA J J, WINTERSGILL M C, et al. NMR, DSC and high pressure electrical conductivity studies on liquid and hybrid electrolytes[J]. Journal of Power Sources, 1998, 81(9):739-747.

The Effect of Plasma Modification on Electrical Properties of CNT Film and Its Nanocomposites

LIU Xiaohua[1,2], XU Fujun[1,2], QIU Yiping[1,2]*

[1] *Key Laboratory of High Performance Fibers & Products, Ministry of Education, Donghua University, Shanghai, 201620, China*
[2] *College of Textiles, Donghua University, Shanghai, 201620, China*

* Corresponding author's email: ypqiu@ dhu.edu.cn

Abstract: Although the large scaled carbon nanotube (CNT) film with dense CNT packaging exhibiting outstanding performances is recognized as a promising nanomaterial for advanced composites, its inactive surface which is lack of oxygen-containing functional groups limits the formation of interfacial bonding and leads to the poor mechanical and electrical properties. In this study, we propose atmospheric pressure helium/oxygen plasma jet to modify the surface of the CNT film. Furthermore, composites with the control and the modified CNT film impregnated in epoxy are fabricated. The gauge factor of CNT film increases from 1.2 to 1.5 after plasma treatment, though the slightly decreased electrical conductivity. The resultant composites revealed the higher sensitivity (gage factor ~ 3.1) with an improvement of 34.8%, and a linear piezo resistive response within a large strain (~ 5%), demonstrated the better strain sensing properties of the CNT film/epoxy composites.

Keywords: Plasma; Carbon nanotubes; Nanocomposites; Electrical properties

1 Introduction

Carbon nanotubes (CNTs), as one ideal reinforcement materials in advanced composites, possess outstanding mechanical, thermal and electrical properties[1]. The commercially available CNT films prepared by floating catalytic chemical vapor deposition (FCCVD), which meet the requirements of good performance and practical operability, are the most efficient way to fully utilize CNTs' excellent performance for macroscopic applications. CNT films not only inherit the CNTs' unique physical characteristic, but also form a network structure which makes stress, electron and phonon transfer better[2]. Moreover, these large scale CNT films with orderly orientation arrangement and high CNT loading can overcome some obstacles during the production of CNT composites, such as aggregation, random orientation and low content of CNTs[3], so in favor of the higher mechanical, electrical and thermal properties of composites. Therefore, CNT film based composites have the functions of conducting electricity, conducting

heat, damping, flame retardant and bullet-proof, and can be applied in ballistic structure, aerospace field and wearable electronic products[4].

However, the quite inactive and smooth CNT surfaces lack of oxygen-containing functional groups leads to its feeble interface bonding strength with matrix and severely limits the full use of CNTs' advantages[5]. Consequently, surface modification of CNT films to promote the chemical bonding between reinforcement and matrix becomes critical to obtain nanocomposites with excellent properties. Traditionally, the common modification methods are physically or chemically treatment of CNT films. Physical modification improves their compatibility with matrix by changing the surface properties of CNTs, such as electrostatic adsorption, coating surfactants or polymers. Nevertheless, chemical modification is a more efficient way which can change the surface structure and morphology of CNTs by initiating chemical reaction, for example acid oxidation, fluorination, free radical addition reaction and plasma treatment[6]. Among these, plasma stands out and attracts the researchers' attention due to the advantages of easy operation, high efficiency, eco-friendliness, and industrializable development[7].

Over the past decade, the research on plasma-modified CNTs has been gradually enriched. For example, JIANG et al.[8] reported He/O_2 plasma functionalized led to 30% and 125% increase in tensile strength and modulus respectively of CNT film/phenylethynyl-terminated polyimide composites, indicating the improved adhesion between CNT film and the polymer. Park and coworkers[9] treated the CNT fibers by 5min oxygen plasma treatment, and found their tensile strength was improved by 40%. However, most of the attention is still focused on the analysis of the mechanical properties of CNT reinforced composites, and the reports on electrical properties of plasma functionalized CNTs-polymer composites are still very few. With the rapid development of intelligent textiles and the important applications of CNT nanocomposites, further exploration of the enhancement effect of plasma on the electrical properties of composites is urgently needed.

In this study, an atmospheric pressure helium/oxygen plasma jet was employed to functionalize CNT films. The effect of plasma modification on the electrical conductivity of CNT film were investigated. In addition, the strain sensitivity of CNT film and CNT film/epoxy composites was systematically analyzed.

2 Experiments

2.1 Materials

CNT films prepared by floating catalyst chemical vapor deposition were purchased from Suzhou Institute of Nano-Tech and Nano-Bionics, Chinese Academy of Sciences. The dimensions of CNT films could reach to tens of meters both in length and in width. The thickness of the film was about 13.7mm with a purity >90%. The building block of CNT film was multi-walled carbon nanotube (MWCNT) with the diameter of ~20nm and around 20 walls. Epoxy resin (JL-235) and hardener (JH-242) were purchased from Jiafa Chem Co., Ltd (Suzhou).

An atmospheric pressure plasma jet Atomflo TM 400 (Surfx technologies, S) was used to treat the CNT films. A 13.56MHz power supply for the discharge was connected to the electrodes via matching network to discharge plasma with a 150W power. The mixed gas source of helium/oxygen was fed at a flow rate of 30/0.3L/min. The treatment time was 0.1s to avoid the etching damage of CNT films caused by plasma[10].

Vacuum-bag molding method (VBM) was applied to fabricate the CNT film/epoxy resin nanocomposite. Firstly, CNT prepregs were manufactured by immersing two layers of CNT films into epoxy resin/alcohol/hardener mixture for 15min. Then put the prepregs flat on the mold layer by layer. With the assistance of a vacuum pump, excess resin between the CNT films was pumped out at 25℃ for 30min. Finally, a solid state of CNT film/epoxy composites were obtained after the processes of the pre-curing at 50℃ for 4h and post-curing at 70℃ for 6h[11].

2.2 Electrical Testing

The CNT film samples for electrical testing were prepared as shown in Fig.1. By linking copper wires at both ends of the sample, the electrical resistance can be recorded with a digital multi-meter (Agilent, 34410A, USA). A XQ-2 tensile testing machine (Shanghai Xusai Instrument Co., China) was used to control the the drawing rate of the sample. The sample of CNT film/epoxy composites were similar to that of films, except the size was about 0.5mm wide[12]. At least five specimens for each sample were tested and the average values were calculated.

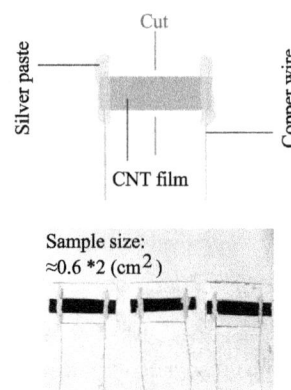

Fig.1 Electrical testing sample of CNT film and the optical images with dimensions

3   Results and Discussions

In Fig.2 (a), the resistance-strain curves of CNT films demonstrated the effect of plasma modification on electrical properties of CNT film. After plasma modified, the electrical conductivity decreased from 833S/cm to

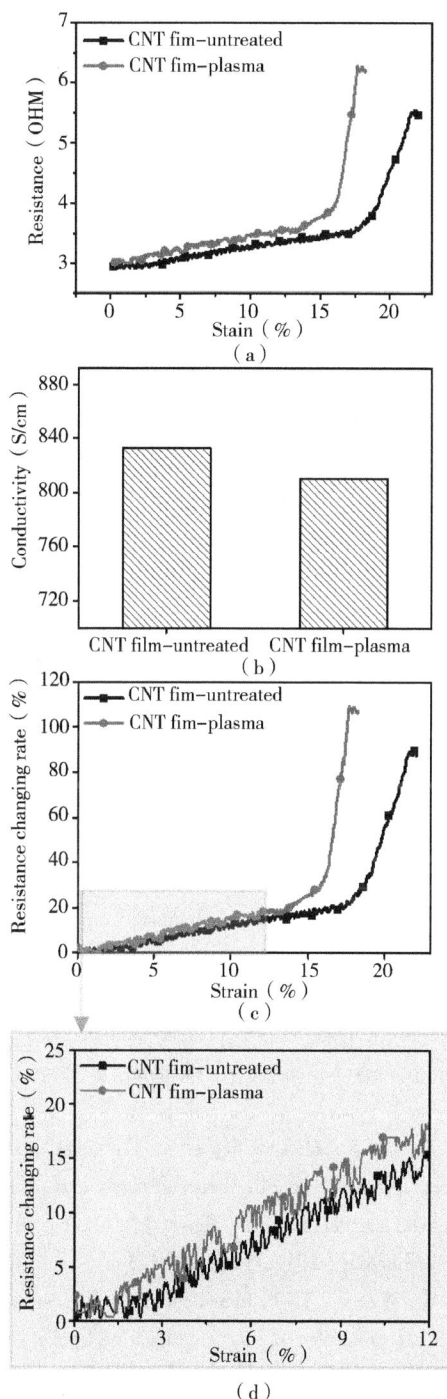

(a)

(b)

(c)

(d)

Fig.2 (a) Resistance-strain curves; (b) comparison of conductivities; (c-d) resistance change ratio-strain curves of untreated and plasma treated CNT films

810S/cm in Fig.2 (b). It was due to the etching effect of plasma jet which induced damage to the CNTs' surface. That meant the ion bombardment and chemical reaction of the plasma treatment attributed to concave surface of the CNTs, leading to a decreased electrical conductivity[13]. Fortunately, due to treatment time is short, the decrease of electrical conductivity of CNT film is very limited.

As presented in Fig.2 (c), the resistance change ratio ($\Delta R/R$) of CNT film was plotted against tensile strain to describe the piezoresistive effect. The results showed that the resistance increased linearly to the tensile elongation within 5% strain. In general, gage factor (GF) was adopted to evaluate the sensitivity of CNT films to the tensile strain, which is the relative change ratio of electrical resistance R to the mechanical strain ε, seeing in Fig.2 (d). It is worth noting that, contrary to the conductivity, the gauge factor (GF) of CNT film increases from 1.2 to 1.5 after plasma treatment. These results can be attributed to the generated chemical bonds on the tube surface of CNT film produced by plasma jet. Then the stronger interaction between the neighboring CNTs than Van Der Waals force emerged. So during stretching, the plasma treated CNT film exhibited a higher GF while received a little more stress than the untreated ones[14-15].

In Fig.3, the resistance change ratio-strain curves of CNT film/epoxy composites indicated the changes in sensing performance caused by plasma treatment. As for the untreated ones, the calculated GF was 2.3. While for the plasma treated CNT film/epoxy composites, the GF increased by 34.8% with a value of 3.1. This value even could rival with that of the conventional metal foil, which is ranged from 2 to 3[16].

The improvement in GF was ascribed to the increased amount of oxygen-containing functional groups on CNT film surface which was incorporated by plasma. The generated C—O group improved the surface polarity and benefited the adhesion between CNT and epoxy, resulting in the stronger film/resin interface bonding[17]. Therefore, the increased interfacial bonding of CNT-epoxy led to the better stress transferability inside the composites during stretching[18].

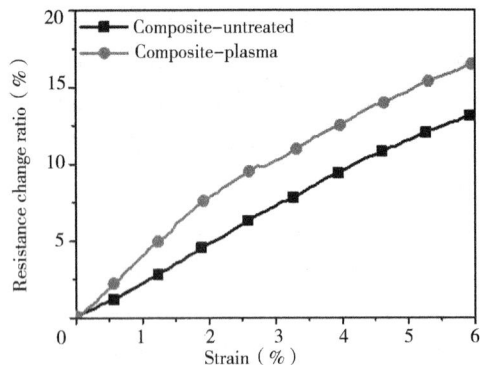

Fig.3 Resistance change ratio-strain curves of untreated and plasma modified CNT film/epoxy composites

According to a charge tunneling model[19] which can describe the piezoresistive effect in CNT film/epoxy composites, the inside better stress transfer could inevitably lead to the increased tunneling resistance between neighboring CNTs. So the composites exhibited more sensitive to tensile strain and an obviously improved GF. But for pristine CNT film/epoxy composites, internal CNT bundles were easy to slip which largely restricted the stress transferring, and few increasement of tunneling resistance occurred. Therefore, according to the above model, the composites revealed a smaller GF when compared with the plasma treated ones. These results also demonstrated that plasma treatment can contribute to better sensing properties of CNT film/epoxy composites.

4 Conclusions

In this study, the effect of O_2/He plasma treatment on the electrical properties of CNT film and its composites were investigated. CNT film showed the improved sensitivity to tensile strain after plasma treatment, though the etching effect on CNT surface led to the slightly decreased electrical conductivity. In addition, the plasma modified CNT film/epoxy composites exhibited a linear piezoresistive response with a higher gage factor than the pristine ones. All these positive outcomes together can establish a new pathway to improve CNT film and its composites which show attractive potential applications in strain sensors.

References

[1] DE VOLDER M, TAWFICK S H, BAUGHMAN R, et al. Carbon nanotubes: present and cuture commercial applications [J]. Science, 2013, 339(6119):535-539.

[2] PUNETHA V, RANA S, YOO H, et al. Functionalization of carbon nanomaterials for advanced polymer nanocomposites: a comparison study between CNT and grapheme[J]. Progress in Polymer Science, 2016, 67:1-47.

[3] ZHU, H. Direct synthesis of long single-walled carbon nanotube strands[J]. Science, 2002, 296(5569):884-886.

[4] XING Y, ZHANG X, CHEN H, et al. Enhancing buckypaper conductivity through co-deposition with copper nanowires[J]. Carbon, 2013, 61:501-506.

[5] KUMAR A, MASCHMANN M, HODSON S, et al. Carbon nanotube arrays decorated with multi-layer graphene-nanopetals enhance mechanical strength and durability[J]. Carbon, 2015, 84:236-245.

[6] TSENG C, WANG C, CHEN C. Functionalizing carbon nanotubes by plasma modification for the preparation of covalent-integrated epoxy composites[J]. Chemistry of Materials, 2006, 19(2):308-315.

[7] OGAWA D, KATO M, MORI J, et al. Dispersion of multi-walled carbon nanotube in tetrahydrofuran functionalized with Ar/O_2, Ar/N_2, and Ar/N_2/H_2 plasma[J]. Surface & Coatings Technology, 2014, 258:605-607.

[8] JIANG Q, LI Y, XIE J, et al. Plasma functionalization of bucky paper and its composite with phenylethynyl-terminated polyimide[J]. Composites Part B: Engineering, 2013, 45(1):1275-1281.

[9] PARK O, YOUNG K, MIN K, et al. Effect of oxygen plasma treatment on the mechanical properties of carbon nanotube fibers[J]. Materials Letters, 2015, 156:17-20.

[10] KIM C, LEE H, MIN B, et al. Transition of carbon nanotubes growth mode on NH_3 plasma-modified Ni films at different plasma powers [J]. Vacuum, 2015, 115: 113-116.

[11] LIU X, XU F, ZHANG K, et al. Characterization of enhanced interfacial bonding between epoxy and plasma functionalized carbon nanotube films [J]. Composites Science and Technology, 2017, 145:114-121.

[12] LIU W, WEI B, XU F. Investigation on the mechanical and electrical properties of carbon nanotube/epoxy composites produced by resin transfer molding[J]. Journal of Composite Materials, 2016, 51(14).

[13] KAISER A, DUSBERG G, Roth S. Heterogeneous model for conduction in carbon nanotubes[J]. Physical Review B, 1998, 57(3):1418-1421.

[14]LI M, WANG Z, LIU Q, et al. Carbon nanotube film/epoxy composites with high strength and toughness[J]. Polymer Composites, 2015:588-596.

[15]SHAO Y, XU F, MARRIAM I, et al. Quasi-static and dynamic interfacial evaluations of plasma functionalized carbon nanotube fiber[J]. Applied Surface Science, 2019, 465: 795-801.

[16]WAN S, ZHANG Q, ZHOU X, et al. Fatigue resistant bioinspired composite from synergistic two-dimensional nanocomponents[J]. ACS Nano, 2017:11(7):7074.

[17]CHETTY R, MANIAM K K, SCHUHMANN W, et al. Oxygen-plasma-functionalized carbon nanotubes as supports for platinum-ruthenium catalysts applied in electrochemical methanol oxidation[J]. Chem Plus Chem, 2015, 80(1): 130-135.

[18]BAO W, MEGUID S, ZHU Z, et al. Tunneling resistance and its effect on the electrical conductivity of carbon nanotube nanocomposites[J]. Journal of Applied Physics, 2012, 111(9):7492.

[19]ZHANG Q, LIU L, ZHAO D, et al. Highly sensitive and stretchable strain sensor based on agents@[J]. Nanomaterials, 2017, 7(12):424.

Physical Densification on the Mechanical and Electrical Properties of Twisted CNT Yarn

ZHANG Qin[1,2,3], XU Fujun[1,2]*, QIU Yiping[1,2]

[1] Key Laboratory of Textile Science & Technology, Ministry of Education, College of Textiles, Donghua University, Shanghai, 201620, China

[2] Department of Technical Textiles, College of Textiles, Donghua University, Shanghai, 201620, China

[3] National Cotton and Textile Quality Supervision and Inspection Center, Aksu, Xinjiang, 843000, China

* Corresponding author's email: fjxu@ dhu.edu.cn

Abstract: The elementary carbon nanotubes (CNTs) have excellent mechanical and electrical properties, showing huge potential on smart textile. However, CNTs are loosely packed in carbon nanotubes assemblies contributing to low density and weak interaction between individual CNTs so that the outstanding properties of CNTs are hard to be fully translated in macroscopic CNT yarn. In this work, we proposed an effective physical densifying method to reduce the interspace to enhance the interaction between CNTs and meanwhile to improve the orientation to the yarn axis. As a result, the mechanical and electrical properties of the densified CNT yarn were both better than that before treatment. The experimental results show the tensile strength is increased by 193.43%, the Young's modulus is increased by 887.5%. Moreover, the electrical conductivity has been improved by 78.9%. Therefore, this densifying method has great potentials in improving mechanical and electrical properties of CNT yarn and this densified CNT yarn with high strength and electrical conductivity can be woven and embedded to textile products.

Keywords: Twist CNT yarn; Physical densification; Mechanical and electrical properties

1 Introduction

Carbon nanotubes (CNTs) with the extraordinary mechanical, electrical, thermal properties has large potential for the application of smart textile including sensor, electric heating, energy-collecting etc[1]. However, the CNTs at nanoscale will cause the threat of health if exposed to human skin. Then the macroscopic CNT yarn is produced to be applied to the textile products[2].

In recent decades, three main methods is proposed to manufacture nanoscaled CNTs to macroscaled CNT yarn for textile application, wet spinning from CNT solutions, dry spinning from CNT arrays in vertical arrangement, direct spinning from CNT aerogels via the floating catalyst chemical vapor deposition (FCCVD) process[3]. However, CNTs are loosely packed in the CNT yarn fabricated by these methods, contributing to low density and weak interaction between individual CNTs so that the outstanding properties of CNTs are hard to be fully translated in macroscopic CNT yarn. It is because the basic component of the spun CNT yarn is the group of bundle where CNTs entangle with each other resulting in the loss of orientation, and the existing interspace between CNTs lead to weak Van Der Waals interaction between adjacent CNTs[4]. Physical densification is an efficient method to improve the interaction between CNTs and orientation of CNT bundles in CNT yarn to enhance the properties of CNT yarn, reducing the gap between macroscale CNT yarn and elementary CNTs[5].

In this work, the CNT film grown by floating catalyst chemical vapor deposition was twisted into cylindrical CNT yarn. We proposed an effective and controllable method of physical densification to treat this twisted CNT yarn, that pulling it out of several drawing dies with smaller diameter to make more compact structure. Then investigated the effect of physical densification on the mechanical and electrical properties of twisted CNT yarn.

2 Experiments

2.1 Materials

The multi-walled CNTs with 25nm diameter and nearly 20 walls were fabricated into CNT film by floating chemical vapor deposition, supplied by Suzhou Institute of Nano-Tech and Nano-Bionics, Chinese Academy of Sciences. The thickness of CNT film is 18.9μm and the width of utilized CNT film is 3mm after cutting. The acetone has a purity of 99.5%. The boiling point of acetone was 56℃ so that it is easy to evaporate.

2.2 The Process of Physical Densification

Fig.1(a) shows the process of twisting CNT film into twisted CNT yarn set as CNTY. Fig.1(b) shows the process of densifying twisted CNT yarn into densified CNT yarn, that the twisted CNT yarn was pulled out of through several drawing dies whose diameter was from 240μm to 150μm indescending order, this yarn was set as P-CNTY. In the drawing treatments, acetone was added as lubricant between CNT bundles to facilitate the densification and orientation of CNT yarn and avoid the damage resulted from surface friction, this another densified CNT yarn with acetone treatment was set as A-P-CNTY. The acetone with low boiling point would evaporate fastly so that we don't need to consider the separation of organic solvent from yarn.

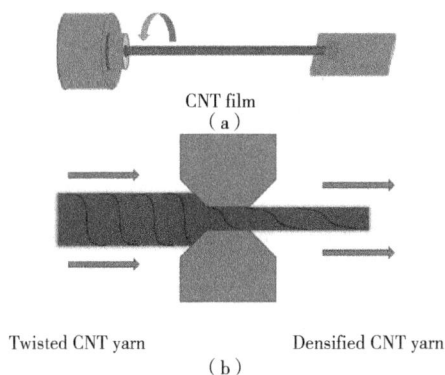

CNT film
(a)

Twisted CNT yarn   Densified CNT yarn
(b)

Fig.1 (a) The process to fabricate twisted CNT yarn; (b) The process of physical densification

2.3 Performance Testing

The fracture sectional morphology of CNTY, P-CNTY and A-P-CNTY were characterized by scanning electron microscope (SEM, Hitachi S-4800). The diameter and twist angle of these CNT yarn above was measured with polarization microscope (Nokon LV100POL). The mechanical properties were tested on a XQ-2 tensile testing machine (Shanghai Xusai Instrument Co., China). The electrical resistance was recorded through a digital multi-meter (Agilent, 34410A, USA) and the density was the mass per unit volume.

3 Results and Discussion

3.1 Mechanical Properties

Fig.2(a) shows that the pristine twisted CNT yarn (CNTY) has a twist angle of 28.5° and diameter of 282μm±5μm. After the CNT yarn was pulled out of the drawing dies with smaller diameter, it would sustain the pressure in radial direction and the tension in axial direction. As shown in Fig.2(b), the twist angle of P-CNTY decreased to 14.5° and the diameter decreased to 185μm±5μm. Moreover, as shown in Fig.2(c), the drawing treatment process with acetone infiltration made more smaller twist angle of 10.5° and diameter of 175μm±5μm compared with P-CNTY. The reduction of diameter indicated that the pristine twisted CNT yarn was densified to more compact structure under pressure, the reduction of twist angle indicated that the pristine CNT yarn was oriented to the yarn axis under tension[6]. Acetone played an important role in physical densification that has small contact angle with CNTs, acting as a lubricant. When add acetone to CNT yarn during drawing process, the wicking effect happened that acetone fastly infiltrated into intertube spacing leading to the reduction in bonding energy between the CNT bundles, further causing larger distance and smaller contact area between CNT bundles to decrease the interaction, that has been demonstrated in previous research[7]. Because of the loss of Van Der Waals' interaction between CNT bundles before acetone volatilizing, the pressure in radial direction and the tension in axial direction made CNT bundles easier to rearrange, renewedly connecting with each other for more condensed structure[5]. As a result, this methold of physical densification with acetone can make A-P-CNTY most compact and oriented structure.

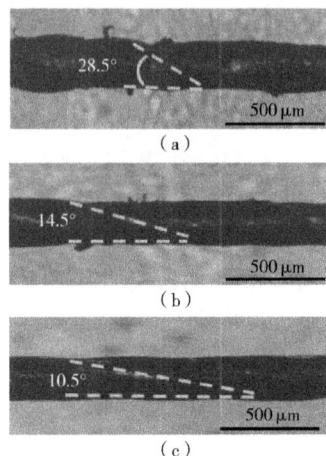

Fig.2 The diameter and twist angle of CNT yarns measured with polarization microscope: (a) CNTY; (b) P-CNTY; (c) A-P-CNTY

Tab.1 recorded the structural parameter of CNTY, P-CNTY and A-P-CNTY. D/d means the densification degree of twisted CNT yarn, D and d are the diameters of pristine CNT yarn and the modified yarn respectively. Because the D/d of A-P-CNTY is larger than that of P-CNTY, A-P-CNTY with smaller diameter. The smaller diameter leads to less defect of A-P-CNTY. The density of CNTY, P-CNTY and A-P-CNTY were calculated by weight dividing volume. Through the physical densification, the density of A-P-CNTY could increase by 118% with a value of $0.465 g/cm^3$ obviously, because the physical densification under the effect of acetone inflitration caused the most condensed structure of A-P-CNTY.

Tab.1　The structural parameter and tensile testing result of CNTY, P-CNTY and A-P-CNTY

Sample	Structural parameter			Performance			
	Diameter (um)	D/d	Density (g/cm^3)	Breakingforce (cN)	Strength (MPa)	Modulus (GPa)	Strain(%)
CNTY	282	1	0.211	855	139	0.78	55.8
P-CNTY	185	1.52	0.413	741	276	6.458	14.33
A-P-CNTY	175	1.61	0.465	966	402	7.839	16.75

The tensile testing results were shown in Tab. 1. The tensile strength of P-CNTY increased by 101.45% with a value of 276MPa, in the meantime, the modules increased by 712.5% from 0.8GPa to 6.5GPa, since the physical densification lead to more compacted and oriented structure of P-CNTY, reinforcing the interaction between CNTs to create higher load transfer and less slide under a given load. Moreover, we could find that the tensile strength and modules of A-P-CNTY increased more dramatically than that of P-CNTY. The tensile strength of A-P-CNTY increased by 193.43% with a value of 402MPa, meanwhile, the modules increased by 887.5% from 0.8GPa to 7.9GPa. The better mechniacal properties of A-P-CNTY than that of P-CNTY resulted from the samller diameter and the higher D/d and higher density of A-P-CNTY shown in Tab.1,

because the effect of acetone inflitration proposed better densification of A-P-CNTY under the same mechanical conditions. Therefore, the interaction between CNTs in A-P-CNTY enhanced more than that of P-CNTY and the defects decreased more in the more compact structure of A-P-CNTY, resulting to higher tensile strength and modulus and breaking force. Even though the elongation of modified CNT yarn decreased to approximately 17% compared to the pristine CNTY, it was still much higher than most of physically densfied CNT yarn in other research, demonstrating great elasticity. Therefore, the mechanical property of twisted CNT yarn can be efficiently enhanced through the physical densification with the acetone as lubricant.

The tensile fracture sectional morphology of CNTY, P-CNTY and A-P-CNTY exhibited in Fig. 3 can further explain the change of mechanical property under physical densification. The tensile fracture sectional morphology of CNTY in Fig.3 (a) clearly showed that the breakage of twisted CNT yarn is not instantaneous because of the incompact structure of CNTY resulting to low load transfer. This would decrese the intrinsic property of CNTs in transition from nanoscale to macroscale CNT yarn. As demonstrated in Fig.3 (b) , the tensile fracture sectional morphology of P-CNTY was more ordered than CNTY, because the twisted CNT yarn was densified to increase the interaction between CNTs, leading to high load transfer and strong mechanical property. The tensile fracture sectional morphology of A-P-CNTY in Fig.3 (c) revealed that its structure is the most compact above all and the breakage of A-P-CNTY is nearly instantaneous. The reason is that A-P-CNTY with the most compact structure possessed stronger interaction between CNTs than P-CNTYs, contributing to higher load transfer and greater mechanical property.

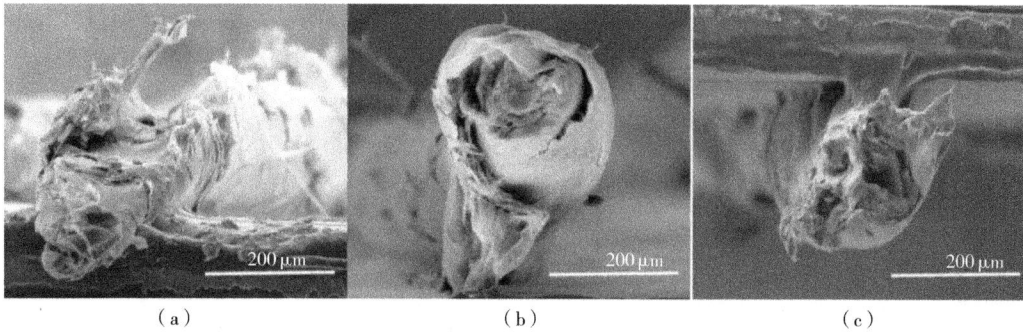

Fig.3   The fracture sectional morphology: (a) CNTY; (b) P-CNTY; (c) A-P-CNTY

3.2   Electrical Properties

The relative resistance and electrical conductivity are showed in Fig.4. The electrical conductivity of P-CNTY increased from 380S/cm to 580S/cm and the electrical conductivity of A-P-CNTY increased from 380S/cm to 680S/cm. The great improvement in electrical conductivity of densified CNT yarn can be attributed to the smaller interstube spacing and more contacting area between CNTs after physical densification, to minimize contact resistance between the CNTs in the highly compacted CNT structure. Because the structure of A-P-CNTY can be modified more densely in physical densification with the acetone as lubricant than that of P-CNTY in physical densification without solvent, the electrical conductivity of A-P-CNTY can be increased as high as 680S/cm, 78.9% higher than that of the pristine CNTY, 17.2% higher than P-CNTY. Moreover, the relative resistance (Ω/cm) of densified CNT yarn is basically stable, increased by approximately 19% compared to the pristine CNTY, the main reason is the reduction of sectional area under the effect of physical densification, according to the formula of $R=\rho L/S$, ρ is the electrical resistivity that is reciprocal to the electrical conductivity, L is the gauge length, S is the sectional area. L is constant, if S decrease more than ρ, then R increase. However, if compared to the twisted CNT yarn with the same length and diameter, the electrical property of A-P-CNTY still had great advantage. Therefore, the physical densification with the acetone as lubricant can improve the electrical property of twisted CNT yarn effectively.

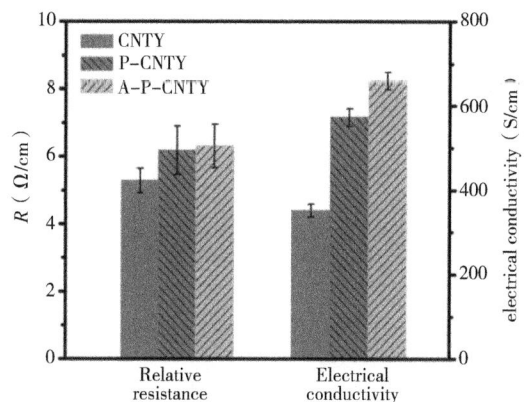

Fig.4   The electrical testing result of CNTY, P-CNTY and A-P-CNTY

4 Conclusions

This study has focused on the effect of physical densification, that mainly including tension and pressure, on mechanical and electrical properties of twisted CNT yarn. Especially through this densified treatment with acetone inflitration, the structure of twisted CNT yarn was modified to more condensed obviously. Therefore, the tensile strength of densified CNT yarn increased by 193.43% and the modules increased by 887.5%. Even though the elongation decreased by 17%, it still revealed great elasticity. The electrical conductivity of densified CNT yarn can be increased as high as 680S/cm, 78.9% higher than the pristine twisted CNT yarn. Thus the physical densification is an effiective methold to improve mechanical and electrical properties of twisted CNT yarn. It is necessary to densify CNT yarn through physical densification in large textile field.

References

[1] LU W, ZU M, BYUN J H, et al. State of the art of carbon nanotube fifibers: opportunities and challenges[J]. Advanced Materials, 2010, 24:1805-1833.

[2] DONALDSON K, AITKEN R, LANG T, et al. Carbon nanotubes: a review of their properties in relation to pulmonary toxicology and workplace safety[J]. Toxicological Sciences An Official Journal of the Society of Toxicology, 2006, 92 (1):5-22.

[3] JIANGTAO D, ZHANG X H, et al. Carbon-nanotube fibers for wearable devices and smart textiles[J]. Adv. Mater, 2016, 28: 10529-10538.

[4] ZHANG X H, LI Q W, et al. Enhancement of friction between carbon nanotubes: an efficient strategy to strengthen fibers[J]. ACS NANO, 2009, 1(4):312-316

[5] YEONSU J, YOUNG S C, et al. How can we make carbon nanotube yarn stronger? [J]. Composites Science and Technology, 2018, 166:95-108.

[6] JUDE C A, KALAYU B B, JANDRO L, et al. Effect of twist on the electromechanical properties of carbon nanotube yarns [J]. Carbon, 2019, 142:491-503.

[7] JING Q, JERONIMO T, JUAN J, et al. Liquid infiltration into carbon nanotube fibers: effect on structure and electrical properties[J]. ACS NANO, 2013, 10(7):8412-8422.

Effects of Extrusion Speed and Spinning Voltage on the Morphology of Fibers Produced via Single-Step 3D Electrospinning

LIU Fei[1,3], ZHOU Mengmeng[1,3], LI Ran[1,3], YANG Yuan[1,3], YI Wenhui[1,3], LIU Wanshuang[4], QIU Yiping[1,2,3,5], JIANG Qiuran[1,2,3]*

[1] *Key Laboratory of Textile Science & Technology, Ministry of Education, College of Textiles, Donghua University, Shanghai, 201620, China*

[2] *Engineering Research Center of Technical Textiles, College of Textiles, Donghua University, Shanghai, 201620, China*

[3] *Department of Technical Textiles, College of Textiles, Donghua University, Shanghai, 201620, China*

[4] *Donghua University Center for Civil Aviation Composites, Donghua University, Shanghai, 201620, China*

[5] *College of Textiles and Apparel, Quanzhou Normal University, Fujian, 362000, China*

* *Corresponding author's email*: jj@ dhu.edu.cn

Abstract: Efforts have been made to produce three-dimensional (3D) electrospun structures for 3D applications in many fields but can hardly maintain the 3D structure, because the layer-by-layer fiber accumulation model has not been changed. In this research, a single-step 3D electrospinning technology has been developed by introducing high conductive silver nanoparticles in the spinning system. It was revealed that 3D fiber bulks with "rope" or "cloud" shapes could be produced with the highest specific pore volume of $2496cm^3/g$. The influence by elevating the extrusion speed was to fill the 3D ropes with more fibers but still maintain the rope morphology. On the contrary, the effect by raising the spinning voltage was to shift the fiber bulk morphology from 3D rope to 3D cloud with increase in the specific pore volume. By simulating the electrostatic field and analyzing the electrostatic forces, the hypothesis for the formation of the 3D structure were proposed as that the silver nanoparticles in the spinning system introduced reversed transfer of negative charges onto fibers and induced the formation of 3D wave structure of fibers and also repulsion between fibers and the collector. This study proved the possibility to form a 3D loose ultrafine fiber bulk via a simple single-step 3D electrospun method, and provided 3D fiber bulks for many potential applications.

Keywords: 3D electrospinning; Ultrafine fibers; Specific pore volume; Extrusion speed; High voltage

1 Introduction

Electrospinning technology is considered as one of the-most effective methods to obtain ultrafine fibers, which are widely used in biomedical, filtration, electronical, sensing fields[1]. The conventional electrospinning process produces two dimensional (2D) fibrous mats with fiber accumulated in a layer-by-layer model, and thus, the fiber gaps are usually less than $5\mu m$ and produce a compact structure with a low porosity. Thereby, the applications of the 2D fiber mats are limited and cannot meet the requirements for the development of three dimensional (3D) products[2].

Efforts have been made to modify the traditional electrospinning technology, including wet electrospinning[3], coarse fiber incorporation[4] and porogen-leaching processes[5]. However, most of the approaches were based on physical blocking and did not change the fiber accumulation model[6].

Previously, we have developed a one-step 3D electrospinning technology, which could produce ultrafine fiber bulk with random fiber orientation and large specific pore volumes more than 20 times higher than the values of 2D electrospun mats[7]. Moreover, the layer-by-layer fiber accumulation model has been replaced by a "electrostatic charge repulsion" model by incorporating surfactant into spinning solutions to induce fast charge transfer. Electrostatic charge reversion occurred once the fibers contact to the fiber collector, and repulsion forces were generated. By this way, the fibers were gathered in a 3D form with a random orientation. However, the surfactant required to produce the 3D structure was around 50% of the spun polymer weight.

It might be the case that the low conductivity of surfactant could make it difficult to achieve high conductivity requirements. In this current research, highly conductive silver nanoparticles (Ag NPs) was employed as the addictive in the spinning solution to provide fast charge transfer aiming to reduce the addictive amount and enhance the morphological shifting. Besides, the influences of the extrusion speed and spinning voltage of this system on the morphological properties were investigated.

2　Experiments

2.1　Materials
Polylactic acid (PLA) granules (6201D) were purchased from Nature Works LLC.. Silver nanoparticle (Ag NP) suspension (particles size: 10–15nm, 1%) was bought from Shanghai Huzheng Nanotechnology co., Ltd.. N, N-Dimethylformamide (DMF), glycerol and chloroform (both AR grade) were ordered from Shanghai Lingfeng Chemical Reagent co., Ltd.

2.2　Electrospinning
The granules of PLA were dissolved in the mixed solvent of chloroform and DMF (chloroform to DMF volume ratio = 9 : 1) at 8% and stirred at 300r/min for 24h. Glycerol was added into the Ag NP suspension at 6% dropwise with shaking for 1min. The suspension was mixed into the PLA solution at 7% with shaking for 5min. The PLA spinning solution was loaded into a syringe which was kept 18cm away from the fiber collector. The spinning was conducted in a sealed chamber which maintained a relative humidity of 30% at 25℃.

2.3　Morphological Evaluation
The macroscopic of the 3D fiber bulks were recorded by a digital camera (OLYMPUS, TG-5), while the micro-scopic morphologies of samples were observed under a scanning electron microscope (SEM, TM-3000, Hitachi, Japan). The fiber diameter was measured from the SEM images by the software of Image J. The mass and volume of each sample were measured, and their specific pore volumes were calculated by the following equation:

$$V_{sp} = \frac{V_p}{m} = \frac{V_t}{m} - \frac{1}{\rho} \qquad (1)$$

where V_{sp} is the specific pore volume, V_p is the pore volume in the fiber bulk, m is the mass of the fiber bulk, V_t is the total volume of the fiber bulk, ρ is the density of PLA as raw material.

2.4　Electrostatic Field Simulation
The electrostatic field was simulated using a multiphysics simulation software (COMSOL Multiphysics® 5.4) under a steady-state condition with the AC/DC module. The space range was defined as 20cm×20cm×30cm. The size of the collector was set at 10cm×10cm×0.1cm. The radius and length of the syringe tip were defined as 0.2cm and 2cm. The initial boundary condition of the syringe tip was set as 16kV to 24kV and the condition of the collector was defined as grounded. The electric field line and the electric potential surface were simulated with 3D drawing under each condition.

3　Results and Discussions

3.1　Effect of Extrusion Speed on the Morphology of Fiber Bulks
Fig.1 shows the digital photos and SEM images of PLA fiber bulked extruded at the speed ranging from 0.8mL/h to 1.6mL/h.

Fig.2 displays the effect of extrusion speed on the specific pore volume of fiber bulks. It is shown that the specific pore volume did not change significantly as the extrusion speed increased from 0.8mL/h to 1.2mL/h. A further rise in the extrusion speed from 1.2mL/h to 1.6mL/h led to a decrease in the specific pore volume from 874cm³/g to 569cm³/g. The total reduction in specific pore volume was around 45%. The reason might be that a higher amount of solution was extruded from the tip of syringe and more fibers could be produced at

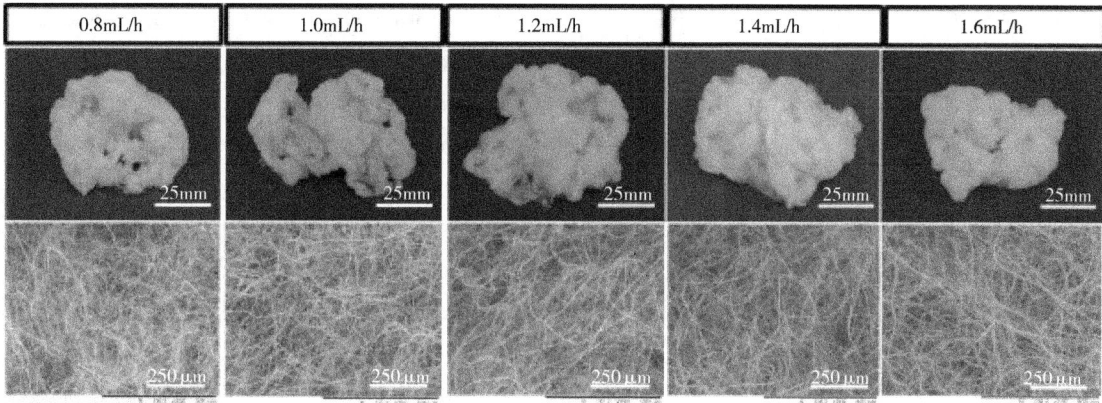

Fig.1 Effect of extrusion speed on the macroscopic and microscopic morphologies of PLA fiber bulks (The magnification of SEM images is 200×)

the same time and formed a more compacted 3D fiber rope.

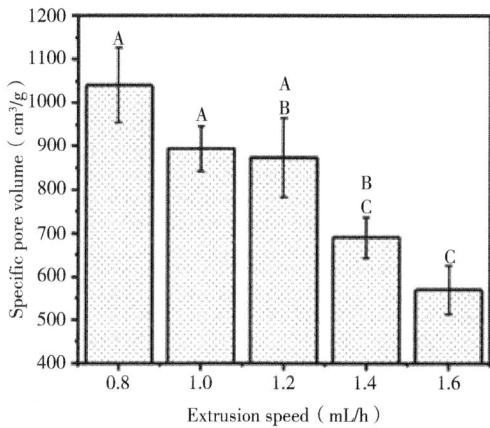

Fig.2 Effect of extrusion speed on the specific pore volume of PLA fiber bulks

3.2 Effect of Spinning Voltage on the Morphology of Fiber Bulks

Fig.3 indicates the changes in the morphology of fiber bulks introduced by the rise in spinning voltage. From 16kV to 20kV, the 3D rope shape was maintained. At 22kV, the rope was obvious expanded, and the 3D shape was formed.

Fig.4 presents the effect of spinning voltage on the specific pore volume of fiber bulks. When the spinning voltages were set at low values around 16kV to 18kV, the specific pore volumes of fiber bulks were similar. As the voltage elevated from 18kV to 22kV, an increase in the specific pore volume was observed from 1041cm^3/g to 1658cm^3/g. Once the voltage raised from 22kV to 24kV, the specific pore volume was increased sharply to 2496cm^3/g, which was about 3 times of the value at 16kV.

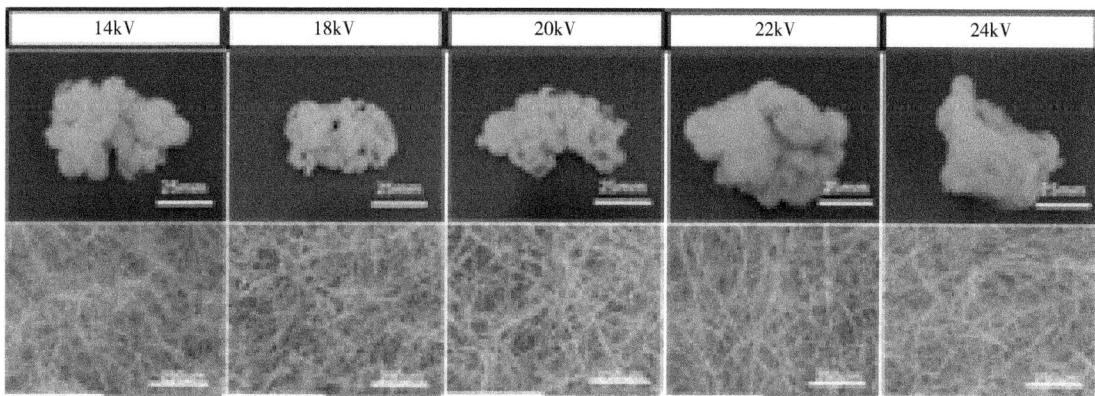

Fig.3 Effect of spinning voltage on the macroscopic and microscopic morphologies of PLA fiber bulks (The magnification of SEM images is 200×)

· 73 ·

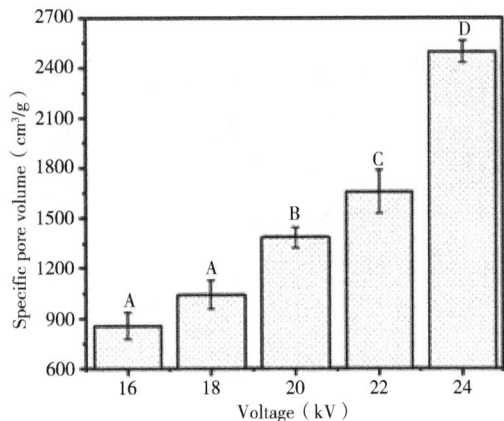

Fig.4　Effect of spinning voltage on the specific pore volume (A) and fiber diameter (B) of PLA fiber bulks.

3.5　Simulation of Electrostatic Field and Force Analysis

The simulation results of the electrostatic fields at different high voltages are shown in Fig.5. The electric potential was highest at the syringe tip labeled with red color. Once approaching the grounded fiber collector, the electric potential was reduced fast [Fig.5(a)]. Within the range of the flow whapping, the electric field lines were relatively dense and became loose and more parallel as moving toward the collector [Fig.5(b)]. Along with the increase in the supplied high voltage, the equipotential surfaces became wider, which meant the range of a higher potential was enlarged.

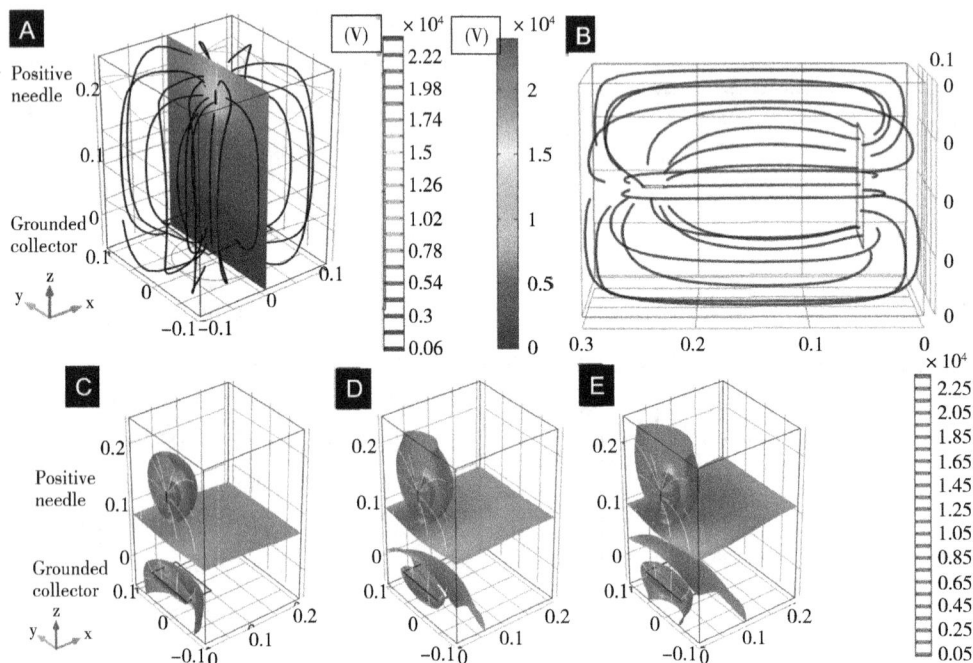

Fig.5　The simulation diagrams of the electrostatic field at 18kV (a)(b) with electric field lines and indication of electric potential from high to low and the equipotential surfaces at (c) 16kV, (d) 20kV and (e) 24kV

Scheme 1 describes the hypothesis of the 3D electrospinning process and the force analysis. Since the conductive Ag NPs have been incorporated in the spinning solution, the amount of the carried positive charges in the jet can be enlarged. Thereby, in the middle spinning section, on a segment of fiber, both positive and negative charges were stored in different positions. The spot loaded with more positive charges subjected to two forces: the repulsion force from the tip of syringe (F1) and the attraction force from the collector (F2). Both forces point to the fiber collector. Similarly, the position accumulated with more negative charges subjects to the attraction force from the tip of syringe (F3) and the repulsion force from the collector (F4). These forces pointed to the tip of syringe. Therefore, the segment of fiber turned to bend and form a "wave" structure. Once the segment of fiber moved to the middle or back spinning regions, the electric field lines were more parallel. By increasing the applied voltage, the electrostatic field was strengthened, and the amount of stored charges were enlarged. Thus, the 3D effects of the fiber bulk were more obvious. As the fibers move to-ward the fiber collector, more negative charges are accumulated, which enhanced the repulsion forces between the fibers and the fiber collector. Hence, the fibers with a wave structure were repelled and apt to form a random oriented 3D structure.

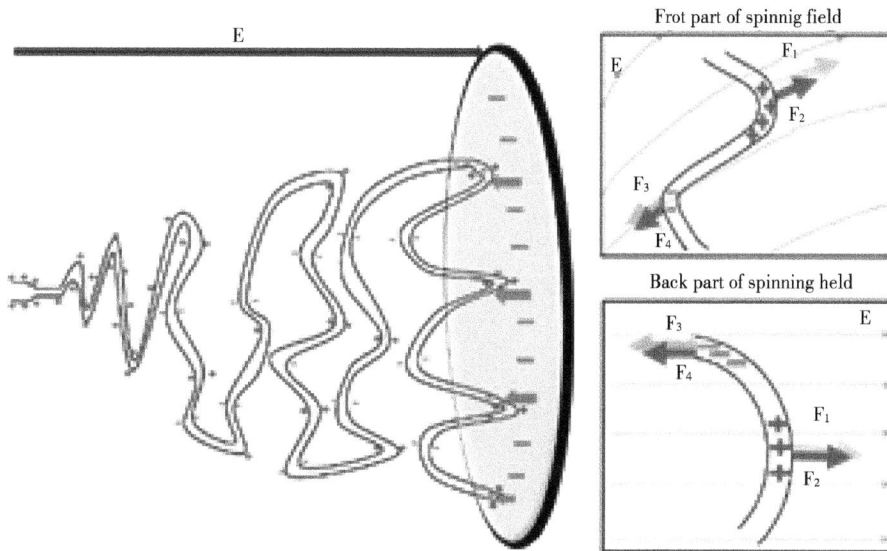

Scheme. 1　The diagram of the charge distribution and force analysis during 3D electrospinning. F1: the repulsion force from the tip of syringe; F2: the attraction force from the collector; F3: the attraction force from the tip of syringe; F4: the repulsion force from the collector

4　Conclusions

In this research, a single-step 3D electrospinning method was developed with involving of high conductive Ag NPs into the spinning system.By changing the extrusion speed and spinning voltage, the morphology could change from 3D rope to 3D cloud. The hypothesis of the 3D electrospinning mechanism has been proposed that the fast transfer of negative charges from the collector was key reason to introduce the generation of wave structure of fiber segments and the repulsion between the fibers and the collector.

Acknowledgements

This research was financially supported by the National Natural Science Foundation of China (51503031) and the Scientific Research Foundation for the Returned Overseas Scholars from the Ministry of Education (15B10127).

References

[1]XUE J J, WU T, DAI Y Q, et al. Electrospinning and electrospun nanofibers: methods, materials, and applications [J]. Chemical Reviews, 2019, 119(8):5298-5415.

[2]SUN B, LONG Y Z, ZHANG H D, et al. Advances in three-dimensional nanofibrous macrostructures via electrospinning [J]. Progress in Polymer Science, 2014, 39(5):862-890.

[3]YOKOYAMA Y, HATTORI S, YOSHIKAWA C, et al. Novel wet electrospinning system for fabrication of spongiform nanofiber 3-dimensional fabric[J]. Materials Letters, 2009, 63(9-10):754-756.

[4]MORONI L, SCHOTEL R, HAMANN D, et al. 3D fiber-deposited electrospun integrated scaffolds enhance cartilage tissue formation[J]. Advanced Functional Materials, 2008, 18(1):53-60.

[5]LIU Y F, LIU R M, WANG X, et al. Electrospun three-dimensional nanofibrous structure via probe arrays inducing [J]. Micromachines, 2018, 9(9):9.

[6]CAI S B, XU H L, JIANG Q R, et al. Novel 3D electrospun

scaffolds with fibers oriented randomly and evenly in three dimensions to closely mimic the unique architectures of extracellular matrices in soft tissues: fabrication and mechanism study[J]. Langmuir, 2013, 29(7):2311-2318.

[7] ZUO W W, ZHU M F, YANG W, et al. Experimental study on relationship between jet instability and formation of beaded fibers during electrospinning[J]. Polymer Engineering and Science, 2005, 45(5):704-709.

Effect of Stacking Sequence on Mechanical Properties of Jute/Glass Reinforced PBS Hybrid Composites

MUHAMMAD Usman Ghani[1], KAHSAY Gebresilassie Abraha[1,2], SHARJEEL Ahmed[3],
SIDRA Saleemi[1], ABDUL Wahid[1], SYED Islam[1], YAO Lan[1]*, QIU Yiping[1]

[1] *Key Laboratory of Textile Science & Technology, Ministry of Education, College of Textiles, Donghua University, Shanghai, 201620, China*

[2] *Department of Textile Engineering, College of Engineering and Technology, Aksum University, Akum, Tigray, Ethiopia*

[3] *State Key Laboratory for Modification of Chemical Fibers and Polymer Materials, Donghua University, Shanghai, 201620, China*

* *Corresponding author's email*: yaolan@ dhu.edu.cn

Abstract: This research work was aimed to investigate the influence of stacking sequence on the mechanical properties of jute/glass fiber reinforced PBS hybrid composite. All the stacks of hybrid composites contained five plies of the fabric. By altering the position and number of jute and glass plies, six hybrid stacking sequences were obtained. Composites containing pure jute and pure glass fiber were also manufactured for comparison. Tensile and flexural tests were carried out according to ASTM D3039 and ASTM D790 for mechanical characterization, while SEM was used to analyze the composite morphological structure after fracture. Maximum tensile and flexural strength of 212MPa and 68MPa was observed for pure glass composites, however, mechanical properties of hybrid composites were found to fluctuate between pure jute and pure glass composites. It was revealed that the strength of jute composites could be significantly enhanced by introducing glass fiber.

Keywords: Jute fabric; Glass fabric; Hybrid composites; Tensile; Flexural; Surface morphology

1 Introduction

Natural fibers are increasingly being used as the reinforced portion in composite laminates due to their lightweight, environmental regulations and reduced price compared to high-performance fibers such as glass and carbon fiber[1]. Because of their cost-effectiveness[2], recyclability[3], and biodegradability[4], natural fiber-reinforced composites have found their applications in buildings, design, packaging, storage and automotive industries. However, their specific strength and modulus are particularly comparable with composites reinforced with glass and carbon fiber[5]. The main issues with vegetable fibers are comparatively low resistance to moisture, fiber wetting and matrix adhesion, all affecting mechanical properties[6]. Chemical surface modification of various vegetable fibers has been carried out to improve adhesion and can be easily found in the literature[7]. A more effective method of enhancing the

properties of these composites is to incorporate different fibers, i.e., to produce a hybrid composite, so their individual properties can be transferred to the final composite, resulting in a material with optimal properties and potentially increasing the range of applications. In this way, the characteristics of the hybrid composites are governed by factors such as matrix type, fibers used, the fiber length, relative fiber contents, interface and how they are dispersed in the composite[8]. Many researchers have reported their research work about hybridization of natural and synthetic fiber. For example, RAMESH et al.[9] studied the sisal/glass and jute/glass hybrid composites and compared mechanical properties. Composites having sisal fibers were observed to have a higher tensile strength in comparison to composites consisting of jute fibers, whereas both showed weaker strength than composites with glass. DHAKAL et al.[10] reported thermal stability, tensile, and flexural properties of the carbon, flax, and flax/carbon hybrid composites. Results indicated that hybrid composites of flax/carbon fiber were found to show enhancement in elongation at break relative to pure carbon composites. Addition of flax fibers reduced the flexural strength of carbon composites owing to their low strength. FIORE et al.[11] hybridized the basalt mats with flax fibers to investigate the durability of hybrid laminates. Results indicated that the hybrid composites quasi-static flexural properties were higher than flax composites.

Many researchers have explored the impact of fiber stacking sequence on hybrid composite mechanical characteristics. Researchers pointed out that stacking patterns of the various constituents in hybrid composites contribute to a vital part influencing the mechanical properties of hybrid composites.

ZHANG et al.[12] reported the impact of stacking sequence on glass (G)/flax (F) composite tensile strength. They were configured as [GF]s, [GGFF]s, and [GGGGFFFF]s. They noted that [GF]s laminate had the highest tensile strength and failure strain, owing to more interaction and different phases between flax and glass layers. RAMNATH et al.[13] produced the composites of jute and glass with various stacking sequence and reported that the properties of the composites could be enhanced by using glass fibers as last layers.

Up to now, no relevant research work has been reported in literature about the hybridization of jute and glass fiber into poly (butylene succinate) (PBS). The objective of this research in this context is to produce hybrid composites of jute/glass PBS with distinct stacks of fiber layers, to study their mechanical behavior viz. tensile, flexural according to ASTM standards. Scanning Electron Microscopy was used to analyze the fractured tensile samples.

2 Experimental Procedure

2.1 Materials

Jute fabric was purchased by plain textiles, with density of $300g/m^2$. Glass fabric that exhibits density of $450g/m^2$ was used for this research. The biodegradable PBS pellets (#1001) with melting temperature of 90℃ was purchased by Dongguan Kaixili Material Co. The density of PBS resin is $1.26g/cm^3$.

2.2 Composite Fabrication

The jute fabric was dried in a vacuum oven for 24 hours at 60℃. First, the sheets of PBS having a thickness (0.2 ± 0.01) mm were prepared by hot press compression molding at 150℃ for 10 minutes. The PBS sheets, along with jute and glass fabrics, were cut according to the mold size of (260mm × 260mm). Then, six hybrid kinds of sandwiches were manufactured by altering the position and number of plies of jute and glass fabric, while each sandwich consists of five plies. Composites consist of pure glass, and pure jute was also manufactured for the comparison. Finally, the prepared sandwiches were pressed in a stainless steel mold, with the thickness of 2.5mm under pressure of 10MPa at 150℃ for 10 minutes and the composite panels were obtained.

2.3 Mechanical Testing

2.3.1 Tensile Test

The tensile property was measured by Instron Machine (model 4302) followed by tensile test standard method ASTM D3039. The specimens for testing were cut out in the warp direction of jute fabric. The specimens had a length of 250mm and width of 25mm. Glass fiber reinforced composite tabs were used to make sure the specimen failure in gauge length and to prevent the slipping while testing. The specimens for the tensile test of various composites are shown in Fig.1. Specimens were placed between the jaws of the machine with a loading rate of 2mm/min. For each configuration, at least three similar specimens were tested, and average results were obtained.

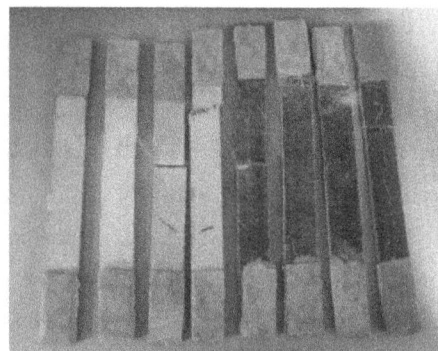

Fig.1　Tensile test specimens

2.3.2 Flexural Test

The flexural property was measured by Instron machine (model 4302) followed by flexural test standard method ASTM D790. Specimens with a size of (127×12.7) mm^2 were cut out from the manufactured composite panels in the direction of jute warp yarns. The specimens for the flexural test of various composites are shown in Fig. 2. The span-to-depth ratio of 16 : 1 was selected for the bending test according to ASTM D790 at a loading rate of 2mm/min. Three specimens of similar size samples for each configuration and average results have been calculated.

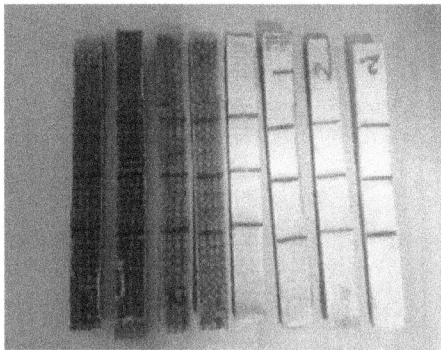

Fig.2　Flexural test specimens

2.4　Scanning Electron Microscopy (SEM)

A scanning electron microscope (HITACHI TM3000) was used to analyze the morphological structure of the composites. For this purpose, a small part was cut out from the tensile test fractured specimens. The specimens were fixed on an aluminum stub, and gold was used for sputter coating for morphological examination. The SEM images were taken with a magnification of X50.

3　Results and Discussions

3.1　Tensile Testing

The results show that the tensile strength of jute composite is lower than the hybrids as well as lower than pure glass composite, as shown in Fig. 3. The glass composite found to have the highest strength of 212MPa, whereas jute composite showed a lower strength of 41MPa. Glass composites tensile strength was higher than all other composites as glass fiber with high strength. It's cleared from the figure that the tensile

properties mostly rely on the strength of the fibers. It can be noted that with the increase of the number of glass fiber plies the tensile strength is increasing which shows the direct relation of tensile strength to the number of glass plies in the composites. It can be observed that the stacking sequence has a significant effect on the properties of hybrid composites. Many researchers have reported that high strength fiber as skin improves the mechanical properties of the composite which is also evident here. The high strength and modulus woven glass fiber provided at the top and bottom layer withstands the applied load whereas core (jute) absorbs and distributes the loads uniformly. The higher tensile strength of hybrid composites is attributed to stronger and stiffer glass fibers. Hybrid composites consist of same jute fabric and glass fabric plies, as in JGJGJ, GJJJG, JGGGJ, and GJGJG, when they are compared, the tensile strength is higher when glass plies were placed on the top and bottom of the sandwich. Tensile fractured specimens of jute composite showed an immediate failure with no or a little fiber pullout where in hybrid configurations, there was extensive fiber pullout or breakage. One reason for this may be due to greater extensibility of glass fibres (2.5−3.0) than jute fibres (1.5−1.8). Delamination was found in hybrid composites of jute and glass at the interface when they were mounted in tension that has been observed in failed specimens.

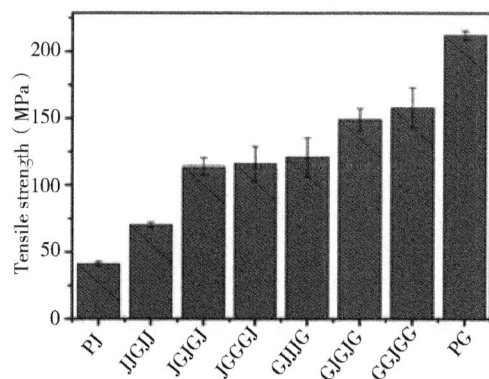

Fig.3　Tensile strength of specimens

3.2　Flexural Testing

Fig. 4 shows the flexural strength of the composites. Generally, three-point bending involves tensile, compressive and shear elements, all of which benefit from the presence of glass fibers. All hybrid composites flexural strengths fluctuated between pure glass composite (68MPa) and pure jute composite (39MPa). It can be noted that the flexural strength of composites (PG, GJJJG, GJGJG and GGJGG), having glass fiber plies on top and bottom is higher than the composites (PJ, JJGJJ, JJGJJ) having jute fiber plies on top and bottom, which proved that the flexural strength mainly depends on the position of glass fiber.

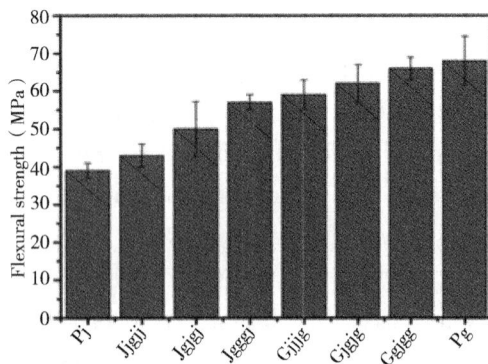

Fig.4　Flexural strength of specimens

3.3　Scanning Electron Microscopy

The tensile fractured of the pure and hybrid composites were observed by Scanning Electron Microscope (SEM) for morphological structure. Fiber and matrix interface has high importance for composite properties. It is suggested that for an effective transfer of stress from the matrix to fiber, there is a need for an excellent interfacial bond, results in obtaining maximized fiber strength in the composite.

Glass fiber stretching and elongation is shown in Fig.5, due to the tensile strength applied. The stretching of fiber shows that the polymer's strength improved because the introduction of glass fiber in PBS composite. The morphology of the composites of jute fiber is shown in Fig.6. From the surface observation of jute fiber composite, it can be seen that there is a little fiber stretching with breakage of fiber. Fig.7 shows the hybrid composite surface morphology. Due to the tensile load, the two kinds of behavior are evident in the hybrid composite surface. One is stretching of glass fiber, and the other is breaking of jute fiber without

stretching.

Fig.5　Pure glass composite

Fig.6　Pure jute composite

Fig.7　Hybrid composite

The jute fiber and matrix bonding are excellent, but there is sudden breakage of the composite which attributed to the brittle nature of the jute fiber.

4　Conclusions

The effect of stacking sequence on tensile and flexural properties of PBS composites reinforced by the woven jute-glass fabric has been analyzed experimentally. The following results are concluded from the findings of this research.

Glass fiber hybridization improved the mechanical properties of the composites insignificantly.

The hybrid laminates displayed intermediate mechanical properties for the pure composites. Tensile strength was found to be mostly dependent on the relative content of each fiber.

Flexural strength increased with the glass fiber content, especially for laminates containing glass fabric plies at the outer layers.

References

[1] SHAHINUR S, et al. Characterization on the properties of jute fiber at different portions[J]. International Journal of Polymer Science, 2015, 2015.

[2] GOPINATH A, KUMAR M S, ELAYAPERUMAL A. Experimental investigations on mechanical properties of jute fiber reinforced composites with polyester and epoxy resin matrices [J].Procedia Engineering, 2014, 97:2052-2063

[3] LILA M K, et al. A recyclability study of bagasse fiber reinforced polypropylene composites[J]. Polymer Degradation and Stability, 2018, 152:272-279.

[4] PLACKETT D, et al. Biodegradable composites based on L-polylactide and jute fibres[J]. Composites Science and Technology, 2003, 63(9):1287-1296.

[5] GUJJALA R, et al. Mechanical properties of woven jute-glass hybrid-reinforced epoxy composite[J]. Journal of Composite Materials, 2014, 48(28):3445-3455.

[6] TSANG F, et al. Effect of γ-irradiation on the short beam shear behavior of pultruded sisal-fiber/glass-fiber/polyester-hybrid composites[J]. Journal of Materials Science Letters, 2000, 19(13):1155-1157.

[7] LI X, TABIL L G, PANIGRAHI S. Chemical treatments of natural fiber for use in natural fiber-reinforced composites: a review[J]. Journal of Polymers and the Environment, 2007, 15(1):25-33.

[8] AMICO S, ANGRIZANI C, DRUMMON M. Influence of the stacking sequence on the mechanical properties of glass/sisal hybrid composites[J]. Journal of Reinforced Plastics and Composites, 2010, 29(2):179-189.

[9] RAMESH M, PALANIKUMAR K, REDDY K H. Comparative evaluation on properties of hybrid glass fiber-sisal/jute reinforced epoxy composites[J]. Procedia Engineering, 2013, 51:745-750.

[10] DHAKAL H, et al. Development of flax/carbon fibre hybrid composites for enhanced properties[J]. Carbohydrate Polymers, 2013, 96(1):1-8.

[11] FIORE V, et al. Effect of external basalt layers on durability behaviour of flax reinforced composites[J]. Composites Part B: Engineering, 2016, 84:258-265.

[12] ZHANG Y, et al. Tensile and interfacial properties of unidirectional flax/glass fiber reinforced hybrid composites[J]. Composites Science and Technology, 2013, 88: 172-177.

[13] VIJAYA RAMNATH B, et al. Determination of mechanical properties of intra-layer abaca-jute-glass fiber reinforced composite[J]. Materials & Design, 2014, 60:643-652.

Fabrication and Mechanical Properties of Apocynum Venetum Fiber Reinforced Polylactic Acid Biocomposites

KAHSAY Gebresilassie Abraha[1,2], MUHAMMAD Usman Ghani[1],
YAO Lan[1]*, QIU Yiping[1], ABDUL Wahid[1]

[1] *Key Laboratory of Textile Science & Technology, Ministry of Education, College of Textiles, Donghua University, Shanghai, 201620, China*
[2] *Department of Textile Engineering, College of Engineering and Technology, Aksum University, Aksum 1010, Ethiopia*

* *Corresponding author's email: yaolan@ dhu.edu.cn*

Abstract: In recent years, due to their favorable properties, the role of natural fiber reinforced polymer composites are growing at a faster rate in the field of engineering and technology. In this study, Apocynum Venetum (AV) fibers and Polylactic Acid (PLA) matrix were used as raw materials to develop and characterize a natural fiber reinforced composite using hot compression molding. Randomly oriented AV fiber mat used as the reinforcement for the biocomposite. Mechanical properties, including tensile and flexural tests of the composites, were conducted according to ASTM standards. Surface morphologies of the fractured surfaces of treated and untreated AV fiber composites have been observed using the Scanning Electron Microscope (SEM). Effects of fiber surface treatment on the mechanical properties of the composites were investigated and discussed in detail. From the test comes about, it has concluded that the treated AV fiber reinforced PLA composite had higher tensile strength, tensile modulus, flexural strength, and flexural modulus than untreated AV fiber reinforced PLA composite. The tensile strength, tensile modulus, flexural strength and flexural modulus of the treated AV fiber reinforced PLA composite are 82MPa, 5.03GPa, 122MPa, and 5.85GPa, while untreated AV fiber reinforced PLA composite showed 63MPa, 4.14GPa, 111.4MPa, and 5.44GPa respectively. AV fiber reinforced PLA biocomposites possess excellent tensile and flexural properties potentially applicable for packaging, biomedical, and automobile industries.

Keywords: Apocynum Venetum (AV) fiber; Biocomposites; PLA resin; Mechanical properties; Surface treatment

1 Introduction

Natural fibre-reinforced polymer composites are attracting the attention of several industrial applications, due to their environmental and economic advantages. Due to these benefits, the generation of bio-composites is expanding[1-2]. Lignocellulose fibres such as flax, hemp, kenaf, henequen, banana, oil palm, and jute have attracted considerable attention as alternatives to synthetic fibres, such as glass and carbon fibers[3-4]. Natural fiber reinforced composites have been used in many applications, such as automotive, aerospace, packaging, and construction, where high load bearing carrying capacity is not required[3].

While natural fibers have advantages over synthetic fibers, natural fibers have several drawbacks that affect their ability and performance in the thermoplastic industry. Some of their major disadvantages are poor adhesion to hydrophobic polymer matrix materials and affinity for hygroscopicity[5-6]. However, the alkali treatment showed a decrease in the lignin content, and the bast fibers were quickly separated, and the strength was uniform. Studies have shown that due to natural fiber reinforcement with polymer, the tensile strength of the composite increase, and after the alkali treatment, the tensile strength of the composite is further improved[7]. In the past, studies have shown up that dousing natural fibers in NaOH solution makes a differencein fulfilling the required compatibility and improveing the mechanical and chemical properties of biocomposites[8-9].

In this research work, apocynum venetum (AV) plants, a small wild shrub obtained from Xinjiang, China, has been used. In recent years, AV fibers used in the textile industry due to their excellent physical and mechanical properties, some for antibacterial textiles made of AV fiber are very popular at home and abroad. Apocynum venetum (AV) fiber is one of the so-called bast fibers and has natural antibacterial properties due to its composition and structure[10]. Only by removing non-cellulose after post-production processing can apocynum venetum be used to obtain usable fibers[11-12]. Herein, chemical degumming has been carried out to produce AV fibers from bast. However, it is difficult to find the work done on AV fiber as a reinforcement material for PLA composite.

In this study, the mechanical properties of treated and untreated AV fiber-based composites were investigated. The hot compression molding machine was used to fabricate the composite material. The effects of alkali treatment on the tensile and bending properties of the developed composites were examined and depicted in detail. The tensile fracture surface of the treated and untreated AV fiber reinforced composites were analyzed using a scanning electron microscope (SEM).

2 Experimental

2.1 Materials

A sample of Apocynum venetum (AV) plants selected from Xinjiang, China. PLA Ploymer matrix (NatureWorks® 4032D) supplied by Zhonghua Suhua Co.,

Ltd. (Guangdong, China). Its melting point is 166℃. Chemicals: sulfuric acid, sodium hydroxide, sodium silicate, sodium sulfate, and sodium polyphosphate, are supplied by Pinghu Chemical Reagent Factory (Zhejiang, China).

2.2 AV Fiber Preparation

As described in the literature section, AV bast fibers contain gummy materials consisting primarily of pectin, hemicellulose and lignin waxes and other impurities. Therefore, the non-cellulosic materials of this raw AV bast need to be eliminated for further industrial use. Chemical degumming is used to extract AV fibers from AV bast. The pith tissue of AV cannot be used to obtain fibers, so after boiling for 1.5 hours in hot water at 100℃, it is separated from the bast parts by hand. Next, the dried bast of apocynum venetum used as raw material, and the AV fiber was extracted using chemical degumming, as shown in Fig.1.

2.3 Fiber Surface Treatment

The AV fibers were immersed in 2% sodium hydroxide (NaOH) solution at room temperature for 2.5 hours and washed several times with water containing a drop of acetic acid to neutralize the excess sodium hydroxide wash. The treated AV fibers were dried in an oven drier at 80℃ for 10 hours.

2.4 Preparation of Web

AV fibers were opened manually and then cleaned and opened using a nonwoven carding machine and obtained AV fiber web. To enhanc the web uniformity, the fibers were carded twice. The formed fiber web was cut into layers according to the mold size and used as reinforcement material to fabricate the composites.

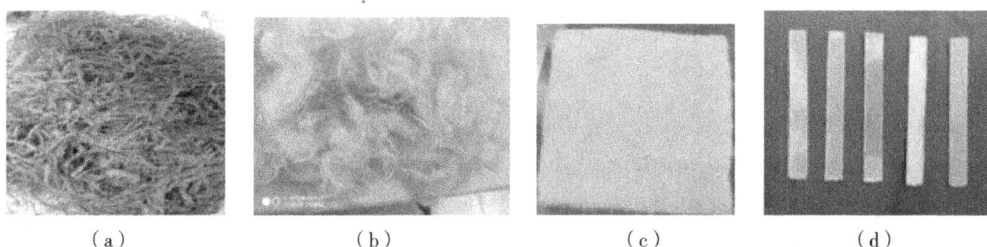

(a)　　　　　　(b)　　　　　　(c)　　　　　　(d)

Fig.1　Specimens for tensile and flexural tests: (a) AV bast fibers; (b) AV fiber; (c) AV fiber web layer; (d) Composite

2.5 Preparation of AV/PLA Biocomposites

First, the web prepared by the nonwoven carding machine was cut into a square piece of 130mm × 130mm, which had the same size as the mold. The PLA resin film was formed from the PLA pellets for 3 minutes using a hot press at a maintained pressure of 3MPa and a temperature of 180℃, respectively. The PLA resin was then cut into sheets of 130mm × 130mm. After preparing a layer of 30% fiber mat and 70% PLA film weight, the PLA film was then held correctly in the mold as a first layer, and the fiber mat applied to the first layer of PLA film. The next second layer of PLA film held on the first layer of the fiber mat. The second layer of fiber mat is then suitably held on the second layer of PLA film. Similarly, the continuous layer can form to the desired thickness, and finally, the entire system is hot pressed and molded on a hot press at 180℃ and pressed at a pressure of 4MPa for 6 minutes. Finally, the composite samples molded into dimensions of 130mm × 130mm. Fig.2 shows the general method of the composite fabrication process.

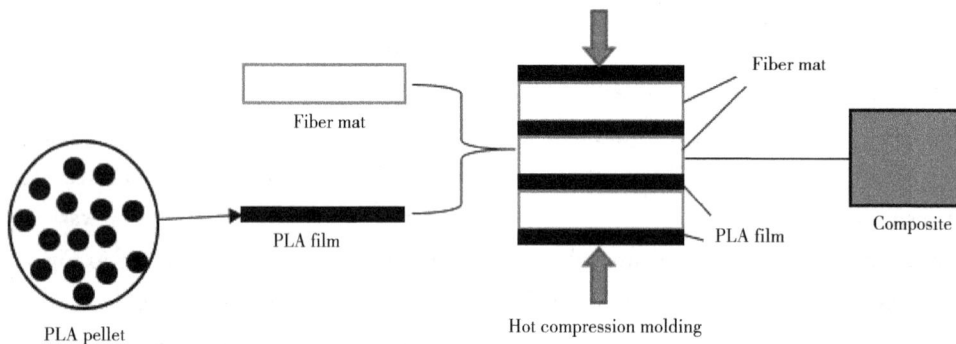

Fig.2 Fabrication procedure of apocynum venetum (AV) fiber reinforced PLA of composites

3 Characterizations

3.1 Tensile and Flexural Strength

Tensile and flexural test samples of the alkali treated AV, and untreated AV fiber mat composites were determined by computer based instruments using an INSTRON 4302 machine according to ASTM D638 and ASTM D790 standards respectively. A 30kN load cell was employed with the crosshead speed of 2mm/min. Test samples having 130mm length and 13mm width were placed in a 65% relative humidity and 23℃ conditioning room for 24 hours before testing. Five rectangular samples of each composite sample were analyzed, and the average of the final results was taken for further analysis.

3.2 Morphological Analysis

After the tensile test, the morphological interface of the fractured composites investigated by scanning electron microscopy (FlexSEM1000 HITACHI). The gold coating of the fractured test was completed before taking the photomicrograph. The device was operated at a current of 100l A and a voltage of 10kV.

4 Results and Discussions

The mechanical properties of the alkali treated, and untreated AV fiber PLA composites were analyzed. Comparison and discussion were done on the results for each composite. Fig. 3 and Fig. 4 shows the stress-strain curves for tensile and bending tests, respectively.

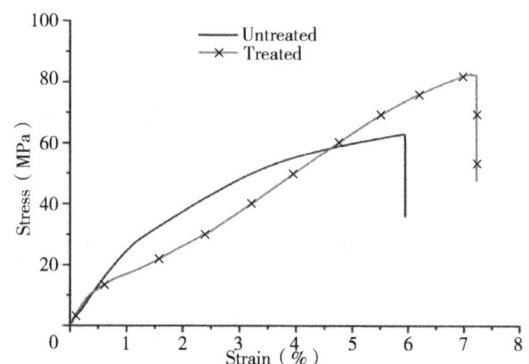

Fig.3 Stress-strain curve for tensile test

4.1 Tensile Properties

The stress-strain curves of the composite are illustrated in Fig.3. A stress-strain diagram was generated to determine the tensile strength and tensile modulus of the composite. As can be seen from the stress-strain graph, the treated AV fiber composites displayed higher tensile strength than the untreated AV fiber composites. The treated AV fiber reinforced composite had a tensile strength of 82MPa, which was higher than that of the composite of the untreated AV fiber reinforced with 63MPa.

Besides, the treated AV fiber composite had a tensile modulus of 5.03GPa, which is 21.5% higher than the tensile modulus of the untreated AV fiber reinforced PLA composite. The results show that alkali treatment can significantly improve tensile properties.

4.2 Flexural Properties

Fig.4 showed the stress-strain curve for the flexural test of composites. The bending properties of composite samples were tested using a three-point bending test method, and the stress-strain curves were obtained with experimental data.

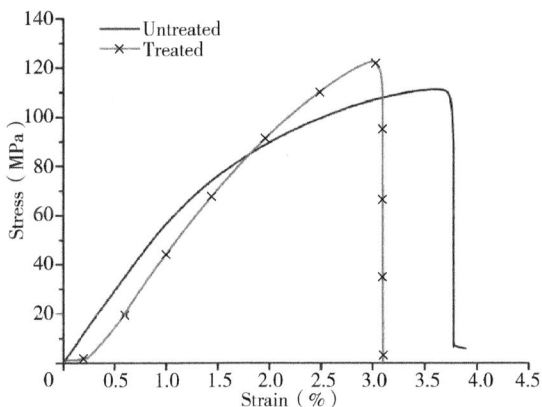

Fig.4 Stress-strain curve for the flexural test

Based on the experimental data, bending strength and modulus of the composites were calculated. As can be seen from the stress-strain chart, the treated AV fiber reinforced tests have higher flexural strength and flexural modulus values than the untreated AV fiber composites. Bending strength and bending modulus of the alkali treated fiber composites were 122MPa and 5.85GPa, which were 9.91% and 7.54% higher, respectively, than the untreated AV fiber reinforced PLA composite. The improved bending properties of the biocomposite after the enhanced treatment of the AV fibers

ensure the excellent fiber-matrix adhesion.

4.3 Morphological Analysis

SEM images of tensile fracture of treated and untreated AV fiber composite samples were shown in Fig.5. Untreated AV fiber reinforced composites showed that there are fiber pull-outs, voids, and weak interfacial bonding between fiber and matrix; while in the case of treated AV fiber reinforced composite shown, the problems have been improved. The composite containing treated AV fiber had good interfacial bonding.

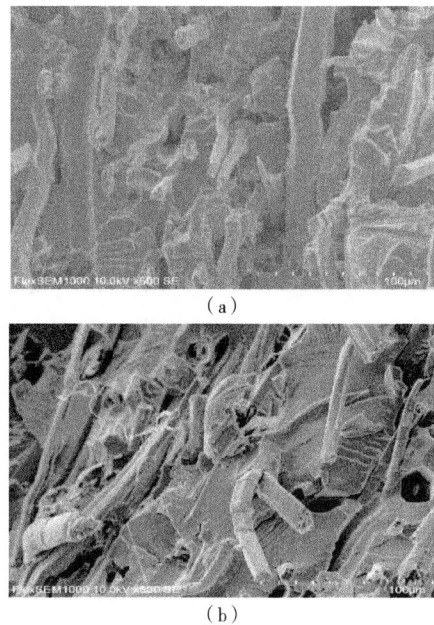

(a)

(b)

Fig.5 SEM micrographs of (a) Untreated AV fiber reinforced composite and (b) Treated AV fiber reinforced composite

5 Conclusions

In this paper, the development of AV fiber reinforced PLA composites is pointed out, and the effect of alkali treatment on the mechanical properties of hot formed composites is studied. The developed samples were mechanically characterized, such as tensile strength and flexural strength, and the conclusions derived from the experimental results. Based on the current results, it noted that the mechanical properties (tensile strength, tensile modulus, flexural strength, and flexural modulus) of the treated AV fiber-reinforced PLA biocomposites are higher than those of the untreated AV fiber-reinforced composites. The results of the bending and tensile properties indicate that the alkali treatment improves the compatibility between the AV fibers and the PLA matrix. The fracture surface morphology of the treated AV fiber composites demonstrates that the fiber matrix interfacial adhesion is better than that of the untreated AV fiber composite.

References

[1] LU N, OZA S. A comparative study of the mechanical properties of hemp fiber with virgin and recycled high density polyethylene matrix[J]. Composites Part B: Engineering, 2013, 45(1): 1651-1656.

[2] NORUL IZANI M A, PARIDAH M T, ANWAR U M K, et al. Effects of fiber treatment on morphology, tensile and thermogravimetric analysis of oil palm empty fruit bunches fibers [J]. Composites Part B: Engineering, 2013, 45(1): 1251-1257.

[3] SATYANARAYANA K G, ARIZAGA G G C, WYPYCH F. Biodegradable composites based on lignocellulosic fibers—an overview[J]. Progress in Polymer Science, 2009, 34(9): 982-1021.

[4] ZHONG Y, KUREEMUN U, TRAN L Q N, et al. Natural plant fiber composites-constituent properties and challenges in numerical modeling and simulations [J]. International Journal of Applied Mechanics, 2017, 09(04).

[5] GEORGOPOULOS S T, TARANTILI P A, AVGERINOS E, et al. Thermoplastic polymers reinforced with fibrous agricultural residues[J]. Polymer Degradation and Stability, 2005, 90(2): 303-312.

[6] WESTMAN MP F L, SIMMONS K L, LADDHA S G, et al. Natural fiber composites: a review[J]. Richland: Pacific Northwest National Laboratory, 2010.

[7] PREET SINGH J I, DHAWAN V, SINGH S, et al. Study of effect of surface treatment on mechanical properties of natural fiber reinforced composites[J].Materials Today: Proceedings, 2017, 4(2): 2793-2799.

[8] SAWPAN M A, PICKERING K L, FERNYHOUGH A. Effect of fibre treatments on interfacial shear strength of hemp fibre reinforced polylactide and unsaturated polyester composites[J]. Composites Part A: Applied Science and Manufacturing, 2011, 42(9): 1189-1196.

[9] ZHU Z, YE C, FU W, et al. Improvement in mechanical and thermal properties of polylactic acid biocomposites due to the addition of hybrid sisal fibers and diatomite particles[J]. International Journal of Polymer Analysis and Characterization, 2016, 21(5): 365-377.

[10] HAN G, WANG L, LIU M, et al. Component analysis and microfiber arrangement of Apocynum venetum fibers: the MS and AFM study[J]. Carbohydrate Polymers, 2008, 72 (4): 652-656.

[11] WANG L, HAN G, ZHANG Y. Comparative study of composition, structure and properties of Apocynum venetum fibers under different pretreatments[J]. Carbohydrate Polymers, 2007, 69(2): 391-397.

[12] LI M, HAN G, YU J. Microstructure and mechanical properties of apocynum venetum fibers extracted by alkali-assisted ultrasound with different frequencies [J]. Fibers and Polymers, 2010, 11(1): 48-53.

Study on Preparation Process and Tensile Properties of New High-Density Biaxial Warp Knitting PVC Tent Materials

LV Linchao[1,2], CHEN Nanliang[1,2], LIU Yiwen[2], HUANG Tianlin[2], LI Beibei[2], JIANG Jinhua[1,2]*

[1] Engineering Research Center of Technical Textiles, Ministry of Education, Shanghai, 201620, China

[2] College of Textiles, Donghua University, Shanghai, 201620, China

* Corresponding author's email: jiangjinhua@ dhu.edu.cn

Abstract: In this paper, the structural design of the new high-density biaxial warp knit fabric was described. On the basis of this fabric, the PVC membranes were laminated on both sides in order to prepare the composite materials, then the tensile mechanism of the composite was analyzed and the orthogonal experiment was designed. The influence of coating process parameters on the tensile properties of the composites was sought to find the coating process that optimized the tensile properties of the composites. Through the analysis of range and the sum of levels, it was concluded that the tensile fracture property of the composite was optimal when the membrane thickness was 0.26mm, the membrane pressing temperature was 160℃ and the membrane pressing time was 160s.

Keywords: Composite materials; Tensile; PVC membrane

1 Introduction

The tent material is a new type of material that has developed extremely rapidly at home and abroad in recent years. It can be widely used in construction, geology, transportation[1], environmental protection, advertising and other industries[2]. As the field of application becomes more widespread, the speed of development is getting faster and faster. At present, the domestic demand is increasing.

Tent fabrics are usually made of polyester and have a small portion of cotton, nylon, acrylic and glassfiber products[3]. Polyester is widely used in base fabrics due to its high strength, durability, good tensile properties and moderate price. The flexible composite material with polyester base fabric as reinforcement has high strength, modulus and dimensional stability. It also has strong bearing capacity and good fatigue resistance. In addition, it has large deformation space compared with thermoset or thermoplastic matrix composites. The new PVC cover material based on polyester industrial fabric gradually replaces the traditional tarpaulin of cotton, vinylon and polyester staple fiber. This phenomenon becomes the mainstream of the development in the world today.

The polyester tarpaulin coated with PVC of our country has many quality problems such as low strength of monofilament, low tear strength[4], low peel strength and poor wear resistance. It will be cracked and contaminated after a period of use without surface finishing[5]. At present, the quality problem of PVC coated polyester tarpaulin has attracted the attention of domestic enterprises, and the membrane structure cover material for construction is being developed in China. In this paper, by designing an orthogonal test, the optimal production parameters of the tensile properties of PVC membrane were found which provided help for the development of the tent materials in China.

2 Experiments

2.1 Technology Design of the Fabric

The knitting process parameters of the high-density polyester biaxial warp knit fabric are shown in Tab.1. The structure diagrammatic of the biaxial warp knit fabric is shown in Fig. 1 and the high-density biaxial fabric sample is shown in Fig.2.

2.2 Materials

High-density polyester biaxial warp knit fabric (textile structure and sample as shown in Fig.1 and Fig.2): warp density is 32 roots per inch; weft density is 32 roots per inch; fabric areal density is $330g/m^2$; fabric thickness is 0.70mm, parchased from Changzhou PGTEX China Co., Ltd. There are three kinds of PVC membrane. The thickness of them is 0.26mm, 0.30mm and 0.34mm respectively. And the areal density is $338g/m^2$, $404g/m^2$ and $432g/m^2$ respectively, parchased from Zhejiang MSD New Materials Co., Ltd.

Tab.1 Weaving process parameters of high-density biaxial warp knit fabric

Number of combs	Raw material specifications	Mat yarn digital
GB1	75D	1-0/2-3/1-0/2-3//
GB2	1000D	0-0/1-1/0-0/2-2//
GB3	1000D	0-0/2-2/0-0/1-1//
MSU	1000D	Full weft insertion

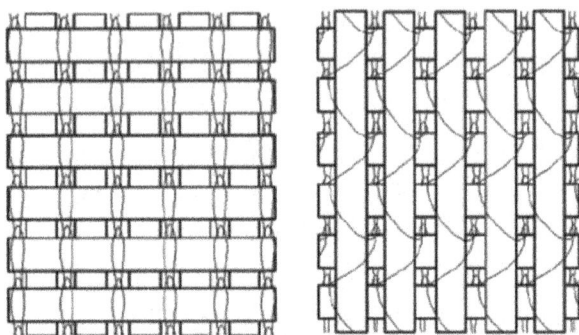

Fig.1 Structure diagrammatic of the fabric

2.3 Laboratory Instruments

INSTRON5980 electronic universal testing machine (Shanghai Hualian Environmental Testing Equipment Co., Ltd.); GZX-GF-101-1 electric heating constant temperature blast drying oven; 350kN XLB-D (Hengchang Instrument Factory); 350×350 type flat panel Vulcanizing machine (Huzhou Shunli Rubber Machinery Co., Ltd.).

Fig.2 High density biaxial fabric sample

2.4 Test Standard

The tensile test of fabrics in this paper refers to GB/T 3923.1—2013 "Determination of tensile properties of textile fabrics—Part 1: Determination of breaking strength and elongation at break (strip method)". The gauge spacing is 200mm, the sample width is 50mm, the clamping length is 50mm, the stretching speed is 100mm/min, and the pre-tension is 5N. In the test, all the samples were tested in the warp and weft directions, and three samples were prepared in the warp and weft directions, and then the average value of the breaking strength was taken three times.

2.5 Methods for Preparing PVC Tent Materials

A manual coating method was used in the test. Place the base on a flat glass table, press the end of the base fabric with iron blocks, and then pour a certain amount of PVC primer sol onto the base fabric evenly, then use the glass rod to evenly scrape the base sol through the base cloth. The fabric is scraped and coated on both sides, and placed in an oven. The oven temperature is 140℃, and the hot drying time is 5 minutes. Finally, the base fabric is double-sidedly laminated with PVC membranes and pressed on a flat vulcanizing machine. After reaching the set time, take out the iron plate together with the composite material, pressurize and cool for 5 minutes, then open the iron plate and take out the finished products.

2.6 Primer Sol Formula

The paste was made of 100 percent of polyvinyl chloride resin, 70 percent of plasticizer and 2 percent of stabilizer, and the mass fraction of PVC binder is 3.3% (mass fraction of total amount of PVC primer sol).

2.7 Experimental Design

The test determines the experimental process parameters according to the factory production process parameters, including the thickness of the PVC membrane, the membrane temperature and the membrane pressing time. Multi-factor optimization was carried out by orthogonal test to determine the comprehensive influence of experimental process parameters on the tensile properties of composites and to find the optimal process. The pressure of the laminating membrane is uniformly 5MPa.

The orthogonal test factor design table is shown in Tab. 2, and the orthogonal test is shown in Tab.3.

Tab.2   Factor design table

Factor	1	2	3
Membrane thickness (mm)	0.26	0.30	0.34
Membrane pressing temperature (℃)	160	170	180
Membrane pressing time (s)	140	150	160

Tab.3   Orthogonal test table

Sample number	Membrane thickness	Membrane pressing temperature	Membrane pressing time
1	1	1	1
2	1	2	2
3	1	3	3
4	2	1	2
5	2	2	3
6	2	3	1
7	3	1	3
8	3	2	1
9	3	3	2

3   Results and Discussions

The test results of the breaking strength of the orthogonal test sample are shown in Tab.4. According to Tab.4, at different membrane thicknesses, laminating temperatures and laminating time, the range in the warp tensile strength of the composites are 831.2, 1105.3 and 410.4, the range in weft breaking strength of composites are 740.8, 1332.8 and 722.3. That is, the influence of three factors on the warp and weft fracture strength from the largest to the smallest is the membrane temperature, the thickness of the membrane and the membrane pressing time.

Tab.4   Tensile fracture strength of samples

Sample number	Tensile strength in warp (N)	Tensile strength in weft (N)
1	4320.3	4299.1
2	4102.5	4393.1
3	3840.3	3838.6
4	4107.8	4276.7
5	4285.2	3864.5
6	3977.7	3648.8
7	4646.0	4118.2
8	4297.5	4227.2
9	4150.8	3873.8

The tensile fracture of the membrane material can be divided into three stages[6]. The first stage is the high modulus zone which is the shortest time. In this stage, the yarn and the fiber of the fabric cause friction because of bending change. The second stage is the low modulus region. The yarn bending in the direction of the force is smaller, and the bending of the yarn in the direction of the vertical force increases. The yarn interlacing point is compressed. The third stage is the high modulus region, and the yarn in the direction of the force is basically straightening. The main manifestations are the elongation and slip of yarns and fibers. The composite tensile curve is shown in Fig.3.

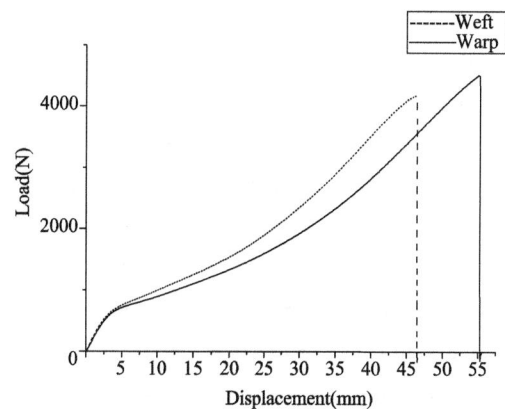

Fig.3   Composite material tensile curve

The mechanical properties of the membrane material mainly depend on the mechanical properties of the base fabric. When the membrane material is subjected to tensile force, it is mainly caused by the force of the base fabric. At the beginning of stretching, the yarn and fiber in the base fabric change from bending to straightening, and the yarn in the non-stretching direction is pressed. During the stretching process, the yarn and the fiber in the direction of the force begin to elongate and become thinner. The fabric is thinned, the sample structure becomes single, and the yarn in the vertical stretching direction is gradually concave due to the tangential sliding resistance, so that the fabric presents a "bow-waist shape". Finally, the yarn breaks from root to root in the direction of the force and causes the entire membrane material to be destroyed.

The sum of the latitude and longitude breaking strength levels of the composite is shown in Fig.4. It can be seen that the tensile strength at break of the warp and weft of the composite material is not consistent with the trend of the three factors. The breaking strength decreases with increasing temperature in the warp and weft direction which may be related to the heat shrinkage of the base fabric. As the temperature increases, the molten PVC penetrates into the base fabric, and part or all of the surface of the yarn is wrapped by the molten PVC. At this time, the undercoat sol is melted by heat and penetrates into the yarn, so that some or all of the fibers in the polyester filament yarn are wrapped by the primer sol. The break strength of fibers and yarns is reduced, and the material breaking strength is reduced. At the same time, the temperature rises, the thermal motion of the macromolecular chain in the PVC membrane is intensified, and the degree of orientation is reduced. Some small molecular substances in the system are volatilized by heat but cannot be discharged in time, so that bubbles and defects in the material increase, the mechanical properties of the material decrease, and the breaking strength decreases. The tensile strength of the warp increases with the increase of the thickness of the PVC membrane, decreases first and then increases with the increase of time. The strength of the latitudinal frac-

ture decreases first and then increases with the increase of the thickness of the PVC membrane, and increases first and then decreases with the increase of time. This may be related to the organization of the base fabric. In the warp direction, as the thickness of the membrane increases, the strength of the membrane itself becomes large, and the breaking strength of the material increases. Due to the isothermal aging, the prolonged time and the elevated temperature have similar effects. That is, the lamination time increases, the PVC melting intensifies and the fibers and yarns are wrapped by the

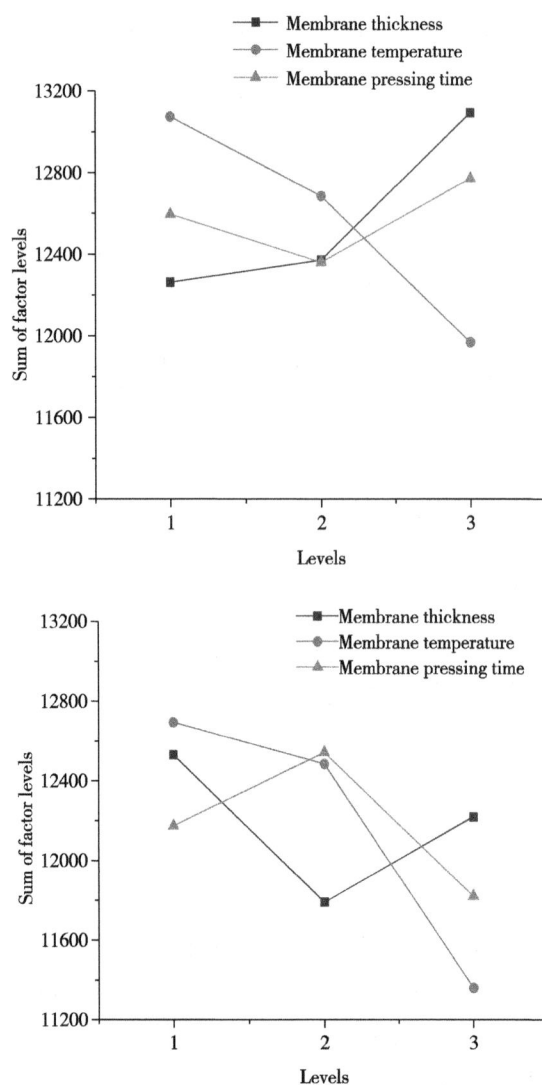

Fig.4 The sum of tensile breaking strength levels

Note The abscissas 1, 2, and 3 represent that the membrane thickness is 0.26mm, 0.30mm and 0.34mm, the membrane temperature is 160℃, 170℃ and 180℃, and the membrane time is 140s, 150s and 160s.

molten PVC. The melting of undercoat sol intensifies, so the fibers and yarns are more closely bonded together. This phenomenon results in the decline of the breaking strength of fibers and yarns. Therefore, the breaking strength of materials decreases. With the further extension of membrane pressing time, the macromolecular chains from PVC membrane to interface and the fabric will probably form bonds with the macromolecular chains such as dipole bonds and hydrogen bonds. The material achieves a new equilibrium and the breaking strength increases.

4 Conclusions

According to the analysis of results, when the membrane thickness is 0.34mm, the temperature is 160℃, and the time is 160s, the sum of the longitudinal tensile strength levels is the largest. When the membrane thickness is 0.26mm, the temperature is 160℃, and the time is 150s, the sum of the latitudinal tensile breaking strength levels is the largest. It is calculated that when the membrane thickness is 0.26mm and the time is 160s, the difference in the strength of the warp and weft fracture strength of the composite material is smaller. Therefore, when the membrane thickness is 0.26mm, the temperature is 160℃, and the time is 160s, the tensile fracture properties of the composite are optimal.

Acknowledgements

This work was financially supported by National Key R&D Program of China (2016YFB0303300), the Fundamental Research Funds for the Central Universities (2232018G – 06), and the Shanghai Innovation Experiment Program for University Students (sh201810255007).

References

[1] TAWFIK B E, LEHETA H, ELHEWY A, et al. Weight reduction and strengthening of marine hatch covers by using composite materials[J]. International Journal of Naval Architecture & Ocean Engineering, 2016, 9(2).

[2] WANG L Y. Membrane structural materials and new covering materials: key technologies to be breakthroughed[J]. Textile and Apparel Weekly, 2006, (18):19.

[3] AVILAFLORES R, MEDELLIN R A. Ecological, taxonomic and physiological correlates of cave use by mexican bats[J]. Journal of Mammalogy, 2004, 85(4):675-687.

[4] CAI Y, SUN P, ZHU H, et al. A Mixed cover meshless method for elasticity and fracture problems[J]. Theoretical & Applied Fracture Mechanics, 2018, 95.

[5] JIAO W H, CHEN N L. Performance advantages of warp-knitted biaxial fabrics as coating substrates[J]. Journal of Donghua University, 2004, 30(6):91-95.

[6] YE H S, REN Z H, YAN Y F. Research on mechanism and tensile properties of PVC menbrane material under different conditions[J]. Materials Review, 2013. 27(S2):219-222+241.

Effect of Plasma Treatment on the Surface Properties of Carbon Fiber Bundles

DI Zhe[1], YAO Lan[1]*, SUN Shiyuan[2], QIU Yiping[1]

[1] *Key Laboratory of Textile Science & Technology, Ministry of Education, College of Textiles, Donghua University, Shanghai, 201620, China*

[2] *Jiaxing Product Quality Inspection & Testing Institute, Zhejiang, 314050, China*

* *Corresponding author's email*: yaolan@ dhu.edu.cn

Abstract: Carbon fiber is widely used in composite materials due to its excellent mechanical properties. However, the surface of the carbon fiber is smooth and chemically inert, which seriously affects the formation of good adhesion with the resins. Plasma treatment, as a usually used fiber surface treatment method, is proved to be an efficient way to improve the adhesion of carbon fiber and resins. In this study, carbon fiber bundles were treated with plasma treatment for different durations. Scanning electron microscopy (SEM) and atomic force microscopy (AFM) results showed that plasma treatment increased the surface roughness of carbon fibers. X-Ray Photoelectron Spectroscopy (XPS) analysis and water contact angle proved that the chemical activity of the carbon fiber surface was improved due to the increase of oxygen-containing polar groups on the fiber surface. Tensile strength test results indicated that the strength of carbon fiber was not affected significantly by the plasma treatment.

Keywords: Carbon fiber bundles; Plasma treatment; Surface properties

1　Introduction

Carbon fiber has been widely used in aerospace, rail transit, automobile and other fields due to the excellent mechanical and thermal properties, such as high specific strength, high modulus and good heat resistance[1-2].

However, the surface of carbon fiber became smooth and lacked chemically active functional groups after carbonization at a high temperature. These characteristics make the bonding between carbon fiber and composite matrix poor, which seriously affects the mechanical properties of the carbon fiber composite[3].

Therefore, more researchers have gradually recognized the importance of surface modification, and conducted many related studies. Currently, electrochemical[4] and chemical treatment[5] sizing techniques[6] as well as the plasma etching are commonly used to modify the surface of carbon fiber. Compared to other treatment types, plasma modification has been widely studied due to the high efficiency, no waste of chemical solution, environmental friendliness, and no significant damage to the properties of the material[7-9].

In this study, T300 carbon fiber bundles were used as raw material and treated with air plasma at low pressure to study the effects of treatment on the surface roughness, chemical elements, wettability and tensile strength of carbon fiber bundles.

2　Experiments

2.1　Materials

T300 carbon fiber bundles were obtained from Japan Toray Industries. Before plasma treatment, the size on the surface of carbon fiber bundles should be removed by Soxhlet extraction[10]. The experimental procedure was as follows.

(1) Assembled Soxhlet extraction device;

(2) The fiber bundles were wound into a circle of appropriate size and put into the Soxhlet extractor.

Poured a certain volume of acetone into the round bottom flask and set the temperature of the constant temperature water bath box to 75℃;

(3) After soaking in pure acetone for 6 hours, the fiber bundles were dried at 80℃ for 4 hours in the oven.

2.2　Plasma Treatment

The plasma treatment process was performed using the vacuum plasma treatment equipment (JXZJY－001). The sample was prepared by fixing the fiber bundles on a square paper frame with the size of 20cm × 20cm. Samples were treated with air plasma at room temperature. The power was set at 200W, the pressure at 30Pa, and the treatment time was 60s, 120s and 180s respectively.

2.3　Surface Morphology and Roughness

2.3.1　Scanning Electron Microscopy (SEM)

SEM (TM 3000) was used to observe the surface morphology of carbon fiber before and after plasma treatment. The fibers were attached to the sample table with double-sided conductive tape and sprayed with gold for observation. The magnification of the fiber image was set to 10k×.

2.3.2　Atomic Force Microscopy (AFM)

The surface topology of carbon fiber before and after plasma treatment were observed by AFM (NTEGRA, NT-MD) with a tapping mode. The fibers were straighten and pasted on the square board with a size of 18mm × 18mm for observation. The scanning area was 5μm×5μm.

2.4　X-Ray Photoelectron Spectroscopy (XPS)

Chemical composition on the surface of carbon fiber after plasma treatment was measured by XPS (Thermo ESCALAB 250Xi, USA). A monochromatic Al Kα X-ray source (1486.6 eV) was used to collect the spectrum, with the power of 150W and the beam spot size of 500μm. The energy analyzer set the transmission energy at 30eV. The data was calibrated and the surface chemical composition was obtained by calculating the relative spectral peak area.

2.5　Contact Angle Test

The contact angles of carbon fiber were collected using the optical contact angle meter (OCAI5EC, Dataphysics, Germany). The hydrophilic sample was prepared by

carding the fibers into a uniform and smooth layer with the size of 40mm×6mm and sticking it in the middle of the glass slide along the longitudinal direction. The hydrophobic sample was prepared in the similar method, but the fiber layer was changed to the size of 45mm× 6mm and stuck in the glass slide along the lateral direction.

2.6　Single-Fiber Tensile Strength Test

XQ-1 single-fiber tensile testing machine was used to test the tensile strength of carbon fiber before and after plasma treatment. The monofilament was separated from the carbon fiber bundle and pasted on the paper frame. The paper frame size is shown in the Fig.1. Then clamp the sample in the test fixture and carefully cut the paper frame along the dotted line in the Fig.1. The tensile speed was 10mm/min and the gauge was 20mm[11]. Samples were tested for 50 times. The 10 maximum and minimum results were removed respectively, and 30 valid datas were obtained as a group.

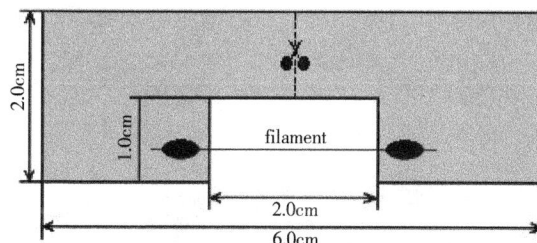

Fig.1　The paper frame for single-fiber tensile strength test

3　Results and Discussions

3.1　Surface Morphology and Roughness

SEM images of carbon fibers surface before and after plasma treatment are presented in Fig.2. Due to the manufacturing process of carbon fibers (CFs), the fiber surface has clear ridges and stripes parallel to the fiber axis. Although the plasma treatment has a certain etching effect on the fiber surface, it can be seen from the SEM images of different treatment times that the effect was not obvious, and the degree was not significantly enhanced with the treatment time.

AFM images of carbon fibers surface before and after plasma treatment are shown in the Fig.3. Compared to the untreated carbon fiber, it can be seen that the sur-

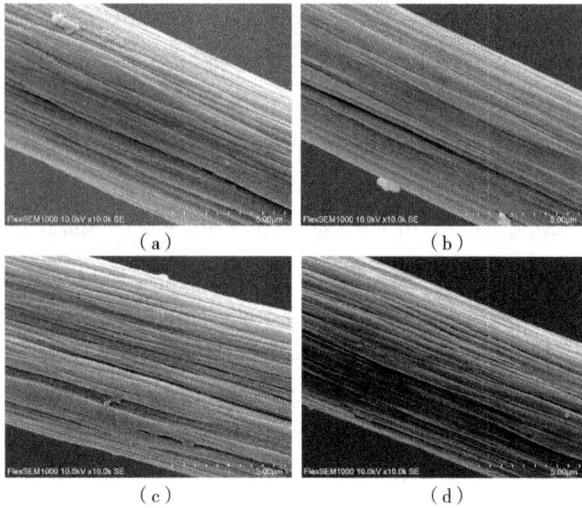

Fig.2　SEM images of CFs at different plasma treatment times: (a) Untreated; (b) Treated for 60s; (c) Treated for 120s; (d) Treated for 180s

face of carbon fiber was significantly rougher after plasma treatment.

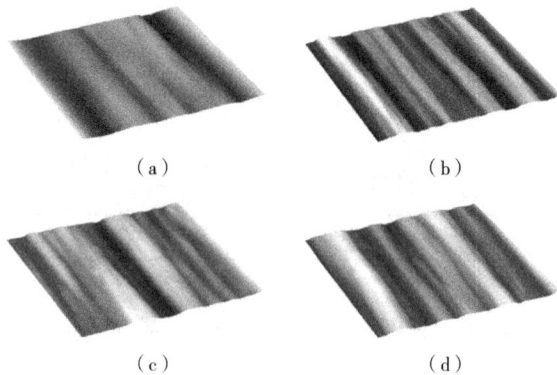

Fig.3　AFM images of CFs at different plasma treatment times: (a) Untreated; (b) Treated for 60s; (c) Treated for 120s; (d) Treated for 180s

Ra (Roughness average) and Rq (Root mean square) (Tab.1) were calculated by AFM analysis software. They are commonly used to characterize roughness. According to the calculation results, Ra and Rq of the treated carbon fibers are larger than those of the untreated carbon fibers, indicating that the plasma treatment increased the roughness of the fiber surface. Rougher surface of carbon fiber leads to larger specific surface area, which is beneficial to increase the mechanical interlocking between the fiber and the resins, thereby improving the interfacial bonding

fastness of the composite.

Compared to the data of 60s, Ra and Rq of 120s are larger, which proves that the surface roughness of carbon fibers increased. It can be attributed to the bombardment of high-energy particles or free radicals in air plasma on the carbon fiber surface[12]. However, the Ra and Rq of 180s are slightly less than those of 120s, indicating a slight decrease in surface roughness. This phenomenon can be explained by the fact that prolonging the plasma treatment time may cause atoms and chains to accumulate together to fill the concave position.

Tab.1　Ra and Rq of untreated and treated CFs

Treatment times(s)	0	60	120	180
Ra(nm)	32.900	48.217	54.807	52.954
Rq(nm)	41.592	57.04	67.49	63.165

3.2　Surface Chemical Composition

The changes of chemical composition on carbon fiber surface before and after plasma treatment were determined by XPS. The relative concentration of atoms for carbon, oxygen, and nitrogen on carbon fiber surface is listed in Tab. 2. The results show that after 60s air plasma treatment, the ratio of oxygen to carbon atoms increased from 0.178 to 0.218, indicating that more oxygen-containing polar groups were introduced on the surface of carbon fiber after plasma treatment, which is beneficial to enhance the chemical bonding between the fiber and the resins. But as time increases, the ratio of oxygen to carbon will decrease. This can be explained by the fact that air plasma sputtering may destroy the intrinsic chains and surface groups of the fiber, and some atoms would be knocked off at the same time[13-15].

Tab.2　Surface chemical composition of untreated and treated CFs

Treatment times(s)	Relative concentration of elements (%)			Atomic ratio	
	C	O	N	O/C	N/C
0	80.99	14.45	4.56	0.178	0.056
60	78.53	17.11	4.36	0.218	0.056
120	81.19	14.56	4.25	0.179	0.052
180	82.68	14.80	2.52	0.179	0.030

3.3 Contact Angle

Good wettability is important for a strong bond between the fiber and resins. The contact angle images of untreated and plasma-treated carbon fibers are shown in Fig.4. After plasma treatment, the contact angle of carbon fiber reduced obviously, and the carbon fiber changed from hydrophobicity to hydrophilicity (Fig.5). This proves that polar groups were introduced into the surface of carbon fiber, which improved the surface activity and wettability of carbon fiber. After 60s treatment, it is not difficult to find that the contact angle decreases most significantly. But the contact angle increases slightly with processing time. The tendency is consistent with the results from XPS.

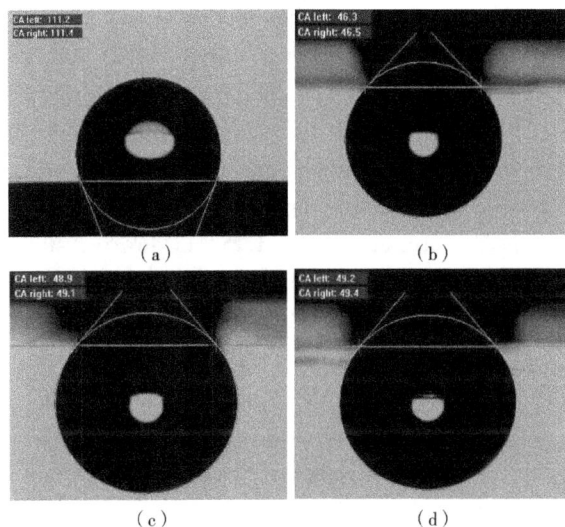

Fig.4　Contact angle images of CFs at different plasma treatment times: (a) Untreated; (b) Treated for 60s; (c) Treated for 120s; (d) Treated for 180s

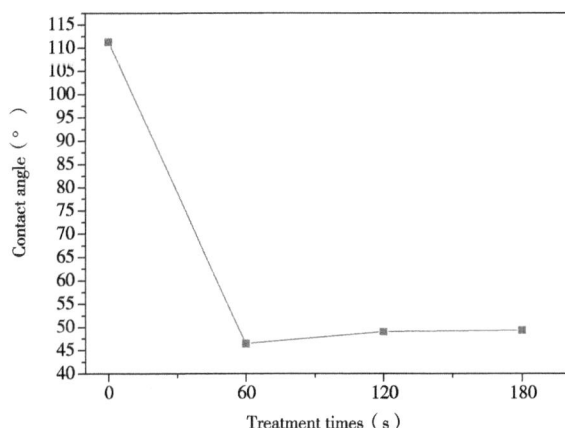

Fig.5　Contact angles of untreated and treated CFs

3.4 Tensile Strength

The tensile strength of carbon fiber treated by air plasma at different time is shown in Fig.6. As treatment time increases, the tensile strength of carbon fiber almost tends to decrease. Compared with the tensile strength of untreated carbon fiber, the tensile strength of carbon fiber with 60s treatment time increased by 2%, and the tensile strength of carbon fiber with 120s treatment time decreased by 6%. But with 180s treatment, the tensile strength of carbon fiber decreased by 10%.

To determine the difference between the test results of treated and untreated samples, the P value of 60s was calculated to be 0.25, greater than 0.05, showing no significant difference between the two groups of data. However, the P value of 120s is 0.02, which is less than 0.05, indicating that the difference between the two groups is significant; the P value of 180s is close to 0, indicating that the difference between the two groups is extremely significant. From the above analysis, it can be concluded that long-time plasma treatment may impair the tensile strength of carbon fiber.

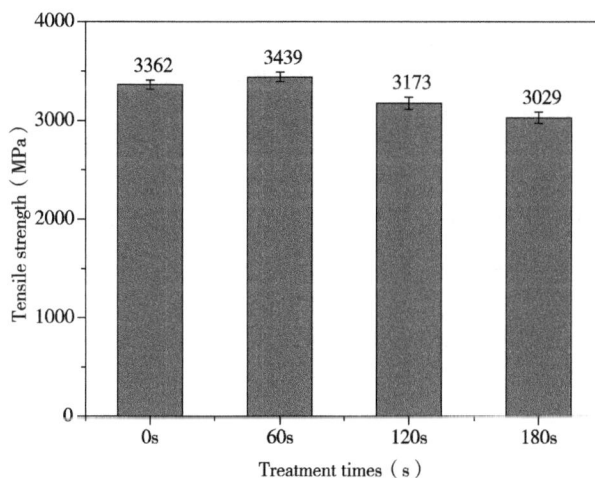

Fig.6　Single fiber tensile strength of CFs after different plasma treatments time

4 Conclusions

Low pressure air plasma treatment has successfully increased the surface roughness and the number of active groups of carbon fiber bundles and improved their wettability. SEM and AFM analysis showed that the plasma modification increased the surface roughness of the fiber, which is beneficial to improve the interfacial bonding strength between the carbon fiber and the resins. Analysis of XPS and water contact angle test proved that air plasma treatment introduced oxygen-containing groups on the surface of carbon fiber, which significantly improved the wettability, making it easier to bond with resins. Tensile strength results indicated that the carbon fiber may be damaged by prolonged plasma treatment.

References

[1]LIU Y, KUMAR S. Recent progress in fabrication, structure, and properties of carbon fibers[J]. Polymer Reviews, 2012, 52(3):234-258.

[2] KARSLI N G, AYTAC A. Tensile and thermomechanical properties of short carbon fiber reinforced polyamide 6 composites[J]. Composites Part B: Engineering, 2013, 51 (Complete):270-275.

[3]PARK S J, JUNG Y, KIM S. Effect of fluorine-oxygen mixed gas treated graphite fibers on electrochemical behaviors of platinum-ruthenium nanoparticles toward methanol oxidation [J]. Journal of Fluorine Chemistry, 2012, 144.

[4] ANDIDEH M, ESFANDEH M. Statistical optimization of treatment conditions for the electrochemical oxidation of PAN-based carbon fiber by response surface methodology: Application to carbon fiber/epoxy composite[J]. Composites Science and Technology, 2016, 134:132-143.

[5]SEVERINI, FEBO, FORMARO, et al. Chemical modification of carbon fiber surfaces[J]. Carbon, 2002, 40(5):735-741.

[6]OZKAN C, KARSLI N G, AYTAC A, et al. Short carbon fiber reinforced polycarbonate composites: effects of different sizing materials[J]. Composites Part B Engineering, 2014, 62:230-235.

[7]XIE Y, WU E, HU R, et al. Enhancing electronic and opto-electronic performance of tungsten diselenide by plasma treatment[J]. Nanoscale, 2018, 10:1039.

[8] GOKUS T, NAIR R R, BONETTI A, et al. Making graphene luminescent by oxygen plasma treatment[J]. ACS NANO, 2009, 3(12):3963-3968.

[9]ZHAO Y, ZHANG C, SHAO X, et al. Effect of atmospheric plasma treatment on carbon fiber/epoxy interfacial adhesion [J]. Journal of Adhesion Science and Technology, 2011,25 (20):12.

[10]CHEN Z, MENG L, FAN D, et al. Study on Soxhlet extraction and removal of carbon fiber surface slurry coating [J]. Synthetic Fiber, 2008(10):21-26.

[11]LI W, YAO S Y, MA K M, et al. Effect of plasma modification on the mechanical properties of carbon fiber/phenolphthalein polyaryletherketone composites[J]. Polymer Composites, 2013, 34(3):368-375.

[12] LIU D, CHEN P, MU J, et al. Improvement and mechanism of interfacial adhesion in PBO fiber/bismaleimide composite by oxygen plasma treatment[J]. Applied Surface Science, 2011,257(15):6935-6940.

[13] FUKUNAGA A, KOMAMI T, UEDA S, et al. Plasma treatment of pitch-based ultra high modulus carbon fibers [J]. Carbon, 1999, 37(7):1087-1091.

[14]MA K, CHEN P, WANG B, et al. A study of the effect of oxygen plasma treatment on the interfacial properties of carbon fiber/epoxy composites[J]. Journal of Applied Polymer Science, 2010, 118(3).

[15]KIM S Y, BAEK S J, YOUN J R. New hybrid method for simultaneous improvement of tensile and impact properties of carbon fiber reinforced composites[J]. Carbon, 2011, 49(15):5329-5338.

Preparation and Properties Study of Chitosan/Polyvinyl Alcohol Blended Fiber Membrane for Medical Dressing

SUN Wei[1], HUANG Liangliang[1], ZHANG Peihua[1]*

[1] *Key Laboratory of Textile Science & Technology, Ministry of Education, College of Textiles, Donghua University, Shanghai, 201620, China*

* *Corresponding author's email*: phzh@ dhu.edu.cn

Abstract: The antibacterial dressing prepared by the electrostatic spinning can play a role in protecting the wound, preventing infection and promoting wound healing, and has broad application prospects. In this paper, chitosan (CS)/polyvinyl alcohol (PVA) blended fiber membranes were successfully prepared by electrospinning. The fiber morphology, thermal properties and material composition of CS/PVA fiber were studied, and the interaction between CS and PVA was analyzed, and the optimum blending ratio was determined. Then glutaraldehyde steam cross-linking of the blend fiber membrane was carried out in order to improve the water resistance of the fiber membrane. At the same time, the effect of different cross-linking time on the water resistance of fiber membrane was investigated. The results show that with the increase of spinning solution concentration, the morphology of the fiber becomes more and more regular, and the fiber diameter increases gradually. The intermolecular interaction between CS and PVA was found by infrared spectroscopy and thermal properties, which improved the spinnability of CS electrospinning. After cross-linking, the water resistance of the fiber membrane was greatly improved, among which the effect of 4 hours cross-linking was the best, and the water resistance of the fiber membrane was increased by 64.89%.

Keywords: Chitosan; Polyvinyl alcohol; Cross-Linking; Water resistance

1 Introduction

Chitosan (CS) is a natural alkaline polysaccharide material, which has antibacterial, biocompatibility and promote wound healing, and is widely used in medical dressings[1]. The micro-nanofiber prepared by the electrostatic spinning technology is similar to the natural extracellular matrix and is widely used in the research of biomedical textiles[2]. CS is soluble in most solutions with lower pH value to form polycationic electrolytes, so it is difficult to carry out electrospinning smoothly. It is necessary to add other polymers with excellent spinnability to the spinning solution for blending[3], usually polyvinyl alcohol (PVA), polyethylene oxide (PEO), because both of them are hydrophilic materials, the composite fiber membrane has good moisture absorption performance, but the fiber is easy to dissolve in contact with the exudation liquid phase of the wound, and the

wet strength is low and the water resistance is poor[4], but there are often more wound exudates in the skin wound. In order to further improve the water resistance of the fiber, the cross-linking treatment is considered, so that it can be better used in medical dressings[5-6].

In this paper, the solution of CS and PVA was mixed according to a certain proportion (CS/PVA = 0/100, 10/90, 20/80, 30/70), and the blended fiber membrane was prepared by electrospinning. The apparent morphology, infrared spectrum and thermal properties of CS/PVA blended fibers with different mass ratios were tested. In order to reduce the hydrophilic properties of CS/PVA blended fiber membranes, the glutaraldehyde (GA) steam cross-linking method was used to cross-link the composite fiber membranes for different periods of time, and the water resistance of the crosslinked blend fiber membrane was tested, and the effect of GA cross-linking time on the water resistance of the fiber membrane was investigated, so as to select the appropriate cross-linking time.

2 Experiments

2.1 Materials

CS (90% deacetylation degree) was provided by State Key Laboratory for Modification of Material Science and Engineering (Donghua University). PLA (1750±50) was supplied by Sinopharm Chemical Reagent Co., Ltd. Glacial acetic acid (analytical pure AR) was provided by Shanghai Lingfeng Chemical Reagent Co., Ltd. GA (25% by mass) was provided by Sinopharm Chemical Reagent Co., Ltd.

2.2 Fiber Membrane Preparation

A certain mass of CS/PVA was mixed according to the mass ratio of 0/100, 10/90, 20/80, 30/70 and then dissolved it in 20% (volume ratio) acetic acid solution to prepare a concentration of 10% (mass volume). The solution was stirred at a constant temperature of 90℃ in a water bath thermostat magnetic stirrer until dissolved and defoaming. Electrospinning was started to prepare blended fiber membrane. The spinning time was 2h, and the spinning conditions were as follows: receiving distance was 20cm, voltage was 15.5kV, spinning speed was 0.8mL/h, flat needle of 18G. After the spinning was completed, a CS/PVA blended fiber membrane was obtained and placed in a ventilated place and dried for use.

2.3 Cross-Linking Treatment of Composite Fiber Membrane

The spinning solution with the best blending ratio was electrospun, continuously spun for 11h, and after drying, 5 parts of 3cm × 3cm samples were taken for cross-linking treatment. An appropriate amount of GA was taken in petri dish and placed at the bottom of glass dryer. Five samples were placed on the plastic scaffold, crosslink at room temperature for 0, 4h, 8h, 16h, 24h. The fiber film which reached the cross-linking time was placed in the oven, dried at 50℃ for 30 minutes, and the residual GA gas was removed.

2.4 Simulated Wound Exudate Configuration

Solution A was prepared according to YY/T 0471.1—2004 to simulate wound exudate for water resistance testing of composite fiber membranes.

2.5 Characterization of Fiber Membrane Properties

2.5.1 Morphology Analysis

Scanning electron microscopy (SEM, TM3000, Hitachi) was performed on the CS/PVA fiber membranes of different mass ratios. The images were processed by Image J software, the average diameter and CV value of the CS/PVA nanofibers with different mass ratios were calculated.

2.5.2 Fourier Transform Infrared Spectroscopy

Four different mass ratios of CS/PVA nanofibers and CS powders were characterized by Fourier transform infrared spectrometer (Spectrum Two, PerkinElmer).

2.5.3 Differential Scanning Calorimetry (DSC)

The thermal properties of four different blend ratio CS/PVA nanofibers were tested by differential scanning calorimeter (power compensation type) (DSC 4000, PerkinElmer).

2.5.4 Parameter Optimization of CS/PVA Blended Fiber Membrane

The mass loss rate can indirectly reflect the water resistance of the material. The lower the mass loss rate, the better the water resistance of the material.

The five kinds of fiber membranes which were crosslinked for different durations were dried to constant weight, and the mass W_0 was recorded, and averaged 5 times. Subsequently, it was placed in solution A for 24 hours, taken out and rinsed 3 times with distilled water, the filter paper was blotted to dryness, dried to constant weight and recorded in mass W_1, averaged 5 times, and the mass loss rate was calculated according to the formula (1).

$$\text{massloss rate} = \frac{W_0 - W_1}{W_0} \times 100\% \tag{1}$$

3 Results and Discussions

3.1 Morphology of CS/PVA Blended Fiber Membrane

Fig. 1 is an electron micrograph of a CS/PVA electrospun fiber membrane with different mass ratios. It can be seen from the figure that when the concentration of the spinning solution is constant, the fiber morphology is good when the mass ratio of CS/PVA is 0/100 and 10/90, and when the mass ratio of CS/PVA is 20/100 and 30/70, a small amount of spindle appeared in the blended fiber membrane. This is caused by the low concentration and high viscosity of chitosan. When the concentration of spinning solution is constant, the viscosity of spinning solution will be increased step by increasing the blending ratio of CS, thus reaching a critical point of spinning.

At the same time, Tab.1 found that with the increasing mass ratio of CS, the average diameter of fiber under different mass ratio increased, but the overall effect was not obvious. The average diameter of CS/PVA fiber with mass ratio of 30/70 was only 3.08% higher than that of CS/PVA fiber with mass ratio of 0/100. However, the effect on the diameter distribution of blend fiber membrane was significant, and the CV value of diameter increased at first and then decreased. This may be due to the increased viscosity of the spinning solution after the addition of CS, and the increase of conductivity, the decrease of surface tension, and the interaction between the three, resulting in less significant changes in the average diameter of the fibers. This also shows that when the mass ratio of CS/PVA is 30/70, it is the best blending ratio, so the CV value is lower.

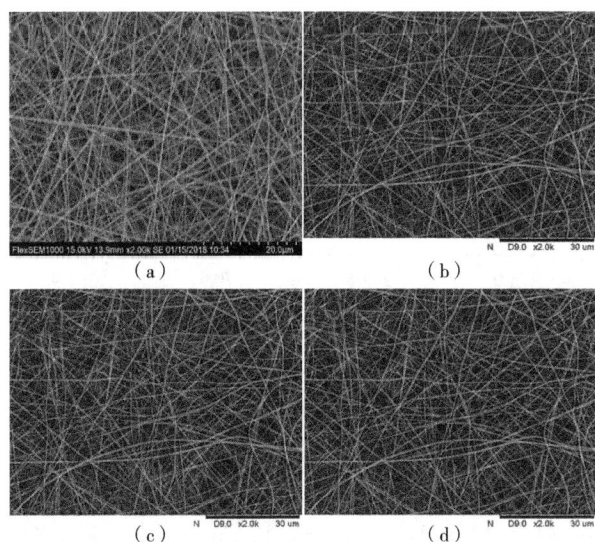

Fig.1　Electron micrograph of CS/PVA fiber membrane with different blending ratios (a) ~ (d) in turn is blend ratio 0/100, 10/90, 20/80, 30/70 fiber)

Tab.1　Diameter statistics of CS/PVA fiber membrane with different blending ratios

CS/PVA mass ratio	0/100	10/90	20/80	30/70
Average diameter(μm)	0.292	0.296	0.298	0.301
CV value(%)	41.01	47.80	40.35	33.29

3.2　Infrared Spectrum of CS/PVA Blended Fiber Membrane

The infrared spectra of the four blended fibers and CS powder are shown in Fig.2. In general, the infrared spectrum of the blended fiber does not change much, but compared with the infrared spectrum of pure PVA and pure CS, especially the infrared spectrum of pure CS, there are obvious differences:

The peak near $3306cm^{-1}$ is the stretching vibration peak of O—H in PVA. As the CS content increases, the peak intensity decreases and widens, and moves to a high wave number. The peak at $2940cm^{-1}$ is the asymmetric stretching vibration peak of C—H in PVA, which gradually decreases as CS increases. The sharp absorption peak at $1090cm^{-1}$ is caused by CO vibration in the PVA molecular chain, and the subsequent infrared absorption peak ($918cm^{-1}$) can be used to judge the crystal strength of PVA, which decreases with the increase of CS, isolated spike becomes a shoulder peak and eventually disappears in the infrared spectrum of pure CS. $846cm^{-1}$ is the vibrational absorption peak of C—H in the PVA molecular chain, which gradually decreases with the increase of CS[7-8].

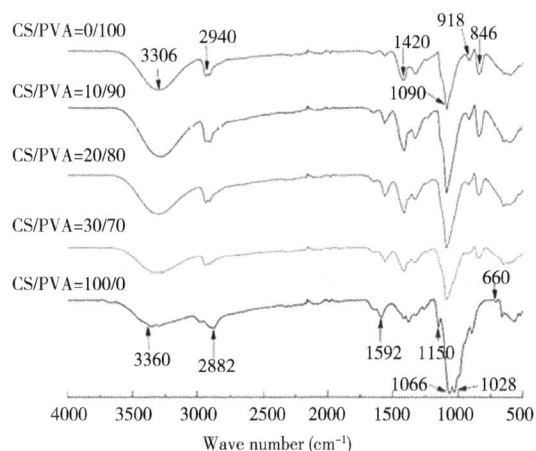

Fig.2　Comparison of infrared spectra of four blended fibers and CS powder CS/PVA fibers

At 1592cm^{-1}, the infrared absorption peak caused by the deformation vibration of the amino group shifts to the right as the mass ratio of the PVA increases, and the peak intensity gradually decreases. 1028cm^{-1} is the characteristic absorption peak of the primary hydroxyl group, and 1150cm^{-1} is the characteristic absorption peak of the secondary hydroxyl group, which disappears after adding PVA[9].

The above situation occurs because the amino group interacts with the hydroxyl group of PVA to form a hydrogen bond between the CS and PVA molecular chains. The formation of hydrogen bonds greatly enhances the interaction between the CS and PVA macromolecular chains, the electron cloud density is averaged, the vibration frequency is reduced, and the peak intensity of the corresponding infrared absorption peak is decreased. At the same time, the regularity of the CS molecular chain is destroyed, and the crystallinity is lowered, so that the combination of the two components is tight.

3.3 Thermal Properties (DSC) of CS/PVA Blended Fiber Membrane

Fig.3 shows the DSC curves for different blend ratio CS/PVA.Tab.2 shows the thermal performance analysis of CS/PVA with different blending ratios. It can be seen from Tab.2 that with the increase of CS content, the T_m of the blended fiber decreases slightly, and the melting enthalpy decreases remarkably. Similarly, the T_d decreases

slightly, and the corresponding enthalpy change is significantly reduced. The above changes are also apparent from Fig.3. Among them, the melting enthalpy of the blended fiber with mass ratio of 10/90, 20/80, 30/70, respectively, decreased by 30.03%, 33.49%, and 67.52%, respectively, compared with the pure PVA fiber, and the decomposition enthalpy was respectively. It fell by 39.61%, 40.86%, and 79.59%. All above shows that there is an interaction between the molecular chains of CS and PVA, which can form hydrogen bonds, disrupt the original regular crystallization region of PVA, make the crystallization region smaller, and the amount of heat absorbed from the outside is reduced when slippage occurs between molecular chains[10].

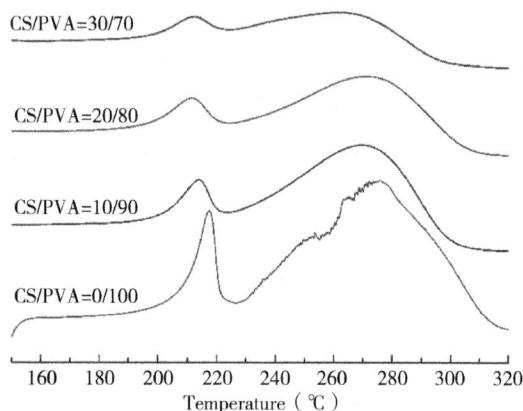

Fig.3　DSC curves of CS/PVA with different blending ratios

Tab.2　Thermal performance analysis of different blending ratio CS/PVA

	CS/PVA mass ratio	0/100	10/90	20/80	30/70
Melting	T_m(℃)	217.6	214.0	211.5	212.2
	Melting enthalpy(J/g)	66.50	46.53	44.23	21.60
Thermal decomposition	T_d(℃)	276.0	269.6	270.9	261.9
	Decomposition and metamorphosis(J/g)	633.6	382.6	374.7	129.3

3.4 Parameter Optimization of CS/PVA Blended Fiber Membrane

The mass loss rate of fiber membrane after treatment by different cross-linking time is shown in Tab.3. After cross-linking for different lengths, the water resistance of the fiber membranes was improved to some extent, which is increased by 64.89% and 45.54%, 48.06%

and 30.08%. With the increase of cross-linking time, the mass loss rate decreased compared with the untreated, then it increased gradually. This may be because the glutaraldehyde vapor cross-linking reaction is mainly concentrated on the surface of the fiber membrane. The longer the cross-linking time took, the more densification the surface of the fiber membrane, and the lower the chance of cross-linking of the inner layer fiber, which will lead to excessive cross-linking.

Tab.3　Design and analysis of water resistance experiment of fiber membrane

Sample serial number	Cross-linking time (h)	Mass loss rate (%)
1	0	44.88±2.87
2	4	9.11±1.82
3	8	19.78±0.09
4	16	18.39±3.72
5	24	28.30±1.76

4　Conclusions

Through the electrospinning method, CS/PVA blended fibers with different mass ratios were successfully prepared. It can be observed by scanning electron microscope that, the fiber morphology was good when the mass ratio of CS/PVA was 30/70, which was the best blending concentration of the spectrum. The infrared spectrum and DSC analysis of the blended fiber membrane demonstrated that there was an interaction between the molecules of CS/PVA, which can form strong hydrogen bonds and significantly improve the spinnability of chitosan electrospinning. The water resistance fiber membrane without cross-linking treatment was poor, and the cross-linking treatment of the blended fiber membrane with glutaraldehyde improves the water resistance of the CS/PVA blended fiber membrane. Among them, the effect of cross-linking for 4 hours is the best, and the mass loss rate of the fiber membrane is only 9.11%.

References

[1] JAYAKUMAR R, PRABAHARAN M, SUDHEESH KUMAR P T, et al. Bimaterials based on chitin and chitosan in wound dressing applications[J]. Biotechnology Advances, 2011, 29 (3):322-337.

[2] LIU Yanbo, SUN Jian, ZHAO Xuefei, et al. Research progress of electrospun fibers in biomedical applications[J]. Industrial Textiles, 2015(9):1-11.

[3] ANA C, Mendes, KAREN Stephansen, et al. Chronakis. Electrospinning of food proteins and polysaccharides[J]. Food Hydrocolloids, 2017(68):53-68.

[4] LI Lei, HSIEH You-lo. Chitosan bicomponent nanofibers and nanoporous fibers [J]. Carbohydrate Research, 2006, 341 (3):374-381.

[5] ZHOU Y S, YANG D Z, NIE J. Effect of PVA content on morphology, swelling and mechanical property of crosslinked chitosan/PVA nanofiber[J]. Plastics, Rubber and Composites, 2019, 36(6): 254-258.

[6] XU Dezeng, SUDAN, CHENG Xue, et al. Preparation of glutaraldehyde cross-linked chitosan/PVA blend fiber[J]. Journal of Dalian Polytechnic University, 2013, 32 (3): 206-208.

[7] SANTOSH B, PALLAVI M, ADIVAREKAR R V. Electrospining of chitosan/PVA nanofibrous membrane at ultralow solvent concentration[J]. Journal of Polymer Research, 2017, 24(6):92-102.

[8] MOJTABA K, HAMID M. Eletrospining, mechanical properties, and cell behavior study of chitosan/PVA nanofibers [J]. Journal of Biomedical Materials Research Part A, 2015, 103(9):3081-3093.

[9] WANG Dan, SHAN Xiaohong, QI Yaoguo. Preparation and Characterization of Chitosan/Polyvinyl Alcohol Nanofiber Membrane [J]. Shanghai Textile Science & Technology, 2016, 44(9):47-50.

[10] LI L, HSIEH Y L. Chitosan bicomponent nanofibers and nanoporous fibers[J]. Carbohydrate Research, 2006, 341 (3):374-381.

A Smart Belt Fabricated Through 3D Printing Technology for Monitoring Hand Gesture

AKTER Farzana[1,2,3*], **SU Liu**[1,2], **ZHANG Yifan**[2,3], **HONG Chengyu**[4]

[1] *College of Textiles, Donghua University, Shanghai, 201620, China*

[2] *Engineering Research Center of Technical Textiles, Ministry of Education, Shanghai, 201620, China*

[3] *Institution of Textiles and Clothing, Hong Kong Polytechnic University, Hung Hom, Kowloon, Hong Kong*

[4] *College of Civil Engineering, Shenzhen University, Shenzhen, 518060, China*

* *Corresponding author's email*：farzanaamin24@yahoo.com, liusu@dhu.edu.cn

Abstract：In this paper, fiber bragg grating (FBG) pressure sensor based smart belt was designed and fabricated using 3D printing technology for monitoring of the hand gestures. The raw material used for the fabrication of this new smart belt was Polylactic Acid (PLA) soft and elastic bandage fabric. During encapsulation process of FBG sensor through 3D printing technology, PLA soft was used with different infill densities that are 20%, 40%, 60%, 80% and 100%. After the FBG sensor encapsulation it was found that this sensor can be successfully embedded into PLA soft material without sacrificing its sensing performance. The change of infill density has no influence on both peak and residual wavelength of FBG sensors during and after the printing process although higher infill density takes longer time to finish the printing process. All FBG sensors printed inside PLA delicate model with various infill thickness esteems show nearly a similar pinnacle and lingering wavelength rise esteems during printing process. Measurements performance of this FBG pressure sensor based smart belt was examined in laboratory cyclic loading tests. In this research we monitored different types of daily performed activities hand gestures like writing gesture, count algorithm gesture, punch gesture and up and down gesture.

Keywords：Fiber bragg grating; 3D printing; Smart belt; Hand gesture

1 Introduction

Hand gestures are commonly used for human-human communications. Hand gesture provides an efficient and natural way for human-computer interaction due to its flexibility and expressiveness[1]. Hand gesture recognition has great potentials for applications in sign language recognition, remote control and virtual reality and has attracted great research interest in past decades[2-6]. Different sensors have been used for gesture recognition, such as camera, radio-frequency identification (RFID), datagloves, IR-UWB Radar, motion feature augmented network (MFA-Net), depth sensor, optical fiber sensor etc[7-9]. In this study, we made a smart belt by using Fiber Bragg Grating (FBG) pressure sensor to monitor gestures of the hand. Recently, Fiber Bragg Grating (FBG) sensors are most popular due it's sensing method for measurements of different physical parameters such as strain, stress, temperature, pressure, and displacement and it's multiplexing capability, small size, ease of encapsulation, high sensitivity, light weight and immunity to Electromagnetic Interferenc (EMI)[10-14] are characterized advantage of FBG sensor. Fabrication and encapsulation methods of different types of optical sensor using FBG sensor are key concerns for the design of a reliable sensing system[15-16].

2 Design and Fabrication Process of FBG Based Smart Belt

2.1 Sensing Principle of FBG Sensor

FBG sensor is an optical based sensing technology developed for the measurement of external strain, temperature, and stress in terms of wavelength shift of grating period. Measurement mechanism of FBGs is mainly based on the principle of Bragg reflection. Fig.1 depicts a schematic figure of working principle of a FBG sensor. It is seen a broadband light is injected into the fiber core and reflected light and transmitted light are motivated at the grating location due to the light inference effect.

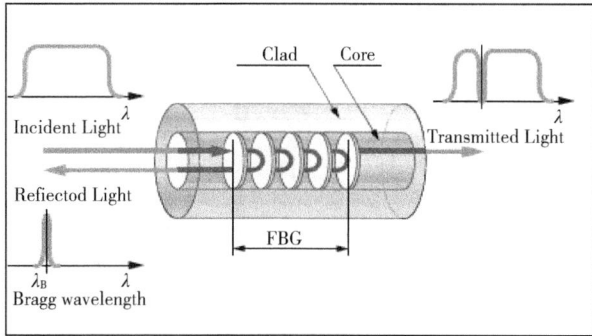

Fig.1 Working principle of Fiber Bragg Grating sensor

The wavelength variation caused by axial strain change $\Delta\varepsilon$ and temperature change ΔT can be given by:

$$\frac{\Delta y}{y} = (1 - P_{eff}) \Delta\varepsilon + (\alpha + \xi) \Delta T \qquad (1)$$

where $\Delta\lambda$ and λ are wavelength change and wavelength value, respectively. P_{eff}, α and ξ are photo-elastic parameter, thermal expansion coefficient and thermal-optic coefficient, respectively. Influence of temperature change should be eliminated to obtain pure strain change of FBG sensors.

2.2 Design and Fabrication of FBG Based Smart Belt

3D printing is mostly realized by Fused Deposition Modeling (FDM) method. The major benefits provided by this technique arises from the potential of building functional components with complex design features and tailored mechanical properties (high strength, stiffness, lower weight, porosity and density) without the requirement of any further tooling and human interface. To fabricate this smart belt we used 3D printing technology's FDM method. In this process 3D printer mainly consists of two driven rollers for feeding filament which were gotten a handle on by warmer up to its softening point and

after then layer by layer statement of this expelled filament to make 3D detecting model. In this process polylactic acid (PLA) soft material was used for printed prototype and its melting temperature 200℃ and the diameter of 1.75mm. The interrogator used for FBG data collection is Sm 125 from Micron Optics and printer brand was Creality 3D and both ends of prototype was used elastic bandage fabric with diameter 25mm and thickness of 0.8mm. Nozzle size, and printing speed were 0.4mm, and 60mm/s, respectively. A schematic diagram of fabrication process is shown in Fig.2. Five FBG sensors were selected for different infill densities with five differents centre Bragg wavelengths 1536nm± 0.3nm, 1552nm ± nm, 1532nm ± 0.3nm, 1539nm ± 0.3nm, 1560nm±0.3nm respectively and length of these FBG sensors was 10mm. Bandwidth @ 3dB, side-lobe suppression ratio (SLSR), and reflectivity are ≤0.3nm, ≥15dB, >90% respectively. The infill densities of prototype sensing components varying at 20%, 40%, 60%, 80%, and 100%. At the point when half printed prototype was done then pause printing and then FBG sensors were legitimately positioned at the upper surface area of the printed model along with elastic bandage fabric right after then remaining half had been completed inside the 3D printer. Measurement of printed acknowledging part model was 2mm, 30mm and 50mm (thickness × width × length).

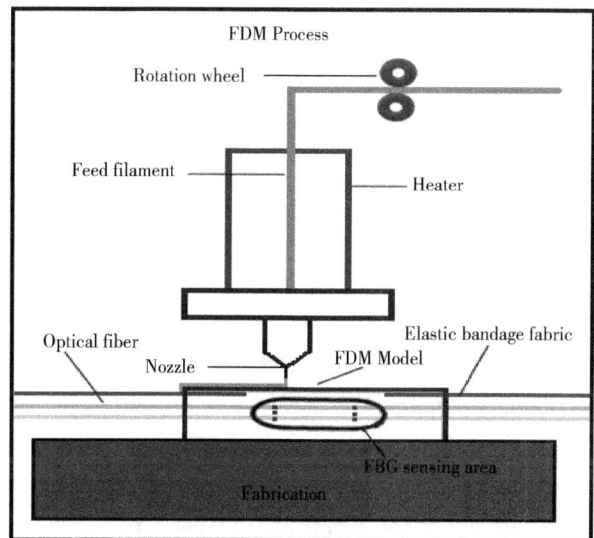

Fig.2 A schematic view of fabrication process

During printing process wavelength change of FBG sensors was collected consistently at a frequency of 10Hz. Fig. 3 displays the FBG based smart belt created utilizing FDM process in this examination. FBG sensor set in the center position [Fig.3(a)] in schematic disgram. This PLA soft prototype was first structured utilizing CATIA [Fig.3(b)]. A solitary FBG sensor was implanted into PLA when half size of the prototype was printed, and the printing procedure needed to stop for

1–2 minutes for the situation and fixation of FBG sensor inside PLA prototype along with elastic bandage fabric [Fig.3(c)]. Grating length the FBG is 10mm, and defensively covered fiber optic was utilized to protect the FBG sensor. The final FBG based smart belt was portrayed by an element of 50mm long, 10mm wide in middle position and 30mm wide in two end position, and 2mm high [Fig.3(d)].

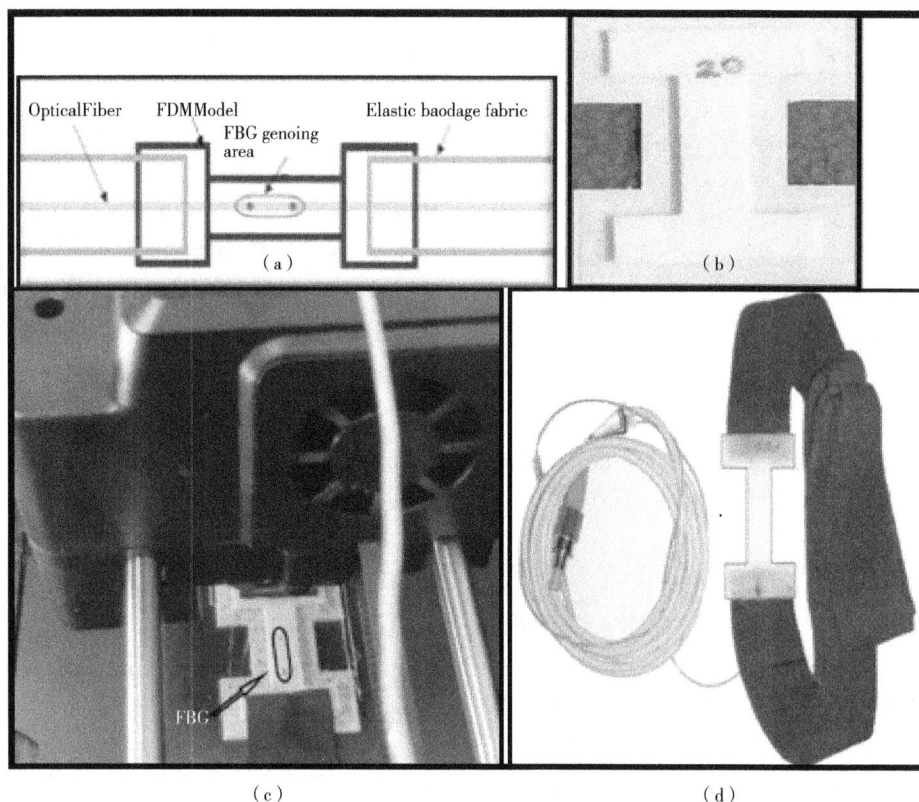

Fig.3 (a) A schematic view of smart belt; (b) Design of PLA prototype; (c) FBG installation using 3D printer; (d) The FBG based smart belt after manufacturing

2.3 Wavelength Shift of FBG Sensor During Printing Process

The reflected wavelength change of FBG sensor during FDM process was collected by an interrogator at a frequency of 10Hz. Total of 9 wavelength peaks are observed for infill densities of 40%, 60%, and 80%, but 7 peak wavelength values are found for infill density of 20% and 100%. Existent of these peak wavelength values are due to the significant thermal expansion when the melted PLA soft material covers the FBG sensors during printing. The reflected wavelength change of

FBG sensor during FDM process was collected by an interrogator at a frequency of 10Hz immediately after FBG sensor was placed inside PLA prototype. The selected infill density was 20%, 40%, 60%, 80% and 100%. Fig.4 describes the change of FBG sensor wavelength before, during and after fabrication of pressure sensor. The wavelength change before printing started is stable, presenting at around 1535.85nm within infill density 20% [Fig.4(a)], around 1552nm within infill density 40% [Fig.4(b)], around 1532.1nm within infill density 60% [Fig.4(c)], around 1540.2nm within infill density 80% [Fig. 4(d)], around 1560.1nm within infill density 100% [Fig.4(e)]. Then the wavelength increases quickly approaching about 1536.65nm, 1552.85nm, 1532.8nm, 1541.1nm, 1560.8nm at 1150 seconds, Wavelength change of the FBG sensor between 1150s and 10000s exhibits significant initial wavelength fluctuation due to the interaction between FBG sensor and melted PLA material. FBG wavelength remains decrease around 1800s to 2000s and finally stabilized at 1535.2nm, 1551.4nm, 1531nm, 1539.1nm, 1559.45nm respectively.

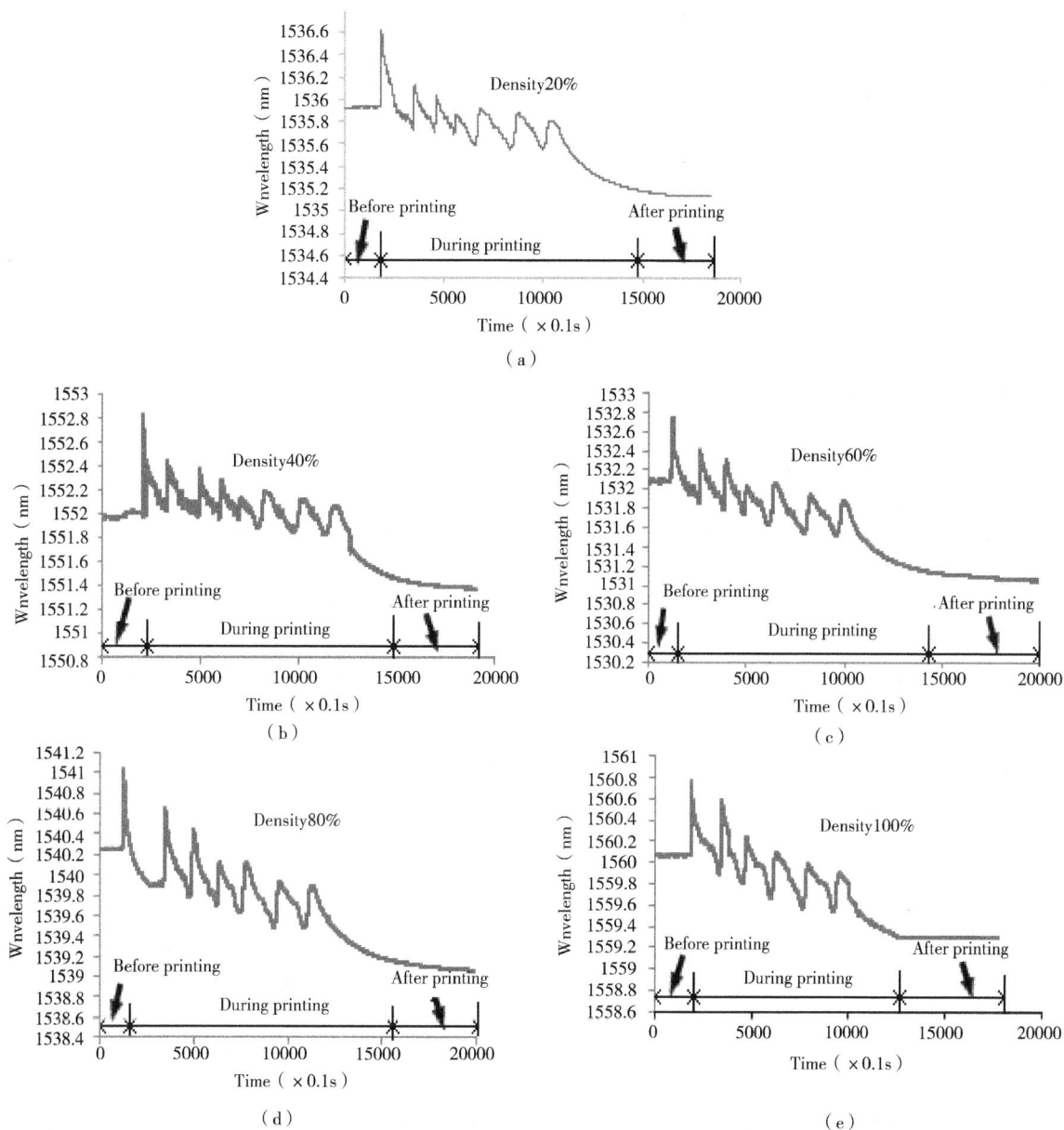

Fig.4 Wavelength variation against time during fabrication process of a FBG pressure sensor inside a 3D printer: (a) Infill density 20%; (b) Infill density 40%; (c) Infill density 60%; (d) Infill density 80%; (e) Infill density 100%

3 Results and Disscusions

3.1 Gesture Monitored by Using Smart Belt

Writing gesture is a basic activity in our daily life. In this study, monitored how much grating wavelength changed along with different infill density. The subject was female and position of the gesture was wrist. Writing gesture were divided into three steps, whole process were performed within 30 seconds, first one

"Open hand position": in this test, the subject was kept straight her hand for 10 second, second one "Hold in pen": in this position kept 10 second, and third one "writing with pen" continuously writing 10 second after wearing smart belt. Fig.5 shows the wavelength change FBG sensing smart belt during wrist position in writing gesture. Maximum grating were changed within 40%, 60% and 80% density around 240nm and 20% and 100% density around 120nm.

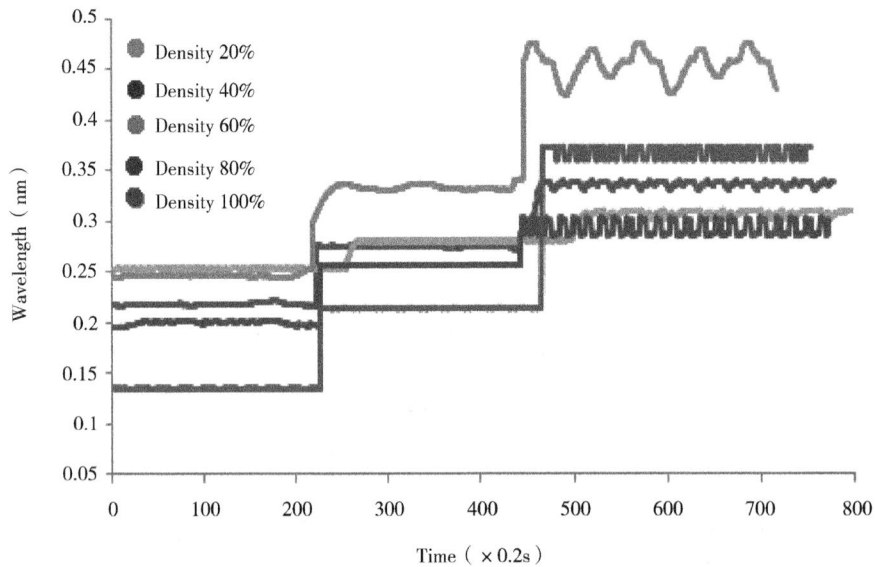

Fig.5　Wavelength change FBG sensing smart belt during writing gesture

4　Conclusions

In this study, a 3D printed FBG pressure sensor based smart belt was designed and fabricated using material FDM method. Mechanical performance of the printed FBG pressure sensor was examined in laboratory calibration tests. Conclusions and main findings of this study are drawn as follows:

(a) FBG based smart belt was successfully fabricated using FDM process by embedding FBG sensor inside a printed PLA prototype along with different infill densities 20%, 40%, 60%, 80%, 100% respectively. This fabrication method is characterized by the advantages of quick fabrication and better protection, avoiding the use of glue or epoxy resin during encapsulation process.

(b) Changing in infill densities appears has no influence on both peak and residual wavelength values during printing process. The required time to embed FBG sensor within a lower density is relatively shorter.

(c) Monitoring gesture by using smart belt data during FDM process indicates that FBG sensor can be successfully embedded inside fused PLA soft material. It indicated that measurement range and sensitivity of FBG pressure sensor are higher within infill densities 40%, 60%, 80% and 20%, 100% are lower.

References

[1] CHEN X, et al. MFA-net: motion feature augmented network for dynamic hand gesture recognition from skeletal data[J]. Sensors, 2019, 19(2):239.

[2] SCHWANKE N L, et al. Differences in body posture, strength and flexibility in schoolchildren with overweight and obesity: a quasi-experimental study[J]. Manual therapy, 2016, 22:138-144.

[3] OHN-BAR E, TRIVEDI M M. Hand gesture recognition in real time for automotive interfaces: a multimodal vision-based approach and evaluations[J]. IEEE Transactions on Intelligent Transportation Systems, 2014, 15(6):2368-2377.

[4] NEVEROVA N, et al. Moddrop: adaptive multi-modal gesture recognition[J]. IEEE Transactions on Pattern Analysis and Machine Intelligence, 2015, 38(8):1692-1706.

[5] PALACIOS J, et al. Human-computer interaction based on hand gestures using RGB-D sensors[J]. Sensors, 2013, 13(9):11842-11860.

[6]ABRAHAM L, et al. Hand tracking and gesture recognition using lensless smart sensors[J]. Sensors, 2018, 18(9): 2834.

[7]KHAN F, LEEM S, et al. Hand-based gesture recognition for vehicular applications using IR-UWB radar[J]. Sensors, 2017, 17(4):833.

[8]ASADZADEH P, KULIK L, et al. Gesture recognition using RFID technology[J]. Personal and Ubiquitous Computing, 2012, 16(3):225-234.

[9]REN Z, YUAN J, ZHANG Z. Robust hand gesture recognition based on finger-earth mover's distance with a commodity depth camera[C]. Proceedings of the 19th ACM international conference on Multimedia, 2011.

[10]ABRO Z A, et al. Development of a smart garment for monitoring body postures based on FBG and flex sensing technologies[J]. Sensors and Actuators A: Physical, 2018, 272:153-160.

[11]KOUSIATZA C, KARALEKAS D, In-situ monitoring of strain and temperature distributions during fused deposition modeling process[J]. Materials & Design, 2016, 97:400-406.

[12]HONG C Y, et al. Comparative study on the elongation measurement of a soil nail using optical lower coherence interferometry method and FBG method[J]. Advances in Structural Engineering, 2010, 13(2):309-319.

[13]SHEN C, ZHONG C. Novel temperature-insensitive fiber Bragg grating sensor for displacement measurement[J]. Sensors and Actuators A: Physical, 2011, 170(1-2):51-54.

[14]SURESH R, TJIN S C, et al. Application of a new fiber Bragg grating based shear force sensor for monitoring civil structural components[J]. Smart Materials and Structures, 2005, 14(5):982

[15]GUAN B O, et al. Simultaneous strain and temperature measurement using a superstructure fiber Bragg grating[C]. IEEE Photonics Technology Letters, 2000, 12(6):675-677.

[16]UMESH S, ASOKAN S. A brief overview of the recent biomedical applications of fiber Bragg grating sensors[J]. Journal of the Indian Institute of Science, 2014, 94(3): 319-328.

Analysis of Cooperation Between China, Kenya and Serbia in the Framework of the World University Union in the Belt and Road Initiative (WTUA)

CHARLES Lagat[1]* , XU Ming[2] , VASILIJE Petrovic[3] , NIKOLA Zivlak[4]

[1] *MOI University, Kenya*

[2] *Donghua University, Shanghai, China*

[3] *University of Novi Sad-Technical Faculty "Mihajlo Pupin", Zrenjanin, 23000, Serbia*

[4] *Emlyon Business School Asia, Shanghai, China*

* *Corresponding author's email*: lagatck@yahoo.com

Abstract: This paper discusses some of the possibilities for cooperation between Donghua University, MOI University from Kenya and University of Novi Sad. These three universities are members of the WTUA. Cooperation in the textile and clothing sector, which has the potential to significantly contribute to the development of the economies of all three countries is considered.

Keywords: The Belt and Road Initiative; World Textile University Alliance; Cooperation between the People's Republic of China, Kenya and Serbia; Textiles and clothing

1 Introduction

In the framework of the Belt and Road Initiative, The Belt and Road World Textile University Alliance (WTUA) was established in 2018, at Donghua University in Shanghai. WTUA was founded by 32 internationally recognized universites in the field of textile and fashion engineering, design, technology and innovation.

This work uses the experiences of East Asian economies, East African countries and Central European countries. It is recommended to use the experience of China, as the world's strongest developing economy and securing jobs for the fast-growing young population in Kenya. It is also recommended to use the Chineese experiences in developing bussines cooperation with Serbian partners and joint enter in the European market.

This paper gives recommendations for the form of cooperation in the textile and clothing sector between China, Kenya and Serbia as part of the promotion of the Belt and Road Initiative.

2 China Textile and Apparel Industry

China textile and apparel industries production value in 2018 could be seen in the following Tab.1. From this table, four sectors related with textile and apparel industry with two minus and two positive, yarn reduced 7.3 percent[1] and cloth reduced 4.9 percent[2].

Tab.1 China's main industry data in 2018

Grain	Cotton	Meat	Yarn	Cloth
−0.6%	7.8%	−0.3%	−7.3%	−4.9%
Services	Information transfer	Technique service	Chemical fiber	
7.7%	37.0%	13.4%	2.7%	
Industry	Manufacture	Energy	High tech	Railroad car
6.2%	6.5%	9.9%	11.7%	183.0%

As the reason for this situation, China's textile and apparel international transition is one of the reasons, those nations labor costs are much lower than that in China, a lot of China Textile and Apparel firms moved into Vietnam, Cambodia, Bangladesh. One of the main reasons is that enterprises are more interested in going abroad to build factories.

2.1 Possibilities of China's Textile and Apparel Firms Move to Europe and Africa

As China has developed some very powerful brand textile and apparel firms, some of them has the interests on abroad, not restricted only in Asian region. Such kinds of investment activities are often appeared in media.

2.1.1 How to Make It Possible to Invest Textile or Apparel Firms in Europe

Obviously, most European region has higher labor costs than China, so normal textile and apparel operation moved from China to Europe is not wise. China firms may seek some opportunities in some East Europe region, which has the advantages in geographic and talent aspects. Recently years, several Chinese firms, such as steel firm and car tire firm and so on, have made huge investment in Serbia. In this April, Professor of Novi Sad University Serbia, Vasilije Petrovic visited Nantong Haimen Home-Textile Zone, China's largest home textile production center, nearly 50% of China bed textile products are made in this zone, the leaders and some firm owners of this zone have showed their interests to make an European base to serve for surrounding markets. So some cooperations between China and Europe in textile and apparel sectors are quite possible.

2.1.2 What Are the Meaning and Challenges to Attract China Textile or Apparel Firms to Africa?

China has already made some textile and apparel investment in Ethiopia, which are in the form of industry zone. Sun Shine Textile Group in Jiangsu province, China is the pioneer in this field, so some Chinese textile and apparel firms followed. Usually in most African countries have got advantage trade conditions to enter European and US markets, so China textile and apparel firms have the interests to move their part of production facilities in African countries. Generally speaking, labor costs, resource availability such as cotton supply, and logistic distance to targeted markets may comparably be favorable aspects, but low skill labor, less developed infrastructures, and different government administration and culture features as well as language problems, often stopped Chinese firms' investment interests.

2.2 Three Party Cooperation Is the Way

International cooperation seems to be trendy nowadays, but how to make them really attractive, which still have a great deal of investigation and research things to do. Thanks to the World University Union In The Belt And Road Initiative (WTUA), China's Donghua University, the largest textile university in the world, Novi Sad University, most powerful science and technology university in Serbian, and MOI University, Kenya, one of advanced African university in textile and apparel field, has built sound relationship to conduct joint research, which will definitely benefit all three involved academic institutions as well as real cooperation between or among the parties involved.

For suggestion, first round investigation for existing Chinese textile or apparel firms or other firms in Serbia and Kenya should be earlier proposed. Second, some special designed materials to attract potential investment should be developed. Third, a joint promotion program to China's textile cluster, such as Nantong Haimen Home Textile Zone, and more similar ones, should be lunched, which hopefully can get some government agency or private firms' support.

3 Kenya Textile and Apparel Sector

Kenya's textile and apparel sector plays a key role in the manufacturing industry and in serving as a source of gainful employment for the fast growing, young population. Kenya has long had a domestic textile and apparel sector, but major growth in foreign investment and exports only arrived with the adoption of AGOA in 2000. Kenya was the first AGOA-eligible country to fulfill the additional requirements for the apparel provision in 2001 to gain access to the US market. This, along with the quotas that existed on Chinese and other Asian exporters as part of the Multi-fiber Arrangement (MFA), made Kenya an attractive location for producing mass market clothing for the US market. Kenya captures more than a third of all apparel exports from Sub-Saharan Africa to the US. Apparel exports grew in spurts from US$ 8.6 million in 2000 to upwards of US$ 332 million in 2014 (Kenya-ATI, 2017).

Kenya has 52 textile mills, of which only 15 are currently operational and they operate at less than 45 percent of total capacity. The existing mills operate using outdated technology and suffer from low levels of skilled labor and low productivity. The cost of electricity (about 25%) is a major cost driver for textile mills, as are the high maintenance and overhead costs due to old equipment. A further cost driver is the need to either use high-cost imported material or low-quality local fiber which requires additional processing[2].

In the apparel sector there are several companies operating in Kenya. Approximately 170 are medium and large, while upwards of 74,000 are small and micro companies. Twenty-one companies operate in the EPZ, employing an average of 1,800 people per company. The Kenya Government recently invested more than Ksh. 10 billion to revive the East Africa Rivatex company factory and have it back on operation. In 2018, the firm received new machines from India as part of the modernization process. According to the managing director professor Thomas Kipkurgat said the new machines would increase the daily production to 40,000 metres of yarn from the initial 5,000 metres. Rivatex factory is a teaching and research facility of Moi University[3].

The major challenges in Kenya's business environment include high electricity prices, limited access to finance, poor roads, challenging logistics, and for non-EPZ companies, complex regulations. The Ministry of Industrialization and Enterprise Development (MOIED) of the government of Kenya is directing its focus towards addressing the primary bottlenecks to competitiveness in the country's textile-apparel sector. The strategic goal is to discover opportunities for growth in order to renew enthusiasm for the textile-apparel sector. A study by the Kenya Association of Manufacturers, World Bank, UK Aid and the Ministry of Industrialization and Enterprise

Development found a dearth in the investment of high-end equipment and technology as a hindrance to the thriving of the country's textile sector. Because of this, Kenya's textile exports failed to compete favourably with those from other countries in the global markets, and small exporters were locked out of preferential trade deals such as the US Africa Growth and Opportunities Act (AGOA) for failing quality thresholds. Other studies have also found that both the supply and distribution chains in Kenya's textile and apparel industry are fragmented, leading to high production costs and eventual retail prices that fail to compete with cheap imports. Save for Ethiopia, Kenya has the highest import-export cost among its Asia and African competitors, including Vietnam, India, Bangladesh, China, South Africa, and Lesotho.

In 2017, the top partnercountries and regions to which Kenya exports textiles and clothing include United States, Uganda, Saudi Arabia, Europe, Tanzania and Nigeria while the countries from which Kenya imports textiles and clothing include China (US$ 278.7), India (US$ 61.4), Pakistan (US$ 54.6), Other Asia couritries (US$ 43.2 b). Exports from East African countries to the US reached about $ 1 billion between October 2017 and September 2018, a 17 percent increase from the same period the previous year. According to the United States Agency for International Development's East Africa Trade and Investment Hub, the apparel dominated the region's sales at 84.4 percent of exports. Kenya exports to Serbia includes vegetable and food products, textile and clothing and electrical products revealed an increase and a comparative advantage for the year 2017[4].

China and Kenya have been cooperating in various sectors such as infrastructure, industrialization, energy, technology transfer, agriculture, peace and security, capacity building, environmental protection, and people-to-people exchanges.

4 Potentials of the Serbian Textile Industry for Cooperation

The textile and clothing industry represents significant

production branches in Serbia, import dependent, export oriented, with tradition in the European and world market.

The textile industry plays an important role in the economy of the Republic of Serbia by number of enterprises, number of employees, and 10% participation in foreign trade. It is recognizable on foreign markets, first of all, on the market of the countries of the European Community[5].

Key chances for the development of the Region[6]:

• Good geo-strategic position of Serbia-road, rail and air traffic network and proximity to the border with the European Union enables the development of the region and the placement of products and services on the markets of neighboring countries;

• International free trade agreements signed by the Republic of Serbia enable easier business conditions in the foreign market, while state and donor programs and projects provide greater chances for the improvement of entrepreneurs operating in this industry;

• Revitalization of production in large textile companies that are bankrupt or in the process of privatization by finding adequate investors who are able to comply with the agreed terms, for a long time;

• Branding the products from the Region.

Serbia is one of the countries included in the BRI and China + CEEC platform. It has a growing collaboration with China and presents a potential hub for CBEC in the Balkan region. In their 2019 E-commerce report concerning Serbia, Statista (Statista, 2019), indicates that revenue in the E-commerce market amounts to 354 million USD, with expected annual growth rate (CAGR 2019—2023) of 9.6% and a market volume of 510 million USD by 2023.

The fashion segment revenue in 2019 amounts to 68 million USD with expected an annual growth rate (CAGR 2019–2023) of 9.4%, resulting in a market volume of 98 million USD by 2023. The market's largest segment is apparel with a market volume of 52 million USD. User penetration is expected to hit 50.7% by 2023. The average revenue per user (ARPU) currently amounts to 87.18 USD, according to Statista (ibidem). According to the Development Agency of Serbia, textile industry is quite relevant in Serbia, employing more than 250,000 workers and exporting more than 5 billion USD, with 1,800 active companies[7].

5 Conclusion

A China, Kenya and Serbia University cooperation under the World University Union in the Belt and Road Initiative (WTUA) would create opportunities for studying and researching in order to address the challenges in the textile sector and spur economic growth. It is recommended to use the experience of China, as the world's strongest developing economy and securing jobs for the fast-growing young population in Kenya. It is also recommended to use the Chineese experiences in developing bussines cooperation with Serbian partners and joint enter in the European market.

References

[1] China's textile and apparel industry current situation and development trend, China industry information, 2019 – 07 – 24 www.chyxx.com.

[2] Kenya Ministry of Industrialization and Enterprise Development, Kenya Apparel and Textile Industry Diagnosis, Strategy And Action Plan, 2017.

[3] https://wits. worldbank. org/CountryProfile/en/Country/KEN/Year/2017/TradeFlow/Export/Partner/all/Product/50 – 63 _ TextCloth, accessed 23/7/2019.

[4] https://countryeconomy.com/countries/compare/serbia/kenya, accessed 14/7/2019.

[5] https://www.pks.rs/ accessed on July 1,2019.

[6] http://www.banat-fashion.rs/accessed on July 3, 2019.

[7] https://ras.gov.rs/ accessed on July 5, 2019.

A Novel Imidazole-Copper (II) Complex as the Latent Curing Agent for Epoxy Resins and Their Application in Glass Fiber-Reinforced Composites

YANG Bo[1,2] , WEI Yi[1,2*] , QIU Yiping[2] , LIU Wanshuang[1,2*]

[1] *Key Laboratory of Textile Science & Technology, Ministry of Education, College of Textiles, Donghua University, Shanghai, 201620, China*

[2] *Collaborative Innovation Center for Civil Aviation Composites, Donghua University, Shanghai, 201620, China.*

* *Corresponding author's email*: weiy@ dhu.edu.cn (Y. Wei) , wsliu@ dhu.edu.cn (W. Liu)

Abstract: In this study, 1-cyanoethyl-2-ethyl-4-methylimidazole (1C2E4MI) was modified by copper chloride to improve its thermal latency towards epoxy resins. Unexpected complexation between 1C2E4MI and copper chloride was discovered. The compositions of the Complex-S was characterized by elemental analysis and inductively coupled plasma optical emission spectrometry. The microanalytical data showed that the ligand-metal ratio value of the Complex-S is 1, rather than the theoretical 4 ratio value. According to the DSC and FTIR results, the complex-S can be deblocked between 140℃ and 160℃. With the Complex-S as a latent curing agent, the thermal and mechanical properties of cured epoxy resins were studied. The resulting epoxy systems showed distinctly prolonged pot life at room temperature. Moreover, the epoxy resin cured with Complex-S has a higher glass transition temperature comparable to that cured with 1C2E4MI. In the practical application for the glass fiber reinforced composites, bending mechanical properties are similar to that of normal epoxy-imidazole system.

Keywords: Epoxy; Glass fiber reinforced composites; Latent curing agent; Imidazole-copper (II) complex

1　Introduction

Epoxy resin has been widely used in different industrial fields, as one of the most significant thermosetting polymers, such as coatings, adhesives, and electronics, owing to their excellent mechanical properties, adhesive capacity, chemical and heat resistance[1-3]. Generally, curing agents of the epoxy resin can be various and abundant, such as amines, anhydrides, carboxylic acid, phenols, thiols, imidazoles, and onium salts[3-7]. However, the latent curing agent plays an important role in one-component epoxy systems, with good storage stability and reactivity. Particularly, compared with epoxy-amine systems, epoxy-imidazole systems have a changeable curing temperature, high glass transition temperature[7-9]. However, a few amounts of imidazole compounds can efficiently initiate the homopolymerization of epoxy groups through both nucleophilic and base catalytic processes[10-13]. Therefore, the disadvantages of epoxy-imidazole systems are poor storage stability and the intrinsically high reactivity at room temperature. To deal with the latency of epoxy systems with imidazole compounds, a great deal of research on blocking the activity groups of the imidazole ring has been performed, such as metal-imidazole complexes[14-18], introductions of substituent groups[18], and the microencapsulation of imidazole with polymer shells[2]. Among imidazole-metal complexes, the ligand-metal ratio value of the complex is 4, in which copper chloride is a common metal reactant[14-18]. Until now, little work has been conducted on the imidazole-copper (II) complex to further improve the latency of epoxy-imidazole systems.

2   Experiments

2.1   Materials

Diglycidyl ether of bisphenol A (DGEBA) with an epoxide equivalent of 190 was purchased by Sanmu Group Inc. 1-cyanoethyl-2-ethyl-4-methylimidazole (1C2E4MI) was purchased from Hubei YCSC Chem Corporation. Copper chloride and anhydrous ethanol were obtained from Sinopharm Group Inc.

2.2   Preparation of Complex-S

1C2E4MI and anhydrous ethanol were added into a flask with magnetic stirring. After stirring for 15min, copper chloride in anhydrous ethanol was slowly added. Then, the solution was heated to 60℃ and held for 4h with constant stirring. After filtration, the isolated solid product was washed by anhydrous ethanol for five times. After dyeing, a pale brown powder was obtained. The solid product was named as Complex-S, shown in Fig.1.

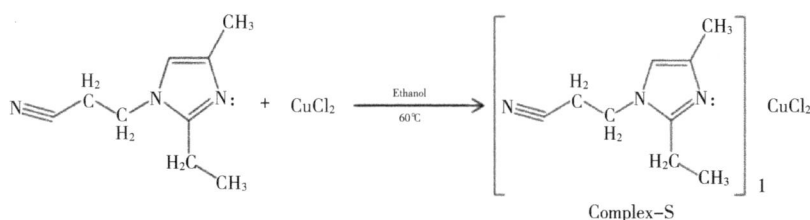

Fig.1   Structure of the Complex-S

2.3   Curing of Epoxy Resins

A certain amount of 1C2E4MI and a certain amount of Complex-S was thoroughly mixed with DGEBA, and then the mixture was poured into an aluminum mold. After degassing in a vacuum oven, the epoxy resin was cured at 120℃ for 1h followed by 160℃ for 1h.

2.4   Preparation of Glass Fiber Composites

Complex-S or 1C2E4MI was firstly dissolved in ethanol, and then the epoxy systems came into being after thoroughly mixed with DGEBA. The glass fiber prepregs were prepared by immersing glass fabrics into the above epoxy systems. After degassing and removing the solvent, the glass fabrics were heated at 80℃ for 5 minutes in the oven. The obtained glass fiber prepregs were layed up in the crossed configuration $(0°/90°)_6$ and cured by hot-press at 120℃ for 1 hour and 160℃ for 1 hour at 0.2MPa to make glass fiber composites.

2.5   Characterization

Elemental analysis was conducted using Perkin Elmer Instruments CHNS-O Analyzer Vario EL Ⅲ. Inductively coupled plasma optical emission spectrometry (ICP-OES), Leeman Prodigy Instruments was used to determine the level of copper in Complex-S. FTIR spectra was recorded using Perkin Elmer Instruments Spectrum GX FTIR spectrometer. Netzsch Instruments DSC 214 at a heating rate of $10℃/min^1$ in the range of 30℃ to 250℃. DMA test was conducted using TA Instruments DMA Q800. Bending properties of the composites were measured on Wance ETM Test Machine following ASTM D790 standard.

3   Results and Discussions

3.1   Structure of Complex-S

Tab.1 shows the appearance and mole ratio of the compositions of 1C2E4MI and Complex-S with the measurement of elemental analysis and ICP-OES. The results show that Complex-S has a metal-ligand ratio value of about 1. For Complex-S, complexation is abnormal, owing to the complex function of both the imidazole and cyano group with transition metals[10-11].

The FTIR spectrum of 1C2E4MI and Complex-S are shown in Fig.2. The bands at $2900cm^{-1}$ and $2250cm^{-1}$ are corresponding to the stretching vibrations of C—H and C≡N, respectively[12]. The band at $1440cm^{-1}$ can be assigned to the combination of imidazole ring vibration and CH_2 bending vibration[12-13]. The band at $1048cm^{-1}$ can be corresponding to the combination of C—C stretching vibration, C—N stretching vibration and C—H bending vibration on the imidazole ring[12-13]. After complexation with copper (II), the band at 560cm^{-1} are observed to shift in the FTIR spectra of Complex-S, which confirms the complexation between 1C2E4MI and copper chloride.

Tab.1 The compositions of 1C2E4MI and Complex-S

| Sample | Color appearance | Elemental analysis | | | | Mole ratiovalue of Copper and imidazole |
		C	H	N	Cu	
1C2E4MI	Dark brown	66.25	7.99	25.76	0.00	—
Complex-S	Pale brown	37.53	5.52	14.21	18.23	1

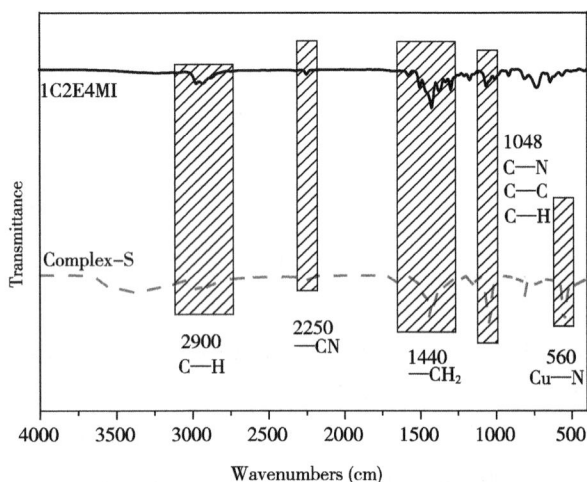

Fig.2 FTIR results of materials and Complex-S

3.2 Thermal Dissociation of Complex-S

Fig.3 shows the thermal dissociation of Complex-S by FTIR and DSC. In Fig.3 (a), the band at 560cm^{-1} are observed to disappear at 160℃, which confirms the thermal dissociation. As shown in Fig.3 (b), a sharp exothermic peak is observed in the DSC curve of Complex-S. The onset temperature and peak temperature of this curve is about 160℃ and 170℃, respectively. In fact, the heating rate would not exceed 10℃/min. Therefore, the thermal dissociation temperature of Complex-S should be between 140℃ and 160℃ [9].

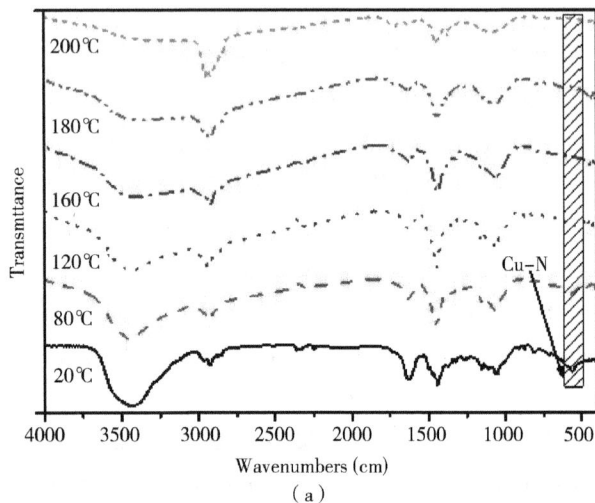

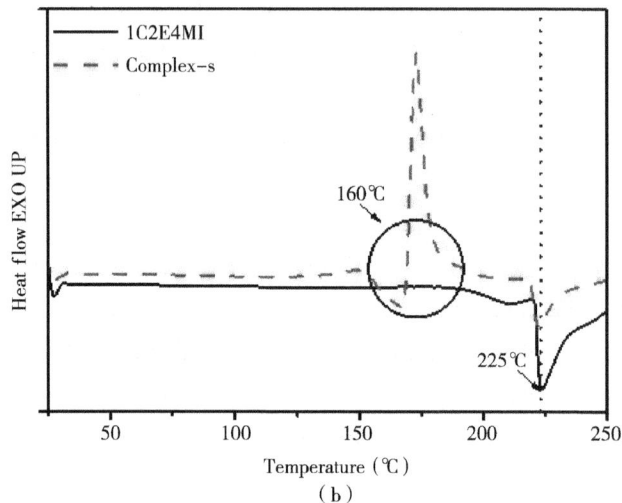

Fig.3 (a) FTIR spectra of Complex-S at the heating rate of 2℃/min at different temperatures; (b) DSC thermograms of 1C2E4MI and Complex-S at the heating rate of 10℃/min

3.3 Curing Behaviors and Thermo-Mechanical Properties

Fig.4 show the DSC curves of two epoxy resin systems. Accordingly, both the onset temperature and peak tem-

perature of DGEBA-Complex-S systems are higher than those of DGEBA-1C2E4MI systems, which indicates the improved latency of DGEBA-Complex-S systems. Notably, the epoxy system with 8% Complex-S shows much lower exothermic heat, indicating that this epoxy system was not sufficiently cured with low Complex-S level. Furthermore, the curves of DGEBA-Complex-S systems are broad and two peeks.

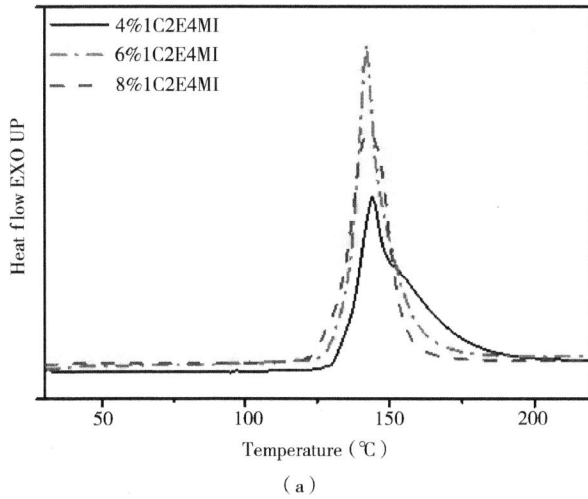

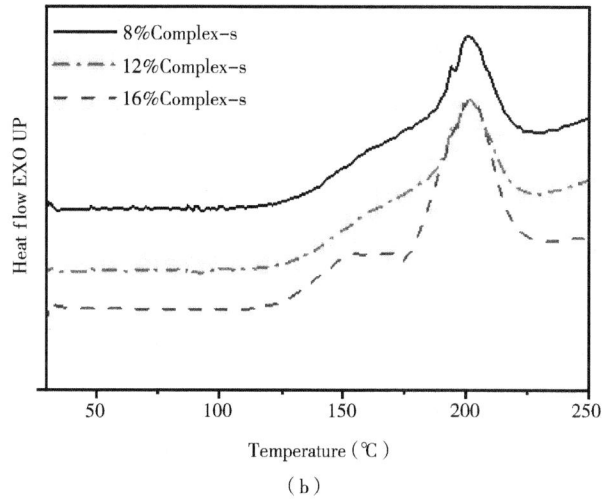

Fig.4　DSC thermograms of DGEBA with different levels of (a) 1C2E4MI and (b) Complex-S at the heating rate of 10℃/min

The curves of storage modulus and loss modulus versus temperature are shown in Fig.5. The epoxy resins cured with 4% 1C2E4MI has the highest Tg of 166℃. The epoxy resin cured with 12% Complex-S shows the highest Tg of 176℃. However, excessive level would result in much more and smaller epoxy networks, which has a detrimental effect on the further formation of epoxy networks, thus reducing crosslink density and Tg. Based on the above DSC and DMA results, epoxy systems with 4% 1C2E4MI and 12% Complex-S are selected in the subsequent study.

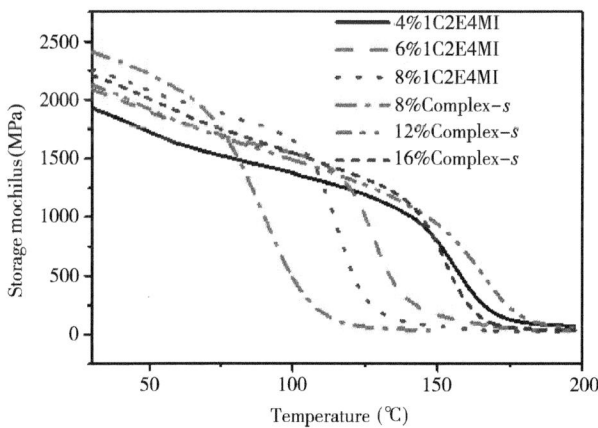

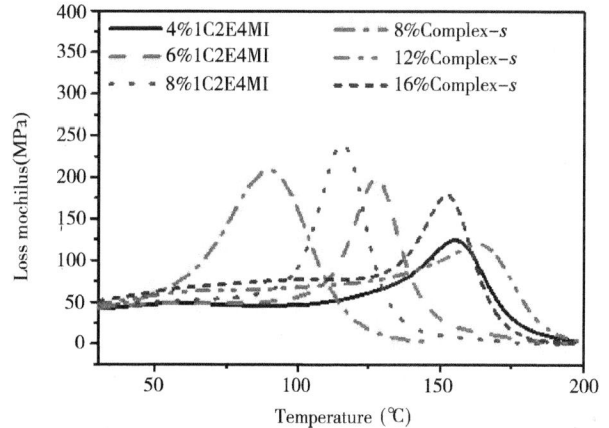

Fig.5　(a) Storage modulus and (b) loss modulus versus temperature curves of DGEBA cured with different levels of 1C2E4MI and Complex-S

3.4　Pot Life

To confirm the effects of Complex-S on epoxy resin system, the fluidity of two epoxy systems at 25℃ was observed, and the results are shown in Fig.6. Accordingly, the DGEBA-1C2E4MI system largely loses fluidity after 6 days, while the DGEBA-Complex-S system still exhibits fluidity after 20 days. The above results indicate that the effects of Complex-S can enhance epoxy-imidazole systems with excellent latency.

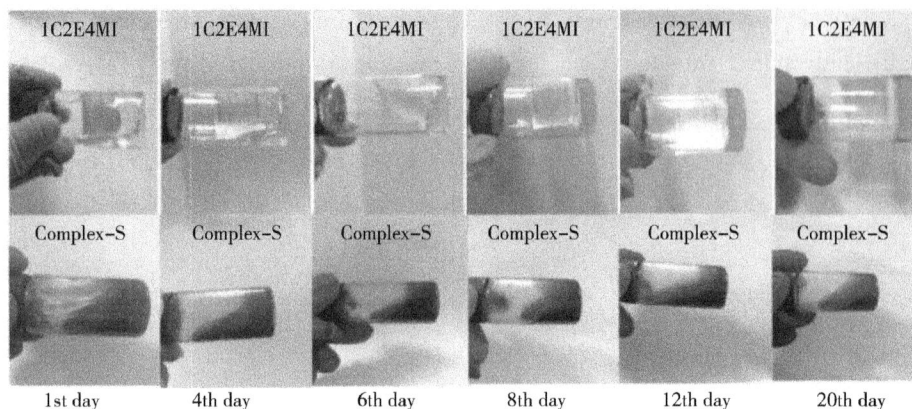

Fig.6   Observation of the fluidity of DGEBA cured with 4% 1C2E4MI and 12% Complex-S

3.5   Mechanical Properties of Composites

In order to investigate bending mechanical properties of fiber-reinforced composites, we performed three-point bending tests in Fig.7. As can be seen, the average bending strength of DGEBA cured with Complex-S is slightly higher than that of DGEBA cured with 1C2E4MI. Furthermore, the average flexural modulus of DGEBA cured with Complex-S is higher than that of DGEBA cured with 1C2E4MI.

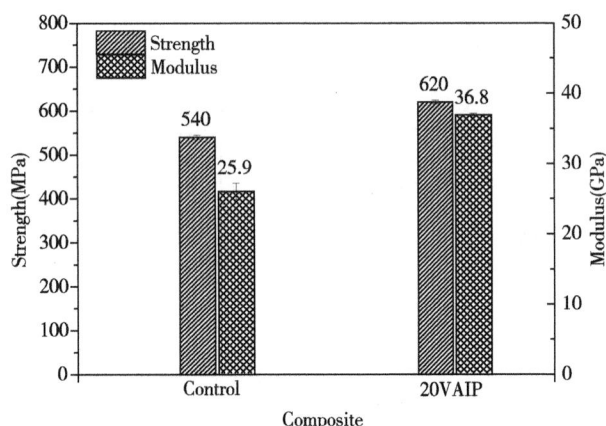

Fig. 7   Three-point bending test results of glass fiber reinforced composites with different epoxy resin systems

4   Conclusions

In summary, abnormal complexation between 1C2E4MI and copper was discovered in this study. The microanalytical data reveals that Complex-S has metal-ligand ratio value of 1. DSC and FTIR study indicate the thermal dissociation temperature of Complex-S is between 140℃ and 160℃. The results of DSC and DMA measurements show that the optimal levels of Complex-S and 1C2E4MI for DGEBA are 12% and 4%, respectively. Notably, the epoxy system with Complex-S shows prolonged pot life compared with that with 1C2E4MI. Owing to the high reactivity at high temperature, prolonged pot life at room temperature, and the high flexural strength and modulus, we believe Complex-S has potential applications as the one-component epoxy system in fiber-reinforced thermosetting composites.

References

[1] AUVERGNE R, CAILLOL S, DAVID G, et al. Biobased thermosetting epoxy: present and future [J]. Chem Rev, 2014, 114: 1082−1115.

[2] LI C M, TAN J J, GU J W, et al. Facile synthesis of imidazole microcapsules via thiol-click chemistry and their application as thermally latent curing agent for epoxy resins [J]. Compos Sci Technol, 2017, 142: 198−206.

[3] JIN F L, LI X, PARK S J. Synthesis and application of epoxy resins: a review [J]. J Ind Eng Chem, 2015, 29: 1−11.

[4] VIDIL T, TOURNILHAC F, MUSSO S, et al. Control of reactions and network structures of epoxy thermosets [J]. Prog Polym Sci, 2016, 62: 126−179.

[5] LIU J, SUE H J, THOMPSON Z J, et al. Nanocavitation in self-assembled amphiphilic block copolymer-modified epoxy [J]. Macromolecules, 2008, 41: 7616−7624.

[6] LU L, FAN J Z, LI G Q. Intrinsic healable and recyclable thermoset epoxy based on shape memory effect and transesterification reaction [J]. Polymer, 2016, 105: 10−18.

[7] ARIMITSU K, FUSE S, KUDO K, et al. Imidazole derivatives as latent curing agents for epoxy thermosetting resins

[J]. Mater Lett, 2015, 161: 408-410.

[8] BARTON J M, BUIST G J, HAMERTON I, et al. Preparation and characterization of imidazole-metal complexes and evaluation of cured epoxy networks[J]. J Mater Chem, 1994, 4: 379-384.

[9] BROWN J, HAMERTON I, HOWLIN B J. Preparation, characterization, and thermal properties of controllable metal-imidazole complex curing agents for epoxy resins[J]. J Appl Polym Sci, 2000, 75: 201-217.

[10] LI S W, WAN Q, KANG Q. Chiral-at-metal Rh(III) complex-catalyzed michael addition of pyrazolones withalpha, beta-unsaturated 2-acyl imidazoles [J]. Org Lett, 2018, 20: 1312-1315.

[11] ARATANI Y, SUENOBU T, OHKUBO K, et al. Dual function photocatalysis of cyano-bridged heteronuclear metal complexes for water oxidation and two-electron reduction of dioxygen to produce hydrogen peroxide as a solar fuel[J]. Chem Commun, 2017, 53: 3473-3476.

[12] VANBAEL M K, SMETS J, SCHONE K, et al. Matrix-isolation FTIR studies and theoretical calculations of hydrogen-bonded complexes of imidazole. A comparison between experimental results and different calculation methods[J]. J Phys Chem A, 1997, 101: 2397-2413.

[13] KING S T. Low-temperature matrix isolation study of hydrogen-bonded high-boiling organic compounds. I. The sampling device and the infrared spectra of pyrazole, imidazole, and dimethyl phosphinic acid[J]. J Phys Chem, 1970, 74: 2133-2138.

[14] BUIST G J, HAMERTON I, HOWLIN B J, et al. Comparative kinetic analyses for epoxy-resins cured with imidazole metal-complexes[J]. J Mater Chem, 1994, 4: 1793-1797.

[15] HAMERTON I, HOWLIN B J, JONES J R, et al. Effect of complexation with copper(II) on cured neat resin properties of a commercial epoxy resin using modified imidazole curing agents[J]. J Mater Chem, 1996, 6: 305-310.

[16] BARTON J M, HAMERTON I, HOWLIN B J, et al. The development of controllable metal-chelate curing agents with improved storage stability[J]. Polym Bull, 1994, 33: 347-353.

[17] BARTON J M, HAMERTON I, HOWLIN B J, et al. Studies of cure schedule and final property relationships of a commercial epoxy resin using modified imidazole curing agents[J]. Polymer, 1998, 39: 1929-1937.

[18] KUDO K, FUSE S, FURUTANI M, et al. Imidazole-type thermal latent curing agents with high miscibility for one-component epoxy thermosetting resins[J]. J Polym Sci Pol Chem, 2016, 54: 2680-2688.

Numerical Simulation of Compression Behaviour of 3D Knitted Spacer Fabrics at the Yarn Level

LOTZ Kevin[1,2], LIU Yanping[1,2]*

[1] Key Laboratory of Textile Science & Technology, Ministry of Education, College of Textiles, Donghua University, Shanghai, 201620, China

[2] Department of Knitting, College of Textiles, Donghua University, Shanghai, 201620, China

* Corresponding author's email: liuyp@ dhu.edu.cn

Abstract: This study aimed to investigate the numerical simulation of a typical spacer fabric by using the real yarn architecture obtained from micro-X-ray computed tomography scanning (μ–CT). In this regard, the complicated deformations and interactions of the component yarns were simulated to identify the authentic compression mechanism. A finite element (FE) model of a unit cell, which comprises of two outer layers (SHELL 181) and forty spacer monofilaments (Beam 188) was established. Multipoint constraint (MPC) approach was used to connect the beam elements with the shell elements. Three additional contact pairs were created, i.e., among spacer monofilaments, between the outer layers and the compression plates, and between spacer monofilaments and compression plates. Finally, a static compression test was simulated, and the results were verified by experimental results. The computational results are in good agreement with the experimental one.

Keywords: Finite element analysis; Simulation; Spacer fabric; Compression mechanism

1 Introduction

Spacer fabric, a three-dimensional (3D) textile, consists of two outer layers and a layer of spacer yarns. The spacer yarns connected and kept apart the two outer layers to form a unique 3D structure[1]. Due to their unique structure, spacer fabrics possess good compressive characteristics[2], good moisture permeability with thermoregulation[3] and excellent energy absorption[2], with a multiple range of applications, including automotive textiles[4], personal protective clothing[5], sport textiles[6], foundation garments[7] and medical textiles[8]. In the past decades, many experimental and analytical studies have been conducted to explore the complex compression mechanisms of spacer fabrics. However, most of the analytical models focused on the deformation behaviour of a single spacer yarn without considering the interactions among yarn components. Moreover, it is not pleasant to analyse the structure effect on the compression behaviour of spacer fabrics by analytical analysis. Consequently, the numerical simulation needs to be carried out to provide a deeper knowledge of the structure and compression properties of spacer fabrics. In this connection, BRISA et al[9]. developed a FE model of a single vertical spacer yarn of thick warp-knitted spacer fabric, by considering the interactions of the spacer yarn with the outer layers, to study the compression elastic behaviour during plane plate compression. Whereas LIU and HU[10] established a FE model to investigate the mechanical behaviour of a typical warp-knitted spacer fabric under compression in terms of its structural feature and mechanical properties of its component by considered all interactions of component yarns in their model. Although some attempts have been made by FE modelling, a clear picture of the complex deformations and interactions of the component yarns of spacer fabrics cannot be drawn yet. This research aims to develop a FE model of a typical spacer fabric by using its real yarn architecture at the yarn level obtained from μ – CT scanning and digital microscopic images. The complex deformations and interactions of the component yarns will be simulated to reveal the authentic compression mechanisms. Finally, the FE model will be verified by the experimental results. It is expected that this study will help to better understand the complex deformation mechanisms of spacer fabrics with optimising the performance of spacer fabrics in design and manufacturing.

2   Compression Behaviour of Spacer Fabric

The warp-knitted spacer fabric used for this study has a thickness of 10.3mm and a density of 53.40kg/m³. The meshed outer layers were knitted with 600D/192F polyester multifilament, and the spacer layer was knitted with 0.22mm diameter polyester monofilament, which connects the two outer layers. Images of the spacer fabric from various directions are illustrated in Fig.1. It can be seen that the two outer layers are connected by the spacer monofilaments in an inclined form [Fig.1 (a)] and that the monofilament loops are mostly covered by the multifilament loops [Fig.1(c)].

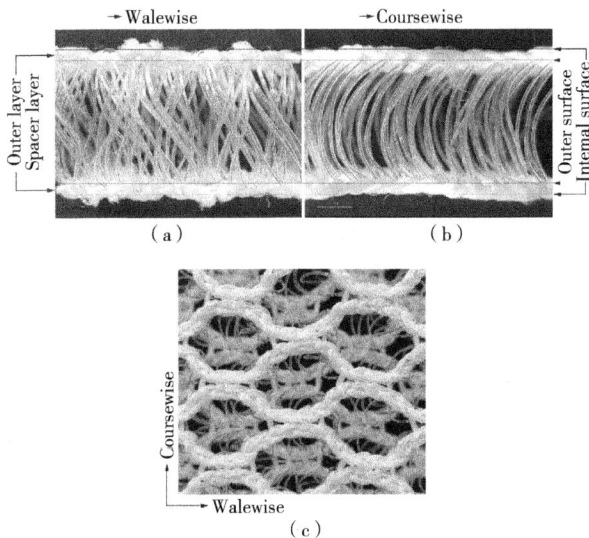

Fig.1   Images of spacer fabric from various directions: (a) walewise direction; (b) coursewise direction; (c) outer surface

Several samples with a size of 10cm × 10cm were tested on an INSTRON 5566 Universal Testing Machine equipped with two circular compression plates of 15 cm in diameter in an environment of 20℃ and 65% relative humidity. The load-displacement curves behave highly nonlinear and three distinct stages, i. e., linear elasticity, plateau and densification, can be observed.

3   Geometrical Analysis

A fabric sample of the size of 2.5cm × 0.8cm was scanned by using a μ-CT system (Scanco/Viva CT 40, SCANCO Medical AG, Switzerland) to obtain a precise 3D reconstruction of the spacer fabric (Fig.2).

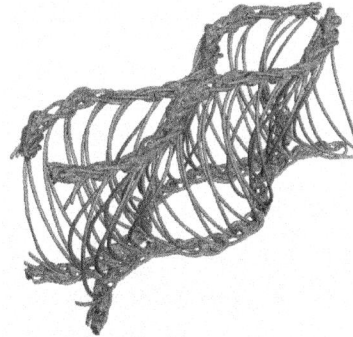

Fig.2   μ-CT reconstruction

3.1   Outer Layers

Due to a resolution limit of the μ-CT system, the outer layers could not be reconstructed well (Fig.2). Therefore, additional images were taken to understand better how the spacer monofilaments are connected with the outer layers [Fig 3(a)]. It can be observed that the spacer monofilaments were knitted into the outer layer and formed an intermeshed monofilament loop [Fig. 3 (a) and (b)], and that the outer layer thickness is irregular [Fig.3(c)]. By neglecting the multifilament thickness, it varies between 0.22mm at the leg and 0.44mm at the head of a monofilament loop [Fig.3(b)], which equals the diameter size of one or two spacer monofilaments.

3.2   Spacer Layer

As seen in Fig.2, the spacer monofilaments are well reconstructed, except the monofilament loops embedded in the outer layers. Since the fabric was initially scanned along its length, the geometric model needed to be sliced along its thickness. The first and last few slices consisting of the outer layer could not be used because of resolution limitations, resulting in an effective spacer layer thickness of 8.41066mm. Then the sliced

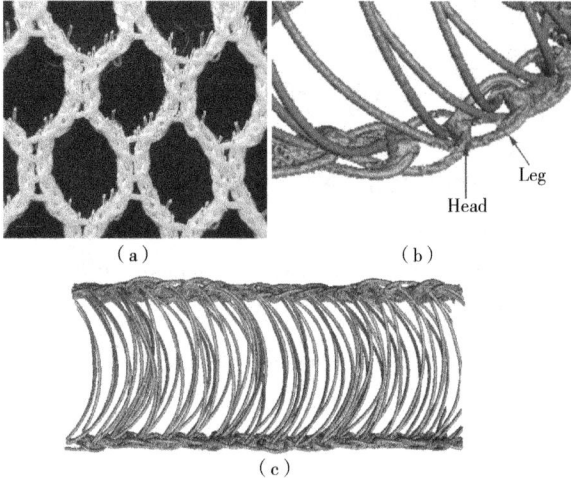

Fig.3 Images of spacer fabric: (a) and (b) internal surface of outer layers; (c) side view of μ–CT reconstruction

images were processed with an image processing software to obtain the accurate coordinates for each spacer monofilament. Fig.4 demonstrates that a unit cell of the spacer fabric consists of 40 spacer monofilaments highlighted by a parallelogram.

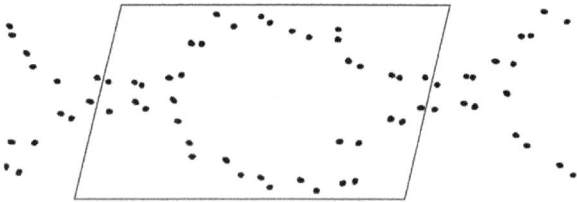

Fig.4 Sliced image

4 FE Analysis

The FE software ANSYS Mechanical APDL 14.5 was used to establish a FE model of the spacer fabric.

4.1 Unit Cell

The outer layers were built up in a simplified way with a constant thickness by considering the wavy outline of the real fabric, still being capable of interacting with the spacer monofilaments. They were meshed by using a shell element SHELL 181, and an effective thickness of 0.5mm was assigned.

The forty spacer yarns were meshed with a beam element BEAM188 by setting a circular section of 0.11mm (equals the radius of spacer monofilament).

To connect the beams with the two shells, the approach of MPC was used. For this, the end nodes of each beam were set as pilot nodes (TARGET 170), while the selected nodes in the shell elements were set as contact nodes (CONTA 175). Then each pilot node was connected to the corresponding contact nodes by force-distributed constrained MPC contact pair.

Finally, two rigid compression plates were created to simulate the static compression test. Each plate was assigned with a pilot node on which the boundary conditions were applied. While the bottom plate is fixed by constraining all the DOFs, a displacement of 7.2mm in Z-direction is applied to the top plate, as shown in Fig.5.

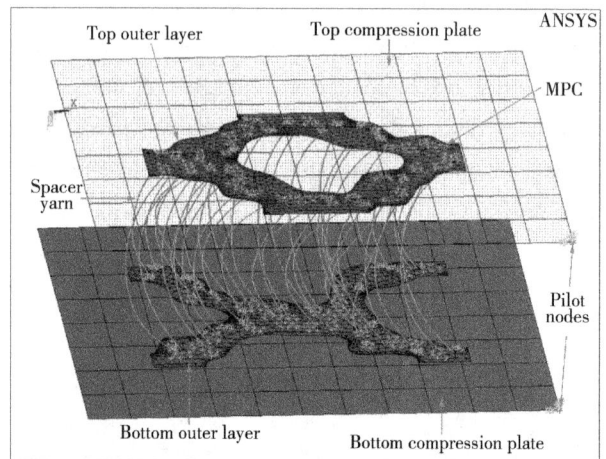

Fig.5 Simulation set-up of the spacer fabric unit cell

4.2 Material Property

Spacer monofilaments behave highly nonlinear during compression. Therefore, nonlinear properties needed to be assigned for the beam elements. For this, a tensile stress-strain test on an Instron 5566 Universal Testing Machine was conducted. In addition, a Poisson's ratio of 0.3[11] and a friction coefficient of 0.28, which was measured by using a portable mechanical yarn friction tester (SDL Atlas Y096A/B), were defined for the beam elements. For the shell elements, linear elastic properties were assigned, i. e., Young's modulus of 13.428MPa, Poisson's ratio of 0.3, and a friction coefficient of 0.28, as the outer layers only undertook small deformation during compression.

4.3 FE Models

4.3.1 Contact Pairs

During the compression test, contacts between spacer

monofilaments and outer layers, between spacer mono-filament and compression plates as well as among spacer monofilaments will occur. Therefore, four contact pairs needed to be created to ensure realistic compression behaviour.

4.3.1.1 First Contact Pair

Contacts between spacer monofilaments and outer layers were established. Two flexible-to-flexible line-to-surface contact pairs were created to simulate the interactions between the beam elements (CONTA 177) and the internal surface layers of the shell elements (TARGE 170). Whereby the beam elements were divided into three sections, a middle section, and two end sections, while the middle section is fully constrained, the two end sections of the size of 0.5 mm can penetrate the shell elements. Additionally, a friction coefficient of 0.28 was defined for this contact pair.

4.3.1.2 Second Contact Pair

Contacts among spacer monofilaments were created. A flexible-to-flexible line-to-line standard self-contact pair (CONTA 176 and TARGE 170) was created to simulate the interactions among spacer monofilaments.

4.3.1.3 Third Contact Pair

Contacts between compression plates and outer layers were created. The two rigid compression plates (TARGE 170) were created laying on the same plane as the external surface layer of the top and bottom outer layers. Then the external surface layers were defined as contact elements (CONTA 174), to form with the compression plates, two rigid-to-flexible surface-to-surface bounded contact pairs without relative motion.

4.3.1.4 Forth Contact Pair

Contacts between compression plates and spacer mono-filaments were created. Tow rigid-to-flexible line-to-surface contact pairs were created to constrain the spacer monofilaments (CONTA 177) from penetrating the compression plates (TARGE 170) during compression. In this connection the spacer monofilaments were divided into three sections, two end sections and a middle section. Only the middle sections were selected as contact elements as they are most likely to contact the compression plates during compression, due to the meshed outer layers.

5 Results and Discussions

5.1 Validation by Experiment

To verify the FE model for simulating the compression mechanism of spacer fabrics, the spacer fabric described in section 2, was compressed on an INSTRON 5566 Universal Testing Machine. The testing machine was set up with two circular plane plates with a diameter of 15cm and a compression speed of 12mm/min. The tested samples had a size of 10cm × 10cm. Several compression tests were conducted to present the compression load-displacement curve of the tested spacer fabric.

Fig. 6 presents the compression load-displacement curves obtained from the experiment and simulation. It can be observed that both curves show three distinct stages, i.e., linear elasticity, plateau and densification. The simulated compression curve is in good agreement with the experimental one and can, therefore, be used to analyse the compression mechanism of spacer fabrics.

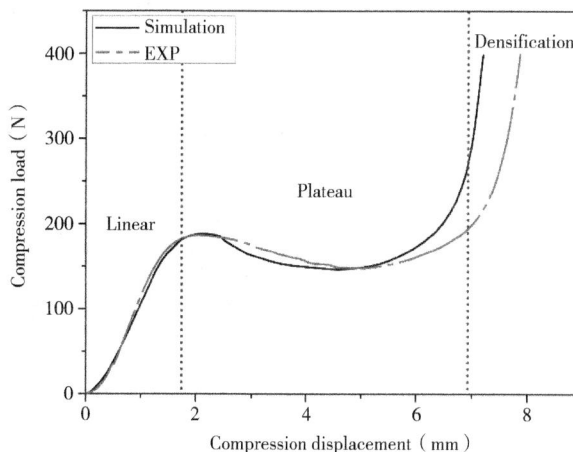

Fig.6 Comparison of the experimental and simulated compression load-displacement curves

5.2 Compression Mechanism

Based on the validated FE model, the compression mechanism of spacer fabrics can be simulated and analysed. In this connection, the validated FE model was used to summarise the compression mechanism for this type of spacer fabric based on the compression load-displacement curves and simulation deformation morphologies. It can be seen from Fig.6, the compression load-displacement curves show three distinct stages, i.e., linear elastic stage, plateau stage, and densification stage. The corresponding simulation deformation morphologies of those three stages are shown in Fig.7.

• In the linear elastic stage, the spacer monofilament end sections start to contact the internal surface of the outer layers. Post-buckling of the spacer monofilaments and constraints of the contacting points leads to a nearly linear load increase with the increase in displacement.

• In the plateau stage, a relatively constant load can be observed with the increase in displacement. All spacer monofilament end sections are contacting the outer layers. The middle section of the spacer monofilament starts to contact either the top or bottom outer layer internal surfaces, due to the inclined form of spacer monofilaments. Free space in the spacer layer becomes less, and contacts among spacer monofilaments lead to large torsion of the spacer monofilaments.

• In the densification stage, the spacer monofilament end and middle sections contacting the outer layer internal surfaces on a large scale. As free space in the spacer layer has been almost removed in earlier stages and the load increases sharply.

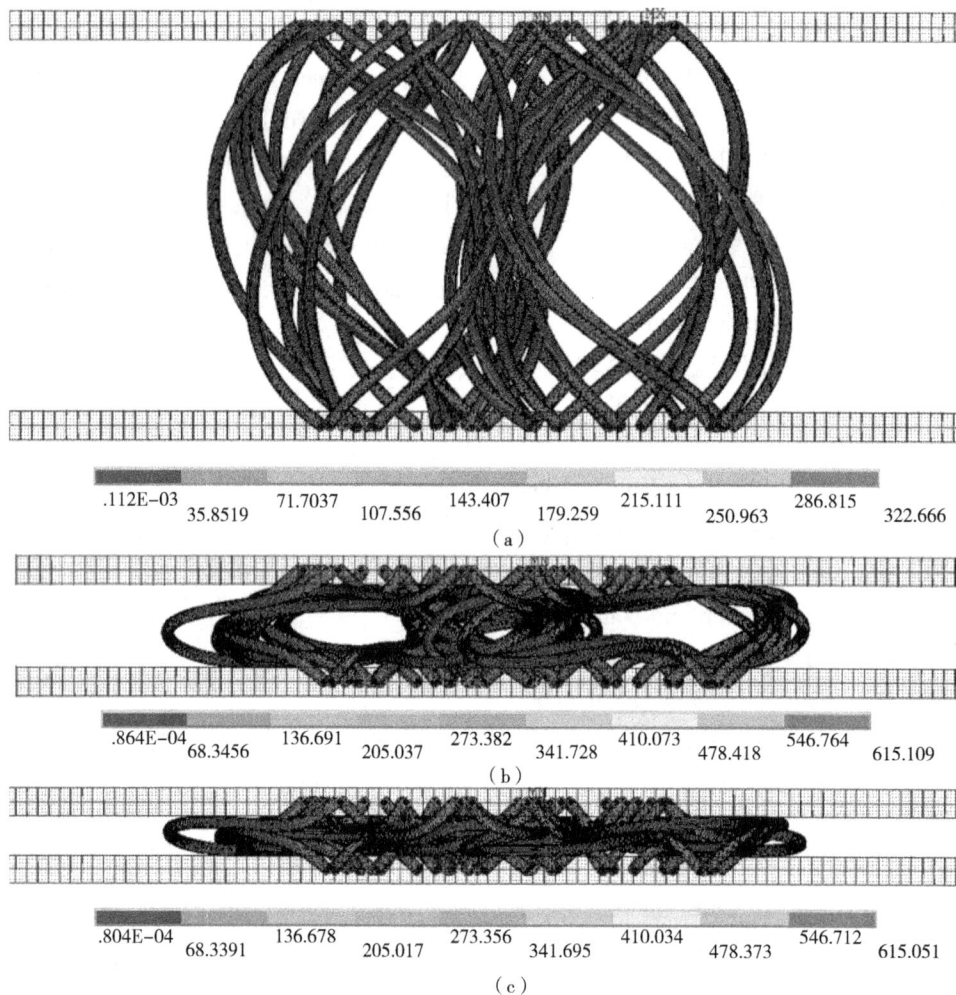

Fig.7　Von Mises stress plot at different compression stages/displacements: (a) Linear/1.78mm; (b) Plateau/6.95mm; (c) Densification/7.2mm

6　Conclusions

The compression mechanism of a meshed spacer fabric was investigated with the FE method at yarn level based on the geometric reconstruction obtained from μ – CT scanning. By FE analysis, the complicated deformations and interactions of the component yarns were simulated to analyse the authentic compression mechanism. The load-displacement curve and simulation deformation morphologies of the validated FE model were used to identify the compression mechanism for this type of spacer fabric. Based on the curve progression of the load-displacement curve, three displacement stages were proposed, i.e., linear elastic stage, plateau stage and densification stage. According to the identified compression mechanism, it can be confirmed that the nonlinear compression behaviour of this type of fabric is due to post-buckling, torsion, contacts between spacer monofilaments and outer layers as well as, contacts among spacer monofilaments. The validated FE model can be used to conduct a parametric study in order to enhance the understanding of the structure-property relationships of spacer fabrics under compression.

Acknowledgements

The work described in this paper is sponsored by the National Natural Science Foundation of China (11702062), Shanghai Pujiang Program (17PJ1400300), Fundamental Research Funds for the Central Universities (16D110120), and initial research funds for Young Teachers of Donghua University (101 - 07 - 0053036).

References

[1] LIU Y, HU H. Compression property and air permeability of weft-knitted spacer fabrics[J]. J Text I, 2011, 102(4): 366-372.

[2] LIU Y, HU H, ZHAO L, et al. Compression behavior of warp-knitted spacer fabrics for cushioning applications[J]. Text Res J, 2011, 82(1):11-20.

[3] DLUGOSCH S, HU H, CHAN A. Thermal comfort evaluation of equestrian body protectors using a sweating manikin[J]. Clothing and Text Res J, 2013, 31(4):231-243.

[4] YE X, HU H, FENG X. Development of the warp knitted spacer fabrics for cushion applications[J]. J of Ind Text, 2008, 37(3):213-223.

[5] MIAO X, KONG X, JIANG G. The experimental research on the stab resistance of warp-knitted spacer fabric[J]. J of Ind Text, 2012, 43(2):281-301.

[6] YE X, FANGUEIRO R, HU H, et al. Application of warp-knitted spacer fabrics in car seats[J]. The J of the Text I, 2007, 98(4):337-344.

[7] PALANI RAJAN T, SOUZA L, RAMAKRISHNAN G, et al. Comfort properties of functional warp-knitted polyester spacer fabrics for shoe insole applications[J]. J of Ind Text, 2016, 45(6):1239-1251.

[8] YIP J, SUN-PUI N. Study of three-dimensional spacer fabrics: Molding properties for intimate apparel application[J]. J of Materials Processing Technology, 2009, 209:58-62.

[9] TONG S, YIP J, YICK K, et al. Exploring use of warp-knitted spacer fabric as a substitute for the absorbent layer for advanced wound dressing[J]. Text Res J, 2015, 85(12): 1258-1268.

[10] BRISA V, HELBIG F, KROLL L. Numerical characterisation of the mechanical behaviour of a vertical spacer yarn in thick warp knitted spacer fabrics[J]. J of Ind Text, 2015, 45(1):101-117.

[11] MOTT P, ROLAND C. Limits to poisson's ratio in isotropic materials[J]. Phys Rev B, 2009, 80(13):132104.

Transverse Impact Behaviors of 3D Angle-Interlock Woven Composite at Subzero Temperatures

ZHANG Jiajin[1], ZHANG Wei[1], ZHANG Junjie[1], HUANG Shuwei[1], GU Bohong[1]*

[1]*College of Textiles, Donghua University, Shanghai 201620, China*

*** *Corresponding author's email*: gubh@ dhu.edu.cn

Abstract: The transverse impact behaviors of 3D angle-interlock woven composites (3DAWC) were characterized from room temperature (20℃) down to −80℃. The transverse impact tests were performed with a modified Hopkinson pressure bar apparatus combined with a self-designed cooling device which can provide a stable subzero temperature environment as low as −100℃. The impact load-displacement curves, peak loads, total energy absorption and impact damage morphologies have been obtained to understand the effect of temperatures and impact intensities. Significant changes in the transverse impact responses of the composites have been found, related first to the impact intensity and then to the subzero temperature. The results also revealed that the failure mechanism changed from ductile failure to brittle failure as the temperature decreases. The matrix crack and fragmentation often occurred on the front surface of the composites, while debonding and fiber breakage happened on the rear.

Keywords: 3D woven composites; Impact behavior; Subzero temperature; Impact intensity

1　Introduction

Carbon Fiber Reinforced Polymer Composites (CFRP) are utilized as critical components in many modern technologies which operate over a wide range of conditions. One of the most widely used CFRP materials is Three-dimensional Woven Composite (3DWC)[1] used as curved beams[2], T-joints and brackets which require load transfer around a bend. Compared to laminated composites, 3DWC have the superiority of high tolerance to structural damage, interlaminar fracture toughness and tensile strain-to-failure values. In addition, complex net-shape structures can be fabricated using modified weaving looms, making it possible to tailor the mechanical properties for specific applications, such as helmet shells and female body armor[3].

It is essential to provide insight into the impact performance of this material to guarantee structure security. Although there have been a few studies performed at room temperature, focusing on low-velocity impact[4-6], bal-

listic impact[7] and transverse impact[8], the subzero temperature properties of 3DWC are not well characterized.

Recently, the most used three-dimensional woven architectures mainly include 3D orthogonal woven structure and 3D angle-interlock woven structure based on different weave patterns of the through-thickness binder yarn. The latter has been studied here in this paper as it possesses good pliability and intriguing structural diversity.

In this work, we prepare the three-dimensional carbon fiber reinforced angle-interlock woven composite and study its temperature effects and the impact intensity effects on transverse impact property and damage mechanism using a modified Hopkinson pressure bar with a self-designed low-temperature environmental device.

2　Experiments

2.1　Materials

The 3D angle-interlock woven fabric is a multi-layered

fabric produced by interlacing two sets of carbon fiber tows in the weaving machine. The weft tows are layer to layer interlocked by the warp tows. 3D angle-interlock woven composite (3DAWC) was fabricated by consolidating the 3D angle-interlock woven fabric (Tab. 1, Suzhou Donghua Fiber Materials Products Co. Ltd.) with the epoxy resin matrix (JC-02A, Jiafa Chemical Co. Ltd.) using vacuum-assisted resin transfer molding [VARTM, Fig.1(a)]. The cured 3DAWC was cut into rectangular specimens along warp direction [Fig.1(b)] by waterjet. As shown in Fig.1(c) and (d), weft yarns kept straight paralleled to each other and warp yarns were in wave patterns.

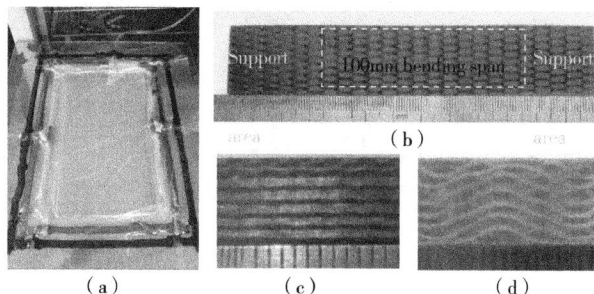

Fig.1　Preparation of 3DAWC specimen: photograph of (a) VARTM process; (b) Specimen for transverse impact test; Cross-section along (c) weft and (d) warp direction

Tab.1　Architectural parameters of 3D angle-interlock woven fabric

Tows	Yarn specification	Linear density (tex)	Layers	Weaving density (end/10cm)	Thickness (mm)	Areal density (g/cm²)
Warp	T300-6K	396	7	40	5	0.47
Weft	T700-12K	792	7	80		

2.2　Transverse Impacts

The transverse impacts at subzero temperatures were performed on a modified Hopkinson pressure bar (HPB) apparatus combined with a self-designed cooling device. As depicted in Fig. 2, the apparatus mainly consists of a nitrogen gas cylinder, a pressure chamber, a striker bar, an incident bar with a hemispherical end, a low temperature environment system, and unlike the conventional split HPB system, no transmission bar. The diameter of the striker bar and the incident bar is 30mm; and their lengths are 400mm and 1800mm, respectively. A specimen was placed at the end of the incident bar in a low temperature environ-

mental chamber, which connected with a liquid nitrogen container and a temperature control device, providing a subzero temperature environment as low as -100℃. The striker bar was accelerated using compressed air and was fired at varying pressures (hereafter called impact intensity): 0. 2MPa, 0. 3MPa and 0. 4MPa. When the striker bar impacted the incident bar, an approximately rectangular compressive wave was produced in the incident bar. Recorded by a strain gauge glued on the midpoint of the incident bar, the original pulse signals under three impact intensities are shown as in Fig.3.

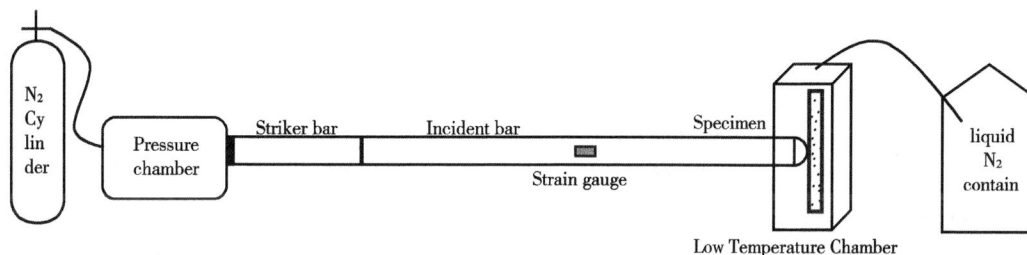

Fig.2　Sketch of a modified split Hopkinson pressure bar apparatus

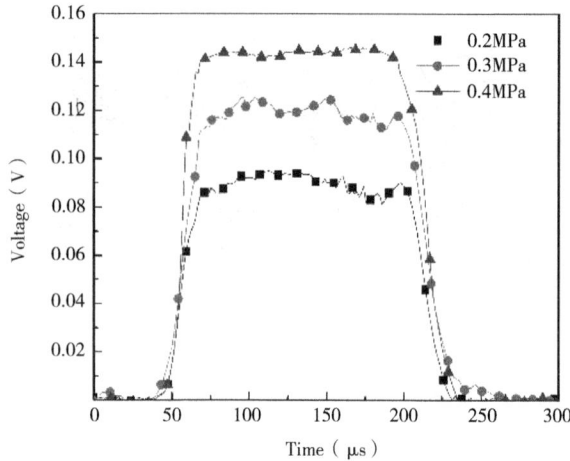

Fig.3 Original pulse signals measured by the strain gauge

Based on the one-dimensional elastic wave propagation theory, impact load $P(t)$ and displacement of the bar $u(t)$ can be determined as[9]:

$$P(t) = EA[\varepsilon_i(t) + \varepsilon_r(t)]$$
$$u(t) = c_0 \int_0^t [\varepsilon_i(\tau) - \varepsilon_r(\tau)]\mathrm{d}\tau \qquad (1)$$
$$c_0 = \sqrt{E/\rho}$$

where $\varepsilon_i(t)$ and $\varepsilon_r(t)$ are strain impulse result from propagation of the incident and reflected waves, respectively. A, E and ρ are cross-sectional area, Young's modulus and mass density of the incident bar, respectively. The pulse duration t_P and interval duration t_i can be calculated by:

$$t_P = 2L_P/c_0 \text{ and } t_i = 2L_i/c_0 \qquad (2)$$

where L_P and L_i are the length of striker bar and incident bar, respectively.

3 Results and Discussions

3.1 Effects of Temperature and Impact Intensity

The displacement/time curves of the incident bar under different impact intensities (0.2/0.3/0.4MPa) and temperatures (20/−20/−50/−80℃) acquired through strain gauge are shown in Fig.4. The stress wave travelled back and forth in the incident bar, causing multiple impacts on the specimen. For each impact, the incident bar moved forward for approximately 160μs and then suspended for 540μs when the stress wave went backward and forward in the incident bar. The displacement increased with increasing impact intensity but kept nearly the same with decreasing temperature when other factors remained

unchanged. But with all the changes, the duration of each impact and interval were kept constant.

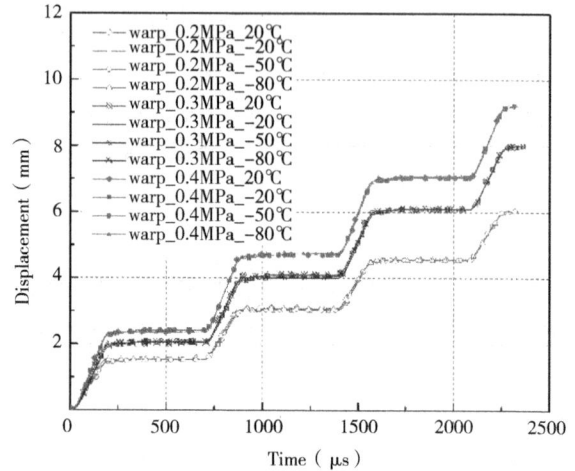

Fig.4 Displacement history under different impact intensities (0.2/0.3/0.4MPa) and temperatures (20/−20/−50/−80℃)

Under the same impact intensity, such as 0.3MPa, the load-displacement curves of different testing temperatures are shown in Fig.5. Peak load tended to decrease with the increasing of impact times owing to damage initiation and propagation of the composites. For example, under −80℃, the first four peak load decreased from about 25kN to around 18kN. The peak load of first four impacts increased together with decreasing temperature as the matrix, cured epoxy resin, became more brittle to withstand larger load.

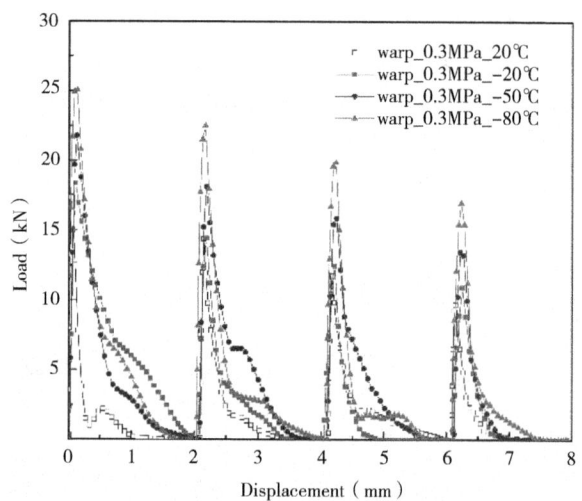

Fig. 5 Load-displacement curves under 0.3MPa at different temperatures (20/−20/−50/−80℃)

Fig.6 illustrate the impact displacement (a), peak load (b) and total absorbed energy of the first four impacts (c) under different impact intensities (0.2/0.3/0.4MPa) and temperatures (20/-20/-50/-80℃).

The three indicators were following the same tendency that they all had positive correlation with impact intensity but negative correlation with temperature.

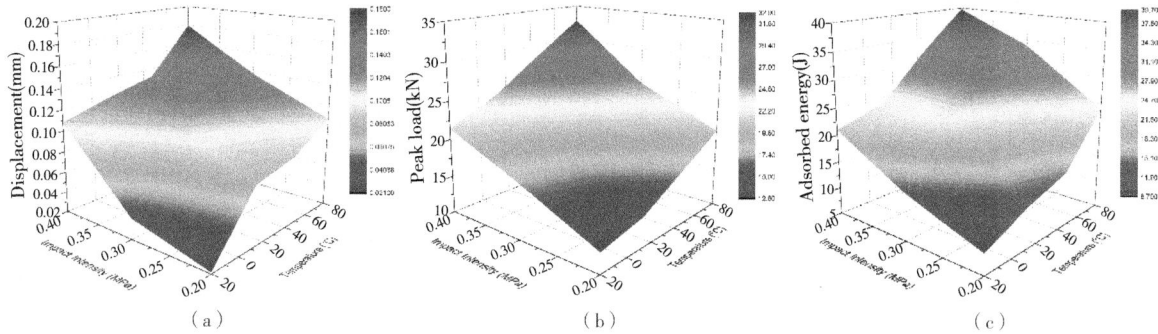

Fig.6　The effect of different impact intensities and different temperatures on (a) Impact displacement; (b) Peak load and (c) Total absorbed energy of first four impacts

3.2　Fracture Morphology and Failure Mechanism

Fig.7 depicts the surface damage morphologies under the same impact intensity, 0.3MPa, at four different temperatures (20/-20/-50/-80℃). With the temperature became lower, the matrix tended to be more fragile. Because the failure mechanism changed from ductile failure to brittle failure as the temperature decreases. The matrix crack and fragmentation often occurred on the front surface of the composites, while debonding and fiber breakage happened on the rear.

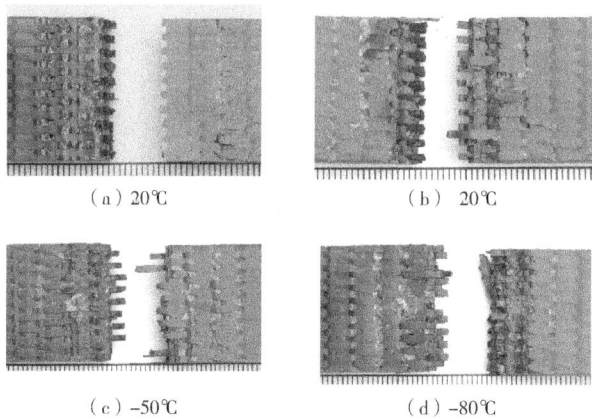

(a) 20℃　　　　(b) 20℃

(c) -50℃　　　　(d) -80℃

Fig.7　Surface damage morphologies under 0.3MPa at different temperatures (a) 20℃; (b) -20℃; (c) -50℃ and (d) -80℃

4　Conclusions

The transverse impact behaviors of 3D angle-interlock woven composite (3DAWC) were studied along warp direction. The modified HTB with a self-designed low temperature device were used to test its transverse impact properties at room and subzero temperatures (20/-20/-50/-80℃). It has been found that the transverse impact responses of the composites are sensitive to the impact intensity and the temperature. The impact displacement, peak load and total absorbed energy of the first four impacts followed the same tendency that they all had positive correlation with impact intensity but negative correlation with temperature. As temperature decreases, the composite presents brittle failure more than ductile failure. The matrix crack and fragmentation often occurred on the front surface of the composites, while debonding and fiber breakage happened on the rear.

References

[1] KAMIYA R, CHEESEMAN B A, POPPER P, et al. Some recent advances in the fabrication and design of three-dimensional textile preforms: a review[J]. Composites Science and Technology, 2000, 60(1):33-47.

[2] REDMAN C, BAYRAKTAR H, MCCLAIN M, Curved beam test behavior of 3D woven composites[C]. International SAMPE Technical Conference, Seattle, WA, 2014.

[3] CHEN X, TAYLOR L W, TSAI L J. 10-Three-dimensional fabric structures. Part 1-An overview on fabrication of three-dimensional woven textile preforms for composites, in Handbook of Technical Textiles[M]. Second Edition. Cambnidge: Woodhead Publishing, 2016: 285-304.

[4] BAUCOM J N, ZIKRY M A, RAJENDRAN A M. Low-velocity impact damage accumulation in woven S2-glass composite systems[J]. Composites Science and Technology, 2006, 66(10):1229-1238.

[5] HART K R, CHIA P X L, SHERIDAN L E, et al. Mechanisms and characterization of impact damage in 2D and 3D woven fiber-reinforced composites[J]. Composites Part a-Applied Science and Manufacturing, 2017, 101:432-443.

[6] WANG M, CAO M, WANG H, et al. Drop-weight impact behaviors of 3-D angle interlock woven composites after thermal oxidative aging[J]. Composite Structures, 2017, 166: 239-255.

[7] MUNOZ R, MARTINEZ-HERGUETA F, GALVEZ F, et al. Ballistic performance of hybrid 3D woven composites: experiments and simulations[J]. Composite Structures, 2015, 127: 141-151.

[8] REN C, LIU T, SIDDIQUE A, et al. High-speed visualizing and mesoscale modeling for deformation and damage of 3D angle-interlock woven composites subjected to transverse impacts[J]. International Journal of Mechanical Sciences, 2018, 140:119-132.

[9] JIANG F, VECCHIO K S. Hopkinson bar loaded fracture experimental technique: a critical review of dynamic fracture toughness tests[J]. Applied Mechanics Reviews, 2009, 62 (6):1469-1474.

Synthesis of Highly Fluorescent Gold-Silver Bimetallic Nanoclusters Mediated by Wool Keratin

ZHANG Xin[1,2], YU Weidong[1,2], LIU Hongling[1,2]*

[1] *Key Laboratory of Textile Science & Technology, Ministry of Education, College of Textiles, Donghua University, Shanghai, 201620, China*

[2] *Department of Technical Textiles, College of Textiles, Donghua University, Shanghai, 201620, China*

*Corresponding author's email: hlliu@ dhu.edu.cn

Abstract: Fluorescent metal nanoclusters have become important scientific research targets in recent years, thanks to their long-term and stable fluorescence properties in the near-infrared region. Compared with single metal nanoclusters, alloy nanoclusters composed of two different metal elements have superior properties in terms of catalysts and biological imaging. Herein, gold-silver bimetallic nanoclusters mediated by wool keratin (Au&AgNCs@ WK) were successfully synthesized for the first time. We optimized the molar ratio of gold to silver and the volume ratio of reducing ligand to chloroauric acid in the reaction system through multiple sets of single factor comparison experiments. It was found that when the chloroauric acid was excessive and the molar ratio of gold to silver was 0.0714, the obtained Au&AgNCs had the best fluorescence performance. The results show that the metal nanoclusters obtained by this method have excellent fluorescence performance and good stability. These studies will lay a solid foundation for the application of bimetallic nanoclusters in other fields.

Keywords: Wool keratin; Bimetallic nanoclusters; Fluorescence; Stability

1 Introduction

In recent years, special metal nanoclusters have attracted a lot of attention due to their molecular-like nature and many novel features[1-3]. Metal nanoclusters typically contain several to hundreds of atoms, the size of which is comparable to the electron Fermi wavelength, which gives them an important role in the transition between a single metal atom and a plasma metal nanoparticle[4]. In this size state, the continuous electron density of the energy state splits into discrete energy levels, giving them peculiar optical, electrical, and chemical properties[5].

Compared with single metal nanoclusters, bimetallic nanoclusters composed of two different metal elements have superior application properties in bioanalysis, photochemistry and industrial catalysis[6]. Therefore, many scholars are also devoted to the study of alloy nanoclusters. The synthesis method of bimetallic nanoclusters is similar to the synthesis method of single metal nanoclus-

ters, and there are many kinds including etching method, reduction method, electrochemical synthesis method, template synthesis method and the like[7-9]. For example, TIAN[10] et al. used egg albumin as a reducing ligand to prepare gold-silver alloy nanoclusters and used them as probes for detecting cyanide ions (CN$^-$). ZHANG's team[11] hydrothermally synthesized gold-silver bimetallic nanoclusters and used them for the selective analysis of mercury ion (Hg^{2+}) and copper ion (Cu^{2+}). However, as of now, the research results on the synthesis of bimetallic nanoclusters always have various disadvantages such as difficulty in preserving ligands, complicated methods, and expensive raw materials. In order to create a simple, economical and environmentally friendly synthesis method, it is crucial to find a cheap and environmentally friendly material.

In this work, we used wool keratin (WK) as a reducing ligand to synthesize gold and silver bimetallic nanoclusters. It is well known that WK can be extracted from discarded wool, and its raw materials are inexpensive and the extraction method is mature[12]. We obtained gold-silver bimetallic nanoclusters with good fluorescence stability by adjusting the synthesis scheme and optimizing the experimental conditions.

2 Experiments

2.1 Materials

70s merino wool was provided by Shandong Nanshan Zhishang Technology Co., Ltd (Shandong). Sodium sulfide nanahydrate ($Na_2S \cdot 9H_2O$), Chloroauric acid tetrahydrate ($HAuCl_4 \cdot 4H_2O$), Silver nitrate ($AgNO_3$), Acetone, Anhydrous ethanol, Urea, and Sodium hydroxide (NaOH) were purchased from Sinopharm Chemical Reagent Co., Ltd. Sodium dodecyl sulfate (SDS) and Sodium chloride (NaCl) from Shanghai Lingfeng Chemical Reagent Co., Ltd.

2.2 Experimental Instruments and Methods

The fluorescence measurements were performed on the QM/TM fluorescence spectrometer (PTI, USA). Using a 100W xenon lamp as the excitation source, the excitation wavelength is 390nm, the scanning range is 500−800nm, and the slit width is 1.0mm. The sonication of the solution was performed by a Jiekang ultrasonic cleaner, model PS-06A, with an ultrasonic frequency of 40kHz.

2.3 Preparation of Wool Keratin (WK) Solution

A mixed solution of Na_2S (0.26M), SDS (0.13M) and urea (9M) was used as a dissolving agent to dissolve 5g of the pretreated wool fiber in a bath ratio of 1 : 10. The wool fibers were treated in a water bath at 60℃ for 12 hours and then centrifuged at 5000r/min for 30 minutes. The resulting supernatant was filtered and dialyzed for 72 hours to become the pure WK solution.

2.4 Preparation of Au&AgNCs@WK

A typical preparation method is as follows: (1) A certain amount of 2.5% WK solution was taken from a refrigerator at 4℃, and it was allowed to stand at 37℃ for 10 min at room temperature. (2) A certain amount of 1 mol/L NaOH solution was added to the WK solution to adjust the pH value of the system. (3) After the pH value of the solution was stabilized, a certain amount of 10mol/L $HAuCl_4 \cdot 4H_2O$ and $AgNO_3$ solution was added dropwise, and treated on an ultrasonic treatment machine for 3 minutes to carry out a chelation reaction. (4) The mixed solution was reacted in a constant temperature and humidity incubator for a certain period of time to obtain Au&AgNCs@WK solution, and the obtained solution was stored in a refrigerator at 4℃ for later use.

3 Results and Discussions

3.1 Effect of Mixing Ratio of WK and HAuCl₄ Solution

In order to explore the effect of the ratio of reducing ligand to gold cluster synthesis agent on the fluorescence properties of Au&AgNCs@WK, four groups of Au&AgNCs@WK were synthesized under the conditions of low silver molar ratio (0.05) and high silver molar ratio (0.25). Each group contained three samples, each containing keratin excess, keratin equivalent to chloroauric acid and excess chloroauric acid. Fig.1 characterizes their fluorescence properties. It can be observed that the gold-silver nanoclusters obtained in the excess of chloroauric acid have the best fluorescence performance regardless of the low silver molar ratio or the high silver molar ratio.

3.2 Determination of the Optimal Gold-Silver Molar Ratio

Fig.2 illustrates a fluorescence spectrum of Au&AgNCs@WK solution synthesized by different gold-silver molar ratios and its fluorescence intensity at 650nm. The fluorescence properties of the synthesized Au&AgNCs@WK were observed only by changing the content of $AgNO_3$ in the system while ensuring that other reaction conditions were unchanged. The $AgNO_3$ solution with 1mol/L was introduced the mixture solution containing WK and $HAuCl_4$ with the addition of 0.1mL incremental growth for each group compared with the previous group. As shown in Fig.2(a), it can be seen that in the range of 500−800nm, pure gold nanoclusters (AuNCs@WK) and Au&AgNCs@WK with different molar ratios have strong fluorescence characteristic peaks at around 650nm, while the pure silver nanoclusters (AgNCs@WK) show a straight line in the fluorescence spectrum.

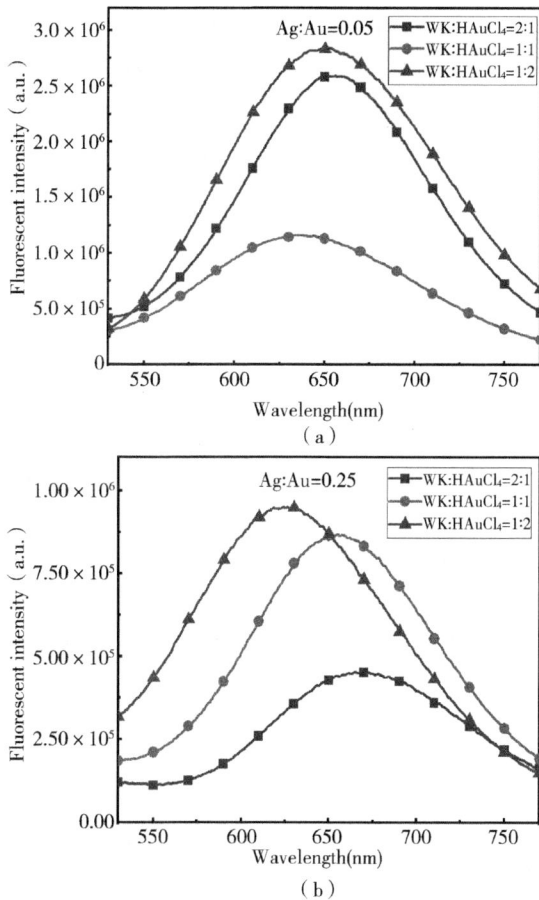

Fig.1 Fluorescence properties of Au&AgNCs@ WK at different $HAuCl_4$ and WK volume ratios

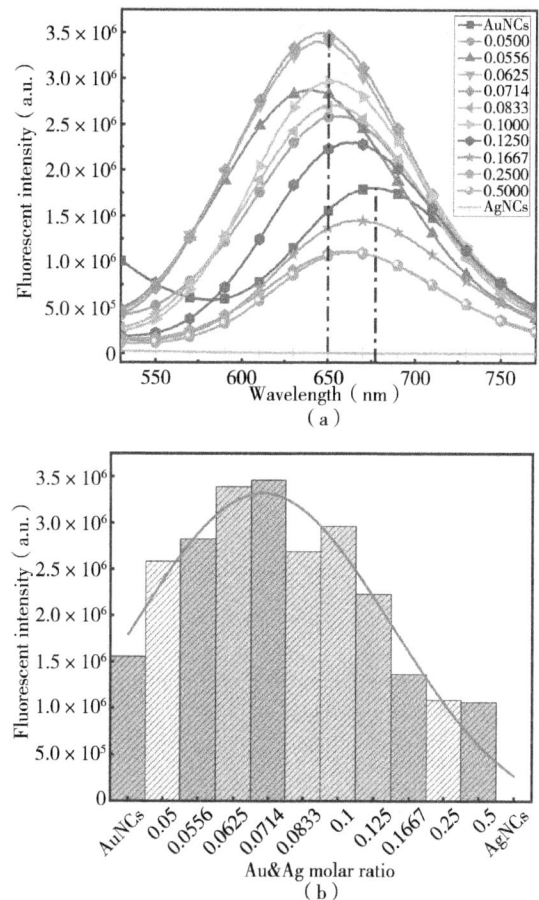

Fig.2 Fluorescence properties of Au&AgNCs@ WK at different Au&Ag molar ratios

There is no obvious fluorescent characteristic peak, indicating that the metal nanoclusters synthesized from pure $AgNO_3$ have no fluorescence properties. And the addition of $AgNO_3$ causes a significant blue shift in the fluorescence characteristic peak of the system. Fig.2(b) shows the fluorescence intensity (λ = 650nm) of Au&AgNCs@ WK in each molar ratio. It can be clearly observed that the fluorescence intensity of AuNCs@ WK is relatively low, while the fluorescence intensity of AgNCs@ WK is 0. With the increase of $AgNO_3$ content in the reaction system, the fluorescence intensity of Au&AgNCs@ WK first increases and then decreases. The addition of silver ions can significantly enhance the fluorescence performance of nanoclusters within a certain range. But when the silver ions exceed a certain amount, at the time, the fluorescence intensity of obtained Au&AgNCs@ WK will decrease. Therefore, the molar ratio of gold and silver in the system is very important, and there is an optimal gold-silver molar ratio of 0.0714.

3.3 Effect of NaOH Solution Content

In the case where the other parameters are unchanged, only the NaOH content, ie the pH value, is changed. The concentration of the NaOH solution was kept constant at 1 mol/L, and gradually increased in units of 0.2mL. We can see from Fig.3(a) that when there is no NaOH in the system, pH = 4.91, which is acidic. The fluorescence spectrum of the solution obtained at this time is a disordered curve with no obvious fluorescence characteristic peak, which indicates that the alkaline environment is essential for the synthesis of Au&AgNCs @ WK with good fluorescence performance. Fig.3(b) shows the fluorescence intensity (λ = 650nm) of gold-silver nanoclusters synthesized under different pH values. The figure clearly shows that as the NaOH content increases, the fluorescence intensity of the obtained

Au&AgNCs@ WK increases first and then decreases, and then remains at a stable level. Among them, when pH = 11.68, the synthesized Au&AgNCs@ WK have the highest fluorescence intensity.

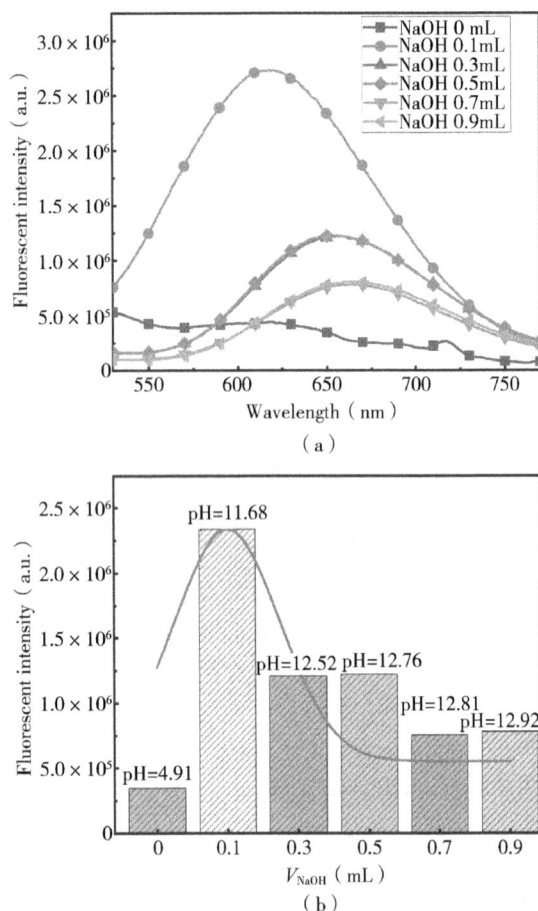

Fig.3 Fluorescence properties of Au&AgNCs@ WK at different NaOH contents

4　Conclusions

In this work, the optimal scheme for preparing gold-silver bimetallic nanoclusters with good fluorescence performance was obtained by adjusting the proportion of various substances in the reaction system and experimental parameters with the aid of ultrasonic treatment. Among them, the optimal gold-silver molar ratio is 0.0714, and the optimal volume ratio of wool keratin solution to chloroauric acid solution is 1 : 2. 0.1mL of NaOH solution (1mol/L) was added to the reaction system so that the pH value of the mixed solution was stabilized at around 11.6, and the gold-silver bimetallic

nanoclusters obtained had the highest fluorescence intensity. Therefore, we have reason to believe that this simple environmentally friendly and mass-produced fluorescent bimetallic nanomaterial can be used in a wide range of applications.

References

[1] DURGADA C V, SHAEMA C P, SREENIVASAN K. Fluorescent gold clusters as nanosensors for copper ions in live cells[J]. Analyst, 2011, 136 (5):933-940.

[2] GUO X, WU F, I Y, et al. Synthesizing a nano-composite of BSA-capped Au nanoclusters/graphitic carbon nitride nanosheets as a new fluorescent probe for dopamine detection [J]. Analytica Chimica Acta, 2016, 942:112-120.

[3] BHOWAL A C, PANDIT S, KUNDU S. Fluorescence emission and interaction mechanism of protein-coated gold and copper nanoclusters as ion sensors in different ionic environments[J]. Journal of Physics D: Applied Physics, 2019, 52 (1).

[4] ALAWA M I, LAI J, XU G. Gold nanoclusters: synthetic strategies and recent advances in fluorescent sensing [J]. Materials Today Nano, 2018, 3:9-27.

[5] LIU H, ZHANG X, WU X, et al. Snochemical synthesis of highly luminescent non-toxic AuNCs and Au@ AgNCs and Cu (II) sensing[J]. Chem Commun (Camb), 2011, 47 (14): 4237-4239.

[6] CHU Z, CHEN L, WANG X, et al. Ultrasmall Au-Ag alloy nanoparticles: protein-directed synthesis, biocompatibility, and x-ray computed tomography imaging[J]. ACS Biomaterials Science & Engineering, 2019, 5 (2):1005-1015.

[7] AHMED H B. Cluster growth adaptor for generation of bactericide Ag-Au bimetallic nanostructures: substantiation through spectral mapping data [J]. Int J Biol Macromol, 2019, 121:774-783.

[8] ZHONG Y, WANG Q, HE Y, et al. A novel fluorescence and naked eye sensor for iodide in urine based on the iodide induced oxidative etching and aggregation of Cu nanoclusters [J]. Sensors and Actuators B: Chemical, 2015, 209:147-153.

[9] ZHOU Q, LIN Y, XU M, et al. Facile synthesis of enhanced fluorescent gold-silver bimetallic nanocluster and its application for highly sensitive detection of inorganic pyrophosphatase activity[J]. Anal Chem, 2016, 88 (17):8886-8892.

[10] TIAN L, LI Y, REN T, et al. Novel bimetallic gold-silver nanoclusters with "Synergy"-enhanced fluorescence for cyanide sensing, cell imaging and temperature sensing [J].

Talanta, 2017, 170:530-539.

[11]ZHANG N, SI Y, SUN Z, et al. Rapid, selective, and ultrasensitive fluorimetric analysis of mercury and copper levels in blood using bimetallic gold-silver nanoclusters with "silver effect"-enhanced red fluorescence [J]. Analytical

Chemistry, 2014, 86 (23):11714-11721.

[12]LIU H, GU T, YU W, et al. Observation of luminescent gold nanoclusters using one-step syntheses from wool keratin and silk fibroin effect [J]. European Polymer Journal, 2018, 99:1-8.

Textile Microstrip Antenna with Artificial Magnetic Conductor for Wearable Applications

LI Yang[1], KUANG Ye[2], YAO Lan[1]*

[1] *Key Laboratory of Textile Science & Technology, Ministry of Education, College of Textiles, Donghua University, Shanghai, 201620, China*

[2] *School of Fashion and Engineering, Zhejiang SCI-TECH University, Hangzhou, Zhejiang, 310018, China*

* *Corresponding author's email*: yaolan@dhu.edu.cn

Abstract: For wireless body area network (WBAN), integrating antennas with body-worn environment is of great importance. In this study, a side-fed 2.45GHz textile microstrip antenna with artificial magnetic conductor (AMC) structure for wearable applications was designed. The antenna was made from all-textile materials due to its low-profile, flexibility and integration simplicity. Simulation and optimization work on the designed antenna has been carried out by HFSS simulation software. Performances of the antenna including the return loss, radiation pattern, and gain were measured. Additionally, the effect of human's body on the antenna performance was investigated to fully evaluate the antenna function under the on-body circumstance.

Keywords: Textile antenna; Wireless body area network (WBAN); Artificial magnetic conductor (AMC); Antenna performance

1 Introduction

In recent years, wireless device has gained its population. Due to the development of communication and electronic technologies, it is possible to integrate such devices into the clothing for wearable applications. Wearable antennas are designed to meet the requirements of such purposes, for instance, healthy and sports monitoring, emergency search and rescue operations[1].

Recently, most researches on wearable antennas include building antenna array[2] and using flexible textile material to fabricate antenna, et al[3]. At the same time, various types of antennas had been developed such as stripline slot antenna, cavity backed antenna, dipole antenna, microstrip antenna, etc[4]. A microstrip antenna was designed in this paper because it is considered as a suitable form of antenna in wearable applications due to its low-profile, small size, light weight, easy conformation, and easy to integrate with clothes[5-6].

Artificial magnetic conductor (AMC) structure was proposed by American scholar SIEVENPIPER D in 1999[7]. With the exploration of AMC, such structure has been widely used to extend the bandwidth of microstrip antennas[8]. A compact low-profile wearable antenna was proposed, which was fabricated using layers of textile and operated within the industrial, scientific, and medical (ISM) 5.8GHz band[9].

In this paper, a low-profile, textile, side-fed antenna with AMC structure for wearable applications in bluetooth 2.45GHz band was proposed. Numerical and experimental investigations revealed that after AMC structure was loaded on the back of the side-fed antenna, its bandwidth broadened. Additionally, t the specific absorption rate (SAR) value decreased, which exhibited that this type of antenna was safer to human's body for wearable applications.

2 Antenna Design

Different from conventional rigid antenna, the substrate of the designed antenna was fabricated from a polyester fabric ($\varepsilon_r = 1.73$, $h = 3\text{mm}$). For the conductive patch, conductive cloth was chosen to replace the conventional mental conductor patch. The design equations for the antenna structure can be derived from the transmission line theory, and the following equations are used[10].

$$W_p = \frac{c}{2f}\left(\frac{\varepsilon_r + 1}{2}\right)^{-\frac{1}{2}} \quad (1)$$

$$L_f = \frac{c}{2f\sqrt{\varepsilon_e}} - 2\Delta L \quad (2)$$

$$\lambda_e = \frac{c}{f\sqrt{\varepsilon_e}} \quad (3)$$

$$\varepsilon_e = \frac{\varepsilon_r + 1}{2} + \frac{\varepsilon_r - 1}{2}\left(1 + 12\frac{h}{w}\right)^{-\frac{1}{2}} \quad (4)$$

$$\Delta L = 0.412h\frac{(\varepsilon_e + 0.3)\left(\frac{w}{h} + 0.264\right)}{(\varepsilon_e - 0.258)\left(\frac{w}{h} + 0.8\right)} \quad (5)$$

where W_p is the width of the patch, L_f is the length of the patch, h is the thickness of the substrate, ε_r is the dielectric constant of the substrate, ε_e is effective dielectric constant, ΔL is the effective length of the antenna.

2.1 Side Fed Antenna

Fig.1 shows the configuration of the side-fed antenna working at 2.45GHz, the optimized dimensions in the unit size of millimeter(mm) are $G = 100$, $L_p = 41$, $W_p = 50$, $L_g = 4$, $W_g = 8$, $W_f = 37.5$, $L_f = 10.5$ and H = 3. The slots were designed to ensure the impedance matching of the antenna.

2.2 AMC Structure

Fig.2 shows the configuration of the AMC structure, which was made up from polyester fabric ($\varepsilon_r = 1.73$, $h = 3\text{mm}$). The optimized dimensions in the unit size of millimeter(mm) are $W_{amc} = 30$, $G_{ap} = 4$ and $H_{amc} = 3$. In the proposed antenna, the ground of the side-fed antenna was replaced by the AMC structure[11].

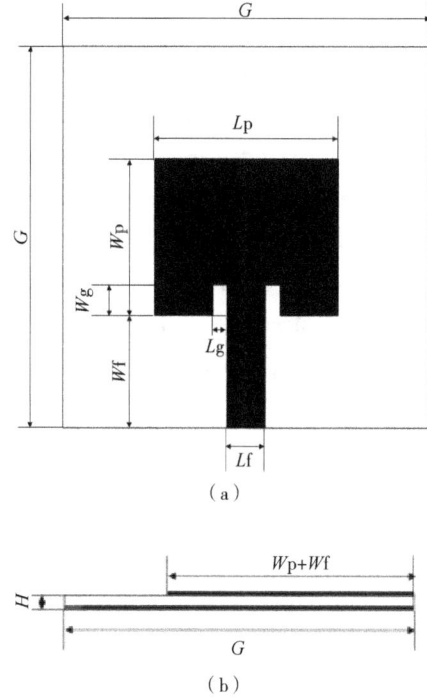

Fig.1 (a) Configuration of side-fed antenna; (b) The side view of the antenna

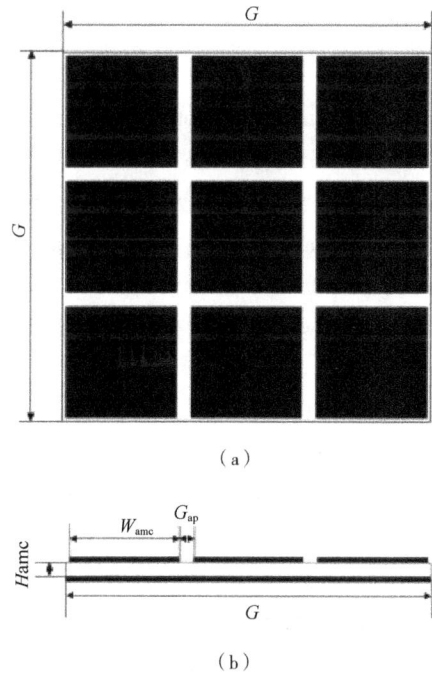

Fig.2 (a) Configuration of AMC structure; (b) The side view of the structure

3 Antenna Performances

3.1 Return Loss

As shown in Fig. 3, return loss results are compared between the side-fed antenna and the antenna with AMC structure. It depicts that after loaded with the AMC structure, the measured resonant frequency of the antenna exhibits a slight shift to the higher frequency (from 2.436GHz to 2.44GHz), which is closer to the designed working frequency. Meanwhile, the bandwidth increased significantly, from 70MHz (2.40GHz to 2.47GHz) to 90MHZ (2.41GHz to 2.50GHz), with a rise of 28.6%.

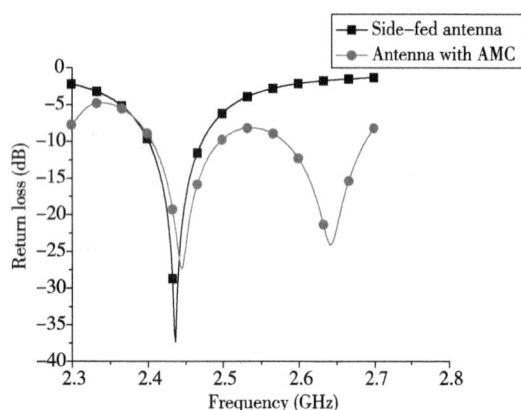

Fig.3　Return loss of the antenna and the antenna with AMC

It is also worth noting that another resonant frequency appeared at 2.64GHz with the bandwidth of 100MHz (2.58 to 2.68GHz). Generally, applying more AMC structure under the antenna can produce more other resonant points, therefore, the bandwidth of the antenna could be broaden, which had been verified in previous researches.

During the optimization process, it was found that the number of AMC unit cells is the primary factor that affects antenna's return loss performance. On the whole, the antenna with AMC structure can better cover the entire bluetooth band (2.4GHZ-2.485GHz).

3.2 Radiation Patterns

The radiation patterns of the proposed antenna at both E-plane (YZ-axis) and H-plane (XY-axis) at the resonant frequency are shown in Fig.4 respectively.

From the simulated radiation patterns results, it is obvious that the textile side-fed antenna provides a gain of 5.57dBi at E-plane and 5.62dBi at H-plane. However,

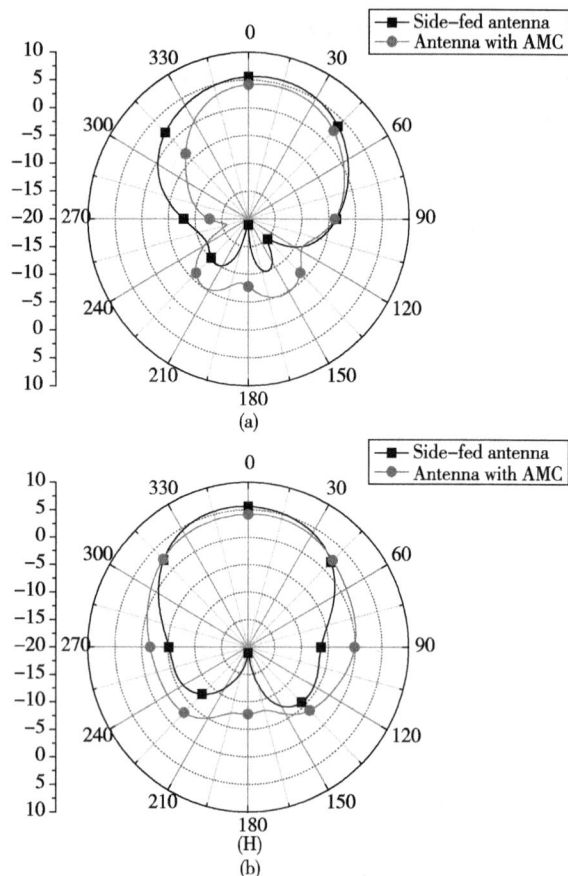

Fig.4　Radiation patterns of the two antennas at (a) E-plane and (b) H-plane (2.45GHz)

after loaded with AMC structure, the antenna gain appears a slight decrease, specifically, 4.17dBi at E-plane (a decrease of 25.13%) and 4.23dBi at H-plane (a decrease of 24.73%). This change could lead to the loss in the substrate of AMC, but the radiation pattern still shows great symmetry. On the whole, we extended the bandwidth of the antenna while reduced the gain, nonetheless, such antenna performance could meet the requirements when put into usage.

3.3 Nearbody Berformance

To confirm that antenna with AMC structure could produce less radiation and do less harm to human's body while wearing, a three-layer human body phantom was built. As is depicted in Fig.5, from the top layer they are air gap (5mm), skin (2mm, $\varepsilon_r = 38.06$), fat (10mm, $\varepsilon_r = 5.28$) and muscle (12mm, $\varepsilon_r = 52.79$), respectively. Also, to simulate the antenna performance under wearing condition, the bending model was also designed with the bending radius $R_x = 49$mm.

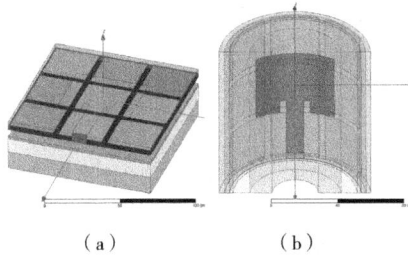

Fig.5 Near body phantom on (a) flat model and (b) bending model

Fig.6 depicts the return loss of the antenna in free space, on human's model and under bending condition. For side-fed antenna without AMC structure, after integrated on human's body model, the resonance frequency exhibits a shift to higher frequency, and the bandwidth appears to reduce significantly. On the other hand, for antennas with AMC structure, the return loss curve shows great agreement under three conditions. Although a slight shift in the resonance frequency happened, the

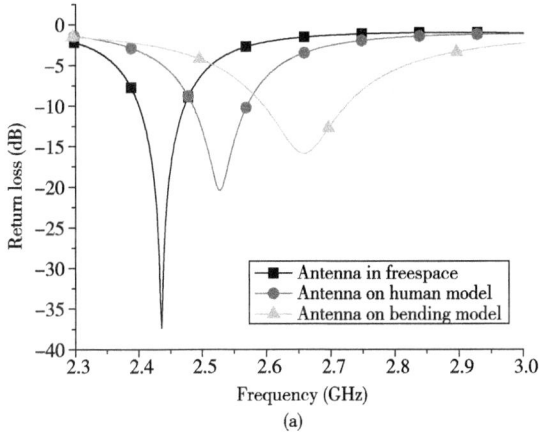

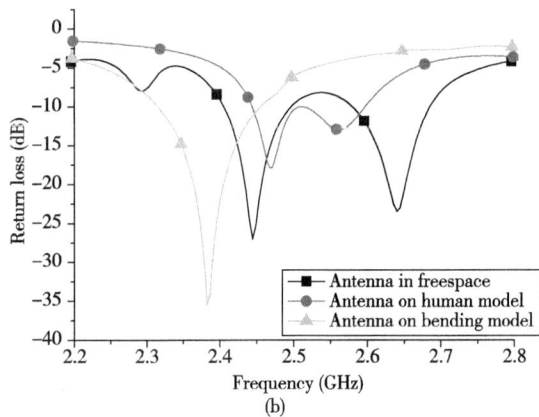

proposed antenna kept a wide impedance bandwidth within the bluetooth band.

3.4 SAR Validation

Through the research and investigation of electromagnetic radiation generated by mobile phones, IEEE, WHO and other organizations have established an important evaluation standard-specific absorption rate (SAR). The maximum safety limit for SAR under the U. S. standard is 1.6W/kg while the European standard is 2W/kg.

The SAR levels were calculated based on the IEEE C95. 1—2005 standard with an input power of 0.1W. The relationship between average SAR value and distance below the antenna was shown in Fig.7, at the same time, the average SAR on the surface are presented in Fig.8.

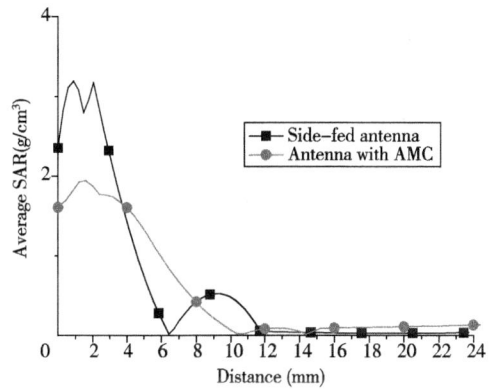

Fig.7 Average SAR value-distance curve of (a) the side-fed antenna and (b) the antenna with AMC structure

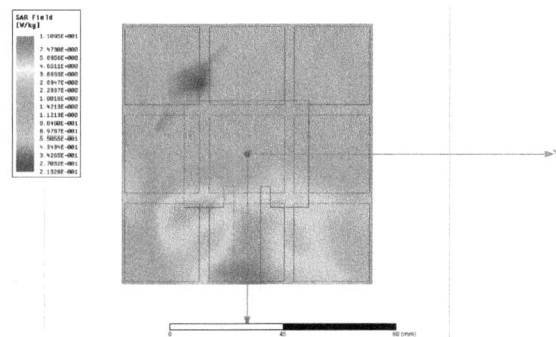

Fig.6 Return loss under three conditions of (a) the side-fed antenna and (b) the antenna with AMC structure

Fig.8 Average SAR value on the antenna with AMC structure

Through the comparison between the two types of the antenna, it is noticed that after loaded with AMC structure, the highest SAR value decreased from 3.1W/kg to 1.9W/kg, complying with 2W/kg, which means the antenna with AMC structure was suitable for wearing applications.

4　Conclusions

In this paper, a textile of 2.45GHz side-fed microstrip antenna with AMC structure loaded on the back side was proposed with all-textile materials. The simulation results showed that using AMC structure to replace the ground of the conventional side-fed antenna in this paper can significantly broaden the impedance bandwidth by 28.6%. At the same time, the radiation patterns still met the requirements at bluetooth 2.45GHz band well.

References

[1]CARLOS M, CUSTODIO P. On-body transmission performance of a novel dual-mode wearable microstrip antenna[J]. IEEE Transactions on Antennas and Propagation, 2018:1-1.

[2]WU Q. Research on wearable microstrip conformal antenna array[D]. Xi'an: Xi'an University of Electronic Science and Technology, 2010.

[3]SALONEN P, HURME L. A novel fabric WLAN antenna for wearable applications[C]. Antennas & Propagation Society International Symposium, 2003.

[4]SILVER S, E. Microwave antenna theory and design[M]. 1949.

[5]ZHONG S S. Theory and application of microstrip antenna [M]. Xi'an: Xi'an university of electronic science and technology press, 1991.

[6]MUNSON R. Conformal microstrip antennas and microstrip phased arrays[J]. IEEE Transactions on Antennas & Propagation, 1974, 22(1):74-78.

[7]SIEVENPIPER D, ZHANG L, BROAS R F J, et al. High-impedance electromagnetic surfaces with a forbidden frequency band[J]. IEEE Transactions on Microwave Theory and Techniques, 1999, 47(11):2059-2074.

[8]LI P. Amc-based wideband circularly polarized microstrip array antenna[D].

[9]ALEMARYEEN A, NOGHANIAN S. On-body low-profile textile antenna with artificial magnetic conductor[J]. IEEE Transactions on Antennas and Propagation, 2019:1.

[10]DEVAMALAR P M B, BAI V T, KAVYA G. Wearable antenna for bio signal monitoring applications using ISM band [C]. International Conference on Advances in Electrical, IEEE, 2016.

[11]AZADEGAN R, SARABANDI K. A novel approach for miniaturization of slot antennas[J]. IEEE Transactions on Antennas and Propagation, 2003, 51(3):421-429.

Effect of Atmospheric Pressure Plasma Treatment on the Properties of Ramie Fiber

YANG Huiling[1], YANG Zhuo[1], YAO Lan[1*], QIU Yiping[1]

[1] *Key Laboratory of Textile Science & Technology, Ministry of Education, College of Textiles, Donghua University, Shanghai, 201620, China*

Corresponding author's email: yaolan@ dhu.edu.cn

Abstract: In this study, the ramie fibers were pretreated with ethanol and then treated by the atmospheric pressure plasma with the power of 120W, 140W and 160W, respectively. The single fiber strength and water contact angle before and after the treatment were tested and compared. The results showed that the fiber strength after treatment did not change significantly, and the water contact angle changed from 55.03° to 113.3°, 114.9° and 115.9°. Moreover, it can be seen that the fiber surface morphology transformed before and after treatment, which was observed by environmental scanning electron microscopy (ESEM). More pits and fragments could be detected on the fiber surface after the plasma treatment, and higher power led to rougher surface. From X-ray photoelectron spectroscopy (XPS) results, it was concluded that the O/C ratio, C—O bond and C=O bond decreased, while the C—C bond increased after the plasma treatment.

Keywords: Ramie; Atmospheric pressure plasma treatment; Surface modification; Mechanical properties; Wetting properties

1 Introduction

Among the methods of surface treatment for fibers, plasma treatment technology has received extensive attention because it does not require large amounts of water and compounds. The surface of the ramie fiber can become hydrophobic from hydrophilic by surface treatment[1]. The atmospheric pressure plasma treatment technology is chosen in this study. At present, this technology has been widely used to improve the surface properties, such as moisture absorption, water repellency and adhesion of materials[2].

2 Experiments

2.1 Materials

The ramie fiber used in the experiments is the degummed fiber provided by the research team of Professor YU Chongwen of Donghua University, with diameters ranging from 15 to 45μm. And the tensile modulus of ramie fiber is 25GPa. The purity of the ethanol used was 99.7%.

2.2 Apparatus and Procedures

The ramie fibers were soaked with ethanol for ten minutes before plasma treatment, and the treated fibers were randomly divided into four groups: untreated group, 120W, 140W, and 160W treated group. The treated group was modified by the APPJ system (Atomflo-F4200N, Surfx Company, USA). The gas is helium with a purity of 99.99%, a flow rate of 30.0L/min. The nozzle spacer is 3mm, and the manipulator speed is 20mm/s. The fiber was treated for 20s.

In order to study the effect of plasma treatment on the ramie fibers, the strength had been tested. The fibers were randomly selected from each of the four experimental samples. The test used Single Fiber Electronic Tensile Strength Tester (XQ – 2, Shanghai Lipu Institute of Applied Science and Technology, China) and a polarizing microscope (LV100P, Nikon Eclipse). The calculating formula for the strength of single ramie fiber is as follow:

$$\tau = \frac{F}{\pi r^2}$$

Where F is the breaking strength and r is the average radius of the ramie fibers. Since the cross-section of the ramie fiber is irregular, it is approximated as a circle. Furthermore, the effects of atmospheric pressure plasma treatment on the properties of ramie fiber were obtained by wettability test, environmental scanning electron microscope (ESEM) and X-ray photoelectron spectroscopy (XPS).

3 Results and Discussions

3.1 Tensile Strength of Control and Plasma-Treated Groups

Fig.1 shows the strength of four groups of ramie fibers. It can be seen that the strength of untreated ramie fiber is 390.5MPa, while the strength of treated groups increase to 398.19MPa, 429.73MPa and 416.32MPa.

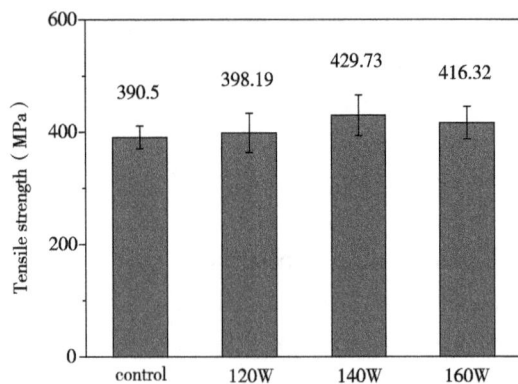

Fig.1　Tensile strength of control and plasma-treated groups

Ramie is a kind of natural fiber with different damaging degree and thickness. So, the fiber strength is not even in the test. After removing the highest and lowest values among the results in each group, 30 datas were selected for statistical analysis using Minitab, and the results are shown in Fig.1[3-4]. The 0-3 levels represent the untreated group, the 120W, the 140W and the 160W treated groups, respectively. The confidence interval is 95%, grouped by the Tukey method. The four groups of fibers all gathered in group A, indicating that there were no significant differences in the four groups, as shown in Tab.1. This proves that there is no obvious effect on the fiber strength after ethanol pretreatment and different power plasma treatments.

Tab.1 Statistical analysis result of fiber tensile strength

C2 (Response Column)	N (Samples)	Average	Group
2	30	429.7	A
3	30	416.3	A
1	30	398.2	A
0	30	390.5	A

3.2 Surface Morphology Analysis

The surface morphology of the four groups of ramie fibers is shown in Fig.2. It can be seen that the surface of untreated fiber in Fig.2(a) is relatively smooth with some natural longitudinal gullies, while the treated groups are rougher. Fig.2(b) was treated with 120W showing visible pits and debris on the surface. As the treated power increasing, the protrusions, pits, and corrugations become rougher and more obvious. The reason is that more ions are sputtered on the surface of the ramie fiber when the power increasing, leading to chemical chain scission. Moreover, small molecular fragments are removed, and the degree of etching increases.

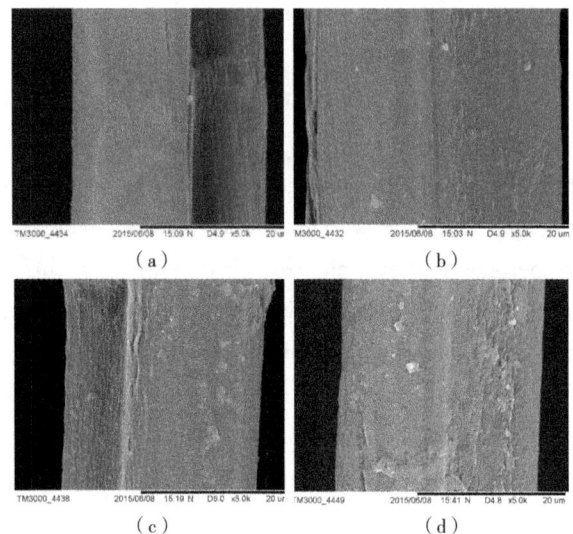

Fig.2　SEM photographs of ramie fibers: (a) Control group; (b) 120W plasma-treated group; (c) 140W plasma-treated group; (d) 160W plasma-treated group

3.3 X-Ray Photoelectron Spectroscopy (XPS)

Tab.2 lists the element contents and O/C ratio on the surface of ramie fiber among the untreated group and the 120W, 140W, 160W atmospheric pressure plasma-treated groups. It can be seen that the O/C ratio after plasma treatment is reduced to some extent. Because reactive groups are grafted on the surface of the fiber under the action of plasma, such as an ethyl group, resulting in an increase of the C element, a decrease of the O element, and a decrease of the O/C ratio. Under the plasma bombardment, chemical bonds are broken. Meanwhile, electrons, ions and groups on the surface are likely to undergo two major chemical reactions. One is the introduction of new functional groups, such as ethyl. At the same time, some macromolecular chains are degraded to produce low molecular fragments[5]. This process is unavoidable, and the reaction formula for introducing an ethyl group is as follow[6-7].

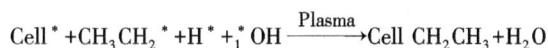

$$Cell + CH_3CH_2OH \xrightarrow{Plasma}$$

$$Cell^* + CH_3CH_2^* + H^* + {}^*_1OH \xrightarrow{Plasma} Cell\ CH_2CH_3 + H_2O$$

In order to further understand the changes in chemical bonds on the surface of ramie fiber before and after treatment, the curve was fitted by Gauss-Lorentz curve fitting method. The C1s peak is deconvoluted into the corresponding C—C bond(285eV), C—O bond (286.5eV), C=O bond (288.1eV), and O=C—O bond (289.4 eV). Tab.3 and Fig.3 show the results of the curve and C1s peak quantification analysis. The data in Tab.3 shows that the content of C—C bond of the untreated fiber was 47.9%, and it improved significantly after treatment. The 120W treated group had the most obvious tendency increasing to 73.6%.

Tab.2 The surface element content of four fiber groups

Groups	Contents(%)			Ratio
	C	O	N	O/C
Control	65.45	32.81	0	0.50
120W	76.18	22.37	0.6	0.29
140W	72.68	26.31	0.4	0.36
160W	74.76	24.04	0.3	0.32

Tab.3 The C1s peak analysis of four fiber groups

Groups	Contents of C1s(%)			
	C—C	C—O	C=O	O=C—C
Control	47.9	41.4	10.2	0.5
120W	73.6	21.9	4.3	0.2
140W	66.2	26.3	7.4	0.1
160W	69.5	24.4	5.9	0.2

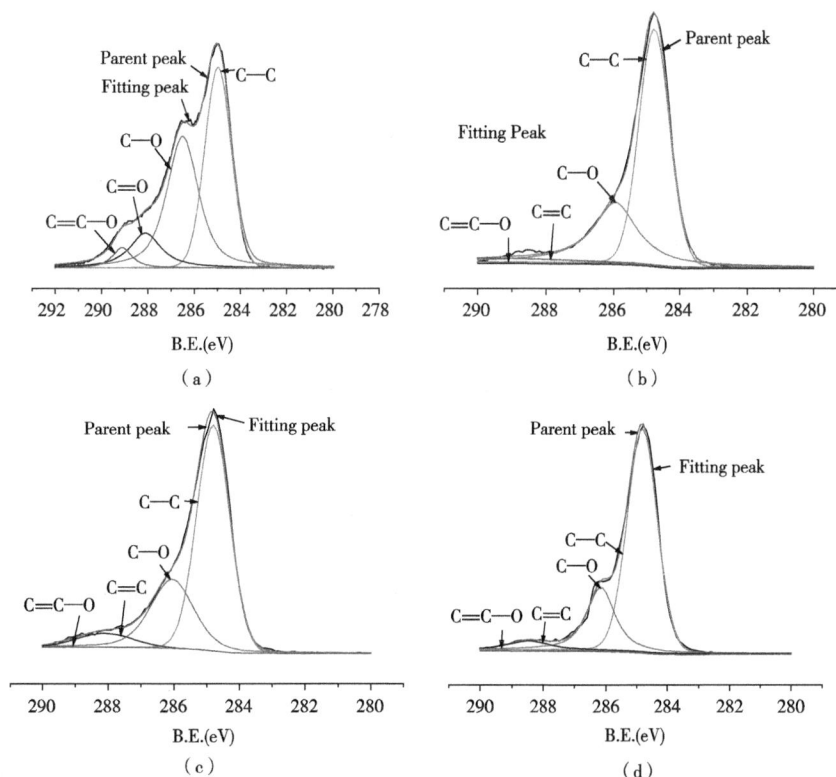

Fig.3 Deconvoluted XPS C1s spectra of ramie fibers: (a) Control group; (b) 120W plasma-treated group; (c) 140W plasma-treated group; (d) 160W plasma-treated group

3.4 Surface Wettability of Fibers

The water contact angle is used to characterize the hydrophilic and hydrophobic properties of the fiber surface. Fig.4 shows the morphology of water droplets on ramie fibers, and Fig. 5 shows the water contact angle values for each group. The testing method differs according to the difference of the hydrophobicity of the untreated and treated fiber surfaces.

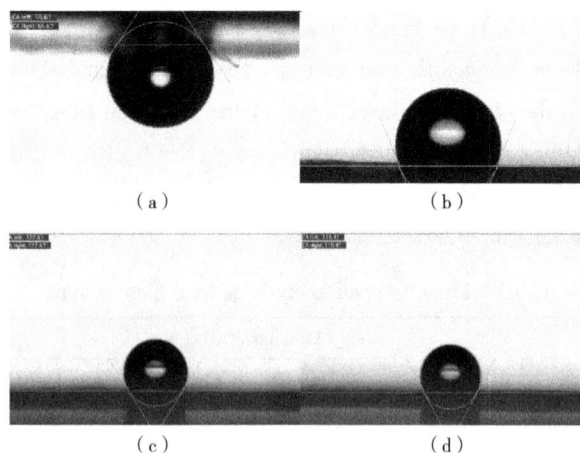

(a)　　　　　　　　　(b)

(c)　　　　　　　　　(d)

Fig.4　Water droplet profile on ramie fibers: (a) Control group; (b) 120W plasma-treated group; (c) 140W plasma-treated group; (d) 160W plasma-treated group

After 120W, 140W and 160W plasma treatment, the water contact angles were increased from 55.03° to 113.3°, 114.9° and 115.9°, respectively. It can be confirmed that the ethanol pretreatment and the plasma treatment changed the surface of the ramie fiber from hydrophilic to hydrophobic.

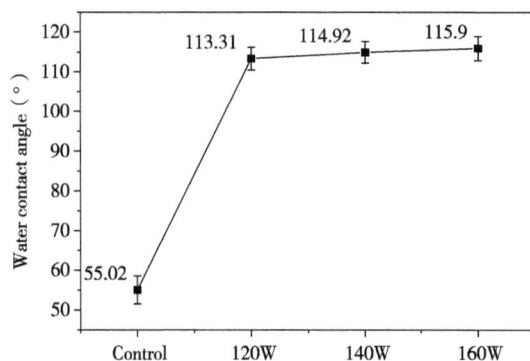

Fig.5　Water contact angle of all groups

A significant analysis was performed on the water contact angle values of the three groups of fibers treated, with a 95% confidence interval, grouped by the Tukey method. If they share the same letter, then there is no obvious difference between them. The results are shown in Tab.4. The fibers treated by 120W, 140W and 160W were in Group A, while untreated fibers were in Group B, indicating that there was no significant difference in water contact angle on the surface of the treated fiber groups, which were all hydrophobic. Instead, the surface of the untreated fiber is hydrophilic. The test results of the water contact angles further verified the results of XPS. During the plasma treatment on ramie fiber, there is indeed an ethyl group grafted on the surface of the fiber, so it is modified from hydrophilic to hydrophobic.

Tab.4　Statistical analysis result of water contact angle in all groups

C2 (Response Column)	N (Samples)	Average	Group
2	5	115.904	A
3	5	114.920	A
1	5	113.310	A
0	5	55.024	B

4　Conclusions

This study mainly discusses the effect of atmospheric pressure plasma treatment power on the properties of ramie fiber. The results showed that there was no significant change in fiber tensile strength before and after treatment. Moreover, the surface of the treated fiber was rougher than the untreated group. The pits and roughness increased with the higher treated power. From X-ray photoelectron spectroscopy (XPS) results, it was concluded that the O/C ratio, C—O bond and C ==O bond decreased, while the C—C bond increased after the plasma treatment. The water contact angle test showed that the ethanol pretreatment and atmospheric pressure plasma treatment modified the fiber surface from hydrophilic to hydrophobic. In summary, the plasma treatment only changes the surface properties of the ramie fibers, and there is no obvious damage or change to the mechanical properties.

References

[1]ZHOU Z, LIU X, HU B, et al. Hydrophobic surface modification of ramie fibers with ethanol pretreatment and atmospheric pressure plasma treatment[J]. Surface and Coatings Technology, 2011, 205(17-18):4205-4210.

[2]HAMAD S F. Exploiting plasma exposed, natural surface nanostructures in ramie fibers for polymer composite applications[J]. Materials,2019, 12(10):15.

[3]LI Y, SUN J, CHENG P, et al. Aging of hydrophobized surfaces of ramie fibers induced by atmospheric pressure plasma treatment with ethanol pretreatment[J]. Journal of Adhesion Science and Technology, 2013, 27(22):2387-2397.

[4]LIU X, CHENG L. Influence of plasma treatment on properties of ramie fiber and the reinforced composites[J]. Journal of Adhesion Science and Technology, 2017, 31(15):12.

[5]YU R, WANG C, QIU Y. Influence of aramid fiber moisture regain during atmospheric plasma treatment on aging of treatment effects on surface wettability and bonding strength to epoxy[J]. Applied Surface Science, 2007, 253(23):9283-9289.

[6]ZHANG Q, JIANG Y, YAO L, et al. Hydrophobic surface modification of ramie fibers by plasma-induced addition polymerization of propylene[J]. Journal of Adhesion Science and Technology, 2015, 29(8):691-704.

[7]YAMADA Y, YAMADA T, TASAKA S, et al. Surface modification of poly (tetrafluoroethylene) by remote hydrogen plasma[J]. Macromolecules, 1996, 29(12):4331-4339.

Mechanical Property of Flexible Envelope Composites for Stratospheric Airships

DING Lei[1,2], WANG Jinxi[2], LIU Yiwen[2], CAO Ying[2], LI Beibei[2], JIANG Jinghua[1,2]*

[1] *Engineering Research Center of Technical Textiles, Ministry of Education, Shanghai, 201620, China*

[2] *College of Textiles, Donghua University, Shanghai, 201620, China*

* *Corresponding author's email:* jiangjinhua@ dhu.edu.cn

Abstract: In this paper, the tensile, tearing and peeling properties of warp and weft Vectran fabrics, and their polyurethane-coated composites were tested. The failure mechanism of stretching, tearing and peeling of envelope materials were discussed and analyzed. The results showed that in Vectran fabrics and their coated composites, the weft tensile strength is higher than the warp strength. The weft tensile strength of Vectran fabric is 13.03% higher than that in the warp direction, for the Vectran coated composites, the weft tensile strength is 12.17% higher than the warp tensile strength. The coating process also has effects on the tensile and tearing of the Vectran composites. The maximum strength (warp and weft) is larger than that of coated composites, and in warp the Vectran fabric is 6.43% higher than its coated composites. In warp the Vectran fabric is 7.34% higher. For tear properties, the weft tearing strength of Vectran fabric is 20.17% higher than that in warp. For Vectran coated composites, and the weft tearing strength is 4.44% higher than that in warp.

Keywords: Vectran; Coated composites; Tensile property; Tearing property; Peeling property

1 Introduction

The stratospheric airship is a new type of near-space multi-functional flight platform that has been developed with the advancement of science and technology. The working height is about 18km to 24 km, mainly relying on uplift to work in the air. Compared with the airplane, it has the characteristics of low manufacturing and cost, good stealth, long air time and large load. It has a wide range of military and civilian values. It is a novel universal spacecraft platform integrating high-altitude observation and communication. As the main structural material of the airship, the skin material has the tensile, tearing and peeling performance directly affecting the application efficiency of the airship, such as the floating height, continuous flight time, payload, service life and so on[1-4].

WAN Zhimin et al.[5] analyzed the effects of ambient temperature and coating thickness on the tensile proper-ties and failure modes of Vectran fabrics. DU Yijun et al.[6] studied the tensile, tear, impact and friction properties of Vectran fabrics and their silicone-coated composites. ZHEN Lei et al.[7] tested and analyzed the trapezoidal and center crack tear properties of Vectran fiber reinforced laminate composite. TAN Huifeng[8] conducted a low-speed impact test on Vectran fabric and its low-temperature silica gel coating composite. The impact response and failure modes of the material were studied. The effects of impact rate, punch size and punch shape on the impact properties of the material were analyzed.

In this paper, the tensile, tearing and peeling properties of Vectran fabrics and polyurethane-coated composites were tested. The performance differences and failure mechanisms were compared to provide references for the application of Vectran fabrics in the stratospheric airship project.

2　Experiments

2.1　Materials

Vectran fabrics are supplied by Kuraray. Polyurethane is a high-elastic soft textile coating water-based polyurethane of Qiancheng Plastic Raw Material Co, Ltd. The material specifications are shown in Tab.1.

Tab.1　Sample specifications

Type of fabric	Fabric structure	Yarn density (D)	Areal density (g/m²)	Thickness (mm)	Weaving density (picks/10cm)	
					Warp	Weft
Vectran fabric	Woven plain	400	91.06	0.2114	100	100
Vectran coated composites	Woven plain	400	154.93	0.2236	100	100

2.2　Sample Preparation

Vectran fabric was cut into 25cm×25cm. In order to ensure the fabric surface is flat to be coated, the fabric folds were removed by using electric iron and fixing the base fabric to the glass plate with clips. After defoaming polyurethane by standing, the Vectran fabric was coated with the polyurethane. Then the fabric was placed in an oven and baked at 50℃ for 1 h.

2.3　Measurements

2.3.1　The Tensile Strength Test

The test was carried out using the MTS Microcomputer Control Universal Material Testing Machine (MTS-E42. 503). The test standard was carried out in accordance with GB/T 1040.3—2006 (Determination of Tensile Properties of Plastics, Part 3: Test Conditions for Films and Sheets). In order to prevent the fabric from slipping out of the machine chuck during stretching, the ends of the fabric are wrapped, which ensures that the fabric does not slip and protect both ends of the fabric from damage by the machine chuck.

2.3.2　The Tearing Strength Test

The tearing performance test was performed using a trapezoidal tearing method according to GB/T 3917.3—2009 (Standard of Tearing Strength of Trapezoidal Sample), as shown in Fig.1, where the tearing speed is set as 100mm/min.

2.3.3　The Peeling Strength Test

The peeling properties of vectran was tested according to FZ/T 01001—2012, with a tensile speed of 100mm/min and a gauge of 30mm. When calculating the peeling strength, the first 20% of the peeling curve is ignored, and the average of the maximum and minimum is taken as the median.

3　Results and Discussions

3.1　Tensile Properties

Fig.1 and Fig.2 show the strength-strain curves of Vectran fabric and its polyurethane coated composites under warp and weft tensile loads respectively. In Fig.1 and Fig.3, the strength-strain of the material is basically linear in the initial stage. When the load increases to the maximum, the load drops rapidly, and some fluctuations appear on the curve until it is completely destroyed.

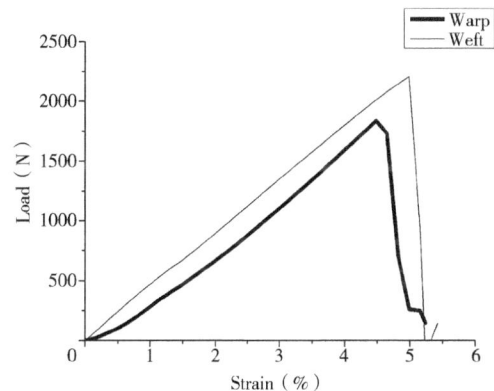

Fig.1　Tensile strength curve of Vectran fabric

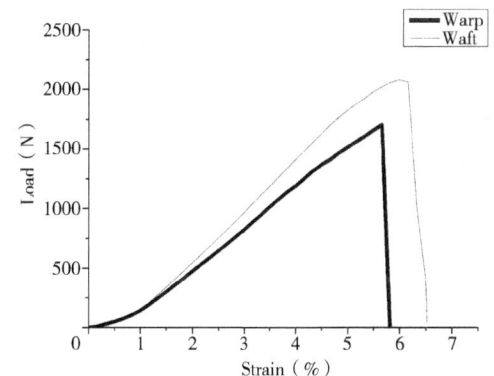

Fig.2　Tensile strength curve of Vectran coated composites

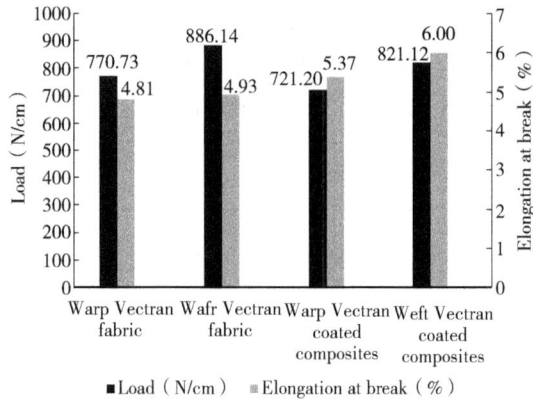

Fig.3 Tensile properties comparison between Vectran and Vectran coated composites in warp and weft

In addition, Fig. 1 and Fig. 2 show that the changing trend of the tensile curves in warp and weft is basically the same. However, the weft tensile strength of Vectran fabrics and their coated composites are generally larger than that of the warp direction, the weft tensile strength of Vectran fabric is 13.03% higher than that in warp. For the Vectran coated composites, the weft tensile strength is 12.17% higher than the warp tensile strength. But the weft and warp density of Vectran fabrics are the same. This paper considers that this is mainly caused by the weaving process. Because the warp yarns will inevitably rub against the machine parts during the weaving process, the strength will be lost to a certain degree.

It can be clearly seen from Fig. 3 that the maximum strength (warp and weft) is larger than that of coated composites, and in warp the Vectran fabric is 6.43% higher than its coated composites. In warp the Vectran fabric is 7.34% higher.

During the stretching process, the transverse fiber slip of the Vectran fabric material is observed, which increases the fiber with the common bearing force. As the tensile load increases, fibers are quickly pulled to be broken gradually, the failure mode of Vectran fabric is mainly characterized by fiber breakage and slip. The tensile of Vectran coated composites is a sudden overall fracture, and the failure mode is mainly characterized by fiber breakage. According to the analysis of the characteristics of woven plain weave fabric and Vectran fiber, the yarn in Vectran fabric is not easy to be fixed, and is subject to be removed. The slight force is easy to produce slip, and the Vectran fiber is not in the same straight state in the coated composites. When subjected to the tensile load, the polyurethane binds the slip of the fiber in the fabric, and when subjected to the maximum load, compared with Vectran fabrics, the fibers that are co-supported are reduced in Vectran coated composites, so the treatment of the coating process causes a certain degree of damage to the Vectran fabric.

3.2 Tearing Properties

In Fig. 4 and Fig. 5, the tearing properties of Vectran fabric and its polyurethane-coated composites are significantly different in warp and weft, the weft tearing strength of Vectran fabric is 20.17% higher than that in warp. For Vectran coated composites, the weft tearing strength is 24.44% higher than that in warp. In addition, the coating also has a great influence on the tearing properties of Vectran fabric. The tearing strength of Vectran fabric is 30.85% higher than Vectran coated composites in warp, and the tearing strength of Vectran fabric is 26.94% higher than Vectran coated composites in weft.

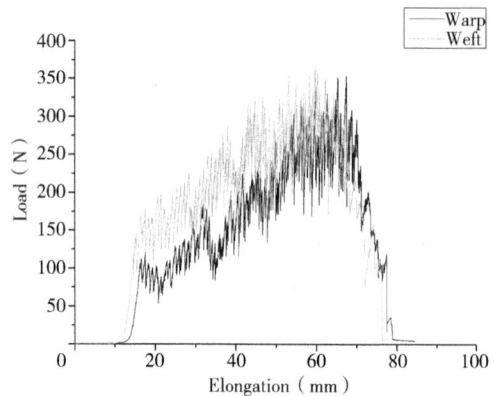

Fig.4 Tear force curve of Vectran fabric

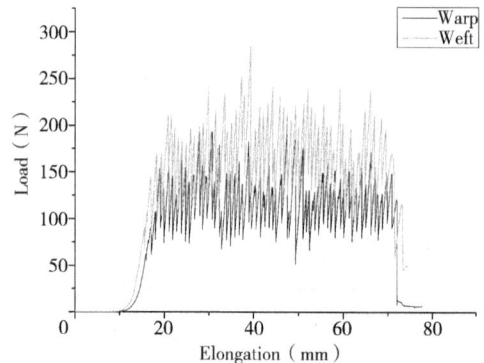

Fig.5 Tear force curve of Vectran coated composites

Tab.2 Average peak tear force of Vectran fabric and Vectran coated composites

Type of fabric	Direction of tearing	Thickness (mm)
Vectran fabric	Warp	213.35
	Weft	267.24
Vectran coated composites	Warp	147.53
	Weft	195.24

Meanwhile, comparing Fig.4 and Fig.5, the peak of the Vectran fabric tear carve has an obvious fluctuation rise. In the initial stage of the curve, the first force-bearing yarn in the force triangle is straightened under the load, and then slides down, the stress that the machine chuck accumulated is instantaneously released, and the force triangle increases with the fiber slip. The first and second fibers are simultaneously stressed, the fibers are aggregated, and the stress of the machine chuck increases instantaneously. When the load reaches a certain level, the fiber at the front end of the tearing triangle begins to break first. When the first fiber breaks, the load is transferred to the next fiber, and the fabric yarn begins to be pulled off one by one. The tension on the chuck of the machine is constantly going through the process of release and loading, which is manifested in the sharp fluctuation on the tearing curve. During this process, the accumulation of fibers continues to increase, and the ability to resist the tearing load is also enhanced, causing the tear curve to fluctuate. The tear curve of Vectran coated composites has a relatively stable fluctuation trend. In the initial stage, the load undergoes a relatively stable rising phase. After the yarn breaks for the first time, the load platform appears within a certain range. In the final stage, the force triangle area becomes smaller. The fibers that bear the load together are reduced, then the fabric is torn. In addition, comparing the tear strength of Vectran fabric and its coated composites, the tearing strength of the Vectran fabric after coating treatment is significantly reduced, because the polyurethane fills the gap between the fabrics, increases the joint between the fibers, and reduces the slip between the fibers. The force triangle is obviously reduced, the number of yarns at the same time reduce, so the tearing strength is greatly reduced

compared with that before the coating.

3.2 Peeling Properties

In Fig.6, the peeling performance of the warp and weft vectran coated composites has reached to 20.66N and 21.05N respectively. There is no obvious difference in warp and weft. In the peeling process of vectran composites, there is a certain gap between the bonding nodes, which need to overcome the greater force in order to peel it off, and the peeling strength increases, which shows that the initial part of the peeling curve continues to rise until it is peeled off. When entering the gap where there are fewer bonding points, the force begins to weaken, and the curve begins to decrease from the rising height, thus forming a "wave peak". When the falling curve meets the dense part of the bonding point, peeling strength suddenly increases. When it is peeled off, at this time, the curve rises from the lower point of decline, forming a "wave valley".

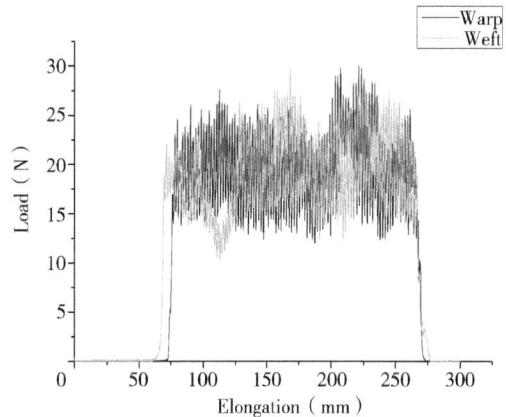

Fig.6 Peeling curve of coated Vectran coated composites

4 Conclusions

In this paper, the tensile, tearing and peeling properties of warp and weft of Vectran fabrics were tested. After the coating process, the fiber in the fabric is fixed, the decrease of fiber slip reduces the number of fibers subjected to the load at the maximum load, resulting in the decrease of the tensile strength of the coated composites. In addition, in Vectran fabrics and their coated composites, the weft tensile strength is higher than the warp strength. It is the wear between the warp and the machine parts in the weaving process cause the loss of tensile strength in warp. The tear resistance of Vectran coated composites is much lower than that of Vectran fabric. In order to improve the tearing resistance, it is necessary to expand its stress triangle. First, the fabric density can be properly increased so that there can be more yarn stress in the stress triangle. Secondly, the tearing resistant microstructure can be designed. The peeling test of Vectran coated composites shows that the peeling resistance of the coated composites still needs to be improved, and the peeling resistance of Vectran coated composites can be improved by means of interfacial modification or adding auxiliaries to polyurethane.

References

[1]LIU Junhu, LIU Zhenhui, JI Xuemei, et al. Research status of stratosphere airship skin materials [J]. Information Recording Material, 2016, (02):1-5.

[2]GU Zhengming. Study on skin material of stratosphere airship [J]. Space Return and Remote Sensing, 2007, (01):62/66.

[3]TIAN Yue, XIAO Shangming. Development status and key technologies of stratosphere airship capsule materials [J]. Synthetic Fiber, 2013, (04):11-15.

[4]TAN Huifeng, LIU Yuxi, LIU Yuyan, et al. Research progress and demand analysis of airship skin materials in adjacent space[J]. Journal of Composite Materials, 2012, (06):1-8.

[5]WAN Zhimin, LIU Yuyan, SONG Yang, et al. Study on tensile and tear properties of Vectran fiber composites [J]. Space Return and Remote Sensing, 2011, 32(04):75-81.

[6]DU Yijun, JIANG Jinhua, CHEN Nanliang. Study on failure resistance of Vectran fiber composites[J]. Glass Fiber Reinforced Plastics / Composites, 2014 (02):27-32.

[7]ZHENG Lei, YI Huaiqiang, WANG Jiayu, et al. Tear properties of Vectran fiber laminated fabric[J]. Shanghai Textile Technology, 2018, 46(01):8-9.

[8]TAN Huifeng, WAN Zhimin, DONG Yabo. Impact response and failure mode analysis of Vectran fabric composites[J]. Space Return and Remote Sensing, 2010, 31(06):9-11.

Effect of Parameters on Morphology and Structure of Electrospun Polystyrene Filament

ABDUL Wahid[1], ZENG Yongchun[1]*, SYED Rashedul Islam[1],
MUHAMMAD Usman Ghani[1], KAHASY Gebresilassie Abraha[1,2],
SHARJEEL Ahmed[3]

[1] *Key Laboratory of Textile Science & Technology, Ministry of Education, College of Textiles, Donghua University, Shanghai, 201620, China*

[2] *Department of Textile Engineering, College of Engineering and Technology, Aksum University, Aksum, 1010, Ethiopia*

[3] *State Key Laboratory for Modification of Chemical Fibers and Polymer Materials, International Joint Laboratory for Advanced Fiber and Low-dimension Materials, College of Materials Science and Engineering, Donghua University, Shanghai, 201620, China*

* *Corresponding author's email: yongchun@ dhu.edu.cn*

Abstract: Polystyrene (PS) fibers have been of increasing interest due to their unique structure and properties. The groove and porous structure of electropun PS filament can make it a promising candidate for high-capacity oil sorbent. The continuous length of PS filament with groove and porous structure produce through conventional electrospinning is reported in this study. PS was chosen as a functional polymer in the process, in which PS tends to produce porous structure on the cross-section of filaments. The morphology and structure of electrospun filaments were observed with the help of Scanning Electron Microscope (SEM). The processing and solution parameter i.e. concentrations of polymer, DMF as a solvent with different amount of LiCl to produce continuous filament and groove structures, and applied voltage are influenced the filament morphology were investigated. The oil sorption experiments show that the PS filament sorbents have the advantage of showing large sorption capacity. It is expected that the continuous filament mats can make a promising candidate for potential applications in those fields such as filtration, separation, and sorption.

Keywords: Conventional electrospinning; Polystyrene filament; Surface structure; Oil application

1 Introduction

Electro-spun microfibers such as porous fibers, groove-fibers, and belt fibers have been of increasing interest because of their unique characteristics like large surface area and large porosity, and better elastic property and therefore find applications in nanocomposites[1] sorption[2] and filtration materials[3]. Many researchers have explored the production of porous fibers using electro-spinning technology. The formation of electrospun fiber, which is involved in different polymer concentrations and solvent mixing ratios, were studied in many works[4-7]. Poly (methy-lmethacrylate) (PMMA) porous fibers were reported to be electro-spun from different solvent systems to compare their surface morphology[4]. The use of chloroform as the solvent of Poly (lactic acid) (PLA) in electrospinning gives rise to circular pores of 100nm diameter confined to the fiber surface[8-9].

PS is one of the most widely used polymers in producing electrospun porous fibers, which shows high liquid sorption capacities and finds application in oil cleanup materials. However, electrospun PS porous structure fibers usually have poor mechanical performance due to the intrinsic property of PS and the porous structure in the fiber surface. On the other hand, previous researchers have produced nonwoven PS porous fibers sheet. But now we have focused on the nonwoven PS grooves structure filament sheet and fewer details of the continuous length of the polystyrene filament were presented. Effects of the processing parameter, conventional electrospinning method and the solution parameters (different amount of the solvents ratio and additive) on the characteristic continuous length and grooves structures are investigated. The continuous length of filament has the advantage of good mechanical property due to the addition of LiCl, and the oil sorption experiment is carried out to compare the sorption capacity of filament sorbents with different amounts of grooves structures. We obtained filament sorbent consists of a large surface area of the grooves structure will have a large prospection for sorption application.

2 Experimental

2.1 Materials

Polystyrene (PS; M_w = 350000g/mol, Sigma-Aldrich) were purchased from Beijing Yili Fine Chemical Co., Ltd., China. N,N-dimethylformamide (DMF; 0.945 - 0.950g/mol at 20℃), were purchased from Sigma-Aldrich. Lithium chloride anhydrous (LiCl) was from Macklin. All of these chemicals were used without further purification.

Homogeneous PS solutions (15%, 20%, and 25%, w/v %) were prepared by dissolving PS pellets in DMF with the addition of organic additive (LiCl; 0.25%, 0.50%, 0.75% and 1.0%, w/v %) for 12 hours stirring at room temperature. All experiments were performed at about 25℃ at a relative humidity of 40%-60%.

2.2 Experimental Setup

In this research, we used a conventional electrospinning method, which was introduced in previous work[10-11]. The conventional electrospinning system is shown in Fig. 1. The steel needle was a blunt-type stainless needle with inner and outer diameters of 0.84mm and 1.27mm. The solutions were fed into the spinneret via corresponding syringe and pump (KDS 220, KD Scientific, Inc. USA). A high-voltage supply (ES - 60P 10W/DDPM, Gamma High Voltage Research, USA) was applied to the spinneret and the collector, which was a rotating cylinder with a linear velocity of 14.24cm/s.

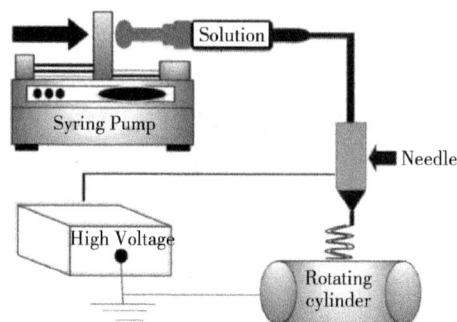

Fig.1　Schematic of conventional electrospinning system

2.3　Testing and Analysis

The morphology of the as-spun filament was detected under a Scanning Electron Microscopy (SEM; Flex SEM 1000, HITACHI, JAPAN) after coating with gold for 30s under an acceleration voltage of 5kV. The average filament diameter was determined by measuring 50 filaments for each image from 3 randomly selected SEM images utilizing Photoshop CS6 (Adobe Systems Inc., San Jose, CA, USA) software.

3　Results and Discussions

3.1　Morphology and Structure of PS Filaments

The SEM images of the electrospun PS filaments are shown in Fig.2. We can see that the sheet contains a large part of PS filaments. These filaments were produced by conventional electrospinning (15%, 20%, and 25%) PS in DMF solvent by stainless steel needle. The processing conditions used were 12 cm spinneret-to-collector distance and 15kV applied voltage. The morphology of 15% PS filament with circular shape was observed in Fig.2 (a). When the concentration of PS increases to 20% and 25%, the morphologies of filaments seem to loose the circular shape and become a little flat, which are shown in Fig.2 (b) and Fig.2(c). The filament diameters vary from about 5μm to 12μm. The microscale filaments produced groove structures on the surface, which are clearly shown in the inserted images. The SEM images of a cross-section view of the electrospun PS filament (Fig.3) show a large part of porous structure in the cross-section.

Fig.2 SEM images of the filaments under different concentration of PS polymer: (a) 15%; (b) 20% and (c) 25% (The inserted pictures show grooves structure on the filament surface)

Fig.3 SEM image of cross-section view of the electrospun PS filaments: (a) 15% PS; (b) 20% PS; (c) 25% PS

3.2 Effects of Parameters on PS Filament Morphology

The PS nonwoven filaments sheet are electrospun with different concentration of polymer under the various relative amount of LiCl shown in Fig.4. With a constant flow rate, we can see that these sheets contain a large part of PS nonwoven filaments. These filaments were generated by conventional electrospinning with different concentration of PS (15%, 20%, and 25%) in DMF solvent. From Fig.4 we can see that the filament morphology is of circular shape at 0.25% concentration of LiCl [Fig. 4 (a)]. However, increasing the concentration of LiCl from 0.5% to 1.0%, the filaments loose the circular shape [Fig.4(b) - Fig.4(d)]. The same trends of the change of filament morphology are observed in 15%, 20% and 25% concentration of PS filament.

Fig.5 shows the SEM images of PS filament morphology structure under various voltages. Other processing parameters were kept unchanged of 12cm distance and 1.0mL of flow rate. The LiCl amount has been an effect of filament morphology structure. We can see that increasing the voltage 1.0% will produce finer filaments. Fig.6 shows the SEM images of PS filaments surface structure in DMF solvent with different concentration of PS polymer. Other parameters were kept unchanged of 12cm distance and 15kV applied voltage. The LiCl amount has been an effect of continuous filament. On the other hand, the grooves structure is strongly dependent on the solvents system. We can see that in [Fig.6(a) - Fig.6(c)], groove structures appear on the filament surface when only use DMF solvent. When using DMF/THF mixed solvents, porous structures can be produced [Fig.6(d) - Fig.6(f)].

3.3 Oil Application of PS Filament

The oil sorption capacities of continuous PS filament sorbents with grooves structure (sample A and B) were investigated. Fig.7 shows that at around 15 minutes the maximum oil sorption achieve. For sample A continuous length of PS filament with small groove structure, the sorption rate is 54.4% in 5 minutes, 77.3% in 10 minutes, and 89.9% in 15 minutes. For sample B that indicates the PS filament with larger groove structure, the sorption rate is 52.26% in 5 minutes, 69.6% in 10 minutes, and 78.6% in 15 minutes. It is clear that higher sorption capacity achieved for the filament sorbents with different concentration of LiCl (a) 0.25% and LiCl (b) 0.50% LiCl.

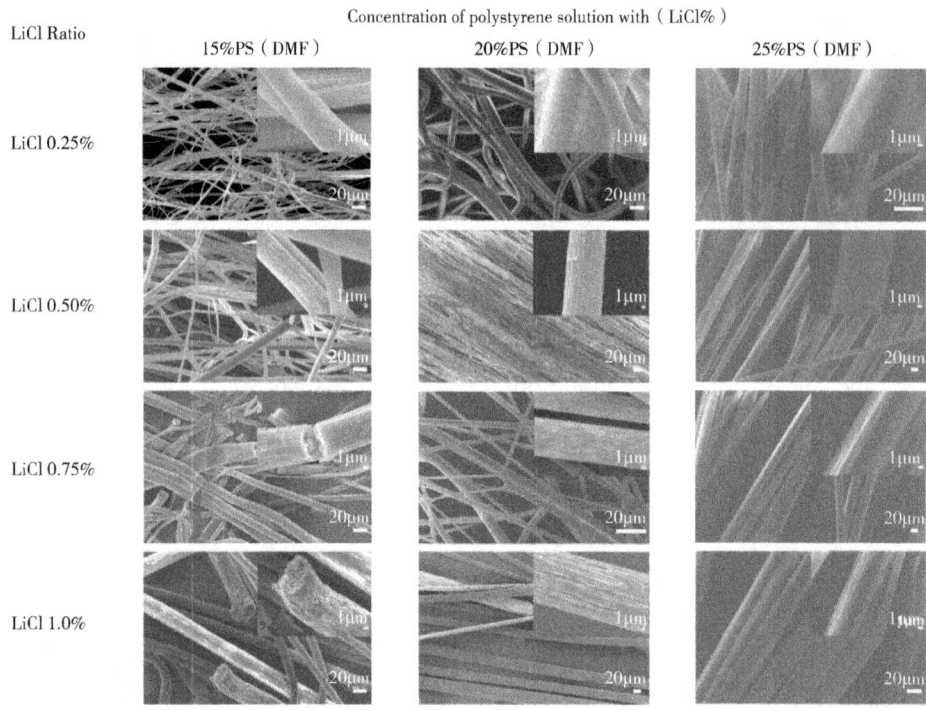

Fig.4　SEM images of the structural morphology with grooves structure under different concentration of PS

(a)　　　　　　　　(b)　　　　　　　　(c)　　　　　　　　(d)

Fig.5　SEM images of the PS filaments morphology structure under different voltages: (a) 5kV; (b) 10kV; (c) 15kV and (d) 20kV

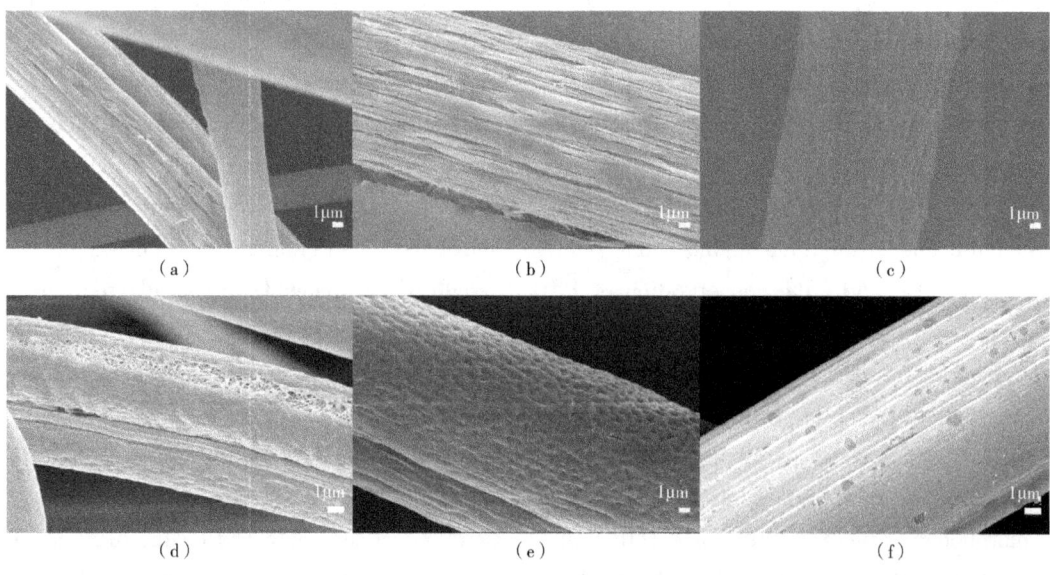

(a)　　　　　　　　(b)　　　　　　　　(c)

(d)　　　　　　　　(e)　　　　　　　　(f)

Fig.6　SEM images of the PS filaments surface structure under single and mixed solvent: (a) 15% DMF; (b) 20% DMF; (c) 25% DMF; (d) 20% DMF/THF; (e) 25% DMF/THF and (f) 30% DMF/THF

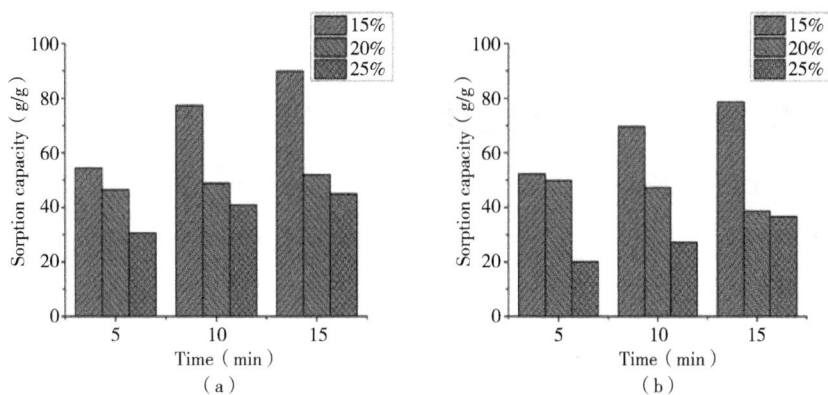

Fig.7 Maximum oil sorption capacities of porous PS

filament sorbent with small grooves structure. PS filament provides more surface area and therefore more grooves on the filament surface. This filament and grooves structure contributes to improved capacity of oil sorption.

4 Conclusions

The microscale PS filament with groove structure has been generated via conventional electrospinning. The mechanism of the filament formation is explained. The effects of different concentration of PS polymer, voltage, the ratio of DMF, DMF/THF solvents, and the addition of LiCl on morphology and grooves structure of the filament were investigated. The results show that polymer concentration and the voltage play important roles to produce a continuous length of filaments. The concentration of (15%, 20%, and 25%) PS polymer at 15kV voltage tends to produce continuous filament.The relative amount of DMF solvent influenced the grooves structure. Around the DMF/THF ration of 50/50 with 0.25% LiCl leads to better porous structure on the filament surface and cross-section. The groove structure filament will be used as an economic and efficient sorbent material of engine oil are highly promising for environmental protection.

References

[1]SHAO C, KIM H Y, GONG J, et al. Fiber mats of poly (vinyl alcohol)/silica composite via electrospin-ning [J]. Materials Letters, 2003, 57(9-10):0-1584.

[2]LIU H, KAMEOKA J, CZAPLEWSKI D A, et al. Polymeric nanowire chemical sensor[J]. Nano Letters, 2004, 4(4): 671-675.

[3]JARUSUWANNAPOOM T, WANNATONG L, JITJAICHAM S, et al. Effect of solvents on electro-spinnability of polysty-rene solutions and morphological appearance of resulting electrospun polystyrene fibers [J]. European Polymer Journal, 2005, 41(3):409-421.

[4]MEGELSKI S, STEPHENS J S, CHASE D B, et al. Micro- and nanostructured surface morphology on electrospun polymer fibers[J]. Macromolecules, 2002, 35(22):8456-8466.

[5] PARK J Y, LEE I H. Relative humidity effect on the preparation of porous electrospun polystyrene fibers[J]. Journal of Nanoscience and Nanotechnology, 2010, 10(5):3473-3477.

[6]FASHANDI H, KARIMI M. Pore formation in polystyrene fiber by superimposing temperature and relative humidity of electrospinning atmosphere[J]. Polymer, 2012, 53(25): 5832-5849.

[7]KIM G T, LEE J S, SHIN J H, et al. Investigation of pore formation for polystyrene electrospun fiber: effect of relative humidity[J]. Korean Journal of Chemical Engineering, 2005, 22(5):783-788.

[8]HUANG C, THOMAS N L. Fabricating porous poly (lactic acid) fibres via electrospinning[J]. European Polymer Journal,2017:S0014305717316294.

[9]NATARAJAN L, NEW J, DASARI A, et al. Surface morphology of electrospun PLA fibers: mechanisms of pore formation[J]. RSC Adv. 2014, 4(83):44082-44088.

[10]XIN Y, HUANG Z H, YAN E Y, et al. Controlling poly (p-phenylene vinylene)/poly(vinyl pyrrolidone) composite nanofibers in different morphologies by electrospinning[J]. Applied Physics Letters, 2006, 89(5):053101.

[11]GODINHO M H, CANEJO J P, PINTO L F V, et al. How to mimic the shapes of plant tendrils on the nano and microscale: spirals and helices of electrospun liquid crystalline cellulose derivatives[J]. Soft Matter, 2009, 5(14).

Study on Mechanical Properties of Three-Dimensional Warp Knitted Super-Spacer Fabric Reinforced Space Membranes

FANG Jialing[1,2], LIU Yining[2], CAO Ying[2], WANG Meiyi[1,2], JIANG Jinhua[1,2]*

[1] *Engineering Research Center of Technical Textiles, Ministry of Education, Shanghai, 201620, China*

[2] *Department of Technical Textiles, College of Textiles, Donghua University, Shanghai, 201620, China*

* *Corresponding author's email: jiangjinhua@dhu.edu.cn*

Abstract: With the wide application of flexible composites in various fields, the prospects of flexible composites are becoming broader and broader. As new types of flexible composites, the three-dimensional warp knitted super-spacer fabric reinforced space membranes used in this paper were made by composite processing of polyester warp-knitted fabric with super-spacer (base fabric) and PVC laminated mesh fabric material. Compared with traditional warp-knitted fabric, warp knitted super-spacer fabric reinforced space membrane has excellent compressive strength and resilience. In this paper, uniaxial tensile properties, tearing properties and bending stiffnesses of the composites with different spacer thicknesses (150mm, 200mm, 300mm) and tensile properties of spacer filaments were tested and compared to analyze the factors affecting their mechanical properties.

Keywords: Super-Spacer; Warp knitting; Spacer fabric; Membrane; Mechanical properties; Flexible composites

1 Introduction

The common warp knitted spacer fabrics have three-dimensional space structures consisting of upper and lower surface fabrics and spacer filaments connecting the upper and lower layers of fabrics. At present, warp knitted super-spacer fabric can selectively change the thickness in the range of 150.0−650.0mm by adjusting the distance between two needle bars to meet customer's requirements for thickness[1], while the thickness of traditional warp knitted spacer fabric can not be changed. Therefore, the warp knitted fabric with super-spacer has excellent resilience, compressive and anti-seismic properties.

Because the single application of warp-knitted fabric with super-spacer can not give full play to its excellent characteristics, the composites which is compounded by warp-knitted fabric with super-spacer and other materials make the warp knitted spacer fabric to have various properties[2], enlarging its application range, and make it more suitable for air cushion bed for medical use[3], military pontoon[4], lifeboat[5]. Three-dimensional warp knitted spacer fabric reinforced space membrane is a new type of flexible composites. At present, there is not enough research on it, but this kind of flexible composite membrane has excellent industrial performance, leaving a broad application prospect and great research value for researchers and industry.

The materials used in this paper were warp knitted super-spacer fabric reinforced space membranes with different spacer thicknesses which were compounded by polyester warp knitted fabric with super-spacer and PVC laminated mesh fabric material. The mechanical properties of warp-knitted flexible composites with super-spacer were investigated by means of uniaxial tensile, tearing, bending stiffness tests on the composites and tensile tests on spacer filaments.

2 Experiments

2.1 Materials

In this paper, three kinds of warp knitted super-spacer

fabric reinforced space membranes were tested. The surface structure of spacer fabrics was shaker stitch/chain.

The specific specifications were shown in Tab.1.

Tab.1 Sample specifications

Parameter	Spacer thickness (mm)	Thickness of single layer(mm)	Warp density (ends/5cm)	Weft density (picks/5cm)	Spacer filaments density (number/m²)
Composite membrane	150	1.41	34	42	29000
Composite membrane	200	1.304	34	43	15600
Composite membrane	300	1.286	34	43	11800
Base fabric	300	0.882	31	47	12000

2.2 Test Instruments

Instron 5967universal electronic strength tester, YG 026MB imported electronic fabric strength tester, LLY-01 electronic stiffness tester.

2.3 Test Methods

2.3.1 Uniaxial Tensile Test of the Composites

The spacer filaments were cut as short as possible to separate the upper and lower layers of warp-knitted super-spacer fabric reinforced space membrane. According to standard GB/T 3923.1—2013, the samples with the size of 200mm×50mm were cut. The testing instrument was Instron 5967 universal electronic strength tester. The clip distance was 100mm, and the tensile speed was 100mm/min. The average values of 5 valid data measured in both warp and weft directions were taken as experiments results.

2.3.2 Tearing Test of the Composites

The spacer filaments were cut as short as possible to separate the upper and lower layers of warp-knitted super-spacer fabric reinforced space membrane. According to standard GB 3919—83, using the tongue (single rip) method, the samples with the size of (220+2)mm × (50+1)mm were cut. Along the length direction from the width of one half, the crack with the width of (100+1) mm was cut. The test instrument was Instron5967 universal electronic strength tester. The clip distance was 100mm, and the tensile speed was 100mm/min. The average values of 5 valid data measured in both warp and weft directions were taken as experiments results.

2.3.3 Test on Bending Stiffness of the Composites

The spacer filaments were cut as short as possible to separate the upper and lower layers of warp-knitted super-spacer fabric reinforced space membrane. According to standard GB/T 18318—2001, the samples with the size of 250mm×25mm were cut. The testing instrument was LLY-01 electronic stiffness tester. The test angle of the instrument was 41.5 degrees. When the sample was pushed to contact with the inclined surface of 41.5 degrees, the average values of 5 valid data measured in both warp and weft directions were taken as the average bending length C. Then the bending stiffness of unit width can be calculated by the following formula:

$$G = m \times C^3 \times 10^{-3} \tag{1}$$

G——Bending stiffness, mN · cm;

m——Mass per unit area of the sample, g/m²;

C——Bending length, cm.

2.3.4 Tensile Test of Spacer Filaments

The PVC reinforced membranes with spacer filaments were used in the test, and the samples with the size of 40mm × 40mm were cut. The upper and lower layers were adhered to the T-shaped clamps respectively, as shown in Fig.1. Two T-shaped clamps were clamped on the upper and lower fixtures of YG026MB imported electronic fabric strength tester respectively. The tensile speed was 100mm/min. Breaking strengths in the direction of spacer filaments were measured. The average values of 5 valid data measured were taken as experiments results.

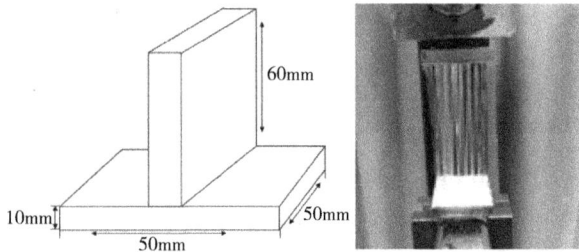

Fig.1 T-shaped clamps

3 Results and Discussions

3.1 Analysis of Uniaxial Tensile Properties of the Base Fabric and Composites

3.1.1 Test Result of Tensile Properties of Three Composites with Different Spacer Thicknesses

The tensile properties of three kinds of composites with different spacer thicknesses were shown in Fig. 2 and Fig.3. From Fig.2, it can be seen that the weft breaking strengths of three kinds of composites with different spacer thicknesses differed little, and the warp breaking strengths of composites at the thickness of 150mm was relatively high. The warp breaking strength of the composites at the thickness of 200mm and 300mm was less than that of weft breaking strength, because the number of yarns that bearing tension in warp directions was less than that in weft directions. The warp and weft breaking strengths of the composites at the thickness of 150mm were similar, which may be due to the larger thickness of the single layer of the composites at the thickness of 150mm than the other two composites. Because the warp density of the composites was less than the weft density, with the increase of coating thickness, slurry penetrated more easily into warp yarns. As a result, the strengths of the warp yarns were strengthened, and the bonds between the base fabric and the PVC laminated mesh fabric material were strengthened. The warp breaking strength of the composites at the thickness of 150mm was greatly improved by the combination of the base fabric and membrane. As can be seen from Fig.3, the warp breaking elongations of the three composites were less than these of the weft breaking elongation, which was mainly due to the increase of the bondage of the warp yarn by the structure of plaiting chain and the

higher flexibility of the weft yarn. The breaking elongation of the composites at the thickness of 150mm was small, because the increase of coating thickness made more slurry penetrate into the yarns and gaps. So that the yarns in the fabric were bonded together.

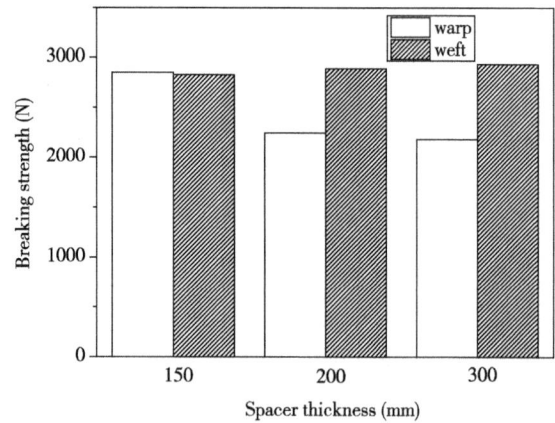

Fig.2 Breaking strengths of three composites with different spacer thicknesses

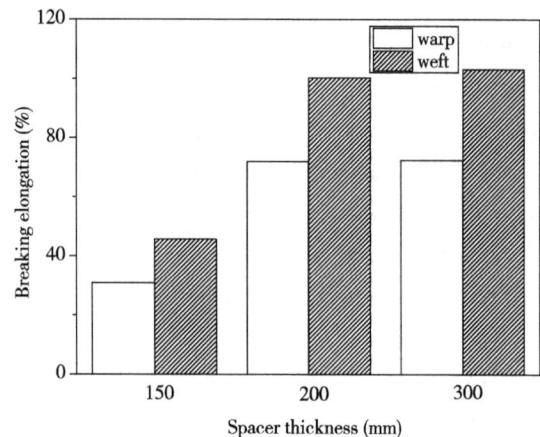

Fig.3 Breaking elongations of three composites with different spacer thicknesses

3.1.2 Test Result of Tensile Properties of the Base Fabric and Composites

The tensile properties of the base fabric and composites at the thickness of 300mm were shown in Fig.4 and Fig. 5.From Fig.4, it can be seen that the warp and weft breaking strengths of spacer fabric were improved after compounding. This was because the slurry increased the bonding force between yarns and fibers, which made the fabric structure more firm. At the same time, excellent property of membrane reduced the opportunity of weak points of yarns after compounding. As can be seen from Fig. 5, the warp breaking elongation of spacer fabric decreased while the weft breaking elongation increased after compounding. As far as coating technology was concerned, coating increased the number of warp yarns per unit area and decreased the number of weft yarns. It meant that the warp yarn was stretched and the weft yarn shrunk. When drawing, the weft yarn had more straightening space and the warp straightening space decreased.

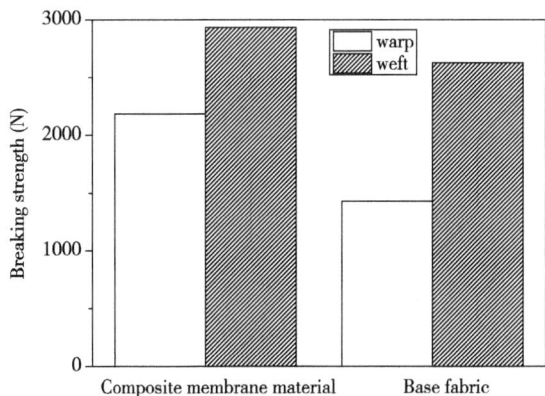

Fig.4　Breaking strengths of the base fabric and composites at the thickness of 300mm

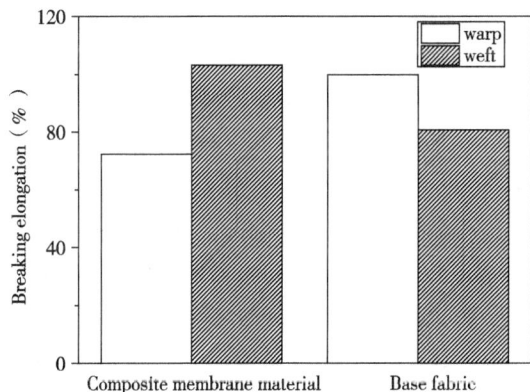

Fig.5　Breaking elongations of the base fabric and composites at the thickness of 300mm

3.2　Analysis of Tearing Properties of the Base Fabric and Composites

The tearing properties of polyester spacer base fabric and composites were shown in Fig. 6 and Fig. 7. From Fig.6, it can be seen that the tearing strength of the composites at the thickness of 150mm was higher than that of other two kinds of membranes, which was due to

the increase of coating and the increase of bonding points and bonding force between yarns. As a result, the slippage of yarns decreased and the tearing strength increased. From Fig. 7, it can be seen that the warp tearing strength of spacer base fabric decreased and the weft tearing strength did not change significantly after compounding. As the slurry entered the gaps of the yarns after coating, the friction between the yarns increased, and the tearing triangle area shrunk. It meant that the number of yarns which was applied to force decreased. Compared with the base fabric, the force in the tearing triangle area was more concentrated, which made the force uneven distribution in the fabric, so compared with the fabric before the coating, the warp tearing strength of the composites decreased.

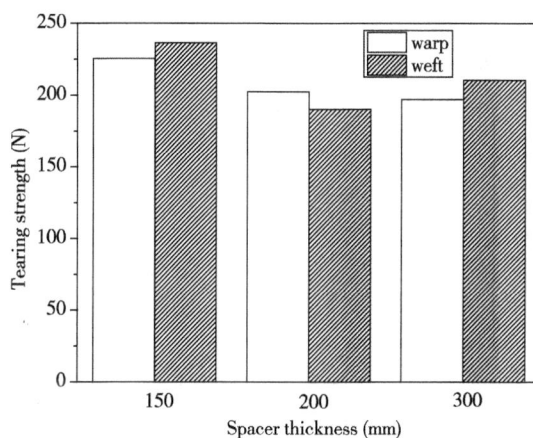

Fig.6　Tearing strengths of three composites with different spacer thicknesses

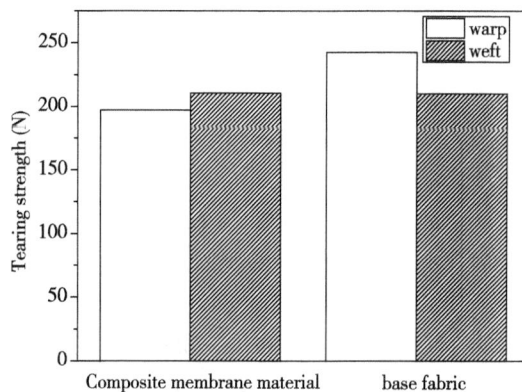

Fig.7　Tearing strengths of the base fabric and composites at the thickness of 300mm

3.3 Analysis of Bending Stiffness of the Composites

In this paper, the bending stiffnesses of three kinds of composites with different spacer thicknesses were shown in Fig.5. From results of the test, it can be seen that the bending stiffnesses of the composites at the thicknesses of 200mm and 300mm were small and the difference of bending stiffness between warp and weft directions was not significant. It meant that the composites at the thicknesses of 200mm and 300mm had good softness. The bending stiffness of the composites at the thickness of 150mm was larger and bending stiffness in the warp direction was larger than that in the weft direction. This was due to the increase of coating amount and more slurry penetrating into the fabric, which made the fabric brittle and hard.

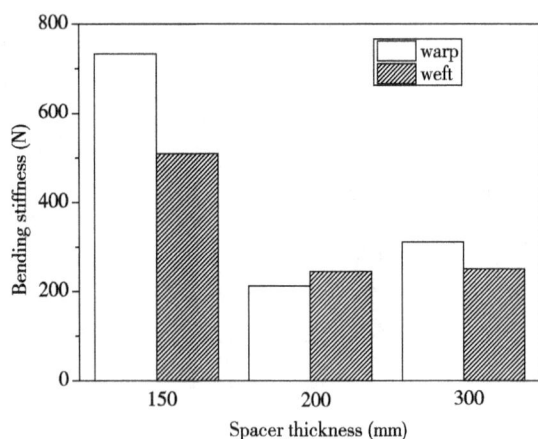

Fig.8   Comparison of bending stiffnesses of three kinds of composites with different spacer thicknesses

3.4 Analysis of Tensile Properties Test Results of Spacer Filaments

In this paper, the specifications and test results of spacer filaments of three kinds of composites were shown in Tab.2 and Fig.9. It can be seen that the breaking strength of the composites at the thickness of 150mm was the largest, that of the composites at the thickness of 200mm was the middle, and that of the composites at the thickness of 300mm spacer was the smallest. This was due to the different density of spacing filaments.

Tab.2   The specifications of spacer filaments with different spacer thicknesses

Spacer thickness (mm)	Spacer filament density (Number of filaments/ 40mm×40mm)	Breaking strength (N)
150	48	711.4
200	30	472.75
300	24	324.15

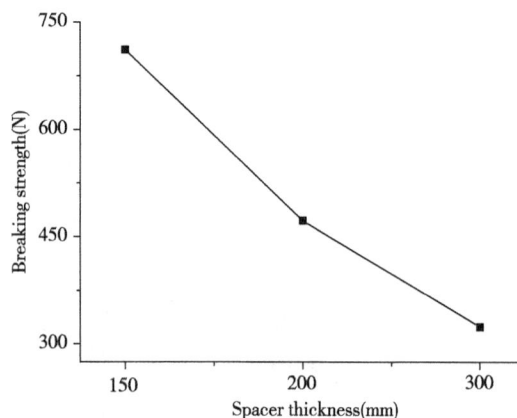

Fig.9   Comparison of breaking strengths of three different spacer thicknesses of spacer filaments

4   Conclusions

In this paper, the uniaxial tensile properties, tearing properties and bending stiffness of the composites at different thicknesses (150mm, 200mm, 300mm) and tensile properties of spacer filaments were tested. It could be concluded that increase of coating thickness decreased the breaking elongation and increased the tearing strength and bending stiffness of warp-knitted spacer fabrics reinforced membranes. After compounding, the breaking strength, the warp breaking elongation and the warp tearing strength decreased. Meanwhile, the weft breaking elongation increased. With the increase of spacer filament density, the breaking strength of the composites' spacer filaments also increased.

Acknowledgements

The authors gratefully acknowledge the funding provided by National Key R&D Program of China (2016YFB0303300), the Fundamental Research

Funds for the Central Universities (2232018G - 06, 2232019G-02) and the National Innovation Experiment Program for University Students (201810255002).

References

[1] ZHANG Xiaohui, MA Pibo, MIAO Xuhong. Development and application of warp knitted spacer fabrics with super large spacing[J]. Industrial Textiles, 2016, 34(5):34-37.

[2] ARMAKAN D M, ROYE A. A study on the compression be-havior of spacer fabrics designed for concrete applications [J]. Fibers and Polymers, 2009, 10(1):116-123.

[3] HEIDE M. Spacer fabrics: trends[J]. Kettenwirk Prax-is, 2001, 35 (1):17-20.

[4] CHEN Zhenzhou. Study on knitting technology of warp knitted spacer fabrics for industrial use [J]. Journal of Textile Science, 1999, 20 (5):303-305.

[5] YE Xiaohua. Structure and properties of functional spacing fabrics[D]. Shanghai: Donghua University, 2006.

Exploration on Waterproof and Moisture Conducting Fabric Based on Computerized Flat Knitting Machine

CAO Honghua[1], LONG Hairu[1]*

[1] College of Textiles, Donghua University, Shanghai, 201620, China

* Corresponding author's email: hrlong@ dhu.edu.cn

Abstract: Waterproof and moisture conductive fabrics are functional textiles with high technical content and high research hotspots. Coating, lamination and high density are usually used to realize these functions. However, the research and achievement obtained by differential capillary effect are almost blank. Based on differential capillary effect, seven different kinds of knitted fabrics were prepared on the flat knitting machine of gauge 12 and their waterproof and moistureconductive properties were tested. Then, the results proved that the waterproof grade can be up to 3, and the unidirectional moisture conduction grade can be up to 2, which can be applied to the upper of shoes, and provide a new idea for the study of waterproof and moisture conductive fabrics.

Keywords: Computerized flat knitting machine; Waterproof and moisture transported fabric; Differential capillary effect; Upper material

1 Introduction

Waterproof and moisture conducting fabrics are functional fabrics that water cannot be immersed in the fabric under certain pressure, but sweat produced by human body can be transmitted from the surface of skin to the surface of the fabric and evaporated, thus avoiding the accumulation of sweat to bring people a sense of wetness and cold, and making the micro-environment between human body and fabric in a comfortable state[1]. As a functional textile with high technical content and research hotspot, waterproof and moisture-conductive fabrics have been widely used in clothing, military, medical and other fields in recent decades[2]. Traditional waterproof and moisture-conductive fabrics use coating, film lamination and high density to realize their functions, which have some shortcomings, such as poor air permeability, high price or poor comfort, complex technology, etc. Moreover, more research has been done on waterproof and moisture-conductive woven fabrics, but less research has been done on related knitted fabrics. The forming technology of computerized flat knitting machine has gradually become one of the hotspots of technology. Therefore, the research of waterproof and moistureconductive fabric based on computerized flat knitting machine has broad market potential and development prospects. According to wicking and differential capillary effect, the knitting and research of waterproof and moisture conductive fabric on E12 computerized flat knitting machine are carried out from the aspects of yarn type, yarn twist, fabric structure, fabric density, and its waterproof and moisture conductive properties are tested, which provides a new idea for the study of waterproof and moisture conductive fabrics and has certain guiding significance.

2 Waterproof and Moisture Conductive Mechanism

Wicking effect refers to the capillary effect between fibers in the aggregate of fibers or the holes in single fibers on liquids. The water in the capillary of yarn and fabric can flow automatically under the additional pressure at the liquid-gas interface in the capillary even without the potential energy difference outside. The wicking is directional and selective, i. e. differential capillary effect. When the linear density of single fiber in inner layer is large, the linear density of single fiber in surface is small, the additional pressure formed by inner layer capillary is small, and the additional pressure formed by outer layer capillary is large, the additional pressure difference will be formed at the junction of inner and outer layers of the fabric, which makes the sweat in contact with the inner layer lead from the inner layer to the outer layer without backflow[3].

The main influencing factors of waterproof and moisture conductivity include yarn type, yarn twist, fabric density, fabric structure. On the basis of wicking effect and differential capillary effect, the effects of yarn combination, twist, fabric structure and density on waterproof and moisture conductivity can be studied, and then, waterproof and moisture conductive fabrics can be available.

3 Design and Knitting

3.1 Structure Design

In order to make the surface waterproof and make the inner layer conducive to moisture conduction, the surface layer should be as tight as possible and the inner layer should be loose[4].

3.1.1 Double-Layer Structure

The surface is designed to be full-knitted weft plain stitch, which makes the surface of the fabric tighter and smoother, and also increases the evaporation area of sweat. The inner layer is knitted by needle drawing method so that the inner density is relatively small, at the same time, part of the yarn in the inner layer tuck in the surface layer to consolidate the two layers. The structure is shown in Fig.1.

3.1.2 Spacer Structure

The spacer is located in the middle of the fabric, it is the conductive layer of sweat. The fibers with strong hydrophobicity and good moisture conductivity are used to form a wick-like water absorption point[5]. The structure is shown in Fig.2.

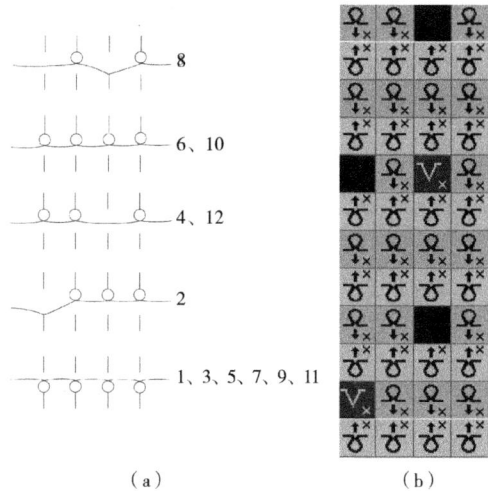

Fig. 1 (a) Loop structure diagram; (b) Computer flat knitting machine pattern

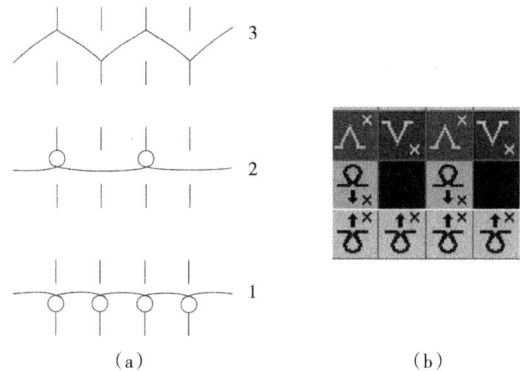

Fig.2 (a) Loop structure diagram; (b) Computer flat knitting machine pattern

3.2 Yarn Selection

Polyester has good moisture conductivity, high breaking strength, good corrosion resistance. Polypropylene has good moisture conductivity, low specific gravity, high strength, good wear resistance, and the polypropylene's moisture regain is close to 0, it hardly absorbs moisture. These properties meet the needs of waterproof and moisture conductive function and upper material. According to characteristics of E12 computerized flat knitting machine, the yarn linear density matches with it is 585D–675D[6]. According to these, 150D/144F polypropylene yarns, 300D/288F polyester yarns, 300D/576F polyester yarns, 300D/96F polyester yarns, 300D/96F polypropylene yarns are selected.

3.3 Twist Sesign of Yarns

After trial weaving on E12 computerized flat knitting

machine, when the yarn is above 40T/10cm, it is almost impossible to knit normally. Therefore, the following twists are added to yarns, and the wicking height is tested by YG（B）capillary effect tester.

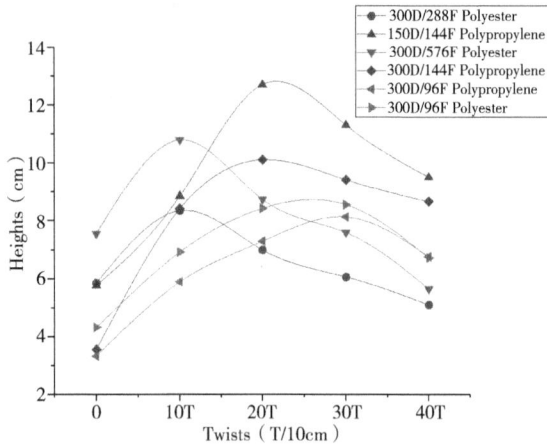

Fig.3　Wicking heights for yarns with different twists

With the increase of twist, the wicking heights increase first and then decrease. There is an optimum twist to make the wicking height the highest and the moisture conduction effect the best. According to differential capillary effect, when the surface yarn type and the inner yarn type are different, the twist of the surface yarn can not be smaller than that of the inner yarn, so as to

ensure the formation of thin capillaries between the fibers in the surface yarn and thick capillaries between the fibers in the inner yarn[5]. Therefore, the twist of inner layer is 10T/10cm, the twist of spacer layer is the twist corresponding to the highest wicking height. In order to study the effect of surface layer twist on the waterproof and moisture conductivity, two kinds of twists of surface yarn are selected for comparison. They are the twist corresponding to the highest wicking height of surface yarn and the maximum twist relatively, so 300D/288F polyester fibers choose 20T/10cm and 30T/10cm.

3.4　Density and Other Parameter Design

Sinking depth refers to the size of loops formed after knitting, reflecting the size of density. After repeated trial knitting, the yarn begins to wear or even break when the sinking depth is less than 72, so the sinking depth can be chosen 72 at least. In order to study the influence of density on the waterproof and moisture conductivity, the surface fabric sinking depths are 72 and 78, and the inner layer sinking depth is 75. The head speed is 40 and the roller speed is 12.

3.5　Knitting Technical Design

Based on the above analysis, the designed fabrics are shown in Tab.1.

Tab.1　Knitting technology of seven kinds of fabrics

Serial number	Structure	Yarn type		Sinking depth	Twist(T/10cm)
1	Double-layer structure	Surface	300D/288F Polyester	72	30
		Inner layer	300D/96F Polyester	75	10
2	Double-layer structure	Surface	300D/288F Polyester	72	20
		Inner layer	300D/96F Polyester	75	10
3	Double-layer structure	Surface	300D/288F Polyester	78	30
		Inner layer	300D/96F Polyester	75	10
4	Double-layer structure	Surface	300D/576F Polyester	72	30
		Inner layer	300D/96F Polyester	75	10
5	Spacer structure	Surface	300D/288F Polyester	72	30
		Spacer layer	300D/144F Polypropylene	72	20
		Inner layer	300D/96F Polyester	75	10
6	Double-layer structure	Surface	150D/144F Polypropylene	72	30
		Inner layer	300D/96F Polyester	75	10
7	Double-layer structure	Surface	300D/288F Polyester	72	30
		Inner layer	300D/96F Polypropylene	75	10

3.6 Finishing Process

After knitting, the finishing process is soaping—drying—heat setting. The purpose of soaping is to remove impurities and oils from fabrics. The soaping process is to soak the fabrics in 5% soap water for 1 hour, bath ratio is 1 : 30, temperature is 50℃, and then wash them three times with clean water. Because of the low melting point of polypropylene, the setting temperature can not exceed 130℃. For fabrics No.5–No.7, taking the setting property of polyester into account, setting temperature is 125℃, for fabrics No.1–No.4,

setting temperature is 175℃, setting time is 60s[7].

4 Testing and Analysis

4.1 Structural Parameters

The final physical parameters of seven fabrics are shown in Tab.2.

4.2 Testing and Analysis of Waterproof Performance

The fabrics are tested in Y813 fabric wettability detector. The test results are shown in Tab.3.

Tab.2 Structural parameters of seven kinds of fabrics

Serial number	Thickness	Square meter weight	Wales density	Courses density	Total density
1	2.006	654.136	42	86	3612
2	1.987	644.401	40	83	3320
3	2.186	622.286	40	68	2720
4	1.973	660.279	41	82	3362
5	2.666	793.068	36	71	2556
6	2.150	620.408	35	72	2520
7	2.280	697.361	39	68	2652

Tab.3 Testing results of seven kinds of fabrics

Serial number	Waterproof grade	Unidirectional moisture conduction index	Unidirectional moisture conduction grade
1	1	16.6799	2
2	1	25.1657	2
3	1	25.2056	2
4	1	135.2375	3
5	1	24.1076	2
6	3	−6.5621	2
7	1	54.7234	2

As shown in Tab.3 above, the waterproof grades of fabrics No.1–No.5 and No.7 are 1, that is, the waterproof of fabric with polyester as the surface layer is poor. Within seconds of contact with the surface layer, the water droplets begin to infiltrate slowly and diffuse into the inner layer, indicating that the moisture absorption of polyester itself and the differential capillary effect have less effect than that of water droplet infiltration power. In particular, although the surface of fabric No.7 is wet when a small amount of water is first dripped into

it, the inner layer is basically dry, because the inner layer is polypropylene fiber, the hygroscopicity of it is very poor, and under the differential capillary effect, the transmission of water droplets to the inner layer is more difficult than the transverse diffusion in the surface layer. When more water drips, it begins to diffuse to the inner layer. The waterproof grade of No.6 fabric is 3, because the moisture regain of polypropylene fiber is almost zero, it hardly absorbs moisture. When the density is large, combining with appropriate structure and differential capillary effect, waterproof fabric can be a-chieved.

4.3 Testing and Analysis of Moisture Conductivity

The fabrics were cut into 8cm×8cm sizes and tested with MMT liquid moisture management testing instrument. There are many indicators measured by the instrument, and the unidirectional moisture conduction index is used to characterize the sweating property of the fabric, which can better reflect the directional wet conductivity of the fabric.

Therefore, the unidirectional moisture conduction index is chosen to compare.

Tab.3 shows the results of the seven kinds of fabrics.

As shown in Tab.3 above, the index of fabric No.2 is higher than that of fabric No.1, but the difference is not significant. Comparing with 30T/10cm, although the radius of capillary formed by the twist 20T/10cm is thicker, the quantity of capillaries may be more, so the unidirectional moisture conduction effect is better. Proper twist can optimize the radius, quantity, distribution of capillary, which is conduct-ive to differential capillary effect; Fabrics No.1 and No.3 show that the index of fabric No.3 is higher than fabric No.1, because when the density of surface fabric is high, the fibers between surface yarns squeeze each other, although it will make the capillary thinner, it will also block capillary, which is not beneficial to differential capillary effect; Fabrics No.1 and No.4 show that the unidirectional moisture conduction grade of fabric No.4 reaches grade 3, while fabric No.1 is grade 2, which indicates that the bigger the difference of linear density of single fiber in two layers the yarn is, the bigger the difference of additional pressure between two layers is, the better the unidirectional moisture conduction is; Fabrics No.1 and No.5 show that the unidirectional moisture conduction index of fabric No.5 is higher than that of fabric 1, because the spacer layer of fabric plays a better conductive role than that of double-layer fabric; Fabric No.1 and No.6 show that the unidirectional moisture conduction index of fabric No.6 is lower than that of fabric No.1, because of high twist and density of surface yarn, polypropylene fibers hardly absorb moisture and water is difficult to penetrate into the sur-face. Therefore, the transverse diffusion of water in the inner layer is easier. After a long period of time, the water content increases continuously, the inner layer is wetted in a large area, only a small part of the remaining water begins to enter the surface layer, and makes the surface layer wet, so its unidirectional moisture conduction performance is poor. Fabrics No.1 and No.7 show that the moisture conductivity of fabric No.7 is higher than that of fabric No.1, because the moisture absorption of polyester fibers in surface layer is better than polypropylene fibers in inner layer. In summary, the order of unidirectional moisture conduction is 4 > 7 > 3 > 2 > 5 > 1 > 6, but there is little difference between them except fabric No.4, they are all grade 2.

5　Conclusions

According to the above test results of waterproof and moisture conductivity, the fabrics with good waterproof and moisture conduction can be obtained by using the differential capillary effect combined with the proper structure, density and twist of the double-layer fabric with polypropylene as the surface layer and polyester as the inner layer. This paper chooses E12 computerized flat knitting machine, when the process is 150D/144F polypropylene as the surface layer, 300D/96F polyester as the inner layer of the double-layer structure, the sinking depth and the twist of the surface layer is re-spectively 72 and 30T/10cm, the sinking depth and the twist of the inner layer is respectively 75 and 10T/10cm, the fabric whose waterproof grade is 3 and unidi-rectional moisture conduction grade is 2 can be knitted. This technology can be applied to shoe upper, which provides a new research idea and development direction for waterproof and moisture conductive fabrics, and has certain guiding significance.

References

[1]TANG Q, WU J Z. Study on moisture conductivity of double-layer knitted fabrics[J]. Shandong Textile Technology, 2007,48(4):49-51.

[2]PANG L Q. Development of waterproof, breathable and anti-bacterial multi-functional composite fabric[J]. Shandong Textile Technology,2016,57(3):8-10.

[3]WANG Q, FENG X W. Differential capillary effect model of fabrics and its application[J]. Journal of Donghua University (Natural Science Edition), 2001,27(3):54-57.

[4] FAN F, QI H J. The relationship between differential capillary effect and pore size properties of fabrics[J].2008 (8):90-92.

[5]XU R C, CHEN L N. Development of directional moisture conductive knitted sports fabric[J]. Knitting Industry,2007 (10):3-5.

[6]SUN W D. Study on knitting technology and performance of shoe upper based on computerized flat knitting machine[D]. Shanghai: Donghua University, 2018.

[7]YANG J, SHEN F. Differential dyeing and finishing of polypropylene/polyester knitted fabrics[C]. "Liansheng Cup" National Symposium, 2013.

Soft Actuated Devices Mechanisms of Textile Materials and Fabrication Process Designs

SUN Maowen[1,2] **LIN Yinglei**[2], **YAN Jianhua**[1], **WANG Lei**[2], **LIU Lifang**[1]*

[1] *College of Textiles, Donghua University, Shanghai, 201620, China*

[2] *Shenzhen institutes of advanced technology, Chinese academy of sciences, Shenzhen, 518055, China*

* *Corresponding author's email*: flily2000@ 163.com

Abstract: Traditionally, soft actuated devices made of electroactive polymers and shape memory alloys have problems of low stress and strain. Actuators made of nylon or spandex are attracting attention because of their wide range of raw materials, low prices, and high power and specific work and may provide significantly benefit to the elderly population on health but it has the disadvantage of low energy conversion efficiency. This presentation gives a review on both the electrothermal performance of materials used in the actuator and fabrication process of nylon and spandex actuator. This article also compares the advantages and disadvantages of shape memory alloys with dielectric elastomer drivers. Further, the difference in stress and strain between the spandex and nylon actuators was compared.

Keywords: Artificial muscle; Nylon; Spandex; Annealing; Training

1 Introduction

Efforts to save human power output and improve external assistance have never stopped; nowadays, humans have gathered more and more attention on the actuator, which can help the elderly and the disabled. Soft actuated devices are different from traditional assistance devices with assembled pump and motor. With their advantages of novel materials and fabrication design process, soft actuated devices are new types of driven methods for wearable robots which can mimic the muscle-like action and provide sufficiently large power and quick response.

The shape memory alloy can completely eliminate the deformation at a lower temperature after heating and restore the original shape before deformation. Some alloys, which have a two-way memory effect, restore the shape of high temperature upon heating and restore the shape of the low temperature upon cooling.

Although the shape memory alloy actuator is simple to structure, its shape variable is small and valuable and its strain only is up to 6%−12%[1].

Artificial muscle, which is made of shape memory alloy and fishing line, has the advantage of low cost and low weight[2], which is electro-variable materials. These materials have the advantages of low actuator voltage, such as polyaniline, and the artificial muscle prepared by polypyrrole has good biocompatibility, which is electro-variable material. Some people polymerize polypyrrole on different conductive yarns and find polypyrrole in PES+2. ×INOX is thicker and more uniform[3]. Wearable flexible artificial muscles can be made by using textile technology and electroactive polymers[4]. Although the electroactive polymer actuator has the advantages that it is small size, small weight, and the like, there is a disadvantage that the actuator force is small. The dielectric elastomer driver (electroactive artificial muscle) has a small reaction time delay, the maximum specific power is, however highly small[5]. Carbon nanotubes and graphene artificial muscle have the advantages that they are low driving voltage, large deformation ability, long cycle life and high stability. A large operating voltage of a few volts produces a large actuation strain.

Lima designed guest-filled, twist-spun actuator, which is fast, high-force and tensile actuation[6]. But carbon nanotube is extremely expensive, which is 1545 per gram from sigma.

Fortunately, in thermotropic material twisted and coiled actuator, such as nylon and spandex, is consist of inexpensive and easily obtained polymer, which provide fast, scalable, long-life tensile and torsional muscle[7]. It can deliver 2000J/kg of specific work[10]. The twisted and coiled actuator can increase the frequency of actuation by means of rapid cooling, which is usually fan[11]. Actuator that plated silver at surface exhibits greater actuation frequency and better drive performance[12]. When the nylon monofilament is formed into a spring shape and heated, on the one hand, the spring shape will have a tendency to return to the original monofilament state, and on the other hand, the nylon monofilament will shrink due to heat shrinkage; the two aspects determine the elongation or contraction. The macromolecular heat shrinkage and the outer spring shape of the spring-like nylon filament are shown in Fig.1.

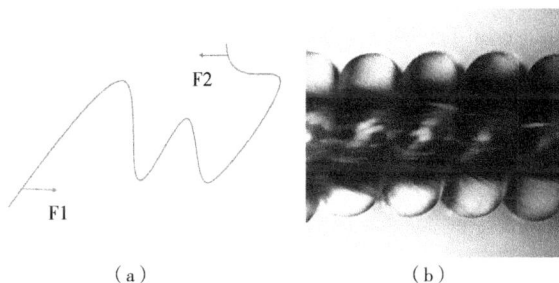

(a)   (b)

Fig.1   Schematic diagram of (a) macromolecular heat shrinkage and (b) spring-like nylon (the diameter of nylon is 0.5mm)

2   Fabrication process

A helical spring-like actuator is developed using polymer fibers that can potentially generate sufficient power for wearable robots[7]. The process of making NTCA is as follows: twist the nylon monofilament until it forms a spring-like shape. During this period, it should be noted that the pre-tension should not be too heavy, so that the nylon filament is broken during the

twisting process, and it should not be too light to be disorderly[7]. At this time, the distance between the adjacent rings is small, and the distance can be increased by increasing the weight so as to be spatially actuation, and the distance between the rings can also be increased by the subsequent training process. In order to maintain the above shape, annealing needs to be carried out in an oven at a temperature above the glass transition temperature and below the melting point; the set time is dependent on temperature, usually one hour[13]. Training to attain fully-reversible actuation and achieve consistency in stiffness, length, and actuation of the muscles at constant load. The fully wound polymer fibers were also obtained by twisting (under a load of 300g) a 1m length of 450μm nylon 6 fishing line with the analog to obtain a 25μm diameter steel wire. The linear resistance of the crimped polymer muscle is $20\Omega/cm$[7]. Joule heating, such as wound wire or surface silver plating or graphene, is a common heating method[8]. The drive can also be controlled by changes in ambient humidity[9]. Another way is to entangle the different mandrels of diameter, so that the resulting TCA strain is large. Actuator made of nylon exhibits greater stress, while actuator made of spandex exhibits greater strain and lower drive temperatures. The performance of the driver made of nylon and the driver made of spandex are shown in the Tab.1. The properties of nylon 66 and spandex are shown in Tab.2.

Tab.1   The performance of nylon and spandex actuator

	Nylonactuator[14]	Spandexactuator[15]
Maximum strains	16.945%	45%
Specific work	732.879 J/kg	1523 J/kg
Training temperature	35~190℃	35~140℃
Actuation temperature	35~180℃	35~130℃

Tab.2   The characteristic of nylon and spandex[19]

	Nylon66	Spandex
Glass transition temperature	82℃	−60℃
Softening point	225℃	170℃
Boiling water shrinkage	4%~10.5%	19%~27%
Melting point	253℃	180℃

The device is capable of producing six identical samples simultaneously and the number of twisters can be measured by the encoder. Five driver samples were made under different load states, and the maximum strain of STCA was finally obtained to be 45% and the maximum specific work was 1532J/kg[15]. Artificial muscles can be used to make robotic hands by alternately flowing hot and cold water through artificial muscles[16-17].

In general, prior to twisting, a highly oriented fiber can be used to make a actuator as long as the diameter is larger than the expansion in the length direction[18]. In other words, both the contraction in the length direction and the expansion in the radial direction result in the generation of the actuation. Artificial muscles have the disadvantage of low energy conversion rate, as shown in the Tab.3.

Tab.3 Energy conversion rate of different types of muscles[7]

	SMA	TCA	Natural muscle
Energy conversion efficiency	1~2%	<1.32%	20%

3　Mechanism

Fiber shrinkage is caused by the absorption of heat from the outside, the dissociation of the amorphous molecular chain, the decrease of the molecular chain, and the shrinkage of the fiber length. The higher the amorphous content and orientation of the fiber are affected by external force or thermal orientation, the more the number of molecules, the greater the degree of regularity of the molecular chain arrangement, and thus the tendency of large shrinkage. According to the fiber heat shrinkage mechanism, the degree of orientation of the fiber macromolecules along the fiber axisis one important structural parameters related to the thermal shrinkage properties of the fiber material. Nylon is used as a thermoplastic fiber; the properties when heated are also related to the ratio of the crystalline region to the amorphous region. When the proportion of amorphous regions is high, the three-state two-transition performance is more obvious[19].

4　Conclusions

We have given a brief overview of soft actuated devices on textile materials and fabrication process. The actuator made of nylon produces stress and strain under hot water or Joule heat conditions due to internal macromolecular shrinkage. Actuator made of nylon exhibits greater stress, while actuator made of spandex exhibits greater strain and requires the lower temperature of actuation.

Acknowledgements

This work was supported by the National Key Research and Development Program of China (2018YFC2000903).

References

[1] GABDULLIN N, KHAN S H. Review of properties of magnetic shape memory (MSM) alloys and MSM actuator designs[J]. Journal of Physics: Conference Series, 2015 (588): 012052.

[2] XIANG C, YANG H, SUN Z, et al. The design, hysteresis modeling and control of a novel SMA-fishing-line actuator [J]. Smart Materials and Structures, 2017, 26(3):037004.

[3] MARTINEZ J G, RICHTER K, PERSSON N K, et al. Investigation of electrically conducting yarns for use in textile actuators[J]. Smart Materials and Structures, 2018.

[4] MAZIZ A, CONCAS A, KHALDI A, et al. Knitting and weaving artificial muscles[J]. Science Advances, 2017, 3 (1):1600327.

[5] JUNG H S, YANG S Y, CHO K H, et al. Design and fabrication of twisted monolithic dielectric elastomer actuator[J]. International Journal of Control, Automation and Systems, 2017, 15(1):25-35.

[6] LIMA M D, LI N, ANDRADE M J D, et al. Electrically, chemically, and photonically powered torsional and tensile actuation of hybrid carbon nanotube yarn muscles[J]. Science, 2012, 338(6109):928-932.

[7] HAINES C S, LIMA M D, LI N, et al. Artificial muscles from fishing line and sewing thread[J]. Science, 2014, 343 (6173):868-872.

[8] MIRVAKILI S M, RAVANDI A R, HUNTER I W, et al. Simple and strong: twisted silver painted nylon artificial muscle actuated by Joule heating [J]. Proceedings of Spie, 2014, 9056: 90560I.

[9] KIM S H, KWON C H, PARK K, et al. Bio-inspired, moisture-powered hybrid carbon nanotube yarn muscles[J]. Scientific Reports, 2016, 6:23016.

[10] HAINES C S, LI N, SPINKS G M, et al. New twist on artificial muscles[J]. Proceedings of the National Academy of Sciences of the United States of Americe, 2016, 113(42): 11709-11716.

[11] TAKAGI K, ARAKAWA T, TAKEDA J, et al. Position control of twisted and coiled polymer actuator using a controlled fan for cooling[C]. Proceedings of Spie, 2017, 10163: 101632V-1.

[12] PARK J, YOO J W, SEO H W, et al. Electrically controllable twisted-coiled artificial muscle actuators using surface-modified polyester fibers[J]. Smart Materials and Structures, 2017, 26(3):035048.

[13] WU L, CHAUHAN I, TADESSE Y. A novel soft actuator for the musculoskeletal system[J]. Advanced Materials Technologies, 2018:1700359.

[14] CHO K H, SONG M G, YANG S Y, et al. Super stretchable soft actuator made of twisted and coiled spandex fiber[C]. Proceedings of Spie, 2017, 10163: 101630W-1.

[15] YANG S Y, CHO K H, KIM Y, et al. High performance twisted and coiled soft actuator with spandex fiber for artificial muscles[J]. Smart Material Structures, 2017, 26(10).

[16] WU L, ANDRADE M J D, ROME R S, et al. Nylon-muscle-actuated robotic finger[C]. Proceedings of Spie, 2015, 9431: 94310I-1.

[17] CHO K H, SONG M G, JUNG H, et al. A robotic finger driven by twisted and coiled polymer actuator[C]. Proceedings of Spie, 2016, 9798: 97981J-1.

[18] HAINES C S, LI N, SPINKS G M, et al. New twist on artificial muscles[J]. Proceedings of the National Academy of Sciences of the United States of Americe, 2016, 113(42): 11709-11716.

[19] YU W D. Textile materials[M]. 2nd edition. Beijing: China Textile & Apparel Press, 2018:17-18.

Study on the Characterization and Measurement Methods of Helical Nanofiber

WANG Han[1], WANG Jun[1,2], CHEN Xia[1]*

[1] College of Textiles, Donghua University, Shanghai, 201620, China

[2] Key Laboratory of Textile Science & Technology, Ministry of Education, College of Textile, Donghua University, Shanghai, 201620, China

* Corresponding author's email: chenxia@ dhu. edu. cn

Abstract: Fabrics made of nanofiber have many excellent properties, and the helical structure makes it more potential for the development and utilization. It is important to measure the helical degree of Nanofiber. At present, it is the fact that nobody set up a system of helical characterizations and scaling the helical degree is very difficult and not convenient. In this paper, four features of helical fiber are put forward from the electron micrograph of nanofiber: helical inner diameter, helical pitch, helical angle, helicity. The measurement method is the image processing technology.

In order to verify that the accuracy of four features and the accuracy of the measurement method is acceptable, the verification experiments is designed. The helical fibers are simulated by computer, their features are preset and compared with the data which is measured by image processing technology. The results show that the preset data is in accordance with the measured data. It verifies the measurement methods of helical nanofiber is feasible. The single helical fiber is separated from the image of the actual fiber web, and its helical features are measured. The result shows that the characterization of the helical degree are accurate and the measurement methods are convenient.

Keywords: Image processing technology; Helical fiber; Nanofiber; Helical characterization; Computer simulation

1 Introduction

Nanofiber technology has been the focus of research recently in the material science filed, including areas such as textiles, chemical synthesis[1], separation, electronics, and medical devices[2], which covers a broad area of industries[3]. The helical character is one of the most common biological shapes in nature. It is used in DNA and many other micro-structures found in biological cells[1, 4]. Fabrics made of nanofiber have many excellent properties[5], and the helical structure makes it more potential for the development and utilization. It is important to scale the helical degree and measure the properties of nanofiber[6].

The character of the fiber can be improved by the degree of helical features because of its three-dimensional-space[7]. Therefore, measuring the features of helical fiber is very important. At present, many scholars focus on how to grow the helical fiber[8], few pay attention to how to measure the helical degree. How to measure it is not only important in the growth process but also is a key to develop the application of helical fiber.

Image processing is a technology which is using computer to analyze the image from cameras, scanners and other equipment. It is easy and convenient to gain the image than other ways to gain the information. In this study, the image of actual helical fiber web is obtained by the scanning electron microscope. As it is shown in Fig. 1. It is difficult to distinguish the helical degree large or not. Up to now, nobody specially devotes the mind to the characterizations and the measurement methods and there is not a system of helical characterizations as well.

Some features are proposed in the process of the growth as a element to adjust the parameter of the helical fiber, but it is not widely used and the measurement method is

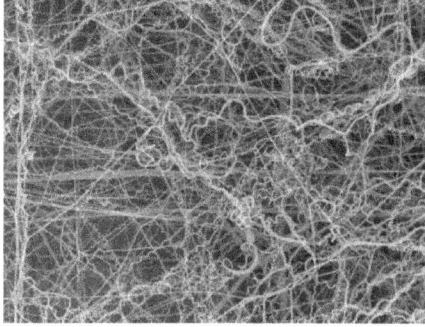

Fig. 1 Actual helical fiber web

difficult. There are two kinds of characterization for the helical degree of the helical fiber. One is the helical angle of a cylinder which is measured by the ruler of the microscope during the process of growth[3-4]. It is difficult to measure and easy to affect the quality of the growth. The other characterization is a mechanical model or a growth model[2]. The model is a hexahedron. The different speeds between the internal surface and the outside surface are used to calculate characterizations of the degree of the helical fiber. The measurement methods are all very difficult.

In this study, four features of helical fiber are put forward from the electron micrograph of nanofiber by image processing technology: helical inner diameter, helical pitch, helical angle, helicity. The image of the helical fiber can be obtained from scanning electron microscope. It is doable and convenient. The image processing technology is used to measure the features from the image in Matlab. It is the measurement method proposed in this study. For it is difficult to verify the accuracy of the features and the accuracy of the method, the verification experiment is designed. In the verification experiment, the helical fibers are simulated by computer, their features are preset and compared with the data which is measured by image processing technology. The results show that the preset data is in accordance with the measured data. The method can be considered accurate and convenient. The four features of helical fiber can be used to measure the helical degree of the fiber in the actual fiber. The measurement method can also be verified that it can apply to different kinds of helical fibers.

2 Model Establishment and Verification Experiments

2.1 Model Establishment

The four features are proposed from the theoretical model. Model establishment can help us easy to understand the meaning of the characterizations of helical fiber. Through the observation on the image of the helical fiber web. The shape of the helical fiber is similar to the curve of cosine function. So principle of Archimedes spiral is applied to the theoretical analysis of helical fiber model. The Archimedes helical curve is a curve in three dimensions. There are two types: cylindrical helical curve and conical helical curve. The cylindrical helical curve is composed of the track of a point which is moving with a uniform speed along the generator of the cylindrical surface. The helical fiber can be considered a cylinder. So the cylindrical helical curve is applied to the formula of the calculation, as it is shown in formula and Fig. 2

$$\begin{cases} x = r\cos(t) \\ y = r\sin(t) \\ z = ct \end{cases}$$

Where: r is the semidiameter of cylinder curve, t is the parameter of polar equation, c is the constant of the curve which can decide the height.

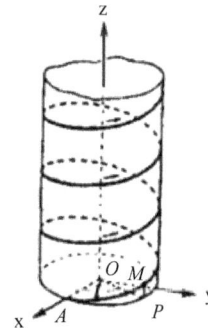

Fig. 2 Cylindrical helical curve

The Archimedes helical curve is in three dimensions, but the image of the helical fiber is in two dimensions. As the image is shown in Fig. 3. So it is necessary to transform the formula to calculate the features of the helical fiber. The transformation of the formula of measuring the features is shown in formula and formula. The formula is on the plane XOZ and the formula(2-3) is on

· 171 ·

the plane *XOY*. The formulas are used in the verification experiments and measurement method. The meaning of the features are shown in Fig. 3.

$$x = r\cos\left(\frac{z}{c}\right)$$

$$[r\sin(t)]^2 + [r\cos(t)]^2 = r^2$$

$$d = 2c\pi$$

$$\alpha = \frac{d}{r}$$

$$k = \frac{L}{D}$$

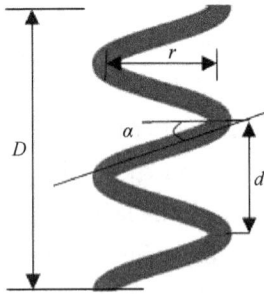

Fig. 3   The features of helical fiber

In the formula, *r* is represented for the inner diameter of the helical fiber, which means the horizontal length of the fiber. The smaller the inner diameter is, the greater the degree of helical features will be. *d* is represented for the pitch of the helical fiber, which means the length of its longitudinal direction. The smaller the pitch is, the larger the degree of helical will be. *α* is represented for the helix angle of the helical fiber, which is between the tangent of the helix on the medium-diameter cylinder and the plane perpendicular to the axis of the thread. The tangent of *α* can be calculated by the ratio of the helical pitch to the inner diameter of the helical fiber. The larger the helical angle is, the smaller the degree of helical fiber will be. In the formula (2-6). *k* is represented for the helicity of the helical fiber, which is the ratio of the total length of the helical fiber to the axial length of the helical fiber. The larger the helicity is, the larger the degree of helical fiber will be. *L* is represented for the total length of the helical fiber. *D* is represented for the length in the axial direction of the helical fiber.

2.2   Verification Experiments

It is difficult to verify the accuracy of the features and the accuracy of the measurement method because there are not the data of the features of the actual helical fiber web and it is difficult to measure the fiber directly. So the verification experiments are designed to measure the accuracy of measurement method. Firstly, the 3D helical fiber is simulated by computer, its four features are preset. The features are shown in Tab. 1. Then the image of 3D helical fiber is changed to the image of 2-dimensional helical fiber. Secondly, four features are measured from the image of simulated fiber by the method of the image processing technology. The measured data is compared with the preset data and the error is calculated and analyzed.

Tab. 1   Features of the 3D helical fiber

Num	Angle (°)	Abs r	Size(mm) d
1	60	15.7	31.25
2	60	11.3	21.82
3	60	13.7	27.97
4	60	11.8	20.65
5	60	16.9	35.7
6	60	14.5	28.76
7	60	7.4	10.8
8	60	15.3	30.95
9	60	9.6	19.78
10	60	16.78	34.6

2.3   Results and Discussions

In the verification experiments, two features are measured because the other features can be calculated from the data of the features measured. The inner diameter and the helical pitch is representative. The result of the verification experiment is in Tab. 2.

As the result is shown in Tab. 2 and Tab. 3, the absolute error and the relative error are calculated by the experiment data and the preset data. They are represented for the miss distance of the measurement method. The result shows that the average of the absolute error is below 0.5 and the relative error is about 2%. The error can be considered in a safe range. The measurement method can be considered accurate and convenient. It can overcome the shortcomings of measurement inaccurate, operation difficult, limitation in the shapes and applications.

Tab. 2　The result of the absolute error

Num	Abs	Size(mm)
	r(AE)	d(AE)
1	0. 5	0. 5
2	0. 34	0. 52
3	0. 2	0. 58
4	0. 3	0. 65
5	0. 6	0. 8
6	0. 5	0. 46
7	0. 2	0. 1
8	0. 4	0. 37
9	0. 1	0. 22
10	0. 5	0. 7
AVR	0. 36	0. 49

Tab. 3　The result of the relative error

Num	Abs	Size(%)
	r(RE)	d(RE)
1	3. 18	1. 6
2	3. 01	2. 38
3	1. 46	2. 07
4	2. 54	3. 15
5	3. 55	2. 24
6	3. 45	1. 6
7	2. 7	0. 93

Continued

Num	Abs	Size(%)
	r(RE)	d(RE)
8	2. 61	1. 19
9	1. 04	1. 11
10	2. 98	2. 02
AVR	2. 652	1. 829

The error as follow is the main and direct source of errors in the experiment:

1. The figure of fiber in the image is made up of pixels. When the fiber is rotated, the number of the pixel will be changed because the direction is converted from the horizontal to the vertical direction. Half is counted as one when calculating the number of the pixels. D and L are the length of the helical fiber, which are calculated by the diameter of the fiber and the number of the pixel of the fiber figure.

2. When the curve is smoothened in the process of measuring the features, the coordinate point of the peak and the valley of the curve will be affected by changing the parameters of the low-pass filter. But the error is small and can be acceptable.

3　Experiment on Actual Fiber

3. 1　Measurement Method of Helical Fiber

In this whole study, image processing technology in Matlab is used to measure the features of the helical fiber. The detailed procedures of measuring method is shown in Fig. 4.

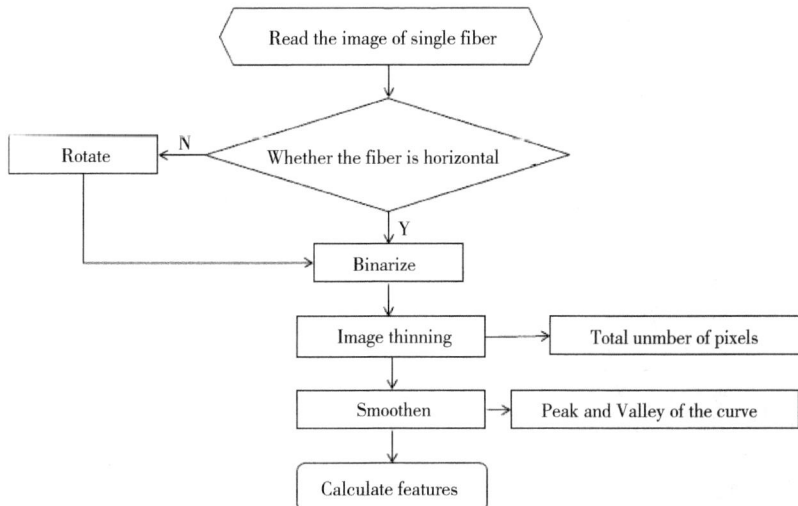

Fig. 4　Measurement procedure

Step1: Extract the single fiber out the actual fiber web and judge the shape of the whole fiber whether it is horizontal or not. The actual fiber web is shown in Fig. 5 and the single fiber is shown in Fig. 6.

Step2: If the fiber is not horizontal as shown in Fig. 6 (a), the angle of inclination will be calculated and the fiber is rotated to be in the horizontal position. It is beneficial to fit it with a curve.

Step3: Transform the image into a binary image and find the figure which is included the largest connected area of the fiber. For it can clear away the hairiness and ensure to get a complete image of the fiber.

Step4: The pixel points of the image make up a matrix. The data in the matrix constitute the coordinates in the coordinate system. The figure of the helical fiber is made up with the white pixel points. Extract the coordinates of the pixel points of the fiber and record the number of fiber pixel points. Thin the figure as much as possible in order that the figure of the helical fiber is made up with a single line of pixel points. Count the number of the white pixel points of the final fiber. The ratio of two numbers is the diameter of the fiber.

Step5: The coordinates of the fiber make up a curve. Smoothen the curve and then obtained the peak and valley of the curve to calculate the features.

3.2 Experimental Process

Firstly, the single helical fibers in Fig. 6 are extracted from the actual multilayer fiber web as shown in Fig. 5. The image of actual helical fiber web is from scanning electron microscope with an amplification factor of 4.5 k. Secondly, the features are measured by the image processing method. The features can be used to analyze the corresponding relationship between the result and the shape of the fiber in the image. At least 50 effective data of the single fibers are obtained, Fig. 5 and Fig. 6 are

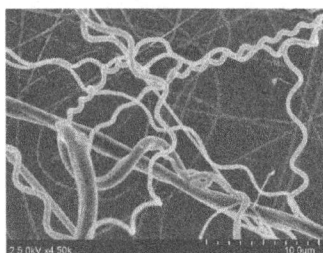

Fig. 5   The actual fiber web

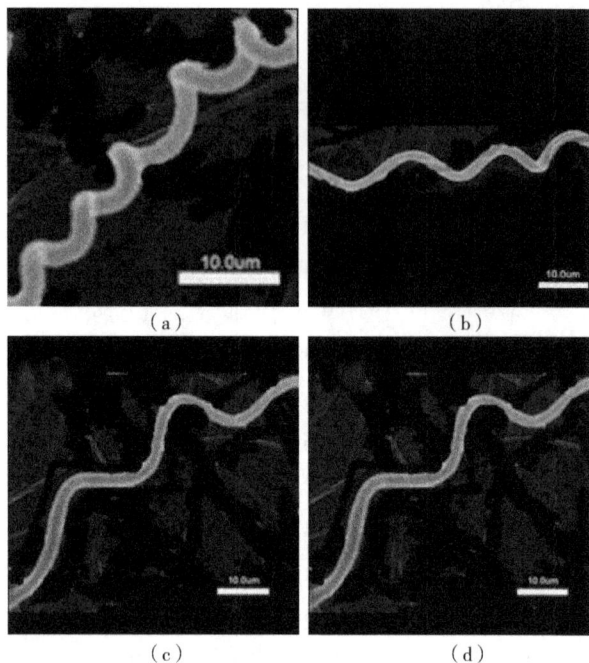

Fig. 6   The single fiber from actual fiber web

the examples to verify that the features can show the helical degree of the helical fiber.

4   Results and Discussions

The helical degree of the helical fiber in this paper is like tightening the twisted wet towel. If the towel is twisted hard, it may be considered high helical degree of the helical fiber.

As it is shown in Fig. 6 and Tab. 4, Fig. 6 is arranged by the helical degree from large to small. The result in the Tab. 4 can be drawn a conclusion that as the helical degree of fiber is smaller, the inner diameter of the helical fiber will be larger, the helical pitch will be larger, the helical angle will also be larger but the helicity will be smaller.

Tab. 4   The result of experiment on actual fiber

Sample	Helicity	Angle(°)	Abs	Size(mm)
			r	d
a	1.97	32.67	10.43	340.89
b	1.96	34.34	18.55	774.4
c	1.82	41.74	26.94	1033
d	1.15	44.85	30.08	1208.17

It can also be concluded that the greater the degree of

helical fiber is, the smaller the inner diameter of the helical fiber is, the smaller the helical pitch is, the smaller the helical angle is and the larger the helicity is.

5 Conclusions

The helical fibers with different features can be simulated by computer. Their preset features are compared with the data which is measured by image processing technology. The results show that the preset data is in accordance with the measured data. The measurement methods of helical nanofiberis verified feasible, accurate and convenient. The measurement method is applied to measure the real image of single fiber which is extracted from the multilayer fiber web. The result shows that the characterization of the helical degree is representative, quantifiable and measurable.

References

[1]KUN Z, YUQING W. Biomimetic study on helical fiber composites[J]. Journal of Materials Science & Technology, 1998.

[2]JOBIN J, HENG M K, MARTIN J, et al. Clinical evaluation of left ventricular function using the cardiac helical fiber model: an echocardiographic study[J]. American Heart Journal, 1985, 110(6).

[3]DOSHI J, RENEKER D H. Electrospinning process and applications of electrospun fibers[J]. Journal of Electrostatics, 1995, 35(2).

[4]LIXIN W, YUHONG C, QINGHUA Q, et al. Helical fiber Pull-out in biological materials[J]. Acta Mechanica Solida Sinica, 2016(03).

[5]RITA AMBRUS, AREEN ALSHWEIAT, ILDIKO CSOKA, et al. 3D-printed electrospinning setup for the preparation of loratadine nanofibers with enhanced physicochemical properties [J]. International Journal of Pharmaceutics, 2019, 567.

[6]HUISI W, CHUNYING G, DI G, et al. Loss characteristics of helical-core fiber[J]. Optoelectronics Letters, 2012(04).

[7]JIANSHAN W, YUAN L, LIXIN W, et al. Numerical study on helical fiber fragmentation in chiral biological materials [J]. Transactions of Tianjin University, 2018(01).

[8]KULPINSKI P. Cellulose nanofibers prepared by the N-methylmorpholine-N-oxide method[J]. Journal of Applied Polymer Science, 2005.

Fully-Recyclable High-Performance Carbon Fiber Reinforced Composites

HAFEEZULLAH Memon[1,2], LIU Wanshuang[1,2*], WEI Yi[1,2]

[1] *Donghua University Center for Civil Aviation Composites, Donghua University, Shanghai, 201620, China.*

[2] *College of Textiles, Donghua University, Shanghai, 201620, China.*

* *Corresponding author's email*: wsliu@ dhu. edu. cn

Abstract: The thermosets possess superior mechanical properties and solvent resistance, however, they fail to be reshaped or recycled once they cured. The fully-recyclable high-performance carbon fiber reinforced composites can be prepared using dynamic imine chemistry. In this study, we synthesized bio-based epoxy curing agent from lignin-derived vanillin and later fabricated carbon fiber reinforced composites from the resin. The chemical structure was confirmed by FTIR and ^{1}H-NMR. The curing behavior and thermomechanical analysis were studied by DSC and DMA, respectively. The mechanical properties of the CFRCs from uncured prepregs and cured prepregs were examined. Finally, gentle reclamation of carbon fiber was realized by depolymerization of the resin through transamination.

Keywords: Carbon fiber reinforced composites; Imine bonds; Full recyclability; SBSS

1 Introduction

Advanced high-performance thermosetting epoxy resin matrix composites have ascertained its importance into high-tech applications owing to their superior mechanical properties i. e. higher specific strength and specific stiffness, high dimensional stability and higher creep/chemical resistance[1]. Their far-reaching consumption has also lead to an influential magnitude of waste, suggesting the regaining and retrieving of carbon fiber from advanced carbon fiber reinforced thermosetting epoxy resin matrix composites[2-3]. But, re-claiming of carbon fiber from three-dimensional permanent crosslinked network structure with good mechanical, thermal and chemical properties without affecting the properties of carbon fiber in a useful nondestructive manner seem prospective research goal[4-5]. It is conflicting demand, to develop advanced high-performance thermosetting composites i. e. stable at extraordinary temperature, pressure and oxidation conditions, while degradable and recyclable under mild conditions[6], without the release of any internal curing material[7].

To answer this debate, an awe-inspiring chemical strategy of structurally dynamic polymers with exchangeable chemical bonds are known as covalent adaptable networks (CANs), as well, has been proposed recently[8]. Changes of chemical crosslinks at different sites of the polymer chains resulting in an overall macroscopic flow of protecting perpetual forfeiture of material's properties.

Herein, we synthesized a novel epoxy curing agent from lignin-derived vanillin which may be cured with commercially available epoxies and have a higher glass transition temperature 120 °C, comparable other properties to existing hardeners. This imine based hardener along with commercially available epoxy was used to fabricate carbon fiber reinforced composites. The CFRCs showed comparable short beam shear and flexural properties to those of their commercial counterparts. Nondestructive reclamation of carbon fibers from the CFRCs was accomplished by depolymerization of the resin into amine solution.

2 Experimental

2.1 Materials

Vanillin was purchased from Sinopharm Reagent Co. Ltd. , China. Isophorone Diamine was provided by Shenzhen Yexu Industrial Co. Ltd, China. Diglycidyl ether of ethylene glycol (EGDGE) was from Shenzhen Vita Chemicals Co. Ltd, China, and the diglycidyl ether of Bisphenol A (DGEBA), was purchased from Jiangsu Sanmu Chemical Industry, China. 2, 4, 6-Tris (dimethyl aminomethyl) phenol (DMP-30) and Tetra-hydrofuran (THF) were purchased from Shanghai Lingfeng Chemical Reagent Co. Ltd. , China. All the chemicals were of analytical grade and were used as received. The carbon fabric (T700-12K) used in this study had the areal density of $408g/m^2$ and was provided by Jiangsu Heng shen Fiber Material Co. , Ltd. China.

2.2 Synthesis of Imine Based Hardener

32g of vanillin dissolved into ethanol was added to 108 g of IPDA and stirred for 3 hours at 60℃ under nitrogen. After evaporation of ethanol and excessive IPDA, the yellow powdered imine based hardener was obtained. The final product was purified using a single-solvent recrystallization process by using ethyl acetate as a solvent.

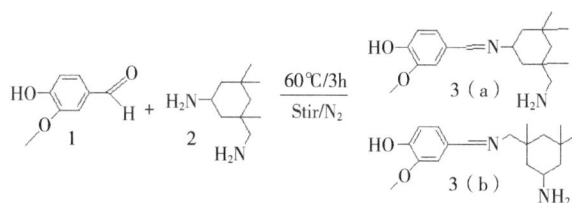

Fig. 1 Synthesis of imine based hardener

2.3 Preparation of Cured Resin Networks

To ease processing, DGEBA and EGDGE were mixed in the weight percent proportions of 60 and 40, respectively. EEW_{DGEBA} and EEW_{EGDGE} were $190g/m^2$ and $154g/m^2$, respectively. Thus the final EEW of the blend was $173.7g/m^2$, determined according to ASTM D1652. In order to achieve fully cured thermosets, 1% DMP-30 was also added into the reaction system. Since amine hydrogen equivalent weight (AHEW) was $101.47g/m^2$, thus, the phr was found to be 58.42. All the samples were pre-cured for 1 hour at 80℃, cured

for 2 hours at 140℃, followed by post-cure for 1 hour at 170℃, and possess uniform appearance, indicating the lack of macroscopic separation.

2.3 Preparation of Carbon Fiber Prepregs

In a 40cm×30cm aluminumplate, 57.2g of imine based hardener (dissolved into THF), 92.8g of the epoxy mixture and 1.5g of DMP-30 were uniformly mixed. At that time, carbon fabrics (26cm×22cm) were immersed in the epoxy solution. The resin content was controlled by the adjustment of the distance of press cudgel to make the resin content up to 40%. The B-stage resin was produced in 80℃ for 7min.

2.4 Fabrication of CFRCs

Eight pieces of carbon fiber prepregs were stacked, then the whole assembly was placed between two aluminum sheets coated with polytetrafluoroethylene (PTFE) and compressed in hot press 80℃ for 1h, 140℃ for 2h, 170℃ for 1h in the press of 0.2MPa. The obtained CFRPs was named as C1 as shown in Fig. 2. Another eight layers of prepregs were cured separately in an oven (80℃ for 1h, 140℃ for 2h, and 170℃ for 1h). After curing, the cured prepregs were stacked together and put on a hot press machine at a pressure of 5MPa for 1 hour. The obtained CFRPs was named as C2.

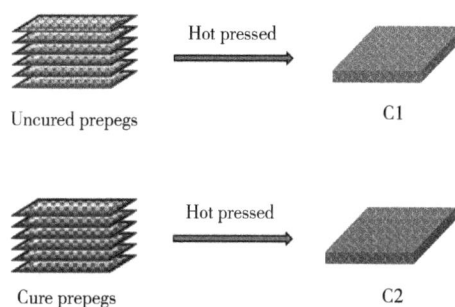

Fig. 2 Demonstration for the fabrication of carbon fiber reinforced composites

2.5 Characterization

The ^{1}H-NMR analysis were done using Bruker Ascend TM 600 spectrometer using DMSO as a solvent. FTIR spectra were analyzed by Fourier-transform infrared spectroscopy by Perkin Elmer at room temperature ranged from $4000cm^{-1}$ to $600cm^{-1}$. The differential scanning calorimetry (DSC) was performed using a NETZSCH DSC 214, under nitrogen atmosphere

(20mL/min) and were heated from 25℃ to 200℃ at a rate of 10℃/min. Dynamic mechanical analyses (DMA) were carried out on a DMA Q800, TA Instruments, New Castle, DE, USA. Surface morphology and cross-sectional analysis of tested coupons were observed on a Hitachi S4800 scanning electron microscope (SEM). Mechanical properties of the epoxy resin and CFRPs were tested on a universal testing machine 203B-TS (Shenzhen Wance). The SBSS and flexural tests were conducted following ASTM D 2344 and ASTM D 790, respectively. Hot press testing machine (HY-10TK, Shanghai Hengshan) was used to prepare CFRP samples.

3 Results and Discussions

3.1 Characterization of Hardener

The results of FTIR and ^{1}H-NMR spectra confirm the structure of synthetic curing agent. FTIR spectrum as shown in Fig. 3, reveals the characteristic absorption bands of the stretching vibration of primary amine and phenol groups of synthetic curing agent at ca. 3430cm^{-1} and phenol of groups of vanillin at ca. 3170cm^{-1}, and a benzene groups ring stretching vibration band at ca.

1520cm^{-1} and 1600cm^{-1} for both synthetic curing agent and vanillin. FTIR spectrum confirms the formation imine since the band at 1640cm^{-1} can be assigned to C=N stretching vibration, indicating the formation of the imine bond. The absence of ca. 1693cm^{-1} and 2952cm^{-1} related to stretching vibration of H and ca. 1663cm^{-1} related to carbonyl and the band at 1199cm^{-1} and 1204cm^{-1} can be assigned to phenolic hydroxyl group.

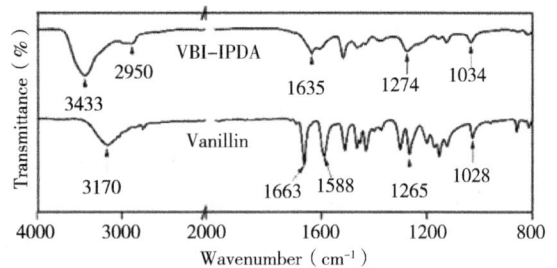

Fig. 3 FTIR analysis of vanillin and imine based hardener

In order to further identify its structure, the ^{1}H-NMR of imine based hardener is presented below in Fig. 4. The resonance peak at δ 8.16 and δ 8.24 are assigned to benzylidenimine (—CH=N—) proton of imine based hardener.

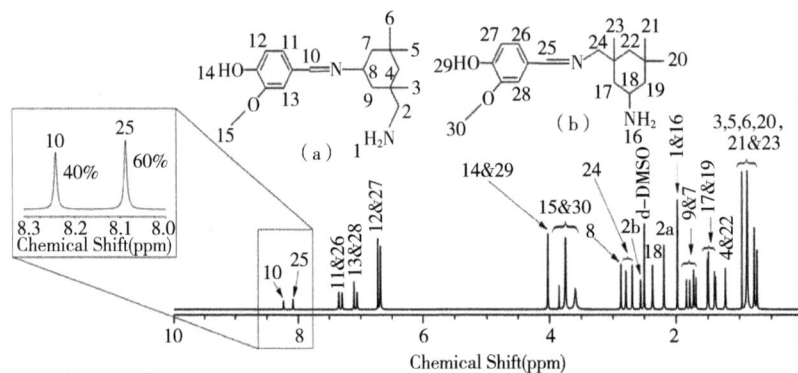

Fig. 4 The ^{1}H-NMR analysis of imine based hardener

Since produced imine was a mixture of two structural isomers, thus it was essential to determine the ratio between both isomers. This was accomplished by analyzing the area under the curve at given positions. Analyzing the ^{1}H-NMR spectrum of imine based hardener, shown in Fig. 4, it can be seen that (a) was produced 40% whereas there was 60% of (b).

3.2 Curing and Thermomechanical Properties of the Resin

The curing of imine based was investigated by DSC in a non-isothermal mode, and is shown in Fig. 5. Since the activities of the two groups (phenolic hydroxyl group and primary amines) are entirely different. The activity of the phenolic hydroxyl group is relatively low, so imidazole accelerator is added. In result, a sharp exothermic peak at which curing agent can react with the epoxy groups in the resin was found.

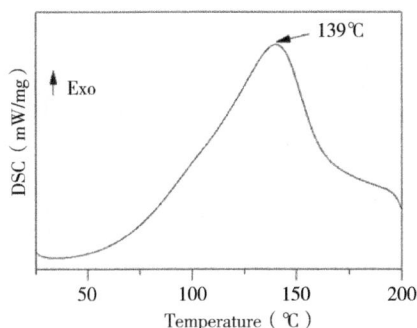

Fig. 5 Non-isothermal differential scanning calorimetric curve of resin

The storage modulus and loss modulus as a function of temperature for the curedimine based resin are shown in Fig. 6. The temperature at the maximum tan δ value is often taken as glass-transition temperature. As can be seen, the Tg value of cured imine based resin is 124℃. The storage modulus at room temperature is around 2500MPa, which is similar to the conventional epoxy and much higher than many reported recyclable epoxy resins.

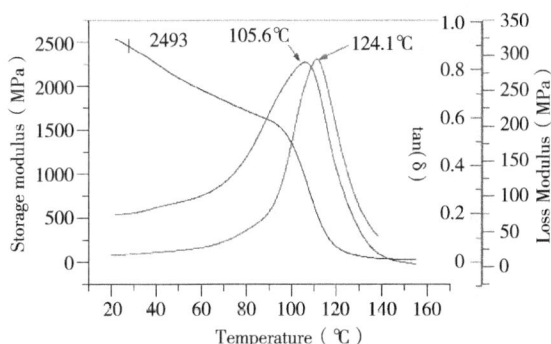

Fig. 6 Thermomechanical analysis of imine based resin

3.3 Enduring Prepregs

Two types of composites were prepared i. e. the composites from uncured prepregs C1 and the composites from cured prepregs C2. Even the carbon fiber prepregs were cured, they can still be hot pressed into C2 by the exchange reaction through dynamic covalent imine bonds in its imine based resin matrix. Moreover, C2

maintains specific mechanical properties. So the carbon fiber prepregs with imine based resin matrix can be stored at room temperature for a long time.

The short beam shear strength of both of the composites-was comparable, as presented in Tab. 1, suggest that for both the resins there had a considerable interface between carbon and resin. Moreover, during the formation of C2 the melt viscosity of the resin was slightly higher during curing reaction occurred in advance. The higher melt viscosity might act as steric hindrance for penetration, thus has slightly decreased the interface.

Tab. 1 SBSS and flexural properties of composites

	SBSS	Flexural strength	Flexural modulus
C1	33.57 ±0.98	654.16 ±14.65	62.14 ±1.66
C2	32.38 ±1.94	309.58 ±9.95	34.20 ±1.87

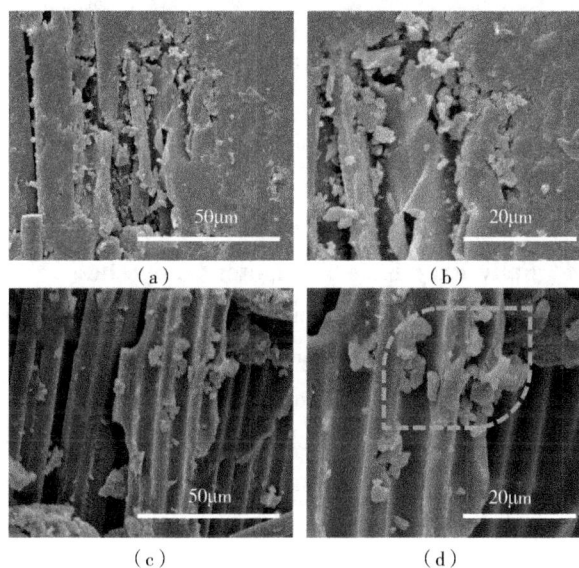

Fig. 7 Surface morphology of fracture surfaces by short beam shear strength test of (a) C1 at 1500×;(b) C1 at 3000×; (c) C2 at 1500×;(d) C2 at 3000 ×

During interlaminar shear strengthtest, the resin from one side has been pulled and attached to the opposite side [Fig. 7(d)], which suggest dynamic bond exchange has occurred between two adjacent cured prepregs.

The mechanical properties of C2 are inferior to C1 in both flexural strength and flexural modulus. This is mainly due to the fact that the prepreg surface which was directly cured without pression is not smooth, so the surface of different prepregs cannot be contacted entirely when hot pressed into a CFRP, resulting in many non-healing voids[Fig. 8(c)and(d)], causes less adhesion between the prepregs, thereby affecting the flexural strength and modulus of the CFRP.

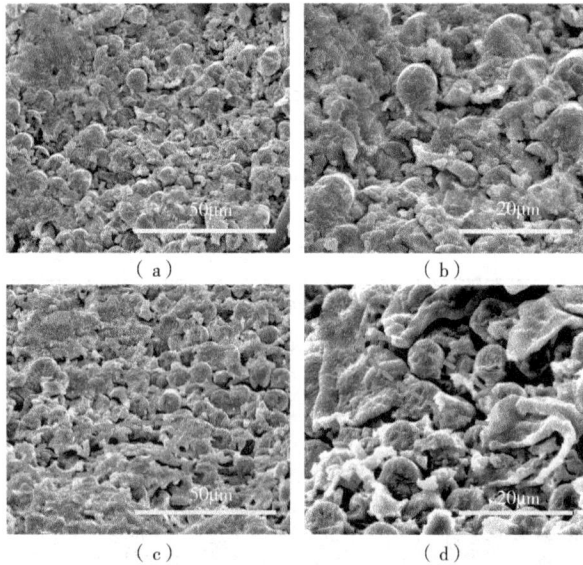

Fig. 8   SEM images of crossectional view for fracture surfaces of (a) C1 at 1500×;(b) C1 at 3000×;(c) C2 at 1500×;(d) C2 at 3000 ×

3.4   Fully Recyclable Thermoset Composites

As shown in Fig. 9, a small piece of eight-layered CFRP was put into IPDA and ethanol solution. The resin matrix in CFRP can be completely degraded by heating at 60℃ for 24h. The obtained carbon fibers were then cleaned in the ethanol and dried in the oven. The microscale morphology of pristine and reclaimed carbon

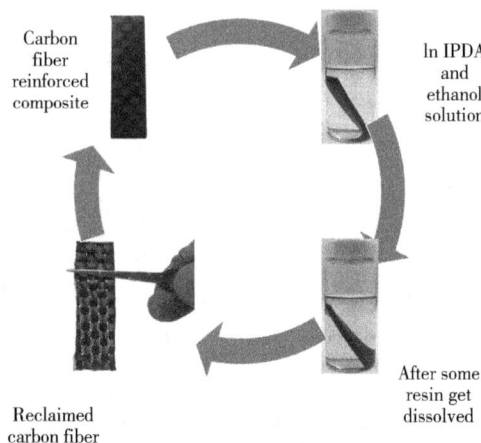

Fig. 9   Demonstration of the full recyclability of carbon fiber reinforced composites

shown in Fig. 10 proves that there is no visible damage or alternation in the fiber dimension. It is also seen that the carbon fiber surfaces become prominent and the whole the resin was dissolved into the solution.

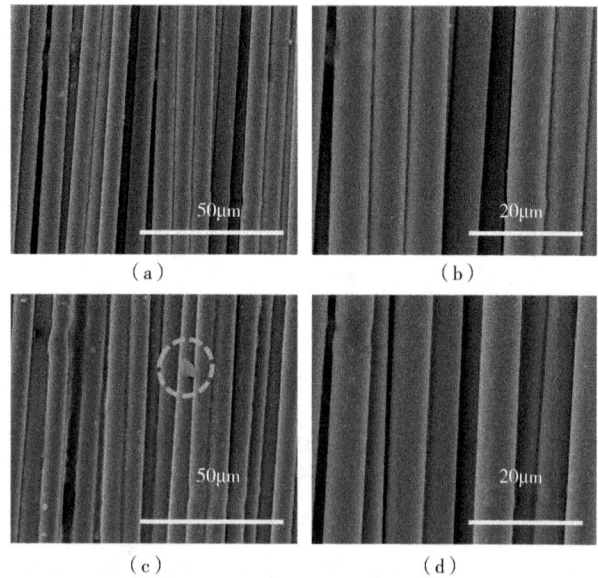

Fig. 10   Surface morphological analysis of (a) pristine at 1500 ×;(b) pristine at 3000×;(c) reclaimed at 1500×;(d) reclaimed at 3000×carbon fiber

It can also be seen that a tiny amount of polymer is attached to the carbon fiber surface in Fig. 10(c).

4   Conclusions

This study focused on the manufacturing of bio-based eco-friendly recyclable thermosetting resin. The epoxy curing agent showed similar properties to the existing commercial curing agents. The glass transition temperature of the resin was above 120℃. Short beam shear strength and flexural properties from uncured prepregs and cured prepregs were studied. These composites are fully recyclable chemically degradable due to transamination reactions by imine bonds. The results suggest that there is a strong potential of these recyclable composites to replace existing nonrecyclable composites.

Acknowledgements

This work was supported by the Shanghai Science and Technology Committee (No. 16DZ112140)

References

[1] PILATO L A, MICHNO M J. Advanced composite materials[M] Berlin: Springer,1994.

[2] PICKERING S J. Recycling technologies for thermoset composite materials—current status[J]. Composites Part A: Applied Science and Manufacturing, 2006,37(8):1206-1215.

[3] PIMENTA S, PINHO S T. Recycling carbon fibre reinforced polymers for structural applications: technology review and market outlook[J]. Waste Management,2011,31(2):378-392.

[4] YANG Y, BOOM R, IRION B,et al. Recycling of composite materials[M]. Chemical Engineering and Processing: Process Intensification,2012,51:53-68.

[5] OLIVEUX G, DANDY L O, LEEKE G A. Current status of recycling of fibre reinforced polymers: review of technologies, reuse and resulting properties[J]. Progress in Materials Science,2015,72:61-99.

[6] GARCÍA J M, JONES G O, VIRWANI K, et al. Recyclable, strong thermosets and organogels via paraformaldehyde condensation with diamines[J]. Science,2014,344(6185): 732-735.

[7] ZHAO Z, ARRUDA E M. An internal cure for damaged polymers[J]. Science, 2014, 344(6184): 591-592.

[8] KLOXIN C J, BOWMAN C N. Covalent adaptable networks: smart, reconfigurable and responsive network systems [J]. Chemical Society Reviews, 2013,42(17):7161-7173.

Recyclable Carbon Fiber Reinforced Composites Enabled by An Imine-Containing Epoxy Resin

LIU Haiyang [1,2], **GAO Jiarui** [1,2], **JIANG Qiuran**[1], **LIU Wanshuang** [1,2*],
QIU Yiping [1,2], **WEI Yi** [1,2*]

[1] *Key Laboratory of Textile Science &Technology, Ministry of Education, College of Textiles, Donghua University, 2999 North Renmin Road, Shanghai, 201620, China*

[2] *Collaborative Innovation Center for Civil Aviation Composites, Donghua University, Shanghai, 201620, China*

[*] *Corresponding author's email*：wsliu@ dhu. edu. cn（W. Liu）, weiy@ dhu. edu. cn（Y. Wei）

Abstract：In this work, a novel imine-containing epoxy resin with recyclability and high performance was facilely prepared through the curing reaction between aldehyde-containing epoxide and diamine hardener. The structure of synthesized aldehyde-containing epoxide was characterized by Fourier-transform infrared spectroscopy, NMR spectroscopy and GC-MS spectroscopy. The results of DMA tests show that the glass transition temperature of the prepared epoxy resin is 125℃. Carbon fiber reinforced composites（CFRPs）was fabricated using this epoxy resin as matrix. The resulting CFRPs can be repaired after bending failure. Moreover, the carbon fibers can be recycled by the degradation of epoxy matrix.

Keywords：Epoxy resins; Carbon fiber reinforced composites; Imine bonds; Recyclability

1 Introduction

For decades, carbon fiber reinforced polymer composites（CFRPs）have become widely employed in aerospace industries, automobile industries, military manufacture, wind energy applications, transportation, sports equipment due to a combination of high modulus, specific stiffness, size stability, strong designability and durability and so on[1]. It should be pointed out that CFRPs could effectively reduce the size and weight of engineering components because of an excellent specific strength[2]. Therefore, their use in lightweight structures will strongly decrease the ratio of energy waste and increase conservation of resources. It is in this sense that constant requirement for fuel-efficient vehicles and environmental protection regulations for low CO_2 emissions will make explosive growth of the CFRPs market[3]. Extensive use of CFRPs generates the huge amount of waste, including leftovers, unused prepregs and end-of-life components, which lead to a series of significant economic and environmental impacts. A problem has aroused wide public concern is that how to retrieve carbon fibers（CFs）from these waste without any damage, owing to the high cost of CFs and their huge volume in CFRCs（up to 70%）[4]. The first choice of getting structural performance is carbon-reinforced thermoset epoxy composites. However, due to the crosslinking structure of thermosetting resin matrices, once these materials were damaged, it could not be repaired, remolded, reshaped or dissolved when the thermoset composites were cured and the high-cost CFs inside could not be recycle[5]. Hence, these waste of thermoset epoxy composites could not be disposed in a environmental and economical way. Therefore, the recycle of CFs and resin matrices in an effective and safe way remains a challenge.

To date, several different recycling methods including mechanical recycling[6], thermal processes[7], and solvolysis[8] have been brought forward. However, these advanced recycling techniques generally destroy the carbon fibers in different extent, which would have a great adverse impact their commercial value. One way to recycle or degrade epoxy resin is introducing dynamic covalent bond[9], including ester bonds, disulfide linkages, sulfonate ester linkages, imine bonds and olefinic bonds. Dynamic covalent bond can be reversibly formed and destroyed under external stimulation, enable the polymer networks to have stress relaxation ability, self-healing ability, reprocessing ability and adaptability. Vitrimers have a high T_g, good mechanical properties and the ability to be manufactured very fast above T_g. Therefore, it is the polymer matrices extremely suitable for the manufacture of fiber reinforced polymer composites. However, if vitrimers have a high T_g and good mechanical properties, the recovery of the broken materials is very low.

Herein, a novel imine-containing epoxy resin with recyclability and high performance was facilely prepared through the in situ formation of schiff base during the curing process between aldehyde-containing epoxide and diamine hardener. CFRPs was fabricated using this epoxy resin as matrix. The repairability of resulting CFRPs and recovery of the carbon fiber were explored.

2 Experiments

2.1 Materials

Deonized water, acetone, dichloromethane, sodium sulfate (anhydrous), sodium hydroxide (NaOH), epichorohydrin (ECH), 4-Hydroxybenzaldehyde (PA) were purchased from Sinopharm Chemical Reagent Co., Ltd., China. 1, 3-Cyclohexanebis (methylamine) (CBMA) was purchased from Sun Chemical Technology (Shanghai) Co., Ltd. Any chemicals were used as purchased without further purification. T700 carbon fiber was purchased from Jiangsu Hengshen Fiber Material Co., Ltd.

2.2 Synthesis of Epoxidated *p*-Hydroxy Benzaldehyde (EPA)

p-Hydroxybenzaldehyde (12.2g, 0.1mol) was dissolved in 4mol/L NaOH (60mL). Epichlorohydrin (27.7g, 0.3mol) was added dropwise to the solution stirred at 0℃. Reaction mixture was stirred 24h at room temperature. The solution was extracted washed three times with dichloromethane (50mL) and the combined organic phases washed three times with deionized water (100mL). The organic phase was dried with anhydrous MgSO$_4$, and then the MgSO$_4$ is completely filtered. The solvent and the excess epichlorohydrin was distilled off under reduced pressure. A yellow liquid was obtained. The synthetic route is shown in Fig. 1.

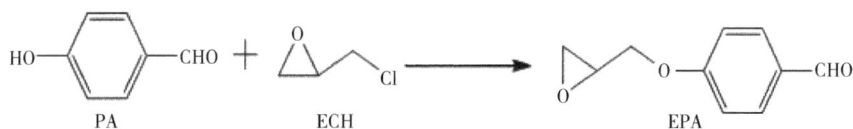

Fig. 1　The synthetic route of the EPA

2.3 Curing Procedure of the Epoxy Resin

EPA (7.1g, 0.04mol) was directly mixed with CBMA (4.2g, 0.03mol) to obtain very high viscosity epoxy at 0℃, and the mixture was cured in oven at 80℃ and 150℃ for 2h, respectively. The obtained faint yellow solid was crushed to get the faint yellow powder by the grinding machine. The powder was pressed in an iron mould at 150℃ for 0.5h at a pressure of 0.3MPa to obtain the cured epoxy resin.

2.4 Preparation of Carbon Fiber Prepregs

As for plain weave CF cloth, EPA (14.2g, 0.08mol), CBMA (8.2g, 0.06mol), acetone (5.8g, 0.10mol) were added into a flask and continuously magnetically stirred atroom temperature under a gentle nitrogen flow for 10min. A pre-cleaned aluminum tray covered with a piece of carbon fiber cloth (40cm×40cm) was prepared in advance. After reacting for 20 minutes, the solution was spread onto the carbon fiber cloth. The pre-polymer was further cured and removed acetone sequentially at 80℃ for 2h and 150℃ for 2h. After that, the carbon fiber prepregs were peeled off from the aluminum tray.

2.5 Preparation of CFRPs

The CFRPs were prepared by hand lay-up and hot-pressing techniques. A carbon fiber prepreg was cut into 4 equal pieces, which were stacked together and put into the interlayer of 2 layers aluminium plate. And the 2 layers aluminium plate including carbon fiber prepregs were put on a hot press machine with a pressure of 0.5MPa at 150℃ for 0.5h. After cutting the composite laminate edges and angle with an electric motor saw, all composite test specimens were easily obtained, grinding and polishing.

2.6 Characterization

Gas chromatography-mass (GC-MS) spectroscopy was performed by using a GCMS-QP2010 Ultra. The GC column oven was initially held at 40℃ for 3min, followed by a ramp at 15℃/min and a hold at 280℃ for 5min under a gentle nitrogen flow. Mass spectrometry was conducted with electron ionization at 70eV, source temperature at 200℃ and interface temperature at 280℃. Fourier- transform infrared (FTIR) spectroscopy was conducted on a Thermo Scientific Nicolet 6700 FTIR spectrometer with a Thermo Scientific Smart ATR sampling accessory. ^{1}H-NMR and ^{13}C-NMR spectroscopy were recorded on Bruker AVANCE III HD 600 MHz spectrometers at 600 MHz and 400 MHz in deuterated solvents (CDCl$_3$). Dynamic mechanical analysis (DMA) was performed on a TA DMA Q800 in the dual cantilever geometry. Heating ramps were conducted at 3℃/min. Differential scanning calorimeter (DSC) was performed on a NETZECH 214 at a heating rate of 10℃/min. Flexural tests were performed on a Wance ETM104B-EX electronic universal testing machine, following ASTM D7264. Scanning electron microscope (SEM) was performed on a Hitachi S4800.

3 Results and Discussions

3.1 Characterization of EPA

The chemical structure of the synthesized epoxy monomers was confirmed by FTIR, GC-MS, ^{1}H-NMR, and ^{13}C-NMR. In the spectrum of pristine PA, the characteristic absorption peak at 3164cm^{-1} and 1664cm^{-1} are due to the stretching vibrations of O—H and C=O in the aldehyde groups, respectively. In the case of EPA, two additional absorption peaks at 1028^{-1} and 915cm^{-1} corresponding to the stretching vibration of oxirane rings in EPA are observed and the stretching vibrations of O—H and C=O disappear in the spectra of in the case of EPA, indicating that O—H in PA were completely epoxided by ECH. The absorption peak at 1687cm^{-1} related to C=O in the aldehyde groups keeps nearly same as it in PA.

The result of GC-MS shows that the purity of obtained EPA is 96.5%, suggesting the good selectivity of the synthesis. EPA was characterized by ^{1}H-NMR and ^{13}C-NMR spectra. As can be seen, the chemical shift of all the peaks match well with the protons and carbons of chemical structures for EPA. The above results indicate that the EPA was synthesized successfully.

3.2 Curing and Thermal Mechanical Properties of CBMA-EPA

EPA was cured with CBMA at a fixed stoichiometric ratio (epoxy/CBMA) of 4/3. The complete cure was confirmed by FTIR. The bands corresponding to the epoxy group at 915cm^{-1} (C—O stretching of the oxirane ring) disappears and stretching band of the hydroxy group (H—O stretching of the oxirane ring) at 3305cm^{-1} appears for the cured epoxy resin, indicating that the curing was complete. This result can also be supported by the data from differential scanning calorimetry (DSC) test. No excess exothermic peak was observed in the DSC curve of cured epoxy resin.

The thermo-mechanical properties of the cured epoxy resin was investigated by DMA. Storage modulus reflects the elastic properties or the energy storage of polymers. As shown in Fig. 2, the storage modulus of CBMA-EPA at room temperature shown in Fig. 2 is around 3500MPa, which is comparable to the conventional epoxy and much higher than many reported recyclable epoxy resins. Furthermore, the storage modulus in rubber region (15MPa at 150℃) confirms the presence of a polymer network, which is attributed to chemically cross-linked systems. The tanδ is defined as the ratio of loss modulus to the storage modulus, and the peak of the tanδ versus temperature curve is often used to determine the glass transition temperature (T_g). The T_g of the cured epoxy resin is 127℃, which is reasonable for the application of epoxy reins. To our best knowledge, the T_g of this epoxy resin is higher than most reported vitrimers based on dynamic covalent bonds.

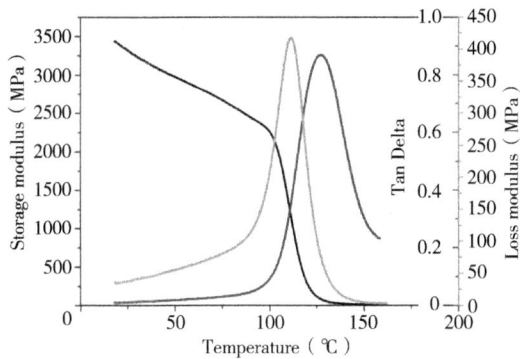

Fig. 2 Storage modulus, loss modulus and tan δ versus temperature curves of the cured epoxy resin

3.3 CFRPs Based on the Imine-Containing Epoxy Resin

As discussed in the introduction, CFRPs have become widely employed in industrial sectors, due to their excellent performance in structural materials. However, the difficulties of CFRPs in repairing and recycling, which are intrinsic to their cross-linked network, limit their fast growth in many applications. In the following sections, the properties of CFRPs based on CBMA—EPA are investigated.

Prepreg is a kind of reinforced materials impregnated in an epoxy resin matrix, which is widely used in the manufacture of thermosetting composite components. The dynamic nature of CBMA—EPA described here would permit the fabrication of a new type of "durable prepreg", since fully cured prepreg sheets can still be used in the manufacture of multilayer composite parts. The "durable prepreg" shown in Fig. 3 have many advantages that is very different from the conventional prepreg. For example, there is no need for protective release films in B-stage. The "durable prepreg" need not to be stored in low-temperature environment (−18℃), having the prepreg a permanent shelf-life and out-life.

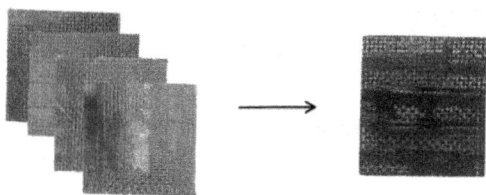

Fig. 3 Photographs of prepregs and corresponding CFRPs based on CBMA-EPA resin

High performance thermosetting composite materials are vulnerable to various kinds of damages, such as impacts, fractures, (micro) cracks and so on. At present, the repair technology of composite materials not only requires special technology, but also needs skilled workers, which costs a lot of manpower and material resources. It may not be repaired for common fractures failures in CFRPs. An approach to improve this situation could be the application of a dynamic CBMA—EPA, which could self-healing partly by hot-press. As shown in Fig. 4, the repaired composites after flexure test have partly recover the flexure strength and flexure modulus because of the damage of the carbon fibers in resin matrix. Therefore, the result indicates that the application of a dynamic CBMA—EPA to repair CFRPs is a feasible way.

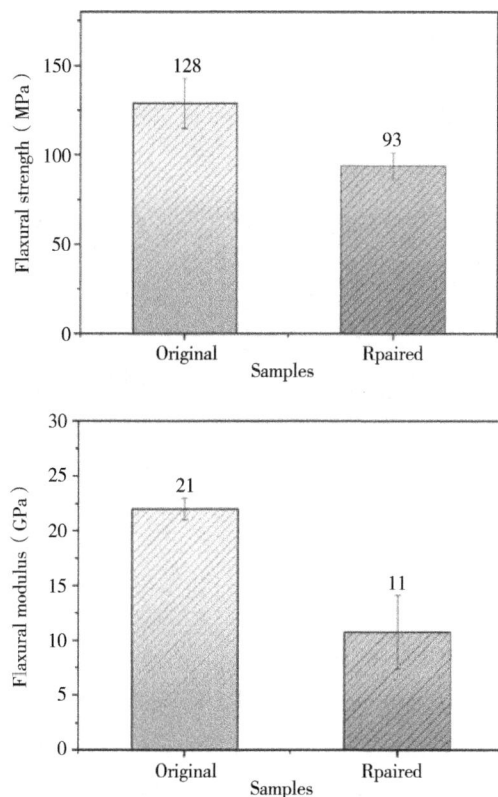

Fig. 4 (a) The flexural strength and (b) flexural modulus of the original and repaired CFRPs based on CBMA—EPA resin

Besides repairability, the carbon fibers in CFRPs can also be recycled by degradation of the CBMA—EPA resin. The recycling process is demonstrated in Fig. 5 (a). A CFRP panel was immersed in CBMA and heated to 50℃ for 12h. The resin matrix would slowly degrade in CBMA through the exchange reactions between the imine bonds in the epoxy and amino groups in CBMA. The carbon fiber fabric can be integrallty recycled and there are no obvious changes were observed in their woven structures. The microscale morphology of target fibers was observed by SEM, and the images shown in Fig. 5 (b) and (c) clearly indicate that no visible damage or alternation in fiber dimension. It is also seen that almost no residual polymer is attached on the recycling carbon fiber surfaces.

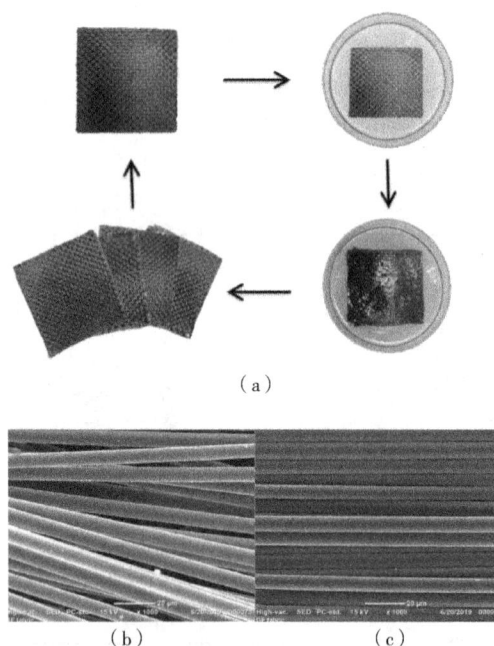

Fig. 5　(a) The recycling process of carbon fiber fabrics; (b) SEM images of the fresh fibers; (c) SEM images of recycled carbon fibers

4　Conclusions

In summary, we demonstrated a novel imine-containing epoxy vitrimer. This epoxy resin displayed excellent mechanical and thermal properties compared to the conventional epoxy materials. In addition, the imine-containing epoxy resin can be used to prepare "durable prepregs" which are no need to store at low temperature. The resulting CFRPs by hot pressing the prepregs are reparable and degradable. The repaired CFRPs show high retention of mechanical properties. Finally, the whole carbon fiber fabrics can be recycled through the degradation of epoxy matrix in CBMA solvent and almost no epoxy residues were observed on the surfaces of carbon fibers.

Acknowledgements

This work was supported by Natural Science Foundation of Shanghai (18ZR1400700) and Fundamental Research Funds for the Central Universities (2232019D3-48).

References

[1] AMAMOTO Y, KAMADA J, OTSUKA H, et al. Repeatable photoinduced self-healing of covalently cross-linked polymers through reshuffling of trithiocarbonate units[J]. Angewandte Chemie, 2011, 50(7) :1660-1663.

[2] BELOWICH M E, STODDART J F. Dynamic imine chemistry [J]. Chemical Society Reviews, 2012, 41(6) :2003-2024.

[3] RUIZ DE LUZURIAGA A, MARTIN R, MARKAIDE N, et al. Epoxy resin with exchangeable disulfide crosslinks to obtain reprocessable, repairable and recyclable fiber-reinforced thermoset composites[J]. Materials Horizons, 2016;3(3) :241-7.

[4] YUAN Y, SUN Y, YAN S, et al. Multiply fully recyclable carbon fiber reinforced heat-resistant covalent thermosetting advanced composites [J]. Nature Communications, 2017, 8 : 14657.

[5] ZHOU Fengtao, GUO Zijian, WANG Wenyan, et al. Preparation of self-healing, recyclable epoxy resins and low-electrical resistance composites based on double-disulfide bond exchange[J]. Composites Science and Technology, 2018, 167:79-85.

[6] COUMAR M S, JINDAL D P, BRUNI G, et al. Synthesis, beta-adrenergic receptor binding and antihypertensive potential of vanillin-derived phenoxypropanolamines [J]. Indian Journal of Chemistry Section B-Organic Chemistry Including Medicinal Chemistry, 2008, 47(6) :903-909.

[7] CUNLIFFE A, WILLIAMS P. Characterisation of products from the recycling of glass fibre reinforced polyester waste by pyrolysis[J]. Fuel, 2003, 82(18) :2223-2230.

[8] FORTMAN D, BRUTMAN J, HILLMYER M, et al. Structural effects on the reprocessability and stress relaxation of crosslinked polyhydroxyurethanes[J]. Journal of Applied Polymer Science, 2017, 134.

[9] GONZALEZ L, FERRAND F, RAMIIS X, et al. Characterization of new reworkable thermosetting coatings obtained by cationic and anionic curing of DGEBA and some Meldrum acid derivatives[J]. Progress in Organic Coatings, 2009, 65 (2) :175-181.

Effects of Core-Shell Polymer Nanoparticles on the Interlaminar Fracture Toughness of Carbon Fiber Reinforced Epoxy Composites

NING Na[1,2], ZHU Siyao[1,2], LIU Wanshuang[1,2]*, QIU Yiping[1], WEI Yi[1,2]*

[1] *Key Laboratory of Textile Science & Technology, Ministry of Education, College of Textile, Donghua University, Shanghai, 201620, China*

[2] *Donghua University Center for Civil Aviation Composites, Donghua University, Shanghai, 201620, China*

* *Corresponding author's email*: weiy@ dhu. edu. cn (Y. Wei), wsliu@ dhu. edu. cn (W. Liu)

Abstract: In this work, soft core-hard shell polymer nanoparticles were synthesized through emulsion polymerization and were used to improve the interlaminar fracture toughness of carbon fiber reinforced epoxy composites (CFRPs). The Mode I and Mode II interlaminar fracture toughness of CFRPs with 10% core-shell polymer particle (CSP) loading in resin were investigated. The Mode I and Mode II fracture toughness of CFRPs modified with CSP was significantly higher than those without CSP, the $G_{IC\text{-}onset}$ Insert, $G_{IC\text{-}onset}$ Pre-crack and G_{IIC} increased by 185%, 76.9% and 43.4%, respectively. The microscopic structure of the fracture surfaces from Mode I fracture toughness test was further studied using SEM. It was demonstrated that the CSP could enhance the fiber-matrix interfacial adhesion, enabling the material to absorb more energy, resulting in reduced crack growth and hence an improvement of the toughness.

Keywords: Carbon fiber reinforced composites; Epoxy resin; Core-shell polymer nanoparticles; Interlaminar fracture toughness; Mechanical properties

1 Introduction

Carbon fiber reinforced epoxy composites (CFRPs) have been widely utilized to manufacture primary and secondary structures in the aviation, aerospace, military and automobile industries due to their high specific strength, specific modulus and in-plane mechanical properties[1-2]. However, the thermosetting epoxy resins are often highly crosslinked and brittle. Therefore, intensive research efforts have been devoted to improve interlaminar fracture toughness of CFRPs. An effective method is to toughen the epoxy matrix.

Various approaches have been used to toughen epoxy resins, including the addition of high toughness modifiers, such as rubbers[3] and thermoplastic polymers[4]. Nonetheless, when using rubbers as toughening agents, losses in tensile strength, modulus and lower glass transition temperature are often observed. One of the approaches to address these issues is the utilization of rigid particles, such as silica[5], carbon nanotubes[6], graphene and its derivatives. Unfortunately, these rigid fillers often do not work well in boosting toughness, especially under high strain. Core-shell polymer particles have been shown to exhibit impressive toughness improvement in brittle polymers without loss of elastic modulus and tensile strength[7-8]. However, there is relatively little work in the literature that discuss the toughness of carbon fiber composites with core-shell particles made of other polymers other than rubber.

In this work, a core-shell polymer nanoparticle (CSP) with a soft poly (butyl acrylate) core and a rigid poly (methyl methacrylate) shell were synthesized via emulsion polymerization. The latex particles with the size about 100nm was transferred from aqueous medium to epoxy resins, subsequently used to modify the mechanical properties of CFRP. The effects of CSP-modified epoxy on the interlaminar fracture toughness and flexural properties of CFRP were studied, and the toughening mechanisms of the modifiers and the epoxy blends were investigated by scanning electron microscope (SEM).

2 Experiments

2.1 Materials

Methyl methacrylate (MMA, Aldrich, 99.5%), butyl acrylate (BA, Aldrich, 99%) and Ethylene glycol dimethacrylate (EGDMA, Aldrich, 98%) were used as monomers without further purification. Sodium 4-dodecylbenzenesulfonate (SDBS, Adamas, 88%) was used as the emulsifier. Ammonium persulfate (APS, Sinopharm, 98%) and sodium formaldehyde sulfoxylate solution (SFS, Macklin, 98%) were used as the redox initiators. 2-Butanone (MEK, Sinopharm, 99%) was used as the transfer solvent.

The carbon fiber used in this research was SYT 45-480 gsm-12K-plain weave provided by Zhongfu Shenying Carbon Fiber Co., Ltd., China. The epoxy resin was a mixture of diglycidyl ether of bisphenol A (DGEBA, Sanmu Group Co., Ltd., China) and neopentyl glycol diglycidyl ether (NGDGE, Baihe Advanced Composites, Ltd., China) with the mass ratio 60 : 40. The curing agent was methyl hexahydrophthalic anhydride (MHHPA, J&K chemical, 98%).

2.2 Preparation of CSP Nanoparticles

PBA—PMMA core-shell nanoparticles with a soft PBA core and a rigid PMMA shell were synthesized through emulsion polymerization. The CSP composition is shown in Tab.1. Synthesis was conducted by charging a 1L jacketed reactorwith DI water and emulsifier at 75℃. The shell monomers were charged after the core monomers.

Tab. 1 Experimental conditions to prepare CSP nanoparticles

Sample	Reactor charge		Core			Shell			Initiator solutions	
	Water (g)	SDBS (g)	BA (g)	EGDBA (g)	MMA (g)	EGDBA (g)	APS (g)	Water (g)	SFS (g)	Water (g)
CSP	238	4.5	91	4.8	91	4.8	0.9	18	0.9	18

2.3 Preparation of Epoxy/CSP Nanocomposite

To obtain a CSP nanoparticle-epoxy resin dispersion, the nanoparticles need to be transferred from an aqueous medium into the epoxy resin. Methyl ethyl ketone (MEK) was chosen as the transfer agent. The obtained CSP-epoxy dispersion was subsequently mixed with the epoxy resin formulation.

A calculated amount of epoxy and hardener having stoichiometric ratio of epoxy : anhydride = 1 : 1 were mixed together. After degassing under vacuum at 60℃ for 1h, the formulation resin was used to prepare the carbon fiber composite.

2.4 Fabrication of the Composite Laminates

The composite laminates used to test were fabricated viavacuum assisted resin infusion (VARI). 8 layers of $(32 \times 32cm^2)$ carbon fabrics were arranged along the warp direction (0^0 orientation). A 30μm thick PTFE non-stick film was inserted at the laminate mid-plane

(between layers 4 and 5) to act as crack initiator. Subsequently, epoxy resin was infused under vacuum at 60℃. The curing was 120℃ for 1h, 140℃ for 2h and 170℃ for 1h.

2.5 Characterizations

The particle size and distribution (PSD) was determined by dynamic light scattering (DLS) measurement using a Malvern Nano-ZS analyzer. Particle imaging was performed using JEOL JEM-2100 transmission electron microscope (TEM). The interlaminar fracture toughness, Mode I Double Cantilever Beam (DCB) and Mode II End Notch Flexure (ENF), were measured according to ASTM D5528 and ASTM D7905. The reported value for each type of test was taken as the average of at least five valid specimens.

The morphologies of the fracture surfaces from Mode I interlaminar fracture toughness were observed on a Hitachi S4800 scanning electron microscope (SEM).

3　Results and Discussions

3.1　Sizes and Morphologies of CSP Nanoparticles

The DLS curves of PBA-PMMA core-shell nanoparticles are shown in Fig. 1(a). As shown in Fig. 1(a), both curves represent mono-dispersed particle size distribution. The curves further illustrated that the shell monomers were

polymerized on top of the core particles, without evidence for secondary particle nucleation. The size of the particles, and particularly their morphology, were better observed by the TEM. Fig. 1(b) further exhibited a light-colored core, and a darker grey shell phase, confirming the formation of the desired.

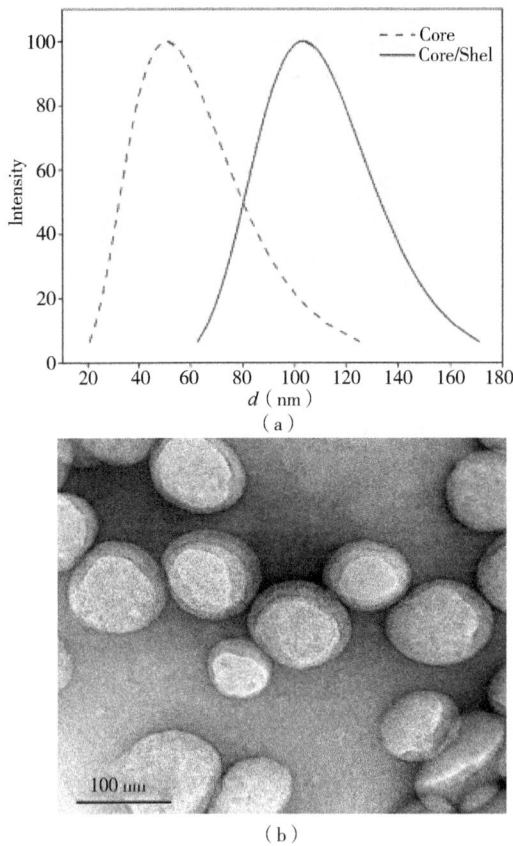

(a)

(b)

Fig. 1　Particle characteristics: (a) The particle size and distributions of PBA/PMMA core/shell latexes; (b) TEM image of PBA/PMMA core/shell latexes

3.2　Mode I and II Interlaminar Fracture Analysis

In order to enhance the interlaminar fracture toughness of CFRPs effectively, 10% CSP-epoxy loading was selected

to prepare composite laminates used for this study.

The Mode I and II interlaminar fracture toughness are important parameters for CFRPs to characterize the propagation of cracks within the composites. In this test, the load-displacement data from five test coupons were collected, averaged, and displayed in Fig. 2 and Fig. 3. The average crack initiation and propagation energy of control specimen having no nanoparticles (CF-Control) and that contained the particles (CF-CSP) are shown in Fig. 2. It was evident that the CF-CSP significantly improved the composite interlaminar fracture toughness, by increasing $G_{IC\text{-}onset}$ insert and $G_{IC\text{-}onset}$ pre-crack 185% and 76.9%, respectively.

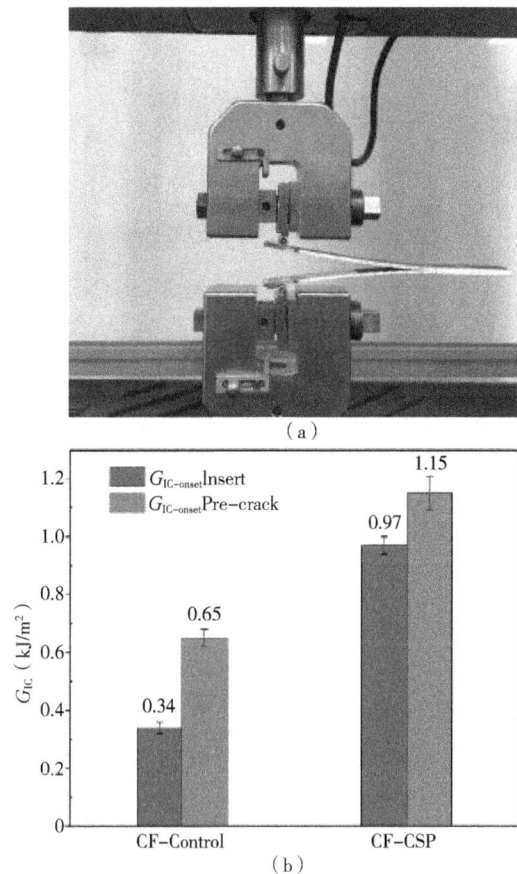

(a)

(b)

Fig. 2　(a)The test setup;(b)Mode I interlaminar fracture toughness for CF-Control and CF-CSP

Mode II interlaminar fracture toughness tests using ENF are unstable so usually only fracture toughness is reported. As shown from Fig. 3, CSP nanoparticles improved Mode II interlaminar fracture toughness, similar to

Mode I interlaminar fracture toughness. Adding 10% CSP nanoparticles increased the G_{IIC} initiation by 43.4%, from 1.82kJ/m^2 for GF-Control to 2.61kJ/m^2 for CF-CSP.

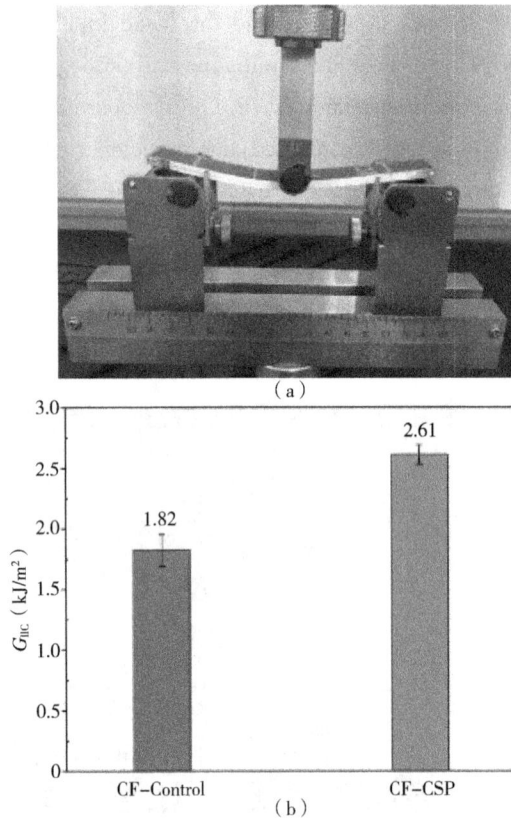

(a)

(b)

Fig. 3 (a) The test setup; (b) Mode II interlaminar fracture toughness for CF-Control and CF-CSP

3.4 Image Analysis

The fracture surfaces of the CF-Control and CF-CSP test coupons were observed using SEM, in order to understand the fracture progress and how the nanoparticles toughened the composite.

In Fig. 4, photographs (a), (c) and (e) show the fracture surface of CF-Control specimen, exposing smooth carbon fiber filaments with little epoxy resin attached to them, and indicating poor fiber-matrix interfacial adhesion. On the contrary, the fracture surfaces of CF-CSP were rough and carbon fibers were covered with matrix resin, as shown in Fig. 4 (b), (d) and (f), indicating better fiber-matrix interfacial adhesion. Moreover, some fiber breakage and pulled-out were observed on the fracture surfaces of CF-CSP [Fig. 4 (b)], owing to the strong interfacial adhesion that allowed more energy to be absorbed, resulting in significantly increased difficulty of crack propagation, and hence an improvement of the fracture toughness.

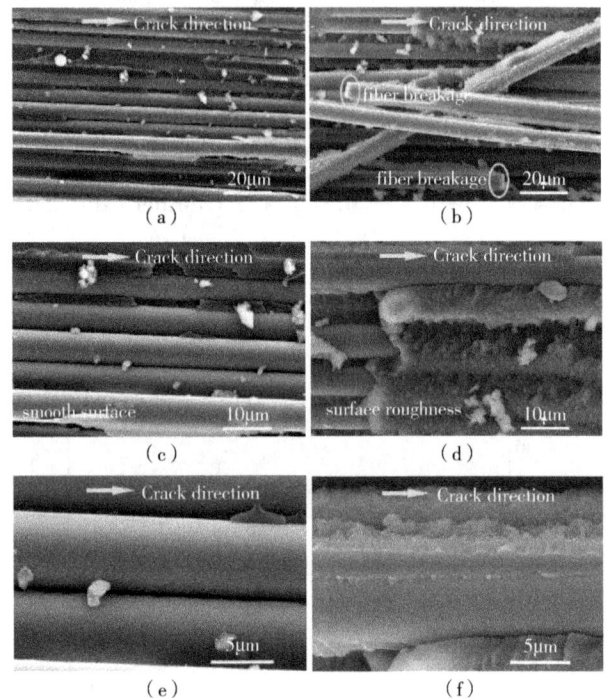

Fig. 4 SEM images of Mode I interlaminar fracture surfaces of CF-Control[(a), (c)and (e)]and CF-CSP[(b), (d) and(f)]

4 Conclusions

A core-shell polymer (CSP) nanoparticle having a soft rubbery core and a rigid polymer shell was used to improve the fracture toughness of CFRPs. The results indicated that the interlaminar fracture toughness was significantly enhanced by the addition of 10% CSP nanoparticles, that the $G_{IC\text{-onset}}$ insert, $G_{IC\text{-onset}}$ pre-crack and G_{IIC} of carbon fiber composites were increased by 185%, 76.9% and 43.4%, respectively, compared to the control specimen having no particles. The toughening mechanism by the nanoparticles was investigated using scanning electron microscopy, and the observation demonstrated that the particles were well-dispersed in the matrix resin with enhanced fiber-resin interfacial adhesion, resulting in an improved interlaminar fracture toughness.

Acknowledgements

This work was supported by Natural Science Foundation of Shanghai (18ZR1400700) and Fundamental Research Funds for the Central Universities (2232019D3-48).

References

[1] TSAI S N, CAROLAN D, SPRENGER S, et al. Fracture and fatigue behaviour of carbon fibre composites with nanoparticle-sized fibres[J]. Compos Struct, 2019, 217(January):143-149.

[2] BECKERMANN G W, PICKERING K L. Mode I and Mode II interlaminar fracture toughness of composite laminates interleaved with electrospun nanofibre veils[J]. Compos Part A Appl Sci Manuf, 2015,72:11-21.

[3] PEARSON R A, YEE A F. Toughening mechanisms in elastomer-modified epoxies[J]. J Mater Sci, 1989, 24(7):2571-2580.

[4] VIJAYAN P P, PUGLIA D, AL-MAADEED M A S A, et al. Elastomer/thermoplastic modified epoxy nanocomposites: The hybrid effect of 'micro' and 'nano' scale[J]. Mater Sci Eng R Reports,2017,116:1-29.

[5] JOHNSEN B B, KINLOCH A J, MOHAMMED R D, et al. Toughening mechanisms of nanoparticle-modified epoxy polymers[J]. Polymer (Guildf),2007,48(2):530-541.

[6] GOJNY F H, WICHMANN M H G, FIEDLER B, et al. Influence of different carbon nanotubes on the mechanical properties of epoxy matrix composites-A comparative study[J]. Compos Sci Technol, 2005, 65(15-16 SPEC. ISS.):2300-2313.

[7] LIU S, FAN X, HE C. Improving the fracture toughness of epoxy with nanosilica-rubber core-shell nanoparticles [J]. Compos Sci Technol, 2016,125:132-140.

[8] JIANG T, REN X, TU Z, et al. Critical rubber layer thickness of core-shell particles with a rigid core and a soft shell for toughening of epoxy resins without loss of elastic modulus and strength[J]. Compos Sci Technol, 2017,153:253-260.

One Thermo-Latent Fast-Curing Epoxy Resin and Its Application in Carbon Fiber Reinforced Composites

LI Yan[1,2], WEI Yi[1,2]*, LIU Wanshuang[1,2]*

[1] Donghua University Center for Civil Aviation Composites, Donghua University, Shanghai, 201620, China

[2] College of Textiles, Donghua University, Shanghai, 201620, China

* Corresponding author's email: wsliu@ dhu. edu. cn (W. Liu), weiy@ dhu. edu. cn (Y. Wei)

Abstract: One thermo-latent and fast-curing epoxy resin system (named as EP-L) was developed based on the mechanism of cationic polymerization. The contents of cationic initiator were optimized by differential scanning calorimetry (DSC). Compared to the commercial thermo-latent epoxy BAC-177 which can only be stored at room temperature for 3 days, EP-L has better latency and can be store at room temperature for more than 7 months. Moreover, EP-L has a fast curing rate and can be fully cured in 2 hour. The cured EP-L shows lower T_g and tensile strength than cured BAC177, but its fracture toughness ($1.11 MPa \cdot m^{1/2}$) is significantly better than that of BAC177 ($0.56 MPa \cdot m^{1/2}$). Finally, the carbon fiber reinforced composite based on EP-L show comparable flexural properties but lower mode II fracture toughness compared with the composite based on BAC−177.

Keywords: Epoxy resins; Thermo-latency; Carbon fiber reinforced composites; Mechanical properties

1 Introduction

Epoxy resin is one of the most important thermosetting resins, and is used extensively as a high performance polymer in composite materials, protective coating, and encapsulation materials in the electronics industry[1] for their excellent properties, such as high tensile strength and modulus, good chemical and corrosion resistance, low shrinkage and easy processability[2-4].

Usually, epoxy resins must be cured for application[5]. Therefore, curing agents (CA) are necessary epoxies to convert them to a three-dimensional network[6]. However, the epoxy systems based on common curing agents show poor storage stability owing to the intrinsically high reactivity[7]. Therefore, latent curing agents have attracted more attention recently. The typical latent curing agent for epoxy is the initiator based on cationic polymerization[8]. Cationic initiators can easily control the initiation and curing of an epoxy system. The epoxy system can remain inactive under normal environmental conditions and become active by external stimulation by

heat or light[6, 9]. So far, many cationic initiators have been synthesized and their importance has been recognized in the fields of organic and polymer synthesis[10]. In this study, one thermo-latent and fast-curing epoxy resin (named as EP-L) was developed based on thermo-triggered cationic polymerization. The curing behaviors, latency, thermal and mechanical properties of EP-L were systematically studied and compared with those of commercial thermo-latent epoxy BAC177. Finally, carbon fiber reinforced composites based on EP-L and BAC-177 were fabricated using vacuum assisted resin infusion (VARI) process. The in-plane (flexural properties) and interlaminar (Mode II fracture toughness) mechanical properties of the composites were investigated.

2 Experiments

2.1 Materials

The epoxy DGEBA was purchased from Sanmu Co., Ltd. Trimethylolpropane triglycidyl ether was purchased from Adamas. The cationic initiator TC3632 was purchased from Kaiji. The one-component epoxy BAC177 was purchased Baihe Hangtai Co. , Ltd. Carbon fiber fabrics (T700, 24K) were purchased from Hengshen Co. , Ltd.

2.2 Preparation of Epoxy Resins

DGEBA and trimethylolpropanetriglycidyl ether were selected for the mixed resin system. The effects of different initiator contents (1%,2% and 3%) on the curing of the resin system were explored.

2.3 Preparation of Carbon Fiber Composites

Carbon fiber reinforced composite was fabricated using VARI process[11]. Firstly, a flat glass plate was cleaned, and a mold release agent was used to the mold surface before layup of bagging materials. Then the bagging materials were laid up. The degassed resin system was infused into the fabrics from one edge to the other end. After injection, the composite was cured using the same manner with the pure epoxy resin.

2.4 Characterization

The differential scanning calorimetry (DSC) thermograms were obtained with a NETZCHE 204 under N_2 flow in the temperature ranges: 20℃ to 250℃ at a rate of 10℃/min[12]. Samples for study on curing kinetics were heated from room temperature to 250℃ at heating rates of 2℃/m, 5℃/m, 8℃/m, 10℃/m, 15℃/min, respectively. The thermal-mechanical properties were measured through dynamic mechanical analysis (DMA) with the rate of 2℃/min and the temperature range was 20-200℃. Tensile tests were performed according to ASTM D638 standard using a Wance ETM104B-EX electronic universal testing machine. Fracture toughness (K_{IC}, critical stress intensity factor; and G_{IC}, critical strain energy release) of the resins were measured according to ASTM D5045-99.

The K_{IC} of the cured specimen was calculated as follows[7]:

$$K_{IC} = \frac{P_{max}}{bd^{1/2}}f(x) \qquad (1)$$

$$x = a/d$$

where P_{max}, d, b, $f(x)$, and a are the critical load for crack propagation, width of the specimen, thickness of the specimen, geometrical factor, and pre-crack length, respectively.

The G_{IC} of the cured epoxy sample was calculated using the following equation:

$$G_{IC} = \frac{(1-v^2)}{E}K_{IC}^2 \qquad (2)$$

where v is the Poisson's ratio of the epoxy (0. 348) and E is young's modulus as determined from the fracture toughness test.

The flexural properties of composite panels were measured according to ASTM D7264. Mode II interlaminar fracture toughness of composite panels are performed according to ASTM D7905. The G_{IIC} of the composite was calculated using the following equation:

$$G_{IIC} = \frac{9P_c\delta a^2}{2b(2L^3 + 3a^3)} \qquad (3)$$

Where b, a, P_c, L are the width of the specimen, the length of crack, the critical load for crack propagation and the displacement.

3 Results and Discussions

3.1 Contents of Resin Systems

The DSC curves of epoxy systems with different initiator contents are shown in Fig. 1 and the data is listed in Tab. 1 Compared with the epoxy systems with 1% and 2% initiator, the resin system with 3% cationic initiators didn't release much more heat and implode during the curing process, but showed faster curing rate. Besides, with the increasing amount of TC3632, the cured epoxy has a higher T_g. Based on the above results, the epoxy system with 3% cationic initiator contents was chosen and named as EP-L.

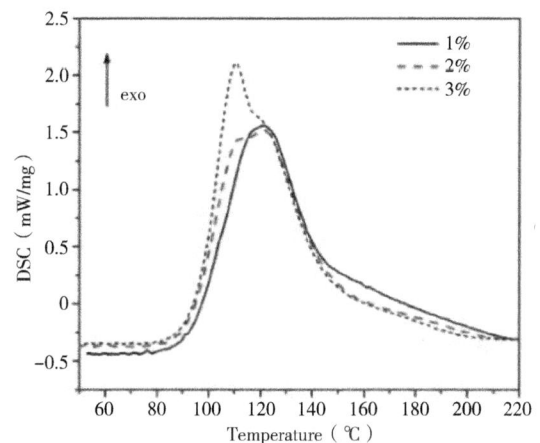

Fig. 1 DSC curves of epoxy resins with different initiator contents

Tab. 1 Data of DSC test of epoxy resins with different initiator contents

Initiator contents	Reaction Time (min)	ΔH (J/g)
1%	4.5	506
2%	4.5	547
3%	3.8	549

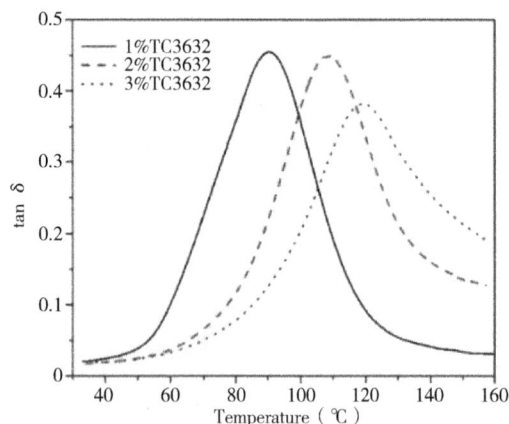

Fig. 2   tan δ versus temperature curve of the epoxy systems with different cationic initiator contents

3.2 Curing Kinetics

The curing kinetics of the epoxy system was investigated by determining the exothermic peak temperatures at different heating rates using the Kissinger method[13-14]. The dynamic DSC curve at different heating rates for EP-L is shown in Fig. 3. The value of calculated E is 130kJ/mol. For an epoxy system, the high activation energy would result in good thermal latency.

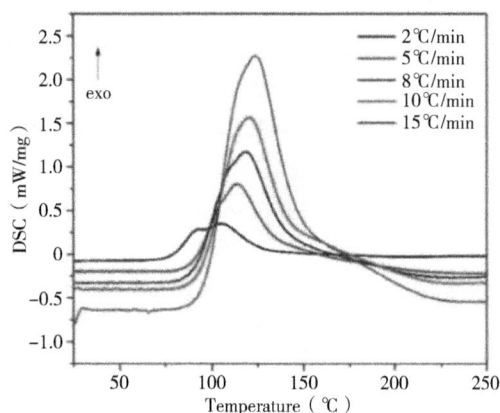

Fig. 3   Dynamic DSC curve for EP-L at different heating rates: 2K/min; 5K/min; 8K/min; 10K/min; 15K/min

3.3 Latency

Thermo-latent and one-component epoxy systems take away the hassle of on-site weighting, blending and degassing[15]. Significantly, EP-L system can be stored

for 7 months and almost keep the same fluidity at room temperature indicating that EP-L system has much better latency than BAC177 system.

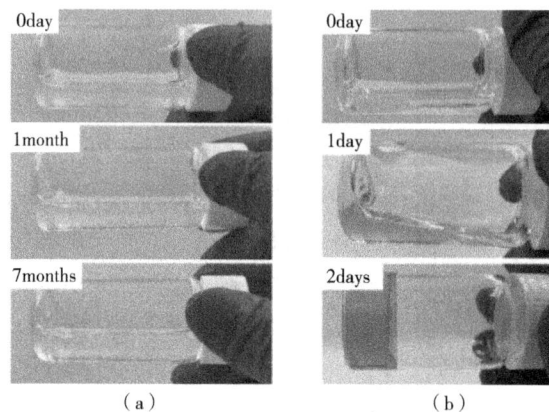

Fig. 4   Viscosity variation of (a)EP-L and (b) BAC177

3.4 Dynamic Mechanical Properties of the Resin System

As shown in Fig. 5(a), the storage modulus of BAC177 was always higher than that of EP-L. As shown in Fig. 5 (b), T_g of cured EP-L and BAC-177 are 148℃ and 156℃, respectively. The above results indicate the cured BAC177 has a higher crosslinking density than EP-L.

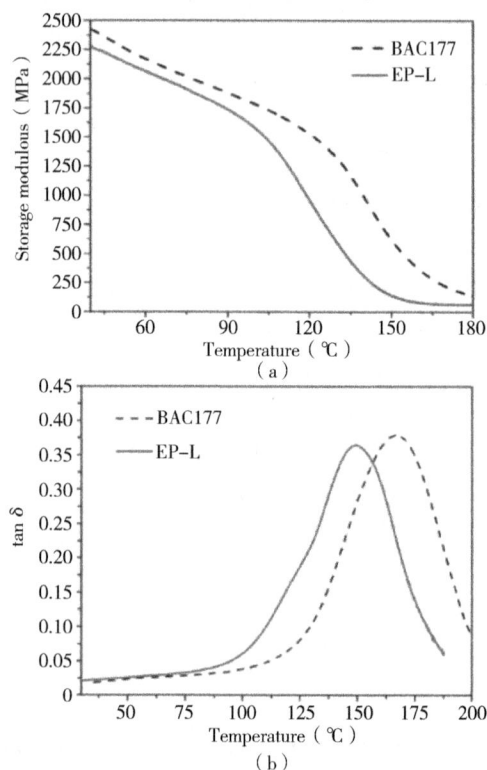

Fig. 5   Dynamic thermomechanical analysis of BAC177 and EP-L: (a) storage modulus; (b)tan δ

3.5 Mechanical Properties

The tensile strength of cured EP-L (63.4MPa) is lower than that of cured BAC−177 (85.9MPa). This is because the high curing rate of EP-L system would cause internal stress which can deteriorate the strength of cured epoxy.

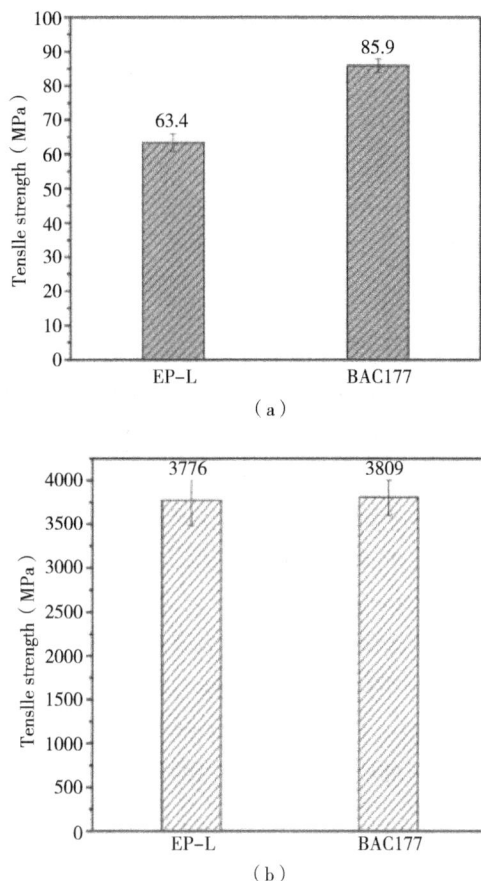

Fig.6 (a) Tensile strength and (b) tensile modulus of EP-L and BAC177

The calculated K_{IC} and G_{IC} are listed in the Fig.9(a) (b). The K_{IC} values of EP-L and BAC177 are 1.11MPa · $m^{1/2}$ and 0.56MPa · $m^{1/2}$, respectively. The G_{IC} values of EP-L and BAC177 are 288J/m^2 and 77J/m^2, respectively. The enhanced fracture toughness is due to its high content of flexible ether segments (—CH_2—O—). Therefore, the cured EP-L tends to form a soft interphase region to enhance the fracture toughness[16].

3.6 Mechanical Properties of Carbon Fiber Composites

The in-plane mechanical properties of carbon fiber re-

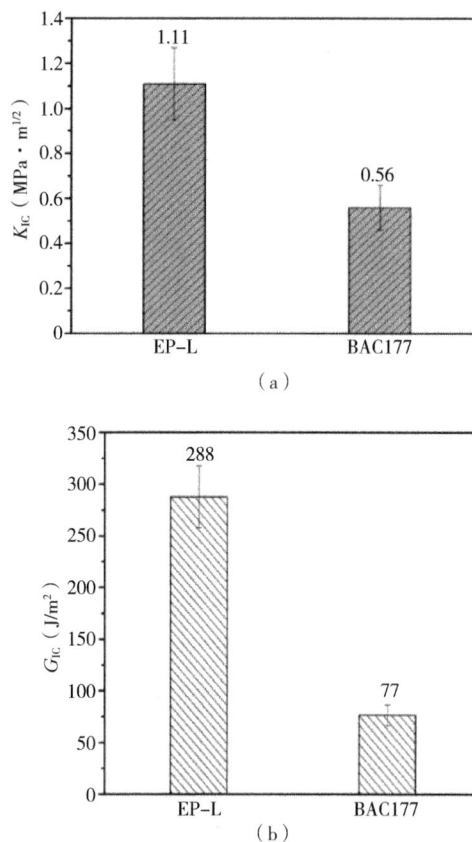

Fig.7 Fracture toughness index (a) K_{IC} and (b) G_{IC} of BAC177 and EP-L

inforced composites were investigated by flexural tests. As shown in Fig.8, flexural strength and flexural modulus of carbon fiber composites based on EP-L is 461MPa and 51.3GPa, respectively, which are comparable to those of composite based on BAC−177. This may be because the carbon fiber plays a dominant role in the flexural properties of carbon fiber composites.

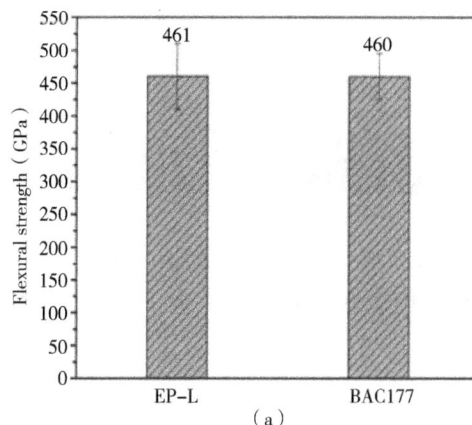

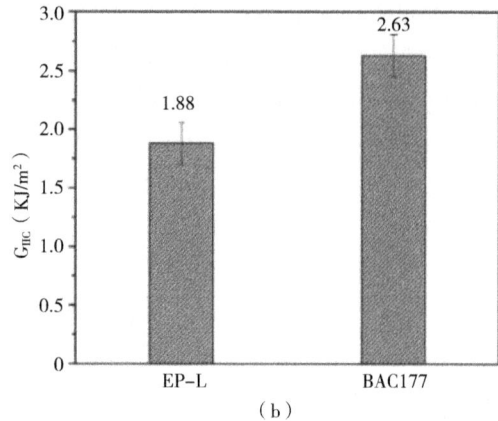

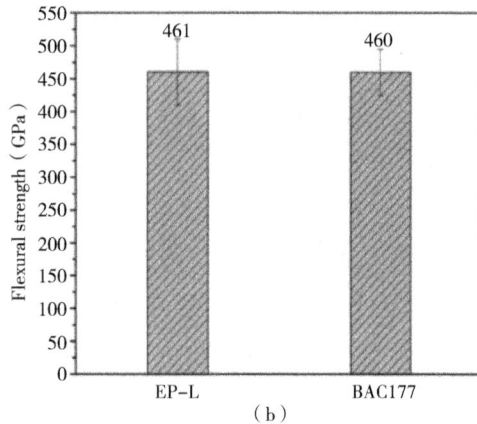

Fig. 8 (a) Flexural strength and (b) modulus of carbon fiber composite based on EP-L and BAC177 matrices

Fig. 9 (a) The test setup; (b) Mode II fracture toughness of two kinds of composites based on EP-L and BAC177

Mode II interlaminar fracture toughness was conducted to study the crack propagation of mode II fracture toughness is interlaminar damage[17]. The values of G_{IIC} of the composite with the matrix of EP-L and BAC177 are 1. 88kJ/m^2 and 2. 63kJ/m^2, respectively. It's known that the interfacial interactions between carbon fiber and epoxy matrix have an important influence on mode II fracture toughness. The lower mode II fracture toughness of the composite based EP-L results from the presence of flexible chains which would decrease the interfacial adhesive between matrix and fabrics[18].

Fig. 9 (a) The test setup; (b) Mode II fracture toughness of two kinds of composites based on EP-L and BAC177

4 Conclusions

In summary, a thermo-latent fast-curing epoxy resin named as EP-L was developed. Compared with commercial latent epoxy BAC177, it showed much better thermal latency and it can be stored at room temperature for at least 7 months. The cured EP-L showed lower T_g and flexural strength compared with cured BAC-177. However, the fracture toughness of cured EP-L is much higher due to the higher content of flexible ether segments in EP-L. The carbon fiber reinforced composites based on two epoxy system showed comparable flexural properties.

Acknowledgements

This work was supported by Natural Science Foundation of Shanghai (18ZR1400700) and Fundamental Research Funds for the Central Universities (2232019D3-48).

References

[1] HARTWIG A, KOSCHEK K, LÜHRING A, et al. Cationic polymerization of a cycloaliphatic diepoxide with latent initiators in the presence of structurally different diols[J]. Polymer,2003(44):2853-2858.

[2] LIU F H, WANG Z G, LIU D, et al. Curing of diglycidyl ether of bisphenol-A epoxy resin using a poly(aryl ether ketone) bearing pendant carboxyl groups as macromolecular curing agent[J]. Polymer Internationai,2009,58(8):912-918.

[3] ISARN I, GAMARDELLA F, FERNÀNDEZ-FRANCOS X, et al. Thermal conductive composites prepared by addition of

several ceramic fillers to thermally cationic curing cycloaliphatic epoxy resins[J]. Polymers,2019,11(1):138.

[4]RIAZ S, PARK S. Thermal and mechanical interfacial behaviors of graphene oxide-reinforced epoxy composites cured by thermal latent catalyst[J]. materials,2019,12(8):1354.

[5]HAN H, JIANG C, HUO L, et al. Mechanical and thermal properties of cationic ring-opening o-cresol formaldehyde epoxy/polyurethane acrylate composites enhanced by reducing graphene oxide[J]. Polymer Bulletin,2016,73(8):2227-2244.

[6]KANG M, JIN F, PARK S. Effect of ozone treatment on fracture toughness of single-walled carbon nanotubes-reinforced epoxy resin initiated by a thermal latent catalyst[J]. Macromolecular Research,2018,26(11):1048-1051.

[7]RIAZ S, PARK S. Thermal and mechanical interfacial behaviors of graphene oxide-reinforced epoxy composites cured by thermal latent catalyst[J]. Materials,2019,12(8):1354.

[8]ISARN I, GAMARDELLA F, MASSAGUES L, et al. New epoxy composite thermosets with enhanced thermal conductivity and high Tg obtained by cationic homopolymerization[J]. Polymer Composites,2018,39(S3):1760-1769.

[9]CRIVELLO J V, LIU S. Photoinitiated cationic polymerization of epoxy alcohol monomers[J].

[10]RIAZ S, PARK S. Thermal and mechanical interfacial behaviors of graphene oxide-reinforced epoxy composites cured by thermal latent catalyst[J]. Materials (Basel, Switzerland),2019,12(8).

[11]LIU Y, YUAN C, LIU C, et al. Study on the resin infusion process based on automated fiber placement fabricated dry fiber preform[J]. Scientific Reports,2019,9(1).

[12]CHEMTOB A, VERSACE D, BELON C, et al. Concomitant organic-inorganic UV-curing catalyzed by photoacids[J]. Macromolecules,2008,41(20):7390-7398.

[13]LIU W S, WANG Z G, CHEN Z, et al. Synthesis and properties of two novel silicon-containing cycloaliphatic epoxy resins for electronic packaging application[J]. Polymers for Advanced Technoles,2012,23(3):367-374.

[14]VYAZOVKIN S, BURNHAM A K, CRIADO J M, et al. ICTAC Kinetics Committee recommendations for performing kinetic computations on thermal analysis data[J]. Thermochimica Acta,2011,520(1-2):1-19.

[15]VIDIL T, TOURNILHAC F, MUSSO S, et al. Control of reactions and network structures of epoxy thermosets[J]. Progress in Polymer Science,2016,62:126-179.

[16]CAROLAN D, IVANKOVIC A, KINLOCH A J, et al. Toughened carbon fibre-reinforced polymer composites with nanoparticle-modified epoxy matrices[J]. Journal of Materials Science,2017,52(3):1767-1788.

[17]LATIF M, PRABHAKAR M N, SONG J. Fabrication of hybrid matrix/silane modified carbon fabric composites and study of their mechanical properties[J]. Journal of Applied Polymer Science,2019,136(26).

[18]XI W. Research on synthesis and properties of a flexible epoxy curing agent[J]. Applied Mechanics and Materials,2015,744-746:1463-1466.

Interlaminar Fracture Toughness of Carbon Fiber/Epoxy Composites Toughened by Polyphenylene Oxide Particles

HUANG Yuan[1,2], QIU Yiping[2], LIU Wanshuang[1,2]*, WEI Yi[1,2]*

[1] *College of Textiles, Donghua University, Shanghai, 201620, China*

[2] *Donghua University Center for Civil Aviation Composites, Donghua University, Shanghai, 201620, China*

* *Corresponding authors' email*: weiy@ dhu. edu. cn（Wei Y.）, wsliu@ dhu. edu. cn（Liu W.）

Abstract: In this study, interlaminar fracture toughness from mode I and mode II deformation were investigated for carbon fiber/epoxy composites toughened by polyphenylene oxide（PPO）particles. PPO particles with different size were used as the interlayer reinforcements. The dispersion state of PPO particles at the interlayer was observed by fluorescence microscope. Mode I and mode II interlaminar fracture toughness were evaluated by standard double cantilever beam（DCB）and end notched flexure（ENF）tests, respectively, acorrding to ASTM standards. The reusults of mechanical tests showed that the introduction of PPO interlayer could improve both mode I and mode II interlaminar fracture toughness of carbon fiber/epoxy composites. Notably, the addion of 10% PPO particles with 10–50μm diameter gave 65% and 40% enhancement in mode I and mode II interlaminar fracture toughness, repectively. The toughening mechanisms of PPO particles was studied by Scanning Electron Microscope（SEM）, including crack deflection, crack termination, particle bridging, etc.

Keywords: Polyphenylene oxide; Interlaminar; Fracture toughness; Interleaf particle

1 Introduction

Carbon fiber reinforced polymer composites（CFRPs）are extensively used[1]. However CFRPs are often of low interlamiar strength, low impact resistance and poor fracture toughness, which greatly limits their uses. Various toughening agents such as reactive liquid rubber[2] and high-toughness thermoplastics[3] have been employed to resolve these problems. Although these materials can effectively improve the fracture toughness of the matrix resin, they may also reduce the composite's service temperature and modulus, especially under hydrothermal conditions. In recent years, using engineering particles of high performance thermoplastics for the interlaminar toughening of composites has proved to be effective, because they remained concentrated in the weaker interlaminar regions and acted as crack arresters, which effectively interrupted or stopped crack propagations[4]. Thermoplastic polymer particles were used for interleaf toughening in the past. The highest toughness epoxy composites were found to be using the engineering particles, such as T800H/3900−2 and IM7/8551−7, and had been successfully used as structures for Boeing 777 and Boeing Bell V − 22 "Osprey"[5]. The effective toughening using interleaf particles overcome many shortcomings of films, nanofibre, and CNTs and have profound research and commercial values.

Polymer for improving interlaminar fracture toughness, it needs to be tough, has a high shear strength, and it requires a ductile way to plastically deform[6]. In this study, particles of a high performance polymer, polyphenylene oxide（PPO）, were tested for interleaf toughening. PPO has good thermal properties（$T_g >$ 210℃）, chemically stable, and has excellent mechanical performance[7-8]. Herein, PPO particles with different size（10−130μm）were used as the interlayer reinforcements for carbon fiber/epoxy composites. The effects of optimized PPO particles on mode I and mode II interlaminar fracture toughness of resulting composites were investigated, and the toughening mechanisms were also illuminated.

2 Experiments

2.1 Materials

PPO 630 (10-200μm) was provided by SABIC Innovative Plastics. Carbon farbic/epoxy prepreg BAC 313FR (200g/m²) was provided by Zhejiang Baihe Advanced Composites. Ltd. The fluorescent yellow acid dye was purchased from Zhejiang Jihua Group Co. Ltd.

2.2 Fabrication of Composite Panels and Test Specimens

Composite panels (280mm×250mm) for both DCB and ENF tests were fabricated according to the prepreg layup of $[(0/90)°]_{16}$, and the stacks were cured using a hot press under a pressure of 0.2MPa and a temperature of 80℃ for 2h. The particles were deposited on the mid-plane by screen-printing. The particle loadings used in this study were 10%. A Teflon film with 30μm thickness was placed in the mid-plane to act as the initial crack for the DCB and ENF test. PPO particles of different sizes were obtained by sieving with 300-mesh, 170-mesh, and 110-mesh screens.

2.3 Characterizations

The dispersion state of PPO particles at the interlayer was observed by fluorescence microscope (FM-400C). Before observation, the composite samples were treated by fluorescent yellow acid dye. The mechanical properties of carbon fiber/epoxy composites were measured on a Electromechanical Universal Testing Machine (203B-TS) equipped with a load cell of 2000N. The interlaminar fracture toughness in Mode I and Mode II were determined by Double Cantilever Beam (DCB) and End Notched Flexure (ENF) tests, according to ASTM D5528 and ASTM D7905, respectively. The Mode I interlaminar fracture toughness G_{IC} was determined by Equation (1):

$$G_{IC} = \frac{3P_c\delta}{2ba} \qquad (1)$$

where P_c is the applied load, δ is the load point displacement, b is the specimen width, a is the delamination length (crack length). The width (b) and thickness of the specimen are 20mm and 3.7mm, respectively. The initial crack length a_0 is 50mm.

The Mode II interlaminar fracture toughness (G_{IC}) was calculated by the compliance calibration method using Equation (2):

$$G_{IIC} = \frac{9P_c\delta a^2}{2b(2L^3 + 3a^3)} \qquad (2)$$

where L is half the span length (50mm), b is the width of specimen, a is the crack length. The width (b) and thickness of the specimen are 20mm and 3.7mm, respectively. The initial crack length a_0 is 30mm.

3 Results and Discussions

3.1 Morphology of PPO Particles in the Composite

To observe the morphology of the PPO particles in the composite, the test specimen was treated with a special fluorescent dye. To perform the treatment, the laminate was cut into 20mm×2mm coupons, and their cross sections were polished to a high glossy finish. The specimens were subsequently placed in a glass flask filled with adequate volume of the fluorescent dye solution, which contained 5g/mL fluorescence yellow acid dye and 5ml/L glacial acetic acid. The flask was heated, and the contents were stirred at 100℃ for 30min to achieve adequate dyeing. Afterwards the specimens were cooled, washed, and dried. Since this process only colored the matrix resin, the morphology of the particles in composite laminates could be observed with clarity under the fluorescent microscope, as shown in Fig. 1.

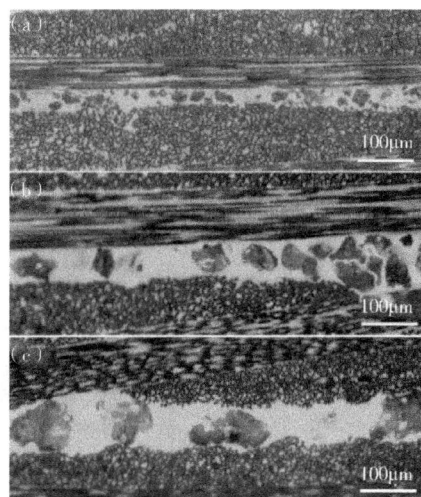

Fig. 1　Fluorescent microscopes of PPO particles with size of (a) 10-50μm; (b) 50-90μm; (c) 90-130μm in composite laminate cross sections

As could be seen from Fig. 1, the PPO particles retained their original shapes well, indicating that the particles did not dissolve or swell in the resin during cure. This is due to the PPO particles being of high glass transition temperature and insoluble in the epoxy matrix resin. It is worth noting that, the interleaf thickness between the two fiber plies was determined by the size of the particles. Moreover, the larger diameter the particles had, the rougher of the interlaminar region. These effects, as could be seen below, would affect the mechanical properties of the laminates.

3.2 Double Cantilever Beam Tests and Mode I ILFT Determination

The Mode I fracture toughness was calculated and presented in Fig. 2, particles in the range of 10–50μm were most effective, which increased G_{IC} by 65%, much higher than the increases of 31% and 18.3% for particle size range of 50–90μm and 90–130μm, respectively.

Some insights might be obtained from Fig. 1 to explain the above observed particle size effect. It could be seen from the figures that, for a fixed level of particle loading, the number of particles per unit area in the interleaf region would increase with decreasing particle size. As a result, for the specimen containing particles of 10–50μm, any cracks would encounter a larger number of particles than those of a specimen with 90–130μm particles, requiring more energy for the crack to propagate further.

To understand the toughening mechanisms, the fracture surface morphologies were observed with SEM, shown in Fig. 3. Fig. 3(a) and (b) revealed that the fracture surface of composite laminate without particles was fairly smooth and clean, suggesting low fracture resistance and fiber de-bonding being the primary failure mode. Contrarily, laminates containing PPO particles [Fig. 3(c)–(f)] showed much different morphology, the rougher fracture surfaces were evidently of higher energy absorption during fracture due to the presence of PPO. Fig. 3(c) revealed a relatively rough fractured surface with the appearance of resin hackles, demonstrating the high-energy absorption plastic deformations. Furthermore, Fig. 3(e) showed that micro-cracks were deflected by the PPO particles embedded in the matrix, effectively making the matrix resin more ductile. Again a closer look at Fig. 3(d) showed micro-cracks been initiated, deflected and terminated by PPO particles, involving more particles in the crack propagation process, and resulting in high resistance to fracture. In addition, the higher magnification image, Fig. 3(f) showed that the PPO particle effectively stopped the propagation of the crack, and interestingly the embedded particle had no fissures around its contour, indicating strong interfacial bonding between the PPO particles and the epoxy matrix resin, similar to what was reported by other researchers.

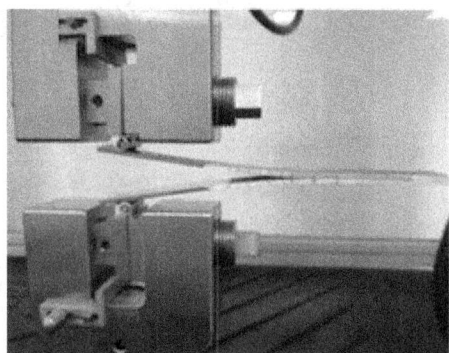

(a)

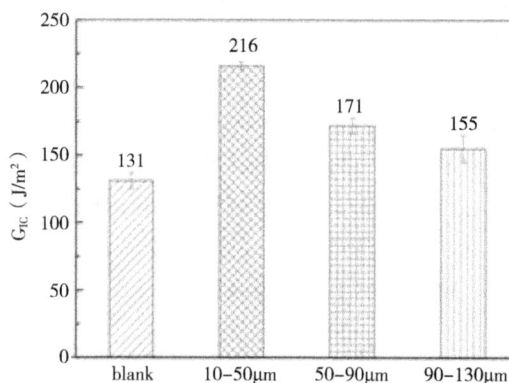

(b)

Fig. 2　Mode I fracture toughness: (a) Interlaminar fracture toughness tests, Load-displacement curves; (b) Different PPO particles size, all at particle loading of 10%

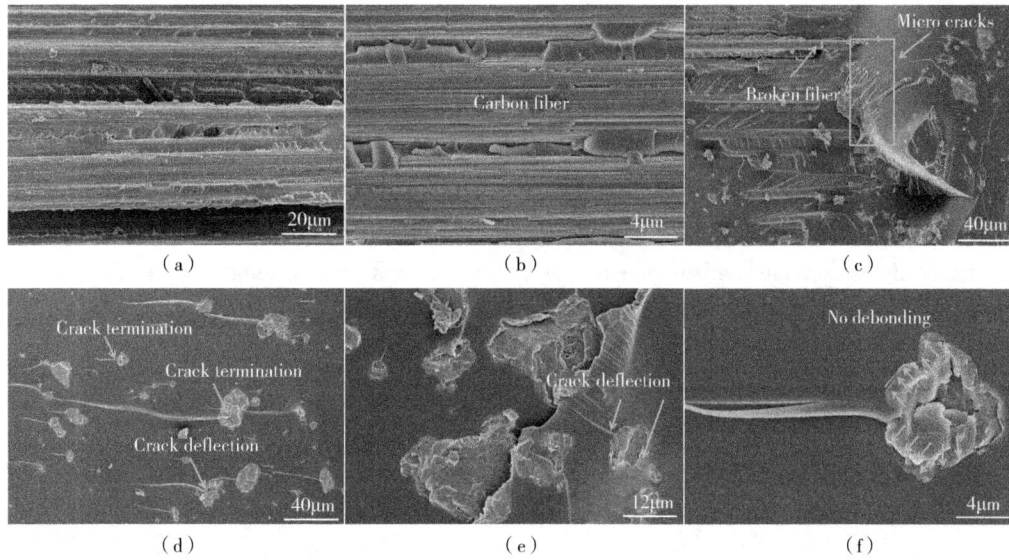

Fig. 3　SEM images of fracture surfaces of DCB specimen at different magnifications; (a)–(b) blank laminates without particles; (c)–(f) l—aminates with particles for the size of 10–50μm and loading of 10%

The SEM observations revealed that the enhanced fracture toughness of interleaf particle containing laminates was attributed to increased plastic deformation created by PPO particles, crack deflection and a chaining effect resulted from the bridging of PPO particles also contributed to the improvement.

3.3　End Notch Flexure Tests and Mode II ILFT Determination

The G_{IIC} values for Mode II interlaminar fracture toughness was calculated and presented in Fig. 4. Composites toughened with different particle sizes are shown in Fig. 4 (b). G_{IIC} increased from 768J/m^2 of the blank specimen to 999J/m^2 with particles in the range of 50–90μm interleaved, and further to 1073J/m^2 with the range of 10–50μm interleaved, As already discussed in section 3.2, smaller particle size is more advantageous when toughening interleaved.

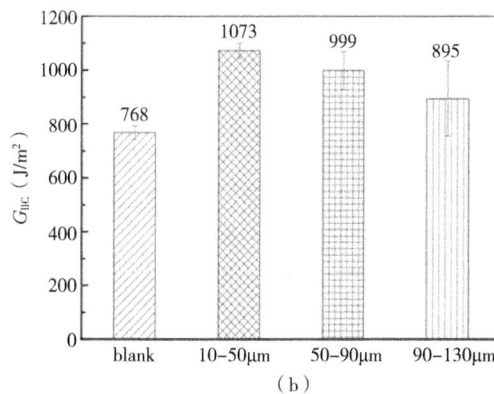

Fig. 4　Mode II fracture toughness; (a) Interlaminar fracture toughness tests, Load-displacement curves;
(b) Different PPO sizes, all at particle loading of 10%

Fig. 5 (a)–(b) show Mode II fracture surfaces of carbon/epoxy laminate without particles, and Fig. 5 (c)–(f) show surfaces of carbon/epoxy laminates with PPO particles. A distinct morphological change from a typical brittle Mode II fracture surface for blank laminates [Fig. 5 (a) and (b)] to a more rough and deformed surface for the particle interleaved laminates was observed [Fig. 5 (e) and (f)]. Brittle fracture from Mode

Ⅱ failure in blank laminates was characterized by a smooth corrugated fracture surface, it is almost made up of pure debonded fibers with little or no resin, defined the main failure was debonding, the interface between matrix resin and reinforced fibers was weak causing poor crack propagation resistance. These micro cracks were created by the crack deflection mechanism due to the addition of PPO particles. The particles created stress concentrations on their balancers and serve as the starting point for the shear bands to form the plastic deformation zone of the PPO toughened matrix requiring a high energy release that contributing to the enhanced interlaminar fracture toughness[9]. The PPO particles behind the crack tip mainly affect the extrinsic toughness of the material through crack deflection and bridging[10].

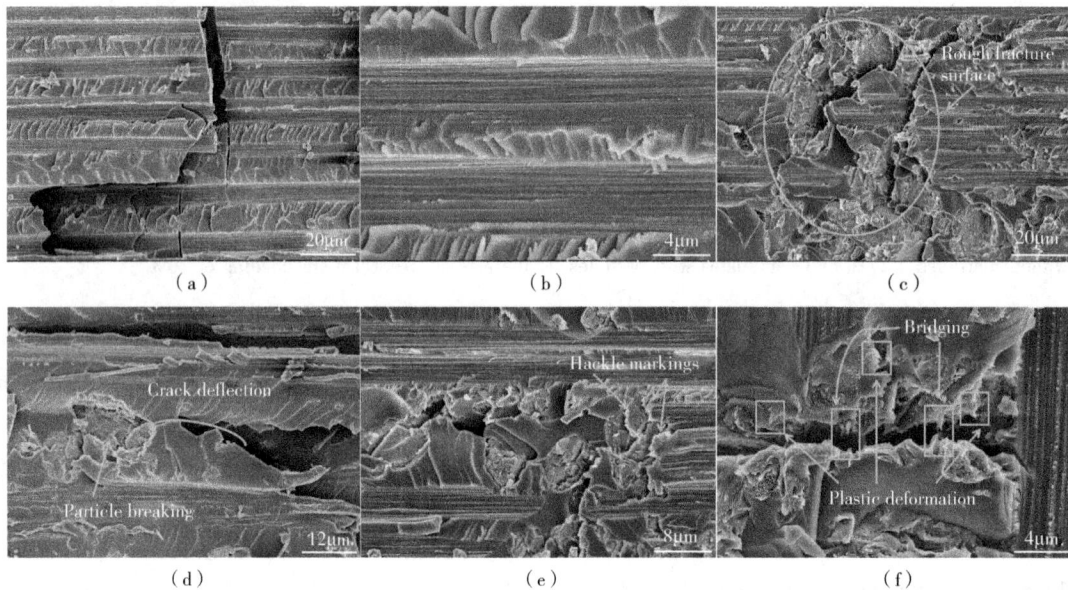

Fig.5 SEM images of fracture surface of an ENF specimen: (a)-(b) Blank laminates; (c)-(f) Particle interleaved laminates with size of 10-50μm and loading of 10%

4   Conclusions

This study demonstrated that the Mode Ⅰ and Mode Ⅱ interlamilar fracture toughness of carbon fiber-epoxy composite could be improved by PPO interleaf particles. Fluorescence microscopy images showed that the PPO particles retained their morphology after the composite was cured. SEM images suggested that the improved toughness by the PPO particles was attributed to plastic deformation, crack deflection and bridging of particles. The study determined that PPO particle size had significant effects on fracture toughness, and suggested the optimum particle size to be 10-50μm. However, it should be beneficiary to further classify the particles in this size range and test their effects in both fracture toughness modes.

Acknowledgements

This work was supported by Natural Science Foundation of Shanghai (18S28147) and Fundamental Research Funds for the Central Universities (19D128105).

References

[1]ZUCCHELLI A, FOCARETE M L, GUALANDI C, et al. Electrospun nanofibers for enhancing structural performance of composite materials[J]. Polymers for Advanced Technologies,2015,22(3):339-349.

[2]CHEN S, CHEN B, FAN J, et al. Exploring the application of sustainable poly (propylene carbonate) copolymer in toughening epoxy thermosets[J]. ACS Sustainable Chemistry & Engineering,2015,3(9):150723114637001.

[3]NASH N H, YOUNG T M, MCGRAIL P T, et al. Inclusion of a thermoplastic phase to improve impact and post-impact performances of carbon fibre reinforced thermosetting compos-

ites—a review[J]. Materials & Design,2015,85,582-597.

[4]LIU D, LI G, LI B, et al. In-situ toughened cfrp composites by shear-calender orientation and fiber-bundle filtration of pa microparticles at prepreg interlayer[J]. Composites Part A: Applied Science and Manufacturing,2016,84,165-174.

[5]ODAGIRI N. Toughness improved high performance torayca prepreg t800h/3900 series[J]. Procinternsampe Symp,1988, 272-283.

[6]GROLEAU, M. R, SHI, et al. Mode Ⅱ fracture of composites interlayered with nylon particles[J]. Composites Science & Technology,1996,56(11):1223-1240.

[7]WANG J, TSOU A H, PASSINO H L, et al. Ppe-g-hdpe in high-performance poly (p-phenylene ether) / polyethylene blends: Synthesis and compatibilization effects[J]. Polymer, 2018,138.

[8]YAN C, LIU L, HUANG Y, et al. Anion-conductive poly (2, 6-dimethyl-1, 4-phenylene oxide) grafted with tailored polystyrene chains for alkaline fuel cells[J]. Journal of Membrane Science,2019,573,247-256.

[9]JOHNSEN B B, KINLOCH A J, MOHAMMED R D, et al. Toughening mechanisms of nanoparticle-modified epoxy polymers[J]. Polymer, 2007,48(2):530-541.

[10]LAUNEY M E, RITCHIE R O. On the fracture toughness of advanced materials [J]. Advanced Materials, 2010, 21 (21):2103-2110.

Waterborne Polyurethane and Silk Sericin and Wool Keratin Sericin Composite Films Reinforced by Ultrasonic Modification

ZHANG Mingyue[1,2], DENG Huihui[3], LIU Hongling[1,2*], YU Weidong[1,2]

[1] Key Laboratory of Textile Science &Technology, Ministry of Education, Shanghai, 201620, China

[2] Department of Technical Textiles, College of Textiles, Donghua University, Shanghai, 201620, China

* Corresponding author's email: hlliu@ dhu. edu. cn

Abstract: In recent years, sericin and wool keratin composite film have been widely used in biomedicine, biomaterials and other fields. Herein, the waterborne polyurethane (WPU) and sericin/wool keratin solutions mixture are composited in different ratios to prepare the waterborne polyurethane/ wool keratin/sericin (WPU-WS) composite films by solvent casting method. The internal structure of the composite films is characterized by infrared spectrometer and ultraviolet spectrophotometer. Ultrasonic modification of WPU-WS composite films was carried out to study the effect of ultrasonic modification time on the structure and mechanical properties of WPU-WS composite films. The results showed that WPU-WS composite films had good tensile properties and ultraviolet absorption capacity. Under the action of ultrasonic, the macromolecular chains of water-based polyurethane, sericin and wool keratin are combined together to make the structure of the composite film more orderly. Ultrasonic modification of WPU-WS composite films was carried out to prepare composites with good physical properties, and the composites were treated on the surface of wool fabrics, which is of great significance for reducing environmental pollution, improving the properties of wool fabrics, expanding the application of protein materials and waterborne polyurethane materials.

Keywords: Waterborne polyurethane; Sericin; Keratin; Composite film; Tensile properties

1   Introduction

Protein films are one of the important materials used in biomedicine and biotechnology. There are various excellent protein materials in nature, such as wool keratin, sericin, silk fibroin, etc. , which can be used to make protein films with adjustable physical and chemical properties through suitable combination of polymers and crosslinking methods[1]. Sericin and silk fibroin contain irregular crimping and beta-folding, and wool keratin is rich in alpha-helices, which, combined with different treatment and blending proportion, yield many excellent properties. When the mixing ratio of wool keratin and silk fibroin to prepare wool keratin silk fibroin composite membrane is 3 : 7, the physical and chemical properties of the composite membrane are optimal[2]. Chen et al. added wool keratin and reconstructed it through molecular network reconstruction in order

to enhance sericin film[3]. And the elongation at break of waterborne polyurethane film is big, but it has low surface free performance, low intensity, mainly through crosslinking reaction and organic polymer hybrid methods such as the modified waterborne polyurethane[4-5], the researchers have so far by the water-borne polyurethane and organic polymer crosslinked to hybrid modification, such as acrylic acid polymer, epoxy resin, organic fluorine and silicone[6-8]. Some researchers also modified waterborne polyurethane with inorganic materials, the most commonly used inorganic materials such as silicon dioxide (SiO_2), titanium dioxide (TiO_2) and green palygorskite[9-11]. In this paper, the structural characteristics of sericin wool keratin were used to composite with waterborne polyurethane, and the molecular crosslinking network structure was formed through structural reassembly, so as to improve the performance of WPU-WS composite film and obtain the composite film with excellent mechanical properties and water resistance. Subsequently, ultrasonic was used to modify WPU-WS composite membrane to explore the influence of ultrasonic modification time on the properties and structure of the composite, which is of potential application value in preparing waterproof and breathable fabric after finishing.

2 Experiments

2.1 Materials

All chemicals are analytically pure and can be used without further purification. Obtain acetone, ethanol, sodium sulfide and sodium dodecyl sulfate from Titan chemical reagent co. LTD. Buy wool and domestic silk cocoons from the Internet.

2.2 Preparation of Wool Keratin Solution

Firstly, the wool was extracted with acetone (65°) and anhydrous ethanol (85°) for 2.5h respectively, and the grease and dirt on the surface of the wool fibers were removed. Secondly, Cut wools into pieces at 1 : 20 bath ratio and add to the mixture of 1.9% sodium sulfide, 42% urea and 0.8% sodium lauryl sulfate at 65 ° for 14h. During the experiment, the wool was thoroughly dissolved after repeated stirring. Filter residue dissolved liquid to remove dissolved wool, the molecular weight of 3500 D dialysis bag for filtering of dissolved liquid dialysis, once every 2h in deionized water, three days later, after using the centrifuge supernatant fluid, wool keratin solution put in big dish, medium speed on the magnetic stirrer, use weighing method to determine the concentration of the protein liquid, eventually concentrated mass fraction of 2% of wool keratin solution, 4℃ refrigerated. Set aside.

2.3 Preparation of Sericin Solutions

The silkworm cocoons were washed with deionized water, then dried in an oven at 65℃, and then cut into pieces of 1.5cm×1.5cm into a sterilizing pot, and then added with appropriate amount of deionized water, boiled in boiling water for 3 hours, and filtered. Then cleaned the silkworm silk twice with deionized water, mixed the cleaning liquid and the sericin solution, ventilated the upper part of the fume hood, rotated and evaporated at 85℃, concentrated to obtain a 2% by weight sericin solution, and stored at −4℃ for refrigeration.

2.4 Preparation of Ultrasonic Modified Membrane

The water-borne polyurethane/sericin/wool keratin composites were mixed at a composite ratio of 80 : 20 respectively, and the glass rod was used to stir them evenly, and the concentration was adjusted to 240g/L. Then, it was placed in the ultrasonic cell shredder, where the ultrasonic frequency was 46 Hz and the ultrasonic power was 50W. After ultrasonic treatment for 0, 6min, 18min, 30min respectively, the mixed solution was poured into the removal template, and the film was formed after standing for 2 days in a constant temperature and humidity environment, labeled as WPU20.

2.5 Infrared Spectroscopy

A certain amount of WPU-WS composite films were taken and scanned 128 times by an infrared spectrometer (Nicolet TM 5700, USA) with a resolution of $4cm^{-1}$ and a scanning range of $4000-660cm^{-1}$ to analyze the molecular structure of the composite films.

2.6 Mechanical Performance Analysis

Fabric thickness meter (YG141N, China) was used to measure film thickness. Three parallel samples were measured and averaged. Unit: mm. The prepared WPU/sericin/wool keratin composite film was cut into the dumbbell shape with standard No. 2 dumbbell cutter, and balanced in a constant temperature and humidity environment for 24h. The mechanical properties of WPU-WS composite film were tested by using multifunctional fabric strength machine (HD026N – 300, China). The clamping distance was 60mm, the tensile speed was 100mm/min, and 5 samples were taken as a group.

2.7 Ultraviolet-Visible Spectrum Analysis

WPU-WS composite film was cut to a size of 4cm × 4cm, and the scanning range was 200−800nm by ultraviolet-visible spectrophotometer (Hitachi U−4100, Japan). Five parallel samples were measured, and the UV absorption capacity of WPU-WS composite films of each proportion was measured by taking the average value.

2.8 Measurement of Contact Angle

A contact Angle measuring instrument (DSA30, Germany) was used to measure the static contact angle of the membrane. The measured sample was fixed on the glass slide and placed horizontally on the test table. At least five different positions of the same fabric were selected and droplets with a volume of 5 microns were added respectively to measure the static contact angle. The data were recorded and the error range was calculated.

3   Results and Discussions

3. 1   The Effect of Ultrasonic on the Structure of Composite Films

Infrared spectroscopy can be used to detect chemical change of secondary structure, the analysis of the effect of ultrasound for composite, after ultrasonic effect of composite membrane amide band I with infrared spectrum is shown in Fig. 1. The composite film showed obvious characteristic peaks at $1650cm^{-1}$ (α-helices) and $1635cm^{-1}$ without regular curling, and at $1619cm^{-1}$ and $1600cm^{-1}$ (β-sheets). With the increase of ultrasonic time, the absorption peak at $1650cm^{-1}$ became narrower and the peak strength increased, and the characteristic peak gradually became obvious at $1635cm^{-1}$. The results showed that the ultrasonic modification time was beneficial to the formation of regular structures such as α-helices and β-sheets. There were characteristic absorption peaks at $1650cm^{-1}$, $1635cm^{-1}$, $1619cm^{-1}$ and $1600cm^{-1}$ of the curves, and the maximum absorption peaks remained unchanged, except that the peak strength changed to different degrees, indicating that ultrasonic treatment did not cause structural changes of the composites, but only played a synergistic role in the aggregation mode and spatial conformation of the composites, as shown in Fig. 1.

3. 2   Mechanical Propertied of Composite Films

In this experiment, WPU20, a composite film with different ultrasonic effects, was tensile tested, and the tensile curve of WPU-WS composite film was shown in Fig. 2. The fracture strength and initial modulus scale showed a trend of first increasing and then decreasing, reaching the maximum at 6min. The final fracture strength and initial modulus were lower than those without ultrasonic, and the fracture elongation showed a trend of first decreasing and then increasing.

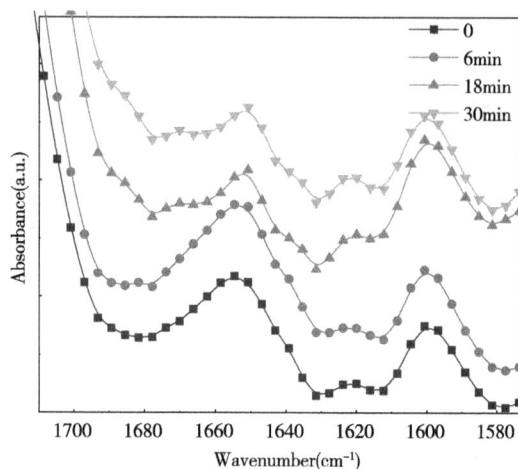

Fig. 1   Infrared spectrum of WPU-WS composite film after different ultrasonic time (wavelength range: $1573-1700cm^{-1}$)

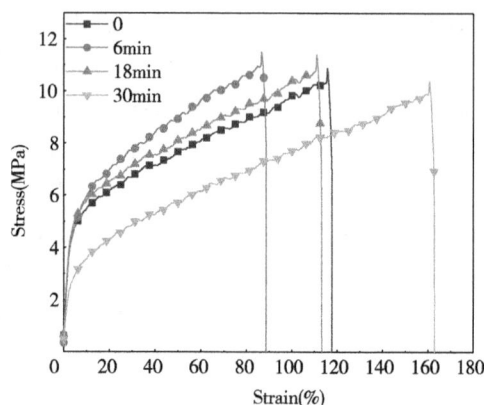

Fig. 2   Stretch curve of WPU-WS composite film after ultrasonic treatment

3. 3   UV Absorbance of Composite Films

Ultraviolet-Visible spectrum can be used for the qualitative and quantitative analysis of inorganic and organic compounds, which is one of the important ways to study the structure and function of materials. In this paper, Ultraviolet-Visible spectrum was used to further explore the structural stability of the composite film, and the UV absorption spectrum of the composite film within the range of 200-800nm was obtained, as shown in Fig. 3. Can be observed with ultrasonic duration increased to 30 from 0, mixed membranes WPU20 ultraviolet absorption ability in 200-800 nm region showed the trend of increased after decreased first, at the time of 6min ultrasonic ultraviolet absorption capacity of the strongest, thus, ultrasonic action time to composite membrane of ultraviolet absorption ability to produce certain effect, this may be due to the ultrasonic cavitation and mechanical action disrupted the density of the composite structure, more chromophores exposed on the surface, so the ultraviolet absorption capacity increase. However, with the increase of ultrasonic time, the interaction between the composites is enhanced, and the chromophore groups will be embedded again, and the ultraviolet absorption intensity will be reduced to some extent.

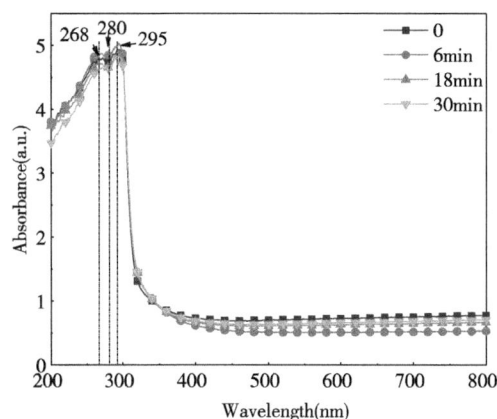

Fig. 3　UV absorption capacity of composite film after ultrasonic treatment for different time

3. 4　Effect of Ultrasonic on Static Contact Angle of Composite Film

According to Tab. 1, with the increase of ultrasonic time, WPU-WS composite membrane surface contact angle showed increasing trend after then, with the increase of ultrasonic action time, this can compact combination effect will be disrupted, carboxyl, ether, hydroxyl and other hydrophilic group exposed on the surface, end surface contact angle below without ultrasonic composite membrane surface contact angle. We speculate that if the ultrasonic time continues to increase, when the rearrangement of the macromolecular structure of the composites reaches a certain balance, the crosslinking between molecular structures will be enhanced, and the crosslinking points will be enhanced. The composites are a kind of molecular network space structure connected by crosslinking points, and the surface contact angle will increase.

Tab. 1　Contact Angle of WPU20 composite film after different ultrasonic time

Ultrasonic time(min)	ContractAngle(°)
0	63. 7
6	68. 8
18	52. 3
30	49. 7

4　Conclusions

The study of ultrasonic modified WPU-WS composite film showed that the breaking elongation of WPU-WS composite film increased with time, while the breaking strength and initial modulus decreased with the increase of ultrasonic time. In addition, the UV absorbance and water resistance of WPU-WS composite films tend to increase and then decrease with the increase of ultrasonic modification time, indicating that appropriate time of ultrasonic treatment can improve the UV absorption capacity and water resistance of the composite film. In this paper, waterborne polyurethane, natural sericin and wool keratin were used as raw materials to prepare WPU-WS composite film by structural reconstruction from the molecular structure. It provides a new reference for the modification of waterborne polyurethane and the utilization of sericin waste resources, which is conducive to environmental improvement, promotes the sustainable development of resources and conforms to the current national environmental protection concept.

References

[1]CHEN L, ZHOU M L, QIAN Z G, et al. Fabrication of protein films from genetically engineered silk-elastin-like proteins by controlled cross-Linking[J]. ACS Biomaterials Science & Engineering,2017,3(3): 335-341.

[2]CHEN H. Preparation and characterization of wool keratin silk membrane[J]. Wool Technology,2016,44 (6): 46-49.

[3]CHEN B, XING Y, YU W, et al. Wool keratin and silk sericin composite films reinforced by molecular network reconstruction[J]. Journal of Materials Science, 2017, 53 (7): 5418-5428.

[4]CHEN X, YANG J, WU Q Y, et al. Preparation and properties of waterborne polyurethane modified by amide-based chain extender[J]. Fine Chemical Industry,2018,35 (11).

[5]MA X, DING B, DUAN Y, et al. Preparation and properties of waterborne polyurethane modified by amino silicone oil [J]. Fine Chemical Industry,2018,35 (5).

[6]LOPEZ A, REYES Y, ASUA J M, et al. High-shear-strength waterborne polyurethane/acrylic soft adhesives[J]. Macromolecular Materials & Engineering,2013,298(6):612-623.

[7]LIM C H, CHOI H S, SI T N. Surface modification with waterborne fluorinated anionic polyurethane dispersions [J]. Journal of Applied Polymer Science,2010,86(13):3322-3330.

[8]LAI X, SHEN Y, LEI W. Preparation and properties of self-crosslinkable polyurethane/silane hybrid emulsion[J]. Journal of Polymer Research,2011,18(6):2425-2433.

[9]TORROPAL A U, ANA M, FERN A, et al. Characterization of polyurethanes containing different silicas[J]. International Journal of Adhesion & Adhesives,2001,21(1):1-9.

[10]LI K, PENG J, ZHANG M, et al. Comparative study of the effects of anatase and rutile titanium dioxide nanoparticles on the structure and properties of waterborne polyurethane [J]. Colloids & Surfaces A Physicochemical & Engineering Aspects,2015,470:92-99.

[11]XIONG J, ZHEN Z, QIN X, et al. The thermal and mechanical properties of a polyurethane/multi-walled carbon nanotube composite[J]. Carbon,2006,44(13):2701-2707.

A Comparative Study of African Traditional Jewelry and Modern African Style Jewelry Expressive Language

WANG Manqian[1*], NELLI Basova[2]

[1] *Department of Fashion and Accessory Design, The School of Fashion, Dalian Polytechnic University, Dalian, 116034, China*

[2] *Southampton International College, Dalian Polytechnic University, Dalian, 116034, China*

* *Corresponding author's email*: V 597077489@ qq. com

Abstract: African traditional jewelry has its own unique characteristics that show the identity of African peoples and is rich in bright colors, totem patterns, and intricate decorative elements. It is believed that today's African style jewelry is the style based on the traditional African jewelry culture and adapted in style to fit into modern fashion design. The language of African traditional jewelry design revealing rich cultural and historical background and expressing African customs, beliefs and traditions has become more concise, refined and more modern. At the same time, modern African style jewelry design has also developed a more profound and versatile expression of the traditional themes as well as expanding the limits of such themes, which now can range from geographical features, nature forms, tribal culture to the expression of strong rhythm and wild nature elements. The author of the article believes that modern African jewelry shows an expressive language that can be described as very distinctive and revealing a strong rhythm.

Keywords: Africa; Traditional jewelry; African style; Expression language

1 Introduction

Jewelry is a means of cultural information transmission and can be seen as a material carrier of cultural representation. 'African traditional jewelry' and 'African style jewelry' are two concepts that are related but different in content. To clarify their difference, we must first understand the connotations of 'traditional' and 'style'. 'Tradition' refers to ideological customs, moral systems, culture and art, etc., which have been passed down from past eras, and are the inheritance of historical development[1]. 'Style' is an artistic concept. It is stable and can reflect the external imprint of the inner characteristics of the times, the nation and the artists' personal spiritual temperament. A work of a specific style can reflect traditional culture and spirit, but are also associated with the background of the creation, influenced by political and economic situation and social ideology[2]. Based on the definition of 'tradition' and

'style', this paper argues that African traditional jewelry can be defined as body decorations showing ethnic, social or regional characteristics of people on the African continent and which has constant artistic features, cultural aesthetics and expression language features developed over the history of the area. African traditional jewelry is mainly influenced by religious beliefs, cultural customs, climatic environment, materials specific for the region and craftsmanship, all of which together make Africa's regional cultural characteristics.

Moving on to African style jewelry, allow us to use a metaphor: if African traditional jewelry can be compared to an old man with the imprints of his life years on him and his apparel, African style jewelry is more like the youth dressed in maverick fashion. African style jewelry belongs to the category of modern design. It is based on the revival of nationalism and post-modern art multiculturalism. It is influenced by traditional jewelry, but it expands the formal expressive language of the traditional jewelry by blending in other African style elements (Fig. 1).

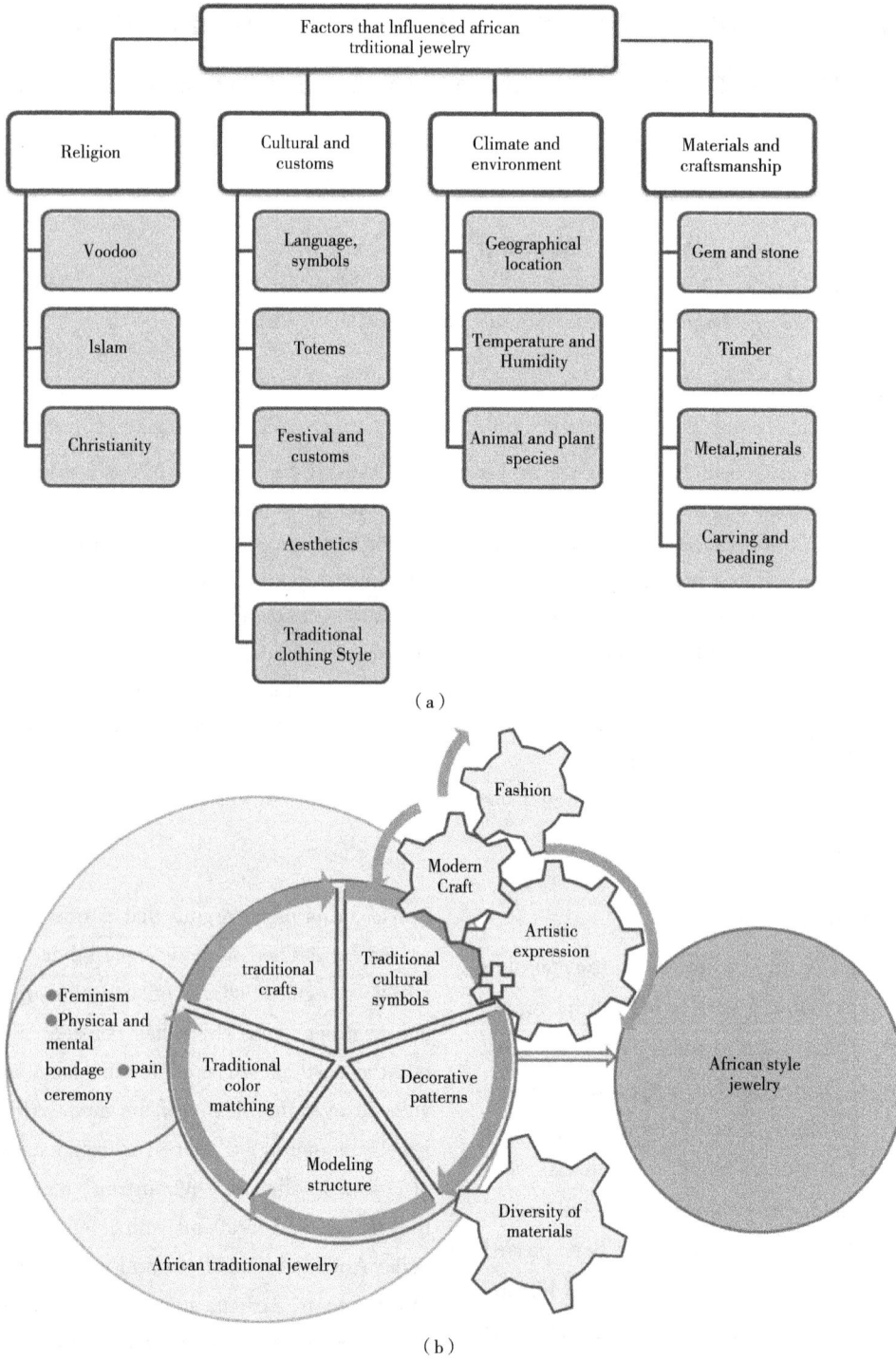

(a)

(b)

Fig. 1 (a) Factors that influenced the development of African traditional jewelry; (b) Graphical presentation of the relationship between African traditional jewelry and African style jewelry

2 Traditional Expressive Language

Africa is well known as a 'tropical continent'. Long long ago, most African regions did not use words, so they needed to use other tools and forms to convey information and preserve their traditional culture[3]. Jewelry was used as an important tool to preserve the traditions. Through long-term cultural exchanges, as well as the spread of religious mythology, African jewelry formed the basic rules of artistic expression and relatively fixed production procedures that allowed the traditional jewelry find its basic style characteristics.

2.1 Characteristic of African Traditional Jewelry

As the main body decoration, African traditional jewelry had big volume and covered large body areas.

The torridity of the climate in the African continent led to a great degree of skin exposure among the population of African countries and tribes. An ancient African's upper body was normally naked while he would wear a pair of pants. Under the influence of this form of clothing, African jewelry achieved its large volume, which plays a key role in shielding or highlighting key body parts. African jewelry's massiveness comes with a special decorative technique which is called 'a balance pendant'. The balance pendant appeared in traditional African ornaments because the size of the jewelry was too large and heavy for human's neck to hold when weighing down in the front, so the decorations at the back of the necklace were added to balance out the weight. Such decoration started also to be considered as an amulet, because people imagined that a balance pendant can protect them; it was like having a shield and eyes in the back. This increased the meaning of this form of decoration and made it popular.

In addition, some Africans can also be seen in exaggerated earrings and with decorations in their lips. For example, the Mursi tribe in Ethiopia decorate their lips with plates since they are about ten. With the plates getting bigger, the lips elongate. Thus, it can be seen that under the influence of special beliefs and adopted aesthetics, in some areas African traditional jewelry got exaggerated to the point of body restraint and even body injury thus demonstrating people's spirit.

2.2 Unusual Body Areas Decorated with Jewelry Brought About Its Unusual Forms

Jewelry in the normal sense refers to decorations of head, ears or hands. Today's usual set of jewelry also appears in the same body areas. However, through the study of African jewelry, we can find that decoration positioning can be very different. Because of the large areas of exposed skin, Africans decorated with jewelry many other body parts. We can see massive jewelry in their navel, on the waist, ankles, arms, etc. For example, in Nigeria, women often wore heavy leg hoops and cuffs. The same can be seen in Zaire women's leg decorations-leggings looking like armor are the demonstration of women's glory[4]. In addition, high-positioned men such as kings and tribal leaders always wore precious golden jewelry. This jewelry was often made into a ring shape and worn on the finger joints. This form of decoration looks very close to the punk style which also has simple expressive language aimed at demonstrating the bravery of the wearer. The same can be seen in knee joint decorations which were also made of gold and beads of various colours. Some special kinds of jewelry can be also found hanging down on the chest or from the shoulders, which dangle on the body when in motion. These help to highlight these body parts to attract a partner of opposite sex.

2.3 Materials and Modeling Representing Nature Worshiping

Some African traditional jewelry has a pure function to nature worship. People were afraid of the unknowable power of nature. So, they wanted to imitate animals that are tenacious, ferocious and strong. Ancient African jewelry reflects the nature worship and beast worship, especially of the animals and plants with strength and vitality. During the hunting process, people have always been impressed by the unparalleled hunting ability and power of African lions, or the height an eagle can fly and spot its prey from. And thus people tried to imitate these animals through body decoration. Ancient Egypt has good examples of this, where images of an eagle, snake or scarab are the main elements on the jewelry of those times[5]. Besides, the natural worship of African jewelry can be also reflected in the natural state of the material. African abundant timber, wheat straw, grass and other plant materials are often directly applied into jewelry in an original natural state. There are also a variety of semi-precious stones. African traditional jewelry often uses jewelry materials such as amber, agate, and lapis lazuli. But African jewelry does not make too many sculpt carvings on these stones, and it is rare to see how to imitate a certain auspicious image by changing its appearance. African traditional jewelry is more keen to preserve the irregular shape of these materials, even deliberately retain the knots, residual edges, cracks of the material, reflecting the charm of the original wildness.

2.4 African Traditional Jewelry Has Strong Social Function and Ceremonial Sense

Jewelry has strong social significance as well as the aesthetic and decorative functions. Teeth and bones of beasts that we can see in African jewelry are meant to demonstrate the bravery and strength of the wearer. A large number of shells combined with semi-precious stones and precious metal materials indicate wealth. In Samburu, the north-central part of Kenya, when boys became warriors, their mothers would put a pair of beads on their ears to celebrate their achievement. Women's age and marital status can also be judged from the earrings, nose rings and other body decorations they wear. Changes in their appearance, such as ear and lip piercing, can be a sign of a new stage in a person's life. In the old times, people could tell whether a Hammer woman is married or not from her necklace, and tell her status in the family from her other jewelry. It can be seen that African traditional jewelry has been directly related to the social status of the wearer and has always had a function of symbolic language.

3 African Style Jewelry

The African style brings the sense of vitality into the world of fashion through its novelty and original style but, at the same time, preserves humanity's most pure understanding of life and nature. Since the beginning of the 20th century, the European avantgarde art community has been influenced by African and primitive art. In the decorative art movement jewelry design, there are a lot of simple modeling and geometric symbolic patterns in which the attribute of African art can be seen. African tribal dance and witchcraft performance masks, wood carvings and other elements have a great influence on modernism style design with its feature of being con-

cise and later influenced the postmodern national style and gradually formed what we now call the 'African style jewelry'.

African style jewelry is directly affected by African traditional jewelry and carries the original wild style and rich cultural history. At the same time, African style jewelry is more flexible in its combination of various fashion elements as well as different characteristics of certain time periods, new materials and production techniques. All this makes the overall artistic and expressive language of African style jewelry rich and diverse.

3.1 Rough and Free Geometric Shape Reflecting the Pursuit of Natural Beauty

From the perspective of modeling elements, African style jewelry often appears in abstract geometric forms. But unlike regular geometry patterns that are common in the modern design, African geometric symbols and elemental lines are irregular. Figures look more like a combination of simple strokes. There is no absolute straight line in nature, and this idea is well represented in African style jewelry. For example, egg-shaped jewelry indicates a desire of married women for fertility. A triangle symbolizes harmonious relationship between a father, mother and their child. Besides, various geometric symbols are rich in the pastoral people of Mali in North Africa, Bama of Cameroon and Guinea in West Africa used geometric forms especially related to their beliefs[6]. These symbols, as cultural elements, also have a certain impact on today's African style jewelry design. We can see from a typical geometric shape in the metal necklace by Maiyet. The shape of the pendant is a simple geometric crescent shape. It does not pursue exquisiteness of lines, but to reflect wild and free nature spirit.

3.2 Traditional Beast Worship and Reproduction of Religious Totem Culture

Pattern is an important element in African style jewelry, the most common pattern there being wild animals of Africa. For example, the antelope and South Africanox. Have always been admired by Africans for their speed and strength, and, when used in jewelry design, are considered to be the representatives of African wildlife.

Wild animal skin patterns such as leopard and zebra prints also appear in jewelry in abstract form, reflecting the wildness and free spirit of Africa. As an important part of traditional jewelry, African masks also often appear in the form of patterns in today's African style jewelry. In Africa, masks represent ancestors' souls and natural elves[7]. They seem to have a mystical meaning in the culture of each of the various tribes in Africa. These features are well reflected in African style jewelry.

3.3 Traditional Crafts and Materials, Reflecting Authentic Rhythm and Sensation

Materials and craftsmanship play an important role in African style jewelry. And a big part of art and fashion jewelry in African style is based on traditional materials and crafts. The variety of materials used is very rich, including animal bones, various stones of many kinds and colours, glass, clay, wood. In the processing of these materials, their natural features, including authentic marks and textures are preserved. Thus, African style jewelry is often made preserving irregular shapes and authentic features such as patterns, textures, or knots that are the attributes of the material itself which makes each piece of jewelry unique.

The most representative jewelry craft in Africa is beading, which is very feminine as it is made and worn by women. Today, beading is still popular on the African continent, and beaded jewelry can be seen in many tourist souvenir shops. In fashion jewelry, beads, together with other jewelry materials, give the designs a new look when used with knitting and through the African style specific rhythm reflected in the relationship between points and lines.

4 Conclusions

Firstly, African traditional jewelry demonstrates a strong spiritual and emotional way of expressing the understanding and feelings of the people of Africa toward the nature, universe, life and gods. It is characterized by exaggerated details, as well as abstract and distorted forms.

Secondly, modern African style jewelry is a jewelry design style with a very artistic and visual language close to the post-modern style while based on the features inherited from the traditional African jewelry. African traditional jewelry and Africa style jewelry have the same connection as the one between heritage and advancement.

Thirdly, African style jewelry can be mainly characterized by rough and free geometric shapes, and its use of African representative animals and traditional mask patterns to represent beast worship and nature worship.

Lastly, most of the materials used in African style jewelry come from nature and undergo simple processing, which is consistent with African traditional jewelry.

References

[1] LIU B W, LI S D, The significance of China's cognitive understanding of African art in a globalized era, African art research[M]. Kunming:Yunnan university press,2010.

[2] WANG H J, Perspective of art[M]. Culture and Art Publishing Press, 2004.

[3] AKIN E, Introduction to music in africa[M]. Lagos:Lagos University Press, 1982.

[4] YU M, The culture spirit of the African traditional jewelry [D]. Tianjin:Tianjin Normal University, 2010.

[5] HELEN S, The encyclopedia of ancient Egypt[M]. Shanghai: Shanghai scientific and technology literature press, 2014.

[6] YUKIMASA M, Zero[M]. Beijing:CITIC press group, 2017.

[7] ZHANG F Y. History foreign arts and crafts[M]. Beijing: Central Compilation & Translation Press, 2004.

Convolutional Neural Networks for Yarn Dyed Fabric Image Recognition

XU Lu[1], ZHANG Ruiyun[1]*

[1] Department of Technical Textiles, College of Textiles, Donghua University, Shanghai, 201620, China

* Corresponding author's email: ryzhang@ dhu. edu. cn

Abstract: In recent years, Convolutional Neural Networks (CNNs) have been widely used in the field of image processing, and have achieved favorable results. In this paper, based on the characteristics of yarn dyed fabric image, on the basis of in-depth understanding and research of convolutional neural network theory and research results at home and abroad, classic network VGG-Net and Inception-v3 are chosen to train for dyed fabric image classification. Experiments are conducted on our own database, 16000 dyed fabric images, which are collected by DigiEye in the best shooting condition. The results show that Inception-v3 achieves a higher excellent accuracy rate of 91. 0% compared with the fine-tuned VGG-Net.

Keywords: Yarn dyed fabric image classification; Convolution neural network (CNN); VGG-Net; Inception-v3

1 Introduction

Nowadays for textile enterprises, especially yarn dyed fabric enterprises, there is production based on samples supplied by customers. After receiving the sample image of the customer, it is necessary to find the corresponding fabric, which often requires a large amount of labor cost for image selection and matching. Therefore, establishing fabric images database and recognition of fabric images can improve product development speed. Scientific and efficient fabric images management can be achieved by using image recognition or image classification techniques. Fabric images classifycation remains challenging in image recognition in computer vision, given that fabric may have similar colors, shapes and texture.

In the past years, a rapid improvement and development have been gained in the field of artificial neural network[1]. The outstanding classification accuracy and operational precision make it an alternative choice when we handle image processing problems. Neural network has numerous characters like unsupervised learning or rich extraction of features, which fairly improves the performance of network. And the convolutional neural network (CNN) makes a big success in large image process. AlexNet[2], VGG-Net[3], GoogLeNet[4] and Inception modules[5] are excellent CNN models in the past few years. These models achieve impressive effect in image process, such as image recognition and classification tasks, object detection and semantic segmentation. In the 1980s and 1990s, some researchers published relevant research work on CNN, and achieved good recognition results in several pattern recognition fields, especially hand-written digit recognition[6-7]. However, CNN at this time is only suitable for the recognition of small pictures, and for large-scale data, the recognition effect is not good. Alex Krizhevsky et al. put forward a deep convolution network architecture in 2012, achieving outstanding performance, which recaused a boom of CNN[2]. Later, plenty of high-quality CNN models were proposed and promoted in the field of computer vision. The winners of ILSVRC 2014 went to VGG-Net and GoogLeNet, which go deeper in their convolution architectures respectively and decrease the top-5 error again. With the deepening of architecture, the CNN model can approximate the objective function in nonlinear growth and gain a better character representation. Present deep learning models can reach a knock down top−5 error, which is even lower than the identification error rate of the human eye.

2　Model and Approach

2.1　Convolutional Neural Network

CNN is a product of neural network development. It belongs to deep feed forward neural network and is often used to deal with image recognition problems. CNN typically include input layer, convolutional layer, pooling layer and fully-connected layer. Each image data of the input layer is convolved with a plurality of convolution kernels in the convolutional layer to generate a new image feature[8]. The pooling layer selects a small area of the generated image feature map, calculates its average value or maximum value, realizes feature aggregation analysis of each position of the feature image, reduces the feature dimension, and prevents overfitting. The last part of the network is generally 1−2 layers of fully-connected layers. The fully-connected layer is responsible for connecting the extracted feature maps, and finally obtaining the final classification result through the classifier.

2.2　VGG-Net

VGG-Net is a typical CNN with high classification and recognition rate[3]. VGG-Net steadily increase the depth of the network by adding more convolutional layers, which is feasible due to the use of very small (3× 3) convolution filters in all layers. VGG-Net explored the important aspect of convolutional networks architecture designits depth, and successfully constructed a 16−19 layers deep convolutional neural network. It has a strong generalization ability. The VGG−16 network model has 16 layers, including 13 convolutional layers and 3 fully-connected layers. The VGG−19 network model has 19 layers, including 16 convolutional layers and 3 fully-connected layers.

2.3　Inception-v3

The Inception-v3 model is a third-generation CNN classifier constructed with an Inception network structure[5]. The network structure consists of 11 Inception modules, which contain a total of 46 layers of network. The image is convolved and pooled (including average pooling and maximum pooling) through 11 Inception

modules. The final fully-connected layer integration feature is input to Softmax layer. The Softmax layer trained through the ImageNet dataset identifies 1000 categories in ImageNet.

2.4　Transfer Learning

In this paper, we use the transfer learning method to retrain the VGG−16, VGG−19 and Inception−v3 models (Fig. 1) in the Tensor Flow deep learning library on the fabric image dataset to classify the fabric image. Transfer learning refers to a deep learning method that uses existing knowledge that has been learned from an environment to solve other new problems that are different from the old one but have a certain relationship. This learning method not only requires a lower number of data sets, but also has shorter training time and higher precision.

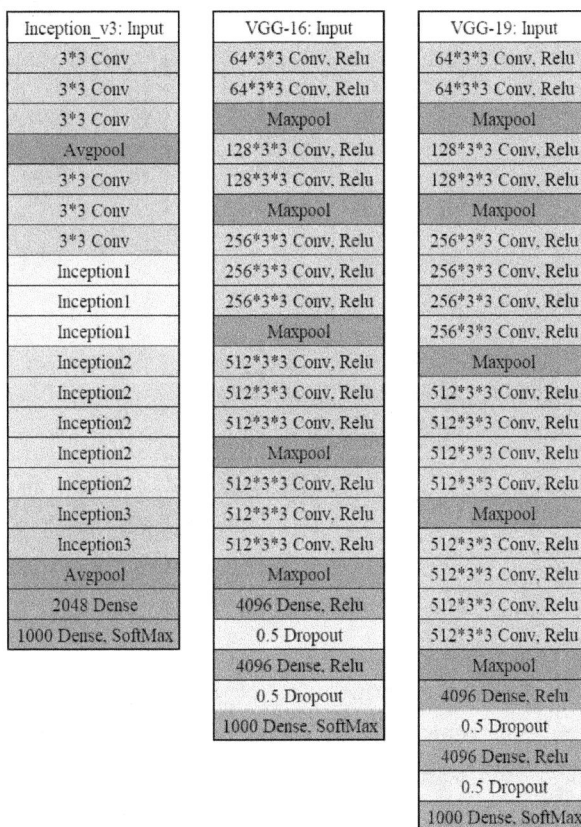

Inception_v3: Input	VGG-16: Input	VGG-19: Input
3*3 Conv	64*3*3 Conv, Relu	64*3*3 Conv, Relu
3*3 Conv	64*3*3 Conv, Relu	64*3*3 Conv, Relu
3*3 Conv	Maxpool	Maxpool
Avgpool	128*3*3 Conv, Relu	128*3*3 Conv, Relu
3*3 Conv	128*3*3 Conv, Relu	128*3*3 Conv, Relu
3*3 Conv	Maxpool	Maxpool
3*3 Conv	256*3*3 Conv, Relu	256*3*3 Conv, Relu
Inception1	256*3*3 Conv, Relu	256*3*3 Conv, Relu
Inception1	256*3*3 Conv, Relu	256*3*3 Conv, Relu
Inception1	Maxpool	256*3*3 Conv, Relu
Inception2	512*3*3 Conv, Relu	Maxpool
Inception2	512*3*3 Conv, Relu	512*3*3 Conv, Relu
Inception2	512*3*3 Conv, Relu	512*3*3 Conv, Relu
Inception2	Maxpool	512*3*3 Conv, Relu
Inception2	512*3*3 Conv, Relu	512*3*3 Conv, Relu
Inception3	512*3*3 Conv, Relu	Maxpool
Inception3	512*3*3 Conv, Relu	512*3*3 Conv, Relu
Avgpool	Maxpool	512*3*3 Conv, Relu
2048 Dense	4096 Dense, Relu	512*3*3 Conv, Relu
1000 Dense, SoftMax	0.5 Dropout	512*3*3 Conv, Relu
	4096 Dense, Relu	Maxpool
	0.5 Dropout	4096 Dense, Relu
	1000 Dense, SoftMax	0.5 Dropout
		4096 Dense, Relu
		0.5 Dropout
		1000 Dense, SoftMax

Fig. 1　Inception-v3, VGG-16 and VGG-19 Network structure diagram

3　Experimental Results

3.1　Establish Database

The collection of yarn dyed fabric images (Fig. 2) was

performed using a DigiEye device[9]. In order to overcome the influence of background, illumination, deformation and other factors, set the standardized parameters of the DigiEye system equipment, select the ANGLE mode under the D65 light source to adopt a shooting angle of 30 degrees, set the aperture to 5. 6, the shutter 1/13, which can better reflect the texture and color effect of the fabric. According to the characteristics of the color fabric, the shooting parameters of the fabric are determined to ensure the clear restoration of the color and texture of the yarn dyed fabric.

Our database consists of 16,000 images grouped into 5 categories, which covers the major types that can be commonly consumed in daily life. We list the 5 different categories here: stripe (4535), plaid (2983), dot (3014), plain (3107), other (2361). The whole categories and samples are shown in Fig. 3. The VGG-16, VGG-19, and Inception-v3 models were compared experimentally. For our performing experiments, images in our database are randomly divided into 80% training and 20% validation for objective and fair.

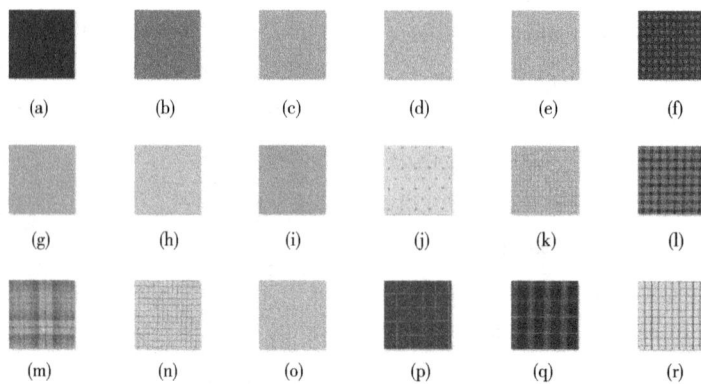

Fig. 2　Examples of yarn dyed fabric images

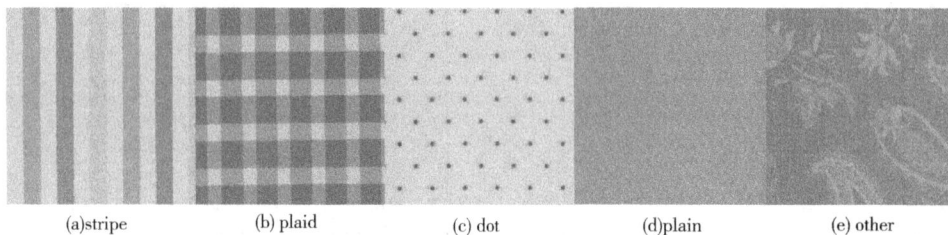

Fig. 3　Examples of yarn dyed fabric images database of 5 categories

3. 2　Evaluation Index

In order to better evaluate the performance of the established deep learning model, this paper intends to use the accuracy and cross entropy cost function as the evaluation indicators of the model.

3. 2. 1　Accuracy

The accuracy indicates the ratio of the number of correctly classified samples to the total number of samples, as shown in equation. The higher the accuracy, the better the model.

$$Accuracy = \frac{(TP + TN)}{(TP + TN + FP + FN)}$$

FN(False Negative) which is judged to be a negative sample, but in fact is a positive sample. FP (False Positive) which is judged as a positive sample, but is actually a negative sample. TN(True Negative) which is judged to be a negative sample, is in fact a negative sample. TP(True Positive) which is judged as a positive sample, is in fact a positive sample.

3. 2. 2　Cross Entropy

The cross entropy represents the degree of closeness between the actual output probability and the expected output probability. The Softmax layer converts the actual output of the neural network into probability through regression processing. Distribution, and then use cross entropy cost function to calculate the close distance coefficient between the actual output probability and the expected output probability. The smaller the coefficient, the more similar the two probability distributions are, and the higher the accuracy of the expected output. For a single neuron network, cross entropy cost function can be expressed as equation:

$$L = - [y\ln\hat{y} + (1 - y)\ln(1 - \hat{y})]$$

It can be seen that the cross entropy can intuitively explain the similarity between the actual output and the expected output: the smaller the cross entropy, the closer the expected output is to the actual output, and the higher the classification accuracy.

3.3 Results

The experiment is based on the TensorFlow frame-work. Fig. 4 and Fig. 5 shows the training accuracy, validation accuracy and cross entropy for each iteration of Inception-v3 model.

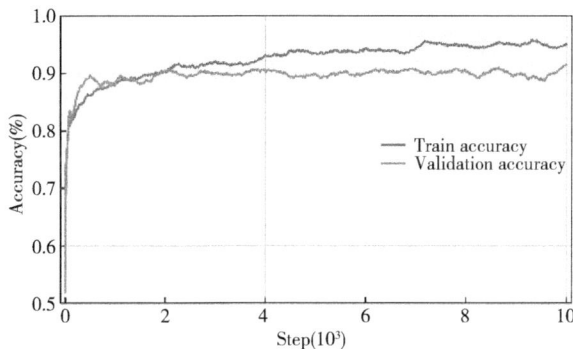

Fig. 4 Train accuracy, validation accuracy of Inception-v3 model

Fig. 4 shows that with the step of training iteration increasing, the training accuracy and validation accuracy of Inception-v3 model keeps upward tendency slowly. The training accuracy is up to 0.960 and validation accuracy up to 0.910 at the end. It can be seen from Fig. 5 that the cross entropy of Inception-v3 model gradually decreases with the increase of the iteration step. At the beginning of training, the cross entropy decreased significantly, indicating that the gap between actual output and expected output decreased continuously. When

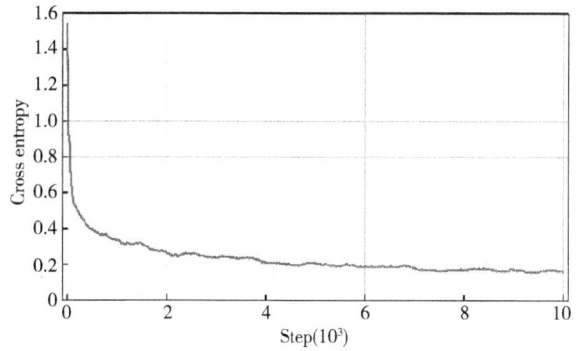

Fig. 5 Cross entropy of Inception-v3 model

the step of training iterations reached 6000, the cross entropy basically tended to be flat, indicating that the actual output is close to the expected output.

Similarly, we recorded the results of VGG-16 network and VGG-19 network at the best level. Tab. 1 lists the comparison of three networks. Three networks' validation accuracy is 0.837, 0.875, and 0.910, respectively. Inception-v3 model performs the best in contrast to VGG-16 network and VGG-19 network. Inception-v3 model is fit for our task of the style recognition in yarn dyed fabrics images.

Tab. 1 Comparison of three networks

Networkmodel	Train accuracy (%)	Validation accuracy (%)
VGG-16	91.8	83.7
VGG-19	93.2	87.5
Inception-v3	96.0	91.0

Tab. 2 shows the recognition results of the five types of fabrics of Inception-v3 model. It can be seen that stripe, plaid, dot and plain four categories of fabric images are easier to identify as the type of other. It shows that Inception-v3 network has deviations from the data set identification with smaller feature differences.

Tab. 2 5 types of fabrics images recognition results of Inception-v3 model

Test type	Prediction type					Accuracy (%)
	Dot	Plaid	Other	Plain	Stripe	
Dot	90	1	6	2	1	90.0
Plaid	2	91	7	0	0	91.0

Test type	Prediction type					Accuracy (%)
	Dot	Plaid	Other	Plain	Stripe	
Other	3	3	89	3	2	89.0
Plain	0	0	3	94	3	94.0
Stripe	0	0	3	1	96	96.0

Continued

4 Conclusions

In this paper, we apply the Inception-v3 model to the recognition of yarn dyed fabric images. In experiments, we verified Inception - v3 network by comparison to VGG-16 network and VGG-19 network. The experimental results show that Inception-v3 achieves a higher excellent accuracy rate of 91. 0% compared with the fine-tuned VGG-Net. This study improves the recognition accuracy of the yarn dyed fabric image. Our approach of automatic recognition of the yarn dyed fabric images is useful for scientific and efficient fabric images management.

References

[1] LI Y D, HAO Z B, LEI H. A review of convolutional neural network research [J]. Journal of Computer Applications, 2016,36(9):2508-2515.

[2] KRIZHEVSKY A, SUTSKEVER I, HINTON G. ImageNet classification with deep convolutional neural networks [C]. Conference and Workshop on Neural Information Processing Systems,2012:1097-1105.

[3] SIMONYAN K, ZISSERMAN A. Very deep convolu-tional networks for large-scale image recognition[C]. International Conference on Learning Representations,2015.

[4] SZEGEDY C, LIU W, JIA Y Q, et al. Going deeper with convolutions[C]. IEEE Conference on Computer Vision and Pattern Recognition,2015:1-9.

[5] SZEGEDY C, VANHOUCKE V, IOFFE S, et al. Rethinking the inception architecture for computer vision[C]. IEEE Conference on Computer Vision and Pattern Recognition,2016.

[6] LAWRENCE S, GILES C L, TSOI A C, et al. Face recognition: A convolutional neural-network approach [J]. IEEE Transactions on Neural Networks,1997,8(1):98-113.

[7] NEBAUER C. Evaluation of convolutional neural networks for visual recognition[J]. IEEE Transactions on Neural Networks,1998,9(4):685-696.

[8] ZHOU F Y, JIN L P, DONG J. Review of convolutional neural network[J]. Chinese Journal of Computers,2017,40(6): 1229-1250.

[9] JIANG L, ZHANG R Y, JI F. Image retrieval system of yarn dyed fabric based on perceptual hashing algorithm[C]. Sino-Africa International Symposium on Textiles and Apparel, 2017:61-65.

Study on Moisture Permeability and Dissipation of Fabrics Imitating Stomata of Plant Leaves

WU Yan[1,2], **MA Yanxue**[1,2]*, **LI Yuling**[1,2], **CUI Yunhua**[1,2], **CHENG Longdi**[1,2]

[1] *Key Laboratory of Textile Science &Technology, Ministry of Education, Shanghai, 201620, China*

[2] *Department of Technical Textiles, College of Textiles, Donghua University, Shanghai, 201620, China*

* *Corresponding author's email: yxma@ dhu. edu. cn*

Abstract: In recent years, moisture absorption fast drying fabrics have been widely used in sports and leisure clothing, but the fast drying function cannot meet the requirements. It is of great significance to design bionic fabrics with good moisture permeability and moisture dissipation for the development of sports fabrics by studying the process of stomatal transpiration and the stomatal structure of leaves. In order to explore the moisture permeability and dissipation of bionic structures, five samples of bionic structure of yarns with different functions of perforation, mesh weave and honeycomb were prepared and tested. The results show that the moisture permeability of bionic structure fabric is better than that of single layer fabric, and the moisture permeability of bionic structure of yarns with different functions of surface-inner layer is worse than that of surface-inner layer fabric. when the moisture content is more, the moisture dissipation of the biomimetic structure is better than that of the single-layer fabric, and within a certain range, the more water content, the greater the moisture dissipation rate. The test basically avoids the influence of moisture absorption and conductivity, and there is little difference in the moisture dissipation of the bionic structure of the yarns with different functions in the surface and the inner layers.

Keywords: Moisture absorption and quick drying; Bionic structure; Moisture permeability; Moisture dissipation

1 Introduction

Skin sweating can be divided into non-sensory sweating and sensory sweating. When no sensory sweating occurs, The initial state of moisture conduction through clothing is vapor. When sensory sweating occurs, the initial state of moisture conduction through clothing is liquid water[1]. When the human body has a large amount of sweat, it will give the human body a feeling of wet and cold, which is mainly due to the fact that sweat cannot be released through the fabric in time. However, the current research mainly focuses on hygroscopicity-conduction, but hygroscopicity and moisture conduction only play a role in promoting and accelerating moisture release. Only hygroscopicity and moisture dissipation are the key steps to transfer water vapor and moisture from the fabric to the surrounding environment.

Domestic and foreign research, from fibers, yarns, fabrics to hydrophilic finishing to improve moisture absorption, conductivity. In terms of fabric structure, through reasonable matching of different functional layers, sweat can only be transferred from the side close to the skin to the outer layer of the fabric, so as to achieve directional water transfer[2]. The design of gradient structure of the fabric originates from the transmission mechanism of the fabric, while the mechanism of moisture permeability and moisture dissipation in the direction of fabric thickness is rare.

Evolution of nature has created the excellent structure of all natural things to adapt to specific survival needs. The unique internal structure of plants determines their superior transpiration capacity. Therefore, the objective of this paper is to design and develop a bionic structure fabric based on the mechanism of plant water transport and the stomatal transpiration principle of plant leaves. The fabric has a good stomatal structure of plant leaves, and its moisture permeability and moisture dissipation performance are improved.

2 Fabric Design

According to stomata and its inferior chamber structure model of plant leaves[3], the bionic fabric was designed. The fabric has two layers of structure, the surface contains a certain size and regular distribution of the pore structure, to imitate the stomata of plant leaves; the inner layer is distributed with the corresponding, to imitate the structure of the lower cavity in the stomata of plant leaves, to provide a huge evaporation surface area, and the surface and inner layer of the fabric are provided with. There is a certain junction structure to form a moisture conduction channel. As shown in Fig. 1.

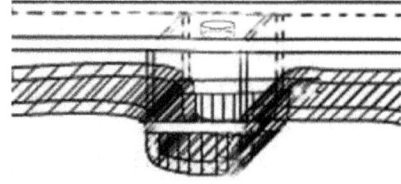

Fig. 1   Diagram of bionic fabric

3 Experiments

3.1 Fabric Preparation

Three bionic double-layer fabrics were fabricated in this experiment. The surface layer was made of mesh weave, the inner layer was made of honeycomb. In order to enhance the characteristics of bionic structure, different yarns with different functions are used in the surface and inner layers of fabrics to imitate the stomatal structure and cavity structure of plants. In order to compare with bionic fabric, the preparation of mesh weave and honeycomb was compared. Therefore, the parameters of the five samples are as follows(Tab. 1).

Tab. 1   Basic parameters of samples

Sample		Raw material		Fabric structure	Yarn count		Fabric density(Root/10cm)
1		C/M		Mesh weave	80s/2		254×169. 5
2		C/M		honeycomb	80s/2		254×169. 5
3	surface	C/M		bionic	80s/2		508×339
	inner	C/M		structure	80s/2		
4	surface	warp C/M	weft M	bionic	warp 80/2	weft 40s	508×339
	inner	warp C/M	weft C	structure	warp 80/2	weft 80s/2	
5	surface	warp C/M	weft C	bionic	warp 80/2	weft 80s/2	508×339
	inner	warp C/M	weft M	structure	warp 80/2	weft 40s	

Note among them, C is cotton yarn, M is coolmax yarn, C/M is cotton and coolmax composite yarn.

3.2 Test Method

The moisture permeability and moisture dissipation of fabrics can evaluate the ability of human sweat to emit into the atmosphere through fabrics. The former simulates senseless sweating, while the latter simulates sensory sweating[4].

3.2.1   Fabric Moisture Permeability Test

According to GB T 12704. 1—2009 "Textile Fabric Hygroscopicity Test Method Part 1 Hygroscopicity Method", each sample is prepared with three pieces, which are balanced at least one day in a constant temperature and humidity room. The average moisture permeability of each fabric sample is measured three times and calculated three times, which is the average moisture permeability of the fabric sample.

3.2.2 Fabric Moisture Dissipation Test

According to the patented "A Floating Textile Dehumidification Rate Testing Device and Method", a 10×5cm-sized test sample is cut. The sample is laid flat on the core suction water cloth of the composite floating board. In the constant temperature and humidity chamber, the water content of the sample is controlled by the feed water cloth extending into the tank at different floating board heights. The higher the floating board height is, the less the water absorption is, and the different sweating states can be simulated. The floating board heights of 0, 1cm, 3cm and 5cm correspond to 1st, 2nd, 3rd and 4th gears. the evaporation per unit area and per unit time, i. e. the rate of moisture dissipation, is measured in g/h. The average value of each fabric sample was measured three times.

4 Analysis and Discussion of Results

4.1 Fabric Basic Performance

Each sample was prepared with 5 pieces, and the average value was measured 5 times. The density was measured 5 times along the warp and weft direction, and the sample was wetted 24h in standard atmosphere before testing. The basic performance test results of five samples are as follows.

From Tab. 2, it can be seen that the density of the fabricswith holes and honeycombs is half less than that of double-layer bionic fabrics, so the thickness and weight of the fabrics with mesh weave and honeycomb are smaller than those with bionic structures. The thickness, weight and density of the fabrics with bionic structures 4 and 5 are similar.

Tab. 2　Basic performance test results of samples

Sample	Fabric thickness (mm)	Weight of fabrics per square meter (g/m²)	Fabric Density(Root/10cm)	
			Warp direction	Weft direction
1	0.2194	69.68	252.4	205.6
2	0.2802	84.84	254.4	197.6

Continued

Sample	Fabric thickness (mm)	Weight of fabrics per square meter (g/m²)	Fabric Density(Root/10cm)	
			Warp direction	Weft direction
3	0.4402	181.4	514.2	388.6
4	0.3948	145.48	508.8	386
5	0.3906	145.28	506.4	388.4

4.2 Fabric Moisture Permeability

Five samples were divided into two control groups. Samples 1-3 were a control group, and samples 3-5 were a control group.

It can be seen from Tab. 3 and Tab. 4 that the moisture permeability rate of bionic structure is higher than that of mesh weave and honeycomb, and the difference is significant. As shown in Fig. 2, first of all, water vapor is accumulated in the lower chamber of the inner layer, and the concentration of water vapor is very high, resulting in a large concentration difference with the external environment[5], which promotes the outward transmission of water vapor. When water vapor reaches the surface layer, most water vapor molecules pass through the voids between yarn and yarn, yarn and fiber[6], except for the voids between yarn and yarn. The vapor molecules pass through the surface holes, which reduces the probability of water molecules collision and makes it much easier for the vapor to escape into the external environment. However, mesh weave and honey-comb do not have such a three-dimensional structure, so its water vapor transport process has no bionic characteristics.

Tab. 3　Test results of moisture permeability of bionic structure and single layer fabrics

Samples	Observation number	Summation	Average	Variance
Sample 1	3	10592.256	3530.752	904.661184
Sample 2	3	11301.744	3767.248	1257.924864
Sample 3	3	14824.416	4941.472	880.143168

Tab. 4　Variance analysis of moisture permeability of bionic structure and single layer fabric

Variance analysis source of difference	SS	DF	MS	F	P-value	F crit
Intergroup	3424863	2	1712431.6	1688.383866	5.58004×10^{-9}	10.9247665
Intra-group	6085.458	6	1014.2431			
Total	3430949	8				

Note　SS represents the sum of squares; DF represents the degree of freedom; MS is the mean square; F is the test statistic; P-value is the significant level observed; Fcrit is the critical value. When $F > F$ crit 0.01, F value is significant at $a = 0.01$ level.

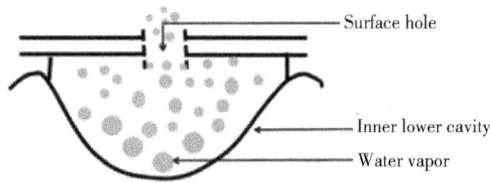

Fig. 2　Water vapor transport in bionic structures

From Tab. 5 and Tab. 6, it can be seen that the moisture permeability rate of the bionic structure differs significantly with the difference of the surface and inner raw materials. Sample 4 contains more cotton fibers in the inner layer and more polyester fibers in the surface layer. Most of the water vapor is first absorbed by the inner layer of cotton fibers. Cotton has a strong ability to absorb water molecules, and the energy needed to escape from the water vapor molecules is large[7]. Sample 5 contains more polyester fibers. When most of the water vapor molecules reach the surface through the voids between the yarns, one part is transferred from the surface voids to the air, the other part is absorbed by the cotton fibers, and the escape of the water vapor molecules also needs more energy. For Sample 3, After a small amount of cotton fibers are absorbed by the surface and inner layers, most of them escape from the holes in the fabric and the voids between the yarn and the yarn, so the moisture permeability of Sample 3 is the highest.

Tab. 5　Test results of moisture permeability of bionic structures with different raw materials in surface and inner layers

SUMMARY Samples	Observation number	Summation	Average	Variance
Sample 3	3	14824.42	4941.472	880.1432
Sample 4	3	12461.64	4153.88	144.8584
Sample 5	3	12744.5	4248.168	1303.293

Tab. 6　Variance analysis of moisture permeability of bionic structures with different raw materials in surface and inner layers

Variance analysis source of difference	SS	DF	MS	F	P-value	F crit
Intergroup	1109862	2	554930.9	715.0268	7.29×10^{-8}	10.92477
Intra-group	4656.589	6	776.0981			
Total	1114518	8				

4.3　Fabric Moisture Dissipation

It can be seen from Tab. 7 that sample 1 and sample 2 (monolayer fabric) exhibit better moisture dissipation at higher float height. When at 1st and 2nd gears, that are, when the water absorption is high, the moisture dissipation rate of sample 3 (bionic structure) is obviously higher than that of monolayer fabric. Moreover, with the increase of float height, the moisture dissipation rate decreases linearly. This may be due to the fact that, first of all, the adsorption force and surface tension of water molecules on the wall deform the concave liquid surface and form different gas-liquid meniscus in the cavity[8].

Tab. 7   The results of moisture dissipation rate of samples

Sample	Moisture dissipation rate(g/h)			
	1st gear	2nd gear	3rd gear	4th gear
Sample 1	0.334	0.316	0.347	0.318
Sample 2	0.328	0.329	0.331	0.340
Sample 3	0.370	0.384	0.339	0.332
Sample 4	0.361	0.350	0.347	0.330
Sample 5	0.387	0.354	0.328	0.302

As shown in Fig. 3, The lower the height of the floating plate, the more water absorbed by the core suction cloth, the more water that can be transferred to the fabric, and the larger the evaporation surface area[9]. On the other hand, if the thickness of the lower layer of the fabric is low, the moisture may partially block the holes, and the evaporation of water vapor is affected, the rate of moisture dissipation will be reduced to some extent. In a certain range, the lower the height of the floating board, the higher the rate of moisture dissipation of the bionic fabric, which means that the water vapor evaporation rate of the bionic fabric will be reduced to a certain extent. The designed bionic structure is more suitable for wearing and using when sweating heavily.

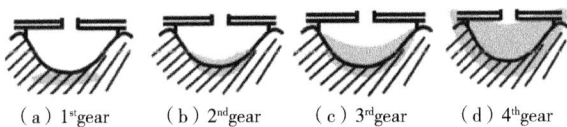

(a) 1st gear   (b) 2nd gear   (c) 3rd gear   (d) 4th gear

Fig. 3   Water content of bionic structure in different gears

It can be seen from Tab. 7 that sample 4, 5 and 3 are all linearly decreasing with the increase of floating plate height, which proves that the bionic structure is more suitable for wearing when sweating heavily. However, because the device test minimizes the influence of moisture absorption and conductivity on moisture dissipa-

tion, the moisture conductivity gradient formed by different functional yarns in the surface and inner layers is not better reflected here.

5   Conclusions

(1) The moisture permeability of bionic fabrics is better than that of single-layer fabrics. The increase of cotton fiber content is not conducive to the release of water vapor molecules in both surface and inner layers of fabrics.

(2) When sweating heavily, the moisture dissipation of bionic fabric is better than that of single-layer fabric, and the moisture conductivity of bionic fabric with different functional yarns on the surface and the inner may have a greater impact on the fast drying.

(3) Moisture permeability and moisture dissipation simulate the ability of sweat emitted from fabrics to the atmosphere without sweating or sweating. The experiment proves that the bionic structure has good moisture permeability and moisture dissipation ability.

References

[1] YAO M, SHI M W, JIANG S C. Study on the theory and practice of fabric moisture conduction. First report: Study on the process and structure of fabric moisture conduction[J]. Journal of Northwest Textile Institute, 2001 (02): 1-8.

[2] ZHANG H M, SHEN L P, LIU H H. Development of single-guide wet three-dimensional woven fabrics[J]. Synthetic Fibers, 2016, 45 (08): 28-31.

[3] WANG T D. Water vapor diffusion between substomatal cavities[J]. Journal of Integrative Plant Biology, 1989 (01): 36-43.

[4] SUI Q. Development and properties of knitted fabrics with moisture conduction and sweat elimination[D]. Qingdao: University, 2018.

[5] ZHANG K P. Bionic microfluidic pump based on stomatal transpiration mechanism[D]. Dalian: University of Technology, 2012.

[6] ZHAI H, XU X L, WANG Q, et al. Study on hygroscopicity and sweat-removing fibers and their working principles[J]. Shanghai Textile Technology, 2004, 32 (2): 6-7.

[7] YU W D. Textile material science[M]. Beijing: China Textile & Apparel Press, 2006: 100-101.

[8] SHI M W, CHEN Y N, YAO M. Study on the theory and practice of wet conduction of fabrics Part 3: Study on ab-

sorption, transmission and evaporation of liquid water in fabrics[J]. Journal of Northwest Textile Institute, 2001 (02): 15-23.

[9] DONG Z J. Reasons for the high rate of plant transpiration [J]. Journal of Chongqing Vocational and Technical College of Industry and Trade, 2010, 6 (04): 41-46.

The Preparation and Performance Evaluation of PCL Electrospinning Membrane

LIU Qinxin[1,2], CHEN Nanliang[1,2], JIANG Jinhua[1,2*]

[1] *Engineering Research Center of Technical Textiles, Ministry of Education, Donghua University, Shanghai, 201620, China*

[2] *College of Textiles, Donghua University, Shanghai, 201620, China*

* *Corresponding author's email*: jiangjinhua@ dhu. edu. cn

Abstract: Electrospinning technology could be used to form membranes applied to the hernia mesh, which would achieve an effect of anti-adhesion. PCL has great biocompatibility and biodegradability that can be used as anti-adhesion material. Use a mixture of acetic acid (AA) and formic acid (FA) as the solvent in PCL electrospinning solution system. When the injector speed was 1. 5mL/h, the spinning voltage was adjusted to 16kV, the distance between the fiber collector and the needle of spinneret was 20cm, the concentration was 10%, the volume ratio of AA : FA was 3 : 7, the electrospinning membrane was a-chieved with a fine construction and good hydrophobicity. Through further study, the membrane can be combined with a warp knitted mesh to form a composite hernia mesh with anti-adhesion properties.

Keywords: PCL; Electrospinning; Membrane; Hydrophobicity

1 Introduction

Hernia is a severe illness which means that an organ or tissue in the human body leaves its normal anatomical site and enters another site through weak points, defects or pores. Hernia does not heal itself. For most patients, surgery is the only cure for hernia. Hernia mesh is widely used in the treatment of hernia surgery[1]. The method of operation is to place the hernia mesh and suture to repair and strengthen the tissue defect[2]. Polypropylene (PP) is the most widely used mesh material at home and abroad. PP is non-toxic, has good physical and mechanical properties and chemical stability. PP mesh is cheap, has good anti-infective ability, can stimulate fibrous tissue proliferation and significantly reduce the recurrence rate of hernia[3]. However, the PP mesh has a rough surface, which could cause abdominal adhesions when it is in direct contact with the organs. Severe adhesions could erodes the intestinal wall and even the intestines[4]. To prevent direct contact between PP mesh and the organs, anti-adhesion material need to be combined with PP mesh. In this study, the anti-adhesive material was prepared by electrospinning using polycaprolactone (PCL). Electrospinning is a spinning technology, using the polymer solution or melt to form fibers and membranes in a strong electric field[5]. Electrospinning can form nanoscale membrane with higher porosity and specific surface area. PCL has good biocompatibility, good organic polymer compatibility, and good biodegradability[6]. It can be completely degraded in 6−12 months in the natural environment[7].

In this study, use acetic acid (AA) and formic acid (FA) as solvent to prepare the PCL spinning solution. The electrospinning effect was changed by adjusting the volume ratio of AA : FA and the concentration of the spinning solution. The effect of electrospinning is mainly evaluated from morphology and hydrophobicity of fiber membrane.

2 Experiments

2. 1 Materials

PCL (SIGMA-ALDRICH Co. , Ltd.); AA (Shanghai

Lingfeng Chemical Reagent Co. , Ltd.); FA (Shanghai Lingfeng Chemical Reagent Co. , Ltd.).

2.2 Electrospinning Test

The spinning solution was formulated according to the preset concentration of the spinning solution and the solvent ratio. After formulation, it was placed in a glass bottle and stirred at 350r/min for 12 hours on a magnetic stirrer (524G, Shanghai, China) to dissolve the solute completely. In the solvent, a transparent viscous solution was obtained. Take a 10mL medical syringe and inhale about 2mL of the stirred solution and replace the original needle of the syringe with a metal needle (size 21). Then, put the syringe into the electrospinning machine (SS series, Beijing Yongkang Leye Technology Development Co. , Ltd.). Use an aluminum foil to receive the electrospinning membrane, and after maintaining the spinning time for 20 minutes, the aluminum foil was taken out, the PCL membrane can be observed on it. In order to eliminate the non-volatile residual solvent, the PCL membrane was put into a vacuum drying chamber at 40℃ (DZF – 6030B, Shanghai Yiheng Technology Co. , Ltd. , China) and was treated for 5 hours.

2.3 SEM Analysis

Scanning electron microscope was used to observe the apparent morphology of the electrospun membrane. The sample needs to be sprayed with gold before the test.

2.4 Hydrophobicity Test

Use a contact angle tester machine (OCA15EC, German Instrumentation Company, Germany) to measure the contact angle between the membrane and the fixed droplets, which could evaluate the hydrophobicity of the fiber membrane. Each sample was measured at 3 points separated by 5mm.

3 Results and Discussions

3.1 Effect of Spinning Solution Concentration on Fiber Morphology and Hydrophobicity of PCL Membrane

4 kinds of PCL electrospinning solution were prepared at a temperature of 25℃ and humidity at 35%, with the solution concentration of 7.5%, 10.0%, 12.5%, and 15.0%. The volume ratio of AA : FA was 3 : 7, the

spinning voltage was set to 14kV, the advancing speed was 1.5mL/h, the receiving distance was 20cm, and the spinning time was 20min. The experimental results were as follows.

Fig. 1 shows the fiber morphology at different solution concentrations. When the concentration was 7.5%, continuous fibers were received, the fiber diameter is the smallest of the four concentration parameters. When the concentration of solution was increased to 10.0%, the fiber was even, and the fiber diameter increased. This is because when the concentration increases, the viscosity of solution increases correspondingly, the entanglement among the molecular chains also increases. The spinning process needs to overcome a larger surface tension, the splitting ability of the jet is weakened, resulting in an increase in fiber diameter[8]. When the concentration was 12.5%, the fiber diameter and the unevenness were increased. The increase in fiber unevenness may be due to an increase in the concentration of the solution, as well as the viscosity. Under the constant voltage, the stretching of the polymer is insufficient, and the conductivity fluctuates greatly, resulting in the increase of unevenness. When the concentration of solution was 15.0%, the diameter and unevenness of the fiber were further increased.

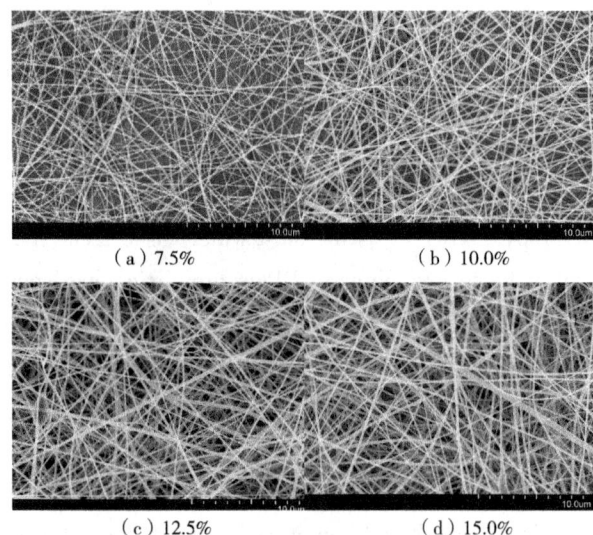

(a) 7.5%   (b) 10.0%

(c) 12.5%   (d) 15.0%

Fig. 1 Effect of spinning solution concentration on fiber morphology

Fig. 2 shows the water contact angle at different concen

trations. The water contact angle of the fiber membrane mainly depends on the fiber material and the surface structure of the membrane. In this study, in order to achieve anti-adhesion, which means cells are not easy to adhere, a fiber membrane with better hydrophobicity would be preferred. Since PCL is a hydrophobic material, and the surface of the electrospinning membrane is dense and smooth, it can be seen from Fig. 3 that the contact angle at each concentration level is greater than 90°, which is hydrophobic. As the concentration increases, the contact angle gradually increases. This is mainly because when the concentration increases, the fiber diameter increases, and the distribution density of the PCL fibers on the aluminum foil per unit time increases, so the contact angle also increases.

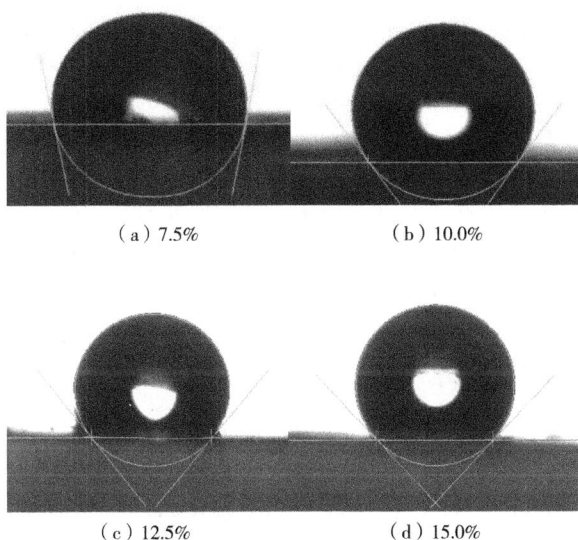

(a) 7.5%   (b) 10.0%

(c) 12.5%   (d) 15.0%

Fig. 2   Effect of concentration on water contact angle

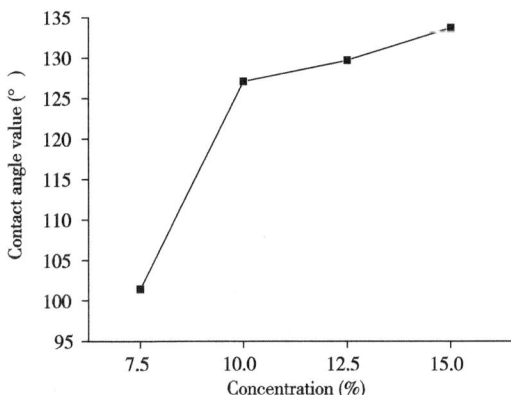

Fig. 3   Contact angle value at different concentrations

It can be seen that when the concentration was 10.0%, the fineness and uniformity of the fibers and the hydrophobicity of membrane were superior.

3.2   Effect of Solvent Ratio on Fiber Morphology and Hydrophobicity of PCL Membrane

4 kinds of PCL electrospinning solution were prepared at a temperature of 25℃ and humidity at 35%, with the ratios of AA : FA were 5 : 5, 4 : 6, 3 : 7 and 2 : 8. The concentration of solvent was 10%, the spinning voltage was set to 14kV, the advancing speed was 1.5mL/h, the receiving distance was 20cm, and the spinning time was 20min. The experimental results were as follows.

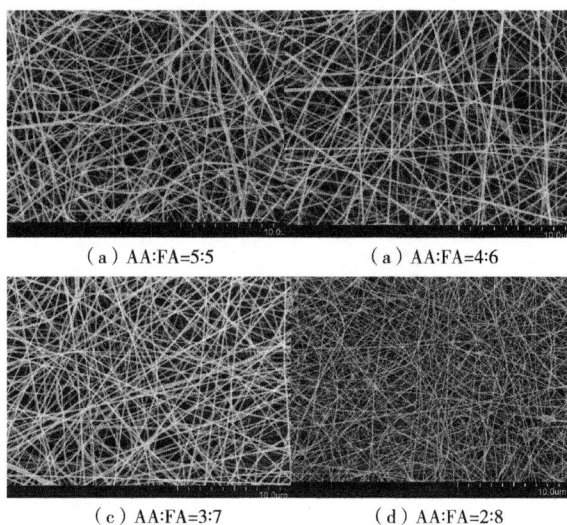

(a) AA:FA=5:5   (a) AA:FA=4:6

(c) AA:FA=3:7   (d) AA:FA=2:8

Fig. 4   Effect of solvent ratio on fiber morphology

Fig. 4 shows the fiber morphology at different solvent ratios. It can be seen that when the proportion of FA in the mixed solvent is low[Fig. 4(a)], the fiber diameter is large; as the proportion of FA increases, the fiber diameter gradually decreased. This is mainly because the fiber diameter is largely affected by the electrical conductivity of the solution system when the concentration and viscosity of solution do not change much. Since the electrical conductivity of FA ($6.4×10^{-5}$) is significantly higher than AA ($1.12×10^{-8}$), as the content of FA in the mixed solvent increases, the charge density of the jet surface increases, the fiber is subjected to a stronger electric field force drawing effect, which results in an decrease of fiber diameter[9]. At the same time, as the proportion of FA increases, the fiber diameter unevenness decreases first and then increases. The reason is presumed to be that when the conductivity of the solution is too small or too large, the jetting of the jet is unstable, resulting in an increase in fiber unevenness. Fig. 5 shows the water contact angle at different solvent ratio. It can be seen from the Fig. 6 that the contact angle is the largest when AA : FA is 4 : 6. This is because the fiber surface is smooth and the membrane structure is dense. When AA : FA is 2 : 8, the fiber surface starts to become rough and the contact angle decreases.

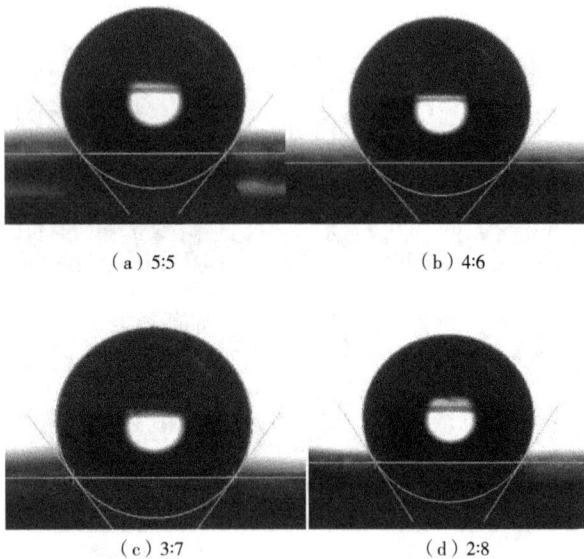

(a) 5:5　　　　　　(b) 4:6

(c) 3:7　　　　　　(d) 2:8

Fig. 5　Effect of AA : FA on water contact angle

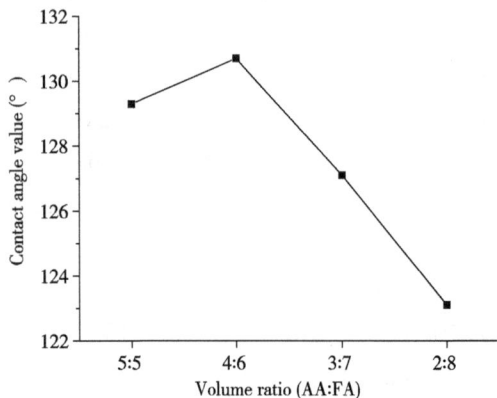

Fig. 6　Water contact angle at different solution ratio

It can be seen that when AA : FA was 3 : 7, the fineness and uniformity of the fibers and the hydrophobicity of membrane were superior.

4　Conclusions

In this study, use AA and FA as solvent to prepare the PCL spinning solution. The electrospinning effect was changed by adjusting the volume ratio of AA : FA and the concentration of the spinning solution. The results show that the solution system can be successfully spun, and the fiber membrane obtained has a compact structure and excellent hydrophobicity. When the advancing speed is controlled at 1. 5mL/h, the distance between the aluminum foil and the needle is 20cm, the spinning voltage is 16kV, the concentration of solution is 10%, the ratio of AA : FA is 3 : 7, the fiber membrane has a good appearance and excellent hydrophobicity. Through further study, the membrane can be combined with a warp knit substrate to form a composite hernia patch with anti-adhesion properties.

Acknowledgements

This work was financially supported by National Key R&D Program of China (2016YFB0303300), and National Natural Science Foundation of China (NSFC11472077), the Fundamental Research Funds for the Central Universities (2232018G-06).

References

[1] CHEN Y M, XI T F, SU J. Effect of ventral hernia patch on endogenous tissue regeneration and tissue defect repair[J]. Chinese Journal of Tissue Engineering Research, 2012, 16 (47): 8875-8879.

[2] CHEN H L, LIU W. Tension free repair technology in elderly inguinal hernia recurrence[J]. Journal of Hubei University for Nationalities: Medical Edition, 2010 (3): 38-39.

[3] KELLY M, MACDOUGALL K, OLABISI O, et al. In vivo response to polypropylene following implantation in animal models: a review of biocompatibility[J]. Int Urogynecology, 2017, 28 (2): 171-180.

[4] GONZALEZ R, FUGATE K, MCCLUSKY D, et al. Relationship between tissue in growth and mesh contraction[J]. World J Surg, 2005, 29 (8): 1038-1043.

[5] ZHANG L L, GAO T T, CHEN S Y, et al. Preparation and characterization of electrospinning oriented micro/nano fibers [J]. Journal of Nantong University, 2019, 18 (1): 50-56.

[6]LAFON O, TRÉBOSC J, HU B W, et al. Observing 13C-13C connectivities at high magnetic fields and very high spinning frequencies[J]. Chemical Communications, 2011, 47 (24) : 6930-6932.

[7]XU R. Preparation and performance evaluation ofPP/PCL anti-adhesion composite hernia mesh[D]. Shanghai: Donghua University, 2017.

[8]CHENG F. Study on preparation and properties of antimicrobial drug loaded wound dressing[D]. Shanghai: Donghua University, 2015.

[9]LUO C J, STRIDE E, EDIRISINGHE M. Mapping the influence of solubility and dielectric constant on electro-spinning polycaprolactone solutions [J]. Macromolecules, 2012 (45) : 4669-4680.

Effects of Weave Structures on Moisture Absorbent and Quick Drying Properties of Woven Fabric

ZHOU Cheng[1,2], MA Yanxue[1,2]*, LEI Min[1,2], LI Yuling[1,2]

[1] Key Laboratory of Textile Science & Technology, Ministry of Education, College of Textile, Donghua University, Shanghai, 201620, China

[2] Key Laboratory of Textile Design and Technology in Textile Industry, Donghua University, Shanghai, 201620, China

* Corresponding author's email: yxma@dhu.edu.cn

Abstract: In order to work out the influence of woven fabric structure on the moisture absorption and quick-drying properties of fabrics, 50% cotton and 50% polyester filament yarns were used as warp and weft yarns to weave five different structures. Subsequently, basic properties including thickness and mass per unit area were tested, also moisture absorption and quick drying including moisture permeability, wetting time, water absorption rate, maximum wetting radius, spreading speed, accumulative one-way transport, overall moisture management capability and moisture dissipation were tested. The characteristic parameters of float and pore were extracted from the woven fabrics structure with different texture morphology on the surface of fabrics, which were applied to analyzing the effects of structure on the basic properties and moisture absorption and quick drying properties. Studies have shown that weave structures with high float concentration and ratio of large pores perimeter pore size had a better moisture absorbent and quick drying properties.

Keywords: Fabric weaves; Float concentration; Ratio of large pores perimeter; Moisture absorption and quick drying properties

1 Introduction

With the gradual improvement of living standards, people put forward higher requirements for the comfort of clothing, and the moisture absorption and quick drying performance of clothing is an important factor affecting wearing comfort of clothing. As a kind of comfort fabrics, moisture-absorbent and quick-drying fabrics are considered as the breathable fabrics. These fabrics feature comfort, functionality and economy, while also meeting the consumer's requirements for the comfort, health, safety and environmental protection[1]. At present, one research was carried out to show that four different weave structures, such as 3/1 twill, five warp satin and eight reinforced satin, 3/1 twill and five warp stain had superior thermal and moisture comfort properties[2]. To find out the basic performance, moisture perspiration performance and cool properties of four fab-

rics, the moisture perspiration functional cool fabrics with plain, twill, grain and through hole plain structure are tested and analyzed. The results showed that the fabric with grain structure was the best[3]. To study the influence of structure parameters on moisture permeability of fabric woven by fine polypropylene fiber with star section, nine fabrics with different structures and tightness had been woven, and a moisture permeability test in the moisture absorption method was performed and compared for these fabrics. The conclusion was that the moisture permeability would be improved with increasing floats in the woven fabric, and would be declined with increasing fabric tightness[4]. A porous complex structured woven fabric was manufactured to maximize the moisture transition ability of the prepared fabric by increasing the absorptive property of the fabric through surface modification using plasma, which is a dry modification method, suggesting that the combination of double complex structures and the plasma treatment helped improve the water absorption[5]. Some of these articles only analyzed and discussed the experimental results according to the phenomena, without explanations from the perspective of fabric structure. Therefore, in this study, five different weave structures were selected to find out the influence of fabric surface textures on moisture absorption and quick drying performance.

2 Experimental Design

2.1 Yarn Materials

Cotton yarns with good hygroscopicity and coolmax© polyester yarns with good moisture permeability were applied with a mass ratio of 1 : 1, obtaining a fold yarns with linear density of 14. 67 ×2 tex. These yarns were used as warp and weft yarns in the test.

2.2 Woven Fabric Design

2/2 basket weave (A1), 3/1 twill(A2), crepe weave (A3), barley corn weave (A4), and square check weave(A5) were selected and shown in Fig. 1. The single variable experimental design method was used to make the other parameters same. The loom set factor of the five woven fabrics[6] is shown in Tab. 1

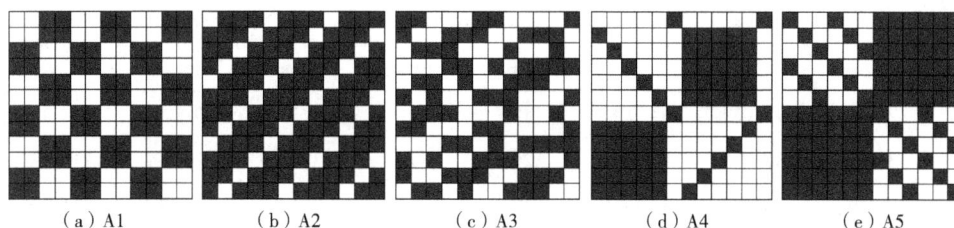

(a) A1   (b) A2   (c) A3   (d) A4   (e) A5

Fig. 1   The five fabric weaves

Tab. 1   The loom set factor

linear density		Fabric count		Covering factor					
Warp(tex)	Weft(tex)	End spacing (end/10cm)	Filling density (filling/10cm)	Warp tightness (%)	Weft tightness (%)	Porter/10cm	Ends per dent	Warp shrinkage (%)	Weft shrinkage (%)
14.67×2	14.67×2	436	426	87	85	105	4	8	4

3 Test Methods

In order to explore the influence of different weave structures on fabric properties, this paper conducted tests of basic properties and wet comfort properties. The thickness and mass per unit area mainly characterize the basic structural characteristics of the fabric; the wetting time and water absorption rate characterize the moisture absorption property of fabrics; the maximum wetting radius, the liquid water diffusion speed, the one-way transfer index and the dynamic transfer of liquid water characterizes the moisture transfer property of the fabric; the moisture permeability and water dissipation characterize the moisture diffusion property of the fabrics.

The test methods are based on various test standards. The thickness test of the fabric refers to GB/T 3820—

1997. The mass per unit area refers to GB/T 4669—2008. The moisture management test refers to GB/T 21655. 2—2009. The moisture permeability refers to GB/T 12704. 1—2009. The moisture dissipation test of fabrics refers to a floating testing device and method to test the moisture diffusion rate of fabrics[7].

4 Results and Discussions

The surface of the woven fabric is abutted by the yarn and the yarn interlacing points to form the texture. The law of interweaving is the structural feature of the texture, visually represented by the interphase distribution of the float and the pore, which plays a decisive role in the transmission, transfer and transportation of various environmental media. Therefore, float concentration and pore perimeter were used to analyze the influence on the moisture absorption and quick drying properties

4.1 Test Results of the Basic Properties

The basic properties test results of five fabrics are shown in Tab. 2.

Tab. 2   Test results of basicpro perties

Indicator	A1	A2	A3	A4	A5
Thickness (mm)	0.346	0.365	0.432	0.438	0.481

Continued

Indicator	A1	A2	A3	A4	A5
Mass per unit area(g/m^2)	165.980	166.510	181.310	169.850	171.810

4.2   Test Results and Analysis of the Moisture Absorption and Quick Drying Properties

4.2.1   The Test Results and Analysis of the MMT

The liquid moisture management test results of fabrics are shown in Tab. 3.

Tab. 3   Test results of MMT

Weaves	Wetting time $T(s)$		Water absorption rate $A(\%/s)$		Maximum wetting radius $R(mm)$		Spreading speed $S(mm/s)$		Accumulative one-way transport O	Overall moisture management capability M
	Top	Bottom	Top	Bottom	Top	Bottom	Top	Bottom		
A1	3.600	26.454	29.089	14.930	10	10	1.3991	0.2903	−65.141	0.0137
A2	4.848	0.324	19.725	41.5392	20	20	1.7569	2.3302	73.4997	0.3357
A3	5.082	0.324	79.623	57.1444	10	10	1.1459	12.6779	724.212	0.881
A4	4.848	0.324	23.002	54.9096	20	20	1.8096	1.7082	290.234	0.5618
A5	3.522	14.286	16.53	36.432	25	25	2.0396	1.3102	128.047	0.2971

It can be seen from the test results that the water absorption rate of five fabrics is: crepe weave > barley corn weave > 3/1 twill > square check weave > 2/2 basket weave. The wetting time and water absorption rate are mainly indicators for evaluating the moisture absorption properties. The shorter the wetting time and the higher the water absorption rate are, the better the moisture absorption properties of the fabrics are. Among these five weave structures, the diffusion radiuses of barley corn, check squares and twill are large. Since the transfer of water molecules in the surface of the fabric is along the axial direction of the yarn, the higher the float concentration in the weave repeat unit is, the less buckling of the yarn due to interlacing will be, which are more conducive to the absorption and transmission of liquid water. The moisture absorption and quick drying properties of fabrics cannot be evaluated by a single indicator of moisture absorption performance or diffusion transmission, but a whole process that is dynamically changing.

4.2.2   The Test Results and Analysis of Moisture Permeability

The moisture permeability of fabric refers to the ability of gaseous water molecules to penetrate the fabric, which has a certain degree of nonlinear correlation with fabric porosity[8]. However, gaseous molecules are affected by the yarn and the size of pores as they pass through the fabric, and then liquefy on the surface of the fabrics[9]. Using the experimental data of the fabric bulk density calculated from Tab. 2 and the test data of moisture permeability, the regression analysis by origin software is shown in equation (1), and the fitting curve is shown in Fig. 2. The equation coefficient of determination R^2 is 0.87, and regression relationship is significant at the level of 0.05.

$$y = -0.0081x + 7293.9 \qquad (1)$$

Being a negative correlation with the fabric density, the moisture permeability of fabrics decreases as the fabric density increases. The smaller the density of fabrics are, the smaller the number of yarns and the more pores between the yarns will be in per unit volume. Under this condition, the water molecules have many transmission channels and are less resistant to fiber yarns, so the moisture permeability of fabrics performs better.

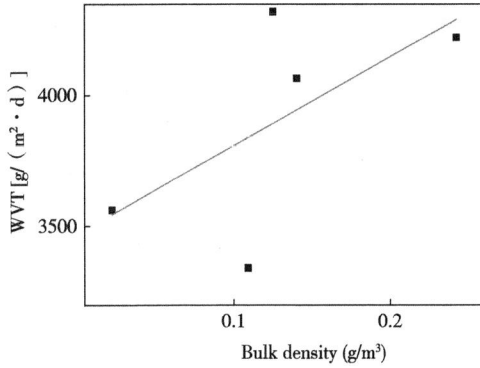

Fig. 2　Relationship between bulk density and moisture permeability

4.2.3　The Test Results and Analysis of Moisture Dissipation

The moisture dissipation of the fabric is equivalent to the evaporation process of liquid water molecules through a porous surface. Tab. 4 shows the distribution of the porosity perimeter ratio no less than $300\mu m$ on five fabrics.

Tab. 4　Ratio of large pore perimeter

Indicator	A1	A2	A3	A4	A5
Ratio of large pore perimeter	0.109	0.022	0.140	0.125	0.242

The regression analysis of the fabric moisture dissipation rate and the large pore perimeter ratio by the origin software is shown in equation (2), and the fitting curve is shown in Fig. 3. The equation coefficient of determination R^2 is 0.86, indicating that the fitting effect of the equation is good. And the regression relationship is significant at the level of 0.05.

$$y = 0.08516x + 0.28435 \quad (2)$$

According to the fitting curve, we can conclude that the larger the pore size and proportion of the pore perimeter are, the better the moisture dissipation rate of the fabrics are. Because the longer the length of the yarn forming the large pores are, the faster the water molecules transfer from the liquid surface to the evaporation surface through the yarn will be. Meanwhile, the structure of large pores has a large saturated vapor pressure, and

the number of the water molecules that can be accommodated around the air will increase.

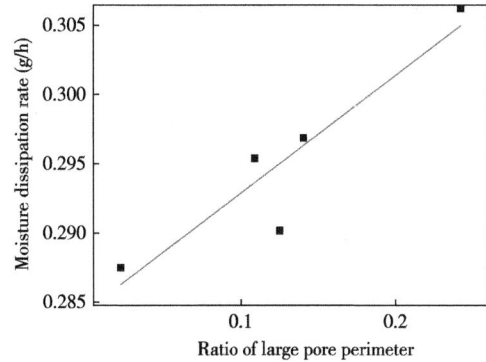

Fig. 3　Relationship between ratio of large pore perimeter and moisture dissipation rate

5　Conclusions

The fabric structures formed by different weaves have different effects on the moisture absorption and quick drying properties of the fabric. The order of moisture absorption and quick drying properties of these five fabrics is: crepe weave > barley corn weave > square check weave > 3/1 twill > 2/2 basket weave.

Different rules of yarn interlace can form different float and pore structures. With the long average float and the high float concentration, the fabric is softer and forms less pores. The other case is the opposite.

With the method of statistical analysis, two important conclusions are shown in the paper. The water vapor transmission of the fabric decreased as the fabric density increases. The moisture diffusion rate of the fabric increased with the increase of the proportion of large pore perimeters.

References

[1] TANG H, JIAN J, XIAO M. Breathable fabric——Development moisture absorption and quick drying functional fabrics [J]. Chinese Dress, 2007(05): 132-135.

[2] ZHENG X Q, SHEN L P. Effect of weave structure on thermal and moisture comfort of fabrics [J]. Synthetic Faber in China, 2018, 47(11): 35-37.

[3] ZHANG H M, SHEN L P. Effect of weave structure on the properties of functional cool lightweight fabric [J]. Shanghai

textile science & technology, 2018, 46(04): 31-33.

[4] JIN G X, ZHU C Y. Influence of structure parameters on moisture permeability of fabric woven by fine PP fiber with star section[J]. Advanced Materials Research, 2012, 502: 292-296.

[5] PARK Y. Development of moisture transition ability on porous complex structured woven fabric with convergence of pattern, porosity, and plasma technology[J]. Fibers and Polymers, 2016, 17(12): 2027-2034.

[6] XIE G Y. Fundamentals of woven fabric design[M]. Shanghai: Donghua university press, 2010.

[7] LI Y L, ZHOU F, MA Y X, et al. The invention relates to a floating textile moisture rate measuring device and method [P]. China: CN109632563A, 2019-04-16.

[8] ZHANG W J, JI F, et al. Study on relat-ionship between capillary characteristic-s and moisture permeability of wool f-abrics [J]. Journal of Textile Reaseach, 2019, 40(01): 67-72.

[9] YAO M, SHI M W. The research on the theory and practice of wet permeability of fabrics II: theoretical equations of wet permeability of fabrics[J]. Journal of Northwest Institute of Textile Science and Technology, 2001(02).

Tensile Properties of Three Dimensional Braided Composites with Holes

SHENG Meihua[1], YAN Shuo[1], HUANG Shuwei[1], SUN Baozhong[1], GU Bohong[1]*

[1] College of Textiles, Donghua University, Shanghai, 201620, China

* Corresponding author's email: gubh@ dhu edu. cn

Abstract: In this paper, the tensile properties of the specimens with braided hole and drilled hole were investigated. The aperture effects on tensile properties were analyzed. The specimens with braided hole are not sensitive to the hole size, and the peak load did not decrease compared with the specimen without hole, its modulus increase, instead. The peak load of specimen with drilled hole decreases with increasing the hole diameter. The tensile load, strength and modulus of the specimens containing braided holes with the same diameter ($\Phi = 10$mm) are larger than those of the specimens with drilled holes. Digital image correlation (DIC) technique was used to collect surface strain distribution of the two kinds of specimens, local strain concentration occurred around the hole. Finite element analysis of specimen with drilled hole (10mm) is carried out. Both stress distribution and strain distribution indicate that shear failure occurred in the specimens with drilled. It lays a foundation for studying the tensile properties of opening braided composites and has important engineering practical significance.

Keywords: 3-D Braided composite; Digital image correlation (DIC); Finite element analysis (FEA); Strain field; Braided holes; Drilled holes

1 Introduction

Three-dimensional braided composites have been widely used in the fields of aero-space, sports and medical equipment in recent years due to their high specific strength, high damage capacity, impact resistance and fatigue resistance, especially its excellent design performance[1-2]. On account of the overlap between different parts, 3-D braided structures often have some holes[3]. For carbon fiber reinforced composite, stress concentration will occur after opening, and damage forms such as fiber breakage and matrix damage will occur around the hole[4-7]. Therefore, the technology of hole making is very important and has been paid more and more attention. A lot of work has been done to reveal the tensile failure process of 3-D braided composites with holes and predict the final failure strength. Prasath et al. [8] studied the sensitivity of DIC parameters (subset size, step size, and ROI) to complex strain fields in the case of open-hole composite plates.

They compared the numerical simulation results with the finite element prediction results and determined the appropriate numerical simulation parameters. Ramji et al. [9] investigated the overall mechanical properties of glass fiber reinforced polymer (GFRP) composite panels under different reinforced structures using DIC technology. They also evaluated the performance of GFRP stiffened plates with different stiffened structures under axial compression. Guo et al. [10] established a finite element model for progressive failure analysis of composite laminates containing a central hole and simulated the failure of composite laminates with holes under uniaxial tension. The numerical results show that the damage model can be used to accurately predict the progressive failure behavior.

However, the above reports are limited to reveal the tensile properties and tensile failure process of laminates with and without holes. This paper is to investigate the tensile properties and tensile failure modes of 3-D braided composites with braided holes and drilled holes, respectively. We compared them with the braided composites without holes. The DIC technique was used to collect surface strain of the specimens and tried to reveal the effect of stress concentration on tensile strength due to opening. Besides, finite element analysis of specimen with drilled hole ($\Phi = 10mm$) was carried out. The simulation results are compared with the results of DIC processing. The simulation results are basically consistent with the results of DIC processing. The result shows that the specimen with drilled hole has a shear failure mode.

2 Tests and Specimens

2.1 Materials Properties

Carbon fiber tows (T700s-12 K, TORAY), epoxy resin (JC-02A) and curing agent (JC-02B) are the main materials. The mechanical properties are shown in Tab. 1, respectively. Among them, the matrix is JC-02A epoxy resin mixed with curing agent JC-02B at a mass ratio of 5 : 4.

Tab. 1 Mechanical properties of fiber and matrix

Material	Carbon fiber	Epoxyresin (JC-02A/B)
E_1(GPa)	230	2.4
$E_2 = E_3$(GPa)	15	
G_{23}(GPa)	5	0.89
$G_{12} = G_{13}$(GPa)	9	
$\nu23$	0.3	0.35
$\nu12 = \nu13$	0.25	
Density(g/cm^3)	1.79	1.13

2.2 Specimens Preparation

2.2.1 Preparation of Specimens with Drilled Hole

The carbon fiber tows were directly braided into an integral preform without making holes by a four-step braiding method[7]. Then, a vacuum assisted resin transfer molding (VARTM) process (shown in Fig. 1) was adopted to make the 3-D braided composites, which was continuously cured at 90℃, 110℃, and 130℃ for 2h, 1h, and 4h, respectively. We drilled out the holes with mechanical method.

2.2.2 Preparation of Specimens with Braided Hole

The preformed holes were directly braided through a circular die of the same size as a circular hole in the braiding process. Thus, in the whole of the preform, including around the holes, the fibers are continuous. During the curing process, the circular mold needs to be applied with a release cloth for later demolding and taking out the metal blocks. After the composite was formed, the drill bit is only in contact with the mold in the mechanical drilling, and the mold of the same diameter is just extruded out of the composite material without damaging the surrounding fibers.

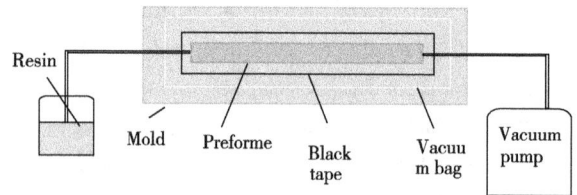

Fig. 1 Schematic diagram of the VARTM process

In this study, there are two kinds of 3-D braided composite specimens (with a braided hole and a drilled hole, respectively), and each type of hole has three different sizes of holes, 5mm, 10mm and 15mm, and each size hole has four test pieces. Fig. 2 is a comparison of specimens with drilled holes and braided holes.

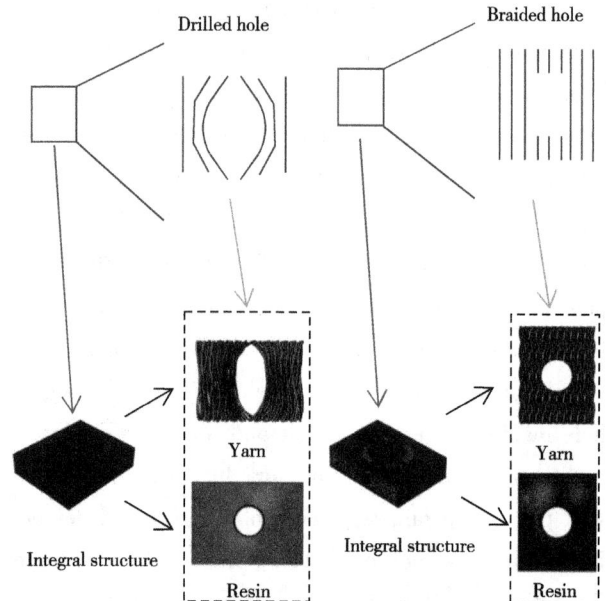

Fig. 2 The comparison of specimens with drilled holes and braided holes

2.3 Tests

Experimental investigations are conducted using the XYB605C MTS (Material Test System) testing machine. The CFRP specimens are subjected to quasi-static uniaxial tensile at a speed of 2mm/min. Using the experimental technique of DIC monitors the CFRP specimen in real time. The relevant experimental devices are shown in Fig. 3. The images of the CFRP specimens deformed during the experiment are captured by the digital cameras. By synchronizing the MTS test system, we can get the corresponding load and displacement values for each image captured by the camera. Then, the acquired image is post-processed by relevant software such as MATLAB to obtain the displacement and strain data on the surface of the specimens.

Fig. 3 Experimental set-up of DIC

2.4 Finite Element Simulation

There is a good repeatability and consistent performance of 3-D braided composite with drilled hole. The tensile properties of the specimens fluctuated little with the same opening method. In this paper, a finite element model of the specimens with drilled hole ($\Phi = 10$mm) was established. In order to reduce the amount of calculation, a small-size microscale structural model was built, as shown in Fig. 4. The micro-scale structural component was composed of yarns and resin. The model was considered as transversely isotropic structure. ABAQUS 6.14 was used for quasi-static simulation of the model. The model was fixed at one end and loaded at the other end. The mesh type is C3D4 and the size is 0.3mm.

Fig. 4 The small-size microscopic structure model

3 Results and Discussions

Fig. 5-7 shows the engineering load-displacement and stress-strain curves measured by MTS (where the number 0 represents the specimen without hole, and 5, 10, and 15 represent the diameter of the hole, which is 5mm, 10mm, and 15mm, respectively. B represents the specimen with braided hole, D represents the specimen with drilled hole).

Fig. 5 (a) shows that the load-displacement curves of 3-D braided composites with braided hole at the different diameters are basically the same. The peak load of the three kinds of specimens (5mm, 10mm, 15mm) are all around 105kN. The corresponding stresses of the specimens without holes and with braided holes (5mm, 10mm, 15mm) are 675MPa, 865MPa, 1015MPa and 955MPa, respectively. As the diameter of the specimen with braided holes increases, the stress does not show a downward trend, but reaches its maximum value when the diameter is 10mm, and all are much larger than that of specimen without hole. The larger the diameter of the braiding hole, the smaller the braiding angle of the yarn around the hole, the average braiding angle is larger than that of specimen without hole. Moreover, the existence of hole increases the average fiber volume fraction of the specimens with braided hole, so the strength of the specimens with braiding hole is smaller than that of specimens without hole.

The engineering load-displacement curves and stress-strain curves of specimens with braided hole and drilled hole ($\Phi = 10$mm) are as shown in Fig. 6. It can be seen that the strength of the specimen with drilled hole is smaller than that of the specimen with braided hole, which are 75kN and 105kN respectively. This is because that the fibers around the hole are not damaged for the specimen with braided hole. That makes the structure around the braided hole relatively compact. The hole of the specimen with drilled hole is drilled mechanically after the specimen is cured. The fibers around the hole are damaged and cut off, the integrity of the structure is destroyed. Therefore, the bearing capacity of the specimen with braided hole is larger than that of the specimen with drilled hole. From Fig. 7, the bearing capacity of 3-D braided composites decreases with increasing the diameter. There was no obvious necking phenomenon before failure both for the two specimens.

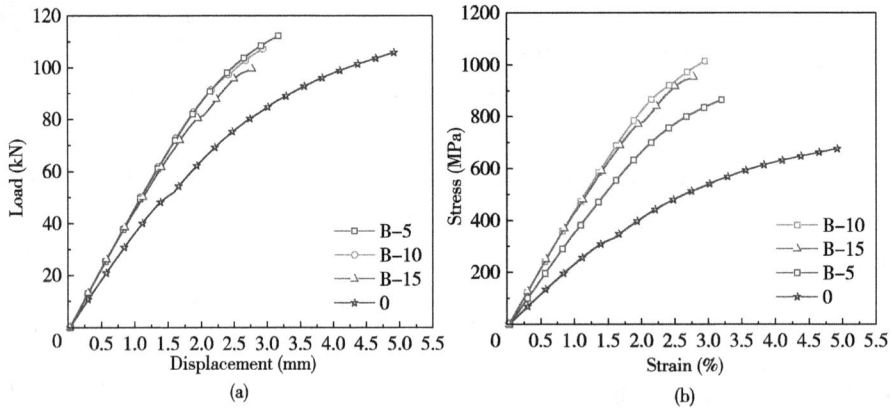

Fig. 5 Tensile curves of 3-D composites with and without braided hole: (a) Load-displacement curve; (b) Stress-strain curve

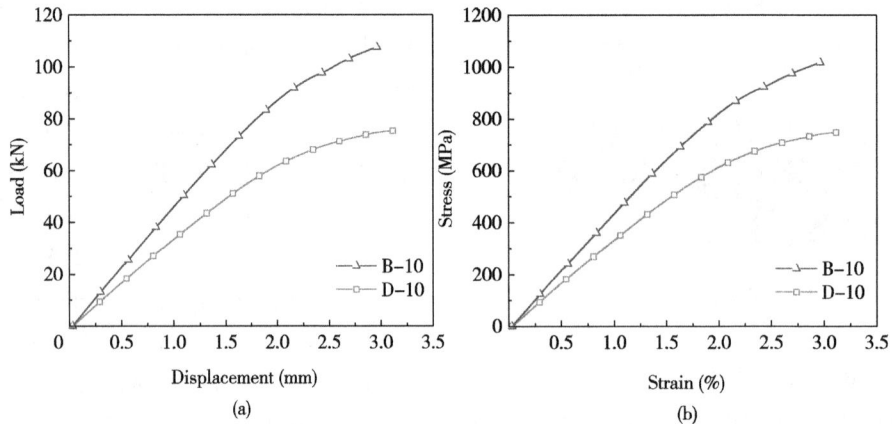

Fig. 6 Tensile curves of 3-D composites with braided hole and drilled hole at the diameter of 10mm

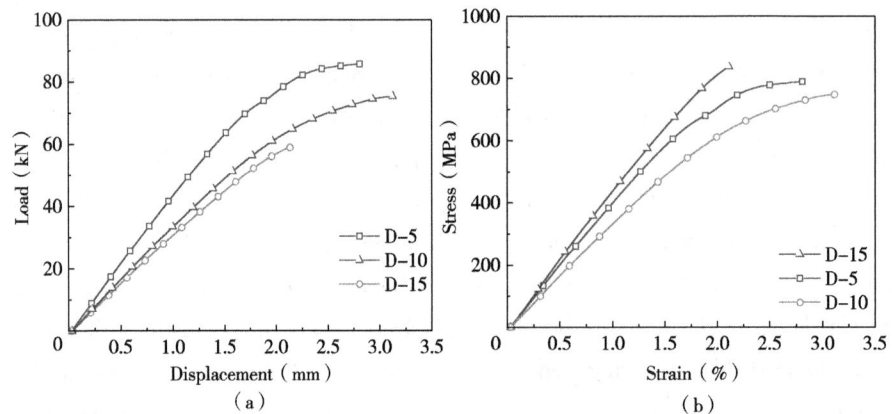

Fig. 7 Tensile curves of 3-D with drilled holes: (a) Load-displacement curve; (b) Stress-strain curve

Fig. 8 shows the strain distributions on the specimen surfaces with drilled hole and braided hole obtained from the DIC. The drilled hole at a diameter of 10mm was analyzed with finite element method, the stress distribution as shown in Fig. 9, and compared it with the result of the DIC picture [Fig. 8 (a)]. The result shows that the specimen with drilled hole has a shear failure mode.

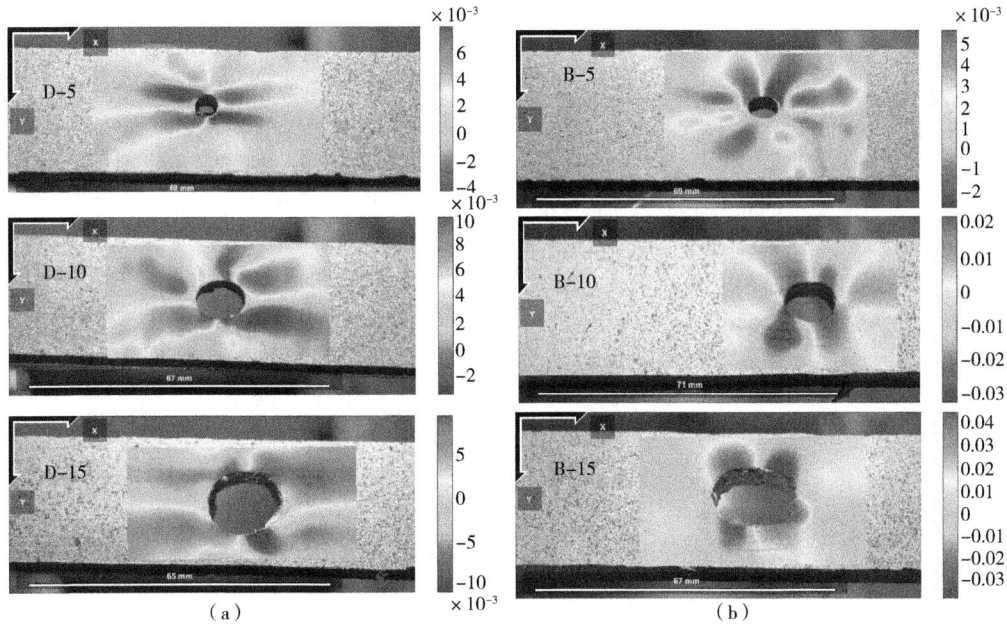

Fig. 8　Strain diagrams of specimens with different diameters: (a) Specimens with drilled holes; (b) Specimens with braided holes

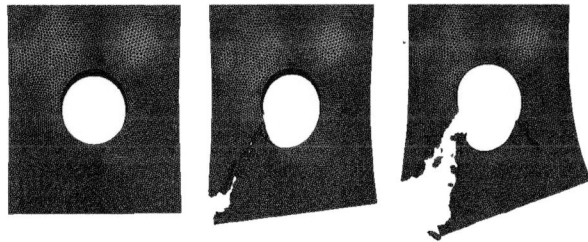

Fig. 9　Finite element analysis diagram (specimen with drilled hole at the diameter of 10mm)

4　Conclusions

The aperture effects on the tensile properties of 3-D braided composites with braided hole and drilled hole were researched. There are three kinds of diameters (5mm, 10mm and 15mm) of the holes. Digital image correlation (DIC) technique was used to collect surface strain of specimens with braided hole and drilled hole. There is local strain concentration around the hole.

The peak load of the specimen with braided hole is not sensitive to the hole size, which do not decrease that compared with the specimen without hole, its modulus increase, instead. The peak load of the specimens with braided holes is all around 105kN. For 3-D braided composites with drilled holes, the peak load decreases with the increases of hole diameter. At the same time, when the diameter of the hole is 10mm, it is found that the tensile load, strength and modulus of the specimen with braided hole are larger than those of the specimen with drilled hole. Finite element analysis of specimen with drilled hole($\Phi = 10$mm) is carried out. Both stress distribution and strain distribution indicate that shear failure occurred in the specimens with drilled.

References

[1] ZHANG C, BUI T. Meso-scale progressive damage modeling and life prediction of 3D braided composites under fatigue tension loading[J]. Composite Structures, 2018, 201: 62-71.

[2] WUH, MUB. On stress concentrations for isotropic/orthotropic plates and cylinders with a circular hole[J]. Composites Structures, 2003, 34: 127-34.

[3] BIAN T, GUAN Z, LIU F. Compressive experiment and numerical simulation of 3D carbon/carbon composite open-hole plates[J]. Archive of Applied Mechanics, 2018, 88: 913-932.

[4] LI C, ZHENG Y, ZHAO H, et al. Finite element calculation of composite material plate with wing connection hole[J]. Journal of Convergence Information Technology, 2013, 8: 467-474.

[5] CHENG L, YING T, KENAN L. Analysis of the opening problem of the composite materials structures with boundary integral[J]. Materials Physics and Mechanics, 2016, 27: 108-112.

[6] OZBAY M, OZER D. The analysis of elasto-plastic stresses in the composite laminate with a circular hole subjected to in-plane loads by means of finite element method[J]. Journal of Reinforced Plastics and Composites, 2005, 24: 621-631.

[7] SUN X, SUN C. Mechanical properties of three-dimensional braided composites [J]. Composite Structures, 2004, 65: 485-492.

[8] KASHFUDDOJA M, PRASATH R, RAMJI M. Study on experimental characterization of carbon fiber reinforced polymer panel using digital image correlation: A sensitivity analysis [J]. Optics and Lasers in Engineering, 2014, 62: 17-30.

[9] KOLANU N, PRAKASH S, RAMJI M. Experimental study on compressive behavior of GFRP stiffened panels using digital image correlation[J]. Ocean Engineering, 2016, 114: 290-302.

[10] GUO Z, ZHU H, LI Y, et al. Simulating initial and progressive failure of open-hole composite laminates under tension [J]. Applied Composite Materials, 2016, 23: 1209-1218.

Preparation and Characterization of Antibacterial Nanofibers of Chitosan Oligosaccharide/Betaine Complex by Electrospinning

JIN Zhao[1], QUAN Zhenzhen[1, 2], ZHANG Hongnan[1], WANG Rongwu[1], YU Jianyong[2], QIN Xiaohong[1 *]

[1] *Key Laboratory of Textile Science & Technology, Ministry of Education, College of Textile, Donghua University, Shanghai, 201620, China*

[2] *Innovation Center for Textile Science and Technology, Donghua University, Shanghai, 201620, China*

* *Corresponding author E-mail address: xhqin@ dhu. edu. cn*

Abstract: Due to their environmental friendliness, natural antibiotics are the mainstream trend today. In our work, two natural antibacterial agents, chitosan oligosaccharide (COS) and betaine, was used as raw materials. The complex of COS with betaine was prepared in weak acidic condition. The complex was characterized by Fourier transform-infrared (FT-IR) and the results showed that the complex was mainly composed of electrostatics interaction between NH_{3+} of COS and COO^- of betaine. The nanofibers were prepared by electrospinning from the mixture solution of PAN and COS/Betaine complex. The results showed that the antibacterial activity is gradually enhanced with the concentration of the complex increased. However, the diameter distribution and uniformity of the nanofibers become wider and worse. Moreover, concentration, pH and temperature are important factors affecting the antibacterial properties of COS/Betaine nanofibers. The optimum temperature for antibacterial property is about 37℃, the optimum pH is about 6 and the optimum concentration is about 5%.

Keywords: Chitosan oligosaccharide; Betaine; Nanofibers; Antibacterial property

1 Introduction

In daily life, people inevitably come into contact with a variety of microorganisms. These microorganisms can grow and multiply under suitable temperature and nutrient conditions, leading to various problems such as material corruption or wound infection that affect people's health[1]. Textiles are easily contaminated by some metabolites. Due to contact the human skin, human secretion, sweat and oil, provide rich nutrients for microbes that will multiply and grow on textiles to spread disease. With the improvement of people's quality of life, the demand for textiles with antibacterial properties is also increasing[2-3].

As we know, COS and betaine are broad-spectrum, green and natural antibacterial agents[4]. In this paper, the complex was mainly composed of electrostatics interaction between NH_{3+} of COS and COO^- of betaine in weak acidic condition, which form a quaternary ammonium salt type chitosan oligosaccharides derivative. In this polymer, NH_{3+} interacts with the anionic component of the cell surface, and the quaternary ammonium group can interact with the phospholipids of the cell membrane, which destroy the microbial membrane and denature the protein. COS/Betaine nanofibers were prepared by electrospinning technique, and their morphology, antibacterial effect and antibacterial suitable conditions (pH, temperature) were characterized.

2 Experiments

2.1 Materials and Chemicals

Polypropylene (PAN), Acetic acid and *N-N* dimethylformamide (DMF) were purchased from Sigma; chitosan oligosaccharide was obtained from Huamaike Biotechnology Co. Ltd (Beijing, China). Betaine was from Bomei Biotechnology Co. Ltd (Anhui, China).

2.2 Preparation of COS/Betaine Complex

COS was dissolved into acetic acid solution 1% (w/v), and the final concentration of COS was adjusted to 10% (w/v), Betaine was diluted to aqueous solution and the concentration was adjusted to 10% (w/v). The same volume of aqueous betaine solution was added to COSAC, stirred for 2h, and then stored for 24h to equilibrate at room temperature. Dried in a freeze dryer to obtain powder.

2.3 Preparation of COS/Betaine Complex Nanofibers

The composite powder was added to 12% PAN solution at room temperature, stirred for 12h. The concentration of the complex in this mixture was adjusted 1%, 2%, 3%, 4%, 5%, respectively. Then, the nanofibers were prepared by electrospinning machine and dried in a 50℃ blast oven for 6 hours to volatilize the solvent.

2.4 Assays for Antimicrobial Activity

Selected *S. aureus* and *E. coli* as test strains, Refer to GB/T 20944—2007 to characterize the antibacterial effect of COS/Betaine complex nanofibers. The nanofibers were tested by the oscillating method. Then, according to the number of colonies in the culture dish of the control group and the test group, the inhibition rate of the sample was calculated according to the formula (1).

$$Y = \frac{W_t - Q_t}{Q_t} \times 100\% \qquad (1)$$

Here, Y represents the inhibition rate (%) of the sample; W_t is the average viable concentration in the control dish (CFU/mL) and Q_t is the average viable concentration in the test culture dish (CFU/mL).

2.5 Characterization

The morphology of the nanofibers with different COS/Betaine complexes were observed by SEM. Then, 50 fibers were randomly selected for statistics to calculate the diameter under different concentration. IR spectra were taken on KBr pellets on a Spectrum Two Fourier transform-infrared (FT-IR) spectro-photometer (PerkinElmer, America) by the method of transmission.

3 Results and Discussions

3.1 Fourier Transform-Infrared Study

As shown in Fig. 1, in the COS and COS/Betaine spectra, the weak absorption band at 2800—2000cm^{-1} was caused by NH$_{3+}$ overtone. Compared with the spectra COS, the band of COS/Betaine had a relatively stronger absorbent. And the absorption bands at 1692cm^{-1} of Betaine and the 1623cm^{-1} of COS spectrum were assigned to the amide I band of COS/Betaine[5].

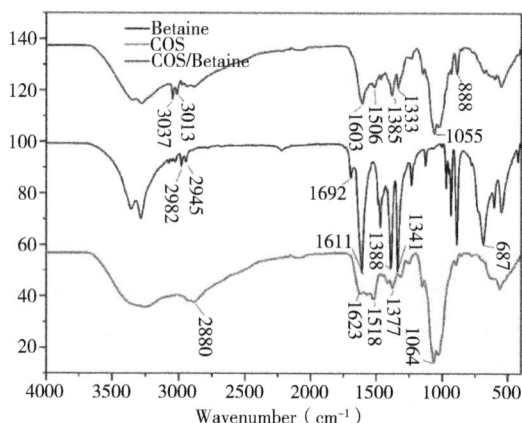

Fig. 1　The FT-IR spectra of Betaine, COS and COS/Betaine

Simultaneously, the absorption band at 1611cm^{-1} of Betaine shifted to the position at 1603cm^{-1} and overlapped with the amide I band, and 1388cm^{-1} shifted to the position of 1385cm^{-1} in the COS / Betaine spectrum. This indicated that there may be the new hydrogen bond was possible formed between COO$^-$ in betaine and NH$_{3+}$ in COS[6-7].

3.2 Characterization of COS/Betaine Complex Nanofibers

Fig. 2 showed the morphology of the nanofibers after 5000 magnification. It can be seen that the diameter distribution and uniformity of the nanofibers become wider and worse with the concentration of the complex increased. The main reason is that the concentration of PAN changed with the COS/Betaine increased. Moreover, COS/Betaine distributed not evenly in the solution, which affected the distribution of the conductivity of the solution. Therefore, the diameter distribution and uniformity of the nanofibers become wider and worse.

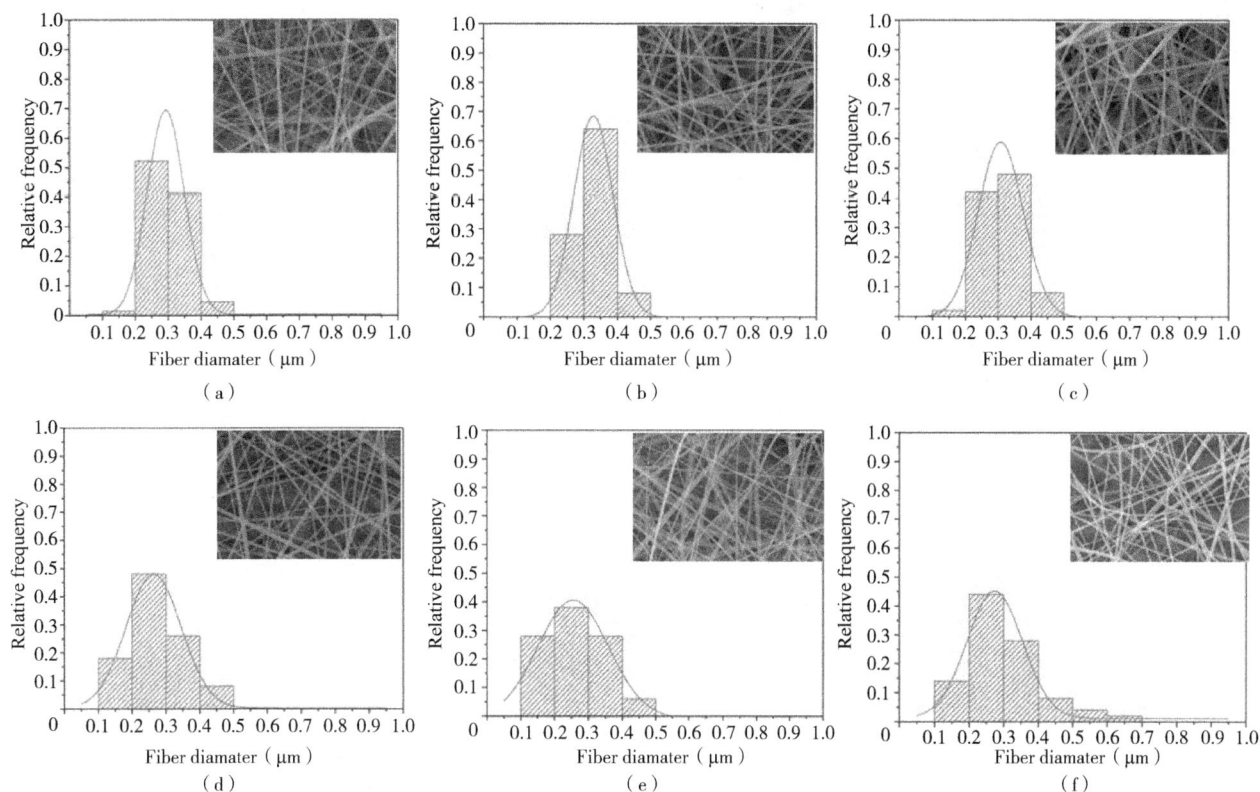

Fig. 2 SEM images of PAN nanofiber membrane at different concentration of COS/Betaine: (a) Pure PAN; (b) 1%; (c) 2%; (d) 3%; (e) 4%; (f) 5%

3.3 Effect of Different Concentrations on the Antibacterial Activity of COS/Betaine Complex Nanofibers

Fig. 3 shows that the bacterio static effect of nanofibers is significantly improved with the concentration of the complex increased. When the concentration was 5%, the anti-bacterial effect against *E. coli* and *S. aureus* reached 97.5% and 95.1%, respectively. The concentration of quaternary ammonium groups and NH_{3+} was increased with antibacterial agent improved. Therefore, antibacterial activity was stronger.

3.4 Effect of Different pH Conditions on Antibacterial Activity of COS/Betaine Complex Nanofibers

The environmental pH in which the microorganisms lived affected their life activities and antibacterial properties. In Fig. 4, (a) *E. coli* and (b) *S. aureus* antibacterial activity at different pH, when the concentration of complex was 3%. it could be seen that the COS/Betaine complex can achieve the best antibacterial effect at pH = 6. The result showed that the antibacterial

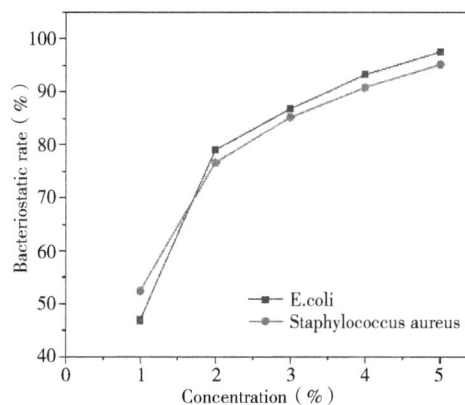

Fig. 3 *E. coli* and *S. aureus* antibacterial activity at different concentration of COS/Betaine

effect against *E. coli* and *S. aureus* reached 88.6% and 87.5%, respectively. The acidic environment provides H^+ to the free amino group of the antibacterial agent, which forms a positively charged protonated ammonium: $H^+ + NH_2 = NH_{3+}$. Therefore, antibacterial activity was enhanced.

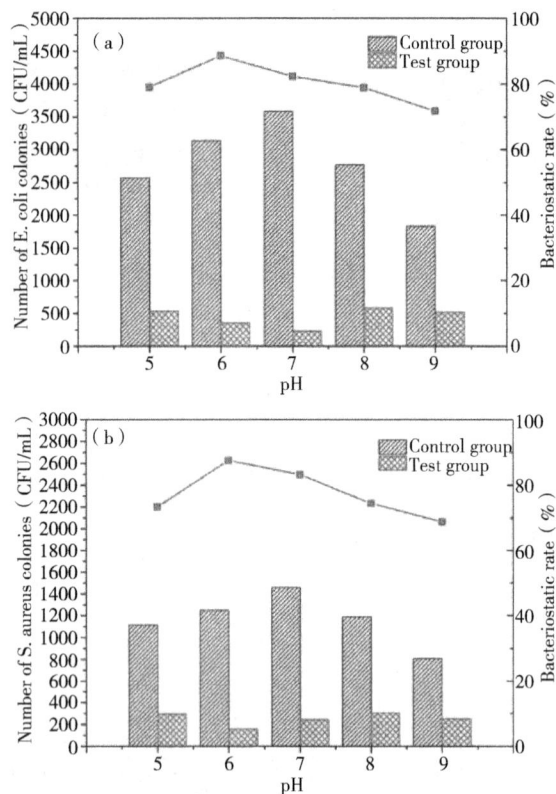

Fig. 4 *E. coli* (a) and *S. aureus* (b) antibacterial activity at different pH

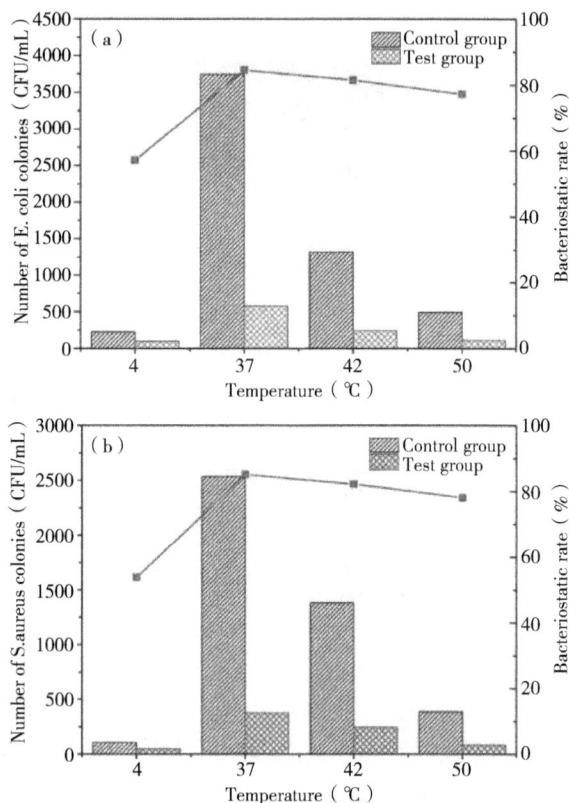

Fig. 5 (a) *E. coli* and (b) *S. aureus* antibacterial activity at different temperature

3.5 Effect of Different pH Conditions on Antibacterial Activity of COS/Betaine Complex Nanofibers

It can be seen that the nanofiber of COS/Betaine complex can maintain a certain antibacterial effect under low temperature conditions, and the growth of bacteria can be inhibited at this temperature. In Fig. 5, *E. coli* and *S. aureus* antibacterial activity at different temperature, when the concentration of complex was 3%. it could be seen that the antibacterial agent achieves the best bacteriostatic effect at 37℃. Although the antibacterial agent still has certain antibacterial activity under high temperature conditions, the antibacterial activity gradually decreases with the increase of temperature.

4 Conclusions

The complex, a quaternary ammonium salt type COS derivative, was formed of electrostatic interaction between NH_{3+} of COS and COO^- of betaine in weak acidic condition. SEM images show that the diameter distribution and uniformity of the nanofibers become wider and worse with the concentration of the complex increased. The experimental results showed that concentration, pH

and temperature were important factors affecting the antibacterial properties of COS/Betaine nanofibers. The optimum temperature for antibacterial property is about 37℃, the optimum pH is about 6, and the optimum concentration is about 5%. Therefore, the antibacterial nanofibers are blended with cotton without affecting their wearability, which gives traditional textiles new functionality and high added value, expanding their application in the field of application, especially in the field of sports.

References

[1]SHIPRA V, MIWAKO Y, KARI M S, et al. The antibacterial lectin RegIIIγ gamma promotes the spatial segregation of microbiota and host in the intestine[J]. Science, 2011, 334 (6053): 255-258.

[2]ALJAZ V, IVAN J, ANGELA S V, et al. Structural properties and antibacterial effects of hydrophobic and oleophobic sol-gel coatings for cotton fabrics[J]. Langmuir, 2009, 25 (10): 5869-5880.

[3]XING Y J, SONG Y, JI Y M, et al. Advances in antimicrobial finishing for textiles based on silver[J]. Journal of Tex-

tile Research, 2008.

[4] DOUGLAS D B, ODÍLIO B G. A novel method for obtaining a quaternary salt of chitosan [J]. Carbohydrate Polymers, 2007, 69(2): 305-310.

[5] WILLIAMS D H, FLEMING I. Spectroscopic methods in organic chemistry[J]. New York: McGraw-Hill, 1995.

[6] LI C X, GUO T Y, ZHOU D Z, et al. A novel glutathione modified chitosan conjugate for efficient gene delivery[J]. Journal of Controlled Release, 2011, 154(2): 177-188.

[7] LIU H. Structural characterization and antimicrobial activity of chitosan/betaine derivative complex [J]. Carbohydrate Polymers, 2004, 55(3): 291-297.

Electrospun Cellulose Acetate Hydrophilic Membrane from Softwood Dissolving Pulp

WU Jiajun[1, 2], WANG Yihan[1], QIU Qiaohua[1, 2], QIN Xiaohong[1, 2*]

[1] *Department of Textile Materials, College of Textiles, Donghua University, Shanghai, 201620, China*

[2] *Key Laboratory of Textile Science & Technology, Ministry of Education, College of Textile, Donghua University, Shanghai, 201620, China*

* *Corresponding author's email:* xhqin@ dhu. edu. cn

Abstract: Cellulose acetate (CA) is made from dissolving pulp, which consists of more than 95% α-cellulose. Compositional analyses by HPLC shows that the softwood dissolving pulp sample consist of 95.7% glucan, 1.7% xylan and 1.4% mannose. In order to get cellulose diacetate (CDA), low temperature heterogenous acetylation was applied to produce cellulose triacetate (CTA) from dissolving pulp, followed by high temperature hydrolysis. The process contains cellulose acetylation with acetic anhydride in the existence of sulfuric acid as catalyst and acetic acid as solvent, substituting hydroxyl with acetyl group on the cellulose molecular chain, and re-substitute hydroxyl back to certain degree of substitution (DS) value by changing hydrolysis conditions. After 16h hydrolysis at 80℃, DS decreased from 2.86 to 2.04 calculated by ^{1}H NMR. With longer hydrolysis time, cellulose acetate is water soluble and it is hard to separate from reaction system. From FTIR, the decreased intensity at $3445 cm^{-1}$(OH stretching), together with the increased intensity and width of the band at $1735 cm^{-1}(\upsilon_{C=O})$, $1375 cm^{-1}(\upsilon_{C-CH3})$ and $1247 cm^{-1}(\upsilon_{C-O-C})$, indicate that the hydroxyl was substituted by acetyl group. Then, CA was dissolved in binary solvent system of acetone/ dimethylacetamide = 2/1 v/v at the concentration of 15% to prepare the sub microfiber membrane by electrospinning. SEM pictures indicate that lower DS CA fiber is thinner than higher DS CA fiber, together with some broken fibers which may due to CA molecular chain broken under longer hydrolysis time. The water contact angle is around 130° for CTA membrane and 46° for the sample of DS=2.04. This unique property broadens the potential use in biomaterials and other applications.

Keywords: Acetylation; Hydrolysis; Cellulose acetate; Electrospinning; Wettability

1 Introduction

Cellulose acetate (CA) is one of the common biopolymers derived from cellulose. Because of its good thermal stability, chemical resistance, biocompatibility and biodegradability, attempts were made to apply as wound dressings[1], drug delivery carrier[2], separation membrane[3], scaffold and others[4]. Typically, the degree of substitution (DS) of CA is around 2.3-2.5, which means there are around five sixths of hydroxyl were substituted by acetyl group on the cellulose molecular chain on average. Increasing hydrolysis time with specific catalyst reduces to cellulose monoacetate of DS = 0.5-0.9, either hydrophilic or water soluble[5].

Using dissolving pulp, or alpha cellulose, as the start-ing material to prepare cellulose acetate is not a new fashion[6-9]. But the key technics for manufacturing are always kept secret, though the basic theories of acetylation and hydrolysis are clear to engineers, within the big companies like Eastman, Celanese, Daicel, Rhodia, et al. Each β-D-glucose monomer unit in cellulose contains three free hydroxyl groups. Almost all the hydroxyl groups should be replaced by acetyl groups, or the DS is above 28 of cellulose triacetate. Typically, the process for preparing CA is acetic acid process, which comprises: (1) pretreatment step wherein cellulose is macerated in acetic acid and a small amount of an acidic catalyst, to make the cellulose structure swollen and give the way for reagents come in afterwards;

(2) acetylation step wherein cooled mixed acid comprising acetic anhydride, acetic acid and acidic catalyst is added; (3) filtration step wherein the unacetylated part was filtered; (4) hydrolysis step wherein cellulose triacetate and dissolved in diluted acetic acid at elevated temperature; (5) precipitation step wherein the CA is precipitated and washed with deionized water followed by drying.

In this paper, CA was prepared from softwood dissolving pulp and hydrolyzed to *DS* around 2. Then, CA was dissolved in binary solvent system of acetone and dimethylacet amide to check the spinnability by electrospinning. The wettability of electrospun mat change from hydrophobic to hydrophilic. It shows potential use in biomaterials or other applications.

2　Experiments

2.1　Materials

Sulfuric acid, acetic acid, acetic anhydride, magnesium acetate, dimethyl sulfoxide and sodium carbonate were bought from Fisher Scientific (USA). Acetone and dimethyl acetamide were bought from Sinopharm Chemical Reagent Co., Ltd (China). Softwood dissolving pulp was offered by own lab.

2.2　Pulp Characterization

Dissolving pulp compositional analyses was measured using a modified version of the NREL standard procedure[10]. A quantity of 300mg powder of pulp was hydrolyzed with 72% H_2SO_4 at 30℃ for 2 hours. The hydrolyzed biomass was diluted to 3% H_2SO_4 and autoclaved at 120℃ for 1.5h. The hydrolysate was filtered and oven-dried to determine the insoluble solids, and the filtrate was collected for the determination of acid soluble lignin by UV spectrophotometer (Lambda XLS, Perkin Elmer) and carbohydrate content analysis using HPLC system (Agilent 1200 series, Agilent).

2.3　Cellulose Acetate Acetylation

Pulp activated in acetic acid : sulfuric acid : pulp = 6 : 0.09 : 1 w/w at room temperature for 0.5h. Remove excess acetic acid to 2 : 1 w/w to reduce the pulp water content. Then, it was acetylated in acetic acid : acetic anhydride : sulfuric acid : pulp = 15 : 3.78 : 0.09 : 1 w/w at 2℃ for 5h.

2.4　Cellulose Acetate Hydrolysis

The acetylated system was filtered through sand core funnel (size M, core size 10-15μm) followed by hydrolysis at 80℃ for 16h. Unhydrolyzed and hydrolyzed samples were precipitated in water until neutral with abundant of water, sodium carbonate and magnesium acetate to remove excess acid. Then drying in the vacuum oven at 60℃ for 24h.

2.5　Cellulose Acetate Electrospinning

CA were dissolved in a mix solvent of acetone/ dimethylacetamide (2/1 v/v) at concentration of 8% for CTA and 15% for CDA. The CDA solution were electrospun at a voltage of 20kV, distance to collector of 15cm, solution flow rate of 0.5mL/h for 2h. Vacuum drying of samples at 60℃ for overnight.

2.6　Electrospun Mat Properties Characterization

Fiber morphology was tested by SEM (KYKY EM6200, China). Fiber diameter was measured by Nano Measurer 1.2. Water contact angle was measured on a contact angle analyzer (OCA15EC, Germany). Samples were dissolved in dimethyl sulfoxide-d6 to measure *DS* by ^{1}H NMR (Bruker Avance 400, Swiss). Chemical composition was analyzed by FTIR (PerkinElmer Spectrum Two, USA).

3　Results and Discussions

3.1　Chemical Composition Analysis

As shown in Fig. 1, the diminishing peak at 3450cm^{-1} (O—H stretching) indicate the reduction of acetyl to hydroxyl group, together with the peaks at 1737cm^{-1} (C=O vibration), 1374cm^{-1} (CαCH$_3$ vibration), 1235cm^{-1} and 1058cm^{-1}(C—O—C vibration). The filter residue after acetylation was much more like cellulose, which should be removed through filtration. The increase of wavenumber of CDA and CTA may be caused by blue shift, indicating the rehybridization of C—H bond[11].

The chemical compositional content analysis was measured by HPLC. Tab. 1 indicates that the softwood dissolving pulp is composed of 95.7% glucan and a small amount of xylan, which is undesired in the acetylation.

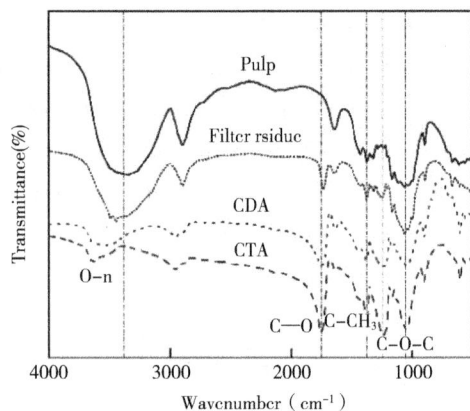

Fig. 1 FTIR spectrum of CA, softwood dissolving pulp and filter residue before precipitation

Tab. 1 Chemical compositional content analysis of softwood dissolving pulp

	Softwood dissolving pup
Glucan (%)	95. 7±0. 6
Xylan (%)	1. 7±0. 2
Lignin (%)	0. 3
Mannose (%)	1. 4±0. 1
Mass Balance	99. 0±0. 7

3.2 *DS* Calculation

DS of each sample was measured by[1]H NMR according to the reported method[12], as shown in Fig. 1.

$$DS = \frac{7 * I_{acetyl, H}}{3 * I_{AGU, H}} \qquad (1)$$

Where $I_{acetyl, H}$ is the integration of the peaks assigned to acetyl's methyl protons of methyl group at 3. 6 – 5. 2mg/kg, while $I_{AGU, H}$ is the sum of integration of the peaks assigned to anhydroglucose ring protons at 1. 7 – 2. 2mg/kg. The *DS* of CTA is around 2. 86 (rounded) after 5h acetylation and reduced to 2. 04 after 16h hydrolysis. The reaction reactivity of O—H on C_3 is much less than that on C_2 and C_6 because of the steric effect.

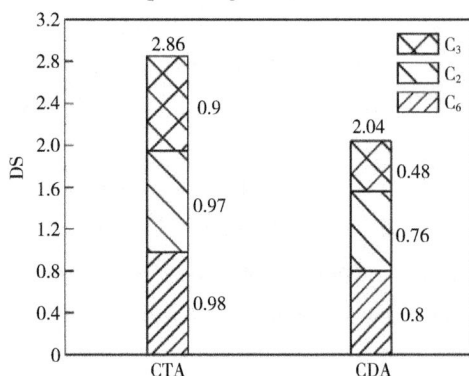

Fig. 2 *DS* of each C on CA molecular chain unit by[1]H NMR

3.3 Electrospun Mat Characterization

Through the SEM image in Fig. 3 (a) and (b), the fiber diameter of CTA ranged from around 0. 2μm to 1. 8 μm and reduced to around 0. 1–03μm for CDA with some broken fibers. This may be caused by the reduction of molecular weight through hydrolysis. The water hydrophilicity increases with lower *DS*. The wettability changed from hydrophobic to hydrophilic through hydrolysis process, which attributes mainly to the increase of hydroxyl replaced for acetyl group. This wettability divergence should be able to be applied in biomaterials such as wound dressings and other applications.

(a)

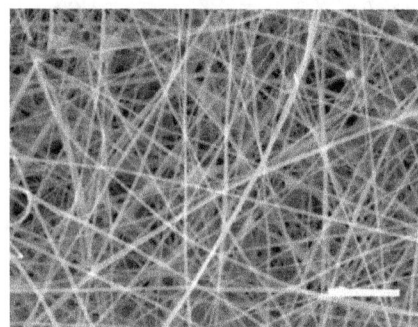

(b)

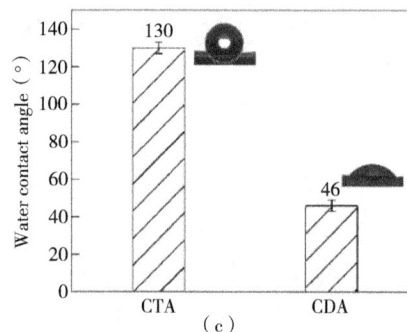

(c)

Fig. 3 SEM of different *DS* of (a) CTA; (b) CDA (The scale bar on the lower right corner is 4μm); (c) Wettability difference of CTA and CDA measured by water contact angle (measured at 10s)

4　Conclusions

The compositional analysis of softwood dissolving pulp was conducted by HPLC. Results show that the pulp consists of 95.7% glucan, 1.7% xylan and 1.4% mannose. Different degree of substitution of cellulose acetate were prepared by low temperature acetylation followed by high temperature hydrolysis from softwood dissolving pulp. DS changed from 2.86 to 2.04 measured by ^{1}H NMR after hydrolysis for 16h. Then, the spinnability of synthetic CTA and CDA dissolved in binary solvent system was checked by electrospinning. The water contact angle is around 130° for CTA membrane and 46° for the sample of $DS = 2.04$. This unique property broadens the potential use of CA in biomaterials and other applications.

References

[1] WUTTICHAROENMONGKOL P, HANNIROJRAM P, NUTHONG P. Gallic acid-loaded electrospun cellulose acetate nanofibers as potential wound dressing materials[J]. Polymers for Advanced Technologies, 2019, 30(4): 1135-1147.

[2] KHOSHNEVISAN K, MALEKI H, SAMADIAN H, et al. Cellulose acetate electrospun nanofibers for drug delivery systems: applications and recent advances[J]. Carbohydrate Polymers, 2018, 198: 131-141.

[3] KANAGARAJ P, NAGENDRAN A, RANA D, et al. Separation of macromolecular proteins and removal of humic acid by cellulose acetate modified UF membranes [J]. International Journal of Biological Macromolecules, 2016, 89: 81-88.

[4] KONWARH R, KARAK N, MISRA M. Electrospun cellulose acetate nanofibers: the present status and gamut of biotechnological applications [J]. Biotechnology Advances, 2013, 31(4): 421-437.

[5] BUCHANAN C M, EDGAR K J, WILSON A K. Preparation and characterization of cellulose monoacetates-the relationship between structure and water solubility[J]. Macromolecules, 1991, 24(11): 3060-3064.

[6] OYA T, WATANABE S. Cellulose acylate, cellulose acylate film, and method for production and use thereof[P]. Google Patents, US 20060222786 A1, 2006.

[7] MITCHELL M G, GERMROTH T C, JOHNSON G I, et al. Process for acetylation of cellulose[P]. Google Patents, WO 1994003497 A1, 1994.

[8] KARSTENS T, HERMANUTZ F. Method for producing cellulose acetate [P]. Google Patents, WO 1998041543 A1, 1998.

[9] COMBS M T, GARRETT T S. Methods for synthesizing acylated cellulose through instillation of an acidic catalyst[P]. Google Patents, WO 2013055717 A1, 2013.

[10] SLUITER A, HAMES B, RUIZ R, et al. Determination of structural carbohydrates and lignin in biomass[J]. Laboratory Analytical Procedure, 2008, 1617: 1-16.

[11] AN X L, LIU H P, LI Q Z, et al. Influence of substitution, hybridization, and solvent on the properties of C—HO single-electron hydrogen bond in CH_3-H_2O complex[J]. Journal of Physical Chemistry A, 2008, 112(23): 5258-5263.

[12] XU J T, SHI Y C. Position of acetyl groups on anhydroglucose unit in acetylated starches with intermediate degrees of substitution[J]. Carbohydrate Polymers, 2019, 220: 118-125.

Finite Element Analyses of Three-Dimensional Angle-Interlock Woven Fabric Under Ballistic Penetration

WEI Qinsong[1], YANG Dan[2, 3], GU Bohong[1], SUN Baozhong[1]*

[1] College of Textiles, Donghua University, Shanghai, 201620, China

[2] College of Garment, Shanghai University of Engineering Science, Shanghai, 201620, China

[3] College of Textile Science and Engineering, Wuhan Textile University, Wuhan, 430200, China

* Corresponding author's email: sunbz@ dhu. edu. cn

Abstract: The ballistic impact damage behaviors of 'through-the-thickness' three-dimensional angle-interlock woven fabric (3DAWF) under ballistic penetration was investigated based on experimental and numerical finite element analysis in this paper. In experiments, the 3DAWF panels were penetrated under 9mm full metal jacket (FMJ) projectiles, the strike velocities and residual velocities of projectiles were recorded to analysis the fabrics ballistic proof properties and ballistic energy absorption mechanisms. A yarn-level mesoscale finite element analysis (FEA) model of 3DAWF under ballistic penetration is designed and established to calculate and demonstrate the energy absorption mechanism of this ballistic event. The comparison of theoretical and experimental results shows a good agreement indicating the validity of the microstructural finite element model of 3DAWF.

Keywords: 3-D angle-interlock woven fabric (3DAWF); Finite element analysis (FEA); Ballistic penetration; Energy absorption; Microstructure

1 Introduction

Three-dimensional angle-interlock woven fabric (3DAWF) consists of weft and warp systems, the weft yarns remain straight, and the warp yarns travel diagonally through-the-thickness direction of the fabric, which constructs a through the thickness self-interlock structure[1]. The angle-interlock structures integrate all threads bundled together, providing excellent intermediate medium to transfer inner response stress when subjected to external dynamic loading[2]. Zahid et al. reported that composites developed from angle-interlock fabric, exhibit different and far better tensile properties in the weft direction as compared to the warp direction[3]. It is also a type of 3D fabric with good mouldability that has the advantages to shape the high mouldable bulletproof structure, such as the helmet[4]. In addition, Luan et al. reported the ballistic impact damage and energy absorption mechanism of three-dimensional angle-interlock

woven composite (3DAWC) based on high strain rate constitutive equations of fiber tows[5].

Here we present a new kind of yarn-level membrane-based microstructure FEA 3DAWF model to reveal the ballistic damage mechanism of 3DAWF and demonstrate the energy absorption mechanism during ballistic penetration. We investigated ballistic behaviors of 3DAWF with tests and numerical analyses to reveal its capabilities for defensive application.

2 Tests

2.1 Target Panel

The 3DAWF employed in this paper is the 5-layer 'through-the-thickness' angle-interlock structure woven by interlacing five adjacent layers of weft yarns with warp yarns shown in Fig. 1. Such a structure will provide more warp yarns in impact direction and enable the fabric flexible. The warp yarns and weft yarns are both the Kevlar yarns K49, manufactured by Dupont De Nemours. Kevlar© is a kind of aramid fiber which has low density, high tensile strength, and high impact resistance. The physical properties of K49 yarns are listed in Tab. 1. The specifications of the 3DAWF are listed in Tab. 2. Tab. 3 lists the parameters of the 3DAWF panel for the ballistic impact tests. The surfaces of tested 3DAWF are presented in Fig. 2.

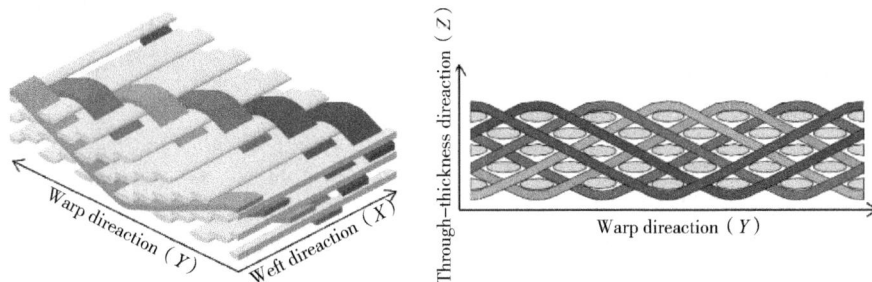

Fig. 1　Schematic of 3DAWF architecture employed in the tests

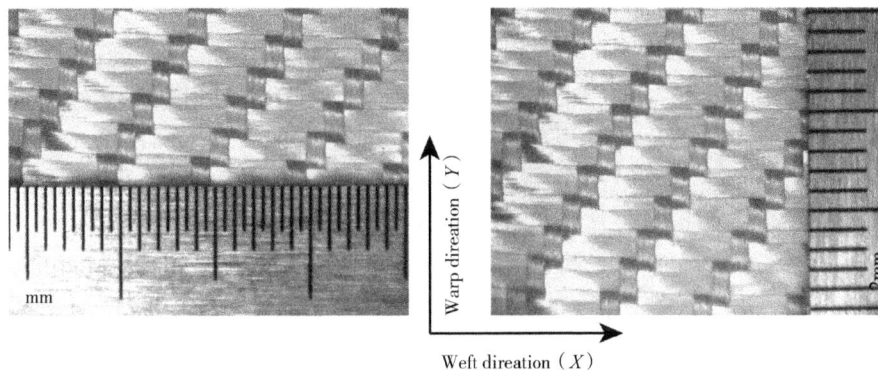

Fig. 2　Surfaces of the tested 3DAWF specimen

Tab. 1　Typical properties of Kevlar© yarns

	PROPERTY	UNIT	TYPE 965 K49
	Denier (Decitex)	Denier(dtex)	1420(1580)
YARN	Specific Gravity	—	1. 44
	Commercial Moisture Regain	%	3. 5
	Breaking Strength	N	309
STRESS-STRAIN PROPERTIES	Breaking Tenacity	cN/tex	196
STRAIGHT TEST ON YARNS	Elongation at Break	%	2. 49
	Initial Modulus	cN/tex	7555

Tab. 2　Specifications of the single-layered 3-D angle interlock woven fabric panel

Length (MM)	Width (MM)	Thickness (MM)	Panel Weight (G)	Usable Area (mm²)
120	120	1. 6	12. 50	80×80

Tab. 3　Specifications of the 3DAWF

Fabric Type	Unit	Direction	3DAWF
Count	dtex	Warp	1580
		Weft	1580
Density	threads/10cm	Warp	120
		Weft	320
Fabric Weight	g/m²		866

2.2 Tests

A series of ballistic impact tests were conducted with 9mm FMJ projectiles to determine the strike and residual velocities of the projectiles. As shown in Fig. 3 (a), the FMJ projectile of diameter 9mm are applied in all the ballistic resistance tests. Fig. 3 (b) is the geometrical model of the projectile in numerical simulation. The projectile, whose weight is 8g. was propelled along a ballistic barrel by using gun powder, and the strike velocity of the projectile could be controlled by adjusting the weight of gun powder. Two laser-diode pairs were used to measure the strike velocities and residual velocities of the projectile before and after ballistic penetration. the schematic diagram of ballistic impact tests are presented in Fig. 5.

Fig. 3　Photograph of the 9mm FMJ projectile and finite element geometrical model

Tested specimens were clamped between two steel square fixture with an inner side length of 8cm. The four sides of the fabric target were fixed by the square fixture, and the dimension of the fixture is shown in Fig. 4. The impact points were designed at the center of the 3DAWF panels shown in Fig. 5. The range of strike velocity is designed as 200m/s to 300m/s to evaluate the ballistic performance of 3DAWF panels.

Fig. 4　Photographs of the fixture

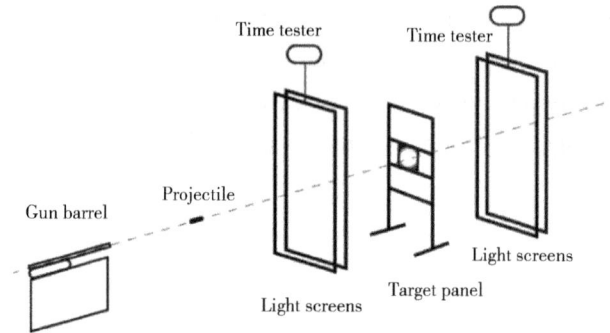

Fig. 5　Schematic representation of ballistic impact tests

3　Numerical Simulation

The full-size microstructure models are established to study the critical importance of 3DAWF architecture in transferring and dissipating the ballistic impact energy during ballistic penetration. Finite element analysis (FEA) was conducted using commercial finite element software LS-DYNA. The homogeneous projectiles with the same weight of 9mm FMJ bullet are employed in FEA and taken as rigid bodies.

3.1　Microstructure Model

Assuming the cross-section of the fiber tow in 3DAWF is a slender rectangle. Fig. 3 and Tab. 3 present the geometrical parameters of the 3DAWF. As shown in Fig. 6, based on the size of the width of fiber tow and woven fabric construction, three-dimensional surfaces with the same width of weft and warp yarns space bending angle are established respectively. The sets of warp and weft yarns are constructed by copying single yarns and arraying them according to the 3DAWF configuration. The warp and weft yarns sets are assembled to form the 3DAWF model as seen in Fig. 6. The whole FEA model for the impact penetration calculations is shown in Fig. 6. The surfaces of the geometrical model and 3DAWF are depicted in Fig. 7. It can be concluded that geometric microstructure models can accurately represent 3DAWF architecture.

3.2　Mesh Scheme

In the yarn-level geometrical model, the microstructure model of the 3DAWF meshed with the four-node Belytschko-Tsay shell element with thickness stretch. The Belytschko-Tsay shell element is one of the fastest elements for thin shell simulations. This, together with its

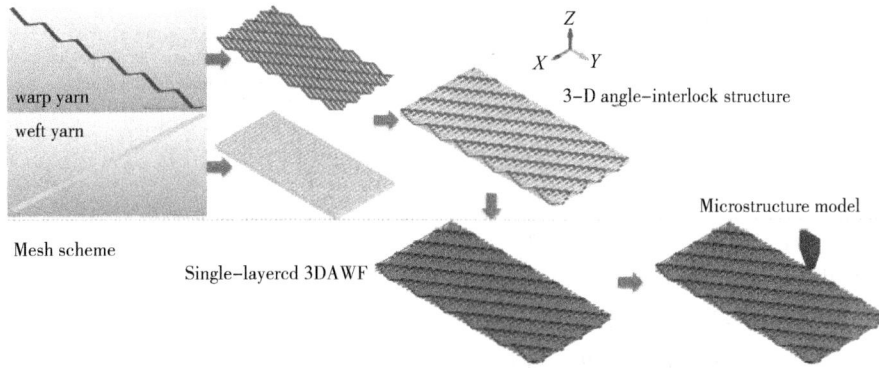

Fig. 6 Schematic process diagram of the modeling

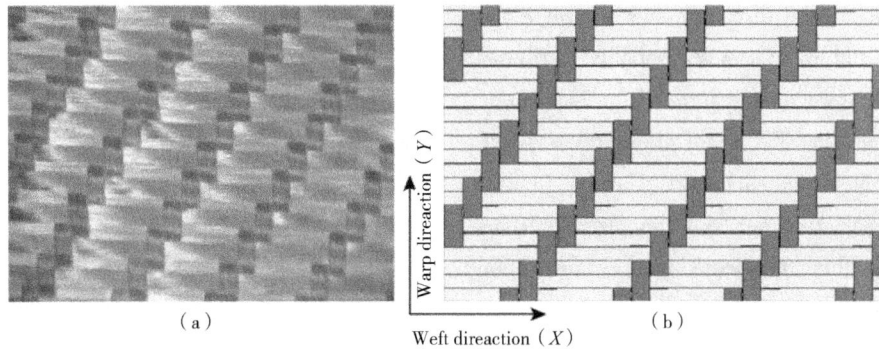

Fig. 7 Surface photographs of the 3-D angle-interlock woven structure: (a) Surface of 3DAWF; (b) Pattern of the geometrical model

robustness, is the reason why it is popular in finite element codes. Readers are directed to the references[6] for an in-depth theoretical background. Surface meshing generates a mesh of plate elements model according to 3D geometry specifications. The thickness of fiber tow is assigned to shell elements that represent the middle surface of the solid part. There are 113848 elements and 143497 nodes in 3DAWF model. The projectile meshes with 1026 hexahedron elements.

3.3 Interaction Property

In impact simulations, the deformations can be very large, and predetermination of where and how contact will take place may be difficult or impossible. For this reason, the automatic contact options are employed as these contacts are non-oriented, meaning they can detect penetration coming from either side of a shell element. The contact search algorithms employed by automatic contacts make them better-suited than older contact types to handling disjoint meshes. In the case of shell elements, shell thickness effects are important when shell elements are used to model nonlinear stretching. In the treatment of thickness, both the slave and master surfaces are projected based on the mid-surface normal projection vectors, as shown in Fig. 8 (a). The surfaces, therefore, must be offset by an amount equal to 1/2 of their total thickness[Fig. 8 (b)].

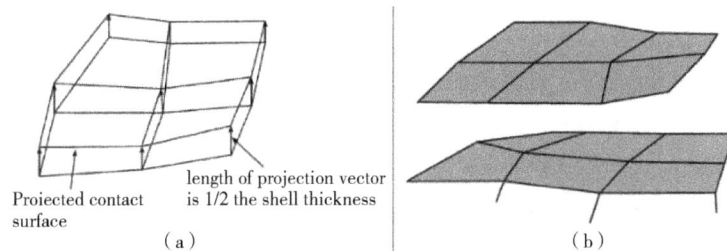

Fig. 8 Schematic diagram of contact-impact algorithm: (a) Contact surface is based on mid-surface normal projection vectors; (b) The slave and master surfaces are offset by one-half the total shell thickness

4 Results and Discussions

For a given striking velocity of the projectiles listed in Tab. 4, the residual velocity can be calculated by FEA model and compared with that in tests. Fig. 9 is the comparison of the stri006Be velocity vs. the residual velocity curves between FEA and tests. An excellent agreement of the residual velocities between FEA and experimental is achieved. The simulation results indicated that the microstructure FEA model agrees well with that in ballistic tests and could be used in the 3DAWF ballistic limit estimation. The tiny difference between the FEA and experimental results most probably attributes to the Kevlar© fiber tows were regarded as a continuum surface with thickness in FEA while they are composed of thousands of filaments in each tow. The un-simultaneous failure of each filament and complex interface friction will lead to the complicated energy absorption mechanism in experimental.

The FEA results of B-2 at the strike velocity 220.7m/s is the closest with the ballistic test as listed in Tab. 4. Moreover, the impact damage morphology of test under the strike velocity of 220.7m/s is accurately predicted by the FEA model, as shown in Fig. 10. So, the FEA model at strike velocity 220.7m/s is taken to analyze the energy absorption mechanism, impact damage evolution, and stress propagation during the impact process.

The velocity vs. time history and the acceleration vs. time history of the projectile during penetration at the strike velocities of 220.7m/s are illustrated in Fig. 11. From the graph, it can be concluded that the projectile takes about 130μs to perforate the 3DAWF target completely. The absolute value of acceleration reaches the maximum value at around 30μs. As illustrated in Fig. 12, at 30μs, warp yarns in the impact zone are straightened from the cured state and stretched by the impact bullet. Weft yarns in the same zone are also stretched to stop the projectile. However, neither warp yarns nor weft yarns are broken. Furthermore, owing to the cylindrical-conically shape of the projectile, the absolute value of acceleration increases at around 70μs. After 120μs, the velocity and acceleration maintain stable because the bullet has fully penetrated the panel.

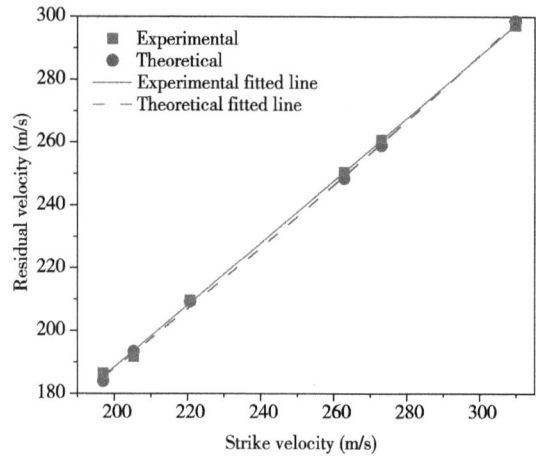

Fig. 9　Strike velocity vs. residual velocity curves in FEA andtests

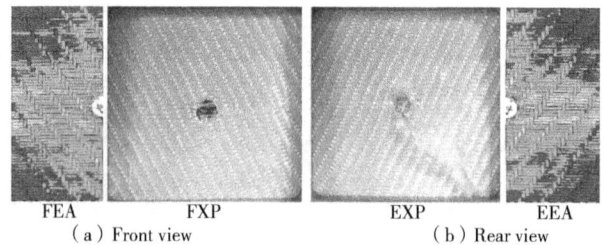

(a) Front view　　　　　　(b) Rear view

Fig. 10　Comparisons of failure morphology impacted by 9mm FMJ bullet at 220.7m/s between tests and theoretical

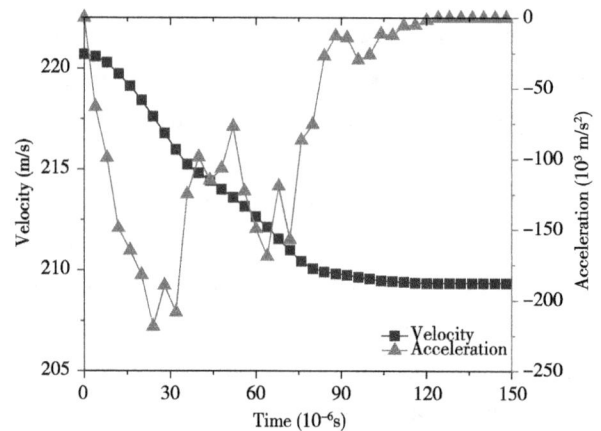

Fig. 11　Velocity vs. time history and acceleration vs. time history of the projectile at the strike velocities of 220.7m/s

Tab. 4　Residual velocity and energy absorbed comparison between tests and FEA

Fabric specimens	No. Strike velocity (m/s)	Experimental residual velocity (m/s)	Theoretical residual velocity (m/s)
B-1	205.3	191.8	193.4
B-2	220.7	209.6	209.3
B-3	273.1	260.7	259.0
B-4	262.9	250.4	248.5
B-5	309.8	297.3	298.6
B-6	197.0	186.5	184.0

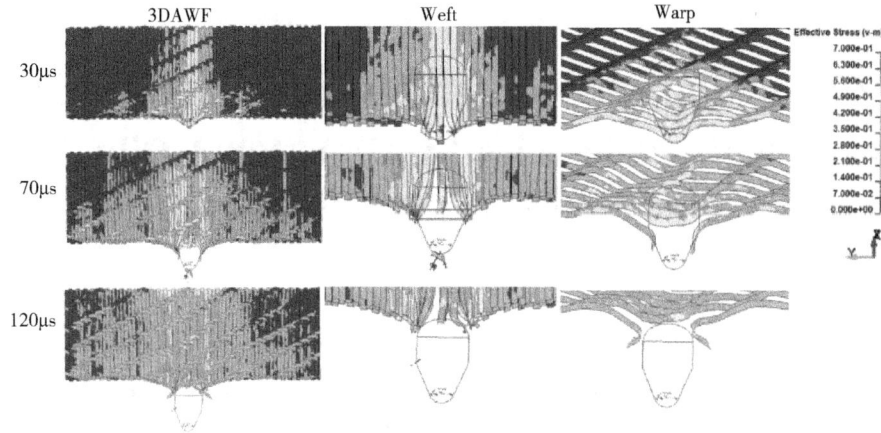

Fig. 12 Ballistic penetration at three different time steps at the strike velocity of 220. 7m/s

Fig. 13 shows the energy absorption of weft and warp yarns during ballistic penetration. As indicated in the curve, the total energy of weft yarns is about three times more than the total energy of warp yarns. In other words, the weft yarns were the dominant part in 3DAWF to absorb the bullet's kinetic energy.

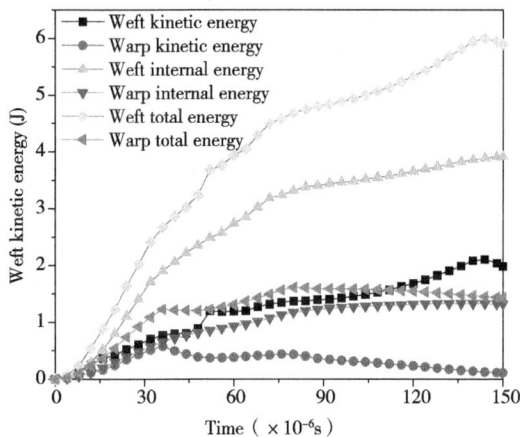

Fig. 13 Yarns kinetic and internal energy vs. time curve under the strike velocity of 220. 7m/s

5 Conclusions

In this study, a yarn-level microstructure FEA model of the 3DAWF was created in LS-DYNA to evaluate the fabric's performance under different ballistic impacts. The FEA model was validated using 9mm FMJ projectile ballistic penetration and shown to agree well with the test data in the predicted residual velocities and failure morphology. It was also observed that the weft yarns absorbed a significant amount of kinetic energy of the bul-

let. The numerical model developed here can thus be applied with confidence for carrying out numerical parametric studies for 3DWAF armour design.

Acknowledgements

This work was supported by the Science and Technology Research Project of Educational Commission of Hubei Province under the grant number Q20181704.

References

[1] CHEN X, POTIYARAJ P. CAD/CAM of orthogonal and angle-interlock woven structures for industrial applications[J]. Textile Research Journal, 2016, 69(9): 648-655.

[2] LUAN K, GU B H. Energy absorption of three-dimensional angle-interlock woven composite under ballistic penetration based on a multi-scale finite element model[J]. International Journal of Damage Mechanics, 2015, 24(1): 3-20.

[3] ZAHID B, CHEN X G. Properties of 5-layer angle-interlock Kevlar-based composite structure manufactured from vacuum bagging[J]. Journal of Composite Materials, 2013, 47(25): 3227-3234.

[4] ZAHID B, CHEN X. Impact performance of single-piece continuously textile reinforced riot helmet shells[J]. Journal of Composite Materials, 2014, 48(6): 761-766.

[5] LUAN K, SUN B, GU B. Ballistic impact damages of 3-D angle-interlock woven composites based on high strain rate constitutive equation of fiber tows[J]. International Journal of Impact Engineering, 2013, 57: 145-158.

[6] BELYTSCHKO T, WONG B L, CHIANG H-Y. Advances in one-point quadrature shell elements[J]. Computer Methods in Applied Mechanics and Engineering, 1992, 96(1): 93-107.

Optimization of Dimension Stability and Bursting Strength of Cotton Knitted Fabrics by Dimethylol Dihydroxy Ethylene Urea Resin Finishing

SHARJEEL Ahmed[1], MUHAMMAD Usman Ghani[2], UMAR Shahbaz[3], NOSHEEN Rasheed[2], QIU Yiping[2], HAFIZ Muhmmad Zahid Farooq[2]*

[1] *State Key Laboratory for Modification of Chemical Fibers and Polymer Materials, International Joint Laboratory for Advanced Fiber and Low-dimension Materials, College of Materials Science and Engineering, Donghua University, Shanghai, 201620, China*

[2] *Key Laboratory of Textile Science & Technology, Ministry of Education, College of Textile, Donghua University, Shanghai, 201620, China*

[3] *School of Biotechnology, Jiangnan University, Wuxi, 214000, China*

* *Corresponding author's email:* 317008@ mail. dhu. edu. cn

Abstract: Application of resins had been used to improve the dimensional stability of cotton knitted fabrics, but this treatment causes in declination of bursting strength of treated fabrics. This research work was carried out to improve the dimension stability and bursting strength of knitted fabrics by use of dimethylol dihydroxy ethylene urea (DMDHEU) and softener. For this purpose, DMDHEU resin finish is prepared with the aid of softener and then applied on three different knitted fabrics (single jersey, fleece, and pique) by surface padding methodology. After the application of resin finish, various tests (dimension stability, skewness, washing, and bursting strength) were carried out to analyze dimension stability and bursting strength. The results show that fabric skewness, spirality, and bursting strength could be improved by using an appropriate type and concentration of the resin. This improved dimensional stability and bursting strength because of locking—OH group of cotton cellulose, letting the yarn to sustain their loop shape even after continual washing and additional processing. Thus, by keeping the loop shape in the knitted framework, dimensional stability is enhanced.

Keywords: Dimensional stability; Cotton knitted fabrics; Resin finishing; Softener; Optimized shrinkage; Spirality; Bursting strength

1 Introduction

Cotton fibers are cheap and easily available as the natural source and useful in many applications, but because of their excellent convenience, cotton knits are prevalent in many fields of life sportswear, casual wear and fit due to their good air permeability and better stretching and retrieval characteristics compared to woven fabrics[1]. However, the most challenging shortcoming of knitted structures is their lower dimensional stability owing to the instability in their loop dimensions. The dimensional stability of knitted fabric depends upon several factors. Fabric shrinkage may result due to fiber swelling under wet conditions and relaxation of internal stresses under different processing stages of cellulosic fabric. Poor dimensional stability may also due to higher spinning tension. The lower-dimensional stability due to the migration of loops and changes in loop shapes in wet or moisture environments[2-3]. The dimensional properties of knitted fabrics are depended upon the loop construction, single jersey knitted fabrics have various forms of dimensional distortion. The fiber type, yarn properties, knitted machine variables, processing, and finishing treatments, mainly influence the dimensional and physical properties of single jersey knitted fabrics[4]. The dimensional instability of the knitted fabric can be regulated by altering the fibres, yarn parameters (twist, bulk, count and finish), the knitting parameters (course per inch, wales per inch, the loop length and fabric weight) and knitting finishes (enzyme and chemical). Dimethylol dihydroxy ethylene urea (DMDHEU) is the most common crosslinking resin used in the textile industry. DMDHEU resin links the—OH group to the cotton fabric polymer chain. This crosslink locks the cellulose group—OH so that the yarn can retain its loop shape even after repeated washing and further processing. The dimensional stability is thus enhanced by keeping the loop shape in the knitted framework[5]. With the application of DMDHEU, the bursting strength of the knitted fabric is effected badly[6]. dimethylene dihydroxy ethylene urea (DMDHEU) resins are applied on knitted fabric with catalyst. A catalyst such as $MgCl_2$ reacts at high-temperature 130-180℃. At this temperature, the color or shade of fabric is badly affected[7-8]. At high temperature, the shade may be fade or dark as compare to its original shade after dyeing. The shade percentage of fabric varies from required shade percentage, so it is difficult to analyze the difference between shade before and after curing of resins at high temperature. The fabrics will be harder and stiffer with the application of resins[9]. Therefore, the softeners are necessary to use with resin to soften and smooth the fabric. Softeners or softening finishes are used to give the fabric a soft feel or touch. With chemical softeners, the fabric can be soft hand (sleek and fluffy), smoothness, flexibility, and better drape and pliability. In textile fabrics, extra smoothness is formed with the application of softeners. Some measurable physical properties such as elasticity, compressibility, and smoothness are also created in the fabric with softeners. Softeners coat the surface of the fabric with themselves. Softeners are chemical compounds, which are electrically charged. They connect one side of these to the fabric, and another side of softeners act as a hydrophobic surface, which provides the excellent softening and lubricity[1]. Fig. 1 explains this phenomenon very well. This study explains the effects of dimethylol dihydroxy ethylene urea (DMDHEU) resin finish on the shrinkage, spirality

and bursting strength of different knitted fabrics such as single jersey, fleece, and pique.

2 Experiments

2.1 Materials

The 100% cotton single jersey, honeycombed pique and fleece knitted fabrics used in this study were used directly as obtained from Masood Textile Mills (MTM), Faisalabad, Pakistan. The Cross – linker DMDHEU (KNITTEX RCT), KNITTEX CATALYST MO/LIQ and Softener (TURPEX ACN) were obtained from Huntsman Textile Effects Pakistan (Private) Limited.

2.2 Preparation of Solution

Finishing solutions were prepared by using a simple mixing method. In this simple process, first 50g and 100g of cross-linker DMDHEU (KNITTEX RCT) were added in two separate containers of 1L; contain deionized water (DI). Then, 25g/L and 50g/L of KNITTEX CATALYST MO/LIQ were added in former containers, respectively. After that, 10g/L of softener (TURPEX ACN) was added and stirred for 30 minutes under room conditions.

2.3 Preparation of Knitted Fabrics

The knitted fabrics (single jersey, pique, and fleece) were impregnated with finishing solution by using padder (Advance System Logic, Pakistan) at a pressure of 5bar and speed of 5r/min. Then, fabrics were dried at 120℃ for 2 minutes and then cured at 170℃ for 3 minutes on Stentor (Roaches by Advanced Dyeing Solutions Limited, UK).

2.4 Characterization

Different physical properties (shrinkage, spirality and bursting strength) of treated knitted fabrics were characterized by following the ISO standards i. e. , dimensional stability (ISO, 2007) was measured on Wascator (SDL Atlas, USA), spirality in fabric (BSI, 1990) and bursting strength (ISO, 1999) were measured on pneumatic bursting strength tester (SDL Atlas, USA).

3 Results and Discussions

3.1 Shrinkage

The results of dimension stability in terms of length and width shrinkage percentage of single jersey pique and fleece without resin finish, with 5% resin finish and with 10% resin finish respectively were shown in Fig. 2.

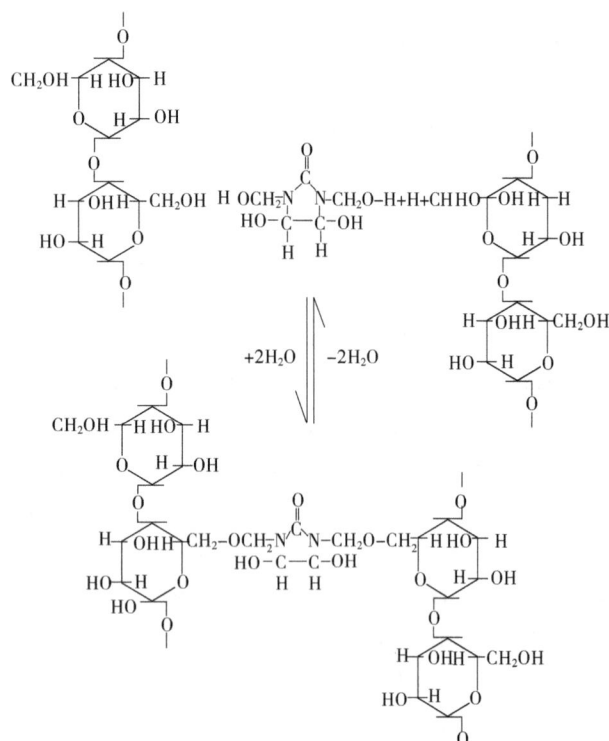

Fig. 1 Mechanism of cross-linking between DMDHEU with cotton

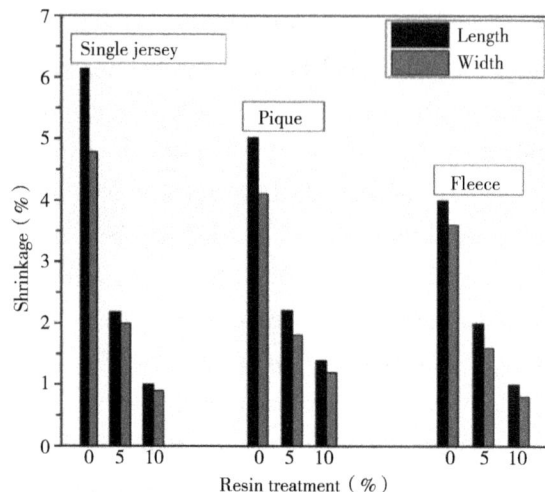

Fig. 2 Effect of different percentage of resin finish on shrinkage percentage of different knitted fabrics

Firstly, the open structure of knitted fabrics is the fundamental reason for its reduced dimensional stability. Secondly, the cellulosic structure includes reactive hydroxyl groups that are susceptible to breaking bonds from one location and creating fresh bonds from another location, resulting in variations in fabric sizes. After application of DMDHEU in various levels on separate knitted structures, a substantial reduction in the shrinkage proportion was noted. Fig. 2 showed that the single jersey was in untreated condition with very high shrinkage percentage, but pique has comparatively lower shrinkage percentage than single jersey but higher than fleece because of its honeycomb-like structure, fleece fabric has lower shrinkage percentage than single jersey and pique fabric due to its compact structure. The most prominent impact was seen on a single jersey where the proportion of shrinkage decreased from 6.2% to 2.1% in the direction of length and width with a concentration of 5% resin. Treatment with 10 percent cross-linker concentration made a further reduction in shrinkage.

Consequently, by raising the concentration of crosslinkers, more reactive hydroxyl groups in the cellulose framework were masked and less shrinking proportion was obtained. In pique fabric, the same trend of shrinking control was noted. Fleece fabric showed 4 and 3.7 percent shrinkage in length and width direction, respectively, as proof of improved dimensional stabilization. The reason for the fleece's better dimensional stability is its compact design with less flexibility and elasticity. In addition, its knits are shorter in length and tighter.

3.2 Spirality

The results of dimension instability in terms of length and width shrinkage percentage of single jersey, pique and fleece without resin finish, with 5% resin finish and with 10% resin finish respectively were shown in Fig 3. Before the application of cross-linker, single jersey fabric showed the highest spirality percentage of 4.5% (more than the acceptable limit). The single jersey's greater proportion of spirality was due to its open composition and reactive cellulose groups. In order to make the single jersey fabric more convenient, long and loose stitches were imparted in its framework, which enhanced the proportion of shrinkage and spirality. Different cross-linker concentrations stabilized the single jersey structure and a significant decrease in the percentage of spirality was noted. Pique and fleece fabrics possess less spirality percentage as compared to the single jersey, which was further reduced by using crosslinker.

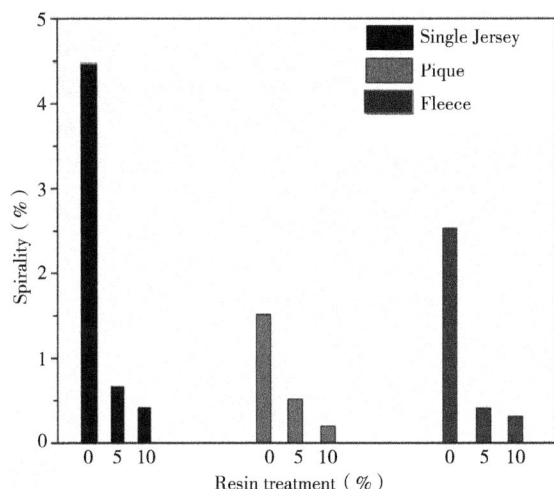

Fig. 3　Effect of different percentage of resin finish on spirality of different knitted fabrics

At 5% resin application, all three fabrics showed around 1% shrinkage in both length and width direction, it was a significant decrease in shrinkage percentage of different knitted structures. At 10% resin application, all three fabrics showed results near 0 shrinkage in both length and width direction, it was also a significant decrease in shrinkage percentage of different knitted structures. This showed that with increasing resin concentration, the shrinkage percentage was decreased and better dimension stability of any cotton knitted structure can be achieved.

3.3　Bursting Strength

The results of bursting strength of single jersey, pique and fleece without resin finish, with 5% resin finish and with 10% resin finish respectively were shown in Fig. 4.

Fig. 4 showed that it was a significant decrease in the bursting strength with the resin application. The bursting strength of all type of knitted fabrics was decreased with the resin finish treatment. The reduction in bursting power of all knitted fabric was due to the capacity of cross-linkers to limit the mobility of fibers in the framework of the fabric through chemical bonding with the reactive cellulose groups.

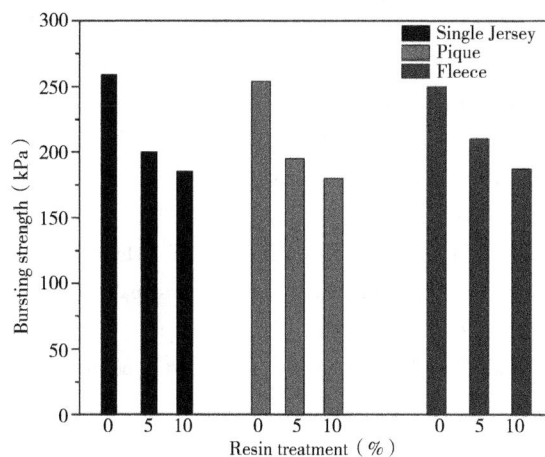

Fig. 4　Effect of different percentage of resin finish on bursting strength of different knitted fabrics

4　Conclusions

The study revealed that fabric shrinkage and spirality were efficiently controlled by the application of crosslinker on the surface of the fabric with the minimum loss of bursting strength. Because of its compactness, fleece fabric has the most dimensional stable structure. The single jersey and pique are dimensionally unstable fabrics owing to loose stitches and open structures. Resin finish application showed the most significant impact on shrinkage and spirality control of single jersey fabric by creating a three-dimensional crosslinking network on the surface of the fabric and by masking the reactive hydroxyl groups present in the cellulosic structure. However, this crosslinking network had prohibited the movement of fiber, which resulted in strength loss of all three knitted fabrics. The loss in bursting strength is controlled by using the softener concentration in finishing the recipe.

References

[1] HUSSAIN T, et al. Optimizing the shrinkage and bursting strength of knitted fabrics after resin finishing[J]. 2013, 35: 1451-1456.

[2] HUSSAIN T, et al. Improving dimensional stability of cotton knits through resin finishing[J]. 2014,9.

[3] LATIF W, et al. The mechanical and comfort properties of cotton and regenerated fibers blended woven fabrics [J]. 2018,30.

[4] KOTHARI V, et al. Spirality of cotton plain knitted fabrics with respect to variation in yarn and machine parameters[J]. 2011,36:227-233.

[5] PAVKO-CUDEN A, HLADNIK A, SLUGA F. Loop length of plain single weft knitted structure with elastane[J]. 2013,8: 110-120.

[6] NG, S. F., HUI P, et al, Dimensional stability of fabrics: resistance to shrinkage and other dimensional changes[J]. 2012:59-69.

[7] SITOTAW D B, Dimensional characteristics of knitted fabrics made from 100% cotton and cotton/elastane yarns[J]. Journal of Engineering, 2018, 2018: 9.

[8] ASHRAF M, et al. Development of a novel curing system for low temperature curing of resins with the aid of nanotechnology and ultraviolet radiation [J]. RSC Advances, 2016, 6 (84): 81069-81075.

[9] W. S, LO T Y, CHOI K F. The effect of resin finish on the dimensional stability of cotton knitted fabric[J]. The Journal of The Textile Institute, 2009, 100(6): 530-538.

Low Temperature Microwave Drying of Cashmere Fiber with Large Load

ZHAN Liuxiang[1], LI Wan[1], PEI Jiahui[1], WANG Gaojun[2], WANG Ni[1]*, LI Yuling[1]

[1] *Key Laboratory of Textile Science & Technology, Ministry of Education, College of Textile, Donghua University, Shanghai, 201620, China*

[2] *Jiangsu Sunshine Co. , Ltd. Jiangyin, 214426, China*

* *Corresponding author's email*: wangni@ dhu. edu. cn

Abstract: The uniformity of low-temperature microwave drying with large-loaded cashmere was analyzed by comparing the tensile properties of fibers in different positions of the containers and the tensile properties of the cashmere dried by hot air convection and low temperature microwave were compared in this study. The results showed that the cashmere fiber loaded in the tray container has a more ideal drying effect with moisture regain decreased from 55% to 10. 8% after 20 minutes. The drying effect is uniform at each position in the three-layer tray, and the $CV(\%)$ of moisture regain, breaking strength and elongation at break are no more than 8%. The strength of the cashmere fibers dried by low temperature microwave is higher than that of the conventional high-temperature hot air, and their elongation at break is increased by 16. 99%.

Keywords: Vacuum microwave; Low temperature; Cashmere fiber; Drying

1　Introduction

Cashmere products are soft, smooth, and comfortable to wear, but because of limited supply and high cost during processing, cashmere has become one of the most luxury fiber with high demand, rare and expensive[1-2]. During the drying processes in textile, the cashmere fibers are mostly dried by hot air convection. Hot air drying has some problems, such as inefficiency, unevenness and excessive fiber damage[3].

Microwave radiation is an environmental friendly and efficient heating method[4-5], it has a different heating mechanism than traditional hot air heating[6]. Microwave heating based on rapid polarization and depolarization of charged groups when the material is subjected to a microwave field[7], thereby causes more uniform and faster heating inside the material[8]. Since the boiling point of water decreases as the vacuum degree increases, the microwave vacuum drying (MVD)[9] is able to dry the material at a lower temperature and in a shorter period[10-11].

In our previous work, it has been proved that low tem-

perature microwave radiation has a good drying effect on cashmere. To promote the industrial application of low temperature microwave drying of cashmere fiber, it is necessary to ensure the efficiency and uniformity of drying. The low drying efficiency will directly lead to the low economic effect of the factory, while the uniformity will affect the processing stability and quality. Based on the previous laboratory research and optimization, the low temperature microwave drying of cashmere with large load was analyzed in details in this paper.

2　Experiments

2.1　Materials

Dyed cashmere fibers were provided by Zhejiang Huayuan Lanbao Co. , Ltd.

2.3　Equipment

YZWZ-3 microwave vacuum machine was manufactured by Nanjing Yanzheng Drying Equipment Co. , Ltd. T98-1088 spin dryer tube was manufactured by Wuhan Sakura Electric Co. , Ltd.

2.3 Pretreatment

In order to simulate the state of cashmere before drying in actual production, cashmere should be pretreated. As shown in Fig. 1, all cashmere samples were dipped in purified water at 20℃ for 3h, and then dehydrated by a spin dryer tube.

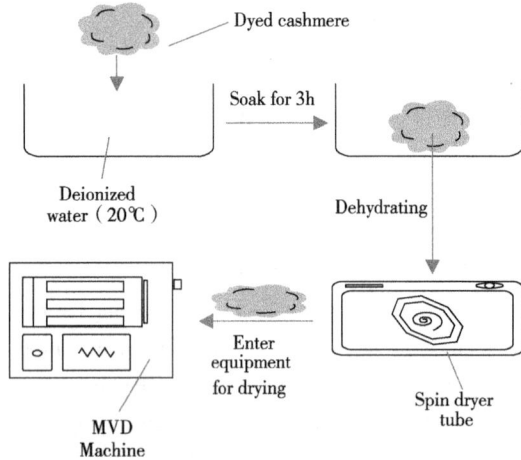

Fig. 1　Pretreatment before MVD

2.4 Drying Experiment of Different Containers

There are two types of containers for loading cashmere: barrel containers and tray containers. As shown in Fig. 2, both containers have a large number of holes that allow hot steam to be quickly removed. The rotating frame in the vacuum microwave machine is a cube with a size of 300mm×300mm×300mm. In order to fit the container with the rotating frame, a grid plastic bucket with a size of 275mm ×200mm ×275mm was selected as the container. The tray container is placed in three layers from top to bottom in the rotating frame with each tray size as 295mm×295mm×85mm. In order to ensure heat dissipation, holes were evenly punched on the pallet.

(a)　　　　　　　　(b)

Fig. 2　Two types of containers: (a) Tray (left); (b) Grid plastic bucket (right)

The cashmere loaded in different containers was subjected to low temperature microwave drying according to the process conditions in Tab. 1.

Tab. 1　Process conditions of cashmere

Container type	Barrel	Tray
Maximum load	1. 1kg	1. 2kg
	Power: 2700W	
Process conditions	Maximum temperature: 50℃	
	Vacuum degree: −0. 09MPa	
Moisture regain before drying	55%	
Drying time	20min	

At the maximum loading quality, the material stacking density of different containers could be calculated by the follows:

$$\rho = \frac{m}{V} \qquad (1)$$

Where: ρ is the stacking density (kg/m³); m is the loading mass (kg); V is the container volume (m³).

2.5 Drying Uniformity of Tray Containers

After the cashmere fibers were dried by low temperature microwave according to the drying process in Tab. 1, the fibers in the tray were sampled as shown in Fig. 3 and the three-layer trays in the rotating frame were sequentially recorded as A, B, and C from top to bottom. Finally the 27 samples are marked as in Tab. 2.

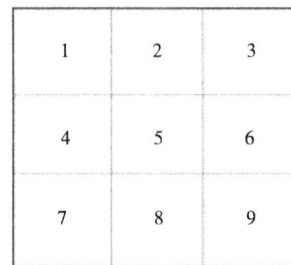

Fig. 3　Tray sampling diagram

Tab. 2　Sampling markers table

Tray	First layer (A)	Second layer (B)	Third layer (C)
Mark	A1, A2, A3, A4, A5, A6, A7, A8, A9	B1, B2, B3, B4, B5, B6, B7, B8, B9	C1, C2, C3, C4, C5, C6, C7, C8, C9

2.6 Moisture Rate Measurement

The cashmere before and after low-temperature microwave drying were weighed separately, and the moisture regain was calculated by the following formula:

$$W = \frac{G_a - G_0}{G_0} \times 100\% \qquad (2)$$

Where, W is the moisture regain (%), G_a is the wet fiber mass (kg), and G_0 is the completely dry fiber mass (kg).

2.7 Mechanical Properties Test

The mechanical properties were tested using LLY-06A Electronic Single Fiber Strength Tester according to GB/T 14337—93. Test conditions: sample clamp dis-tance is 20mm, pre-tension is 0.2cN/dtex, and the tensile speed is 20mm/min. Each sample was measured 100times.

3 Results and Discussions

3.1 Drying Effect of Different Containers

The stacking density of cashmere loaded in different containers and the low temperature microwave drying effect are shown in Tab. 3.

Tab. 3 Low temperature microwave drying effect of different containers

Container Type	Moisture regain before drying (%)	Load before drying(g)	material stacking density (kg/m³)	Load after drying(g)	Water loss(g)	Moisture regain after drying (%)
Barrel	55	1100	90	835.2	264.8	17.0
Tray	55	1200	54	863.5	336.5	10.8

In maximum loading state, the tray container carries more material than that of the barrel container, and the material stacking density in the tray is only 60% of that in the barrel. The two containers are loaded with cash-mere fibers with the same moisture regain for the same process of low temperature microwave drying. The mois-ture regain after drying of the barrel-loaded fiber is 17%, which is much higher than that of fiber loaded in tray as 10.8%.

The results show that the tray container not only has a higher maximum load than that of the barrel container, but also has a higher drying efficiency significantly. In the barrel container, the fiber is pressed tightly in the barrel, so that the stacking density of fiber is too large. When the fiber is dried by low temperature microwave, the outer layer fiber has better heat transfer due to the hole near the barrel wall, while the internal hot steam is not easily diffused to the outside, making the drying ef-ficiency relatively low. Compared to barrel containers, the fibers in the tray container are looser and the stac-king density is much smaller. During the drying process, the thermal vapor generated inside the fibers can be well evacuated, so the drying efficiency is much higher than that of the barrel container.

There are also some differences in the drying effect of the trays in different layers, and the water loss in differ-ent layers is shown in Tab. 4. It can be seen that the fi-ber in the lowermost tray has the highest water loss, which possibly due to the water vapor is instantaneously liquefied when the vacuum is removed after the drying, and is attached to the upper wall of the vacuum micro-wave dryer to form drops of water to the uppermost fi-ber. It may also be related to the microwave distribution in a vacuum microwave dryer.

Tab. 4 Water loss in different layers

Tray	Empty pallet mass (g)	Total mass after loading (g)	Mass after drying(g)	Water loss(g)
First layer (A)	745.6	1145.6	1037.7	107.9
Second layer (B)	746.1	1146.1	1033.5	112.6
Third layer (C)	747.6	1147.6	1031.6	116.0

3.2 Uniformity of Low Temperature Microwave Drying

After died by low temperature microwave, the moisture regain, breaking strength and elongation at break of cashmere fibers loaded in tray containers are shown in Fig. 4 and Fig. 5 respectively, and the CV (%) of each index at different positions are shown in Tab. 5. It can be seen that the breaking strength, elongation at break and moisture regain of cashmere fibers at different positions in the tray are not different obviously, and the maximum CV (%) of each index is only 7. 88%. This means that although the shape of the tray is square, the effect of low temperature microwave drying of tray-loaded cashmere fiber is relatively uniform.

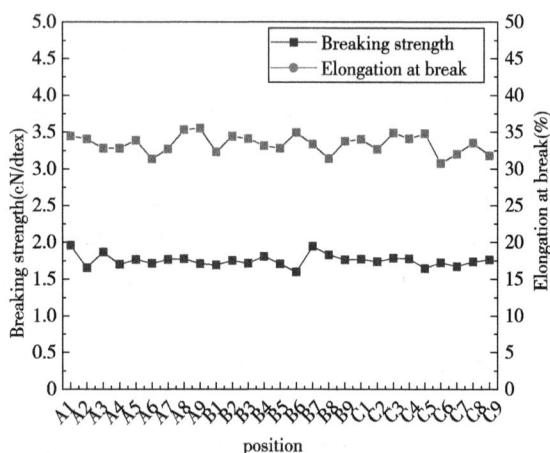

Fig. 4 Uniformity of mechanical properties at different positions

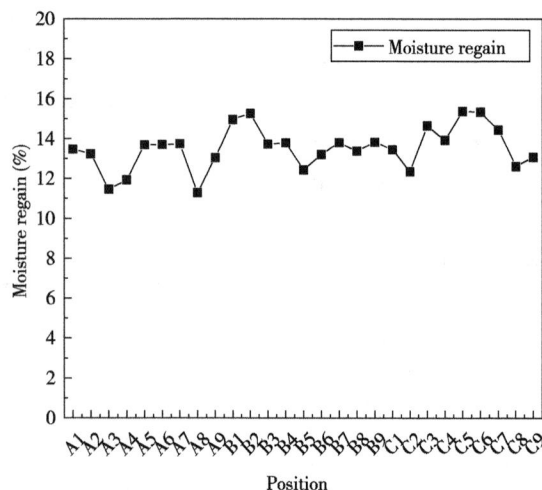

Fig. 5 Uniformity of moisture regain at different positions

Tab. 5 CV(%) of each index at different positions

Index	Breaking strength (cN/dtex)	Elongation at break(%)	Moisture regain (%)
CV(%)	4. 52	3. 73	7. 88

3.3 Effect of Low Temperature Microwave Drying on Mechanical Properties of Fiber

The mechanical properties of cashmere after hot air drying and low temperature microwave drying are shown in Tab. 6. Compared with hot air dried cashmere fiber, the breaking strength of cashmere fiber dried by low temperature microwave drying has almost no loss, while the elongation at break is obviously improved with the rate of change as 16. 99%. The microwave frequency is 2450MHz, and microwave quantum energy are $1. 62 \times 10^{-24}$ J. The bond energy level of Van der Waals bond and the rotational energy level of free water molecule are 10^{-24} J/bond and $1. 6 \times 10^{-23}$ J respectively, so the free water molecules can resonantly absorb microwave. Microwave drying adjusts the aggregate structure of cashmere fibers, improves the elasticity of macromolecules and increases the breaking elongation of fibers.

Tab. 6 Mechanical properties of fiber

Drying method	Breaking strength (cN/dtex)	Change rate of strength (%)	Elongation at break (%)	Change rate of elongation (%)
Hot air	1. 77	—	28. 55	—
Low temperature Microwave	1. 75	−1. 13	33. 40	16. 99

4 Conclusions

This study proposed a novel and environmental friendly method for drying cashmere by using a combination of vacuum and microwave, and analyzed the uniformity of this processing with large load.

Compared with the barrel container, the tray not only has a smaller stacking density, but also has a better drying effect with more moisture regain reduction. Moreover, the maximum CV(%) of moisture regain, breaking strength and elongation at break of each position in the three-layer tray were no more than 8%, which shows the uniformity of drying effect of tray-loaded cashmere. Interestingly, compared with traditional high temperature hot air drying, the mechanical properties of cashmere fiber dried by low temperature microwave were improved obviously.

References

[1] WANG L, SINGH A, WANG X. A study on dehairing Australian greasy cashmere[J]. Fibers and Polymers, 2008, 9(4): 509-514.

[2] MCGREGOR B A, TUCKER D J. Effects of nutrition and origin on the amino acid, grease, and suint composition and color of cashmere and guard hairs[J]. Journal of Applied Polymer Science, 2010, 117(1): 409-420.

[3] FENG H, YIN Y, TANG J. Microwave drying of food and agricultural materials: basics and heat and mass transfer modeling[J]. Food Engineering Reviews, 2012, 4(2): 89-106.

[4] CHEN L, WANG L, WU X, et al. A process-level water conservation and pollution control performance evaluation tool of cleaner production technology in textile industry[J]. Journal of Cleaner Production, 2017, 143(1): 1137-1143.

[5] HASANBEIGI A, PRICE L. A technical review of emerging technologies for energy and water efficiency and pollution reduction in the textile industry[J]. Journal of Cleaner Production, 2015, 95(1): 30-44.

[6] KATOVIC D. Microwaves in textile finishing, yes or no[J]. Journal of Textile Science & Engineering, 2012, 1(01): 1-4.

[7] RATTANADECHO P, MAKUL N. Microwave-assisted drying: a review of the state-of-the-art[J]. Drying Technology, 2016, 34(1): 1-38.

[8] KATOVIC D, VUKUSIC S B, GRGAC S F. The effect of microwave drying on warp sizing[J]. Textile Research Journal, 2008, 78(4): 353-360

[9] PU Y Y, SUN D W. Combined hot-air and microwave-vacuum drying for improving drying uniformity of mango slices based on hyperspectral imaging visualisation of moisture content distribution[J]. Biosystems Engineering, 2017, 156(1): 108-119.

[10] ZIELINSKA M, ZIELINSKA D, MARKOWSKI M. The effect of microwave-vacuum pretreatment on the drying kinetics, color and the content of bioactive compounds in osmo-microwave-vacuum dried cranberries (vaccinium macrocarpon)[J]. Food and Bioprocess Technology, 2018, 11(3): 585-602.

[11] PU Y Y, SUN D W. Vis-NIR hyperspectral imaging in visualizing moisture distribution of mango slices during microwave-vacuum drying[J]. Food Chemistry, 2015, 188(1): 271-278.

A Study on the State of Mixed Method Application in Natural Dye Analysis: In the Year of 2018

AGULEI Karen Desta[1]*, **JOSPHAT Igadwa Mwasiagi[1,2]**

[1] *Department of Manufacturing, Industrial and Textile Engineering, School of Engineering, Donghua University, Shanghai, 201620, China*
[2] *Moi University, P. O. Box 3900, Eldoret, Kenya*

* *Corresponding author's email: prisskarena@ gmail. com*

Abstract: Research methods are defined as methods or techniques used for conducting research. They play a vital, critical and pivotal role in collection, analysis and interpretation of data in the engineering field. The two basic methodological research approaches are quantitative and qualitative methods of research. However, debatable questions have at present escalated anticipating whether quantitative or qualitative methods can singly be used to address issues such as why and how changes occur during natural dye analysis. Furthermore, studies have stated that details of qualitative data can in a way provide insights not available through quantitative surveys and vice versa, but not offset the weakness of both methods. These uncertainties have thus given rise to a new methodological concept named mixed method methodological design. Using Good Reporting on a Mixed Method Study (GRAMMS) framework, articles published by Elsevier and Researchgate in 2018 were reviewed in regards to mixed methods application in natural dyes analysis. Out of 7122 articles, only 15 articles met the inclusion criteria. Additionally, all authors with exception on one, neither mentioned the use of mixed methods in their study no gave reasons for using either quantitative or qualitative approach. This proposes the need for researchers to adopt mixed methods research since it's underdeveloped. This research has thus given insight on the state of mixed method application in natural dyes analysis.

Keywords: Quantitative method; Qualitative method; Mixed method; Natural dye analysis

1 Introduction

Qualitative research (Qa) can be defined as a philosophical approach of searching the cognitive content of humans i. e. search of peoples' perceptions via aggregation of verbal description or textual data[1]. On the other hand quantitative research (Qu) expressed as a quantity is a phenomena that projects how results/outcomes are determined by deducing reasonable causes[2]. Although a considerable amount of literature has been published on quantitative and qualitative research, there is little empirical investigation of their combined application in natural dye experimentations. Mixed methods, a developing phenomenon movement is defined in various ways by different authors[3-5]. In summary, it is basically the integration or synthesis of quantitative and qualitative research in one single study using different experimental designs. Research establishes that this method if grounded, can potentially countervail imperfections of Qa and Qu (if incorporated at any stage of data collection), strengthen the study and reveal individual and contextual factors influencing the observed patterns[6]. In the engineering field, where the phenomena is developing, it is termed as a third methodological movement and synthesis of intellectual and practical quantitative and qualitative data[3, 7]. Hence the need for its progress assessment in natural dye analysis.

Natural dye researchers have employed various kinds of quantitative and qualitative methods of research. The analysis encompasses optimization of conditions in which the experimenter has little or farfetched knowledge on the optimum conditions. For such analyses with uncertainties, Pedro et al, 1996 recommends use of sequential designs[8], such as embedded mixed method approach. However, for the choice of survey method in mixed method approach, the design should be driven by research questions[2, 9]. Studies have been documented concerning the integration of the methods but data about the efficacy and quantitative analysis of the mixed method methodology in natural dye researches is non-existent. This research thus examines the emerging role of mixed methodology in the context of natural dye analysis while adopting GRAMMs framework.

2　Experiments

2.1　Criteria of Data Review

The review focused on reviewed journals articles from Elsevier and research gate journals that were published in 2018 and Sage Journals such as Journal of Mixed Methods Research and Textile Research Journal. To make the scope manageable, the focal area was publications that employed mixed method in the study of natural dye analysis, rather than only quantitative or qualitative methods. Furthermore, journals with the word mixed methods in their abstract were considered for analysis. The inclusion and exclusion criteria was studied that entailed natural dye analysis (Extraction, various applications in different fields and usage on fabrics) and employed mixed method methodology of study. Non-English articles (say journals, reviews, guidelines, protocols) and literatures (like water waste management, non-composites and water treatments) were excluded. Furthermore, the search strategy employed using two search engines namely Research gate, and Science direct (Sage journals). The search terms used were mixed methods, natural dye analysis, quantitative and qualitative analysis, combined qualitative and qualitative analysis in natural dye analysis, qualitative methods, and qualitative methods, natural dyes-cotton. The appraisal of data extracted was by categorization into 3 sets namely None (those which reported no qualitative research; Basic (contained basic information) and Extensive (contained quantitative and qualitative data) deemed fit for analysis.

3　Results and Discussions

3.1　Using Science Direct Search Engine

Fig. 1 illustrates the sequence of analysis for the papers retrieved that sought to answer two major questions that is:1) Why the author chose mixed method approach and when mixing occurred? As can thus be seen in Fig. 1, the general references (considering only review articles) obtained using the search term mixed methods was seven thousand ninety five articles for the year of 2018 and twenty seven accepted articles for 2019. With further specification by including natural dyes, the updated search resulted into five hundred and ninety one reviews.

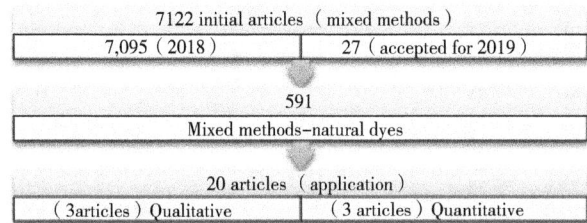

7122 initial articles (mixed methods)	
7,095 (2018)	27 (accepted for 2019)

591	
Mixed methods-natural dyes	

20 articles (application)	
(3articles) Qualitative	(3 articles) Quantitative

Fig. 1　Procedure for literature reviewed

According to the review criteria, only twenty articles met the inclusion. Analysis of the twenty articles established that one author out of the twenty one authors titled the study as mixed methods. Seven articles employed one approach either qualitative method (employing texts, images and diagrams) or quantitative method of analysis as shown in Tab. 1. Validation of methods used in the articles was in accordance to[10] the results. However, out of the 20 articles, none of the authors employed mixing method approach in their study whereas the remaining authors never mention whether their studies involved Qa or Qu methods.

Tab. 1　Analysis of 20 published articles

S/No.	Author	Type of Data
1	[12]	Qualitative data
2	[13-14]	Quantitative data
3	[15]	Qualitative data
4	[16]	Quantitative, green methodology
5	[17]	Quantitative

3.2 SAGE Journals (Journal of Mixed Methods Research)

For this category, science direct search in Journal of Mixed Methods Research using mixed method search term for the year of 2018, obtained 31 publication.

None of the publications met the criteria mentioned in 2.1, hence they were not considered in the analysis. Further analysis using the search term natural dyes generated over 154 articles. Only eight of the articles as tabulated in Tab.2 met the criteria selection.

Tab.2 Sage reviewed journals for the year of 2018

S/No	DOI	A few examples of type of data		Mixed method
		Quantitative data	Qualitative	
1	[18]	Amount of treatment, Statistical analysis, Frequencies	Figures	Sequential exploratory
2	[19]	Clustering method, colour histogram	Colour themes, fabric images, saliency analysis	Sequential transformative
4	[20]	Aqueous plant extracts, calorimetric data	Dyed fabrics, colour, antimicrobial effect	Sequential exploratory design
5	[21]	Extracted components	antioxidant & antimicrobial	Concurrent triangulation
6	[22]	(B-CD/citric acid treatment), K/S values, fastness tests	Modified fabric	Concurrent embedded
7	[23]	K/S values, antibacterial, diff. con. of extract, oxygen index value, fastness tests	Spectrums, colour, SEM images flammable test, images	Sequential exploratory design
8	[24]	Thermal & water vapor resistance, air permeability	Images	Sequential transformative

The study established that all authors neither mention the use of mixed methods in their study to gave reasons for using either of quantitative or qualitative approach. The study confirmed findings that established uneven or unequal application of research methods[2]. With exploring the data, only 8 articles out of 154 stated various natural dye application. The general observation, however was that none of the articles specified the use of mixed methods in their study. Therefore the discernment of mixed methods tabulated was adopted from literature review[5, 11]. From the data collected, it can be concluded that application of mixed methods in natural dye research is underdeveloped.

4 Conclusions

Several quantitative and qualitative methods currently exist for natural dye researches, but the involvement of mixed methods approach in natural dye research is still wanting. In addition, data collection in natural dye analysis entails uncertainties hence the need to use mixed method experimental approach.

This study reveals that researchers only implied the employment of Qa and Qu in their data collection but didn't mention the reason for their choice of approach. This work is still developing. However, for concrete analysis, the author recommends widening the scope of study, a comparison study between the Qa and Qu against mixed method approach, more time and work be focused on single studies of qualitative and quantitative analyses so as to ascertain the existence of the utilization of mixed method approach in the natural dye application.

Acknowledgements

The authors acknowledge the financial aid rendered by Moi University African Centre of Excellence II in Phytochemicals, Textile and Renewable Energy (ACE 11/PTRE) throughout the research.

References

[1] VASS C, RIGBY D, PAYNE K. The role of qualitative research methods in discrete choice experiments: a systematic review and survey of authors[J]. Journal of Medical Decision Making, 2017, 37 (3): 298-313.

[2] BORREGO M, ELLIOT P D, CATHERINE T A. Quantitative, qualitative, and mixed research methods in engineering education[J]. Journal of Engineering Education, 2009: 53-66.

[3] O'CATHAIN A, MURPHY E, NICHOLL J. Why, and how, mixed methods research is undertaken in health services research in England: a mixed methods study[J]. BMC Health Services Research, 2007, 7 (85): 1-11.

[4] CRESWELL J W, VICKI L P C. Designing and conducting mixed methods research[M]. 2nd Edition. Thousand Oaks, CA: Sage Publications, 2007: 1-443.

[5] TEDDLIE C, TASHAKKORI A. Major issues and controversies in the use of mixed methods in the social and behavioral sciences. in Mixed methods in social and behavioral research [M]. Second Edition. Thousand Oaks, CA: Sage Publications, 2003: 3-50.

[6] TAGUCHI N. Description and explanation of pragmatic development: quantitative, qualitative, and mixed methods research[J]. Journal of System, 2018: 1-10.

[7] CHAUDHARY N, BRENT K J. State of mixed methods research in engineering education: in-depth examination of JEE articles[C]. 2016 IEEE fronties in education conference proceedings, 2016.

[8] ARAUJO P W, RICHARD G B. Experimental design 11. optimization[J]. Trends in Analystical Chemistry, 1996, 15 (2): 63-70.

[9] CRESWELL J W, VICKI L P C, GUTMANN M, et al. An expanded typology for classifying mixed methods research into designs: in advance mixed methods research designs In handbook of mixed methods in social and behavioral research [M]. 2003: 159-196.

[10] KOTHARI C R. Research methodology, methods and techniques[M]. 2nd Edition. New Delhi: New Age Iternational, 2004: 1-401.

[11] CRESWELL J W. Quantitative, qualitative and mixed methods approach in research design[M]. 3rd Edition. CA: Sage Publication Ltd., 2009: 200-224.

[12] AYODHYA D, VEERABHADRAM G. A review on recent advances in photodegradation of dyes using doped and heterojunction based semiconductor metal sulfide nanostructures for environmental protection[J]. Materials Today Energy, 2018, 9 (9): 83-113.

[13] BUJDÁK J. Molecular aggregation of organic dyes controlled by the properties of layered nanoparticles[J]. Journal of Photochemistry and Photobiology, 2018, (03): 1-104.

[14] KAUR G, SINGH G, SINGH J. Photochemical tuning of materials: A click chemistry perspective[J]. Materials Today Chemistry, 2018, 8: 56-84.

[15] GOBALASINGHAM N S, THOMPSON B C. Progress in polymer science direct arylation polymerization: a guide to optimal conditions for effective conjugated polymers [J]. Progress in Polymer Science, 2018, 83: 135-201.

[16] KSHATRIYA R, JEJURKAR V P, SAHA S. In memory of Prof. Venkataraman: recent advances in the synthetic methodologies of flavones[J]. Tetrahedron, 2018, 74 (8): 811-833.

[17] MAI S, PLASSER F, DORN J, et al. Quantitative wave function analysis for excited states of transition metal complexes[J]. Cordination Chemistry Reviews, 2018, (361): 74-97.

[18] CONTI S, VEXLER A, HAGOEL L, et al. Modified citrus pectin as a potential sensitizer for radiotherapy in prostate Cancer[J]. Textile Research Journal, 2018: 1-10.

[19] LIU S, JIANG Y, LUO H. Attention-aware color theme extraction for fabric images [J]. Textile Research Journal, 2016: 1-14.

[20] LEE Y, KIM A, PARK Y, et al. Colorimetric assay and deodorizing/antibacterial performance of natural fabrics dyed with immature pine cone extract[J]. Textile Research Journal, 2017, 88 (7): 731-743.

[21] JANARTHANAN M, KUMAR M S. The properties of bioactive substances obtained from seaweeds and their applications in textile industries[J]. Journal of Industrial Textiles, 2017, 48 (1): 361-401.

[22] ZHANG W, JI X, WANG C. Dyeing of polyester/cotton blended fabric with cationic dyes via b-cyclodextrin modification[J]. Textile Research Journal, 2018: 1-13.

[23] TELI M D, PANDIT P. Development of thermally stable and hygienic colored cotton fabric made by treatment with natural coconut shell extract[J]. Textile Research Journal, 2017, 48 (1): 87-118.

[24] ZIMNIEWSKA M, PAWLACZYK M, KRUCINSKA I, et al. The influence of natural functional clothing on some biophysical parameters of the skin[J]. Textile Research Journal, 2018, 89 (8): 1381-1393.

Investigation of Rheological, Thermal and Mechanical Properties of Recycled Poly (ethylene terephthalate)/ Hyperbranched Polyester Blended Fibers

SAEED A M Haroon[1,2], ELTAHIR A Yassir[1,2], XIA Yumin[1], HE Yong[1], WANG Yimin[1, *]

[1] State Key Laboratory for Modification of Chemical Fibers and Polymer Materials, College of Materials Science and Engineering Donghua University, Shanghai, 201620, China

[2] Faculty of Industries Engineering & Technology, University of Gezira, Wad-Medan, P. O. Box 20, SUDAN

* Corresponding author's email: yw@ dhu. edu. cn

Abstract: To investigate the effect of hyperbranched polyester (HBPET) and concentration on the rheology, thermal and mechanical properties of recycled polyethylene terephthalate (RPET) fibers. Different amounts of hyperbranched polyesters (HBPET), 0.5% and 1% were added to the RPET. The influence of HBPET on the rheological, thermal and mechanical properties of produced fibers was investigated. Thermal stability and rheological behavior of the pure recycled PET (RPET-0) and RPET-0.5 and RPET-1 blend prepared by melt compounding were tested by thermogravimetric analysis (TGA), Differential Scanning Calorimetry (DSC) and parallel-plate rheometer. RPET-0.5 and RPET-1 blend were in a good agreement with improved rheological characteristics and led to significant enhancement in thermal stability. Decrease in the complex viscosity (η) of the blends was observed with increasing content of HBPET. On the other hand, it was found that mechanical properties of the (RPET-0.5 and RPET-1) fibers were improved with respect to pure recycled PET (PET-0) fibers. Moreover the crystallinty of blended fibers was also increased with an increasing of (HBPET) content.

Keywords: Complex viscosity; Recycled PET; Hyperbranched polyester; Thermal and mechanical properties

1 Introduction

Hyperbranched polymers (HBPs) have been discovered at the end of 1980s. After the linear, branched, and crosslinking polymers,[1-2] Since rheological plays key roles in the properties of the resulting products, more sophisticated control of these factors may facilitate even wider technological applications.

Poly (ethylene terephthalate) (PET), as a high-strength and high-modulus thermoplastic polyester, is widely employed in many applications such as synthetic fibers films and beverage, food, other liquid containers and parts in auto-motives and electronics due to its superior thermal and mechanical properties, low permeability, and chemical resistance[1]. However, during the recycling processes PET undergoes chemical, mechanical, thermal and oxidative degradation. Degradation of RPET renders it unsuitable for many applications.

The HBPET additives are able to behave as lubricants during processing and as self-compatibilizing toughening agents in the final blend formulation. MULKERN et al[2] T J studied polystyrene/hyperbranched polyester blends; they found that a significant drop in the blend viscosity occurs immediately on addition of HBP. MONTICELLIO et al[3] and FAN Z et al[4] studied the blends of polyamide and hyperbranched polymers, they found that the hyperbranched polymers strongly modified the rheological behavior of polyamide.

In this article, HBPET was used as rheological modifier for recycled PET, melt rheological, thermal and mechanical properties of produced fibers were investigated.

2　Experimental

2. 1　Blends Preparation and Characterizations

Before preparing the blends, RPET and HBPET were dried and mixed together with 0. 5% and 1% of HB-PET, and then melts-blended in a SHJ-20 type self-wiping co-rotating twin-screw extruder with six heating sections (Nanjing Giant Machinery Co. ,China) operating at a screw speed of 100r/min and temperatures of 250℃, 255℃, 260℃, 260℃ ,and 180℃ from the first section to the end. The produced pellets subjected to melt rheological measurements using a HAAKE MARS, Modular Advanced Rheometer system (Germany) with parallel-plate rheometer in oscillation mode under a nitrogen atmosphere at 280℃. Then thermal stability was performed using theromgravimetric analysis (TGA) on a simultaneous thermal analyzer (Netzsch TG209F1). The scans were run from room temperature to 600℃ at rate of 20℃/min under nitrogen flow. Mechanical properties of the produced fibers such as tensile strength, modulus and breaking elongation were measured at 25℃, 65% RH; use ASTM D 3822 with a XL-2 Yarn Elongation Tester, from Shanghai New Fine Instrument CO. LTD. The orientation factor (f_s) were measured using a sonic velocity orientation instrument model SCY-Ⅲ, which was manufactured by Donghua-kaili Chemicals and Fiber Technology Corporation, Shanghai, China

3　Results and Discussion

3. 1　Complex Viscosity

As shown in Fig. 1 after adding 0. 5% of HBPET (RPET-0. 5), the zero-shear viscosity (viscosity extrapolated to a frequency of 0) of recycled PET was changed from 4142Pa · s (no of HBPET) to 1471Pa · s (0. 5% of HBPET). With increasing the amount of HBPET in the composite a continuous reduction of the complex viscosity was observed at a concentration of 1% it was reached to 626Pa · s (1% of HBPET). This behavior has been reportedin previous publications[2, 5]. The decrease of complex viscosity is due to the good dispersion interaction between recycled PET and HB-PET.

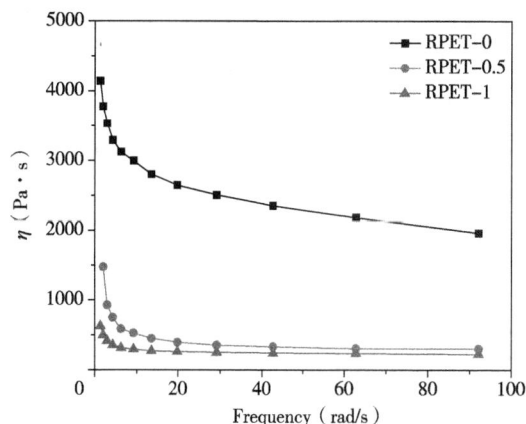

Fig. 1　Complex viscosity of all samples vs. frequency($T=280℃$)

3. 2　Thermal Stability

As can be seen in Fig. 2, the thermogravimetric temperature of the RPET-0. 5 and RPET-1 shift to higher temperature than that of RPET-0. This fact indicates that there is a strong interaction between the HBPET and RPET. Similar results of high thermogravimetric temperature of PET/Silica nanocomposites.[6] Moreover, it can be found that there is no significant difference in char residue of the RPET-0. 5 and RPET-1 than that of RPET-0. These additional weights may be of undecomposed of HBPET within this range of the temperature. However, it can be concluded that HBPET could enhance the thermal stability of the composites.

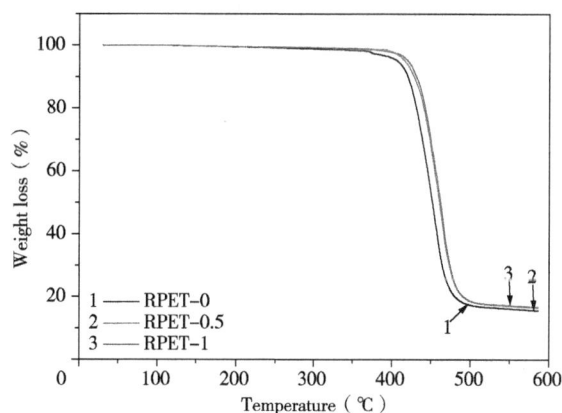

Fig. 2　Thermogravimetric curves all samples

3. 3　Mechanical Properties

Addition of the HBPET led to significant increase in tenacity and initial modulus[Fig. 3(a) and (b)]. The highest tenacity value was observed to be 3. 7cN/dtex for RPET-1 at draw ratio of 3, while it was 3. 0cN/dtex for RPET-0 at same draw ratio. Apparently, addition of HBPET acted as lubricant within the recycled PET and due to the large interaction between the HBPET and recycled PET molecules and improve mechanical properties. Furthermore, the HBPET layers dispersed uniformly in recycled RPET and restricted the movement of RPET macromolecules. This is consistent with the general observations that the introduction of an organoclay into a polymer matrix increases its strength and modulus. [7]

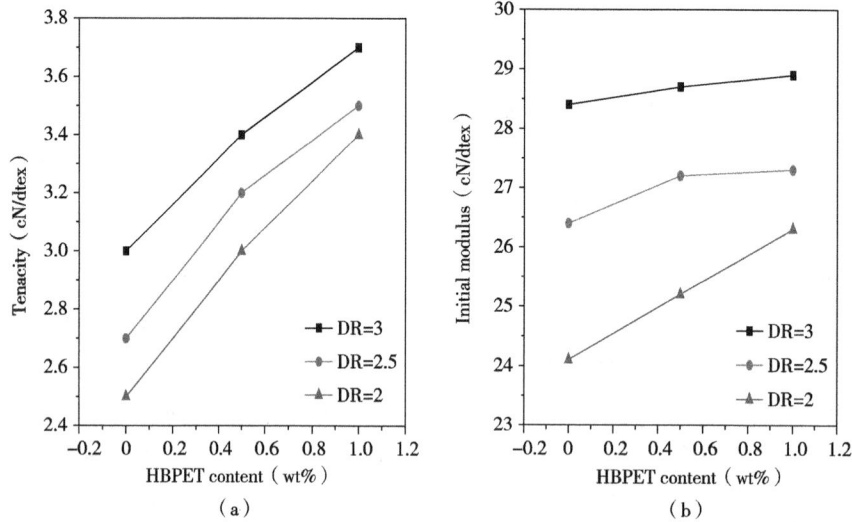

Fig. 3 The relationship between: (a) Tenacity and HBPET content; (b) Initial modulus and HBPET content at different draw ratio

3.4 Orientation Factor

Certain typical orientation factor (f_s) values of all fibers prepared at varying draw ratios are summarized in Tab. 1 and the changes of f_s with draw ratio and contents of HBPET are also shown in Fig. 4(a) and Fig. 4(b) respectively. As expected, f_s values of all samples increased significantly with the increase of draw ratio, which indicates that the drawing gives rise to more ordered non-crystalline structure in the fibers[8].

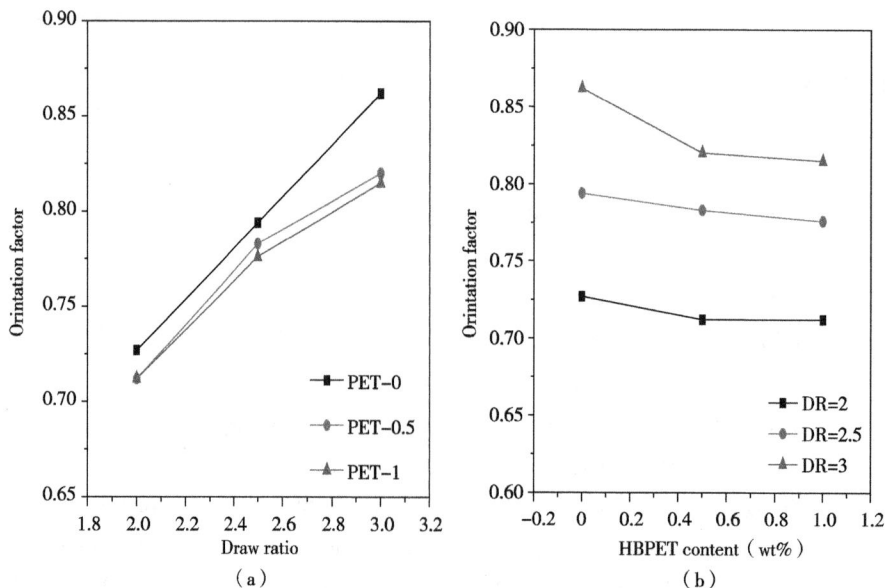

Fig. 4 (a) Orientation factor and draw ratioThe relationship between; (b) Orientation factor and HBPET content of all samples The ralationship between

Tab. 1 The mechanical properties and orientation factor of different samples

Sample	D. R	Linear density (dtex)	Tenacity (cN/dtex)	Breaking elong ation (%)	Modulus (cN/dtex)	*fs*
RPET-0	3	79	3.0	9.6	28.4	0.862
RPET-0	2.5	82	2.7	11.7	26.4	0.794
RPET-0	2	90	2.5	15.2	24.1	0.727
RPET-1	3	75	3.7	8.5	28.9	0.815
RPET-1	2.5	78	3.5	10.2	27.3	0.776
RPET-1	2	79	3.4	12.2	26.3	0.712
RPET-0.5	3	73	3.4	8.5	28.7	0.820
RPET-0.5	2.5	72	3.2	10.5	27.2	0.783
RPET-0.5	2	71	3.0	14.2	25.2	0.712

The results confirmed that the degree of orientation of RPET-1 and RPET-0.5 fibers was lower than that of RPET-0 fibers. Moreover, the orientation of RPET-1 and RPET-0.5 fibers had no distinct change as the HBPET content increase[Fig. 4(b)]. It was suggested that the addition of HBPET and indeed weakened the disorientation ability of molecular chains and improved the dimensional stability of the fibers, which were in agreement with the previous study.[9]

4　Conclusions

The influence of HBPET on the rheological, thermal and mechanical properties of produced fibers was investigated. It was found that the viscosity of recycled PET, initially Newtonian, becomes pseudo-plastic when the HBPET is added. Moreover, It was found that the tensile strength and initial modulus of the RPET-0.5 and RPET-1 blend fibers were increased, the tensile mechanical properties of the blend fibers are also improved with increases in DR, and this was attributed to the development of a more ordered crystalline structure.

References

[1] GOKKURT T. Investigation of thermal, rheological, and physical properties of amorphouspoly (ethylene) terephthalate)/organoclay nanocomposite films[J]. J Appl Poly Sci, 2013, 129(5): 2490-2501.

[2] MULKERN T J N, TAN C B. Processing and characterization of reactive polystyrene/hyperbranched polyester blends[J]. Poly, 2000, 41(9): 3193-3203.

[3] MONTICELLI O, et al. On blends of polyamide 6 and a hyperbranched aramid[J]. Macro Mater and Eng, 2003, 288 (4): 318-325.

[4] FAN Z. et al. Blends of different linear polyamides with hyperbranched aromatic AB(2) and A(2)+B-3 polyesters[J]. J Poly Sci Part a-Poly Chem, 2009, 47(14): 3558-3572.

[5] ALI X, et al. Study of blends of linear poly (ether ether ketone) of high melt viscosity and hyperbranched poly (ether ether ketone)[J]. Poly Inter, 2011, 60(4): 607-612.

[6] GU X H, et al. Preparation and characterization of poly(ethylene terephthalate) incorporated with secondary-modified montmorillonite[J]. Iran Poly J, 2014, 23(4): 249-255.

[7] CHANG J H, et al. Poly(ethylene terephthalate) nanocomposites by in situ interlayer polymerization: the thermo-mechanical properties and morphology of the hybrid fibers[J]. Poly, 2004, 45(3): 919-926.

[8] BASERI S, et al. Effect of drawing temperature on mesomorphic transitions of oriented poly (ethylene terephthalate) fibers exposed to supercritical CO_2[J]. J of Poly Res, 2011, 18(6): 2033-2043.

[9] WEIZHEN X, et al. Study on PET fiber modifiedby nanomaterials: improvement of dimensional thermal stability of PET fiber by forming PET/MMT nanocomposite[J]. J Appl Poly Sci, 2005, 96(6): 2247-52.

Pollen as Non-Prey Source for Phytoseiid Predators of Whiteflies (Hemiptera: Aleyrodidae): A Case Study to Improve Cotton Yield and Quality

AHMAD Rehan[1]*, TURAZIA Syeda Eishah[2], GHANI Muhammad Usman[3]

[1] *Department of Entomology, University of Agriculture, Faisalabad, 38000, Pakistan*

[2] *Department of Zoology, Wildlife and Fisheries, University of Agriculture, Faisalabad, 38000, Pakistan*

[3] *Key Laboratory of Textile Science & Technology, Ministry of Education, College of Textile, Donghua University, Shanghai, 201620, China*

* *Corresponding author's email: rehanahmad189. ra@ gmail. com*

Abstract: Whiteflies are one of the devastating pests of cotton and also vectors of many dangerous viruses decreasing the yield up to 40%. It has been observed that whiteflies are now becoming resistant to many chemical pesticides and also there are serious effects of chemicals on quality of cotton. Now the trend is moving towards biological control of whiteflies. Different studies and experiments have shown that population of phytoseiid predators increases markedly and thus the predatory efficacy is also increased by the use of pollens of different horticultural crops as a supplementary food source. The present study discussed the influence of pollen on predatory potential of phytoseiid mites. Pollens of narrowleaf cattail (T. latifolia) were used as a pollen supplement. Experiments were conducted on cotton leaves using four treatments to check the effect of pollen supplement on predatory effectuality of predatory mites. It was seen that pollen application enhanced predatory potential of phytoseiid mites and reduction of whiteflies was increased almost two times (from 28% to 51% egg mortality in case of without pollen and with pollen respectively). From the results it is concluded that pollen supplement strategy is a best replacement of repeated inundative predator release and chemical control of whiteflies maintaining both yield and quality of the crop.

Keywords: Cotton quality; Pollen as supplementary food; Population dynamics; Predatory mites; Textile problems

1 Introduction

Whitefly is a tiny whitepest and important threat to textile industry. It sucks the cell sap from leaves and also acts as vector of cotton leaf curl virus which drastically decreases the quality and quantity of final product. This pest has become resistant to several pesticides so there is a need for suitable alternate of chemical control. Biological control is an important natural service provided by natural enemies for the control of different kind of pests including whiteflies. Biological control sometimes depends upon the availability of alternative food, which can increase the survival and effectiveness of natural enemies. It has been observed that plant-based products such as pollen and nectar can be used as supplementary food for many polyphagous natural predators[1]. Phytoseiidae are very important predators of different kinds of phytophagous mites, soft bodied insects and different root knot as well as free living nematodes and thus can assume a significant job in securing greenhouse vegetables as well as flowers as a natural control factor[2]. Many species of generalist predators' group can survive on pollen of different plants. Alternate and supplemented food sources are very essential for the survival and effectiveness of phytoseiid predators as biocontrol factors[3]. Cattail pollen has been utilized in numerous predatory mites examines since it is a decent dietary source and is exceptionally simple to gather in huge amounts resulting in improved effectiveness in biological control[4]. In this study we considered cattail pollen as supplementary diet to study its effect on predatory potential of predatory mites of phytoseius genus against different stages (egg, 1st instar and 2nd Instar) of B. tabaci.

2 Experiments

2.1 Materials

Mite cells were developed by using petri dishes. Water soaked cotton was placed within a petri dish and fresh cotton leaves taken from field were trimmed to round form and then were placed on cotton. Purpose of water-soaked cotton was to restrict escape of mites from the leaf surface. Lid of the mite cell contained a small hole to maintain internal environment according to the surroundings.

2.2 Arthropod Collection

Predatory mites belonging to phytoseius genus were collected from the field directly from brinjal plants (S. melongena) and red roses (R. macdub) planted in (Vegetable Area) and (Floral Area), University of Agriculture, Faisalabad and were shifted to the mite cells with the help of fine camel hair brushes[5]. Different stages of whitefly were also collected from the fields of cotton (G. hirsutum) and these specimens were used to check the predatory efficacy of phytoseius predators. Fifteen specimens of each egg, 1st and 2nd instar stage was applied separately in different treatments for this experiment.

2.3 Collection of Pollens

Cattail pollen were collected from Gojra canal side near Samundari, Faisalabad and these freshly collected pollen were applied at a rate of 2.5 mg/cell in treated mite cells to study the effect on predatory efficacy of phytoseiid mites against eggs, and instars of whitefly.

2.4 Conditions for Experiment

Cells were placed in 25℃±2℃ and 65%±5% R H.

2.5 Treatments

A total of seven treatments (T_1 = 2 mites without pollen; T_2 = 3 mites without pollen; T_3 = 4 mites without pollen; T_4 = 2 mites with pollen supply; T_5 = 3 mites with pollen supply; T_6 = 4 mites with pollen supply and T_7 as control treatment) along with three replications

were considered.

2.6 Collection of Date

Data was collected using microscope and counting killed or damaged individuals of B. tabaci. Data was collected after 12h, 24h and 36 h. After each data collection, numbers of prey were again maintained to fifteen per cell till last data collection.

2.7 Statistics

Data was analyzed using simple ANOVA using CRD design. Tukey test was used for pairwise comparison of different treatments.

3 Results and Discussions

3.1 Mortality After 12 Hours

This study mainly focused on influence of cattail pollen on predatory potential of phytoseiid mites on B. tabaci. In results of feeding potential after 12 hours, efficacy of predator was slightly enhanced due to the application of cattail pollen.

Percentage feeding potential increased from 37.78%, 34.04%, 32.59% to 67.41%, 59.26%, 54.07% in case of eggs, 1st instar and 2nd instar respectively (Fig. 1). In feeding potential of predatory mite mortality of eggs was more as compared to 1st and 2nd instars. Feeding potential of T_6 was much higher as compared to other treatments because of availability of pollen and greater number of predators as compared to other treatments.

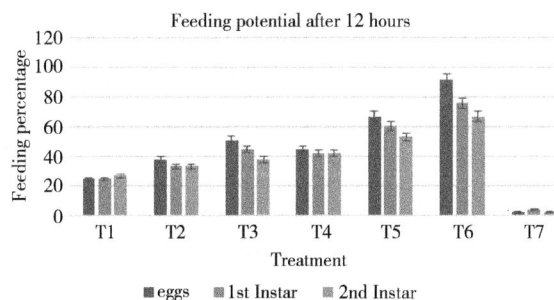

Fig. 1　Maximum mortality of B. tabaci was due to T_6

3.2 Mortality After 24 Hours

In case of feeding potential after 24 hours, it was seen that mortality of B. tabaci was much greater in case of treatments applied with pollen as compared to treatments which were without pollen source. Mortality raised from

32.22%, 27.78%, 25% to 53.34%, 45%, 42.23% in case of eggs, 1st and 2nd instar respectively (Fig. 2). After 24 hours mortality on eggs, 1st and 2nd instar of B. tabaci was highly significant ($P_{Value} = 0.00$).

Feeding potential after 24 hours

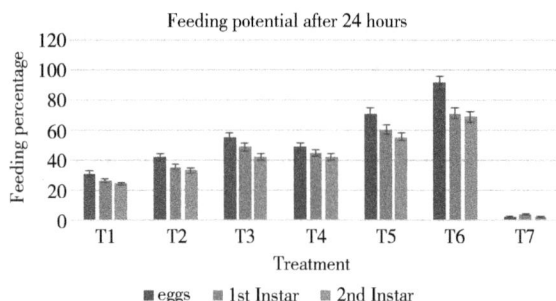

Fig. 2 Maximum mortality of B. tabaci was due to T_6

3.3 Mortality After 36 Hours

After 36 hours it was seen that mortality increased from 45.19, 37.78, 34.41 to 70.37, 58.52, 55.56 in case of eggs, 1st instar and 2nd instar due to application of cattail pollens (Fig. 3).

Feeding potential after 36 hours

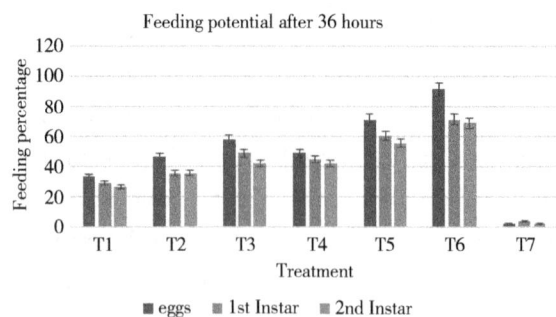

Fig. 3 Maximum mortality of B. tabaci was due to T_6

It can be seen that there is a little difference between T_1 and T_4, T_2 and T_5, T_3 and T_6 in case of 2nd instar showing that there is a little influence of cattail pollen of feeding potential of phytoseiid predator.

3.4 Effect of Pollen on Predatory Potential

It was seen that cattail pollen increased the feeding potential of phytoseiid mites which may be due to the fact that these predacious mites favor mix diets and in the presence of cattail pollen, their survival, lifecycle has been enhanced which then positively influenced the population and predatory potential of mites[6]. Maximum feeding potential was seen with T_6 which was mainly due to the reason that it was favored with both

higher number of predators and pollen supply and pollen supply enhances the predatory potential of phytoseiid mites[7]. It was also observed that mortality was more in case of egg stage as compared to 2nd instar. It also decreases from 2nd instar to 4th instar and adult whitefly. Although in this experiment effects of pollen on development, survival and reproduction were not considered but it also influences these characteristics markedly. An increased feeding potential of phytoseiid mites may be due to the better nutritious nature of cattail pollens[8]. Due to availability of cattail pollens lifecycle of phytoseiid mite was influenced positively and it was seen that pollen was more favorable for mite as compared to available host which increased the potential of mite as a biocontrol due to increased survival[9]. Development of phytoseiid predators is very low when fed on larvae but it increased when pollens were applied[10]. Cattail pollen results in decreased mortality, increase in longevity and fecundity rate, a decrease in developmental period of phytoseiid mite which then results in improved biological control[3-4]. The acceptability of these phytoseiid mites on cattail pollen and taking advantage from nutrition of pollen make these predators as more profitable species to be utilized in biological control of whiteflies[11] and this profit was observed in current study where the feeding potential was increased from 31.11% to 48.89% in case of eggs, where number of mites were same but only difference was the application of pollens to the predatory mites. There was overall positive effect of pollen supply to phytoseiid predators.[12]. This study coincides with current results in which T_6 proved itself as best treatment to control whitefly mainly due to higher predators in that treatment and available pollens. When extra food is applied the predatory population goes on increasing as a result pest population decreases[13]. Predator, along with eggs and young instars of whitefly, feed on pollen provided. The results showed that when extra food is provided the control of whiteflies increased significantly. Thus, with provision of pollens as extra food, control of whiteflies by A. swirskii increases sharply, this study also supports current experiment. Predatory potential on B. tabaci was higher when the release rate was higher (75 A. swirskii/m^2) as compared to other release rates which coincide with this study where maximum predatory potential was seen by T_3 and T_6 containing maximum numbers of predatory mites per cell[14]. Predatory potential was maximum in case of egg stage ($\geqslant 30\%$) and it was decreased when feeding on 1st instar ($\leqslant 27\%$) was checked and again decreased to a very low level when 2nd instar ($\leqslant 10\%$) in case of whitefly[5]. The after effects of current examination are upheld by this investigation as in present research it was seen that least mortality was observed on 2nd instar and maximum mortality was on eggs and 1st instar stage.

4 Conclusions

This study has focused on the effect of pollen application on the feeding potential of phytoseius predators. It was seen that there was a little increase in the predatory potential of predators with the application of cattail pollen and control of whitefly was increased from 50% to almost 85% in case of feeding on eggs by treatments with 3 individuals of predators.

References

[1] SAMARAS K, PAPPAS M L, FYTAS E, et al. Pollen suitability for the development and reproduction of amblydromalus limonicus (Acari: Phytoseiidae)[J]. BioCont, 2015, 60: 773-782.

[2] DOGRAMACI M, KAKKAR G, KUMAR V, et al. Swirski mite (suggested common name) amblyseius swirskii athias henriot (arachnida: mesostigmata: phytoseiidae)[J]. Eeny, 2016, 565: 1-5.

[3] HUANG N, ENKEGAARD A, OSBORNE L et al. The banker plant method in biological control[J]. Critical Rev Plant Sci, 2011, 30: 259-278.

[4] LEE H S, GILLESPIE D R. Life tables and development of Amblyseius swirskii (Acari: Phytoseiidae) at different temperatures[J]. Exp App Acarol, 2011, 53(1): 17-27.

[5] CUTHBERTSON, A. G. S. The Feeding Rate of Predatory Mites on Life Stages of Bemisia tabaci Mediterranean Species [J]. Insects. J Ins Sci, 2014, 5: 609-614.

[6] GERSON U, WEINTRAUB P G. Mites (Acari) as a factor in greenhouse management[J]. Ann Rev Entomol, 2012, 57: 229-247.

[7] PARK H H, SHIPP L, BUITENHUIS R, et al. Life history parameters of a commercially available Amblyseius swirskii (Acari: Phytoseiidae) fed on cattail (Typha latifolia) pollen and tomato russet mite (Aculops lycopersici)[J]. J Asia-Pacific Entomol, 2011, 14: 497-501.

[8] PARK H H, SHIPP L, BUITENHUIS R. Predation, development, and oviposition by the predatory mite Amblyseius swirkii (Acari: Phytoseiidae) on tomato russet mite (Acari: Eriophyidae)[J]. J Econ Entomol, 2010, 103(3): 563-569.

[9] DELISLE J F, BRODEUR J, SHIPP L. Evaluation of various types of supplemental food for two species of predatory mites, amblyseius swirskii and neoseiulus cucumeris (acari: phytoseiidae)[J]. Exp Appl Acarol, 2015, 65(4): 483-494.

[10] BUITENHUIS R, SHIPP L, SCOTT-DUPREE C. Intraguild versus extra-guild prey: effect on predator fitness and preference of amblyseius swirskii (athias-henriot) and neoseiulus cucumeris (oudemans) (acari: phytoseiidae)[J]. Bull Entomol Res, 2010, 100: 167-173.

[11] KUMAR V, WEKESA V W, AVERY P B, et al. Effect of pollens of various ornamental pepper cultivars on the development and reproduction of Amblyseius swirskii (Acari: Phytoseiidae)[J]. Florida Entomol, 2014, 97: 367-373.

[12] GHASEMZADEH S, LEMAN A, MESSELINK G J. Biological control of Echinothrips americanus by phytoseiid predatory mites and the effect of pollen as supplemental food[J]. Exp Appl Acarol, 2017, 73(2): 209-221.

[13] NOMIKOU M, SABELIS M W, JANSSEN A. Pollen subsidies promote whitefly control through the numerical response of predatory mites[J]. BioCont, 2010, 55: 253-260.

[14] CALVO F J, BOLCKMANS K, BELDA J E. Control of Bemisia tabaci and Frankliniella occidentalis in cucumber by Amblyseius swirskii[J]. BioCont, 2011, 56: 185-192.

Bioconversion of Crude Glycerol into Bacterial Cellulose-A Potential Green Raw Material for Textile Industry

MAMOONA Sattar[1, 2], ZOU Xiaozhou[2], CHEN Lin[2], HONG Feng[1, 2] *

[1] *Key Lab of Science & Technology of Eco-textile, Ministry of Education, Shanghai, 201620, China*

[2] *Group of Microbiological Engineering and Industrial Biotechnology, College of Chemistry, Chemical Engineering and Biotechnology, Donghua University, Shanghai, 201620, China*

* *Corresponding author's email*: Email: fhong@ dhu. edu. cn

Abstract: Bacterial cellulose (BC), a linear polymer and extra cellular polysaccharide of acetic acid bacteria (Komagataeibacter xylinus), is a potential eco material to replace cotton and wood pulp as the primary source of cellulose to make viscose fibers. In this study, crude glycerol (by-product from biodiesel industry) was used as a sole carbon source for cost effective production of BC by static fermentation of K. xylinus ATCC 23770 for 14 days in five different culture media containing mannitol, glucose, commercial glycerol and two different crude glycerol samples as carbon source. The dry yield in crude glycerol-based medium[(1. 35±0. 049) g/L] was comparable with that in mannitol-based medium[(1. 44±0. 05) g/L)] and significantly higher than that in glucose-based medium[(0. 98±0. 074) g/L]. FTIR spectra revealed that all the BC pellicles obtained were pure cellulose regardless of the carbon source used in the medium. Mechanical properties (Young's modulus) of the BC pellicles obtained from glycerol-based media were comparatively better than those in glucose-based medium. The work demonstrates that the waste stream of biodiesel industry, crude glycerol, is not only a cheaper carbon source for BC production but also a competent substrate giving enhanced yield and mechanical properties as compared with the relatively expensive sugars (mannitol and glucose).

Keywords: Bacterial cellulose; Eco material; Sustainability; Static fermentation; Crude glycerol; Biodiesel industry

1 Introduction

Cellulose is one of the most abundant natural polymers on the earth. Although plants are the main source of cellulose on the planet, but several types of bacteria (Komagataeibacter, Sarcina, and Agrobacterium), algae and fungi are capable of producing cellulose as an exopolysaccharide[1]. Bacterial cellulose (BC) is linear polymer formed by $\beta-1$, 4 glycosidic linkage of glucose monomers. Compared with plant cellulose, BC holds desirable properties i. e. high degree of polymerization and crystallinity (compared with cotton ~ 70%), fine assemblage of nanofibers, incredible tensile strength in wet state, pronounced water holding capacity, biodegradability and excellent biocompatibility enabling it to be a competent material in textile, paper and packing material, food industry, medical and advanced functional materials[2].

The concept of sustainability and renewable development in textile industry emphasizes on reducing cost, protecting the environment by eco-friendly practices, and recycling the renewable resources. The increased consumption of cotton and wood is leading to occupation of cultivated land, huge pesticide use, deforestation and other environmental issues, which compel textile industry to synthesize alternative regenerated and synthetic fibers e. g. viscose, tencel, rayon, polyester[1]. Unlike plant based cellulose, BC does not need chemical treatment for separation of lignin, hemicellulose and pectin which ensures it to be a green material for manufacturing textile materials[3]. Although BC has wide range of applications, but relatively high production cost restricts its large-scale production. One of the major part of the culture media is the carbon source and approach of bio-refinery (using wastes and by-products of other industries as a feedstock) is a remedy to cope with cost competitiveness[4]. In this context, waste products from various industries like wheat straw, beet molasses, sugar-cane molasses, corn steep liquor, several fruit juices and residues from agro-forest industries have been used as carbon source[5-6].

Crude glycerol from biodiesel industry, an inevitable by-product of transesterification of oils and one of the low-cost carbon sources, is attractive feedstock for fermentative industries. It is estimated that 1ton of biodiesel processing yields 100kg of waste glycerol. In 2015, 1 Mt of crude glycerol had been produced, out of which 0.8Mt was recorded as surplus. It is predicted that by 2020, the production of crude glycerol would reach 41.9 billion liters. A number of bacterial strains important in fermentation industry are capable of using glycerol as sole carbon source including Komagataeibacter xylinus. Various researchers used commercially available glycerol as a sole carbon source or mixed with other carbon sources for BC production and suggested that glycerol gives comparatively higher yield than glucose[4,7-10]. However, to date just one report of using crude glycerol as a sole carbon source by strain K. saccharivorans is available, proposing that industrial waste glycerol can be a good carbon source for BC production[11].

In this study, two crude glycerol samples; one from processing of animal oil (ACG) and the other from plant oil (PCG), were used as a sole carbon source for production of BC by K. xylinus ATCC 23770 in comparison with analytical grade pure glycerol. Moreover, mannitol as a sugar alcohol was used as positive control and glucose was used as negative control in the study. The BC pellicles harvested were examined for mechanical strength and Fourier transform infrared spectroscopy (FTIR).

2 Experiments

2.1 Microbial Strain and Culture Media

K. xylinus ATCC 23770 obtained from American type

culture (Manassas, VA, USA) was used for fermentation[12]. Glucose (Glu), mannitol (Man), and glycerol (Gly) used as carbon source were analytical grade while animal fat based crude glycerol (ACG) and plant oil based crude glycerol (PCG) were obtained from Yihai Co., Ltd, China. The seed culture for inoculum was prepared in a medium supplemented with $10g/L^{-1}$ glycerol, 5g/L peptone and 3g/L yeast extract. In the comparison of five different carbon sources, same basal medium containing 25g/L of one of the five carbon sources mentioned above was used. The pH of all the media was initially adjusted to 5.0 with 0.1 mol/L sulfuric acid.

2.2 Cultivation of BC Pellicles

5mL of seed culture in log phase was inoculated into 250mL Erlenmeyer flasks containing 100mL medium. The flasks were statically incubated at 30℃ for 14 days. BC membranes obtained after cultivation were purified by washing them with 0.1mol/L NaOH solution for 2h followed by several rounds of washing with deionized water at same temperature and time conditions. The yield of purified and oven-dried (at 105℃) BC pellicles was determined gravimetrically.

2.3 Characterization of BC

Mechanical properties of hydrated BC pellicles were tested as previously[13]. FTIR of freeze-dried samples was performed to evaluate the chemical structure of BC pellicles formed in different media[14].

Statistical analysis:

All the data given are mean ± SD and were statistically analyzed by paired student t-test ($p < 0.05$ was considered to be statistically significant).

3 Results and Discussions

3.1 BC Yield in Crude Glycerol in Comparison with Other Carbon Sources

Fig. 1(a) represents the absolute dry yield of BC in five different media supplemented with different carbon sources. The yield in glucose based medium (0.98g/L) was significantly lower ($p < 0.05$) than those from mannitol (1.44g/L), glycerol (1.33g/L) and ACG (1.35g/L) based media. The yield in PCG based medium was slightly lower than ACG medium but not significantly different

($p>0.05$). Moreover, the yield of BC against the consumed carbon source in each medium for glucose is significantly lower than all glycerol based media as shown in Fig. 1(b).

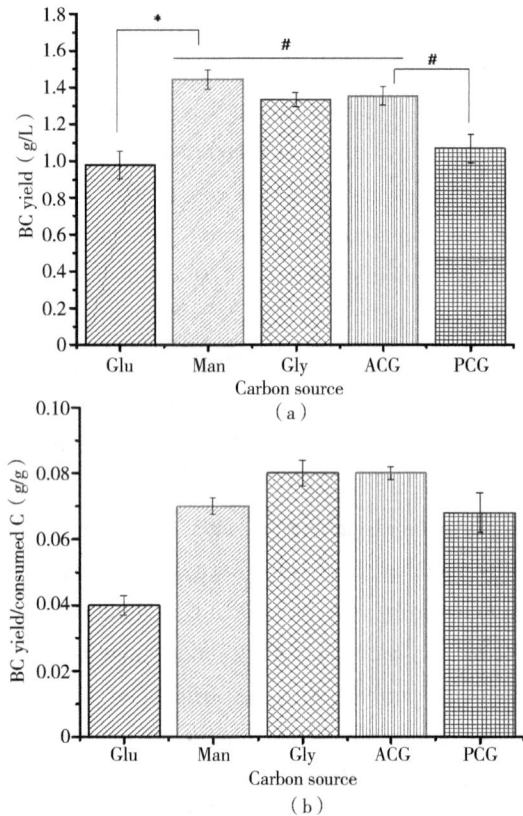

Fig. 1 (a) BC yield; (b) BC yield in consumed carbon source (g/g) (* refers to significant difference, # refers to no significant difference, C refers to carbon source)

The results are in good agreement with previous researches focusing on the improved BC yield in the presence of glycerol as a carbon source. It is reported that for long term fermentation glycerol and mannitol are preferable carbon sources, as the gluconic acid accumulation in glucose medium followed by drop in pH of medium influences the yield[7-8,10,15]. In comparison of effect of different alcohols on BC production, mannitol is stated to enhance the BC yield[16]. Furthermore, enhanced BC yield in biodiesel based crude glycerol medium was observed by Carreira et al(2011)[6].

3.2 Characterization of BC

3.2.1 Tensile Strength
The mechanical strength is an important feature for any textile material. Although tensile properties of BC are strain specific but the cultivation system and carbon source are important factors influencing it. The difference in tensile properties can be associated with various features including fiber density, crystallinity and fiber distribution[14]. Owing to the previous reports, BC pellicles harvested from ATCC 23770 possess relatively poor tensile properties[13]. Fig. 2 shows that the Young's modulus (0.4MPa) and fracture stress (0.15MPa) of BC pellicles from glucose medium are significantly lower than the samples from other media. Whereas, in the ACG and PCG medium tensile properties are comparable with that of pure glycerol. It implies that crude glycerol can be a favorable carbon substrate for ATCC 23770.

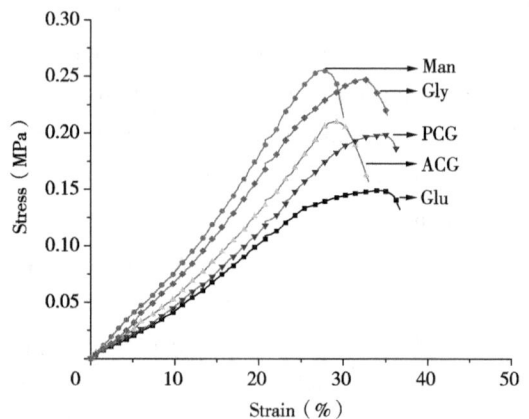

Fig. 2 Tensile stress-strain curves for BC in five different carbon sources

3.2.2 Fourier Transform Infrared Spectroscopy
Fig. 3 demonstrates the FTIR spectra of BC pellicles obtained from different media. The peaks of 1158cm^{-1} depict the glycosidic linkages of cellulose[12]. The peaks of 895cm^{-1} and that at 1427cm^{-1} refer to —CH and —CH$_2$ bends, while at 710cm^{-1} and 750cm^{-1} indicate Iβ and Iα specifically. The vibration of —OH in cellulose causes the peaks at 3350cm^{-1}. The spectra reveals that irrespective of the carbon source used, cellulose structure is highly conserved. The results coincide with previous reports that chemical properties of BC produced by K. xylinus are independent of carbon substrate[10,17].

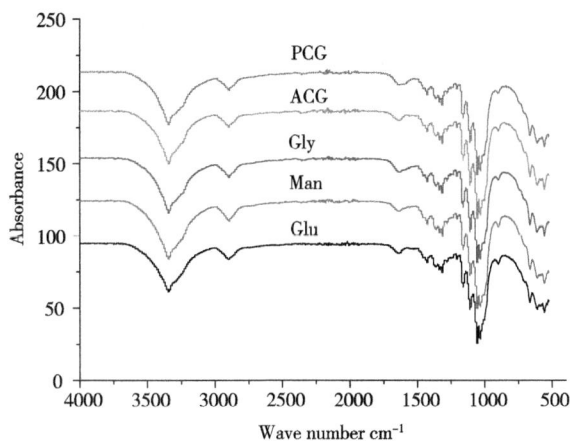

Fig. 3　FTIR spectra of BC obtained in five different carbon sources

4　Conclusions

The present study validates that the crude glycerol from biodiesel industry can serve as a preferable carbon substrate for K. xylinus ATCC 23770. Glycerol based media improved not only the yield but also comparable tensile properties with conventional expensive carbon sources (mannitol and glucose), making it desirable for further applications including biomedical textile. Further studies could lead this approach to combat the cost competitiveness for large scale production of this valuable material. Additionally, the detailed compositional analysis of waste glycerol from various processing lines can be helpful for bioconversion of crude glycerol as a renewable resource into bacterial cellulose.

Acknowledgements

The investigation is funded by the Fundamental Research Funds for the Central Universities (2232019A3-08).

References

[1]COSTA A, ROCHA M A V, SARRUBO L. Bacterial cellulose: an ecofriendly biotextile[J]. Int J Text Fashion Technol, 2017, 7: 11-26.

[2]KESHK S M. Bacterial cellulose production and its industrial applications[J]. Bioprocess Biotech, 2014, 4(2): 1-11.

[3]FERNANDES M, GAMA M, DOURADO F, et al. Development of novel bacterial cellulose composites for the textile and shoe industry[J]. Microb Biotechnol, 2019, 12(4): 650-661.

[4]TSOUKO E, KOURMENTZA C, LADAKIS D, et al. Bacterial cellulose production from industrial waste and by-product streams[J]. Int J Mol Sci, 2015, 16(7): 14832-14849.

[5]HONG F, QIU K Y. An alternative carbon source from konjac powder for enhancing production of bacterial cellulose in static cultures by a model strain Acetobacter aceti subsp xylinus ATCC 23770[J]. Carbohyd Polym, 2008, 72(3): 545-549.

[6]CARREIRA P, MENDES J A S, TROVATTI E, et al. Utilization of residues from agro-forest industries in the production of high value bacterial cellulose [J]. Bioresour Technol, 2011, 102(15): 7354-7360.

[7]KESHK S, SAMESHIMA K. Evaluation of different carbon sources for bacterial cellulose production[J]. Afr J Biotechnol, 2005, 4(6): 478-482.

[8]MIKKELSEN D, FLANAGAN B M, DYKES G A, et al. Influence of different carbon sources on bacterial cellulose production by Gluconacetobacter xylinus strain ATCC 53524 [J]. J App Microbiol, 2009, 107(2): 576-583.

[9]VAZQUEZ A, FORESTI M L, CERRUTTI P, et al. Bacterial Cellulose from Simple and Low Cost Production Media by Gluconacetobacter xylinus[J]. J Polym Environ, 2013, 21(2): 545-554.

[10]JUNG H I, JEONG J H, LEE O M, et al. Influence of glycerol on production and structural-physical properties of cellulose from Acetobacter sp V6 cultured in shake flasks [J]. Bioresour Technol, 2010, 101(10): 3602-3608.

[11]GAYATHRI G, SRINIKETHAN G. Crude glycerol as a cost-effective carbon source for the production of cellulose by K. saccharivorans[J]. Biocat Agri Biotechnol, 2018, 16: 326-330.

[12]CHEN G Q, CHEN L, WANG W, et al. Manufacture of a novel anisotropic bacterial nanocellulose hydrogel membrane by using a rotary drum bioreactor[J]. Carbohyd Polym, 2019, 211: 281-288.

[13]YUAN H B, CHEN L, HONG F, et al. Evaluation of nanocellulose carriers produced by four different bacterial strains for laccase immobilization [J]. Carbohyd Polym, 2018, 196: 457-464.

[14]CHEN G Q, WU G, ALRIKSSON B, et al. Scale-up production of bacterial nanocellulose using submerged cultivation [J]. J Chem Technol Biotechnol, 2018, 93(12): 3418-3427.

[15]JOZALA A F, DE LENCASTRE-NOVAES L C, LOPES A M, et al. Bacterial nanocellulose production and application: a 10-year overview[J]. Appl Microbiol and Biotechnol, 2016, 100(5): 2063-2072.

[16]LU Z G, ZHANG Y, CHI Y, et al. Effects of alcohols on

bacterial cellulose production by Acetobacter xylinum 186 [J]. World J Microbiol Biotechnol, 2011, 27(10): 2281-2285.

[17] CHEN G Q, WU G, CHEN L, et al. Comparison of pro-ductivity and quality of bacterial nanocellulose synthesized using culture media based on seven sugars from biomass [J]. Microb Biotechnol, 2019:1-11.

Modeling Surface Roughness for Prediction and Evaluation of Plain-Woven Fabric

ALEMAYEHU Kura[1], Sampath V R[1] *

[1] *Ethiopian Institute of Textile and Fashion Technology, Bahir Dar University, Bahir Dar, 1037, Ethiopia*

* *Corresponding author's email*: kuraalemayehu@ gmail. com

Abstract: Modeling helps to determine how the structural parameters of the fabric affect the surface of a fabric and also identify the way they influence fabric properties. Moreover, it is helpful for estimating and evaluating without complexity and time consuming experimental procedures, and the results available quickly, tangible, accurate and reliable, and project relevant. In this research preparing the regression model was developed that utilized for prediction and evaluation surface roughness of plain-woven fabric and various types of woven fabric. The model was developed based on nine different half-bleached plain woven fabrics with three weft Yarn count 42tex(14Ne), 29. 5tex(20Ne) & 14. 76tex(40Ne) and three weft thread density(18ppc, 21ppc &24ppc) and then the surface roughness of plain-woven fabric was tested by Kawabata (KES-FB4) testing instrument. The Design-Expert© 11 software was used for developing model equation and analysis of variance (ANOVA). The effects of count and density on the roughness of plain-woven fabric were found statistically significant at the confidence interval of 95%. Surface roughness values increase with weft yarn count coarseness increase, while it decreases as the weft yarn gets finer and finer. Surface roughness values decreased as the pick density increases and the vice versa. Correlation between the measured value by KES-FB4 and the calculated value by the model equation are strongly correlated at 95% (R^2 of 0. 97). This model can be used to select a suitable fabric for various end applications and it was also, used for tests and predicts surface roughness of plain woven fabrics.

Keywords: Surface roughness; Regression modeling; Design expert; Prediction; Plain woven fabric

1 Introduction

Nowadays, consumers demand clothing which not only looks good but also feels comfortable. Consumers choose comfort as the most important attribute that they seek in apparel products, which is followed by easy care and durability. As comfort is definitely an individualistic sense it is very difficult to define, design or determine it[1]. Evaluating fabric touch can be a great interest in the industry in order to match the quality needs of the consumer and the parameters for the manufacturing process. One of the most important characteristics of the fabric which affects the comfort properties of cloth is the constructional specification. Parameters such as thickness, weight per square meter, the pattern of weave thread density, crimp(%), and yarn count can be counted as the most effective parameters[2].

Roughness is a descriptive term for a fabric surface which has the feel of sand paper.

Smoothness and roughness of fabric materials are important fabric tactile properties for engineering design of many textile products including medical textiles, hygiene and healthcare products, sportswear, underwear, plain woven, lingerie, and other consumer products having special requirements is sensitive surface tactile properties[3-5].

Modeling is the process of perception of textiles by the skin fills the gap between two contemporary existing solutions: objective and subjective assessment of handling properties of fabrics[6]. Numerous mathematical models involving the human body, clothing, and environment provide useful tools for identifying key parameters in material design and for predicting clothing performance under extreme environmental conditions[2].

The evaluation of fabric surface roughness is possible by using either contact or non-contact methods. In this regard, many devices and techniques have been developed and employed. The Kawabata Evaluation System for Fabrics (KESF), Fabrics Analysis by Simple Tests, and Fabric Touch Tester (FTT) systems are available for measuring the fabric handle related characteristics under the contact methods. But, as far as the tactile responses are concerned, all the low-stress mechanical characteristics directly or indirectly stimulate the touch pressure roughness and other mechanoreceptors of human skin[6-8].

Recent years there have been huge advances in the accuracy, realism, and predictive capabilities of tools for the theory and simulation of materials. Predictive modeling has now become a powerful tool which can also deliver real value. Most of the researchers were focused on experimental methods for characterizing the surface roughness of fabrics but, their focus on modeling the roughness of a commonly used plain-woven fabric is limited and hence most industries are suffering to knowing the level of surface roughness of their product. In this research, a regression model was developed based on the geometrical parameter of fabrics. Thereby the designers in the weaving looms have the ability to design a plain-woven and various types of woven fabrics with specific surface roughness; simply by applying changes in fabric structural parameters (such as weft yarn density and weft yarn linear density) and a laboratory personnel can simply calculate surface roughness of a given fabrics by using the model equations.

2 Experiments

2.1 Materials

Nine 100% cotton plain woven fabrics were produced with different structural parameters; with three different weft density (PPC) and three different weft yarn count while the other parameters are kept in constant such as warp density, warp count, tension, speed, and RH% as shown in Tab.1 All the fabric specification is mentioned as shown in Tab.1 Then each fabric was treated with combined pretreatment process. The chemicals used were so-dium hydroxide 3%, hydrogen peroxide 4%, sodium silicate 2%, wetting agent 0.5% and EDTA 0.5 on the weight of the fabric and one to ten liquor ratio.

Tab.1 Construction parameters of plain woven fabric

Fabric code	Weave type	Warp density (EPC)	Warp count (tex)	Weft density (PPC)	Weft count (tex)
FK$_1$	Plain	24	29.5	18	14.76
FK$_2$	Plain	24	29.5	21	14.76
FK$_3$	Plain	24	29.5	24	14.76
FK$_4$	Plain	24	29.5	18	29.5
FK$_5$	Plain	24	29.5	21	29.5
FK$_6$	Plain	24	29.5	24	29.5
FK$_7$	Plain	24	29.5	18	42
FK$_8$	Plain	24	29.5	21	42
FK$_9$	Plain	24	29.5	24	42

2.2 Experimental Design

A central composite design (CCD) was selected to determine the experimental conditions as the inclusion of axial experimental points allowing for a larger spread of conditions to be examined, which is beneficial when the required complexity of the model is not known for accurate predictions to be made[9]. The experiment has 8 non-center and 5 center points and the total run is 13 with five numbers of replications as shown in the Tab.2.

Tab.2 The experimental design with two factors and three levels

Code	Run	Factor 1 Count (Ne)	Factor 2 Density (PPC)	Response1 SMD
FK$_2$	1	14.76	21	1.31542
FK$_5$	2	29.5	21	1.90625
FK$_8$	3	42	21	2.32167
FK$_1$	4	14.76	18	1.38958
FK$_5$	5	29.5	21	1.90625
FK$_5$	6	29.5	21	1.90625
FK$_9$	7	42	24	2.32167
FK$_5$	8	29.5	21	1.90625
FK$_4$	9	29.5	18	2.13792
FK$_5$	10	29.5	21	1.90625
FK$_3$	11	14.76	24	1.11375
FK$_6$	12	29.5	24	1.52
FK$_7$	13	42	18	2.56625

2.3 Experimental Procedure

Five test specimens 20. 0cm×20. 0cm are prepared for measuring surface roughness by Kawabata Evaluation System (KES-FB4) from each produced samples and conditioned at 65%±2% relative humidity and 20℃± 2℃ for a minimum of 24h before testing as per ASTM-D1776 standard[10]. The data were statistically analyzed and evaluated using Design-Expert software analysis of variance (ANOVA) was done.

2.4 Developing An Empirical Model

Several statistical approaches are now available to researchers to analyze multiple outcomes or informants[11]. Design-Expert provides different prediction equations (model) in terms of actual units and coded units. The coded equations are determined first, and the actual equations are derived from the coded. To get the actual equation each term in the coded equation is replaced with its coding formula.

$$X_{coded} = \frac{X_{actual} - \overline{X}}{(X_{High} - X_{Low})/2} \quad (1)$$

Assumptions:

All the fibers have the same properties.

Fabric produced at constant tension force.

Fabric surface hairiness is ignored.

Normal yarn elongation(%) is maintained.

Twist factor of the yarn is maintained.

The experimental results from the forming trials performed according to the matrix by central composite are tabulated in Tab. 2. These values feed to Design-Expert software to develop the model for SMD of fabric by using count and density of the plain-woven fabric.

$$SMD = \beta_0 + \beta_1 A + \beta_2 B \quad (2)$$

2.5 Model Validity Test

It is always necessary to examine the fitted model to ensure that it provides an adequate approximation to the true system and verifies that none of the least-squares regression assumptions are violated. Proceeding with the exploration and optimization of a fitted response surface will likely give poor results unless the model provides an adequate fit[9,11-12].

2.6 Model Test

A plain fabric consists of different structural parameter which has different weft densities and weft counts were used for model test against surface roughness measured values by KES-FB4. Structural parameter analysis (density & count) was done for the fabrics which are used for model validation. Count of weft yarn from the fabric was measured as per ISO 7211-5; density of weft yarn was measured using ISO 7211-2standard[13-14]. The average value of each measurement was used for calculating surface roughness of the fabrics by developed SMD equation as shown in Tab. 4. Finally, calculated and the measured values were checked their correlations graphically.

3 Results and Discussions

3.1 Effects of Count and Density on the Surface Roughness

The data which were collected from the KES-FB4 under the response column is normally distributed as shown in Fig. 1. From the box plot in Fig. 2, it is instrument of surface roughness values in Tab. 2 observed that the collected data have no out layers either an upper limit or lower limit. This implies that the collected data are normal and it can be used for further statistical analysis.

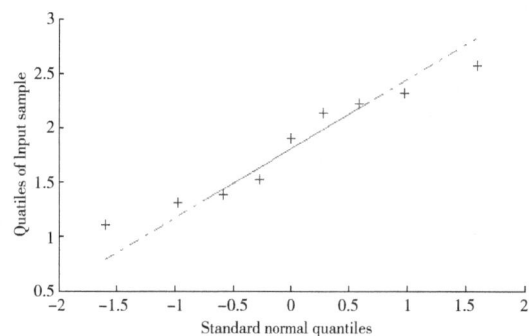

Fig. 1 The QQ-plot of the input data vs. standard normal

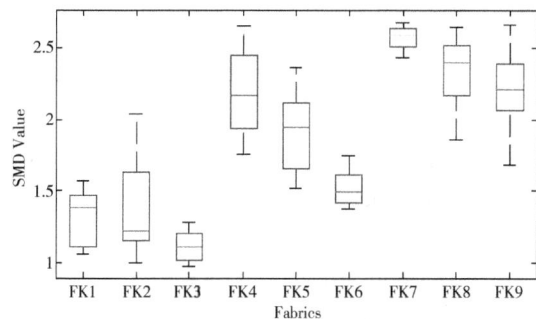

Fig. 2 The box plot of the data

ANOVA results of the linear models presented in Tab. 3

indicates that the model can adequately be used to describe the surface roughness of the fabrics based on the fabric parameters viz. count and density of weft yarn. The F-value is 166. 83 ($P<0.0001$) which implies that the model is significant for surface roughness. There is only a 0. 01% chance that an F-value this large could occur due to noise. A P-value is the indicator of the significance of the test. Values of less than 0. 05 ($P<0.05$) indicate the significance of the model terms. Both the model terms count and density is statistically significant at 95% of the confidence interval since they have a P-value of 0. 0001 and 0. 0002 respectively.

Tab. 3   ANOVA table for linear model

Source	Sum of Squares	df	Mean Square	F-value	p-value	Decision
Model	2. 14	2	1. 07	166. 83	$P<0.0001$	Significant
Count	1. 92	1	1. 92	299. 98	$P<0.0001$	Significant
Density	0. 2160	1	0. 2160	33. 69	$P<0.0002$	Significant
Residual	0. 0641	10	0. 0064			
Lack of Fit	0. 0641	6	0. 0107			Not−significant
Cor Total	2. 20	12				

The effect of weft yarn count on surface roughness values of fabrics was observed that surface roughness values increase with weft yarn count (coarser), while it decreases as the weft yarn get finer and finer as shown in Fig. 3. Also, the surface smoothness of the fabrics increases as the pick density of the fabrics increases and the surface roughness of the fabric increases as the weft thread density decreases as shown in Fig. 3. This was due to the fact that as the thread density of weft yarn increases the pick and valley on the fabric surface decreases.

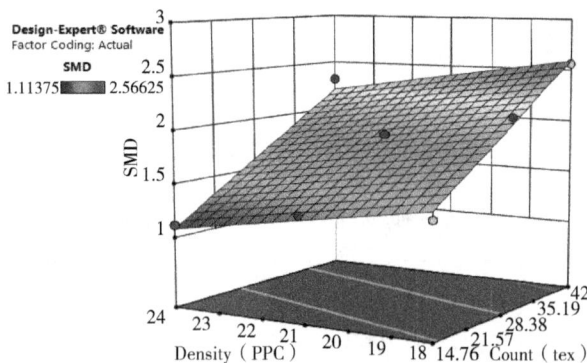

Fig. 3   The effects of both density and count on the surface roughness of the fabric

3. 2   Model Equation for Surface Roughness

The actual model equation was developed by using surface roughness values of the nine samples which were measured by KES-FB4 instrument.

The equation in terms of actual factors (count & density) can be used to make predictions about the response for given levels of each factor. Here, the levels should be specified in the original units for each factor.

$$SMD = + 1. 98837 + 0. 041492 \times Count - 0. 063241 \times Density. \tag{14}$$

3. 3   Model Validity Test

The model validation test was done by checking the correlation between the measured data obtained from the experimental method (KES−FB4) and the calculated (estimated) data obtained from the developed actual model equations (SMD). As it is shown in Fig. 4, the proposed model equation can properly correlate the experimentally measured data from KES−FB4 at the confidence interval of 95% (R^2 of 0. 97).

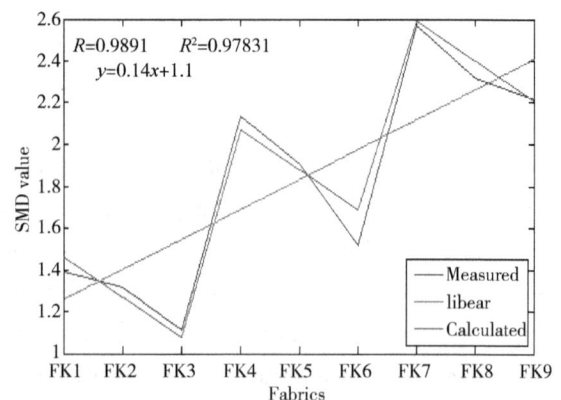

Fig. 4   Correlation between measured SMD by KES−FB4 and calculated SMD by the model equation

The model efficiency was tested by using three different fabrics which are not used for the model equation extraction. The fabric's properties were studied and identified the weft density and count by using the ISO 7211-5 and ISO 7211-2 standard.

3.4 Model Test

The fabric's properties of the fabric that were used for the model test which was 100% cotton half-bleached and parameter of construction was shown in Tab. 4. The correlation between the surface roughness values from KES-FB4 and the surface roughness values from the developed model equation were found strongly correlated at the 95% degree of freedom as shown in Fig. 5.

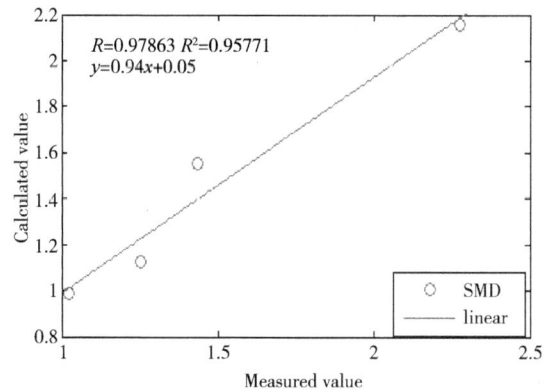

Fig. 5 Correlation between measured SMD by KES-FB4 and calculated SMD by model equation

Tab. 4 Fabrics parameters for model test

Fabric code	Weave type	Warp density (EPC)	Warp count (Ne)	Weft density (PPC)	Weft count (Ne)	Measured (SMD)	Calculated (SMD)
MT$_1$	Plain	32	28	32	28	1.25	1.12644
MT$_2$	Plain	20	20	20	20	1.437	1.5533
MT$_3$	Plain	21	36	21	36	2.277	2.154
MT$_4$	Plain	28	18.5	28	18.5	1.023	0.9859

4 Conclusions

Even though there were different structural parameters that affect the surface properties of the fabrics, it is possible to control the surface behavior of the fabric with the developed model. The weft count and density were used for the model equation which can be used prediction and evaluation of surface roughness of woven fabric. The model statistically significant and can adequately be used to describe the surface roughness of the fabrics. The surface roughness increases with count increases and the surface roughness decrease as the density of the weft thread increases. The model was validated and tested the correlation between measured by KES-FB4 and calculated by the developed model equation reveals that the model was strongly correlated with the confidence interval of 95% (R^2 of 0.95).

References

[1] SONG G. Improving comfort in clothing[J]. Elsevier, 2011.

[2] PENSE-L, GUILABERT C, BUENO M, et al. Sensory evaluation of the touch of a great number of fabrics[J]. Food Quality and Preference, 2006, 17(6): 482-488.

[3] AKGUN M. The effect of fabric balance and fabric cover on surface roughness of polyester fabrics[J]. Fibers and Polymers, 2013, 14(8): 1372-1377.

[4] AKGUN M. Assessment of the surface roughness of cotton fabrics through different yarn and fabric structural properties [J]. Fibers and Polymers, 2014, 15(2): 405-413.

[5] MAO N, WANG Y, QU J. Smoothness and roughness: characteristics of fabric-to fabric self-friction properties[C]. The Proceedings of 90th Textile Institute World Conference, Beijing: China Textile & Apparel Press, 2016.

[6] CLASSEN E. Comfort testing of textiles[J]. Advanced Characterization and Testing of Textiles: Elsevier, 2018:59-69.

[7] HU J. Fabric testing[J]. Elsevier, 2008.

[8] KAWABATA S, NIWA M. Objective measurement of fabric mechanical property and quality: its application to textile and clothing manufacturing[J]. International Journal of Clothing Science and Technology,1991, 3(1): 7-18.

[9] MYERSRH, MONTGOMERY D C, ANDERSON-COOK C M. Response surface methodology: process and product optimization using designed experiments [J]. John Wiley & Sons, 2016.

[10] TESTING A S F, Standard practice for conditioning and tes-

ting textiles[J]. Materials,2015.

[11] NORMANDS-LT. Some old and some new statistical tools for outcomes research[J]. Circulation, 2008, 118(8): 872-884.

[12] MONTGOMERY D C. Design and analysis of experiments [J]. New York: John Willy and Sons inc. 2001.

[13] Canadian General Standards Board. CAN/CGSB 4. 2 No. 6 M89/ISO 7211/2 : Textiles-woven fabrics construction-methods of analysis-part 2: determination of number of threads per unit length [J]. Canadian General Standards Board, Ottawa, Ontario, Canada, 1984.

[14] Canadian General Standards Board. CAN/CG SB-4. 2 No. 6-M89/ISO 7211-5: textiles-woven fabrics-construction-methods ofanalysis-part 5: determination of linear density of yarn removed from fabric[J]. Canadian General Standards Board, Ottawa, Ontario, Canada, 1984.

Study on the Weld Strength and Fatigue Properties of Glass Fiber Reinforced PET Injection Molding Composites

MIAH Md. Sohag[1*], YU Jianyong[1], XU Mengyao[2], ISLAM Syed Rashedul[1], SARKER Sagar[1], YANG Yuqiu[1]

[1] *Key Laboratory of Textile Science & Technology, Ministry of Education, College of Textile, Donghua University, Shanghai, 201620, China*

[2] *School of Material Science and Engineering, Tongji University, Shanghai, 200092, China*

* *Corresponding author's email*: sohagdonghua@ gmail. com

Abstract: Glass fiber reinforced Polyethylene terephthalate PET composites have high melting point, strong mechanical properties, high temperature resistance, corrosion resistance, with also wide range of applications and recyclability. These composites are inevitably subjected to internal and external influences during injection molding, such as weld, temperature, and fatigue life. Three different glass fiber reinforced PET composites were selected for the study. Their tensile properties at different temperatures and different crosshead displacement speeds were measured for different fiber contents. The dynamic mechanical analysis and SEM observation were also accomplished to characterize the results. Finally, the fatigue properties of the material were evaluated using the time-temperature superposition. Experiments show that at different temperatures and tensile speeds, the weld strength of glass fiber composites is reduced by about 50%−60% compared to tensile strength. As the fiber content increases from 15% to 30%, the weld strength of the material can be reduced by 10%; the tensile speed increases from 0. 2mm/min to 20mm/min, the tensile strength of GF PET(30%, Normal) increasesby 15%−25%, and the weld strength of GF PET 30% (Welded) and GF PET 15% (Welded) increases by 50% at 100℃. The tensile strength and welding strength of glass fiber reinforced composites are inversely proportional to the test temperature. GF PET 30% (Normal) have the longest fatigue life, followed by 15% welded, and GF PET 30% (Welded) materials have the shortest fatigue life.

Keywords: Glass fiber-PET composite; Injection molding; Weld strength; Time-temperature superposition

1 Introduction

The continuous advancement and development of science and technology have made the use of thermoplastic products more and more extensive, and are involved in the fields of automobile, medical, aerospace and electronics. Taking automobiles as an example, it is well known that plastics can make cars light weight. The application of plastics in the automotive field is mainly divided into three categories: exterior parts, interior parts and functional structural parts[1-2]. However, the most extensively used thermoplastic PET melts at around 250−255℃, has excellent mechanical properties, good weather resistance, good film formation, and has the highest heat distortion temperature and long-term use temperature in thermoplastics. Therefore, it is widely used in the automotive field. On the other hand, PET becomes more brittle and has poor stability due to crystallization near T_g(80℃), and its impact resistance is weak, which limits its development in the industrial field[3].

Another drawback of the PET, weld marks, an important defect in the injection molding process, which has attracted wide attention of researchers[4]. The weld line is caused by the fusion of two or more layers of material, which forms a distinct line after cooling. The presence of weld lines on the one hand destroys the external features of the material and on the other hand attenuates its intrinsic strength, especially tensile strength and flexural strength[5]. Therefore, it is strongly expected that the accelerated testing methodology is established for the long-term life prediction of composite structures with weld-lines exposed under the actual environment of temperatures, fatigue and stretching rate.

In this paper, through three different kinds of glass fiber reinforced PET injection molding composites were prepared for tensile test in different crosshead speeds and different temperatures. The study focused on the weld joint damage caused by the tensile strength of the material, combined with the condition of composite materials in practical application. The influence of the stretching speed, temperature, tensile strength, the welding strength was further analyzed along with the dynamic mechanic analysis. Finally, the applicability of the time temperature equivalence principle[6] of glass fiber reinforced PET injection molding composites in tensile mode was verified, and the tensile fatigue of glass fiber reinforced PET injection molding composites was evaluated.

2 Experiments

2.1 Materials

In this study, three different glass fiber reinforced polyethylene terephthalate (GF PET) injection molding composite materials were prepared in the lab of Kyoto Institute of Technology, Japan. The 30% GFPET normal (N30) was selected, and the fiber premixing was mainly carried out by using an impregnation device to form a glass fiber content of 30% reinforced polyester thermoplastic pellets, then they were molded into a non-welded dumbbell specimen by injection molding machine which has only one sided casting port. The 30% GF PET weld (W30), and the 15% GF PET weld (W15), respectively with a glass fiber content of 30% and 15% of reinforced polyester thermoplastic pellets were injection molded with double sided casting port into a dumbbell-shaped specimen containing a weld line. The injection molding process parameters of the three composite materials are shown in Tab. 1, and the injection molding method is shown in Fig. 1 (a).

Tab. 1 Injection molding method

Temperature(nozzle→hopper)	Injection pressure	Injection speed	Holding pressure	Holding time	Cooling time	Molding temperature
250-240-260-270℃	20MPa	50mm/s	15MPa	5s	15s	40℃

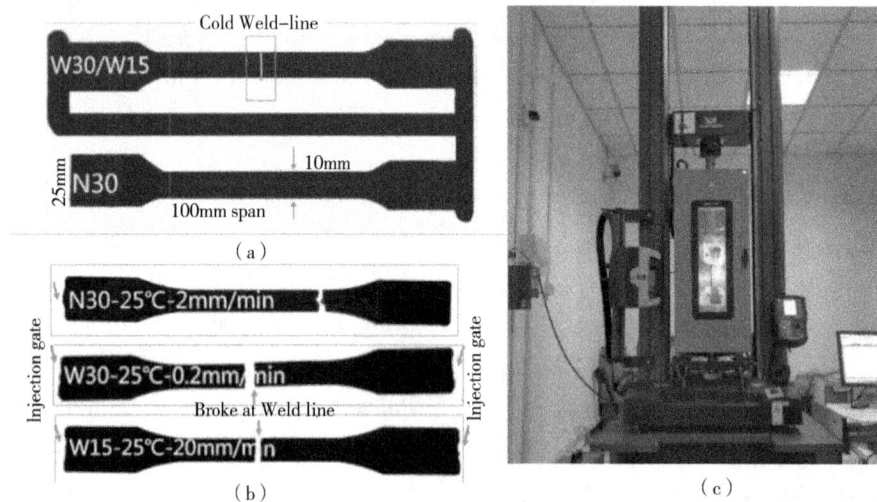

Fig. 1 (a) Injection molding method with single and double injection gates; (b) Tensile broken specimens of Normal and welded injection molding; (c) Instron universal tensile testing machine with temperature control chamber

2.2 Characterization

The tensile properties of glass fiber reinforced PET injection molding composites were determined according to the standard GB/T 1447—2005 "Fiber reinforced plastic tensile properties test method", and selected type I specimens (i. e. dumbbell type).

The shape of the sample is shown in Fig. 1 (a). The tensile test of the three injection-molded composites were accomplished at five different temperatures (temperature gradient settings were: 25℃, 40℃, 60℃, 80℃, 100, with three different tensile speeds of 0.2mm/min, 2.0mm/min, and 20mm/min. The Instron universal tensile test machine (model INSTRON 5967) was used for tensile test as shown in Fig. 1 (b). Dynamic mechanical analysis tests were conducted by using a TA instruments DMA Q800 analyser with extension type clamp at 0.2Hz, 2Hz and 20Hz frequency from room temperature up to 180℃, at a rate of 3℃/min to analyse the viscoelastic behaviour of the composites.

3 Results and Discussions

3.1 Effect of Weld Strength on PET Composite

According to the tensile test results and load-displacement curves of the three materials, we can observe the relationship between the fracture load and the displacement of the same glass fiber composite under different tensile speeds and different temperature gradients. The stretching speed range was from 0.2mm/min to 20mm/min and the temperature was from 25℃ to 100℃.

Observing the fracture patterns of the three glass fiber composites, we found that the N30 (normal) composites broke at different position of the specimens when the fracture point was close to one side; and for W30 (weld) and W15 (weld) injection molded composites, all of which break-position was at the weld line location. This also proves that the weld line is an important factor that weakens the tensile strength of the glass fiber composite. Fig. 1 (b) shows the fracture image of specimens. The tensile test results of the samples are shown in Fig. 2. This figure describes the load-displacement curves of the three different glass-fiber composites during the stretching process at different temperatures.

Tensile properties were tested for N30 (normal), and the breaking strength was denoted tensile strength, while for W30 (weld) and W15 (weld) it was called the weld strength due to the existence of weld lines.

According to Fig. 2 and Fig. 3, N30 (normal) showed the same change rule under other temperature gradients. The weld strength of GF PET W30 material at different temperatures and different stretching speeds is much smaller than the tensile strength, and the reduction range is about 50%–60%.

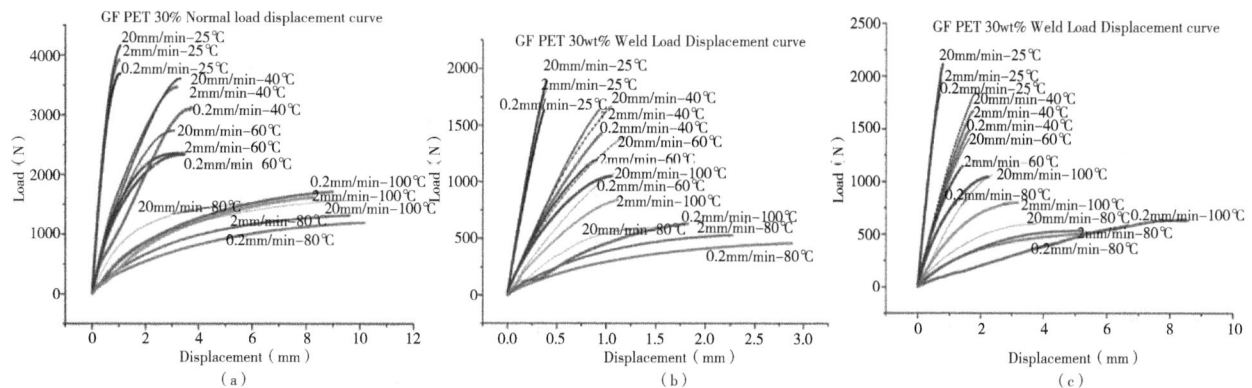

Fig. 2 Load-displacement curve of (a)normal 30% GF-PET; (b) 30% weld; (c) 15% weld for 0.2mm/min, 2.0mm/min, 20mm/min stretching speed at different temperatures (20℃, 40℃, 60℃, 80℃, 100℃)

During the injection molding process, the melt enters the cavity through two injection ports and they are in contact with each other in the center of the cavity by "head-to-head". After the intersection, cooling produces a weld line. The polymer chains at the weld lines are not sufficiently entangled and dispersed, resulting in weak adhesion and weakening the intermolecular forces at the weld marks[5, 7].

Fig. 3 shows the variation of the weld strength of the composite with the fiber content. From Fig. 3 (a) and (b), it can be seen that the weld strength of the glass fiber composite is inversely proportional to the fiber mass fraction. Among them, as the fiber content increases from 15% to 30%, the weld strength of the material at 25℃ and 40℃ decreases greatly, about 10%; when the temperature is greater than 60℃, the weld strength decreases very small and unstable, only about 2%-5% lower. The increase in glass fiber content may improve the tensile properties of the material, but when the fiber content increases to a certain extent, it will weaken the tensile strength of the material.

According to Fig. 3 (c), the stretching speed is increased from 0. 2mm/min to 2mm/min, the tensile strength of the N30 (normal) composite increases by about 5% - 10%, while for W30 (weld) and W15 (weld), the weld strength of composites increases by about 10% - 20%; when it continues to increase to 20mm/min, the tensile strength of 30% normal increases by 15% - 25% compared to 0. 2mm/min. As the tensile speed increases, the tensile strength and weld strength of the glass fiber composites increase. The main reason is that the segmental motion of the polymer is a mechanical relaxation phenomenon, and the external force causes the relaxation time reduction. When the temperature is higher than 80℃, the tensile strength and welding strength are increased again. Probably the materials have started crystallized at 100℃, and the tensile strength thereof has increased compared with 80℃ stage as it is the glass transition temperature of PET.

3. 2 Time-Temperature Superposition Principle for Determining Fatigue Properties of Glass Fiber Reinforced PET Composites

In the conventional fatigue analysis of composite materials, we often use the time-temperature equivalent rela-

tionship in the mechanical relaxation process[6, 8]. In this work, according to the comparison of the tensile strength of glass-reinforced PET composites at different temperatures and different tensile velocities, the establishment of WLF master curve and the relationship between the displacement factor and the temperature are analyzed, and the time-temperature equivalent relationship of the glass-reinforced PET is obtained, and the fatigue life of the material is predicted. In the range of 25℃ to 80℃ the increase in temperature causes a significant decrease in tensile strength and weld strength of the glass fiber composite, and a drop of 70% at 80℃ compared to 25℃. The specific steps are as follows: (1) The relationship between the tensile speed logarithm (mm/min) and the isotherm is fitted; (2) Select 25℃ as the reference temperature, fit the polynomial regression equation, and transform the tensile strength curve under different temperature gradients to the main curve by shift factor to generate the WLF main curve; (3) Verify that the relationship between the shift factor and temperature satisfies the empirical formula. The shift factor refers to the horizontal or vertical distance at which the tensile strength curve at each temperature is moved to the reference temperature main curve, and the relationship between the temperature and the temperature can be expressed by the formula (1):

$$E(T, t) = E\left(T_0, \frac{t}{a_t}\right) \tag{1}$$

Where T_0 represents the reference temperature; t represents time; T represents temperature; and a_t represents horizontal shift factor.

According to Ferry's second condition for the applicability of the time-temperature superposition principle: the relationship between the shift factor and temperature needs to satisfy the WLF equation or the Arrhenius equation[9] see equation (2).

$$\lg a_t = \frac{\Delta E}{2. 303R}\left(\frac{1}{T} - \frac{1}{T_0}\right) \tag{2}$$

We found that the relationship between the shift factor and temperature which is related to the activation energy of the glass-reinforced PET and the molar constant R, and both ΔE and R are constant values. We get the relationship between different temperature shift factors and temperature, as in equation (3):

$$\frac{\lg a_{t1}}{\lg a_{t2}} = \frac{T_2(T_0 - T_1)}{T_1(T_0 - T_2)} \tag{3}$$

According to Ferry (1980), in Tab. 2, for N30 and W15 composites, the error between the standard values of $\lg a_{t1}/\lg a_{t2}$ is less than 20%, so the two materials meet the time-temperature superposition.

Tab. 2 Three glass fiber composites $\lg a_{t1}/\lg a_{t2}$ values

T_1, T_2	Standard value $\dfrac{T_2(T_0 - T_1)}{T_1(T_0 - T_2)}$	GF PET N30 $\lg a_{t1}/\lg a_{t2}$		GF PET W30 $\lg a_{t1}/\lg a_{t2}$		GF PET W15 $\lg a_{t1}/\lg a_{t2}$	
		Test value	SD	Test value	SD	Test value	SD
40,60	0.46	0.45	2.5%	0.30	34.1%	0.45	2.6%
40,80	0.31	0.34	9.4%	0.20	36.6%	0.33	6.8%
60,80	0.67	0.75	12.8%	0.64	3.4%	0.73	10.4%

According to the WLF master curve obtained in Fig. 4, further perform polynomial fitting were done to make the tensile strength of the glass fiber composite material close to 0. The time scale achieved by the WLF master curve is beyond the reach of current instruments—that is, we can estimate the fatigue life of three glass fiber composites. The N30 (normal) have the longest fatigue life, followed by W15 (weld), and W30 (weld) composites have the shortest fatigue life.

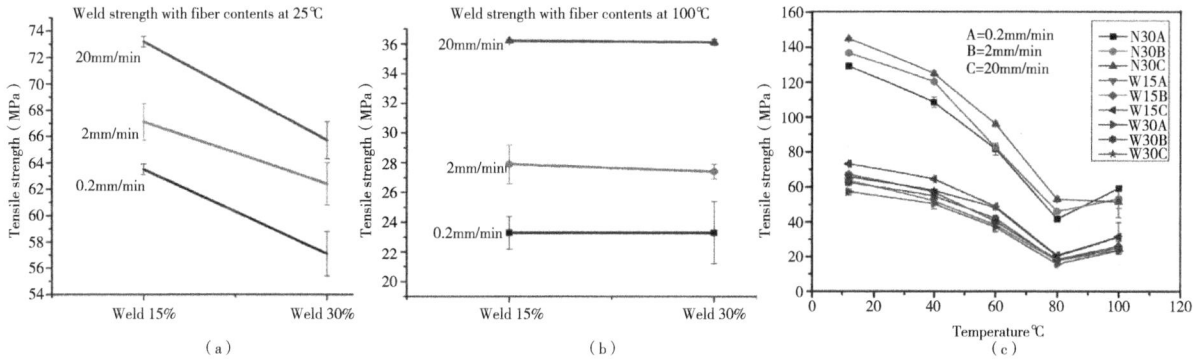

Fig. 3 Tensile strength of GF-PET at different temperature and stretching speed: (a) Tensile strengths for 15% weld and 30% weld at 25℃ and (b) at 100℃; (c) Tensile strengths of three composites

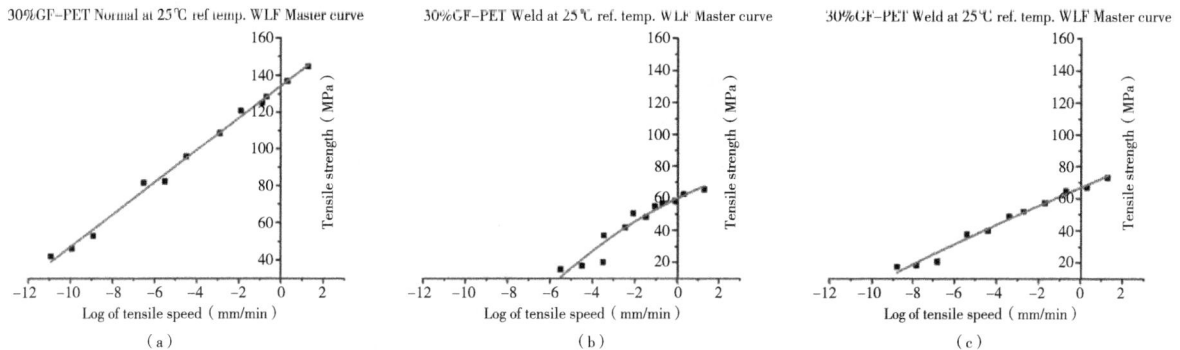

Fig. 4 WLF master curve of GF-PET for three composites

3.3 DMA Analysis

Dynamic mechanic analysis shows the higher storage modulus and tanδ at higher frequency of the strain. As the frequency increases from 0.2Hz to 20Hz, the tanδ or T_g value increases which comply with the tensile tests values at higher speeds (Fig. 5). The glass transition temperature changes in a higher frequency due to the short period of time for the polymer relaxation.

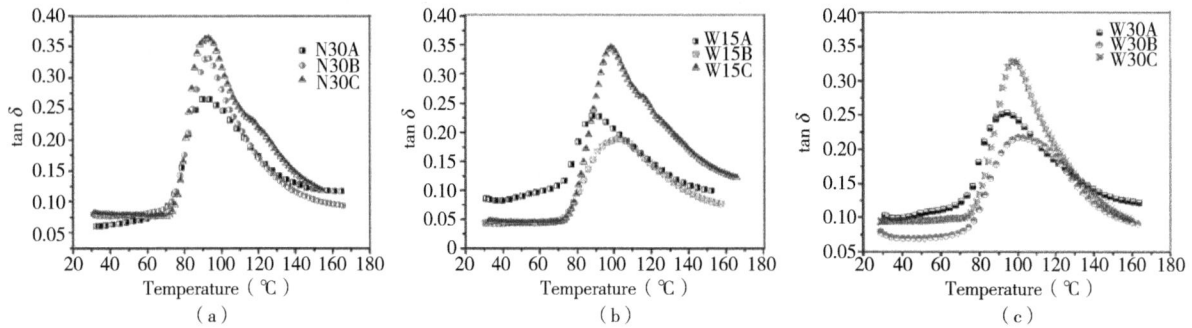

Fig. 5   Tan delta curves at different frequency [(a)=0.2Hz;(b)=2.0Hz;(c)=20Hz] in DMA tests for three composites

4   Conclusions

In this research, the tensile properties of three glass fiber reinforced PET injection molding composites at different tensile speeds and temperatures were systematically studied. The specific conclusions are as follows:
(1) Comparing the glass fiber reinforced PET injection molding composites with or without weld lines, it is found that the weld strength is significantly lower than the tensile strength at different temperatures and different tensile speeds, with a decrease of about 50% – 60%. (2) As the fiber content increases from 15% to 30%, the material weld strength can be reduced by about 10%. The tensile strength of N30 increases by 15% – 25% when crosshead speed increases from 0. 2mm/min to 20mm/min. The tensile strength and weld strength of the composites are inversely proportional to the test temperature. (3) The time-temperature equivalent relationship is applicable to the glass fiber composite under tensile conditions. Using the time-temperature superposition conversion, it is possible to predict the fatigue life of the material, the 30% normal glass fiber reinforced PET injection molding materials have the longest fatigue life, followed by 15% weld, and 30% weld materials have the shortest fatigue life.

References

[1] HASHEMI S. Temperature, strain rate and weld-line effects on strength and micromechanical parameters of short glass fibre reinforced polybuylene terephthalate(PBT) [J]. Polymer Testing,2011(30):901-810.

[2] WANG Guilong, ZHAO Guoqun, WANG Xiaoxin. Effects of cavity surface temperature on mechanical properties of specimens with and without a weld line in rapid heat cycle molding[J]. Materials and Design,2013(46):457-472.

[3] DZULKIPLI Azieatul Azrin, AZUDDIN M. Study of the effects of injection molding parameter on weld line formation [C]. Advances in Material & Processing Tech Conference, Procedia Engineering,2017(184):663-672.

[4] OZCELIK Babur,KURAM Emel,MUSTAFA Topal M. Investigation the effects of obstacle geometrice and injection molding parameters on weld line strength using experimental and finite element methods in plastic injection molding[J]. International Communications in Heat and Mass Transfer, 2012 (39):275-281.

[5] BANIK Nabanita. A review on the use of thermoplastic composites and their effects in induction welding method[J]. Materials Today:Proceedings,2018(5):20239-20249.

[6] KOYANAGI Jun,NAKADA Msayuk,MIYANO Yasushi. Prediction of long-term durablity of unidirectional CFRP[J]. Journal of Renforced Plastics and Composites, 2011, 15 (30):1305-1313.

[7] DAIRNIEH I S,HAUFE A,WOLF H Jet al. Computer simulation of weld lines in injection meolded poly(methyl methacrylate) [J]. Polymer Engineering and Science, 1996, 15 (36):2050-2057.

[8] NAKADA Masayuki,MIYANO Yasush. Formulation of time- and temperature dependent strength of unidirectional carbon

fiber reinforced plastics[J]. Journal of Composite Materials, 2012,47(15):1897-1906.

[9]NAKADA Masayuki,MIYANO Yasush,CAI Hongneng,et al. Predication of long-term viscoelastic behavior of amorphous resin based on the timetemperature superposition principle [J]. Mech Time-Depend Mater,2011,15:309-316.

Preparation and Thermal Insulation Properties of Kevlar/ Polyimide 3D Woven Fabric Composites

ZHENG Liangang[1, 2], XIAO Yuanxin[1, 2], XU Fujun[1, 2*], QIU Yiping[1, 2]

[1] *Key Laboratory of Textile Science & Technology, Ministry of Education, College of Textile, Donghua University, Shanghai, 201620, China*

[2] *Department of Technical Textiles, College of Textiles, Donghua University, Shanghai, 201620, China*

* *Corresponding author's email*: fjxu@ dhu. edu. cn

Abstract: With the development of science and technology, the requirements for performance of material in aerospace, military, transportation and other fields have been continuously improved. Composite materials with light weight, high strength, high temperature resistance, ablation resistance and good mechanical properties have attracted extensive attention. Three-dimensional woven fabric has the characteristics of good integrated structure and easy to be designed, which provides an idea for the researchers to fabricate the products with the above excellent properties. In this paper, based on the structural design, polyamide acid (PAA), the precursor of polyimide (PI), was applied to three-dimensional fabric. The PAA was transformed into PI by heat treatment to prepare the three-dimensional woven spacer Kevlar fiber reinforced polyimide composites (K/PICs). The results show that the composite material has good mechanical properties, and the weight is light, the unit volume density is about a quarter of the wood block, is the one-fifth that of glass fiber/epoxy resin composite of the same structure. At the same time, the composite material has good thermal insulation performance, when exposed to 100℃ environment, it can cut off nearly 50% of the heat, is superior to the same conditions of PE foam. This composite material has a great application prospect in the field of protection of thermal insulation.

Keywords: Three-dimensional spacer fabric; Kevlar fiber; Light weight; Polyimide; Thermal insulation properties

1 Introduction

Three-dimensional spacer connective fabric is a kind of fabric with hollow structure, which is woven as a whole and connected by vertical yarns between up and down layers. Due to its good integrated structure, light weight and designability of structure, it has been widely concerned by researchers[1-3]. As is shown in Fig. 1, (a) is the physical structure and (b) is the schematic structure of three-dimensional spacer composites. The yarns include warp, weft and piles yarns. The warp yarns are flexed, the weft yarns are straight, and the orientation of the pile yarns in the surface layer is the warp direction. As the yarns in three directions can be replaced by other kind of yarns with different characteristics, and the surface layer's warp density, weft density, core col-umn height and its distribution density can be adjusted, it can be made into composite materials that can meet different requirements through structural design[4].

The heat insulator is a material that insulates or reduces the flow of heat in a particular direction. Traditional insulation material were produced by laminating process[5-7] or made of foam material, However, they usually has some problem that cannot meet the requirement, such as high weight, poor interlaminar shearing resistance, and the mechanical properties were weak. As the requirement of light materials in the field of aerospace and automotive is increasing, it is necessary to manufacturing lightweight materials that have good mechanical properties and thermal insulation properties. In this study, Therein forced body of composites were prepared by using the three-dimensional loom, and the lightweight composite material with certain thermal insulation properties were designed and prepared by controlling the hollow structure. Until now, there are no reports on the study of three-dimensional woven spacer Kevlar fiber reinforced polyimide composites.

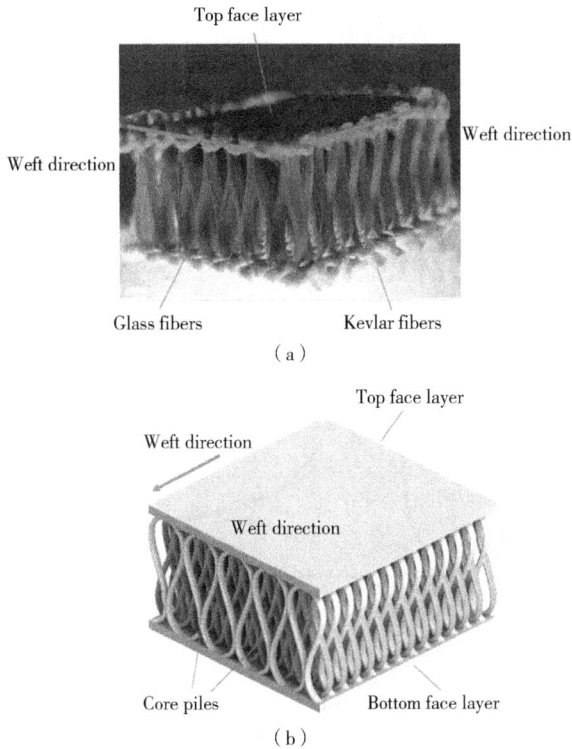

Fig. 1　The physical (a) and schematic (b) structure of three-dimensional spacer composites

In this paper, Kevlar-129 fiber as the main raw material, the preparation process and compress properties of three-dimensional woven spacer Kevlar fiber reinforced polyimide composites was explored, and the properties of thermal insulation between the composites and the foam material was studied and compared.

2　Experiments

2.1　Materials

Fig. 2 shows the main steps of the preparation process of the K/PICs. The selected aramid fiber, Kevlar-129 fiber (Type964c) was provided by DuPont Co, Ltd. The 3D spacer fabrics were woven by a 3D weaving loom. Kevlar-129 fibers were adopted as the warp and weft yarn to weave its top and bottom fabric face sheets. E-glass fibers (EDR13-300-386) were adopted as pile yarns. E-glass fibers were supplied by CHINA JUSHI

Co., Ltd. By hand paste method, the prepared PAA solution was added to the surface of aramid fabric through dropper, After the infiltration is complete, the PAA was heated through controlling the temperature gradient to obtain the composite material.

Fig. 2　Preparation and process of the composites

2.2　Methods

2.2.1　Fouriertransform Infrared Spectroscopy (FT-IR)

In order to determine the formation of PI at the set temperature, FT-IR was also carried out using a Perkin-Elmer FT-IR (Spectrum100, Waltham, MA, USA) over the range of $400 \sim 4000 cm^{-1}$. To observe whether PI is bonded on the surface of aramid fiber.

2.2.2　Compression Performance of the Composites

The composite material was cut into 40mm×40mm samples according to GB 1448—2005, and the compression performance was tested on XS(082) strength test machine. The compression results are analyzed.

2.2.3　Thermal Properties Analysis

Thermal properties of composite materials were tested by infrared thermal imager(Fotric, model 225, ZXF Laboratories), and compared with PE foam in the same shape.

3　Results and Discussions

3.1　FT-IR

Fig. 4 shows the results of the FT-IR spectra of 4000−

400cm^{-1} in the pure Kevlar yarn and the yarn from the K/PICs, respectively. FTIR spectrographs of Kevlar fiber exhibited a sharp absorption peak at 3316cm^{-1} due to hydrogen-bonded N—H groups. The absorption band of Kevlar fiber at $1,700 \text{cm}^{-1}$ is relatively strong, and the vibration absorption peak at $1,640 \text{cm}^{-1}$ is the stretching vibration characteristic absorption of C=O of Kevlar fiber. For the FTIR spectrographs of K/PICs, the peak of 1776cm^{-1} (carbonyl, C=O), 1710cm^{-1} (C=O) and 1370cm^{-1} (C—N—C) indicate the existence of imide ring structure. From the comparison of the two different yarns, there were big differences could be found in FTIR spectrographs meaning that PI has formed on the fabric surface. In addition, the peaks at 2930cm^{-1} may indicate that a few PAA were not fully converted to PI.

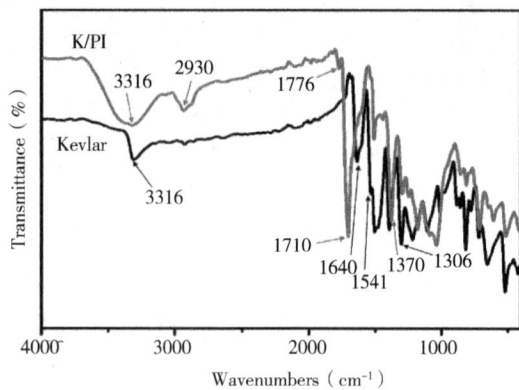

Fig. 3　FT-IR spectra of Kevlar and KF/PI composites

3.2　Compress Properties

The sample was cut into the size to be compressed according to the standard requirements. Fig. 4 (a) is the volume density of the sample to be tested. It can be seen that among the materials of the same volume, this composite material has the characteristics of light weight. The compression performance of the sample was tested on Xusai strength tester, and the results are shown in Fig. 4 (b). It can be found that when the strain is around 6%, the stress reaches a peak of 520kPa. The elastic buckling of the material occurs before the elastic deformation of the structure reaches the peak load. After the buckling failure, the load will suddenly drop, followed by a longer deformation platform and the curve remains flat and parallel to the deforma-

tion axis.

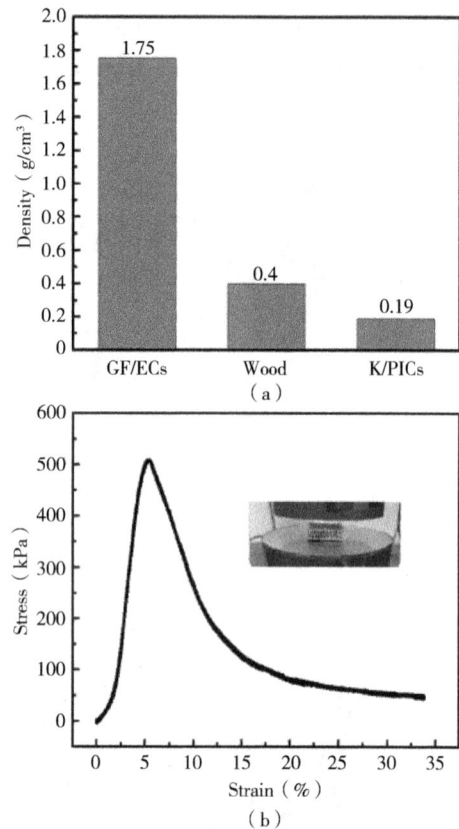

Fig. 4　(a) Density contrast of three different materials; (b) Compressive stress-stain curve of K/PICs

3.3　Failure Mechanisms

Through compression test, it can be seen that the composite has certain mechanical properties. The damaged specimen was observed under XK-ST900 Continuous Variable Ploidy Microscope (XK-ST900 CVPM). In the compression test, pile yarns is the main part to bear the load in the compression process. As shown in Fig. 5, (b) is the view of pile yarns in weft direction and (d) is the view of pile yarns in warp direction under XK-ST900 CVPM. It can be found that after compression the core yarns were not broken, but became relatively fluffy. When observed under higher magnification, it can be found that the resin and the yarn were separated, the binding of the resin on the yarns were weakened, and the single fiber in the core yarn was separated from each other. The pile yarns cannot bear the pressure at the same time, resulting in the decrease of the overall compressive strength.

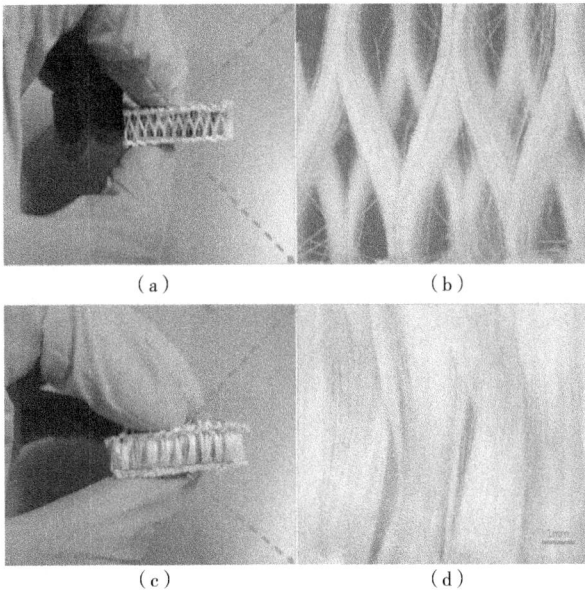

Fig. 5 Microscopic view of section of specimen after compression failure

3.4 Thermal Insulation Properties

The heat insulation performance of the material was tested in the environment where the temperature of the heat source is maintained at 100℃, and the results were shown in Fig. 6. It can be seen from the figure that the surface temperature of the material was basically maintained at (54±1)℃ when the stable state was reached, and the heat insulation degree was close to 50%, which was lower than (62±2)℃ of the foam material. It can be concluded that the heat insulation performance of the composite material is superior than that of the foam material under the same conditions.

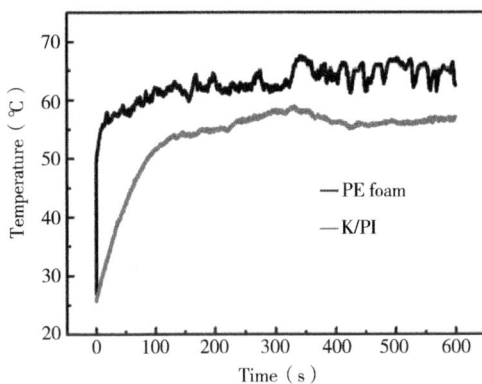

Fig. 6 Thermal insulation properties of K/PICs

4　Conclusions

In this paper, the preparation of three-dimensional woven spacer Kevlar reinforced polyimide composites has been realized. The compressive mechanical properties of the material were studied, when the strain was around 6%, the stress reached a peak of 520kPa. By comparing and analyzing the heat insulation performance of material and foam, it was found that the material has better thermal insulation performance, which provides a new method for manufacturing this thermal insulation material with the special structure.

Acknowledgements

This work was financially supported by Shanghai Natural Science Foundation (Grant No. 12ZR1440500), and Specialized Research Fund for the Doctoral Program of Higher Education of China (Grant No. 20120075120016). This work was also funded by the State Key Laboratory for Modification of Chemical Fibers and Polymer Materials, Donghua University and the Fundamental Research Funds for the Central Universities.

References

[1] LI M, WANG S, ZHANG Z, et al. Effect of structure on the mechanical behaviors of three-dimensional spacer fabric composites[J]. Applied Composite Materials, 2008, 16(1): 1-14.

[2] LI D S, ZHAO C Q, JIANG L, et al. Experimental study on the bending properties and failure mechanism of 3D integrated woven spacer composites at room and cryogenic temperature[J]. Composite Structures, 2014, 111:56-65.

[3] LI D S, ZHAO C Q, JIANG N, et al. Fabrication, properties and failure of 3D integrated woven spacer composites with thickened face sheets[J]. Materials Letters, 2015, 148:103-105.

[4] NEJE G, BEHERA B K. Investigation of mechanical performance of 3D woven spacer sandwich composites with different cell geometries[J]. Composites Part B: Engineering, 2019, 160:306-314.

[5] BISWAS K, DESJARLAIS A, SMITH D, et al. Development and thermal performance verification of composite insulation boards containing foam-encapsulated vacuum insulation panels[J]. Applied Energy, 2018, 228:1159-1172.

[6] DI X, GAO Y, BAO C, et al. Thermal insulation property and service life of vacuum insulation panels with glass fiber chopped

strand as core materials[J]. Energy and Buildings, 2014, 73: 176-183.

[7] WANG Y, CHEN Z, YU S, et al. Improved sandwich struc-tured ceramic matrix composites with excellent thermal insula-tion[J]. Composites Part B: Engineering, 2017, 129:180-186.

An Experimental Investigation of Modified Kevlar Plain Weave on the Ballistic Performance

SAID Yehia[1], HASSAN Omar[1], MORSI Loaa[1], ZHOU Yi[1]*

[1] Key Laboratory of Textile Fiber & Product (Wuhan Textile University), Ministry of Education, Wuhan, 430200, China

* Corresponding author's email: yi. zhou@ wtu. edu. cn

Abstract: Yarn to yarn sliding force plays a vital role in absorbing impact energy for plain fabrics. This paper reports the methods and results of an investigation on the mechanisms that enable higher yarn pull-out force of woven fabrics with the incorporation of knits. The experimental results suggested that the insertion of single jersey and angle-interlock knitted structures on plain weave gives an approximately 200% increase in junction rupture force over the original plain construction. With rib knitted structures inserted, the structure-modified fabrics showed a junction rupture force up to over 15 times higher than simple plain weave. It was even found that the yarns failed rather than pulled out in multiple yarn pull-out tests. This is because knitted structures tend to become self-locked and consequently restrict yarn displacement when subjected to external loading. The ballistic tests were performed using a gas gun. The gas gun propels a spherical projectile at impact velocities from 0 to 170m/s; the loss of the projectile kinetic energy was used to characterize the performance of each sample target. It was found that plain weave with single jersey insertions absorbs around 22% more energy than plain weave. The insertion of the rib knitted structure leads to an increase of 44. 8% in the loss of projectile kinetic energy. The improvement in ballistic protection of the structure modified plain weave allows less material to be used without using any chemical treatment, leading to lighter and softer anti-ballistic liner.

Keywords: Ballistic; Pull-Out; Kevlar; Knitted structure

1 Introduction

Rapid developments of weapons manufacturing increase the danger of law enforcement personnel day by day, Soft body armors have been used for protection without obstructing their body movement freedom during various situations[1]. Usually, it is made from highperformance textile fibers in different fabric formation construction. Recently, many developments were continued to improve body armor. New materials were developed, which are lighter, more flexible and give particular protection against attacks. Dupont's Kevlar© is a polymer of amides which is used in ballistic applications due to its high strength to weight ratio. Flexible, woven fabrics are used for ballistic protection in body armor. These fabrics defeat the projectile through a combination of mechanisms, including yarn uncrimping, stretching,

breakage, and pull-out from the fabric[2-3]. Plain and basket weave show higher resistance more than twill and satin weaves because of its low rigidity and the uneven distribution of the weaving points. As the more even weaving points are the higher resistance is, so plain weave shows the best results for the woven fabric. At high velocities, ballistic damage in fabric armor occurs through localized fabric loading and yarn uncrimping, followed by fiber plastic deformation and fracture[4, 8]. At lower velocities, however, fabric damage occurring by yarn un crimping and translation[4, 8], which we can refer to the yarn pull-out. So, the pullout test can be considered as a premature indication of the fabric performance, the higher the pullout result, the higher ballistic resistance. The force required to pull the yarn from the fabric structure was the sum of the frictional forces between the yarn sets at all intersecting points[1]. NILA-

KANTAN et al discovered that during impacting the main energy dissipating mechanisms are the pull-out and yarn sliding forces[5]. So we can consider it as beside ballistic performance dependence on material properties such as elastic modulus, yarn linear density, fabric's thread density or the yarn strength itself, it also depends on the fabric yarn to yarn sliding friction force, but according to a previous study, the excessive inter-yarn friction could lead to premature yarn rupture during impacting and eventually reduce the energyabsorbing ability of the fabric[6-7]. The importance of yarn pull-out mechanisms can also be inferred by studies on surface modifications to ballistic fabrics. The working principle is to change yarn crimp in a plain fabric so that the gripping force is increased. Some researchers inserted leno structures into the plain weave so that only a small section of yarn path is undulated. Leno weaves, which are also called cross weaves, are open fabrics with warp and weft threads crossing with two adjacent warp yarns crossing over each other and wrapping around a weft yarn. Plain weave with leno-weave fabrics were tested and results showed higher results of the pullout test by about 30% than normal plain weave, and according to results, more designs were inserted to the woven fabrics. the main aim of this research is to increase the pull-out and ballistic resistance of plain weave fabric by the insertion of knitted structures such as single jersey, rip and angle-interlock with the sacrificing of fabric appearance or evenness, in order to increase the crimp of the weft yarns which leads to more energy absorption. Tests were done to prove that there is an improvement compared to the neat plain weave.

2 Fabric Design

As mentioned before that some researchers inserted leno structures into the Plain weave to improve its properties, the results for the pullout test were higher than in case of normal neat fabric, but it was not higher enough to provides significant results. There the idea of adding more structures into the fabric in order to increase the yarn crimp by special weaving techniques, which led to the combining between the woven and knitted designs. Plain weave structure with a density of 7 picks and

ends/cm is manufactured using Kevlar 29 with a 1500 D linear density and with a weight of the fabrics varies from $250-270g/m^2$ is used for the armor's vests as, the tighter the structure is, the higher resistance the fabric is, plain weave structure fabrics were manufactured on a retrofitted semi-automatic sampling loom with the usage of needles to insert the knitted structures in order to increase the yarn crimp. Three knitted structures were inserted, single jersey, rib, and interlock into the plain weave in a form of a line or two lines with a distance of 9cm in between as illustrated in Fig. 1.

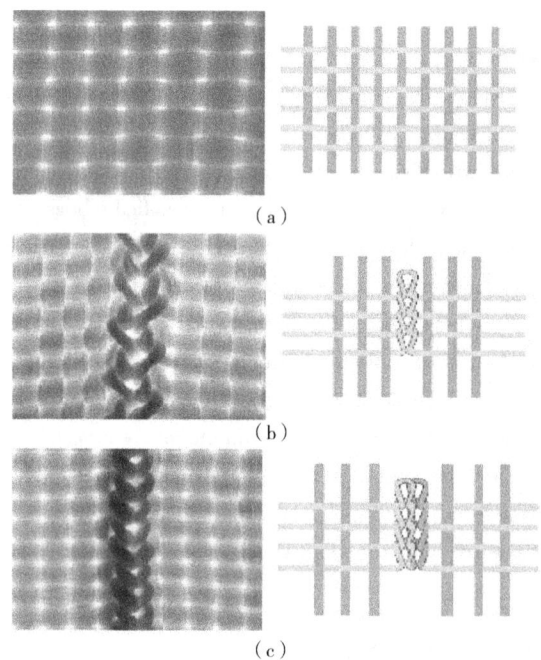

Fig. 1 Optical micrographs of (a) Plain weave; (b) Plain weave with one wale of single jersey knitted structure on the warp direction; (c) Plain weave with rib knitted structure on the warp direction

Tab. 1 Sample descriptions

Samples	Description
PW	Plain weave
PWSJ	Plain weave with one wale of single jersey knitted structure on the warp direction
PWR	Plain weave with rib knitted structure in the warp direction
PWI	Plain weave with one wale of interlock knitted structure on the warp direction

The mechanism of single jersey loops' structure was done from the technical back and towards the technical face side of the fabric with one needle, rib structure with the use of two needles to draw two loops face and back in an alternatively sequence in the same wale, and finally interlock structure derived from the rib structure by the use of two needles but in two neighbored wales. Yarns are gripped and intermeshed together in order to provide highly crimped path referred to the loop.

3 Experimental Setup

3.1 Yarn Pull-Out Test

Pull-out test for Kevlar yarns was undergone to regulate the impact of the modifications inserted to the plain weave and their effect on the pull-out force and to determine the increase on the yarn gripping force. The testing machine for the pull-out test was "YG028 Universal testing machine" with a load of 500N. Samples' size was $(60\times120)mm^2$, and yarn's tails were left from both the top and bottom sides. A small slot was left in the bottom jaw for the yarn to be pulled from the bottom while other tails were clamped in the bottom jaw. The upper jaw grips the selected weft yarn and moves at a constant rate of 250mm/min.

3.2 Fabric Ballistic Test

3.2.1 The Penetration Test

When the bullet is fired, if it fully or partially passes the armor it is called penetration. A projectile with weight of 2 grams, with a spherical shaped diameter of 8mm shot by a gas gun with an initial velocity 0 to maximum velocity of 170m/s was used to measure the ability of the fabric to absorb the impact energy of the projectile as a simulation to real life bullet shooting.

4 Results and Discussions

4.1 Yarn Pull-Out

4.1.1 Single Yarn Pull-Out

When yarn is pulled, yarn tension will reach a value called the junction rupture force (JRF) or peak load force[1, 16-17], which determines the amount of projectile kinetic energy dissipated by frictional interaction during a ballistic event. The gradient before the JRF depends on the fabric extent in plain deformation and yarn uncrimping. The JRF value depends on such factors as

yarn count, fabric density, yarn to yarn friction, pull-out rate, and clamping condition. The greater the force more than the JRF causes the yarns to slip and the curve becomes oscillatory, which is described as yarn stick-slip. Fig. 2. shows an exemplary load-displacement curve from a single yarn pull-out test performed on Kevlar PW.

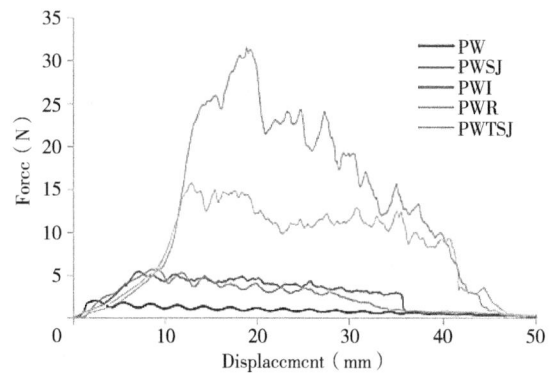

Fig. 2 The load-displacement curve of single-yarn pull-out on PW and PW with the knitted insertions

By studying the knitted loop shape, the intermeshing is formed by entangling the heads and feet on consecutive loops, creating four pairs of contact. When the loop-forming yarn is stretched, the normal components of the interactive force between the legs and feet are increased, thus, increasing the friction between them. In comparison to the single areas of friction points in case of the woven fabrics, the fabrics with knitted structures insertions have a greater ability to resist the yarn pull-out upon impact. One wale of single jersey, interlock structures, and rib structure were investigated in comparison with PW. Results showed that the deformation and the tightness occurring during yarn stretching causes compressing in the top and bottom pairs of the loop which greatly increases the interactive force between the head and feet, which leads to more resistance to the pull-out force. As shown in Fig. 2 and Fig. 3 the insertion of single jersey and angle-interlock knitted structures on plain weave gives an approximately 200% increase in junction rupture force over the original plain construction, When the loading force is applied on the inclined loops of PWR, its overlapping profile produces a resistant force against yarn pull-out up to over 15 times higher than simple plain weave.

4.1.2 Multiple Yarn Pull-Out

Upon projectile impacting, the force of the projectile often distributed on more than one yarn depend on projectile size and load, causing multiple yarns to be pulled-out. As shown in Fig. 3 the values of the JRF for double, triple, and quadruple on the plain weave yarn pull-out are around 260%, 389% and 489% that of single yarn pull-out, as the friction will be distributed between many yarns and the uncrimping between more warps and wefts will be more difficult to be achieved which also gave same effect with the modified knitted structures.

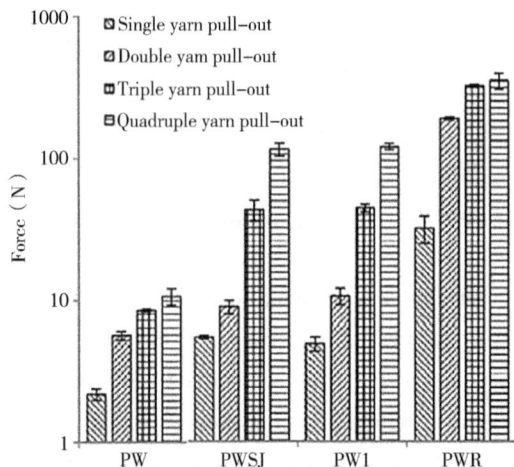

Fig. 3 Junction rupture force (JRF) of yarn pull-out tests for plain weave (PW) and structure modified fabrics.

4.2 Ballistic Test

4.2.1 Energy Loss

The samples were clamped and shot by a projectile in the center of the sample. Impact and residual velocities of each sample were measured and by calculating the difference between the two velocities we get the amount of energy absorbed by the fabric samples during the ballistic test as shown in Fig. 3.

Results show that the plain weave with single jersey insertions absorbs around 22% more energy than plain weave, while the insertion of the rib knitted structure leads to an increase of 44.8% in the loss of projectile kinetic energy. But the more wales inserted in the structure the less energy absorbance happen, which can be explained as with increasing the number of knitted

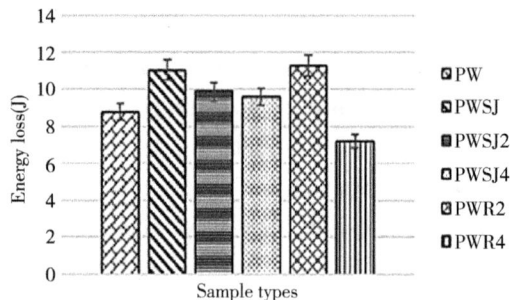

Fig. 4 An average energy loss of different types of fabrics

structure inserted wales, an increases in the ability to resist the projectile during impacting but with an excessive tightness which prevents the yarn elongation leads to quick yarn failure, hence less energy will be absorbed.

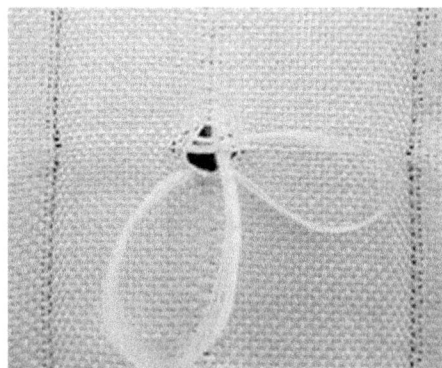

Fig. 5 Ballistic impacted fabric and windowing effect on PWSJ2

5 Conclusions

The aim of this research is to investigate the influence of the ballistic performance of different insertions of knitted structures on the Kevlar© plain weave. single yarn pull-out test showed an increase in the force required by up to 200% with the insertion of the single jersey, and interlock structures, while it showed an increase of 15 times more with the insertion of the rip structure more than the normal plain weave. This proves the theory that upon insertion of knitted structures to woven fabrics, the loop undergoes stretching upon impact and consequently deformation of the loop structure rather than the slippage of the yarn from the fabric and thus locking the yarn in the fabric and thus improving the resistivity of the fabric to resist yarn pull-out. with the consideration that the pull-out test is a premature indication of the fabric ballistic performance[10] , interlock knitted structure gave almost the same pull-out result as single jersey knitted structure, so ballistic tests were performed on the single jersey and rip structures only. The ballistic test was performed, the penetration test results showed an increase in the energy absorbed by structure samples of the single jersey insertions by around 22%, while the insertion of the rib knitted structure showed an increase of 44. 8% energy absorbance more than plain weave, because of the inclined appearance of the rip structure formed by two alternative loops back and face that allow more resistance to pullet impacting compared to the face loop of the single jersey structure. It can be concluded from this investigation that the ballistic resistance ability of a plain fabric could be greatly improved by inserting knitted structures, indicating the possibility of further exploring the potential of textile-based technologies for ballistic protection lighter, flexible, and without using any chemical treatments providing alternatives for the engineering design of soft body armor.

References

[1] KEITH M K, JOHN E K, et al. Yarn pull-out as a mechanism for dissipating ballistic impact energy in kevlar & reg; KM-2 pabric part I: quasi-static characterization of yarn pull-out[J]. Textile Research Journal, 2004, 74 (10), 920–928.

[2] CARR D J, Failure mechanisms of yams subjected to ballistic impact[J]. J. Mater. Sci, 1999, 18, 585–588.

[3] JACOB M J, Van D, J L, et al. Ballistic protection mechanisms in personal armor [J], J. Mater. Sci, 2001, 36, 3137–3142.

[4] CHEESMAN B A, Bogetti T A, et al. Ballistic impact into fabric and compliant composite laminates[J]. Comp. Struct, 2003, 61, 161–173.

[5] NILAKANTAN G, MERRILL R L, KEEFE M. Experimental investigation of the role of frictional yarn pull-out and windowing on the probabilistic impact response of Kevlar fabrics [J]. Composites, Part B, 2015, 68: 215–229.

[6] TAN V B C, SHIM V P, ZENG S X. Modeling crimp in woven fabrics subjected to ballistic impact[J]. Int J Impact Eng, 2005, 32: 561–574.

[7] ZENG S X, TAN V B C, SHIM V P W. Modeling inter-yarn friction in woven fabric armor[J]. Int J Numer Meth Eng, 2005, 66: 1309–1330.

[8] SHIM V, TAN V, TAY T E, et al. Modeling deformation and damage characteristics of woven fabric under small projectile impact[J]. Int. J. Impact Eng, 1995, 16, 585–605.

Characterization of New Natural Cellulosic Fiber from Ethiopian Yucca Elephantine Plant Leaves

AKLILU Azanaw[1], ADANE Haile[1], ROTICH K. Gideon[1]*

[1] *Department of Textile Chemistry, Ethiopian Institute of Textile and Fashion Technology, Bahir Dar University, 1037, Bahir Dar, Ethiopia*

* *Corresponding author's email*: rotichgideon2016@ gmail. com

Abstract: Natural fibers are increasingly being used because of ecological concerns of man-made fibers. Cotton is leading the way for the most frequently utilized natural fiber trailed by leaf fibers as sisal and bast fibers as jute and flax. These alternative natural fibers are an essential source of fibers which could be used in industrial textiles. The aim of the current work was to extract and evaluate fibers from Ethiopian Yucca elephantine plant leaves. The fibers were extracted by two methods: water retting and chemically using sodium hydroxide (NaOH). The extracted fibers were evaluated for their breaking strength, breaking elongation, fineness, diameter and their moisture content. The functional groups of the fibers were checked with FTIR while its thermal properties were evaluated by TGA. It was observed that the extracted fibers had tensile strength of 5.7cN/tex (water retted) and 7.55cN/tex (3% NaOH extracted) similar with hemp and sisal fibers. Thermal analysis showed that the fiber is stable up to 290℃.

Keywords: Cellulosic fibers; Fiber retting; Chemical extraction; Fiber physical properties

1 Introduction

Natural cellulosic fibers are increasingly being used for technical textiles due to their advantages of being a renewable natural resource, biodegradable, low cost, good specific physical properties and low density[1-4]. There exist a wide variety of wild plants that can be used as a source of cellulosic fibers. One of the potential source of strong natural fiber is Yucca elephantine plant leaves as shown in Fig. 1.

Fig. 1　Yucca elephantine plant

Fiber extraction from cellulosic sources can be done mechanically, with water retting[5], alkaline extraction or with acid extraction[6-8]. The extraction process has major impact on the final product quality[9]. Alkali treatment leads to fibrillation causing break down of the composite fiber bundle into smaller fibers, which means that this treatment reduces the fiber diameter[10]. Once the non-cellulosic parts have been decomposed, the fibers are washed and subjected to mechanical combing process which removes the broken down soft tissues followed by drying to obtain the fibers[11].

The aim of this study was to extract and characterize cellulosic fibers from Yucca elephantine plant leaves using water retting and chemically using NaOH. The extracted fibers were characterized on their breaking tensile strength, breaking elongation, fineness, diameter and their moisture contents. Thermal analysis were also used to characterize the extracted fibers.

2 Materials and Methods

2.1 Materials

Yucca elephantine plant leaves were harvested from rural areas in Ethiopia. The removal of non-fiber contents from the leaves was done by both chemical (NaOH) and water retting methods. The chemicals used were of analytical grade.

2. 2 Methods

2. 2. 1 Water Retting

Water retting process was conducted by placing the raw leaves in water at room temperature for 26 days in abarrel[12] during retting, the pectinolytic microorganism present in water broke down the non-fiber material thus loosening the fibers[13-14]. Untreated river water was used because of the presence of these microorganisms. The fibers were then washed in plenty of water to remove the remaining green slime residue. Subsequent separation of fibers was done by employing a traditional combing process with the aid of fine, long metal wire comb.

2. 2. 2 Chemical Extraction

NaOH was used in fiber extraction to dissolve the lignocellulose material between fibers and separate structural linkages between lignin and cellulose. This method is frequently utilized for obtaining cellulosic fibers by extraction and isolation of the fiber bundles with elimination of non-cellulosic compounds[15-17]. Different concentrations of NaOH (3%, 5%, 10%) at boiling temperature and MLR of 1 : 20 were used for the extraction for 2h[15]. The fibers were washed with excess water to ensure the remaining NaOH was totally removed. This was followed by fiber individualization by combing process and removal of the digested non-fiber parts after which the fibers were dried and characterized.

2. 3 Fiber Characterization

The physical properties of fibers extracted from Yucca elephantine plant leaves were investigated for their potential as a new source of textile fibers. The following tests were carried out.

2. 3. 1 Fiber Diameter and Microscopic Structure

Leica biological microscope model 2086C was used to establish the structure and the diameter of the extracted fibers. The sample was prepared and the procedures were done in line with the ASTM D76 standard test method.

2. 3. 2 Fineness

Fiber fineness was evaluated according to ASTM D1577-

07(2012) standard. The length of the extracted fibers was measured and the fibers weighed on an electronic balance before their fineness calculated using equation (1) and reported in form tex.

$$Fineness(\text{Tex}) = \frac{Mass(\text{g})}{Length(\text{m})} \qquad (1)$$

(1) Tensile Strength of Fibers

The tensile strength test was carried out using KBS single fiber strength tester as per the ES ISO 5079 standard method. Throughout testing, the gauge length was set at 25mm and the test performed at a constant speed of 75mm/min. The test was done in standard condition of 21℃ and R. H. of 65%.

(2) Fiber Length

The length of the extracted fibers from the two extraction methods was measured. To determine the fiber length, 20 sample fibers were taken from the extracted fiber for each type. The fiber length was measured by ruler and the average reported.

(3) Moisture Content

The moisture content of the samples was determined by drying the fibers in an oven at 105℃ for 4h before weighing them on an electronic weighing balance. The percentage of moisture presence per unit weight of each extracted fiber was evaluated.

(4) Thermal Analysis

Perkin Elmer TGA 4000 model was utilized to analyze the thermal properties of the extracted fibers. The tests were conducted in line with the machine guidebook and 2g of the fiber was taken for measurement.

3　Results and Discussions

3. 1　Fiber Diameter

Fiber diameter was evaluated using an electron microscope. Fig. 2 shows the diameters of the extracted fibers. The water retted fiber had a diameter of 242μm which was lower than 3% NaOH extracted fibers (397μm). This shows that microorganism in water was more efficient in digesting the fiber constituents than the 3% NaOH thus lower diameter. The chemically extracted fibers had varying diameter depending on the concentration of the NaOH used. As the concentration of alkaline increased, the diameter of the extracted fiber decreased as observed in Fig. 3. This could be attributed to the fact that at higher concentration, the alkaline digested the non-fiber contents more effectively thus reducing the fiber diameter[17].

Fig. 3 shows the micro structure of the extracted fibers. The fibers were generally uniform and of equal diameter from end to end. This uniformity is an important aspect especially for fiber spinning quality and its flexibility.

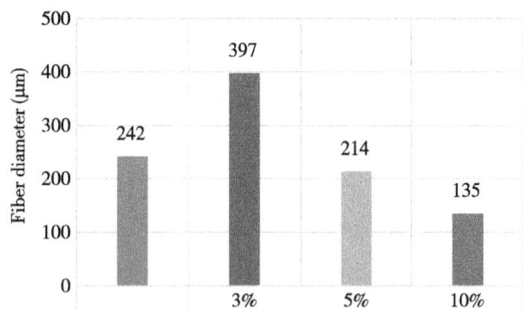

Fig. 2　Fiber diameter

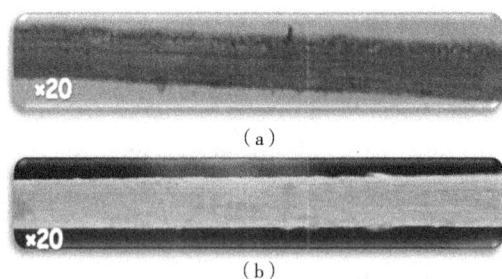

(a)

(b)

Fig. 3　Microscopic structure: (a) Water retted and (b) NaOH extracted fiber

3. 2　Fineness

The linear density of the fiber was calculated in terms of tex units. As seen from Fig. 4, water retted fibers had a fineness of 5 tex while for NaOH extracted fibers, the fineness varied depending on the concentration used. As the NaOH concentration increased from 3% to 10%, the fiber fineness decreased from 5. 96 tex to 4. 2 tex as shown in Fig. 4. This could be attributed to efficient removal of non-fiber content by higher concentration of alkali.

3. 3　Tensile Strength and Elongation

Fig. 5 shows the strength and elongation of the extracted fibers. The 3% NaOH extracted fibers had higher fiber strength than water retted fiber but for elongation it was

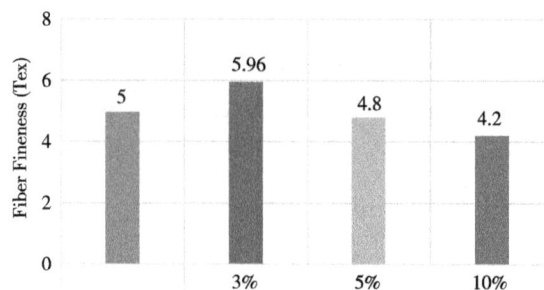

Fig. 4　Fiber fineness of the extracted fibers

vice-verse. It can also be seen that increasing the concentration of NaOH caused a decrease in tensile strength while elongation increased. This could be as a result of increased removal of non-fiber parts reducing the load bearing capacity of the fiber but increasing the fiber elasticity.

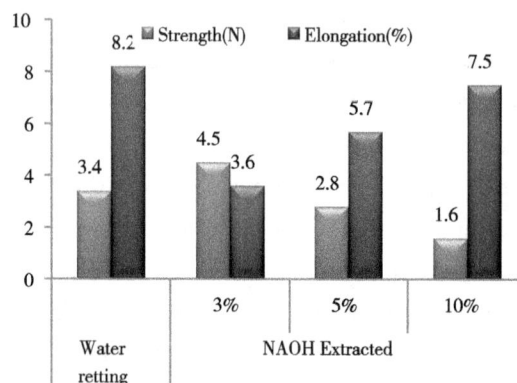

Fig. 5　Tensile strength and elongation of extracted fibers

Tab. 1 shows the comparison of tenacity of the extracted fibers with other natural fibers. It can be seen that the strength of the extracted fibers are comparable with already established natural fibers like hemp (strength 4−7cN/dtex). The elongation of the extracted fibers was on the higher side when compared with already established natural leaf fibers.

3. 4　Fiber Length

Length is the most important fiber property that determines its quality and spinning ability. The average length of the extracted fibers was 98. 5cm and was not affected by the extraction method used. The length of the fiber was basically determined by the length of the raw leaves which means that the longer the leaves, the longer the fibers extracted.

3.5　Moisture Content and Moisture Regain

Moisture content of lignocellulosic fibers relies on a number of factors, such as composition, age and climatic conditions for growth of the parent plant[18]. The moisture content and regain of the extracted fibers were evaluated and the results are shown in Fig. 6.

Tab. 1　Comparison of tensile strength[19]

Natural fibers	Tenacity (cN/dtex)	Elongation (%)
Yucca elephantine fibers		
Water retted fibers	5.7	8.2
3% NaOH	7.55	3.6
5% NaOH	4.7	5.7
10% NaOH	3.8	7.5
Other natural fibers		
Ramie	10	2
Jute	2.5	1.8
Hemp	4–7	1.6
Sisal	3.6–4.5	2–3
Kenaf (bast)	2	2.7–6.9
Coir	1	30
Flax	2.3–2.4	1.2–1.6

As seen from Fig. 6, the water retted fibers had the highest moisture content and regain as compared to the chemically extracted fibers. For the chemically extracted fibers, as the concentration of the NaOH increased, the moisture content and regain on the extracted fibers decreased.

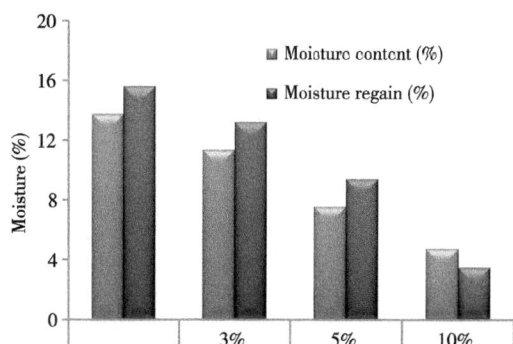

Fig. 6　Moisture content and regain of extracted fibers

3.7　Thermal Analysis of Extracted Fibers

The thermal analysis was carried out on a TGA machine and the resulting curve is shown in Fig. 7. Initial degradation of the extracted fibers started at 110℃ which resulted in a weight loss which is presumably due to the vaporization of water in the fiber. The water retted fibers had the highest initial loss in weight due to its method of extraction. It can also be seen that the thermal degradation of the extracted fibers started at around 290℃ typical of all the natural cellulosic fibers and ended at about 350℃. Overall, the water retted fibers had the highest weight loss of about 70%. For chemically extracted fibers, the loss was dependent on the concentration used. As the NaOH concentration increased, the weight loss reduced and the onset degradation temperature increased. This could be attributed to the elimination of non-fiber parts by high concentration NaOH.

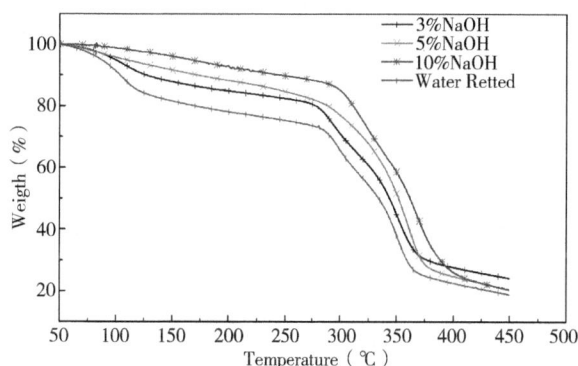

Fig. 7　Thermal analysis of the extracted fiber

4　Conclusions

In this study, cellulosic fiber was extracted from Yucca elephantine plant leaves by using both water retting and chemical extraction methods. From the results, the extracted fibers had good tensile strength of 5.7cN/tex (water retted) and 7.55cN/tex (3% NaOH extracted). Thermal analysis showed that the extracted fibers start to degrade at a temperature of 290℃ thus can be used below this temperature. With higher strength, cost-effective and renewable source, the extracted fiber can be used to make technical textile products like packaging material (bags), carpet backing, ropes, yarns and composite reinforcement.

Acknowledgements

This work was supported by Ethiopian institute of textile and fashion technology (EITEX).

References

[1]SAMRAT Mukhopadhyay,YUSU Arpac,Ulkusendurk. Banana fibers-variability and fracture behavior[J]. Journal of Engineered Fibres and Fabrics, 2008. 3(2):39-45.

[2] FORTUNATIE, PUGLIA D, Monti M, ETAL. Cellulose nanocrystals extracted from okra fibers in pva nano composites[J]. Journal of Applied Polymer Science, 2013. 128 (5).

[3]MOHAMMED L, et al. A review on natural fiber reinforced polymer composite and its applications [J]. International Journal of Polymer Science, 2015. 2015:1-15.

[4]SENTHIIL P V,AKASH Sirsshti. Studies on material and mechanical properties of natural fiber reinforced composites [J]. International Journal of Engineering and Science, 2014,3(11): 18-27.

[5]SARAVANAKUMAR S S, et al. Characterization of a novel natural cellulosic fiber from prosopis juliflora bark[J]. Carbohydrate Polymers, 2013, 92. 1928-1933.

[6]AZANAW A, et al. , Extraction and characterization of natural cellulosic fibers from carissa edulise plant stems[J]. International Research Journal of Advanced Engineering and Science, 2018. 3(1):49-52.

[7] ASHISH A H, PRADYUMKUMAR V K, POOJA M K. Green fibre-agave americana[J]. Journal of Basic and Applied Engineering Research, 2015, 2(1):1-6.

[8]DESALEGN A, ROTICH K G. Extraction and characterization of Ethiopian palm leaf fibers [J]. Research Journal of Textile and Apparel,2018, 22(1): 15-25.

[9]MSAHIL S, SAKLI F, DREAN J. Study of textile potential of fibres extracted from Tunisian Agave Americana L[J]. AUTEX Research Journal, 2006, 6(1): 9-13.

[10]HULLE A, KADOLE P, KATKAR P. Agave Americana leaf fibers[J]. Fibers, 2015. 3(1):64-75.

[11]MOHANTY A K, MISRA M, DRZAL L T. Surface modifications of natural fibers and performance of the resulting biocomposites: an overview [J]. Composite Interfaces, 2001,8(5):313-343.

[12]FIORE V, VALENZA A, DI Bella G. Artichoke (Cynara cardunculus L.) fibres as potential reinforcement of composite structures[J]. Composites Science and Technology, 2011, 71(8):1138-1144.

[13]TAMBURINI E, et al. Characterization of bacterial pectinolytic strains involved in the water retting process[J]. Environmental Microbiology, 2003. 5(9):730-736.

[14]DI C M, et al. Effects of selected pectinolytic bacterial strains on water-retting of hemp and fibre properties[J]. Journal of Applied Microbiology, 2010. 108(1):194-203.

[15]NAILI H, et al. Extraction process optimization of Juncus plant fibers for its use in a green composite[J]. Industrial Crops and Products, 2017. 107:172-183.

[16]FIORE V, SCALICI T, VALENZA A. Characterization of a new natural fiber from Arundo donax L. as potential reinforcement of polymer composites [J]. Carbohydrate Polymers, 2014, 106:77-83.

[17]BOOPATHI L, SAMPATH P S, MYLSAMY K. Investigation of physical, chemical and mechanical properties of raw and alkali treated Borassus fruit fiber[J]. Composites Part B: Engineering, 2012, 43(8): 3044-3052.

[18]AQUINO E M F, et al. Moisture effect on degradation of jute/glass hybrid composites [J]. Journal of Reinforced Plastics and Composites, 2007, 26(2): 219-223.

[19]MSAHLI S, et al. Mechanical behavior of Agave Americana L. fibres: correlation between fine structure and mechanical properties[J]. Applied Sci, 2007, 7(24):3951-3957.

Recycling of Low Density Polyethylene into Composite Reinforced with Pineapple Leaf Fibers for Wall Tile Application

NEGASI G. medhin[1], ROTICH K. Gideon[1]*

[1] Department of Textile Manufacturing, Ethiopian Institute of Textile and Fashion Technology, Bahir Dar University, 1037, Bahir Dar, Ethiopia

* Corresponding Authors e-mail: rotichgideon@ yahoo. com

Abstract: Plastic has been a dominant material for packaging in recent years but due to its non-biodegradability it is causing environmental pollution. Among the plastic used, low density polyethylene is used abundantly. This plastic can be removed from environment by recycling into useful product by reinforcing with natural fibers to manufacture composite materials. Natural fibre based composites are eco-friendly and low cost. This research aims at manufacturing a composite by reinforcing recycled low density polyethylene with pineapple leaf fibres (PALF). PALF was extracted manually and the fiber treated with 5% NaOH to improve the fiber-matrix interaction. Wall tile composites were manufactured by melt-mixing method followed by compression moulding. The effect of fiber length and fiber proportion on the composite properties were investigated using their tensile, flexural, impact and water absorption tests. The study showed that the optimum fibre proportion and fiber length for the best performance of the composite was achieved at 30% fiber weight ratio and 30mm fiber length, respectively. The maximum tensile strength of $1562N/mm^2$, flexural strength of $454.9N/mm^2$ and impact strength of $225.2J/mm^2$ were obtained. Water absorption increased with the increase in fiber proportion and fiber length, respectively.

Keywords: Pineapple leaf fibre; Low density polyethylene; Composites; Fiber treatments; Tensile strength; Flexural strength; Water absorption; Wall tiles

1 Introduction

Plastic has been a dominant material for packaging in recent past but due to its non-biodegradability it is causing environmental pollution. Among the plastic used, low density polyethylene is used abundantly. The waste plastic bottles can be burned, reused or recycled. Burning of the plastic waste produces lethal fumes whereas reuse is not an attractive alternative due to contamination. For this reasons, recycling to other products turns out to be a more attractive choice[1]. Waste plastics can also be recycled chemically in many ways such as glycolysis[2], hydrolysis, alkalosis, methanolysis, ammonolysis and aminolysis[3-4].

There is increase awareness of natural reinforced composite because of their properties of biodegradability, non-carcinogenic and being cost-effective[5-6]. Researchers are looking for new sources of composite reinforcing materials that have similar properties to synthetic fibers[7]. This is because synthetic fibres reinforced polymers are expensive and have environmental impact. Therefore, natural fibers are preferable because it's a renewable resource, thus providing a better solution of sustainable supply[8]. As a matrix material, LDPE has been extensively used with natural fiber in composite preparation. There are many plant fibres available which has potential to be applied as composite reinforcing materials such as pineapple leaf fibers, kenaf, coir, abaca, sisal, cotton, jute, bamboo, banana, palmyra, hemp and flex. Pineapple leaf fibre (PALF) is one of the waste materials in agriculture sector[9]. Pineapple leaves are considered as agricultural by-product which can be used for producing natural fibres.

This research aims at using manually extracted pineapple leaf fibers to reinforce recycled low density polyethylene (LDPE). The manufactured composite was tested for its tensile strength, flexural strength, impact resistance and water absorption.

2　Materials and Methods

Recycled low density polyethylene was sourced from Addis Ababa while urea, sodium hydroxide and hydrochloric acid were used of analytical grade. Pineapple leaf was collected from southern part of Ethiopia.

2.1　Extraction of Pineapple Leaf Fibre

The fibre was extracted from pineapple leaf using wet retting method. The pineapple leaf was immersed in urea solution for one week. The urea solution was prepared by dissolving 10g/L of urea. The fibre was removed from the pineapple leaf with blunt knife to remove the skin leaves still attached to the fiber surface. After that, the extracted fibres are washed with water and air dried for 24 hours.

2.2　Chemical Treatment of Pineapple Leaf Fiber

Prior to composite preparation, the fibre was treated with sodium hydroxide solution in order to improve the fiber-matrix interface. The fibre was treated with 5% NaOH solution for one hour at room temperature. The fibre was further dried in an air blast oven at a temperature of 60℃ and stored in a dry environment for composite preparation.

2.3　PALF-LDPE Composite Preparation

Randomly oriented pineapple fiber LDPE composites with varying fiber length and fiber volume fraction were prepared by a melt mixing process. Composite tiles of size (150×200×8) mm were prepared using a closed mold. The mold was polished with oil to avoid LDPE from sticking to it. The specimens of required dimensions were cut from the tiles, smoothed by sand paper, and used for testing as shown in Fig. 1.

Tensile testing of pineapple fibers was carried out in an Instron universal testing machine Model 1121 at a crosshead speed of 1mm/min. The diameters of the fiber specimens were measured using an optical Leica microscope.

2.4　Tests

2.4.1　Tensile Test

Tensile tests were performed on Instron 5567 at a cross

Fig. 1　Pineapple fiber reinforced low density polyethylene wall tiles

head speed of 50mm/min. The samples were prepared for this test according to ASTM D638 standard.

2.4.2　Flexural Test

The tests were done on a universal testing machine. The specimens were prepared according to ASTM D790. The specimens were tested with a support span depth ratio of 16. The specimen was then placed on two support spans fixed at 100mm.

2.4.3　Impact Test

Charpy-type impact tests on unnotched specimens were performed using a pendulum impact testing machine JBS-300N model. The test specimens were prepared according to ASTM D570 with dimension of 50mm long, and the cross-sectional area of 24mm². For evaluation of tensile, flexural, and impact properties, five specimens were tested and average values reported.

2.4.4　Water Absorption Test

Water absorption tests were carried out in accordance with ASTM D570. Samples of each composite grade were oven dried before weighing. The weight recorded was reported as the initial weight of the composites. The samples were then immersed in distilled water maintained at room temperature (25℃) for 24 hours. After the time elapsed, the samples were removed from water, pat dried and weighed. The amount of water absorbed by the composites (in percentage) was calculated using equation (1).

$$W(\%) = \frac{W_t - W_o}{W_o} \times 100 \qquad (1)$$

3　Results and Discussions

3.1　Characterization of PALF

The physical properties and mechanical properties of extracted PALF are shown in Tab. 1

Tab. 1　Physical properties of pineapple leaf fiber

No	Properties	Values
1	Average length（mm）	300. 5
2	Average diameter（μm）	59. 73
3	Moisture content（%）	10. 99
4	Tensile strength（cN/tex）	32. 679
5	Elongation at break（%）	2. 08

3.2　Tensile Strength

3.2.1　Effect of Fiber Loading on Tensile Strength

As seen from Fig. 2, tensile strength increased with the increase of fiber proportion from 10% to 30%, from 800N to 1200N, respectively. After 30% fiber loading, the strength dropped to almost the same value in 10% fibre loading. These increased of strength actually mean that the LDPE with reinforcement were becoming stiff and could withstand higher stress at the same strain portion. The fibre served as reinforcement because the major share of load has been taken up by the crystalline fibrils resulting in extension of the helically wound fibrils along with the matrix[10]. Besides, > 30% of fibre was a bit excessive that the LDPE matrix was hard enough to flow through every fibre thus leaving voids and fibres were more easily expose to environmental degradation. In practical, this composition is hard to produce and the composite is brittle. To conclude, these ultimate stresses before break basically decreased because the interfacial adhesion between fibre and LDPE was not good, fibre to fibre interaction was preferred by the system. Fibre agglomerations happened thus causing dispersion problems in LDPE, which lead to decrement in tensile strength.

3.2.2　Effect of Fiber Length on Tensile Strength

From Fig. 3 it can be observed that when the fiber length is increased from 10mm to 30mm, there is an enhancement in strength by about 14% due to the stress transfer between the matrix and fiber. When the fiber length is increased beyond 30mm, there is only a 3.4%

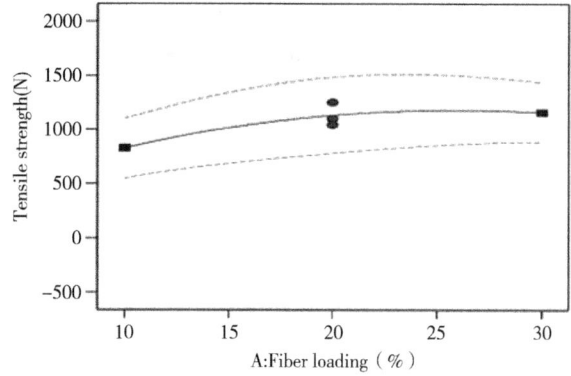

Fig. 2　Effect of fiber loading on tensile strength

increase in tensile strength and modulus wiich is almost unaffected. This indicates that the mechanical properties level off beyond 30mm fiber length. The plateauing off is associated with poor dispersion of fiber in the matrix and fiber to fiber entanglements at higher fiber length.

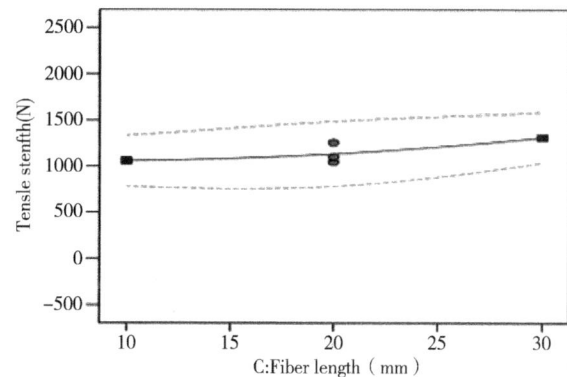

Fig. 3.　Effect of fiber length on tensile strength

3.3　Flexural Property

The Flexural strength for PALF and LDPE composite is shown in Fig 4. From this figure, the flexural strength increased gradually with fibre loading. The flexural strength of the composite increased linearly with fibre composition. Increase in fibre content from 10% to 30% increases the flexural strength by about 42%. However, further increase in fiber content above these value there is a lowering of flexural strength by about 15%. The decrease in flexural strength at higher weight percentage of fibre proportion may be due to the increased fibre-to-fibre interactions and dispersion problems[10]. PALF in a composite system will fail when the stress is initiated at the defective cells as a result of stress concentration. Consequently, the PALF can withstand bending forces which comprise of compressive forces and tensile stress.

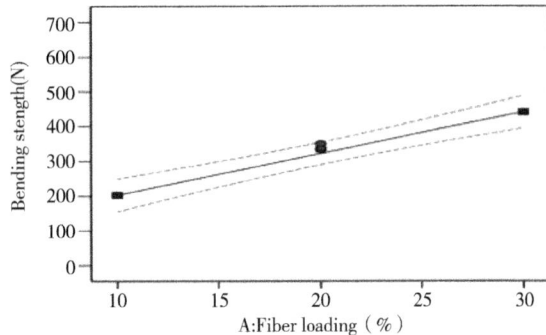

Fig. 4　Effect of fiber loading on flexural property

3.3.1　Effect of Fiber Length on Flexural Strength

The dependence of flexural properties of the composites on fiber length is shown in Fig. 5. Here, same trend of higher flexural strength is shown in 30mm fiber length when compare to the fibers which are shorter and also fibers which are above 30mm composites. The flexural strength of the PALF composites containing 30mm long fibres was 23% higher than that of PALF composites with 10mm length fibre. However, the flexural strength showed a decreasing trend for composites having a fibre length of greater than 30mm. The optimum flexural strength and modulus of the PALF composites was obtained at a fibre length of 30mm.

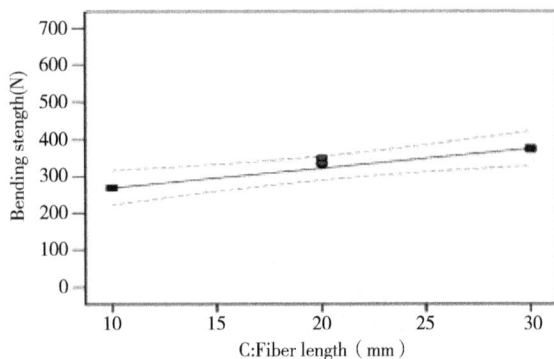

Fig. 5　Effect of fiber length on flexural strength

3.4　Impact Strength

3.4.1　Effect of Fiber Loading on Impact Strength

Fig. 6 depicts the charpy impact strength (IS) of unnotched samples of treated PALF composites. The IS increases with the amount of fibres added until a plateau is reached at 30% fibre weight. At this fibre loading (30%), the IS value is about 20% more than that of the pure LDPE as the fibre bridges crack and increases the resistance to propagation of the crack. However, at higher percentage of fibre proportion, above the optimal percentage (30%), the IS decreases by about 4% than the 30% due to the fact that the addition of more fibres creates regions of stress concentrations that require comparatively less energy to initiate a crack.

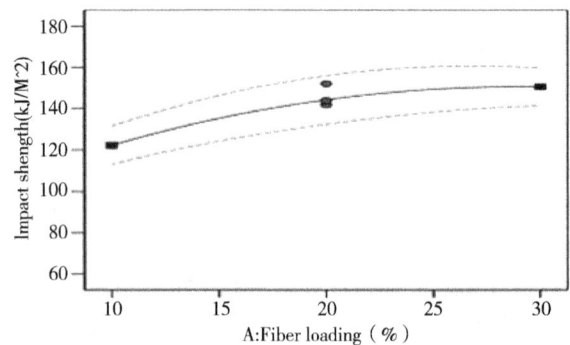

Fig. 6　Effect of fiber loading on impact strength

PIAH et al[11] reported that the energy-absorbing mechanism in the composites includes utilization of energy required to debond the fibers and pull them completely out of the matrix when there is a weak interface between fibre and matrix. In practical interest, a significant part of energy absorption during impact takes place through the fibre pull-out process.

3.4.2　Effect of Fiber Loading as a Function of Fiber Length on Impact Strength

The work of fracture (impact strength) of PALF—LDPE composites at 30% loading as a function of fiber length is shown in Fig. 7. It is seen that a comparatively higher impact strength is observed for composites of fiber length 30mm (critical fiber length).

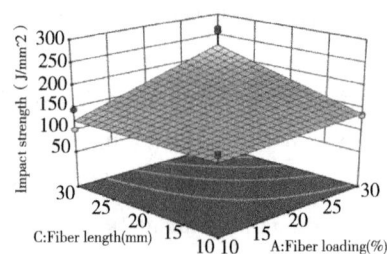

Fig. 7　Effect of fiber loading as a function of fiber length on impact strength

3.9 Water Absorption

After 24h immersion in water, there was a noticeable effect of fiber content on water absorption test results as shown in Fig. 8. The lowest water absorption rate was a-chieved at 10% fiber loading. There was only a slight reduction in the rate of water absorption when the length of the fiber was increased from 10mm to 30mm. When the volume of the fiber increased from 20% to 30%, the rate of water absorption was increased because of more lignocellulosic fibers was added in composite thus more hydrogen bonds formed between molecules of water and O-H group of the fibers. HANERr and ZAHZRI[12-13] also found that the rate of water absorption increased with increase of fiber content.

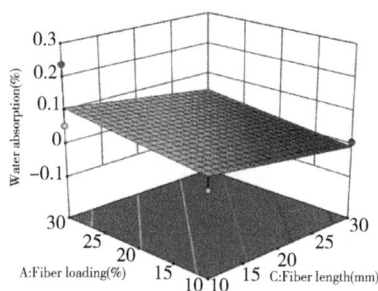

Fig. 8 Effect of fiber loading as a function of fiber length on water absorption

At lower fiber length, the water absorption was low due to less formation of surface interaction between the water and fiber. When fibers greater than 30mm size is used in composites, it leads to the formation of voids and mi-cro cracks, which meant that more water diffused into the composites[14].

4 Conclusions

The results of this study showed that a useful composite with good properties could be successfully developed u-sing treated PALF as reinforcing agent for the LDPE matrix. The optimum length of the fiber required to ob-tain PALF—LDPE composites of maximum properties was found to be 30mm. The tensile strength of PALF—LDPE composites increased drastically up to the opti-mum level of fiber weight fraction. But in the case of flexural strength, it increased linearly with the weight fraction and fiber length up to the optimal level i. e 30% and 30mm beyond these there is a leveling off on the flexural strength. The impact strength also increased linearly with the weight fraction of the fiber. The com-posite with 30% fiber content exhibits an impact strength of 225.2J/mm^2. The amount of water absorbed by the composites increases with increase in the PALF weight fraction and slight reduction when the length of the fiber was increased

References

[1] REIS J M L, CHIANELLI-JUNIOR R, CARDOSO J L, et al. Effect of recycled PET in the fracture mechanics of polymer mortar[J]. Constr Build Mater, 2011,25(6): 2799-2804.

[2] BARBOZA E S, LOPEZ D R, AMICO S C, et al. Determi-nation of a recyclability index for the PET glycolysis[J]. Re-sour Conserv Recy, 2009,53(3): 122-128.

[3] YEHIA F Z,AL-SABAGH A M, ESHAQ G H, et al. Greener routes for recycling of polyethylene terephthalate[J]. Egypt. J. Pet. , 2016. 25: 53-64.

[4] MAYANK R P, VIJAYKUMAR S, JIGAR V P et al. Pet waste management by chemical recycling: a review[J]. J Polym Environ, 2010. 18: 8-25.

[5] DEVI L U, BHAGAWAN S S, THOMAS S. Mechanical properties of pineapple leaf fiber-reinforced polyester compos-ites[J].J. Appl. Polym. Sci. , 1997,64(9): 1739-1748.

[6] CYRAS V P, IANNACE S, KENNY J M, et al. Relationship between processing and properties of biodegradable compos-ites based on PCL/starch matrix and sisal fibers[J]. Polym Composite, 2001, 22(1): 104-110.

[7] BARKOULA N M, GARKHAIL S K, PEIJS T. Biodegrada-ble composites based on flax/polyhydroxybutyrate and its co-polymer with hydroxyvalerate[J]. Ind Crop Prod, 2010,31 (1): 34-42.

[8] CHOUW N, YAN L, YUAN X. Improving the mechanical properties of natural fibre fabric reinforced epoxy composites by alkali treatment[J]. J Reinf Plast Comp, 2012. 31(6): 425-437.

[9] ARIB R M N, SAPUAN S M, HAMDAN M, et al. A litera-ture review of pineapple fibre reinforced polymer composites [J]. Polym Polym Compos, 2004, 12(4): 341-348.

[10] MUKHERJEE P S, SATYANARAYANA K G. Structure and properties of some vegetable fibres [J]. J. Mater. Sci. , 1986, 21(1): 51-56.

[11] PIA M R, BAHARUM A, ABDULLAH I. Mechanical properties of bio-composite natural rubber/high density po-lyethylene/mengkuang fiber (NRHDE/MK) [J]. Polym Polym Compos, 2016, 24(9): 767-774.

[12] HUNER U. Effect of water absorption on the mechanical properties of flax fiber reinforced epoxy composites [J]. Adv. Sci. Technol. Res. J. , 2015, 9(26).

[13] BADRI R N, ZAHARI W, ARDYANANTA H, et al. Mechanical properties and water absorption behavior of polypropylene/ijuk fiber composite by using silane treatment [J]. Procedia Manuf, 2015, 2: 573-578.

[14] DHAKAL H N, ZHANG Z Y, RICHARDSON M. Effect of water absorption on the mechanical properties of hemp fibre reinforced unsaturated polyester composites [J]. Compos Sci Technol, 2007, 67(7-8): 1674-1683.

Study on the Fluorescence Characteristics and Pyrolysis Mechanism of Natural Indigo Dye

JU Zixin[1], LIU Yanping[1]*

[1] *Engineering Research Center, Technical Textiles, Ministry of Education, Shanghai, 201620, China*

* *Corresponding author's email*: liuyp@ dhu. edu. cn

Abstract: Natural indigo is a kind of vat dye with a widely uses for more than 5,000 years. Indigo is a planar molecule and contains a large conjugated structure, which can produce strong fluorescence. In this study, the fluorescence characteristics of natural indigo and its pyrolysis mechanism were analyzed by recording the excitation and emission spectra of indigo in DMF of different concentrations. Additionally, the pyrolysis products of indigo were obtained at 350,400,450,500 and 550℃, respectively, by using a synchronous thermal analyzer. The pyrolysis products of indigo were also dissolved in DMF to obtain five solutions with 50μg/mL concentration. The pyrolysis mechanism of indigo was discussed by measuring and comparing the excitation and emission spectra of indigo and its pyrolysis products. The results illustrated that when the indigo standard solution was excited at 380nm, there was a distinct fluorescence peak at 485nm. As the concentration of the indigo solution increased, indigo has two different luminescence phenomena, aggregation-caused quenching and aggregation-induced emission, in the aggregate state. With the increase of temperature, indigo began to pyrolysis at 400℃, which causing four fluorescence peaks at 407, 429,450 and 480nm. The intensities of these four fluorescence peaks increased with the increase of pyrolysis temperature. By comparing the excitation and emission spectra of indigo and its pyrolysis products in solution, the fundamental causes of fluorescence characteristics of different concentration of indigo in DMF were analyzed, and the pyrolysis mechanism of indigo was also explored.

Keywords: Indigo; Fluorescence analysis; Fluorescence quenching; Pyrolysis

1 Introduction

Fluorescence isthe property of a substance that produces light when it is being acted upon by radiant energy. The fluorescence analysis can reveal various properties of molecules, which is a common method for substances analysis with the advantages of high sensitivity, less samples and convenience. It is widely used in quantitative analysis and qualitative identification of substances.

Natural indigo (C. I. 73000) is a natural dye extracted from plants, such as the Indigofera tinctorial, Knotweed and Isatis tentoria. It is one of the earliest and most popular vat dyes and has wide application in the food, pharmaceutical and printing industries. It has been used in dyeing in India, China, and Egypt for 5, 000 years[1-7]. Indigo is a dark blue dye at ambient temperature and pressure with molecular formula $C_{16}H_{10}N_2O_2$. In-

digo has highly thermal stability which sublimates at 300℃ and decomposes at 390℃. As shown in Fig. 1, Indigo is a planar molecule in which two intramolecular hydrogen bonds are formed between the adjacent carbonyl group and the imino group, the hydrogen bonds and carbon-carbon double bonds from two five-membered rings. Therefore, indigo has a strong conjugated effect, which can produce strong fluorescence[8-9]. The absorption and fluorescence of indigo solution have been reported in experiment and calculation so far, in which both studies did not investigate the variation of fluorescence spectra of indigo solution with concentration and pyrolysis temperature[10-11].

In this study, the fluorescence characteristics of natural indigo and its pyrolysis mechanism were studied by a steady state and transient state fluorescence spectrome-

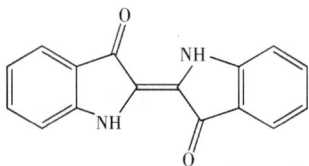

Fig. 1　Chemical structure of indigo

ter. The fluorescence characteristics of natural indigo were analyzed by recording the excitation and emission spectra of standard indigo solution of different concentrations. In addition, the pyrolysis products of indigo were obtained at different temperatures of 350℃, 400℃, 450℃, 500℃ and 550℃, respectively, by using a synchronous thermal analyzer. The pyrolysis mechanism of indigo was discussed by measuring and comparing the excitation and emission spectra of indigo and its pyrolysis products in DMF. It is expected that the results could provide the reference for the research of qualitative identification, quantitative analysis and thermal performance of indigo dye.

2　Experiments

2.1　Materials

Pure natural indigo was purchased from Chengdu Pure Chem Standard Co., Ltd., which used as received. Natural indigo dye was kindly provided with Shanghai Naturalism Biological Technology Co., Ltd. N, N-dimethylformamide (DMF, 99.5%) of analytical grade was purchased from Sinopharm Chemical Reagent Co., Ltd.

2.2　Instrumentation

The pyrolysis products of indigo were collected by using STA8000 (PerkinElmer, America). A certain amount of indigo and its pyrolysis products were weighed by using an AL-104 Electronic Balance (Mettler Toledo, Switzerland), and then dissolved the samples in the DMF solution. Transferred this solution to a 50mL volumetric flask and bring to volume by DMF solution, placed the prepared solution in a KQ-500DE CNC Ultrasonic Cleaner (Kunshan Ultrasonic Instrument Co., Ltd.) for 10 minutes to mix evenly. As shown in Fig.2, the fluorescence spectra of indigo in DMF solution were determined by a QM/TM Steady State and

Transient State Fluorescence Spectrometer (PTI, USA). The excitation and emission slit widths were set to 5nm, and the excitation and emission wavelengths were measured in the range of 260~460nm and 400~680nm.

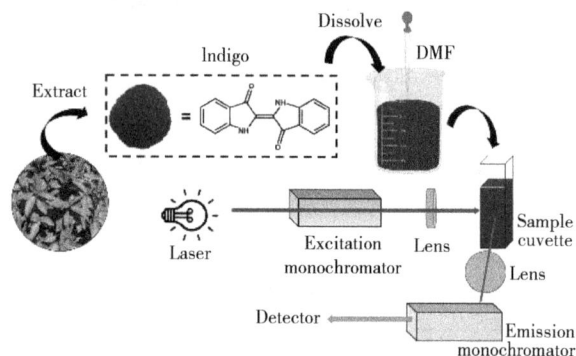

Fig.2　The process of measuring the fluorescence spectrum of indigo

3　Results and Discussions

3.1　Fluorescence Characteristics of Indigo Solution

The fluorescence spectra of 50μg m/Lsolutions of indigo in DMF were measured by the method of 2.2 in the experiment. The emission and excitation spectra of indigo solution are shown in Fig.3 and the three-dimensional projection and three-dimensional contour fluorescence spectrum of indigo solution are presented in Fig.4. We can see from that indigo has three characteristic absorption peaks at 281mm, 323mm, and 397nm in the ultraviolet region. That is because the aromatic rings, carbon-carbon double bonds and carbonyl groups in the indigo molecule are chromophores, and the imino groups are autochromes. When energy is absorbed, the aromatic rings and carbon-carbon double bonds produce a $\pi \rightarrow \pi^{*}$ transition, and the carbonyl groups produce a $n \rightarrow \pi^{*}$ transition. The absorption wavelength generates bathochromic shift in the spectra, because the autochromes is connected to the chromophore. Consequently, indigo has three characteristic absorption peaks at 281nm, 323nm, and 397nm in the ultraviolet region. However, the electrons in the π^{*} orbit are unstable and will quickly return to the ground state and emit fluoresce, which produces a fluorescence peak of 485nm.

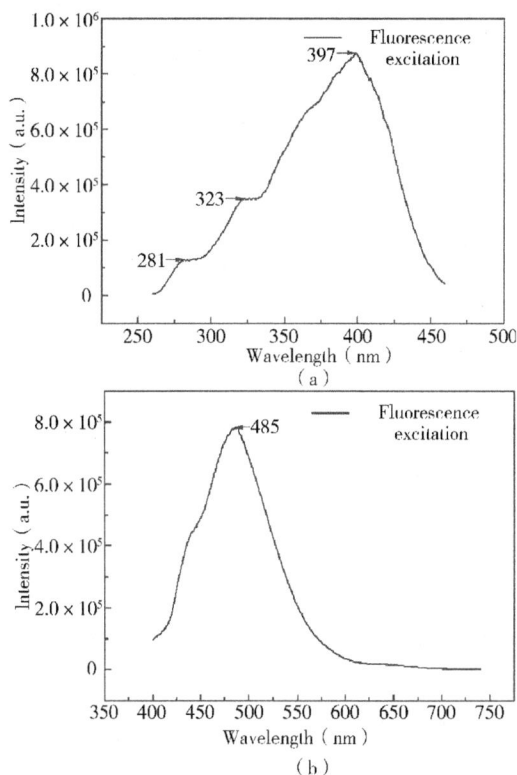

Fig. 3　(a) The excitation and (b) emission spectra of indigo in DMF, $T = 293K$

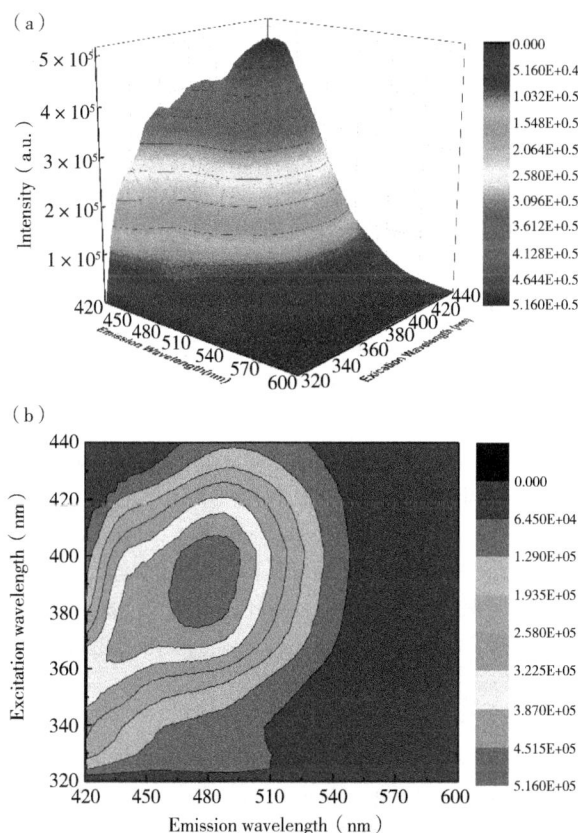

Fig. 4　(a) Three-dimensional projection and (b) contour fluorescence spectrum of indigo in DMF

3.2　Fluorescence Spectra of Indigo Solutions with Different Concentrations

The solutions of indigo of 10－100μg/mL in DMF were obtained, respectively. Fig. 5 shows that the intensity of the fluorescence peak of indigo gradually increases as the concentration of the solution increases, and the fluorescence peak changes from 440nm to 488nm. When the concentration of the solution increases to 80μg/mL, the intensity of the maximum fluorescence peak began to decrease. That is because indigo has a strong π—π interaction in the aggregate state, which causes the decay of the excited state to be dissipated in a non-radiative relaxation mode, and produces the fluorescence quenching. As the concentration of the solution increased to 100μg/mL, the fluorescence peak at 660nm has been increasing. It is because in the aggregated state, the steric hindrance of the indigo molecule increases to suppress intramolecular rotation, which promotes radiation transition and leads to fluorescence enhancement. Thus, indigo may have two different luminescence phenomena, aggregation-caused quenching (ACQ) and aggregation-induced emission (AIE), in the aggregate state.

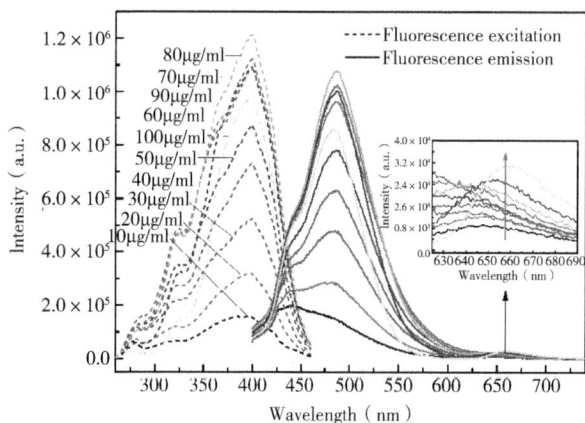

Fig. 5　The emission and excitation spectra of indigo in DMF with different concentrations

3.3　Fluorescence Spectra of Indigo Solutions with Different Pyrolysis Temperature

Indigo sublimes at about 300℃ and decomposes at 390℃. When natural indigo is heated to 300℃, or just above 300℃, a gas phase of indigo is obtained which can be easily separated from impurities remaining in the solid phase. When the temperature of the gas phase of indigo is brought below 300℃, indigo desublimes and reappears in the solid state[12-13]. Indigo and its pyrolysis products were obtained at 350℃, 400℃, 450℃, 500℃ and 550℃, respectively, by using a synchronous thermal analyzer. The products were dissolved in DMF to obtain five solutions with concentration of 50μg/mL, and their fluorescence spectra were measured by 2.2 method. The fluorescence spectra of solutions of different pyrolysis products of indigo has exposed clearly in Fig. 6. As presented in Fig. 6, when the pyrolysis temperature is below 400℃, the position of the fluorescence peak of the indigo solutions shift slightly. While the pyrolysis temperature reaches at 400℃, the indigo molecules begin to decompose, at which time the carbon-carbon double bond is broken, the nitrogen heterocycle is also opened, and the fluorescent emission group are destroyed, causing four fluorescence emission peaks at 407nm, 429nm, 450nm and 480nm respectively. The intensities of these four fluorescence peaks increased with the increase of pyrolysis temperature.

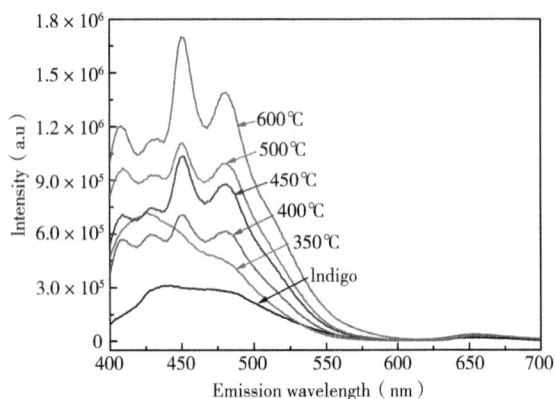

Fig. 6　Fluorescence spectra of indigo solutions with different pyrolysis temperature

4　Conclusions

Indigo is a planarmolecule with a large conjugated structure, which can produce strong fluorescence. When it absorbed energy, the aromatic rings and carbon-carbon double bonds produce a $\pi \rightarrow \pi^{*}$ transition, the carbonyl groups produce a $n \rightarrow \pi^{*}$ transition. So that indigo has three characteristic absorption peaks at 281nm, 323nm and 397nm in the ultraviolet region and produces the fluorescence peak at 485nm. As the concentration of the indigo solutions increases, indigo may have two different luminescence phenomena, aggregation-caused quenching (ACQ) and aggregation-induced emission (AIE), in the aggregate state. At about 300℃, indigo can be purified by sublimation. When the pyrolysis temperature reaches at 400℃, the fluorophores of indigo is destroyed and there are four fluorescence peaks at 407nm, 429nm, 450nm and 480nm were observed. The intensities of these four fluorescence peaks increased with the increase of pyrolysis temperature.

References

[1] HE B, PUN A B, ZHEREBETSKYY D, et al. New form of an old natural dye: bay-annulated indigo (BAI) as an excellent electron accepting unit for high performance organic semiconductors[J]. Journal of the American Chemical Society, 2014, 136(42): 15093-15101.

[2] BOUZIDI A, YAHIA I S, El-SADEK M S A. Novel and highly stable indigo (C. I. Vat Blue I) organic semiconductor dye: Crystal structure, optically diffused reflectance and the electrical conductivity/dielectric behaviors[J]. Dyes and Pigments, 2017, 146: 66-72.

[3] NAMGUNG S, PARK H A, KIM J, et al. Ecofriendly one-pot biosynthesis of indigo derivative dyes using CYP102G4 and PrnA halogenase[J]. Dyes and Pigments, 2019, 162: 80-8.

[4] GARCIAMACIAS P, JOHN P. Formation of natural indigo derived from woad (Isatis tinctoria L.) in relation to product purity[J]. Journal of Agricultural and Food Chemistry, 2004, 52(26): 7891.

[5] SHIN Y, SON K, YOO D I. Indigo dyeing onto ramie fabric via microbial reduction: Reducing power evaluation of some bacterial strains isolated from fermented indigo vat[J]. Fibers and Polymers, 2016, 17(7): 1000-1006.

[6] MOTAGHI Z. The comparison between a natural reducing agent and sodium dithionite in vat, indigo and sulphur dyeing on cotton fabric[J]. Advanced Materials Research, 2012, 441: 207-211.

[7] MIYOKO K, RYOKO Y. Characteristics of color produced by awa natural indigo and synthetic indigo[J]. Materials, 2009, 2(2): 661-673.

[8] STEINGRUBER E. Indigo and indigo colorants[M]. Ullmann's Encyclopedia of Industrial Chemistry, 2000.

[9]SUSSE P, STEINS M, KUPCIK V. Indigo: Crystal structure refinement based on synchrotron data[J]. Zeitschrift Für Kristallographie, 1988, 184(3-4): 269-273.

[10]RONDAO R, MELO J S D, SCHABERLE F A, et al. Excited state characterization of a polymeric indigo[J]. Physical Chemistry Chemical Physics, 2012, 14: 1778-1783.

[11]JACQUEMIN D, PERPETE E, CIOFINI I, et al. Accurate simulation of optical properties in dyes[J]. Accounts of Chemical Research, 2009, 42(2): 326-334.

[12]BECHTOLD T, MUSSAK R. Handbook of natural colorants [M]. Environmental Aspects and Sustainability, 2009.

[13]OVARLEZ S, GIULIERI F, CHAZE A M, et al. The incorporation of indigo molecules in sepiolite tunnels[J]. Chemistry-A European Journal, 2009, 15(42): 11326-11332.

Innovative Application of Puff Printing in Modern Garment Design

SUN Zhaojie[1], MAO Dan[1]*

[1] College of Fashion and Design, Donghua University, Shanghai, 200050, China.

* Corresponding author's email: miranda2007@ 126. com

Abstract: Printing is widely used in fashion design. With the progress of society and the innovation of technology, stereo printing on textiles appeared, which breaks through the traditional way printing can be and creates larger space for fashion design. Puff printing, as the most widely used method of stereo printing on textiles, is popular among consumers and fashion designers. However, the application of it is too general and lacking of innovation as well as the making method for different types of garments. In order to solve the above problems, this paper based on the research of the theory and the application of "puff printing", putting forward the feasible design project of ready-to-wear and creative series. The results show that the three-dimensional effect of puff printing can offer reference ideas for modern garment design; the combination of the two is also conducive to the market-oriented application of foaming printing.

Keywords: Stereo printing on textiles; Puff printing; Fashion design

1 Introduction

With the liberation of personality of current age, the development of clothing has begun to enter the era of pluralism. Since the early development of the cloth printing, solvent-based ink printing, water slurry and glue printing, a variety of new printings have emerged. In order to realize the consumer's pursuit of the three-dimensionality of garment printing, three-dimensional printing has been produced.

2 Overview of Puff Printing

By the physical aspect, "three-dimensional printing" is applying a principle to print pattern on the fabric. And the principle is that the various parts of the object are different in light intensity to cause the distinction between light and dark. That is, the "semi-anti-dyeing" and "imprinting" methods are combined to divide a pattern into two colors, which are printed on the fabric in a partially overlapping manner, and the background color is set off additionally to produce a "stereo" feeling. From a chemical point of view, three-dimensional printing is a method of printing a printing paste made of a polymer synthetic agent and a dye which can be naturally expanded at a certain temperature and time, while the printed pattern bulges out the surface of the fabric[1]. And the puff printing is a kind of three-dimensional printing.

2.1 Definition of Puff Printing

Puff printing is a printing method originating in the United States, which utilizes foaming agent, additive, coloring agent and thermoplastic high-polymer resin emulsion. After printing, it is dried into film and high-temperature melting to decompose the foaming agent, and the air is released to expand the color paste film to form a three-dimensional printing. And the resin is used to attach the paint and display color[2]. Puff printing effect is shown in Fig. 1.

2.2 History of Puff Printing

In 1979, FABLICS AMERIA CORP (textile company) published the first industrial report, announcing that they produced an expanded puff print with flocking embroidery effect. In 1981, Japan's Otsuka Seiki Co.,

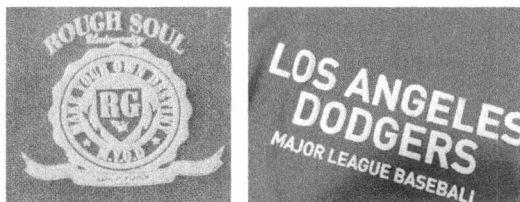

Fig. 1   Puff printing effect

Ltd. exhibited New Dyfoam W-400 foaming adhesive at the Beijing Textile Industry Exhibition[3].

China began to develop it in the early 1980s. At that time, we had initially mastered the production technology of foamed printed fabrics, but most of the foamed printing pastes were imported raw materials, and the foamed printing paste was introduced with the production of polystyrene foam. At present, puff printing products have a good sales market in Guangzhou, Beijing, Shanghai, Wuhan and other places of China.

3   Theoretical Research on Puff Printing

Most of the research results in the 1990s and early 2000s came from factory researchers who focused on the technical aspects and proposed the selection principle of foaming temperature and equipment based on a series of investigations on the choice of blowing agents, printing paste components and the foaming conditions. However, after 2014, there has been little research on puff printing. The application of it in modern fashion design is even more unattended, so that such a technology that can bring abundant artistic effects has not been fully used in fashion design, which is a waste of resources.

4   Application Method of Puff Printing Technology in Garment Design

4.1   Process Flow and Design Points of Puff Printing

The process flow of puff printing is divided into 9 steps: Pattern design-black and white draft depiction—photosensitive plate making—color matching proofing—formulating color paste—printing—drying—foaming fixation—finished product inspection.

4.1.1   Pattern Design of Puff Printing

Three-dimensional puff printing has certain requirements on the pattern. The more complicated the pattern, the worse the printed effect is. Therefore, overlapping colors and large area patterns should be avoided as much as possible, and those can be replaced with snowflakes or dry pens. There should be gaps between the patterns to avoid too much concentration and color overlap, otherwise the effect of puff printing would not be reflected, and appearing a block panel knot[4]. Therefore, the complicated pattern should be simplified with fine lines. And the the pattern contour spacing should be large.

Due to these requirements, puff printing mostly chooses basic fashion styles pattern on clothing with little innovation, and it has not played its due role in modern clothing design. At present, the application form of puff printing in clothing is shown in Tab. 1

Tab. 1   The application form of puff printing in clothing

Sort of apparel	Application characteristics	Sample pictures
T-shirt	Mainly letters and lines, outdated	
Children's garments	Mainly cartoon pattern and geometric figure, rich in color	
Women's panties	Monochrome printing which combine pattern with letter	

4.1.2 Multiple Material Applications of Puff Printing

Compared with traditional printing methods, puff printing has strong three-dimensional effect, wear resistance, good color fastness and wide application. It can be applied to the creative printing of pure cotton or polyester/cotton fabrics. It is also possible to combine the puff printing with the new printing such as diamond printing and illuminating printing to form different stereoscopic effects of the pattern. For example, the pearlescent puff printing, the golden light puff printing and the silver puff printing new technology are all based on the color foaming. Created on the top, so that the fabric has both a distinct three-dimensional sense and the noble sense of gold and silver jewelry.

As the technology matures, puff printing has been applied to the leather industry, and high-end foam printed leather can also be developed, whose products are extremely unique.

4.2 Comparison of Puff Printing, Foaming Printing and Velvet Embroidery

The principle, stereoscopic, characteristics and printing methods of foam printing, foaming printing and velvet embroidery are shown in Tab. 2.

Tab. 2 Comparison of puff printing, foaming printing and velvet embroidery

Type	Principle	Stereoscopic	Characteristics	Methods
Puff printing	A foaming agent and a thermoplastic resin are added to the printing paste, and the foaming agent decomposes at a high temperature to release air, then the ink is expanded to achieve the three-dimensional effect	Three-dimensional	Visually embossed; Under the microscope, the foamed printed fabric has a sponge cake profile in cross section.	Physical foaming method, Chemical foaming method
Foaming printing	Using air as a thickener to replace part of the water, relying on a surfactant to introduce air into the colorant. The volume of the colorant is then increased, and the printing paste is applied to the fabric	Flat	The printing part is soft to the touch, good in color fastness, no fire oil pollution in the printing process, not easy to plug the net, chemicals in the processing and dyes can be used effectively	Blowing air method, mechanical agitation method, blowing air and agitation combined foaming method[5]
Fleece printing	There are many gas microcapsules in the printing paste. The volume of the microcapsules expands when heated, and they squeeze, overlap and irregularly distribute each other, resulting in a embossing effect[6]	Three-dimensional	looks like a velvet embroidered, with gorgeous appearance, can't be ironed, Under the microscope, the cross-section of the velvet printed fabric is a tiny sphere, which is soapy	Physical foaming method

In comparison, the puff printing has a visually embossed effect, which is more novel with future technological sense and funny design. It can be used for children's wear, fashion brand clothing, or design applications of different themes. At the same time, puff printing is widely used in pure cotton and pure polyester fabrics, which is resistant to washing and rubbing and has good practical properties.

5 Puff Printing Design Practice

5.1 Pattern Design Inspiration of Puff Printing

The design practice was inspired by the story of the traditional Chinese female hero "Mulan". As a representative of the typical figure of " the saying women are inferior to men is wrong", Mulan appears to be in line with modern trends and can promote Chinese traditional culture in the situation of increasing female status today.

When it comes to the technical level, as mentioned in the theoretical research section, puff printing has certain requirements on the pattern. Therefore, simple patterns should be used as much as possible to make the effect better. Based on the above reasons, when using the white pattern to draw the pattern, the lines are as clean and tidy as possible, and the large-area pattern is replaced by the point-like distribution, which achieved the ideal artistic effect as well as solving the possible problems in puff printing technology.

Materials of pattern design is shown in Fig. 2. Process of pattern adjusting is shown in Fig. 3.

Fig. 2　Materials of pattern design

Fig. 3　Process of pattern adjusting

5.2　Experiment of Foaming Time at Different Temperatures

Based on the designed puff printing pattern, the experiment of foaming time at different temperatures is carried out. The fabric used is black polyester fabric. The experimental results are shown in Tab. 3.

Tab. 3　Experimental record of foaming time at different temperatures

Temperature (℃)	Time (min)	Foaming effect	Conclusion	Product
160	10	Unfixed, unfoamed	160℃ temperature is too low to foam	
	20	Unfixed, unfoamed		
	30	Unfixed, unfoamed		
170	10	Unfixed, unfoamed	170℃ temperature is too low to foam, but fix	
	20	Start fixing, not foaming		
	30	Further fixed, not foamed		
180	10	Start fixing, not foaming	180 degrees Celsius is a temperature suitable for foaming but it is necessary to control the time	
	20	Further fixed, not foamed		
	30	Successfully foamed and started burnt		
190	10	Basically fixed, not foamed	As the temperature increases, the speed of foaming becomes faster, and the time is controlled to prevent burnt	
	20	Foaming is basically formed		
	30	Foaming start burnt		
200	10	Foaming begins to form	The temperature of 200 degrees Celsius is already high, and it can be foamed successfully in a short time	
	20	Foaming is basically formed		
	30	Foaming has been burnt		

The experimental results show that the temperature of 160℃ and 170℃ is on the low side, so it is not suitable for manual foaming. When the temperature is above 180℃, the foaming time becomes shorter with the increase of temperature, but it needs to be controlled around 15 minutes, otherwise the foaming would be burnt.

5.3　Innovative Application of Puff Printing in Ready-Made Clothes and Creative Clothing Design

Based on the above puff printing pattern as the ma-terial, further realize the original application of puff printing in ready-made clothes (take T-shirt as an example) and creative clothing design after successful print test. The product of print test is shown in Fig. 4. The color matching scheme is mainly black, white and red. In the ready-to-wear series, three T-shirts are designed according to the current fashion trend, and the pattern is comprehensive applied with integrity, matching and disassembly. In the creative series, five sets of clothing are completed with the use of the elements of

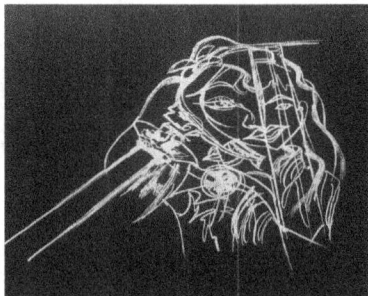
Fig. 4 The product of print test

traditional Chinese clothing(such as girdle and stand-up collar) and puff printing pattern. The effect drawing of ready-to-wear series is shown in Fig. 5. The effect drawing of creative series is shown in Fig. 6.

Fig. 5 The effect drawing of ready-to-wear series

Fig. 6 The effect drawing of creative series

The significance of design practice lies in exploring the possibility of using puff printing technology in fashion design, improving the utilization rate of puff printing technology in fashion industry, and highlighting the traditional original methodology so as to provide a new research approach and technical support for the printing form in clothing.

6　Conclusions

Through the study and practice of puff printing, the following conclusions are drawn.

(1) Foam printing has broad application prospects. In addition to its own independent applications, it can also be combined with a variety of new printing to produce more rich results.

(2) The effect of puff printing is restricted by various prerequisites. Only by designing patterns which meet both technical and aesthetic requirements can make puff printing with suitable height and clarity.

(3) The combination of modern fashion design and puff printing pattern can be conducive to the market-oriented application of puff printing.

References

[1] LI Y. Study on stereo printing technology and its appropriate pattern[J]. Shandong Textile Science & Technology, 1987 (01): 16-18.

[2] SHEN H, WANG X Y. Technology and method of T-shirt printing[J]. Progress In Textile Science & Technology, 2008 (01): 50-52.

[3] LAI M L, LIU D X, ZHANG C J, et al. Study on chemical foaming stereo printing paste and printing technology[J]. Guangzhou Chemical Industry, 1986(04): 7-12.

[4] YI X P. Study on stereo foaming printing technology[J]. Dyeing and Finishing, 1999(04): 27-29+35.

[5] BANDYOPADHYAY B N, SUN K. Application of foam in textile chemical wet processing-foam printing [J]. Textile Technology Overseas, 1983(05): 20-23+16.

[6] LIU Y Q. Unique clothing printing technology[J]. Screen Printing Industry, 2003(21): 72-75.

Human Parsing Transfer via Generative Adversarial Network

YU Li[1], ZHONG Yueqi[1,2]*

[1] *College of Textiles, Donghua University, Shanghai, 201620, China*

[2] *Key Laboratory of Textile Science & Technology, Ministry of Education, College of Textiles, Donghua University, Shanghai, 201620, China*

* *Corresponding author's email*: zhyq@ dhu. edu. cn

Abstract: Human parsing, which focuses on the fine-grained segmentation for body parts and clothes, can be used to analyze human images. In this paper, we propose a human parsing transfer which can transform the input human parsing with the desired pose and body shape. By given a body segmentation of the person X and a human parsing of another person Y wearing the desired clothes, we use a dual-path auto-encoder to generate the synthesized human parsing, which describes the person X wearing the desired clothes from Y. With the help of the paired training strategy and careful network design, our method can robustly generate high-quality results with the attributes of the desired clothes while the original pose and body shape are still retained. Our method is useful for many practical applications such as photo editing and virtual try-on.

Keywords: Human parsing transfer; Generative adversarial network; Self-supervised learning

1 Introduction

Recently, deep learning[1] technology has achieved a big success in the computer vision area. As an important visual task, human paring[2], which is one of fine-grained semantic segmentation[3], has attracted great interests for researchers. Given a human image, human paring is trying to classify each pixel into a certain category (such as body parts or clothes). Therefore, pixel-level content understanding for human images is provided by human parsing. It is close to body segmentation[4], which only provides body parts labels (such as head, arms, and torso) but totally ignores garment information. Body segmentation includes the information of body shape and human pose, whereas human parsing implies the relation between body parts and clothes.

Although some works[5-7] are able to predict accurate human parsing results, the studies[8-11] on the transformation of human parsing are limited. The human parsing transfer tries to automatically edit the input human parsing based on a certain condition. It is similar to neural style transfer[12] which aims to transform an input image in the style of the conditioned image. Human parsing transfer has great potentials for many practical applications, such as photo editing[13], person image generation[8-9] and virtual try-on systems[10, 14].

Generative Adversarial Network (GAN)[15], which has been widely used in the image generating, is the mainstream approach for human parsing transfer. Fashion-GAN[9] transforms the input human parsing according to a language description of the desired outfit. It encoded the human attributes and textual descriptions and then generate the desired human parsing via a GAN. Swap-Net[10] uses a warping module to generate human parsing in target pose conditioned on a body segmentation. This method only used a single image and its augmentation (random affine transformations) as a training sample which is convenient for training, but the quality of the result is poor for large pose change.

In this work, we propose a network to transform human parsing with the desired pose and body shape by given a body segmentation as a condition. Our model enables the result to retain the garment information (such as the class and attribute of the garment in original human parsing). It is a crucial preprocessing step for synthesizing person image in clothing since it provides spatial constraint to ensure the structural coherence of the synthesized image.

2 Methods

2.1 Human Parsing Transfer

Given a human parsing (denoted as P) and a body segmentation (denoted as B), our human parsing transfer can generate a plausible human parsing (denoted as P') which portrays the same person from B wearing the desired clothes from P. We achieve it via a dual-path auto-encoder network, as shown in Fig. 1. The model takes the human parsing P and the body segmentation B as the inputs.

For the human parsing P, we use the same definition in look into person dataset[6], which annotated images with 20 categories. For the sake of simplicity, we ignore the sunglasses and hat classes. Thus the human parsing P has 18 channels and each channel represents a binary mask for the corresponding class. For the body segmentation B, the definition is slightly different from the existing work[4]. Despite head, torso, arms and legs, we add hair class for B which cannot be inferred by the human parsing P.

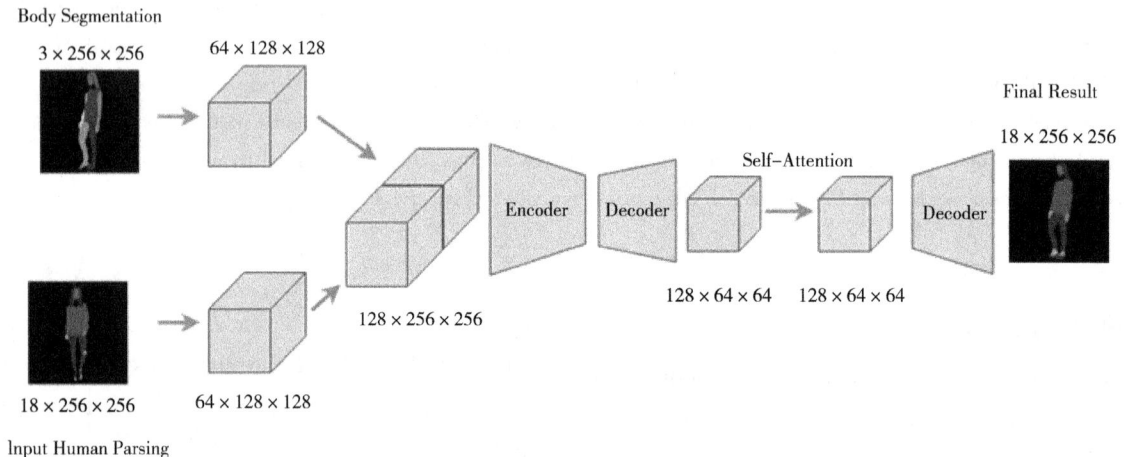

Fig. 1　The network architecture of our human parsing transfer

Since it is hard to collect a dataset for supervised learning, we use paired images of the identical person wearing the identical clothes in two different poses as the training sample (denoted as $\{x, y\}$). In the training stage, we use the human parsing of one image x as P_x and the body segmentation of the other image y as B_y. Thus the human parsing of the image y (denoted as P_y) is the ground truth. Hence, we use the cross entropy loss as training loss. Compared with performing augmentations on a single image[10] for training, our paired training strategy makes the network more robust for large pose changes.

2.2 Implementation Details

There is no existing dataset for training our task directly. Therefore, we adopt self-supervised learning by u-sing existing algorithms to generate a suitable dataset. We use LookBook dataset[19] and Multi-View Clothing (MVC) dataset[20] since they all contain the paired images. Then we use existing algorithms to predict these images to obtain the human parsing and body segmentation. We obtain human parsing via CE2P[7] model. We obtain the body segmentations via both CE2P model and DensePose-RCNN[21] (since our body segmentation includes hair classes).

We use Adam optimizer[22] with $\beta_1 = 0.5$, $\beta_2 = 0.99$ and a learning rate of 0.0002 for our human parsing transfer. We use instance normalization[23] instead of batch normalization and all up sampling layers are transposed convolutions[24].

3 Results and Discussions

We compared our human parsing transfer with the warping module in SwapNet[10], which only performing augmentations on a single image for training. We also verify the impacts of paired training, self-attention module and total variation regularization by the following three experiments. 1) Ours (w/o Paired): similar to SwapNet, we perform augmentations on a single image for training our network. 2) Ours (w/o Self-Attn): we replace a convolutional layer with the self-attention module. 3) Ours (w/o TV): we remove the total variation regularization when training our network.

All these methods were trained for 68K steps. The qualitative comparisons are shown in Fig. 2. Both the warping module in SwapNet and our method without paired training always fail to deal with large pose changes (the last row of Fig. 2). Without the self-attention module, the clothes sometimes cover the region should belong to the arms (the second row of Fig. 2). It indicates that the self-attention module helps the network to capture the human structure. Without the total variation regularization, the networks occasionally generate results with checkerboard artifacts (the second row of Fig. 2). Additionally, we found SwapNet would incorrectly preserve the hair from the model parsing (the first row of Fig. 2) since its body segmentation does not contain the hair class.

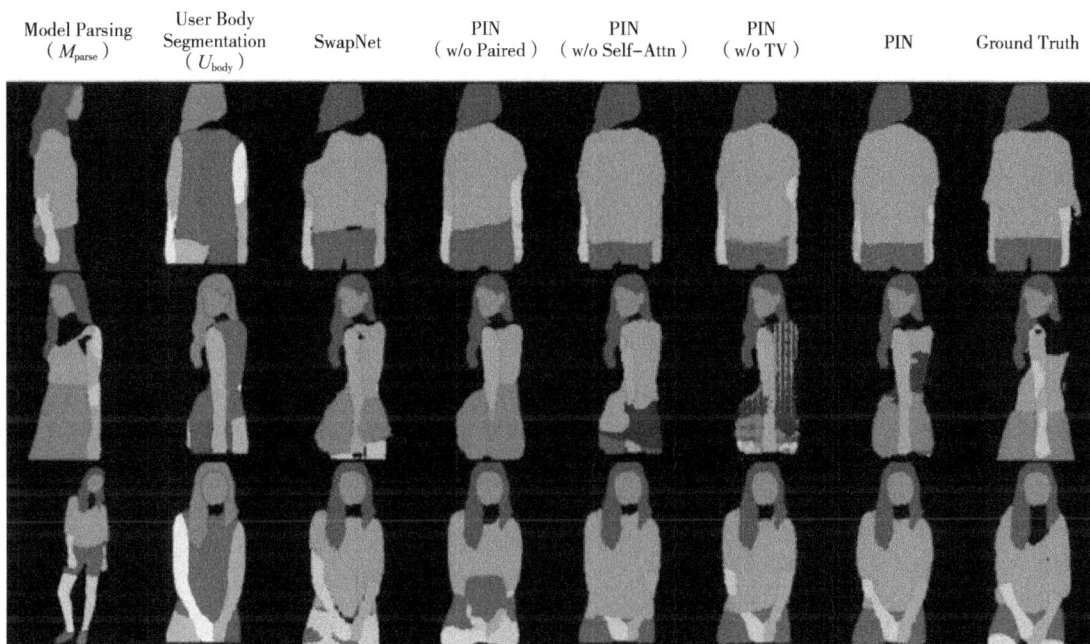

Fig. 2 The qualitative comparisons with other methods

We also evaluated the quantitative performance of these methods by using paired training samples includes two images of a person wearing identical clothes in different poses. To be specific, we random select 5000 paired samples from Deep Fashion dataset[25]. Then the human parsing results of each sample are still obtained by CE2P[7], one as input, and the other as ground truth. We use mean pixel accuracy (mean acc.) and mean region intersection over union (mIoU)[26], which are common metrics for semantic segmentation task, to evaluate the synthesized parsing results. The results are reported in Tab. 1, our method achieves the best results for both mean acc. and mIoU, which indicated our model generates more accurate human parsing than others. Even with fewer training parameters (about 30× smaller than SwarpNct), our mcthod improves the mean acc. by 6.11% and the mIoU by 7.86%. Both paired training strategy and self-attention module are crucial for our method. Total variation regularization also slightly improves our results.

Tab. 1 Quantitative comparisons of different methods for synthesized parsing

Method	mean acc.	mIoU	Param ($\times 10^6$)
SwapNet	66. 29%	56. 88%	98. 5
Ours (w/o Paired)	65. 15%	55. 28%	3. 3
Ours (w/o Self-Attn)	64. 50%	56. 92%	3. 3
Ours (w/o TV)	68. 58%	59. 99%	3. 3
Ours	70. 34%	61. 35%	3. 3

4　Conclusions

We propose a human parsing transfer to transform the human parsing into a desired pose and body shape by providing a body segmentation. To achieve it, we train a dual-path auto-encoder with self-supervised learning. The paired training strategy make the model more robust, especially for large pose change. We further improve the results via total variation regularization and self-attention module. Our qualitative and quantitative experiments demonstrate our methods can generate higher quality results. By using the paired sample to evaluate our method, the mean pixel accuracy reaches 70. 34% and the mIoU reaches 61. 35%.

5　Acknowledgments

This work was supported by the National Natural Science Foundation of China (Grant No. 61572124).

References

[1] LECUN Y, BENGIO Y, HINTON G. Deep learning[J]. Nature, 2015, 521(7553): 436.

[2] TANGSENG P, WU Z, YAMAGUCHI K. Looking at outfit to parse clothing [J]. ArXiv Preprint ArXiv, 2017, 1703:01386.

[3] ZHAO B, FENG J, WU X, et al. A survey on deep learning-based fine-grained object classification and semantic segmentation[J]. International Journal of Automation and Computing, 2017, 14(2): 119-135.

[4] VAROL G, ROMERO J, MARTIN X, et al. Learning from synthetic humans[C]. Proceedings of the IEEE Conference on Computer Vision and Pattern Recognition, 2017: 109-117.

[5] ZHAO J, LI J, NIE X, et al. Self-supervised neural aggregation networks for human parsing[C]. Proceedings of the IEEE Conference on Computer Vision and Pattern Recognition Workshops. 2017: 7-15.

[6] LIANG X, GONG K, SHEN X, et al. Look into person: joint body parsing & pose estimation network and a new benchmark[J]. IEEE Transactions on Pattern Analysis and Machine Intelligence, 2018: 1-1.

[7] LIU T, RUAN T, HUANG Z, et al. Devil in the details: Towards accurate single and multiple human parsing[J]. ArXiv Preprint ArXiv, 2018,1809: 05996.

[8] LASSNER C, PONS-MOLL G, GEHLER P V. A generative model of people in clothing[C]. Proceedings of the IEEE International Conference on Computer Vision,2017: 853-862.

[9] ZHU S, FIDLER S, URTASUN R, et al. Be your own prada: fashion synthesis with structural coherence[C]. IEEE International Conference on Computer Vision, IEEE Computer Society, 2017: 1689-1697.

[10] RAJ A, SANGKLOY P, CHANG H, et al. SwapNet: image based garment transfer [C]. European Conference on Computer Vision, Springer, Cham, 2018: 679-695.

[11] HAN X, WU Z, HUANG W, et al. Compatible and Diverse Fashion Image Inpainting[J]. ArXiv Preprint ArXiv, 2019,1902:01096.

[12] GATYS L A, ECKER A S, BETHGE M. Image style transfer using convolutional neural networks[C]. Proceedings of the IEEE Conference on Computer Vision and Pattern Recognition, 2016: 2414-2423.

[13] HSIAO W L, KATSMAN I, WU C Y, et al. Fashion++: minimal edits for outfit improvement [J]. ArXiv Preprint ArXiv,2019,1904:09261.

[14] DONG H, LIANG X, WANG B, et al. Towards multi-pose guided virtual try-on network [J]. ArXiv Preprint arXiv, 2019,1902:11026.

[15] GOODFELLOW I J, POUGET-ABADIE J, MIRZA M, et al. Generative adversarial nets [C]. International Conference on Neural Information Processing Systems,MIT Press, 2014: 2672-2680.

[16] MAHENDRAN A, VEDALDI A. Understanding deep image representations by inverting them[C]. Proceedings of the IEEE Conference on Computer Vision and Pattern Recognition, 2015: 5188-5196.

[17] ZHANG H, GOODFELLOW I, METAXAS D, et al. Self-attention generative adversarial networks[J]. ArXiv Preprint ArXiv,2018,1805:08318.

[18] MIYATO T, KATAOKA T, KOYAMA M, et al. Spectral normalization for generative adversarial networks[J]. ArXiv Preprint ArXiv,2018,1802:05957.

[19] YOO D, KIM N, PARK S, et al. Pixel-level domain transfer[C]. European Conference on Computer Vision, Springer, Cham, 2016: 517−532.

[20] LIU K H, CHEN T Y, CHEN C S. Mvc: A dataset for view-invariant clothing retrieval and attribute prediction [C]. Proceedings of the 2016 ACM on International Conference on Multimedia Retrieval, ACM, 2016: 313−316.

[21] ALP Güler R, NEVEROVA N, KOKKINOS I. Densepose: Dense human pose estimation in the wild[C]. Proceedings of the IEEE Conference on Computer Vision and Pattern Recognition, 2018: 7297−7306.

[22] KINGMA D P, ADAM B A J. A method for stochastic optimization[J]. ArXiv Preprint ArXiv,2014,1412:6980.

[23] ULYANOV D, VEDALDI A, LEMPITSKY V. Improved texture networks: Maximizing quality and diversity in feed-forward stylization and texture synthesis[C]. Proceedings of the IEEE Conference on Computer Vision and Pattern Recognition, 2017: 6924−6932.

[24] RADFORD A, METZ L, CHINTALA S. Unsupervised representation learning with deep convolutional generative adversarial networks [J]. ArXiv Preprint ArXiv, 2015, 1511:06434.

[25] LIU Z, LUO P, QIU S, et al. Deepfashion: powering robust clothes recognition and retrieval with rich annotations [C]. Proceedings of the IEEE Conference on Computer Vision and Pattern Recognition, 2016: 1096−1104.

[26] LONG J, SHELHAMER E, DARRELL T. Fully convolutional networks for semantic segmentation[C]. Proceedings of the IEEE Conference on Computer Vision and Pattern Recognition, 2015: 3431−3440.

A Review About Cotton Leaf Curl Virus; Devastating Effects on Yield and Quality of Cotton and Its Control Strategies

TU RAZIA Syeda Eishah[1], AHMAD Rehan[2*], GHANI Muhammad Usman[3]

[1] *Department of Zoology, Wildlife and Fisheries, University of Agriculture, Faisalabad, Pakistan*

[2] *Department of Entomology, University of Agriculture, Faisalabad, Pakistan*

[3] *Key Laboratory of Textile Science & Technology, Ministry of Education, College of Textiles, Donghua University, Shanghai, 201620, China*

* *Corresponding author's email*: rehanahmad189. ra@ gmail. com

Abstract: From the last few decades, cotton leaf curl virus (CLCuV) (Begomovirus: Geminiviridae) is considered to be the most severe menace to cotton crops in Asia and Africa. This virus is transmitted by whitefly (Aleyrodidae: Homoptera) and is capable of casing devastating effects in the fields of cotton which negatively affects the economy of Pakistan and all other suffering countries. Researchers are still trying to study the disease and its after effects right from its appearance from 1967. The heaviest outbreak of cotton leaf curl virus (CLCuV) was seen in Pakistan during the early 1990s where it covered almost all cotton fields and devasted the cotton and textile industry of Pakistan. Losses of about an average of 8. 5 million bales occurred during these years and there was an average of 30%–35% yield reduction. Now works are being done to decrease the threat by making resistant cotton cultivars against CLCuV. Different methods are being used for this including grafting, delayed sowing whitefly mediated transfer. According to the concepts of the disease triangle, it is obvious that metrological factors affect the epidemiology. Different managemental practices like changing sowing dates in accordance to whiteflies and metrological factors, using a balanced nutritional diet, cultural practices, vector (whitefly) control strategies, using systemic poisons on cotton seed to make the seedlings resistant for the early weeks. Many scientists are studying how to introduce resistance in cotton by the methods of transcriptional gene silencing. Genetic engineering and biotechnological tools can be helpful in controlling this cotton disease in the near future.

Keywords: Bemisia tabaci; Cotton leaf curl virus; Cotton quality; Gossypium hirsutum; Textile problems

1 Introduction

Cotton (Gossypium hirsutum L.) is the best money harvest of Pakistan which has a place in Gossypium Genus and Malvaceae family. According to 2017 world ranking Pakistan was the 4th largest county in cotton production following China, India and USA and 1st in the exportation of yarn[1]. Sowing date can affect the infection level by CLCuV as sowing after 15 April, level of disease percentage increases[2]. Cotton leaf curl infection (CLCuV) results in enormous economic misfortunes. It is the most significant reason setting up essential breaking point[3]. In this review, we are going to discuss the CLCuV in relation with whitefly, its different control measures and influence on cotton lint quality and yield.

2 Cotton Leaf Curl Disease and Whitefly

Although all begomoviruses are transmitted by a solitary species of whitefly, there is vector specificity. Although 'B' biotype of B. tabaci could transmit each of the 15 begomoviruses, different biotypes could not transmit some begomoviruses and some viruses were transmitted with more noteworthy proficiency by certain biotypes. Along these lines, it creates the impression that probably some begomoviruses are transmitted by specific biotypes. This may clarify why during first CLCuD pandemic in Pakistan, there was no infestation seen in Sindh region[4]. An alternate biotype of *B. tabaci* was brought into Sindh that can more proficiently spread begomoviruses to cotton[5]. According to genetic information, entomologists have classified *B. tabaci* into 24 morphologically indistinguishable species. Taxonomy of begomoviruses will explore the reason for vector specificity with proposed species of whitefly.

3 Symptoms of CLCuV on Cotton

Symptoms include thickening and yellowing of smaller veins mainly present downside the leaf surface on younger leaves and curling of the leaf upward or downward. Thickening of both smaller and main vein can take place(Fig. 1)[1].

Fig. 1　Enation and veins thickening due to CLCuV

4 Outcomes of Disease on Yield and Quality of Fiber

When an attack is severe during the seedling stage, it causes retardation of flowering, boll formation, maturing of the plant which ultimately decreases the quality of fiber and the final outcome of cotton seed. Almost 40.6% reduction in plant height, 33.8% to 40% in boll weight and 3.9% reduction in ginning outcome take place due to the severe attack of CLCuV. It also causes a reduction of 72.5% in the production of cotton bolls on a single cotton plant[6].

There occurs a drastic reduction of 3.44% and 10% on staple length and staple strength respectively due to CLCuV[8]. CLCuD influences the quality attributes of fiber(Fig. 2). It also influences ginning turnout rate, staple length, fiber consistency record, fiber pack quality, fiber fineness and development proportion[9]. The misfortunes that happen due to CLCuD rely upon the infectivity and variety. Damage due to CLCuD varies on different parts of the plant which eventually brings about a decrease of the yield. It can diminish different attributes like fiber length 3.44%, fiber quality 10%, prolongation rate up to 10% boll weight 33.8%, 73.5% in boll per plant, GOT% up to 3.93%, seed record 17.0% and yield per plant 64.5%[8]. Central cotton research insti-

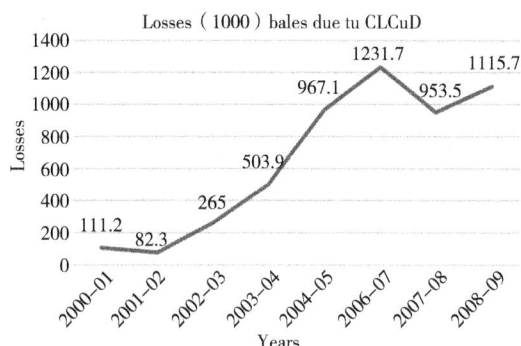

Fig. 2　Bale losses due to CLCuD[7]

tute, Multan conducted several types of research during 2017−2018 to check the influence of CLCuD on characteristics of fiber and results are given below[2](Fig. 3 and Fig. 4).

From the graphs it can be seen easily that the fiber characteristics of healthy plants are much better that the inoculated plants and also the severity of the inoculum have shown its influence in the results.

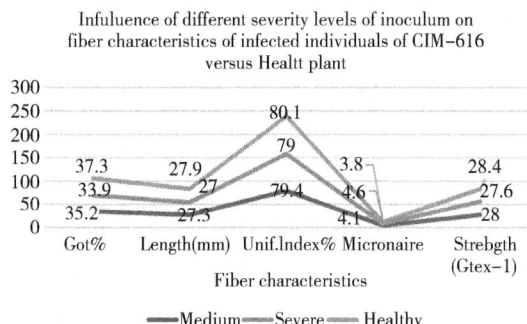

Fig. 3　Influence of CLCuD on CIM−616[2]

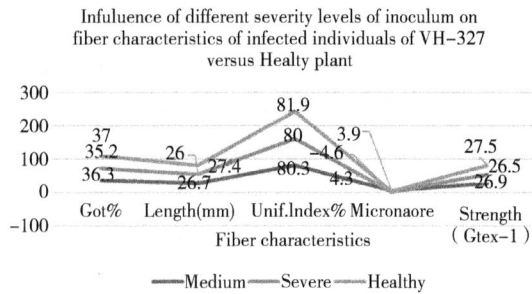

Infuluence of different severity levels of inoculum on
fiber characteristics of infected individuals of VH-327
versus Healty plant

Fig. 4   Influence of CLCuD on VH-327[2]

5   Epidemiology

Critical connection exists among temperature, PAN evaporation and CLCuV. Cultivated hosts and weeds as functional reservoirs of the virus and the sites of infections are those which contained more populations of whiteflies. These areas as well as other vectors become a cause of the secondary spread of the virus to other hosts which enter in the field during the entire developing season[10]. Percentage of infestation by virus increases with increase in temperature and there is a non-significant correlation between infestation and whitefly population, while poor relationship between humidity and week connection with rainfall and the advancement of the disease[11]. There was a negative correlation between infestation rate and velocity of wind and the lowest temperature of the air. The only positive correlation seen was between infestation rate and age of the plant. Infestation due to CLCuV gradually decreased moving to elder crops[10].

6   Conventional Control Strategies

By maintaining population of whiteflies, we can maintain the level of infestation by CLCuV. Cultivation of a variety which is resistant to the infection is a good management practice. Eradication of alternate hosts must be done in nearby areas of cotton production zones. The disease is not seed transmitted yet utilization of sound seed, corrosive delinting and treatment of seeds with the chemical are suggested as preventive tools. Plant debris must be removed and burnt before the sowing of next crop. Weeding and crop rotation are good managemental practices. Legitimate utilization of water system and synthetic fertilizers increases the plant's ability to resist the infestation by a virus. Managing production technologies according to proposals of rural specialists or scientists is good practice to check the disease[12].

7   Modern Genetic Engineering and Molecular Control Approaches

Certain siRNA has been recognized potential against various strains of cotton leaf curl infection. Out of 54 putative siRNAs, 27 qualified as exceedingly potential siRNAs for focused gene silencing[12]. Conventional breeding and molecular techniques are being utilized to make cotton resistant against CLCuV. To produce better and durable resistant in cotton, there is a great need to introduce multiple resistant genes having minute impacts in cultivated cotton varieties. Gene introgression and interspecific hybridisation can be used to introduce resistance from wild cotton into developed cotton. Multiple crosses including direct and back crosses were conducted by NAZEER et al. to move resistance from G. arboreum ($n = 26$) into G. hirsutum ($n = 52$) and finally BC1, BC2 and BC3 generations were assessed for resistant against CLCuD. Less infection was observed in BC1 showing the abnormal state of resistance while disease occurrence expanded in BC2 and BC3 generations(Fig. 5). The consequences of this investigation demonstrated that obstruction against CLCuD is managed by single genes with overwhelming impacts[13]. Resistance against CLCuD has been produced by using different viral genes. Transgenic cotton utilizing truncated AC1 gene sequences has additionally been created with resistance against CLCuD. Cotton plants over-exploiting N-terminal or C-terminal sequences of the AC1 quality demonstrated protection from CLCuD by restraining replication of the virus genome and related beta satellite. Almost 72% and 81% of resistance were observed in gene inserted plants[14]. Sohrab et al. transformed cotton with antisense βC1 gene by using variety Coker 310 and Cauliflower mosaic virus-35S promoter and then confirmed the transformation using PCR. After the observation they found transformed cotton with no symptoms throughout the season and thus were concluded as resistant varieties[15].

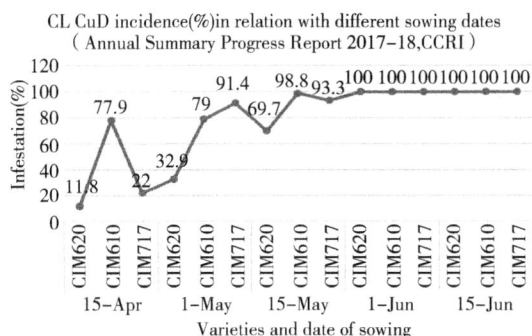

CL CuD incidence(%)in relation with different sowing dates
(Annual Summary Progress Report 2017-18,CCRI)

Fig. 5　Effect of different sowing dates on CLCuD[2]

Utilization of various viral genes for developing resistance is impeded because of difficulties due to cotton transformation and colossal assorted variety of CLCuV isolates under field conditions. Various methodologies utilizing viral qualities have not been effective in making CLCuV resistant plants for use under field conditions. Studies referenced above uncover that creating 100% CLCuD resistant cotton was not obtained. A couple of virus-contaminated plants in the field gives inoculum for epidemics.

8　Conclusions

If Burewala species spread to other cotton developing zones of the world, it will end up being a significant issue. Until now, no variety offers resistance towards Burewala species and accentuation ought to be given for creating resistance towards this species. Resistance genes from wild cotton species ought to be utilized which offer resistance towards the whitefly vector. But, due to the tetraploid nature of cultivated cotton, resistance from G. arboreum is hard to move because these species are diploid. Consolidating different resistance genes with minor impacts with the help of classical breeding can be helpful to produce long lasting resistance in cultural varieties. Endeavors ought to be made to oversee whitefly through bio-pesticides, biocontrol agents and other molecular methodologies.

References

[1] AHMAD S, NOOR-UL-ISLAM, MEHMOOD A, et al. Screening of cotton germplasm against cotton leaf curl virus [J]. Pak J Bot,2010,42:3327-3342.

[2] CCRI Annual Report. 2017-18. http: //www. ccri. gov. pk/reports. html

[3] KHAN A I, HUSSAIN M, RAUF S, et al. Inheritance of cotton leaf curl virus in cotton (Gossypium hirsutum L.) [J]. Plant Protect Sci,2007,43:5-9.

[4] PANHWAR G, PANHWAR R, SOOMRO G A, et al. Survey of cotton leaf curl virus (CLCV) in Sindh [J]. J Biol Sci,2001,1:134-135.

[5] DE BARRO, LIU P J, BOYKIN S S, et al. Bemisia tabaci: a statement of species status [J]. Annu Rev Entomol,2011, 56:1-19.

[6] MAHMOOD T, ARSHAD M, TAHIR M, et al. Response of upland cotton genotypes to leaf curl viruses infection [J]. Pak J Phytopath,1994,6:147-151.

[7] NAWAZ B, NAEEM M, MALIK T A, et al. A review about cotton leaf curl viral disease and its control strategies in pakistan [J]. Int J Inno Approach Agric Res,2019,3:132-147.

[8] AHMED Z. Prospects and bottlenecks of cotton crop in Pakistan [J]. The Pak Cotton Grower,1999,3:6-7.

[9] VERMA P, RAO A R, SINGH P J. In silico prediction and designing of potential siRNA to control cotton whitefly Bemisia tabaci Gennadius vectored cotton leaf curl virus (CLCuV) [J]. 2018.

[10] FAROOQ J, FAROOQ A, RIAZ M, et al. Cotton leaf curl virus disease a principle cause of decline in cotton productivity in Pakistan (a mini review) [J]. Can J Plant Prot, 2014,2:9-16.

[11] KHAN M A, MIRZA J H, AHMED S. Relationships of environmental conditions conducive to cotton leaf curl virus disease development [J]. Pak J Phytopath,1998,10:5-8.

[12] KUMAR A, SAIN S K, MONGA D. Study on Correlation between Population of Viruliferous Whitefly and the Percent Intensity of Cotton Leaf Curl Disease in Cotton [J]. Int J Curr Microbiol App Sci,2019,8:922-937.

[13] NAZEER W, TIPU A L, AHMAD S, et al. Evaluation of cotton leaf curl virus resistance in BC1, BC2, and BC3 progenies from an interspecific cross between Gossypium arboreum and Gossypium hirsutum [J]. PloS One, 2014, 9 (11):111861.

[14] HASHMI J A, ZAFAR Y, ARSHAD M, et al. Engineering cotton (Gossypium hirsutum L.) for resistance to cotton leaf curl disease using viral truncated AC1 DNA sequences [J]. Virus Genes,2011,42:286-296

[15] SOHRAB S S, KAMAL M A, ILLAH A, et al. Development of cotton leaf curl virus resistant transgenic cotton using antisense szC1 gene [J]. Saudi J Biol Sci,2014,23: 358-362.

Effect of Phosphorylation on the Thermal Properties of Jute Extracted CNF

MOHAMMED Kayes Patoary[1, 2], LIU Lifang[1, 2*], AMJAD Farooq[1, 2]

[1] *College of Textiles, Donghua University, Shanghai, 201620, China*

[2] *Innovation Center for Textile Science and Technology, Donghua University, Shanghai, 201620, China*

* *Corresponding author's email*: lifangliu@ dhu. edu. cn.

Abstract: The thermal properties of phosphorylated CNF (Cellulose Nanofibers) at multiples curing times have been investigated by thermogravimetric analysis (TGA) in this study. Three different phosphorylated CNFs were analyzed. All the phosphorylated CNF exposed high char formation around 38% indicates better thermal properties comparing with original fibers. Phosphorylation has done by using $NH_4H_2PO_4$ with the presence of urea at high temperature, that introduced phosphate group in CNF surface and CNF become notably flame retardant, but affected negatively when phosphorylation duration has varied, though in all cases, the charring effect of CNF was enhanced comparing with original fibers. FTIR reveals that hemicellulose, lignin, and other impurities have been decreased prominently. As well as, by visual examination a gel-like CNF has been observed, indicating a high degree of nanofibrillation with increasing surface area. After all, mean diameters approximately 9nm± 2nm with having the high surface area and competitive thermal properties around 290℃ greater than tempo oxidize CNF makes it particularly useful for nanocomposites and biomedical fields.

Keywords: Jute; Cellulose nanofibrils; Phosphorylation; Ultra-sonication; Thermal properties

1　Introduction

With the divert choice tonano range, cellulose nanofibers extracted from cellulose being studied broadly because of its tremendous structure and properties such as high elastic modulus, high aspect ratio, high crystallinity, and low thermal expansions which makes it favorable in wide variety range of applications including nano papers, foams, aerogels, nanocomposites and so on. The properties and structures of CNF are varied with the variation of origin such as woods, cotton, banana, hemp, wheat straw, jute, etc. and the extraction processes such as high-pressure homogenization, acid hydrolysis, and ultra-sonication[1]. Though jute is the most consumed natural's fibers called as golden fibers in Bangladesh, cultivated mostly in Bangladesh and some other regions of India[2], which is mostly used for food packaging, geotextile, industrial products, etc. because of low cost, environment friendly behavior, bio-degradability and so on, but interestingly very few research has done regarding jute extracted CNF. With containing the foremost component of 61%−72% cellulose by mass[3] that made jute easy to catch by fire and damaged readily at a typical atmosphere[4]. By introducing phosphate group on the surface of the fibers via phosphorylation which is widely appreciable alternate after the restriction of halogenated FRs (Flame Retardancy) due to environmental concern gives the materials flame-proof properties. The aim of this paper is to study the effect of thermal properties of jute extracted CNF at different phosphorylation times with combining the ultra-sonication as mechanical treatment so that it can add further value in the field of bio composites.

2　Experiments

2.1　Materials

Jute was tages used as raw materials were collected from

a farm (Shanghai, China). NaOH, H_2O_2, urea, and $NH_4H_2PO_4$ were purchased from Shanghai Lingfeng Chemical Reagent Co. Ltd. (Shanghai, China). Provided chemicals were used directly without further conditioning or purification.

2.2 Phosphorylation of Residue Jute

In the beginning, the chopped fibers were bleached for 90 min at 55℃, with an aqueous solution of 16%. Then filtered until the pH becomes neutral and phosphorylation has done[6]. In brief, the pulverized pulp was soaked with a weight ratio of 0.5 : 0.75 : 0.6 : 0.224 (raw fiber : deionized (DI) water : urea : $NH_4H_2PO_4$). The compositions were then dried and cured at 165℃ for 10min, 15min and 20min in hot air for making three different samples and marked as HP10, HP15, and HP20. Untreated reagents were removed by continuous filtration. Lastly, the fibers were treated for 1h by NaOH with maintaining the pH 12 - 13. Excess NaOH removed by repeated filtration.

2.3 Preparation of CNF by the High-Intensity Ultra-Sonication Method

0.5% pretreated cellulose fiber was diluted with DI water then placed in a JY92 - IIDS ultrasonic cell disruptor for 30min at 1000W of 20 - 225kHz in frequency for conducting ultra-sonication[7] with maintaining an ice/water bath throughout the process. A portion of the obtained suspensions after ultra-sonication was centrifuged for 10 minutes at 6000rpm to separate the sediments from the rest and rapidly freeze-dried for further process. Ultra-sonicated CNF was labeled as CNF10, CNF15, and CNF20.

2.4 Characterization

The changes in the dispersion of treated and untreated fibers were observed by visual examination.

Transmission electron microscopy (TEM) images obtained from JEM - 2100 (JEOL Co. Ltd) at accelerating voltage of 60kV. 20μL diluted NC suspension was dropped onto a copper grid and excessive water was drained and then it was used as a background with 2% uranyl acetate to heighten the microscopic resolution. For scanning electron microscope (SEM, Coxem EM - 30plus, South Korea) images, samples were placed in

a metal stud using double-sided tape and coated with a fine layer of gold using a sputter gold coater before subjected to the SEM analysis. The diameters of the CNF were determined by using nano measurer software.

TGA (Thermogravimetric analysis)/DTG analysis has done by TGA 4000 (PerkinElmer) analyzer with the freeze-dried of 3 - 5mg samples by maintaining a heating range from 30℃ to 700℃ at a constant rate of 10℃/min under a nitrogen environment with a gas flow rate at 20mL/min.

Freeze-dried fibers were examined at the range of $450cm^{-1}$ to $4000cm^{-1}$ by attenuated total reflectance Fourier transform infrared spectroscopy (ATR-FTIR) using a NEXUS - 670 FTIR spectrometer.

3 Results and Discussions

3.1 Visual Examination

All the CNF samples were placed motionlessly for a certain period of time after ultra-sonication including raw fibers as shown in Fig. 1. From visual observation, it was clear that CNF was sufficiently dispersed and converted into gel form suspensions which indicated a high degree of nanofibrillation and improvement of surface area. Whereas, raw fibers were aggregated at the bottom after a while.

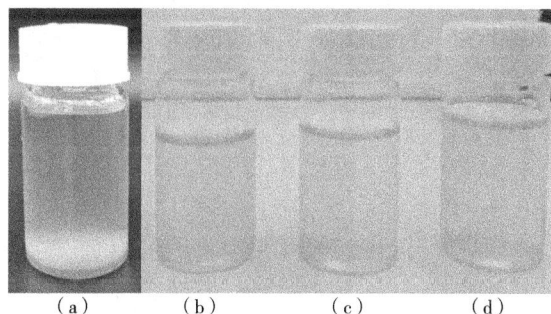

Fig. 1　(a) Raw fibers; (b) CNF10; (c) CNF15; (d) CNF20

3.2 Morphological Analysis by SEM and TEM

Fig. 2 and Fig. 3 show the SEM and TEM micrographs of the untreated and extracted CNF fibers respectively. Whereas before ultra-sonication the dia of the fibers were around 100μm with an aggregated multiple branches and impurities have been showing up, however, the TEM images of CNF fibers after the ultra-sonication have a web-like structure with negligible branches of aggregated bundles of nanofibers having a mean diameter of (9 ± 2) nm, where approximately 5% nanofibers revealed the diameter more than (14 ± 2) nm with a length of hundreds of nanometers to few microns. Although a certain amount of small gaps among the individualized nanofibers can be observed in the aggregated areas which is a lower hydrogen bonding indication after ultra-sonication.

Fig. 2　SEM images of jute fibers

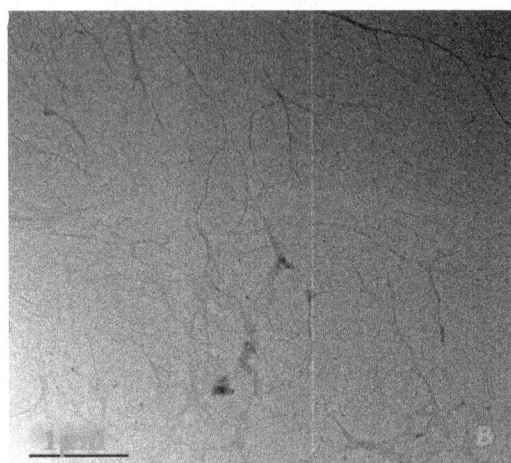

Fig. 3　TEM images of extracted CNF

3.3　Thermal Stability Analysis

From TGA and DTG graph, a devious curvature was exposed up to 100℃ for both treated and untreated fibers due to the evaporation of bound molecules of moisture and other low weight particles from the surface of the fibers[8]. Around 300℃, raw jute was started degrading whereas extracted CNF with different curing time de-

clined earlier around 280℃ to 290℃ respectively.

As well as $T_{\max}$ on the DTG curve were 388℃ for raw fibers, on the other hand, for CNF10 it was 343℃, and rest of the CNF showed a negligible different from CNF10 (Fig. 4). Because of non-cellulosic elements present on original fibers which act as obstacles to initiate its thermal degradation, but for the CNF due to the larger surface area with the presence of fewer impurities like lignin, hemicellulose makes it free from such interruptions[9]. On the other hand, it was obvious by observing char percentage from the graph, the residues values for original fibers was around 15%, whereas extracted CNF exposed the values near 38% which indicated the flame retardancy of fibers because higher char indicates fewer impurities, but among the three treated fibers CNF10 was more thermally stable than others and thermal stability for CNF20 become decline (Fig. 5). Nanofibrillation diminished due to excessive cross-linking of cellulose chains along phosphate groups with increasing phosphorylation and the inner crosslinking between microfibrils, as well as with increasing of times urea reduction occurred which is a key element that used as a spacer to prevent cross-linking between cellulose and microfibrils as well as act to prevent proton release from $NH_4H_2PO_4$, is also a reason of cellulose degradation[6].

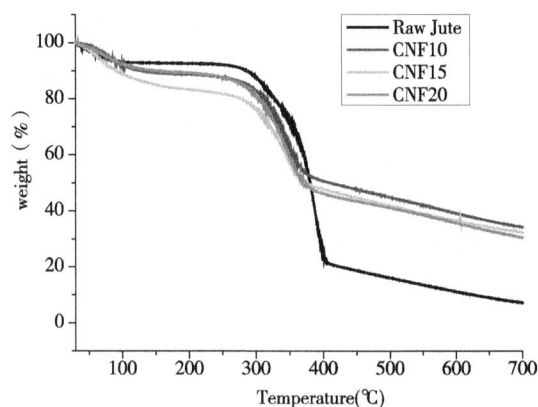

Fig. 4　TGA curves of pristine jute

3.4　FTIR Analysis

The comparable curve for untreated and treated fibers with variable conditions has revealed from FTIR analysis (Fig. 6). From band at 1240cm^{-1} detects the presence

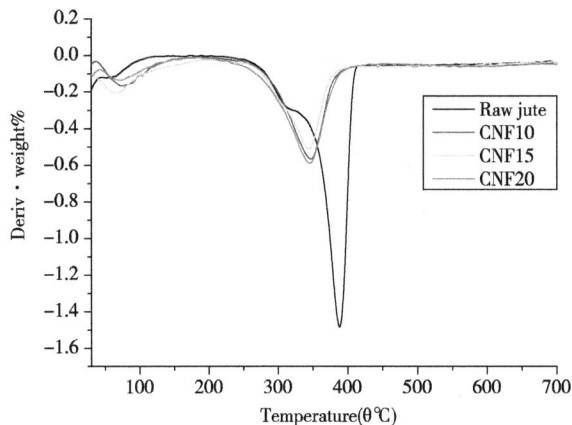

Fig. 5 DTG curves of extracted CNF

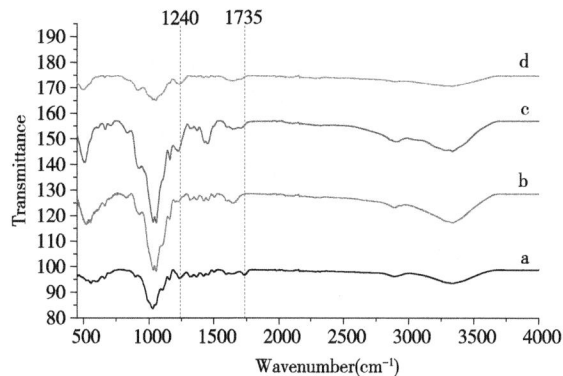

Fig. 6 FTIR spectra of (a) untreated jute; (b) CNF10; (c) CNF15 and (d) CNF20

of lignin which intensity is higher for raw but completely absence for rest of the samples realm[10]. As well as at 1735cm⁻¹ obvious peaks showed for raw fibers but absence in CNF which is the corresponding peak to the vibration of acetyl and uronic ester groups of hemicellulose or indicates the linkage of carboxylic groups of ferulic and p-coumaric acids presents in lignin[10]. Overall the dominated absorption peaks at 3400cm⁻¹, 2900cm⁻¹, 1430cm⁻¹, 1370cm⁻¹, 897 – 890cm⁻¹, 1030cm⁻¹ or 1160cm⁻¹ and 675–557cm⁻¹, are coincided with —OH groups, CH_2 groups, intermolecular hydrogen attraction at C_6 groups, C—O bonds in the polysaccharide aromatic ring[11], C—O—C groups from glycosidic units or β – glucosidic linkage[12], C—O stretching and bending vibration of intermolecular O—H group under different treatment, indicating the cellulose structure[10].

4 Conclusions

By comparative analysis of thermal properties it's being manifested that though phosphorylated duration negatively affect the cellulose nanofibers, but comparing with tempo oxidized CNF which can degrade at 200℃, our extracted CNF has much higher thermally stable properties and can be used as a promising reinforcing materials in packaging industries wherein the processing of thermoplastic polymer has done above the 200℃ temperature[13]. After ultra-sonication, TEM confirmed the presence of nanofibers had a mean diameter around

9nm±2nm with fewer impurities which are also supported by FTIR analysis. On the other hand, no chemical reagents were used during the extraction process, resulted CNF is more compatible in biomedical and pharmaceutical fields[14].

5 Acknowledgments

The authors disclosed receipt of the following financial support for the research, authorship, and/or publication of this article: the work was supported by National Key R&D Program of China (2018YFC2000900) and Fundamental Research Funds for the Central Universities (2232018A3-04).

References

[1] NECHYPORCHUK O, BELGACEM M N, BRAS. Production of cellulose nanofibrils: a review of recent advances[J]. Industrial Crops and Products, 2016(93):2-25.

[2] CAO X, DING B X, YU J, et al. Cellulose nanowhiskers extracted from TEMPO-oxidized jute fibers[J]. Carbohydrate Polymers, 2012, 90(2): 1075-1080.

[3] THANGAVEL G, MOHANTY S, NAYAK S K. A review of the recent developments in biocomposites based on natural fibers and their application perspectives[J]. Composites Part A: Applied Science and Manufacturing, 2015,77:1-25.

[4] BASAK S, SAMANTA K K, CHATTOPADHYAY S D, et al. Flame retardant and antimicrobial jute textile using sodium metasilicate nonahydrate[J]. Polish Journal of Chemical Technology, 2014,16(2):106-113.

[5] HORROCKS A R, KANDOLA B K, DAVIES P J, et al. Developments in flame retardant textiles-a review[J]. Poly-

mer Degradation and Stability, 2005,88(1):3–12.

[6] NOGUCHI Y, HOMMA I, MATSUBARA Y. Complete nanofibrillation of cellulose prepared by phosphorylation[J]. Cellulose, 2017,24(3):1295–1305.

[7] CHEN W, YU H, LIU Y, et al. Isolation and characterization of cellulose nanofibers from four plant cellulose fibers using a chemical-ultrasonic process[J]. Cellulose, 2011,18 (2):433–442.

[8] C. S J C, GEORGE N, NARAYANANKUTTY S K. Isolation and characterization of cellulose nanofibrils from arecanut husk fibre[J]. Carbohydrate Polymers, 2016,142:158–166.

[9] MARIANO D S R, SOUZA D M C, MAMEDE J N. Preparation and characterization of nanowhiskers cellulose from fiber arrowroot (maranta arundinacea) [J]. Materials Research, 2015,18:225–229.

[10] FONSECA A S, PANTHAPULAKKAL S, KONAR S K, et al. Improving cellulose nanofibrillation of non-wood fiber using alkaline and bleaching pre-treatments [J]. Industrial Crops and Products, 2019,131.

[11] XUE Y, HAN F, XU C, et al. Effects of preparation methods on the morphology and properties of nanocellulose (NC) extracted from corn husk [J]. Industrial Crops and Products, 2017,109:241–247.

[12] GHANADPOUR M, CAROSIO M, LARSSON P T, et al. Phosphorylated cellulose nanofibrils: a renewable nanomaterial for the preparation of intrinsically flame-retardant materials[J]. Biomacromolecules, 2015,16(10):3399–3410.

[13] LU H, GUI Y, ZHENG L, et al. Morphological, crystalline, thermal and physicochemical properties of cellulose nanocrystals obtained from sweet potato residue [J]. Food Research International, 2013,50(1):121–128.

[14] GUISE C, FANGUEIRO R. Biomedical applications of nanocellulose. in natural fibres: advances in science and technology towards industrial applications [J]. Dordrecht: Springer Netherlands,2016.

Escalation of Polyethylene Oxide (PEO) Nanofibers Through Triangular Groove Rotor in the Centrifugal Electrospinning Process

NAVEED Tayyab[1,2], BAJWA Usman Khalid[1], FAROOQ Omer[3], XIE Haoyang[1], YU Zhicai[1], ZHANG Xi[1], WANG Xin[1], ZHONG Yueqi[1,4]*, QIU Yiping[1,4], GUO Jiansheng[1,4]

[1] *College of Textiles, Donghua University, Shanghai, 201620, China*

[2] *Department of Textiles and Technology, University of the Punjab, Lahore, 54590, Pakistan*

[3] *Allied Science College, Gujranwala, 52250, Pakistan*

[4] *Key Lab of Textile Science and Technology, Ministry of Education, shanghai, 201620, China*

* *Corresponding author's email: zhyq@ dhu. edu. cn*

Abstract: In recent years, the advancements in textiles have gained attention due to the cost-effectiveness and production efficiencies. Therefore the purpose of this study was the manufacturing of polyethylene oxide (PEO) nanofibers through triangular and rectangular groove structure rotors, accumulated in the centrifugal electrospinning process. Moreover, the variation in fiber diameters was noticed by varying concentration. The subsequent PEO fibers were characterized through SEM. It was pragmatic that the diameter of PEO fibers changed with the variation in concentration. The results implied that the triangular groove rotor structure was an effective method for yarn production of PEO nanofibers then the rectangular groove rotor structure.

Keywords: PEO nanofibers; Centrifugal electro spinning (CES); Triangular rotor

1 Introduction

Recently, the use of advance textiles has been increased and attained attention due to the high demand in health care, and safety of the world environment[1]. Therefore, textile companies have not only been focusing on new product developments but also on the process efficiencies and cost-effectiveness[2]. Currently, the fibers contrived from polymers through many techniques i. e. electrospinning, melt-blowing and self-assembly, etc[3]. In all techniques, electro-spinning (ES) is considered to be the most efficient procedure for the production of nanofibers[4]. The nanofibers have successful applications in many fields such as biomaterials and composites[5]. Nonetheless, the production of nanofibers is still not cost-effective and non-significant[6]. Thus innovation in utensils and implements are continuously needed to overcome such types of industri-

al constraints[7]. Nanofibers through ES has encountered with more impediments like solution conductivity, high-voltage electric field and an environmental aspect[8]. While nanofibers through the centrifugal electrospinning (CES) of polymers, is recognized considerably because of its simple working principle[9]. The other parameters that affect the CES process are the concentration of polymer, rotational speed, electric voltage, nozzle size, temperature (for melts), evaporation rate, and collector distance, etc. [10]. Although all parameters are obligatory for configuration, however, solution concentration and rotational spinning speed are the primary factors[11]. Since the fibers are produced with narrower diameter while fiber morphology has an elusive impact with the rotational speed of the machine[12].

Many authors have proven the maxes and scams for the optimization of ultrafine fibers[13-16]. However, authors have not found any study associated with the effect of rotor structure design in the CES process. Thus in the present study, the authors have used an electrospinning machine through both centrifugal and electrostatic force with newly proposed high-speed rotor structure. A polymer spinning solution was fed to the nozzle, controlled by the metering pump and dropped down in the center of the spinning rotor. The centrifugal force throws the spinning solution and it deposited on the collector and forming dried nanofibers. In this study, the PEO nanofibers prepared from rotors (rectangular groove structure rotor and triangular grooved structure rotor) have been compared and analyzed under different conditions. Furthermore, the effect of process parameters on fiber diameter and its uniformity obtained from both rotor structures was also examined.

2 Experiments

2.1 Materials

Polyethylene oxide (PEO) $M_W = 100000$, was attained from Shanghai Macklin Biochemical Co. Ltd. The metering pump was coped from Shanghai Angel Electronics Co Limited and DC generator was attained from the Scholl-run factory of Fudan high school. The solutions to the CES experiment were arranged using polyethylene oxide (PEO). PEO powder was dissolved into distilled water in a beaker and stirred with the help of magnetic stirrer at 80℃. It takes 4 hours to make a spinning solution with different concentrations i. e. 6%, 7%, 8% and 9%.

2.2 Structure of Spinning Rotor

Fig. 1 indicates two types of rotors i. e. rectangular groove structure rotor (conventional method) and triangular groove structure rotor (anticipated method). PEO nanofibers accomplished through both the rotors were compared and analyzed. Tab. 1 displays the fundamental scheme of the production of PEO nanofibers. The two-process variables were selected in three levels of each variable i. e. percentages of concentrations, rotor speeds, and the flow rate.

2.3 Sample Preparation

The dissolved PEO solution was prepared and sucked through the vessel meter, and flow rate of the polymer solution was changeable with the metering pump and kept constant (mL/h). The spinning rotor was rotated smoothly through the motor. Thus the liquid dropped down under the action of centrifugal force and electric field force. The development of jet was collected on the circular collector and finally, the continuous PEO nanofibers were obtained. The receiving distance (between the needle and the circular collector) was fixed at 30cm. The factors i. e. the spinning solution concentration, rotor speed, and liquid flow, were considered and examined according to the single-factor experiment. Three levels (shown in Tab. 1) were selected for each parameter. The fabricated material (samples) was acquired on the aluminum foil. The whole spinning process was completed in 1h.

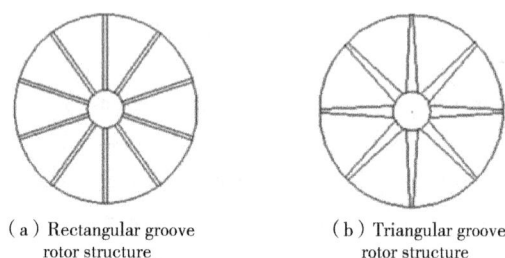

(a) Rectangular groove rotor structure   (b) Triangular groove rotor structure

Fig. 1 Two types of rotor structures

Tab. 1 Production scheme of PEO nanofibers

Level	solution concentration (%) (A)	Rotor speed (R/min) (B)
1	6	4600
2	7	5500
3	8	6400

2.4 Characterization

The morphology of nanofibers was characterized by means of FE-SEM (Scanning electron microscope) instrument. All the samples were coated with the gold prior to the observations. 100 different fiber points of nanofibers were randomly selected from the FE-SEM images. The diameter of the selected nanofibers was measured through the measurement software. The nano measure software was used for the collection of SEM images data. The significance of the images has been described next.

3 Results and Discussions

3.1 Influence of Solution Concentration

PEO nanofibers were fabricated at constant operational conditions of rotational speed, and liquid flow rate in order to determine the influence of solution concentration. The centrifugally electrospun PEO nanofibers were characterized by SEM. The effect in fibers was noticeable with three different solution concentrations. At concentration of 6%, there were large number of droplets and a small number of beads in the fiber. They gave rise to non-continuous fiber. When the concentration was escalated to 7%, a reduction in number of droplets and beads was noticed that caused a lengthier, incessant fiber with the progress in fiber morphology. With the 8% solution concentration, the consequential fibers were established into more advanced and incessant form. Moreover, the fiber diameter increased with the proliferation of solution concentration.

Thus, due to the insufficient chain stretch, the formed fibers were thicker. Fig. 2 has shown SEM images and corresponding fiber disseminations of PEO nanofibers with different solution concentrations (6% to 8%). Fig. 3 displays that with the proliferation of solution concentration the thickness of spun fibers augmented. Thus once the solution concentrations have a high range, i. e. 8% or more, the highly-viscous solution yields the fiber with a thicker breadth. It was due to the higher surface tension that resisted the elongation caused in an insufficient drawing under a certain centrifugal force and electric field strength.

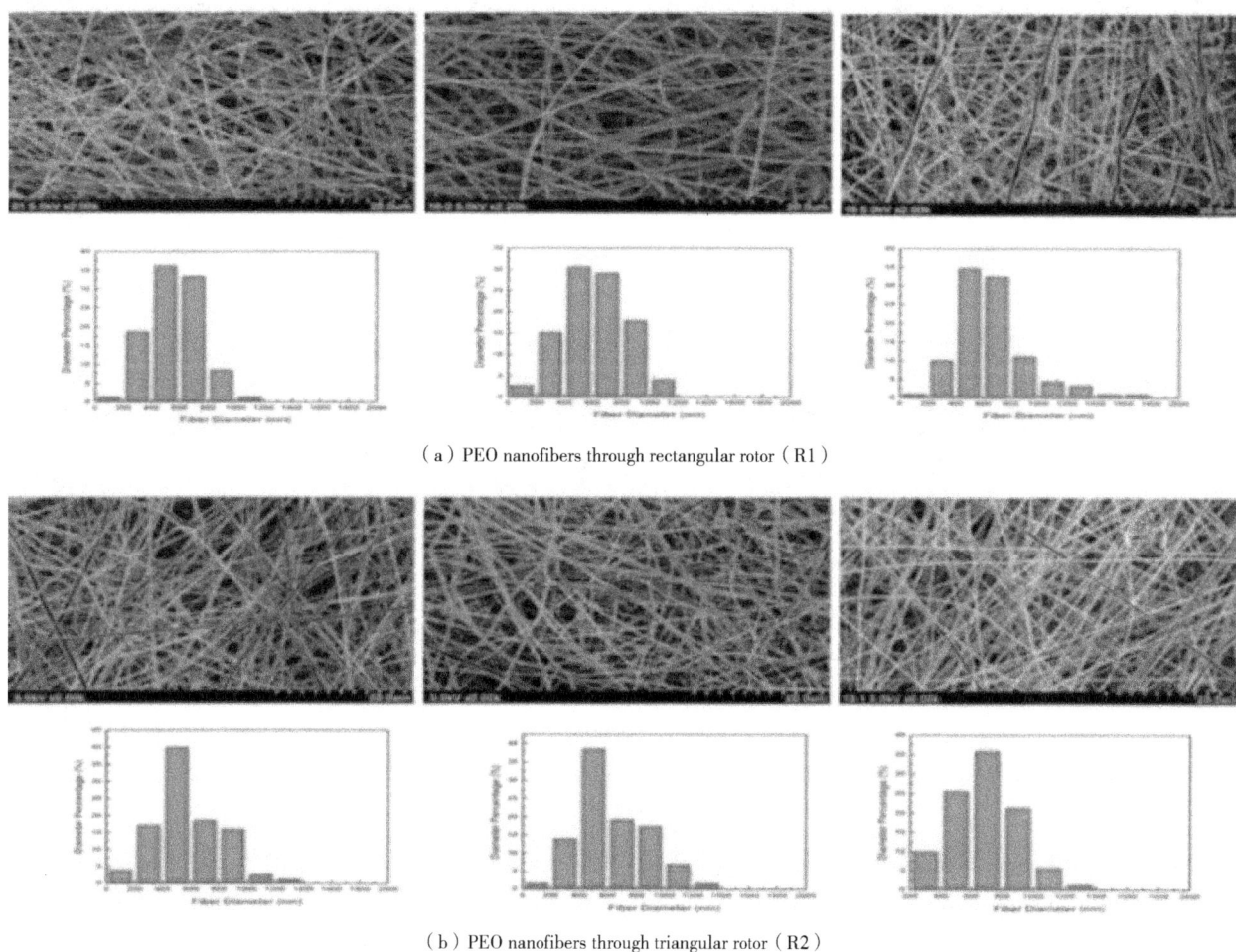

(a) PEO nanofibers through rectangular rotor (R1)

(b) PEO nanofibers through triangular rotor (R2)

Fig. 2 SEM images and diameter of PEO nanofibers at 4600r/min centrifugal electrospun with different solution concentrations (6%, 7%, and 8%)

3.2 Influence of Rotational Speed

Fig. 4 shows the SEM images and fiber (diameter) distributions of PEO nanofibers in different rotational speeds (4600~6400r/min). With the rotor speed lower than 4600r/min, the fibers were thicker and fineness was not uniform. Since the spinning rotor rotates at a slow speed and the small droplets received a little force while throwing them out in the spinning rotor. The droplets thrown and dropped were smaller. The droplet area was large, and the electrical energy required generated the jet increased, resulting in the increase of fiber diameter. When the speed of rotor increased to 5500r/min, the fiber was thinner and more uniform.

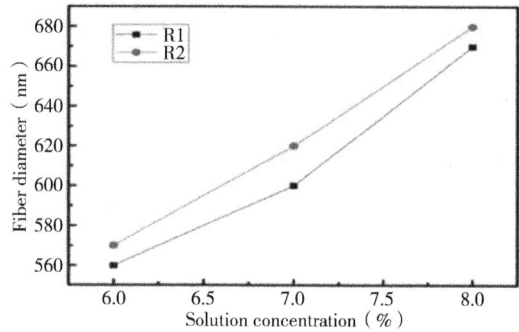

Fig. 3　Influence of solution concentration and fiber diameter

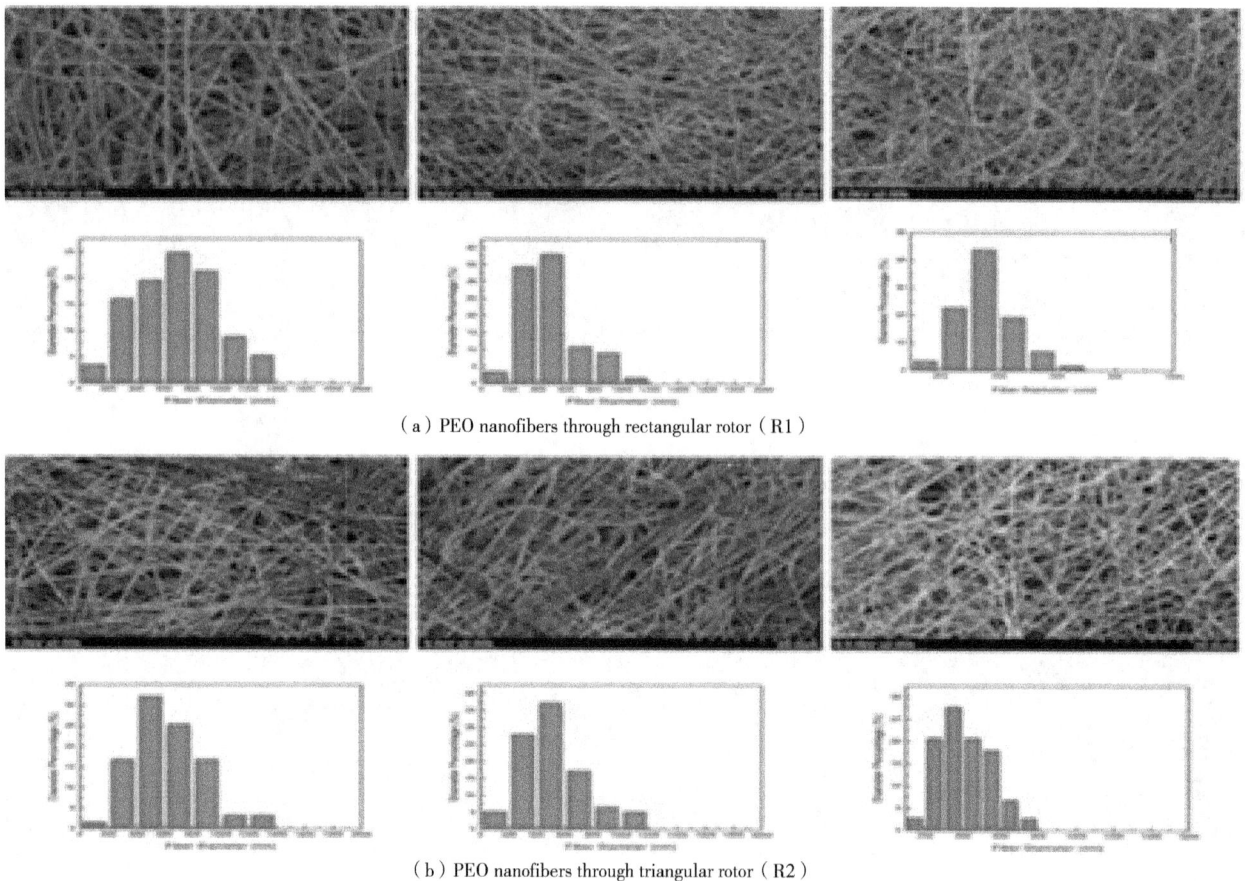

(a) PEO nanofibers through rectangular rotor (R1)

(b) PEO nanofibers through triangular rotor (R2)

Fig. 4　SEM images and diameter of PEO nanofibers centrifugalelectrospun at different rotational speeds (4600r/min, 5500r/min and 6400r/min)

When the spinning rotor rotated at a high speed, the centrifugal force of the small droplets being thrown out was greater. Moreover, the falling of a number of small droplets on the spinning rotor resulted in small droplet surface area. The diameter of the fiber decreased with the increase in rotational speed of the spinning rotor. At the further higher rotational speed of the rotor, i. e. reached to a critical value, the fiber began to crack, and then the jet became bead-like and the diameter of the fiber increased. It produced more non-uniform beads and feeble fibers. Thus the fiber has the best effect at rotor speed of 5500r/min.

Rotational speed has a critical role in the determination of the liquid dropped in the drawing process. To evaluate the effect of rotational speed on fiber morphology, PEO nanofibers with varying rotational speed were fabricated at constant operational conditions of liquid flow, solution concentration and electric field. Fig. 5 has shown that the diameter decreases with the increase in rotational speed. It was observed that the diameter of spun fibers decreased with the increase of rotor speed (Fig. 5). Thus with the increase of rotational speed, the centrifugal force increased.

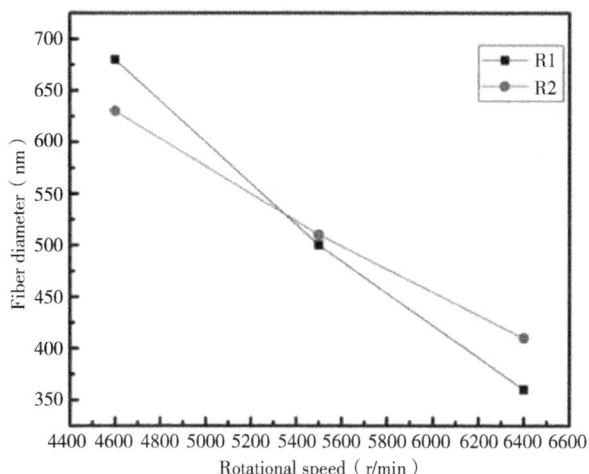

Fig. 5　Influence of rotational speed and fiber diameter

3.3　Influence of the Spinning Rotor Structure

Fig. 6 has displayed the SEM image and distribution of fibers prepared from both the rotors. SEM images have shown that the diameters of PEO nanofibers spun with a triangular groove structure of the spinning rotor have finer and more uniform results than the rectangular groove structure rotor. Thus, the proposed triangular groove structure rotor has better results.

4　Conclusions

PEO yarn production was examined and enhanced through conventional (rectangular rotor structure) and newly proposed (triangular grooved rotor structure) in the CES technology. The consequences revealed that the diameter of the PEO nanofibers with triangular grooved rotor structure was more even and uniform as compared to the rectangular rotor structure. Moreover, it had processed low cost and large-scale production of nanofibers. The highest quality of PEO fibers was obtained at 8% solution concentration where spinning rotor speed of 5500r/min. Thus the successful implementation of the triangular grooved rotor shows an effective approach to assist the conventional spinning industry in PEO yarn production.

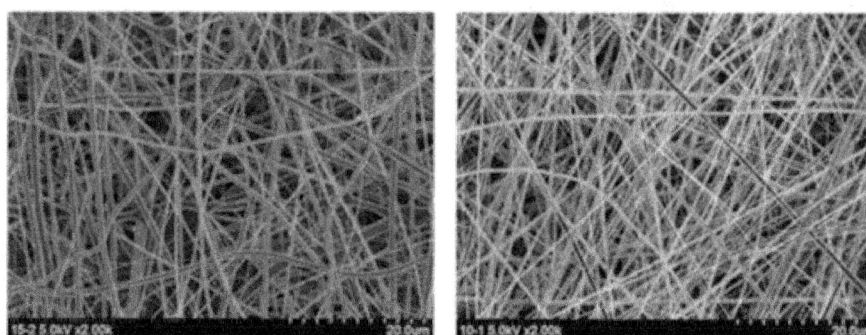

(a)

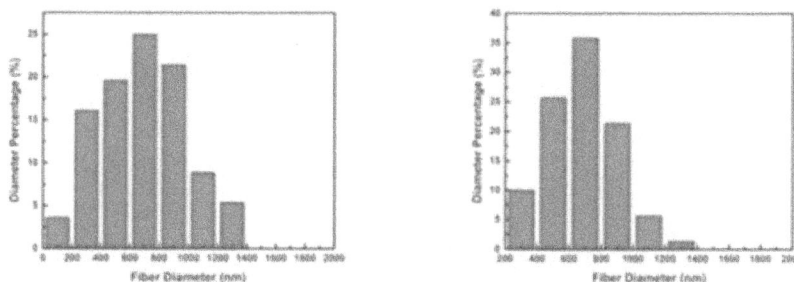

(b)

Fig. 6　Comparison of SEM images and effect of two rotor structures

Acknowledgements

The research is supported by National Natural Science Foundation of China (61572124) and Fundamental Research Funds for the Central Universities (Grant number CUSF-DH-D-2018040).

References

[1] SANDRA VŽ, SANKAUSKAITE A, STYGIENE L, et al. The investigation of barrier and comfort properties of multifunctional coated conductive knitted fabrics [J]. Journal of Industrial Textile, 2016, 45(4): 585-610.

[2] MIRAFTAB M. Comparison of air permeability and moisture management properties of the jersey, interlock, and pique knitted fabrics [J]. The Journal of the Textile Institute, 2012, 2: 1-5.

[3] TAN D, ZHOU C, ELLISON CJ, et al. Melt blown fibers: influence of viscosity and elasticity on diameter distribution [J]. Journal of Non-Newtonian Fluid Mechanics, 2010, 165: 892-900.

[4] LI M, LONG Y Z, YANG D, et al. Fabrication of one dimensional superfine polymer fibers by double-spinning [J]. Journal of Materials Chemistry, 2011, 21: 13159-13162.

[5] HEIDI S G, GIBSON P, KRIS S, et al. Protective textile materials based on electrospun nanofibers [J]. Journal of Advance Materials, 2002, 34: 44-55.

[6] EICHHORN S J, SAMPSON W W. Statistical geometry of pores and statistics of porous nanofibrous assemblies [J]. Journal of the Royal Society Interface, 2005, 2: 309-318.

[7] NAVEED T, HUSSAIN A, and ZHONG Y, Reducing fabric wastage through image projected virtual marker (IPVM) [J]. Textile Research Journal, 2017, 88 (14): 1571-1580.

[8] MARY L. A, SENTHILRAM T, SUGANYA S, et al. Centrifugal spun ultrafine fibrous web as a potential drug delivery vehicle [J]. Express Polymer Letters, 2013, 7: 238-248.

[9] HUTTUNEN M, KELLOMAKI M. A simple and high production rate manufacturing method for submicron polymer fibres [J]. Journal of Tissue Engineering and Regenerative Medicine, 2011, 5: 239-243.

[10] BADROSSAMAY M R, MCLLWEE H A, GOSS J A, et al. Nanofiber assembly by rotary jet-spinning [J]. Nano Letters, 2010, 10: 2257-2261.

[11] LUO C J, STRIDE E, EDIRISINGHE M. Mapping the Influence of Solubility and Dielectric Constant on Electrospinning Polycaprolactone Solutions [J]. Macromolecules, 2012, 45: 4669-4680.

[12] ZHANG C, YUAN X, WU L, et al. Study on morphology of electrospun poly (vinyl alcohol) mats [J]. European Polymer Journal, 2005, 41: 423-430.

[13] ZHANG X, LU Y. Centrifugal spinning: an alternative approach to fabricate nanofibers at high speed and low cost [J], Polymer Reviews, 2014, 54: 677-701.

[14] XIA L, JU J, XU W, et al. Preparation and characterization of hollow Fe_2O_3 ultra-fine fibers by centrifugal spinning [J]. Materials and Design, 2016, 96: 439-445.

[15] WEITZ RT, HARNAU L, RAUSCHENBACH S, et al. Polymer nanofibers via nozzle-free centrifugal spinning American Chemical Society [J]. Nano Letters, 2008, 8 (4): 1187-1191.

[16] VALIPOURI A, HOSSEINI RAVANDI S A, PISHEVAR A R. A novel method for manufacturing nanofibers [J]. Fibers and Polymers, 2013, 14 (6): 941-949.

Comparison Between the Three-and Four-Component Low Temperature Treatments for Dyed Cotton Warp Yarn Preparation

GUAN Yue[1,3], ZHANG Ziyun[1,3], GHULAM Mustafa[1,3], ZHANG Xijuan[1,3],
LIU Wanshuang[4], QIU Yiping[1,2,3,5], JIANG Qiuran[1,2,3]*

[1] Key Laboratory of Textile Science & Technology, Ministry of Education, College of Textiles, Donghua University Shanghai, 201620, China

[2] Engineering Research Center of Technical Textiles, College of Textiles, Donghua University, Shanghai, 201620, China

[3] Department of Technical Textiles, College of Textiles, Donghua University, Shanghai, 201620, China

[4] Donghua University Center for Civil Aviation Composites, Donghua University, Shanghai, 201620, China

[5] College of Textiles and Apparel, Quanzhou Normal University, Fujian, 350000, China

* Corresponding author's email: jj@ dhu. edu. cn

Abstract: The conventional sizing processes consume a large amount of sizing agents and require for corresponding desizing processes, which add the costs and elicit severe water pollution. In this research, two low temperature treatments in a three-and a four-component baths were used for the preparation of dyed cotton warp yarns. The treatment effects on morphology, hairiness, mechanical properties, abrasion resistance and decoloration were investigated and compared. The results indicated that both treatments could substantially reduce the amount of harmful hairiness, enhance the yarn strength and slightly reduce yarn elongation at a similar level. The abrasion resistance has been elevated, but the four-component treatment were more efficient. No decoloration was observed after the treatments. On the contrary, the color depth was increased. This research proved that the three-and four-component low temperature treatments are applicable for the cotton warp yarn preparation and the four-component treatment can provide a better treatment efficacy. These treatments can be used for not only greige cotton yarns but also dyed cotton yarns without eliciting any decoloration.

Keywords: Low temperature; Dyed cotton yarn; Sizing; Hairiness; Decoloration

1 Introduction

The sizing process provide warp yarns with enhanced strength, abrasion resistance and reduced hairiness tolower the warp breaking rate and increase the weaving productivity[1]. Thus, this process is essential to produce fabrics, especially when staple yarns are used. The consumption of sizing agents causes additional costs to the low margin textile products.[2]. To promote a sustainable development of the textile industry, it's important to replace the traditional sizing process with more economical, environmentally friendly and efficient processes for warp yarn preparation.

A low temperature dissolution method for cellulose in a sodium hydroxide (NaOH)/urea aqueous bath was reported to be efficient at a low temperature around $-13\,^\circ\!C$ to $-15\,^\circ\!C$[3]. Based on this concept, a new low temperature sizing process was developed with the NaOH/urea aqueous bath for the treatment of cotton warp yarns without any addition of sizing agents[4]. It was proven that the strength and abrasion resistance of yarns could be elevated to the comparable levels with the traditional methods.

Recently, Huajin Jin et. al. reported that a new four-component NaOH/thiourea/urea aqueous bath was more efficient to dissolve cellulose at low temperatures[5]. The portion of cellulose that can be dissolved in the three-component solution was only 5. 0%, while the four-component solution could raise the dissolution amount to 6. 0%[6]. Therefore, in this current research, we proposed a hypothesis that this four-component bath might be more efficient for the cotton yarn preparation. Besides, greige cotton yarns were used and then the dyeabilities the original and treated yarns were compared. It is still unclear whether the low temperature treatment systems can be applied for the dyed cotton yarns. Hence, in this current research, the three-and four-component treatments for cotton warp yarn preparation were compared and feasibility to apply these methods to dyed cotton yarns was proven.

2　Experiments

2.1　Materials

To prove the feasibility of applying the developed treatments on dyed cotton yarns, the cotton yarns (20tex) pre-stained by a reactive dye (Reactive Blue 19, CAS2580-78-1) were provided by the Guangzhou Esquel Group. The chips of NaOH (≥ 98.0%, premium level) and the granules of urea (≥99.0%, analytical purity) were bought from the Shanghai Titan Scientific Co., Ltd. The powders of thiourea (chemically pure) was purchased from the Sinopharm Chemical Reagent Co. Ltd.

2.2　Yarn Treatment

The three-component treatment bathwas prepared by dissolving NaOH and urea in distilled water at a weight ratio of 12 : 7 : 81, while the four-component treatment bath was prepared similarly with NaOH, urea and thiourea in distilled water at a weight ratio of 8 : 8 : 6.5 : 77.5[11]. Both types of treatment baths were pre-cooled to −15℃. The cotton yarns were fixed on steel frames, immersed in treatment bathes for 5min, washed by distilled water 3 times to neutral and dried at 70℃ for 30 min. In the following description, the original yarns were labeled as C, the yarns treated in the three-component bath were indicated as T3 and the samples prepared in the four-component bath were represented as T4.

2.3　Characterization of Yarn Properties

The photos of yarns were recorded by a digital camera (Cannon, Power Shot SX40HS) in the Standard illuminant Box (YG982, QuanzhouMeibang Instrument Co., Ltd. China) The hairiness of yarns was tested on a yarn hairiness tester (YG172A, Shanxi Changling Textile

Mechanical & Electronic Technological Co., Ltd. China) at 30m/min. The strength and elongation of the yarns were measured on an electronic single yarn strength tester (YG 061, Laizhou Electron Instrument co., Ltd. China) with a gauge length of 500mm at a crosshead speed of 500mm/min. The abrasion resistance of yarns was evaluated on a yarn cohesion tester (Y731, Changzhou Textile Instrument, China) equipped with friction blades (90mm in length) at a reciprocating velocity of 90 times/min. The friction cycles were recorded at rupture. To evaluate the changes in the color depth of yarns, the original and treated yarns were parallelly arranged to form a single yarn layer and two layers of yarns were fixed on a frame orthogonally to each other to prepare a $4 \times 4cm^2$ square. The K/S values of samples were tested on a Datacolor 850 spectrophotometer (America, USAV).

2.4　Statistical Analysis

The obtained data were analyzed by a one-way analysis of variance with Turkey's pair wise multiple comparisons. The confidence interval was 95%. A statistically significant difference was shown when the p-value was less than 0.05, and the compared data were labeled with different letters.

3　Results and Discussions

3.1　Effect of the Treatments on the Hairiness of Yar

Fig. 1(a) displays the morphologies of the original and treated yarns. A large amount of long fiber endsprotrudes from the body of the original yarn, while the lengths and amounts of fiber ends reduce substantially after the three-and four-component treatments. The yarn hairs above 3mm are considered as harmful, because they may induce yarn entanglement, prevent shedding and even elicit the breakage of yarns[7]. After the three-and four-component treatments, the hairiness numbers of the benign yarn hairs were substantially reduced by 89.6% (T3) and 90.5% (T4), and the values of the harmful yarn hairs decreased 82.9% (T3) and 88.6% (T4) (Fig. 1 B). During the treatments, the low molecular weight components, such as pectin, lignin, hemicellulose, and small cellulose, were dissolved or partially dissolved from cotton fibers. Thereby, some of the fiber ends might be ruptured during treatments, and the harmful hairs were reduced.

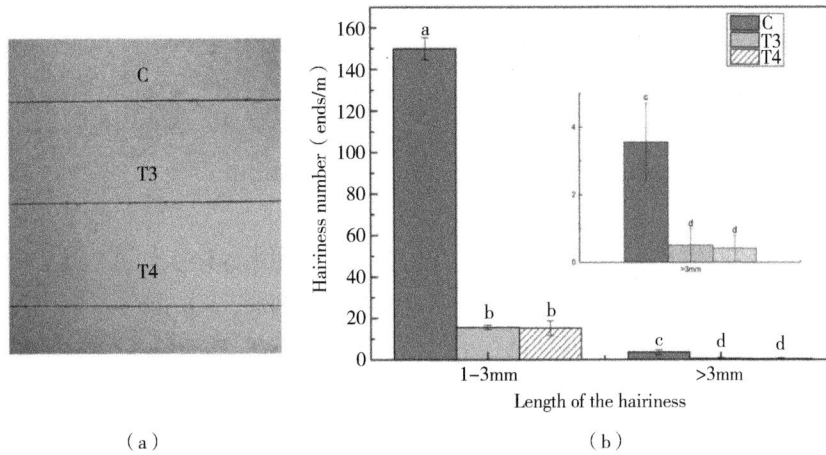

Fig. 1　Effect of the treatments on the hairiness of yarns. (a) the morphological changes of yarns by treatments; (b) the changes in hairiness number by treatments. C: original yarn; T3: the yarns treated in the three-component bath; T4: the yarns treated in the four-component bath.

3.2　Effect of the Treatments on Mechanical Properties of Yarns

As shown in Fig. 2(a), the three-and four-component treatments could enhance the yarn tenacity by 13.1% (T3) and 16.2% (T4), while the elongations were reduced by 16.9% (T3) and 18.6% (T4). The reso-lidified low molecular components on fiber surfaces could bind fibers and build connection among fibers, which facilitated load transfer. Therefore, the load distribution could be more efficient and even. With a small amount of the resolidified low molecular components, the yarn tenacity could be enhanced.

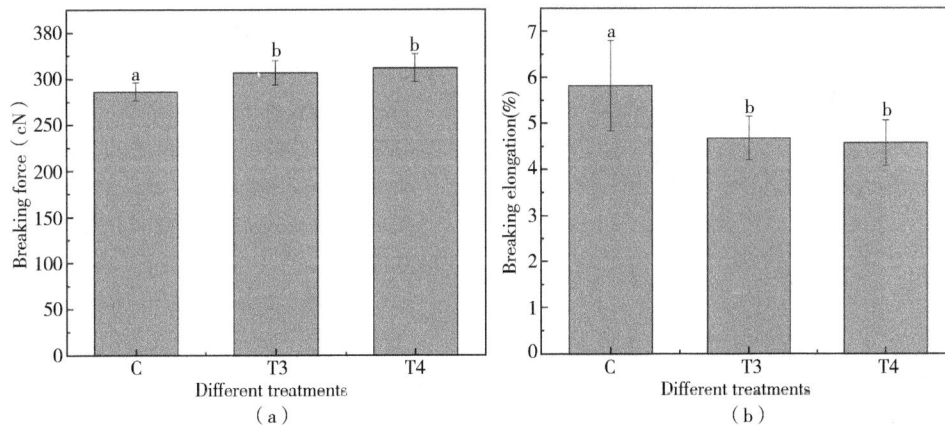

Fig. 2　Effect of the treatments on mechanical properties of yarns: (a) Breaking force of yarns; (b) Breaking elongation of yarns

3.3　Effect of the Treatments on Abrasion Resistance of Yarns

Fig. 3 displays the efficacy of the treatments to enhance the abrasion resistance of yarns. The friction cycles of the yarns treated in the three-and four-component baths increased 41.7% (T3) and 94.5% (T4), respectively.

For the original cotton yarns, the abrasion resistance was provided by the limited friction force among fibers. After the treatments, the resolidified components not only offered a thin coating layer on the out surface of yarns but also built the connections among fibers, which substantially enhanced the friction force among fibers.

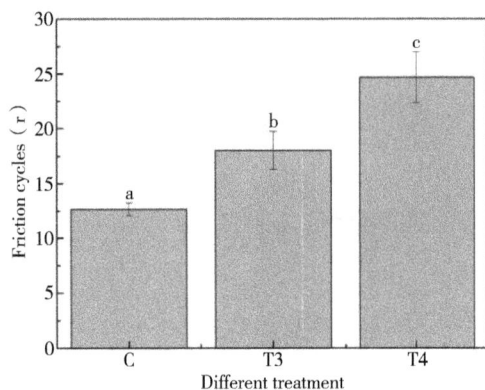

Fig. 3　Effect of the treatments on abrasion resistance of yarns

3.4　Effect of the Treatments on the Decoloration of Yarns

The digital photos and the K/S values of the original and treated yarns are shown in Fig. 4. After the treatments, the changes in color depth of samples were subtle, but could still notice that the colors of treated samples were deeper[Fig. 4(a)], which proved that nodecoloration was elicited after the treatment. It was consistent with the results of the K/S values[Fig. 4(b)]. The three-and four-component treatments could raise the K/S values around 6.0% (T3) and 10.0% (T4), but the efficacies were similar. The low treatments

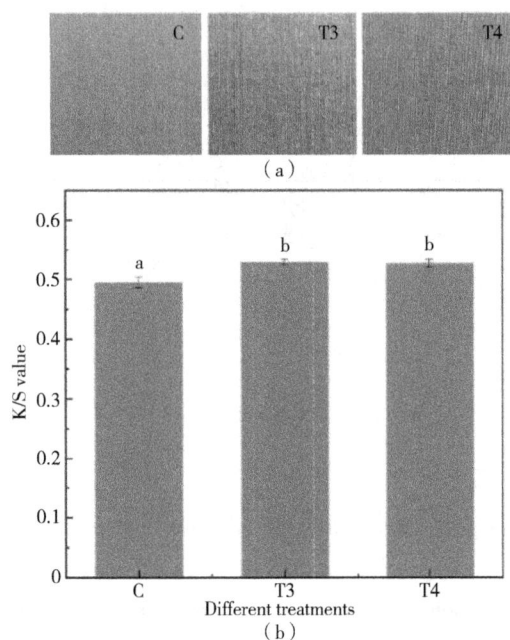

Fig. 4　Effect of the treatments on the decoloration of yarns:
(a) The digital photos of the original and treated yarns;
(b) The K/S values of the original and treated yarns

could remove a portion of the pectin, lignin, hemicellulose, cellulose and waxes, which have different affinities to dye molecules. During the treatments, some hydrogen bonds were dissociated leading to the swelling of cotton fibers. The cross sections of fibers changed from a kidney shape to a round shape and the color of yarns became brighter[8].

4　Conclusions

This research compared a three-and four-component low temperature treatments for the preparation of dyed cotton warp yarns. The results indicated that this work proved the penitential of these two low temperature treatments to replace the conventional sizing processes.

Acknowledgements

The financial supports of this work were provided by the National Natural Science Foundation of China (51503031) and the Scientific Research Foundation for the Returned Overseas Scholars from the Ministry of Education (15B10127).

References

[1] AMIT Madhu, CHAKRABORTY J N. Recovery and reuse of immobilized α-amylase during desizing of cotton fabric[J]. Research Journal of Textile and Apparel, 2018, 22(3): 271-290.

[2] CAI J, ZHANG L, LIU S, et al. Dynamic self-assembly induced rapid dissolution of cellulose at low temperatures[J]. Macro-molecules, 2008, 41(23): 9345-9351.

[3] ZHANG S, LI F X, YU J Y, et al. Dissolution behaviour and solubility of cellulose in NaOH complex solution[J]. Carbohydrate Polymers, 2010, 81(3): 668-674.

[4] JIANG Q R, CHEN S, DENG X, et al. A sustainable low temperature yarn reinforcing process to reduce water and energy consumptions and pollution in the textile industry[J]. Journal of Cleaner Production, 2019, 210: 646-652.

[5] JIN H J, ZHA C X, GU L X. Direct dissolution of cellulose in NaOH/thiourea/urea aqueous solution[J]. Carbohydrate Research, 2007, 342(6): 851-858.

[6] YAN L, CHEN J, BANGAL P R. Dissolving cellulose in a NaOH/thiourea aqueous solution: a topochemical investigation[J]. Macro-molecular bioscience, 2007, 7(9-10): 1139-1148.

[7] KESHK S M A S. Effect of different alkaline solutions on

crystalline structure of cellulose at different temperatures [J]. Carbohydrate Polymers, 2015, 115(2): 658-662.

[8]CAI J, ZHANG L N, CHANG C, et al. Hydrogen-bond-induced inclusion complex in aqueous cellulose/LiOH/urea solution at low temperature[J]. Chem Phys Chem, 2007, 8(10): 1572-1579.

Effect of Phosphorus, Antimony Trioxide and Zinc Borate Flame Retardant on PVC Materials

HUANG Li[1,2], **CHEN Nanliang**[1,2], **WANG Meiyi**[1,2], **JIANG Jinghua**[1,2], **HAO Enquan**[3], **ZHANG Renbiao**[3]

[1] *Engineering Research Center of Technical Textiles, Ministry of Education, Shanghai, 201620, China*

[2] *College of Textiles, Donghua University, Shanghai, 201620, China*

[3] *Zhejiang MSD New Material Co. ,Ltd. ,Haining, 314419, China*

* *Corresponding author's email*: jiangjinhua@ dhu. edu. cn

Abstract: With the increasing demand for PVC film in the market, customers' requirements for their special performance are also increasing. Among them, flame retardant and smoke suppressing is one of them. Of course, it is also the research target of this subject. This project uses DOP as a plasticizer for PVC film, a phosphorus-based flame retardant (liquid flame retardant) and antimony trioxide (solid flame retardant), and zinc borate as a smoke suppressant to form a film. DPK-Sb_2O_3-ZB constitutes a ternary compounding System. The best formula for flame retardant is obtained by designing orthogonal experiments. And the best formula is: PVC : C-PVC 70 : 30, DOP : DPK 50 : 10, Sb_2O_3 : ZB 6 : 10. The obtained film was subjected to basic mechanical properties test such as tensile fracture. And the mechanical properties of the film were found to be excellent.

Keywords: PVC film; Flame retardant; Smoke suppression; Compound-synergy effect; Flame retardant mechanism

1 Introduction

Polyvinyl chloride (PVC) is one of the most widely used chemical materials, whether it is used in the chemical, light industry, building materials industry, or in the electromechanical, textile and other industries. However, PVC materials are easy to burn and to produce a large amount of toxic fumes in the combustion. So it is of special significance for the study of smoke suppression of PVC[1]. As the market demands for its performance, the study of PVC materials should be deepened. The flame retardant and smoke suppression effect achieved by a single flame retardant and smoke suppressant has not been able to meet the needs of the market. Therefore, the study on the compounding system of various flame retardant and smoke suppressant has been favored by many researchers. A large number of studies have shown that the flame retardant effect of the phosphorus-based flame

retardant is excellent, and the smoke suppressing effect of Sb_2O_3 and ZB is very obvious[2-4]. It can be used in soft PVC, and it is one of the commonly used methods to study the flame retardant effect by the vertical combustion method. In this paper, DPK—Sb_2O_3—ZB ternary compounding system is studied. Different ratios of PVC : CPVC, DOP : DPK and Sb_2O_3 : ZB on the flame retardant and smoke inhibition properties and mechanical properties of PVC membranes were studied.

2 Experiments

2.1 Materials

The ground cloth was produced by Zhejiang MSD New Material Co. ,Ltd. Warp and weft linear density : 1000 D; Warp density: 18 picks/inch; Weft density: 18 picks/inch. Reagents: PVC powder, CPVC powder, DOP, ESO, Ba—Zn, $CaCO_3$, Sb_2O_3, zinc borate, liquid flame retardant (phosphorus), glue, slurry.

2.2 Main Equipment

Flat vulcanizingmachine (Huzhou Shunli Rubber Machinery Co. Ltd.); Fabric flame-retardant tester (Wenzhou Fangyuan Instrument Co. Ltd.); MTS material testing machine; Instron universal material testing machine(Instron Corp. Canton); SEM.

2.3 Test Conditions

The flame retardant test is carried out according to the vertical burning method in the textile performance test method GB/T 5455—2014; the tensile fracture strength test mainly refers to the strip method in ASTM D751—2005. The test conditions are: temperature 20℃, relative humidity 50% The tear strength test mainly refers to the trapezoidal tear in GB/T 3917.2—2009; the peel strength test mainly refers to GB/T 3917.2—2009, and the sample size is 182mm×50mm.

2.4 Experiment Procedure

Mix PVC resin with plasticizer (DOP), stabilizer, lubricant and flame retardant on the open mill for 8min, the front roll temperature is 170℃, the back roll temperature is 180℃, and then place in the automatic tablet press, at 160℃, 5MPa hot press for 3 min, 10MPa hot press for 5 min, then take the PVC film out and cold press for 3 min. After the mixing part is completed, cut it into A4 paper size. Finally, the PVC film and the sized substrate were calendered and laminated on a flat vulcanizer.

2.5 Characterization

The surface topography of the sample was observed on an environmental scanning electron microscope. In order to enhance the conductivity of the sample, the sample was subjected to steaming treatment before the test.

3 Results and Discussions

3.1 Orthogonal Test Analysis

Epoxy soybean oil (ESO): 2phr, plasticizer + flame retardant = 60phr, PVC + CPVC = 100. Determine (a) PVC : CPVC, (b) plasticizer: flame retardant (DPK), (c) Sb_2O_3 : ZB. Each factor level: A: A_1 = 100 : 0, A_2 = 85 : 15, A_3 = 70 : 30, B: B_1 = 45 : 15, B_2 = 50 : 10, B_3 = 55 : 5, C: C_1 = 6 : 10 C_2 = 8 : 15, C_3 = 10 : 20, according to these levels and factors, 9 kinds of formulations were randomly combined. This experiment uses L9 (3^4) orthogonal table, the orthogonal experimental scheme is as follows, and the fourth column is blank column.

According to Tab. 1, the damage carbon length of the PVC film of the 9 formulas is kept within 5cm, which indicates that the flame retardant property of the film is excellent, and at the same time, the tensile strength of the film is generally maintained at about 1200N while ensuring excellent flame retardant properties. Due to different ratio of flame retardant and smoke suppressant added in each formula, the tensile strength of PVC film is different. Generally speaking, in the flame retardant system, the flame retardant effect gradually increase with the increase of particulate matter. Decreasing, as the content of Sb_2O_3 and ZB increases, the

Tab. 1　Flame retardant properties and mechanical properties analysis table

Formulations	Column NO.				Results		
	1(A)	2(B)	3(C)	4	Damaged length(cm)	Breaking strength(N)	Elongation(%)
1	1	1	1	1	4.12	1397.2	15.4
2	1	2	2	2	4.63	1143.1	15.3
3	1	3	3	3	4.73	1331.6	13.0
4	2	1	3	3	4.50	1223.2	12.7
5	2	2	1	1	4.67	1178.7	16.6
6	2	3	2	2	4.52	1171.0	17.3
7	3	1	2	2	4.60	958.0	16.8
8	3	2	3	3	4.17	1338.6	13.3
9	3	3	1	1	4.69	1123.2	12.7

tensile strength of the system decreases. Using MAT-LAB to analyze and considering the damage length, breaking strength, and elongation, the optimal formula can be obtained: PVC : CPVC 70 : 30, DOP : DPK 50 : 10, Sb_2O_3 : ZB 6 : 10. According to the formula, a new PVC composite material was prepared, and the flame retardant effect and mechanical properties were all optimized to the best.

3.2 SEM Analysis

Fig. 1(a) shows the surface structure of the PVC film after combustion. It can be seen that the surface of the film has formed a dense carbon layer with different shapes and irregularities. During the combustion of PVC, Sb_2O_3 and ZB react chemically, forming a dense carbon layer to prevent air from entering the system, and also preventing the combustion system from exchanging heat with the outside world. Fig. 1(b) shows that the surface of Sb_2O_3—ZB particulate matter. The particulate product of the Sb_2O_3—ZB produced by the reaction coats the surface of the combustible material, thereby preventing the combustible material from continuing to burn. Fig. 1(c), (d) are EDS diagram. It can be seen that the P and Sb elements are uniformly distributed on the surface of the film, and the contents of Sb and P are higher than those of other elements other than Cl, which means that the flame retardant has been well mixed into the PVC.

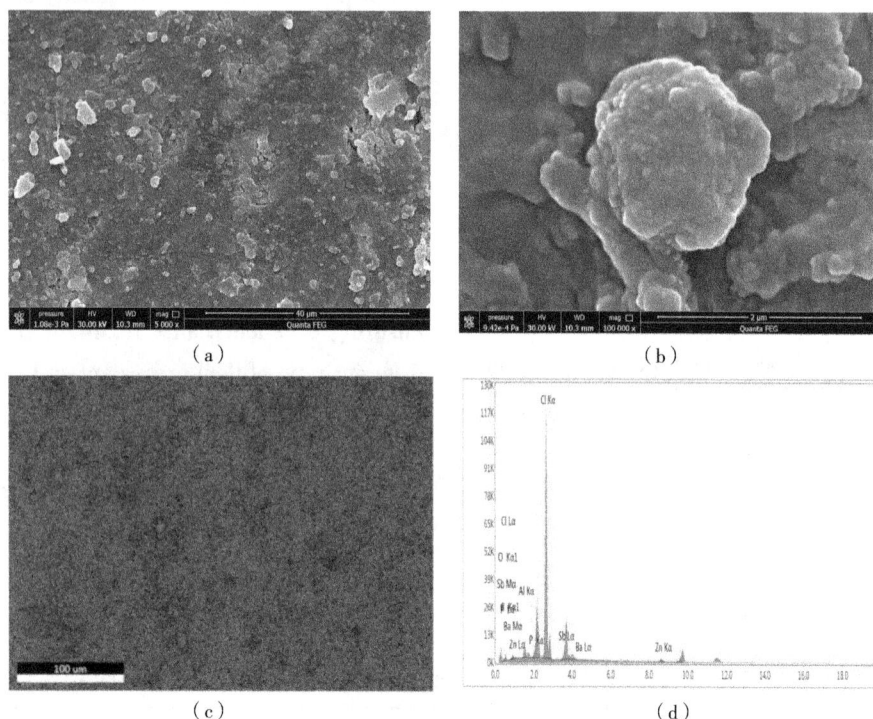

Fig. 1   SEM of surfaces of PVC/DPK—Sb_2O_3—ZB: (a) Surface of burnt PVC film; (b) Surface of Sb_2O_3—ZB particulate matter; (c) Element overlay of PVC/DPK—Sb_2O_3—ZB system; (d) Sum Spectrum of PVC/DPK—Sb_2O_3—ZB system

3.3 Effect of DPK, Sb_2O_3 and ZB on Flame Retardant and Smoke Suppression of PVC

As can be seen from Fig. 2, samples 1, 4, 7: as the mass of Sb_2O_3 and ZB increases, the carbon length decreases. Samples 2, 4, 9: the more DPK, the shorter the damage carbon length, the better the flame retardant effect. In the ternary composite system of PVC/ DPK—Sb_2O_3—ZB, the flame-retarding mechanism of DPK and Sb_2O_3 : ZB is completely different. DPK acts as the main flame retardant and plays a leading role. Sb_2O_3 and ZB act as auxiliary flame retardants, the flame retarding effect of DPK is more obvious than Sb_2O_3 and ZB's. DPK mainly plays a role in the condensed phase, it forms phosphoric acid as a dehydrating agent, and promotes carbon formation. The formation of carbon reduces the heat conduction from the flame to the condensed phase. Phosphoric acid can absorb heat because it prevents CO oxidizing to CO_2 and reduces the heating process to form a thin glassy or liquid protective layer on the condensed phase, thereby it reduces oxygen diffusion and heat and mass transfer between the gas phase and the solid phase, and inhibits the carbon oxidation process[5-6]. While Sb_2O_3 acts in the gas phase, the HCl generated in the initial stage of PVC combustion cracking is absorbed by Sb_2O_3 and ZB to eliminate the catalytic effect of HCl on the continued cracking. The chemical reaction that may occur in this process is:

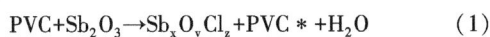

$$PVC+Sb_2O_3 \rightarrow Sb_xO_yCl_z+PVC*+H_2O \qquad (1)$$

On the one hand, $Sb_xO_yCl_z$ formed by the reaction make the HCl which is removed by heating absorbed, thereby avoiding the degradation of PVC chains by HCl. The effect is to increase the stability of the main structure. On the other hand, the vaporized $Sb_xO_yCl_z$ is heavier than HCl gas, and it is more concentrated on the surface of PVC, so the isolation effect of air is enhanced and the flame retardancy is increased, thereby achieving flame retardant and smoke suppression effect[7]

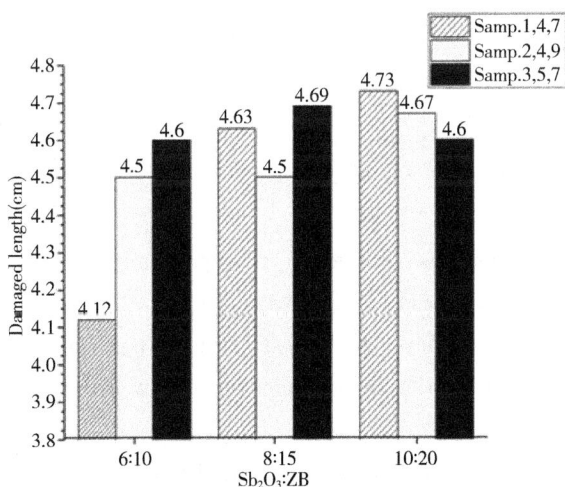

Fig. 2　Flame retardant effect comparison chart

4　Conclusions

DPK, Sb_2O_3 and ZB can be compounded as an ideal flame retardant and smoke suppressant PVC composites.

The best ratio is: PVC : CPVC (70 : 30), DOP : DPK (50 : 10), Sb_2O_3 : ZB(6 : 10). DPK is low-smoke, non-toxic, low-halogen, halogen-free, low in cost. The anti-smoke effect of Sb_2O_3 and ZB is excellent, so the compounding system has a very broad market prospect and practical value.

Acknowledgements

This work was financially supported by National Key R&D Program of China(2016YFB0303300), the Fundamental Research Funds for the Central Universities (2232018G - 06, 2232019G - 02), and the Shanghai Innovation Experiment Program for University Students (sh201810255010).

References

[1] TIAN C M, YE X, QU H Q, et al. Influence of Al (OH)₃ and Mg (OH)₂ on flexible PVC as flame retardants and smoke suppressants [J]. Journal-Hebei University Natural Science Edition, 2004, 24: 263-267.

[2] SHEN K K, SPRAGUE R W. Recent studies on the use of zinc borate as a flame retardant and smoke suppressant in PVC[J]. Journal of Vinyl Technology, 1982, 4(3): 120-123.

[3] SHEN K K, KOCHESFAHANI S, JOUFFRET F. Zinc borates as multifunctional polymer additives[J]. Polymers for Advanced Technologies, 2008, 19(6): 469-474.

[4] JIA P, ZHANG M, LIU C, et al. Effect of chlorinated phosphate ester based on castor oil on thermal degradation of poly (vinyl chloride) blends and its flame retardant mechanism as secondary plasticizer [J]. Rsc Advances, 2015, 5 (51): 41169-41178.

[5] PAN Y T, WANG D Y. One-step hydrothermal synthesis of nano zinc carbonate and its use as a promising substitute for antimony trioxide in flame retardant flexible poly (vinyl chloride)[J]. Rsc Advances, 2015, 5(35): 27837-27843.

[6] QI Y, WU W, HAN L, et al. Using TG-FTIR and XPS to understand thermal degradation and flame-retardant mechanism of flexible poly (vinyl chloride) filled with metallic ferrites [J]. Journal of Thermal Analysis and Calorimetry, 2016, 123(2): 1263-1271.

[7] PI H. Studies on structure development of poly (vinyl chloride)/flame-retardant and smoke-suppressant system during thermal decomposition and mechanism of flame retardancy and smoke suppression[D].

Plating Stitch Applied to A Three-Dimensional Triboelectric Nanogenerator for Powering Wearable Electronics

DONG Shanshan[1], LIU Yanping[1]*

[1] Department of Knitting Technology, College of Textiles, Donghua University, Shanghai, 201620, China

* Corresponding author's email: liuyp@ dhu. edu. cn

Abstract: Triboelectric nanogenerator (TENG) has attracted a lot of attention in recent years due to its potential as a way to solve energy shortages. And the key to developing a TENG is a method for effectively combining triboelectric layer and electrode layer. In this work, a three-dimensional structure TENG that achieved the combination of triboelectric layer and electrode layer by using plating technique was developed. It was mainly divided into two parts: 3D spacer fabric part and tubular part based on plating stitch, and they were alternately arranged to form a stable structure. The spacer fabric part can offer a good resilience for the whole fabric, helping to cause repeated contact-separation cycles in the tubular part. Specially, in the tubular part, polyephylene (PE) yarn and nylon 66 yarn were selected as negative and positive triboelectric materials respectively, while Ag-coated nylon (Ag) yarn was selected as electrode. The Ag yarns were tightly integrated with the PE layer and nylon 66 layer by using plating technique and located on the outer surface of the two layers, thereby forming a double-electrode mode TENG that can convert compressed mechanical energy into electrical energy. Under the pressure of 50kg (equivalent to the weight of an adult woman), the open circuit voltage and the short circuit current of the TENG reaches about 200mV and 20 nA, respectively, within an effective area of 40cm^2. In addition, the TENG is flexible, breathable, lightweight and washable, suitable for power wearable devices. Furthermore, it is a one-piece power textile and can be fabricated directly on a computerized flat knitting machine, showing great potential for mass production. In short, our study provides a simple and efficient method to make a TENG.

Keywords: Plating stitch; One-piece structure; Mass production

1 Introduction

Wearable electronics have developed rapidly in recent years, and with the improved quality of people's life, the comfort of wearable electronics has become increasingly important[1]. As a potential energy source for wearable device[2], triboelectric nanogenerators (TENGs) also need to be made more comfortable[3], especially when they are used in intelligent clothing. Textile based TENGs (t-TENGs) have been proved to be more suitable for wearable electronics due to their good flexibility, breathability and durability[4-7]. There are many t-TENGs have been reported so far, in most of which the triboelectric layer and electrode layer are integrated through external processes[8-11]. For example, a 3D spacer fabric based TENG was made by coating graphene ink as an electrode and coating polytetrafluoroethene (PTFE) textile auxiliaries as negative tribopolarity layer[12], which was time consuming and not suitable for mass production. Though a core-shell-yarn-based TENG can be fabricated directly on industrial textile machines, the most critical core-shell-yarn should be made in advance through weaving method[13].

In this work, plating stitch was used to integrate friction layer and electrode layer in a 3D spacer fabric to make a three-dimensional TENG. Plating stitch is a knitted structureof which the technical face and technical back reveal different yarns[14], and it can be made on a knitting machine directly by adjusting the feeding angles of the two different yarns. Therefore, a conductive yarn and a yarn for triboelectrification can be knitted in this way to form a fabric that has two sides with different functions, for one side as an electrode layer and another side as a triboelectric layer. Polyephylene (PE) yarn and nylon 66 yarn were selected as negative and positive triboelectric materials respectively, and Ag-coated nylon (Ag) yarn was selected as conductive materials. Combining technologies of 3D spacer fabric and plating fabric, The TENG was knitted on a computerized flat knitting machine directly with these commercially available yarns, minimized the production process.

2 Experiments

2.1 Materials

Nylon 66 multifilament (140 D) was bought from Foshan Nanhai Lishui Chemical Fiber Co., Ltd. PE multifilament (400 D) was provided by Honeywell (China) Co., Ltd. Ag multifilament (280 D) was bought from Qingdao Tianyin Textile Technique Co., Ltd. Nylon/spandex (70/20 D) multifilament was obtained from Caota Town, Zhuji City, Zhao Boxiang socks factory. Nylon 66 monofilament (30 D) was got from Wuxi Jintong High Fiber Co., Ltd.

2.2 Fabrication of the TENG

This TENG has a designed structure that the plating stitch is applied to a 3D spacer fabric to form the key functional areas, which consists of two alternately arranged parts: 3D spacer fabric parts and tubular fabric parts. Fig. 1 schematically shows the structure of the TENG. The 3D spacer fabric part, which is made of nylon/spandexmultifilament and nylon 66 monofilament, has good compression-recovery performance to provide continuous contact-separation cycles for the whole fabric. The tubular fabric part consists of two parallel plating stitch layers, one of which is made of nylon 66 multifilament and Ag multifilament and another is made of PE multifilament and Ag multifilament. Nylon 66 and PE materials have opposite triboelectric properties, and Ag has good electrical conductivity. The whole fabric was knitted on a STOLL computerized flat knitting machine (ADF 530 - 32 W, Reutlingen, Germany) directly.

2.3 Microscopic Observation

To observe the surface characteristics of the plating stitch, a stereo microscopic (NIKON SMZ745T) was used to shoot the surface of the fabric.

2.4 Electrical Performance Testing

The electrical output of the TENG was measured under external compression forces applied via a strength meter Instron 5967. The electrical output of the TENG was measured by a 1/2 digit multimeter (Keithley DMM7510 7, USA).

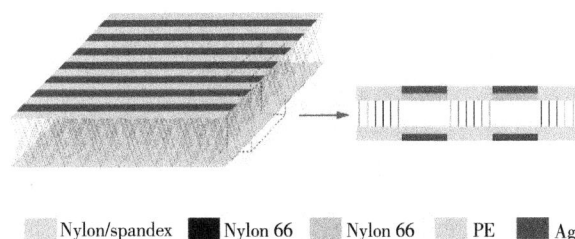

Nylon/spandex ■ Nylon 66　Nylon 66　PE ■ Ag

Fig. 1　Design and structure of the three-dimensional TENG and its side view

3 Results and Discussions

3.1 Fabrication of the Three-Dimensional TENG

This three-dimensional TENG was fabricated directly on a computerized flat knitting machine, and importantly, plating technique was used to combine triboelectric layer and electrode layer in this study. Fig. 2(a) shows the principle of plating technique. For plating stitch made of nylon 66 multifilament and Ag multifilament, the yarn guide of nylon 66 is set a little higher and behind the yarn guide of Ag, leading the difference of the two angles between yarn and needle bed. Because the angle between Ag and needle bed ($\angle \alpha$) is smaller than the angle between nylon 66 and needle bed ($\angle \beta$), Ag yarn will be hooked first by the needle and the loop of Ag yarn will appear on the technical face of the fabric. The surface of this plating stitch is shown in Fig. 2(b). It can be seen that the nylon 66 yarn is well covered by Ag yarn, which means the electrode layer and triboelectric layer are clearly distributed on the technical face and back of the plating stitch fabric, forming exactly the structure required for a TENG. The total size of the fabric including all spacer fabric parts and tubular fabric parts is 6. 5cm×6. 2cm.

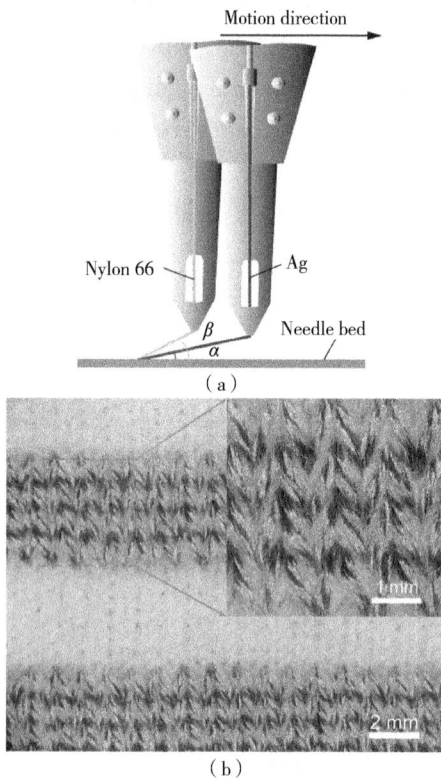

(a)

(b)

Fig. 2　Plating stitch applied to the TENG: (a) Principle of plating technique; (b) Microscopic image of the surface of plating stitch layer made of nylon 66 multifilament and Ag multifilament

3. 2　Electrical Performance Measurement

Working principle of this TENG is shown in Fig. 3(a). Nylon 66 and PE layers in the tubular fabric part are kept apart in the initial state. When the fabric is pressed by external force, the two layers will touch and rub. Nylon 66 tends to lose electrons, while PE is inclined to get electrons. Thus, equal amount of opposite charges will accumulate on the surface of the two layers after friction. When the external force disappears, the two layers begin to separate due to the good resilience of the 3D spacer fabric part. Andelectric potential between the two layers increases as the distance between the two layers increases. Electrons will flow from the low potential layer to the high potential layer through the closed circuit connected to the two electrodes to balance the electric potential difference, so current is generated. Similarly, when the fabric is pressed again, electric potential difference between the two triboelectric layers

will reduce and a reversed current is generated.

The electrical output of the TENG was tested under the pressure of 500N with different frequencies (0. 5Hz, 0. 8Hz and 1Hz), which are close to the force generated by an adult woman walking or running. As shown in Fig. 3(b) and Fig. 3(c), the electrical signal increases obviously with increasing frequency, which can be used for motion sensors. Open circuit (OC) voltage reaches about 200mV under the frequency of 1Hz, while short circuit (SC) current reaches about 20nA. According to the Gauss theorem, the OC voltage (V_{OC}) can be calculated as follows[15].

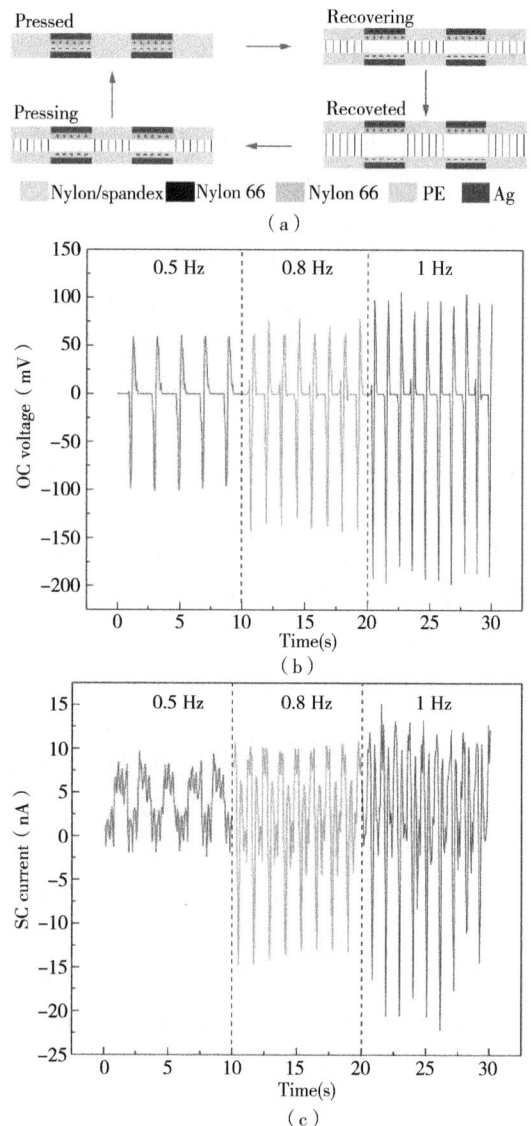

(a)

(b)

(c)

Fig. 3　Working principle and output performance of the TENG: (a) Working principle of the TENG; (b) OC voltage and (c) SC current of the TENG with compression frequencies at 0. 5Hz, 0. 8Hz and 1Hz

$$V_{OC} = \frac{\sigma x(t)}{\varepsilon_0} \quad (1)$$

where σ is the surface charge density, $x(t)$ is the distance changing with time between the nylon 66 layer and PE layer and ε_0 is the vacuum permittivity.

3.3 Mass Production of the TENG

The materials used in this work are allcommercially available, and this TENG was made through traditional knitting technique without any additional procedures, so it can achieve mass production. Take the STOLL computerized flat knitting machine we used in this study for example, when the weaving speed is set to a medium speed of 0.6m/s, it can product about 0.3m of this TENG (0.5m wide) per hour. And with the highest weaving speed of 1.2m/s, the productivity even can be doubled theoretically.

4　Conclusions

In this work, plating stitch was used to make a three-dimensional TENG with a size of 65cm×6.2cm. Plating technique can knit a fabric with different materials in its technical face and technical back, which is exactly what a TENG needs. With this method, mass production of textile based TENGs can be achieved. Under the pressure of 500N, the electrical signal of the TENG changes obviously as the compression frequency changes. The OC voltage and the SC current reaches about 200mV and 20nA, respectively, at the frequency of 1Hz. With this feature, the TENG can be applied to motion sensors, such as a speed monitor. The electrical signal is not strong enough now for powering other electronic devices. In the future, plating stitch is expected to applied to more different TENGs, getting better electrical output and being used for more fields.

Acknowledgements

This work was supported by the Fundamental Research Funds for the Central Universities (16D110120) and initial research funds for Young Teachers of Donghua University (101-07-0053036).

References

[1] SEUNG W, GUPTA M, LEE K, et al. Nanopatterned textile-based wearable triboelectric nanogenerator[J]. ACS Nano, 2015, 9(4): 3501-3509.

[2] FAN F, TIAN Z, WANG Z. Flexible triboelectric generator [J]. Nano Energy, 2012, 1(2): 328-334.

[3] PU X, LI L, SONG H, et al. A self-charging power unit by integration of a textile triboelectric nanogenerator and a flexible lithium-Ion battery for wearable electronics[J]. Advanced Materials, 2015, 27(15): 2472-2478.

[4] WANG Z, RUAN Z, NG W, et al. Integrating a triboelectric nanogenerator and a zinc-Ion battery on a designed flexible 3D spacer fabric[J]. Advanced Science News, 2018, 2: 1800150.

[5] ZHAO Z, YAN C, LIU Z, et al. Machine-washable textile triboelectric nanogenerators for effective human respiratory monitoring through loom weaving of metallic yarns[J]. Advanced Materials, 2016, 28(46): 10267.

[6] QIU Q, ZHU M, LI Z, et al. Highly flexible, breathable, tailorable and washable power generation fabrics for wearable electronics[J]. Nano Energy, 2019, 58: 750-758.

[7] CHEN J, GUO H, PU X, et al. Traditional weaving craft for one-piece self-charging power textile for wearable electronics [J]. Nano Energy, 2018, 50: 536-543.

[8] JAO Y, YANG P, CHIU C, et al. A textile-based triboelectric nanogenerator with humidity-resistant output characteristic and its applications in self-powered healthcare sensors [J]. Nano Energy, 2018, 50: 513-520.

[9] DUDEM B, KIM D, YU J. Triboelectric nanogenerators with gold-thin-film-coated conductive textile as floating electrode for scavenging wind energy[J]. Nano Research, 2018(1): 101-113.

[10] DUDEM B, MULE A, PATNAM H, et al. Wearable and durable triboelectric nanogenerators via polyaniline coated cotton textiles as a movement sensor and self-powered system[J]. Nano Energy, 2019, 55: 305-315.

[11] LEE S, KO W, OH Y, et al. Triboelectric energy harvester based on wearable textile platforms employing various surface morphologies[J]. Nano Energy, 2015, 12: 410-418.

[12] ZHU M, HUANG Y, NG W, et al. 3D spacer fabric based multifunctional triboelectric nanogenerator with great feasibility for mechanized large-scale production[J]. Nano Energy, 2016, 27: 439-446.

[13] ZHONG J, ZHANG Y, ZHONG Q, et al. Fiber-Based Generator for Wearable Electronics and Mobile Medication [J]. ACS Nano, 2014, 8(6): 6273-6280.

[14] SUN F. Study of single plating principle on large diameter circular weft knitting machine[J]. Journal of China Textile

University, 2000(2): 91-94.

[15] NIU S, WANG S, LIN L, et al. Theoretical study of contact-mode triboelectric nanogenerators as an effective power source [J]. Energy & Environmental Science, 2013, 6 (12): 3576.

Fabrication and Photothermal Conversion Properties of Flexible Fluorescent Solar Thermal Collector with Spacer Fabric Composite

ZHU Jingjing[1], JIA Hao[1], BAI Zhiqing[1], LI Yao[1], GUO Jiansheng[1, *]

[1] *Key Laboratory of Textile Science & Technology, Ministry of Education, College of Textiles, Donghua University, Shanghai, 201620, China*

* *Corresponding author's email*: jsguo@ dhu. edu. cn

Abstract: Solar thermal collector is recognized as one of the most efficient methods to utilize solar thermal energy. Recently, flexible solar thermal collector (FSTC) based on flexible warp-knitted spacer fabric composite draw some researcher's attention due to its unique three-dimensional structure and low manufacturing cost, especially when it is used for facades and roofs of buildings. This study proposed a FSTC by modified spacer filaments with wave-guiding fluorescent materials for improving the temperature and thermal collect efficiency. Field-emission scanning electron microscopy (FE-SEM) results shown that the interfacial adhesion between fluorescent coating and spacer filament was improved after spacer filaments were treated with NaOH solution. Compared with FSTC without fluorescent coating in spacer filament, the as-fabricated FSTC with fluorescent coating exhibited exceptional sunlight harvesting properties. To be specific, the stable collection temperature of the coated FSTC can reach to 92℃ at a solar radiation around 1000W/m^2, which is 4.5℃ higher than that of FSTC without fluorescent coating. Therefore, this novel color-tunable FSTC has great potential application in the field of integration of solar energy and architecture.

Keywords: Flexible solar thermal collector; Fluorescent materials; Spacer fabric composite

1 Introduction

Solar energy is one of the most abundant renewable energy sources on earth surface[1-2]. Researches show that the solar spectrum mainly distributes from 0.25μm to 2.5μm, accounting for 95.6% of the solar energy reaching the earth surface through the earth's atmosphere[3]. Thus, transforming sunlight into thermal energy is a good way to utilize solar energy and solve environmental problems.

It is reputed that the infrared spectrum of solar radiation can directly heats objects without photo-thermal conversion, while UV and visible light, accounting for about 57% of solar radiation has no heating effect[4]. Therefore, converting UV and visible sunlight into thermal energy through photothermal conversion materials is essential. Up to date, photothermal conversion materials have been developed rapidly, which are mainly classified into metals, metal oxides, metal sulfides, colorants, paintings, semiconductors, quantum dots and carbon materials[5-8].

Recently, the fluorescent collectors for solar energy conversion have attracted much interest because of their potential of concentrating sunlight from a wide angle of incidence onto a smaller solar absorbing plate[9-11]. Fluorescent materials can absorb a particular solar spectrum and emit for red-shifted wavelength range, which has a strong thermal effect compared with absorption light[12]. Jia et al. proposed a new textile-based device coated with fluorescent dyes, showing that different dyes can cause different heat effect[13].

In thiswork, a fluorescent solar thermal collector with Coumarin 40# based on spacer fabric composite is designed and manufactured. The morphology of surface coating and properties of materials have been systematically investigated. Additionally, outdoor experimental results shown that FSTC coated with fluorescent materials exhibits exquisite photothermal conversion performance and thermal insulation property. This study provides a possibility for the fabrication of flexible high solar thermal efficiency collectors with various colors.

2 Experimentaland Methods

2.1 Materials

The warp-knitted spacer fabric was manufactured on the Raschel warp-knitting machine with polyester monofilaments. Two type of spacer fabric with the same specification but different colors were manufactured. The photographs and parameters of spacer fabrics are shown in Fig. 1 and Tab. 1.

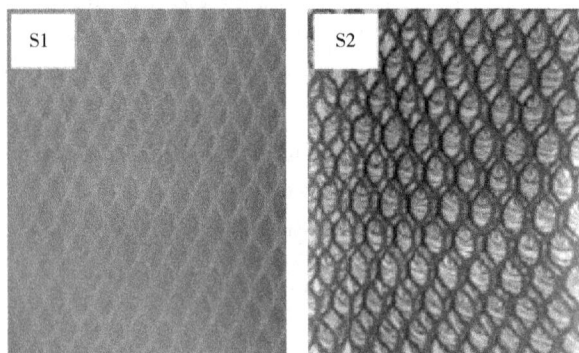

Fig. 1   Photographs of spacer fabric

Tab. 1   Specification of spacer fabrics

Sample	1	2
Color	White	Black
Thickness(mm)	7	7
Material	Polyester	Polyester
Diameter of spacer filament (mm)	0.18	0.18
Stitch density (stitch/cm^2)	30	30

Coumarin 40#, purchased from Shanghai Hushi Pharmaceutical Technology Co. Ltd., was chosen as the fluorescent materials to modify the spacer fabric. PDMS purchased from Guangzhou Boqiao Co. Ltd., used as surface encapsulation material owing to its good adhesion with spacer fabric and flexibility after curing. Be-

sides, the selective absorption plate, purchased from Shenzhen Zhenyuan energy-saving equipment Co. Ltd., was selected as the solar energy absorbing plate under the spacer fabric composite to fabricate an entire solar energy harvesting system. Alumino silicate fiber cotton layer with the thickness of 2cm was used as thermal insulation layer, which thermal conductivity is 0.03W/(m·K).

2.2 Fabrication of FSTC with Fluorescent Coating

Spacer fabric was emerged in 10% NaOH solution for 2h and then washed with deionized water for three times. To obtain uniformly fluorescent solution, 0.5g Coumarin 40# particles and 2mL hyperdispersant silok @ 7455 were added into 50mL 15% PVA aqueous solution and stirring for 30min at 80℃. Then, the solution was evenly sprayed on the space fabric filaments by a facile air spraying method. After that, the coated spacer fabric quickly dried in an oven at the temperature of 120℃ to evaporate solvent. Moreover, transparent PDMS fully mixed with curing agent at a ratio of 1:10 was spread on a mould with the thickness of 1mm. Next, the coated spacer fabric was placed in the mould for 24h at room temperature before being taken out.

2.3 Characterization Methods

The morphology of spacer filament modified by NaOH solution and fluorescent coating were examined by FE-SEM.

It is necessary to evaluate the range of solar absorption spectra of absorbing plate and fluorescent materials for designing ahighly efficient solar collector. Hence, the absorbance of solar selective absorption plate and fluorescent spectra were measured by a fluorescent spectrometer and a dual-beam ultraviolet-visible-near-infrared (UV-VIR-NIR) spectrophotometer with integrating sphere attached.

The transmittance of spacer fabriccomposite was also measured by the UV-VIR-NIR spectrophotometer. According to ASTM D1518-14, the thermal resistance of each flexible composite was measured by textile thermal resistance instrument (YG606E).

To investigate the photothermal conversion properties of FSTCs, an outdoor experimental testing system was constructed. As shown in Fig. 2. The size of test panel was

15cm in length and 15cm in width. Thermocouples (PT100) was set on the top surface and below the absorption plate for testing the temperature of glazing layer and absorbing plate. Simultaneous solar radiation intensity was recorded by a Pyranometer (SOLAR-1) at an interval of 5min.

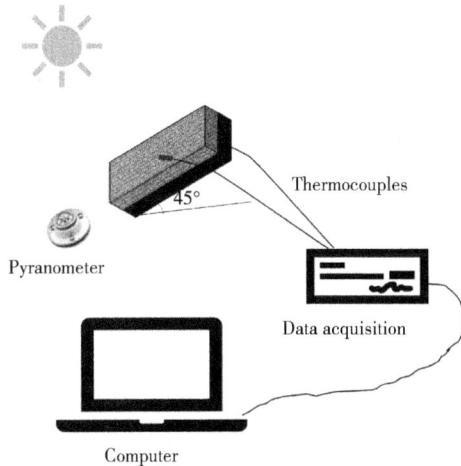

Fig. 2　Outdoor experimental testing system

3　Results and Discussions

3.1　Morphology of Spacer Filaments

FE-SEM micrographs of untreated spacer filament and treated spacer filament are shown in Fig. 3. We can see that the surface of spacer filament treated with NaOH solution exhibits a lot of small pits and the fluorescent coating is uniformly coated on the surface of spacer filament. This is because the surface of filament treated with alkali is rougher than that of untreated, making it easier for fluorescent pigment to adhere to the surface of filament. In addition, alkali treatment only corrodes the surface of spacer filament and has no considerable effect on the strength of spacer filament.

3.2　Properties of Materials

3.2.1　Absorption Properties of Solar Absorbing Materials

Fig. 4 reveals that commercial solar selective absorption plate has high absorption rate in the visible and near-infrared waveband, as well as low absorption rate in far-infrared range, which can effectively reduce heat loss from absorbing plate.

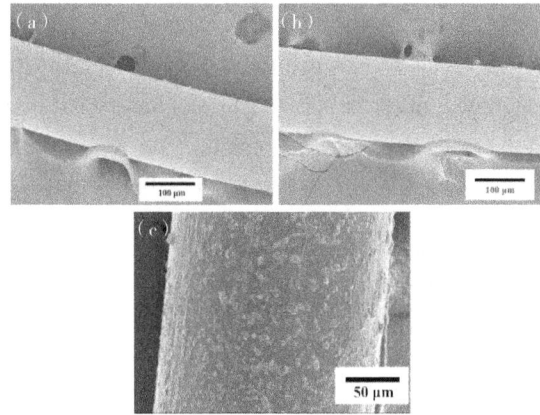

Fig. 3　FE-SEM images of (a) Spacer filament; (b) Spacer filament treated with NaOH solution; (c) Spacer filament coated with fluorescent materials

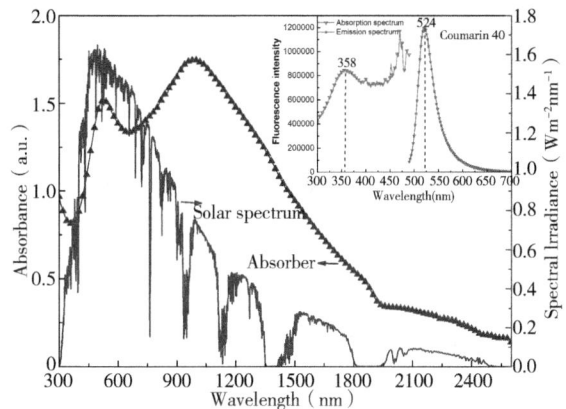

Fig. 4　Absorbance of solar selective absorption plate and fluorescent spectra of Coumarin 40#

However, solar selective absorption plate displays a relatively lower absorption in ultraviolet waveband of 350–450nm, which also has a huge solar radiation intensity. Based on this defect, coumarin 40# was chosen from a large amount of fluorescent materials to improve thermal performance of FSTC. As shown in Fig. 4, coumarin 40# has high excitation band ranging from 350nm to 500nm and emission band in the range of 500nm to 550nm, which is just in the range of absorption peak of the selective absorption plate. Therefore, this combination design can make up low absorption band of the selective absorption plate and improve thermal collection efficiency.

3.2.2　Transmittance and Thermal Conductivity of Spacer Fabric Composite

The transmittance of spacer fabric shown in Fig. 5 demonstrates that the transmissivity of composites is slightly lower than that of spacer fabrics. Moreover, the light transmittance of black spacer fabric is lower than that of white fabric at the same parameters. This may be due to the higher absorption effect of black color.

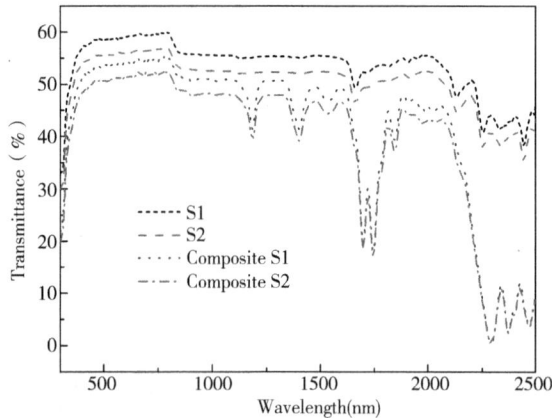

Fig. 5　Transmittance of spacer fabric and composite

Further, heat transfer coefficient of composite S1 and composite S2 are 9.16W/(m² · K¹)and 9.28W/(m² · K)respectively, indicating that this kind of composite has good thermal insulation property.

3.3　Photothermal Conversion Properties of FSTC

Temperature is an index to characterize photothermal performance of solar collector. The changes of temperature and solar radiation as a function of time of FSTC based on composite S1 and composite S2 are shown in Fig. 6.

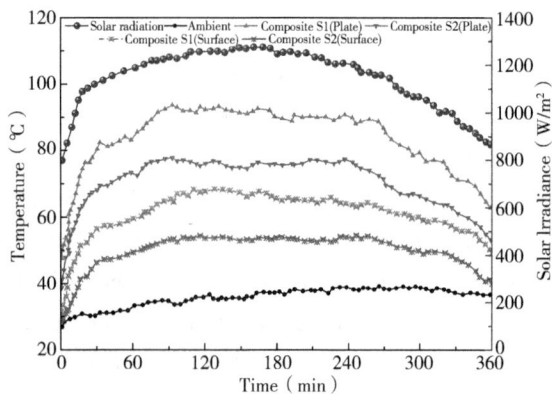

Fig. 6　Temperature and solar radiation variation with time of FSTC based on composite S1 and composite S2

It is notable that the temperature of selective absorbing plate and upper surface of the FSTC based on composite

S2 were both higher than that of FSTC based on composite S1. The result indicates that the black spacer fabric can absorbs sunlight and increases the temperature of absorbing plate. On the other hand, black color has intensity thermal radiation, causing the temperature of upper surface for composite S2 up to around 65℃, which is about 12℃ higher than that of composite S1.

In order to investigate photothermal conversion performance of fluorescent solar thermal collector, outdoor experiments on the fluorescent collector based on the fluorescent black spacer fabric composite (composite S3) also carried out. The results are shown in Fig. 7.

Compared with FSTC based on composite S2, the selective absorption plate's temperature of FSTC based on composite S3 is relatively higher and the temperature of upper surface is much lower. The absorbing plate of fluorescent collector reached to 92℃ at the solar irradiance of around 1000W/m². Mean temperature difference of absorbing plate and upper surface between FSTC based on composite S2 and composite S3 were about 4.5℃ and 7.2℃, respectively. Besides, the mean temperature difference between upper surface and absorbing plate of fluorescent collector was about 24.1℃. Those results show that the spacer fabric composite coated with coumarin 40# not only increases the photothermal conversion efficiency of FSTC, but also impedes the heat loss from upper surface.

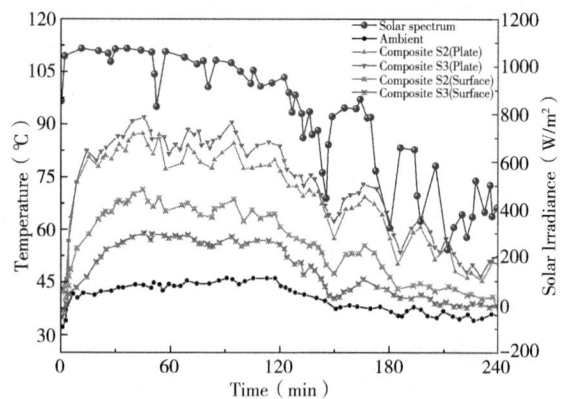

Fig. 7　Temperature and solar radiation variation with time of FSTC based on composite S2 and composite S3

4　Conclusions

In this work, we fabricated flexible fluorescent solar

thermal collectors with spacer fabric composite. The spacer filament of spacer fabric coated with fluorescent materials by air spraying method. FE-SEM images shown that the spacer filament can be coated evenly by the fluorescent materials after treated with NaOH solution. The analysis of absorbance spectra for selective absorption plate and coumarin 40# shown that this combination design can make up low absorption band of the selective absorption plate and improve thermal collection efficiency.

Photo thermal conversion experimental of FSTC shown that the temperature of fluorescent collector can reach to 92℃ at a solar radiation around 1000W/m², which is 4.5℃ higher than that of FSTC without fluorescent coating. Therefore, this novel color-tunable FSTC has great potential application in the field of integration of solar energy and architecture.

References

[1] SAXENA A, SRIVASTAVA G, TIRTH V. Design and thermal performance evaluation of a novel solar air heater[J]. Renewable Energy, 2015, 77: 11-501.

[2] KITTIDACHACHAN P, DANOS L, MEYER T J J, et al. Photon collection efficiency of fluorescent solar collectors [J]. CHIMIA International Journal for Chemistry, 2007, 61: 6-780.

[3] GRANQVIST C G. Solar energy materials[J]. Advanced Materials, 2003, 15: 803-1789.

[4] MUHAMMAD Iqbal. An introduction to solar radiation[D].
Canada: Academic Press, 2012.

[5] LI Y, FU Z Y, SU B L. Hierarchically structured porous materials for energy conversion and storage[J]. Advanced Functional Materials, 2012, 22(22): 4634-4667.

[6] MICHALET X, PINAUD F, BENTOLILA L, et al. Quantum dots for live cells, in vivo imaging, and diagnostics[J]. Science, 2005, 307(5709): 538-544.

[7] WU Y, KOBAYASHI A, HALDER G J, et al. Negative Thermal Expansion in the Metal-Organic Framework Material Cu₃(1, 3, 5-benzenetricarboxylate)₂[J]. Angewandte Chemie International Edition, 2008, 47(46): 8929-8932.

[8] ACCARDI-DEY A, GSCHWEND P. Assessing the combined roles of natural organic matter and black carbon as sorbents in sediments [J]. Environmental Science & Technology, 2002, 36(1): 21-29.

[9] STAHL W, WITTWER V, GOETZBERGER A. Thermal conversion with fluorescent concentrators[J]. Solar Energy, 1986, 36: 27-35.

[10] GOETZBERGER A. Thermal energy conversion with fluorescent collector-concentrators [J]. Solar Energy, 1979, 22: 8-435.

[11] DEBIJE M G, VERBUNT P P C. Thirty years of luminescent solar concentrator research: solar energy for the built environment[J]. Advanced Energy Materials, 2012, 2: 12-35.

[12] JIA H, ZHU J, LI Z, CHENG X, et al. Design and optimization of a photo-thermal energy conversion model based on polar bear hair[J]. Solar Energy Materials and Solar Cells, 2017, 159: 51-345.

[13] JIA H, ZHU J, LI Z, GUO J. Optimization design of a flexible absorption device for solar energy application[J]. E-Polymers, 2017, 17.

A Promising Approach to Predict Areal Density of 1×1 Rib Fabric Using Mathematical and Fuzzy Inference Model

SMRITI Shamima Akter[1], BELAL Shah Alimuzzaman[1], FARZANA Nawshin[2],
HAQUE Abu Naser Md Ahsanul[2, 3], FARHA Farial Islam[4, 5]*

[1] Department of Fabric Engineering, Bangladesh University of Textiles, Dhaka, 1208, Bangladesh

[2] Department of Textile Engineering, Daffodil International University, Dhaka, 1207, Bangladesh

[3] Deakin University, Institute for Frontier Materials, Geelong, Victoria, 3216 Australia

[4] Key Laboratory of Textile Science & Technology, Ministry of Education, College of Textiles, Donghua University, Shanghai, 201620, China

[5] Department of Textile Engineering, Ahsanullah University of Science and Technology, Dhaka, 1208 Bangladesh.

* Corresponding author's email: farial_fara143@ yahoo. com

Abstract: Areal density being the representative parameter for knitted fabrics, is always difficult to obtain accurately in finished state based on the prediction of different parameters; especially in case of mass scale production. To address this challenge, the value of a new factor 'K_y' has been enumerated by mathematical model establishing from yarn count, stitch length and areal density (measured in fully relaxed state) as input variables. A total of 35 samples of one of the commercially popular knitted fabric namely 1×1 Rib were developed consisting of yarn having different counts ranging from 16's to 44's; followed by adjusting five different stitch length (2. 5–4mm) for each count in order to calculate the constant "K_y". Fuzzy inference system as a proficient modelling tool has been adopted to prognosticate the value of areal density using the same factors which can easily interpret the knowledge of experts into a set of rules in inference system focusing on modes of reasoning that are fairly accurate rather than exact. Moreover, the prediction accuracy through K_y factor and fuzzy logic were compared in terms of co-efficient of determination (R^2) and Mean Absolute Error (MAE)%. It was found that both of this promising ways of estimating areal density of knitted fabric possess the ability to elevate productivity along with less time and effective cost in industrial environment.

Keywords: Areal Density; 1×1 Rib fabric; K_y factor; Mathematical model; Fuzzy inference model

1 Introduction

With the growing market demand of knit fabrics since 1970s owing to higher level of comfort ability; the challenge to provide quality fabrics with a reasonable price for the manufacturer is also being intensified. Areal Density, playing a vital role to maintain knit fabric's quality as well as reasonable cost, is indeed a critical task to obtain accurately as loop distortion can be occurred by take down mechanism, spreader pressure even finishing processes[1]. Till now, a number of researches were carried out based on several knit structures to predict areal density through verifying different knitting parameters along with establishing the prime constants namely K_c, K_w and K_s symbolized as stable state constants for course per unit length, wales per unit width and stitch density per unit area respectively[2-3]. KUMAR et al.[4] established various U constants of 100% cotton weft-knitted double cardigan structure to predict the dimensional properties through artificial neural network model.

Although, this K factors being familiarized for more than 40 years among the technologists are being used generally, the real life problems to work with this values in order to predict finished GSM (an expression of Areal Density) are necessarily it's extreme time consumption, yet frequent erroneous data due to inefficiency of workers. Recently, Cotton Incorporated, USA has introduced a new factor namely 'K_y' based on the fabric yield. The factor for the yield was derived from the relationship that says the ounces per square yard in the reference state are inversely proportional to the product of the yarn count (Tex) and the stitch length (l). Based on this relation, the derivation of K_y constant for calculating GSM of knitted fabric can be expressed as per Equation (1).

$$K_y = \frac{GSM x l}{Tt} \qquad (1)$$

However, Cotton incorporated found $K_y = 15.670$ for overflow jet dyed, compacted plain single jersey fabric but no details comment for K_y value was discussed to standardize this factor in general for knit fabrics[5]. On the other hand, several modeling in particular mathematical, statistical regression and intelligent; are gathering much more attention to predict knit fabric properties because of their scientific fundament, clear conceptual methods and accuracy[6-8]. Meanwhile, Fuzzy Inference system being considered more proficient modeling tools than other artificial intelligent techniques such as ANN, ANFIS or statistical regression due to its fuzzy logic base that can easily translate the experience of experts into a set of inference system based rule and focuses on modes of reasoning which are approximate rather than exact; It can be also implemented easily than other models[9].

In this current research, an innovative approach was taken to establish two effective and accessible models through statistical analysis and fuzzy inference system for predicting areal density of 1×1 rib finished fabrics for a particular process route. Furthermore, the value of Ky factor of 1×1 rib fabric was also developed from the mathematical model which could be used as an effective prediction tool.

2 Experiments

2.1 Yarn and Fabric Sample

In this work, 35 samples, in total, were developed by using seven commonly used yarn count to cover the pos-

sible range of 1×1 rib fabric on a 40inch diameter and 18gauge circular double jersey knitting machine. The fabrics for each yarn count were produced with five optimum values of stitch length inmm (l) which were derived by using Equation 2.

$$l = \frac{\sqrt{Tt}}{TightnessFactor(K)} \qquad (2)$$

The detail specifications of all samples have been shown in Tab 1. All the samples were maintained with a constant take-down tension all the time, were dyed and finally finished by stentering and compacting following the same process parameters. The knitted samples were subjected to a relaxation treatment to bring them to the 'fully relaxed state' using ISO 139: 1973 and ISO 6330: 1984 methods.

2.2 Development of Fuzzy Knowledge Based Intelligent Model

In this work, Fuzzy prediction model was constructed by using triangular membership functions for both input and output variables where stitch length (SL), yarn count (YC) were considered as input variables and GSM of 1×1 rib knitted fabrics as output variable. The proposed fuzzy prediction model of fabric GSM with its membership function was developed by using a Fuzzy logic Toolbox from MATLAB (version 8.2.0.701). For fuzzification, different linguistic subsets of input and output variables (Tab. 2) were selected in such a way that the fuzzy expert system could trace small changes in areal density with any variation of input variables and its inference mechanism was based on Mamdani max-min system where total 24 rules out of 56 were used on the basis of expert knowledge and prior experience to make the model simple and easier (Fig. 1).

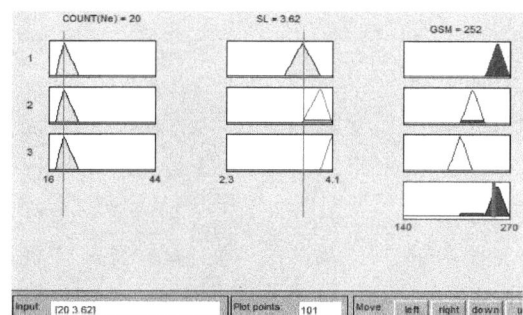

Fig. 1   Operation of fuzzy inference rule based system

Finally, the centre of gravity (COG) defuzzification method was used for converting the fuzzy output into non-fuzzy crisp numeric value[9].

Tab. 1 Data for each count and stitch length of all samples in 1x1 rib structure of both state

No.	Yarn count			Stitch length, l	Tt/l	Average GSM	
	Actual	Calculated				Finished fabric	Fully relaxed fabric
	(Ne)	(Ne)	(tex)	(mm)		(g/m²)	(g/m²)
S1	16	15. 46	38. 2	3. 95	9. 67	247	281
S2	16	15. 46	38. 2	4	9. 55	164	264
S3	16	15. 46	38. 2	4. 05	9. 43	167	293
S4	16	15. 46	38. 2	4. 1	9. 32	165	275
S5	16	15. 46	38. 2	4. 15	9. 2	266	268
S6	20	20	29. 53	3. 52	8. 39	261	250
S7	20	20	29. 53	3. 57	8. 27	270	254
S8	20	20	29. 53	3. 62	8. 16	258	253
S9	20	20	29. 53	3. 67	8. 05	267	230
S10	20	20	29. 53	3. 72	7. 94	247	225
S11	26	25. 71	22. 97	3. 07	7. 48	225	222
S12	26	25. 71	22. 97	3. 12	7. 36	235	215
S13	26	25. 71	22. 97	3. 17	7. 25	227	207
S14	26	25. 71	22. 97	3. 22	7. 13	223	202
S15	26	25. 71	22. 97	3. 27	7. 02	218	193
S16	30	29. 47	20. 04	2. 86	7. 01	215	202
S17	30	29. 47	20. 04	2. 91	6. 89	221	205
S18	30	29. 47	20. 04	2. 96	6. 77	215	199
S19	30	29. 47	20. 04	3. 01	6. 66	218	176
S20	30	29. 47	20. 04	3. 06	6. 55	230	167
S21	34	33. 12	17. 83	2. 69	6. 63	219	191
S22	34	33. 12	17. 83	2. 74	6. 51	224	184
S23	34	33. 12	17. 83	2. 79	6. 39	221	180
S24	34	33. 12	17. 83	2. 84	6. 28	209	174
S25	34	33. 12	17. 83	2. 89	6. 17	195	182
S26	40	40. 32	14. 65	2. 46	5. 96	180	192
S27	40	40. 32	14. 65	2. 51	5. 84	139	149
S28	40	40. 32	14. 65	2. 56	5. 72	139	142
S29	40	40. 32	14. 65	2. 61	5. 61	172	178
S30	40	40. 32	14. 65	2. 66	5. 51	166	165
S31	44	44	13. 42	2. 34	5. 74	173	148
S32	44	44	13. 42	2. 39	5. 62	172	142
S33	44	44	13. 42	2. 44	5. 5	159	136
S34	44	44	13. 42	2. 49	5. 39	145	125
S35	44	44	13. 42	2. 54	5. 28	165	135

Tab. 2 Linguistic fuzzy sets for input-output variables

	Range	Linguistic fuzzy set
Input variables		
Stitch length(mm)	2. 3–4. 1	Very Very Low (VVL), Very Low (VL), Low (L), Medium (M), Medium High (MH), High (H), Very High(VH), Very Very High (VVH)
Count (Ne)	16–44	Very Very Coarse(VVC), Very Coarse(VC), Coarse(C), Medium (M), Fine (F), Very Fine (VF), Very Very Fine(VVF)
Output variables		
Areal density (g/m2)	140–270	Level 1, Level 2, Level 3, Level 4, Level 5, Level 6, Level 7, Level 8, Level 9

3 Results and Discussions

3. 1 Acquired Value of K_y Factor for 1×1 Rib Fabric

Analyzing Fig. 2, it is obvious that the value of K_y factor being related to the slope of the straight line equation of $y = 37.662x - 64.173$; is 37. 662 in fully relaxation state, where y carries the value of GSM and x carries quotient value of count and stitch length.

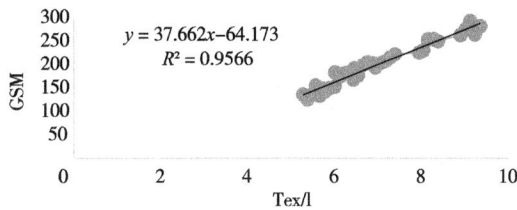

Fig. 2 Representation of all values of relaxed state GSM against Tt/l for (1×1) rib fabric

The explored value of Ky constant from mathematical and Fuzzy intelligent model for prognosticating areal density of 1×1 rib structure were validated by the same experimental data. Among 35 samples, experimental results of 10 samples, which were not used for developing fuzzy models, were used to verify the proposed models by enumerating coefficient of determination (R^2) and Mean absolute error (MAE)% between the real and prognosticated values of 1x1 rib fabric. Comparison of prediction performance of K_y constant and the fuzzy intelligent model is shown in Tab. 3.

Tab. 3 Comparison of prediction performance for fuzzy model and mathematical model

No.	Stitch length (mm)	Yarn count (Ne)	Actual fin. GSM	Fuzzy model Predicted GSM	Fuzzy model Absolute error (%)	Mathematical model Predicted GSM	Mathematical model Absolute error (%)
T1	3. 52	20	261	255	2. 299	284. 36	8. 95
T2	3. 62	20	258	252	2. 326	276. 5	7. 17
T3	3. 07	25. 71	225	240	6. 667	253. 6	12. 72
T4	3. 27	25. 71	218	228	4. 587	238. 1	9. 23
T5	2. 91	29. 47	221	225	1. 810	233. 4	5. 63
T6	3. 01	29. 47	218	225	3. 211	225. 7	3. 52
T7	2. 69	33. 14	219	226	3. 196	224. 6	2. 54
T8	2. 89	33. 14	195	198	1. 538	209. 0	7. 19
T9	2. 66	40. 32	166	162	2. 410	186. 7	12. 44
T10	2. 54	44	165	165	2. 299	179. 1	8. 56
Mean absolute error (MAE)%					2. 80		7. 80
Co-efficient of determination (R^2)					0. 954		0. 959

3.2 Analysis of Prediction Accuracy of K_y Factor and Fuzzy Intelligent Model

The correlation between the actual and predicted values of fabric GSM by K_y constant and fuzzy intelligent model have been illustrated in Fig. 3 and Fig. 4 respectively. It was observed that the coefficient of determination (R^2) from the fuzzy model and mathematical K_y constant were obtained to be 0.954, 0.959 and the mean absolute error (MAE)% valued 2.8% and 7.8% respectively which clarified comparatively good agreement of Fuzzy intelligent model.

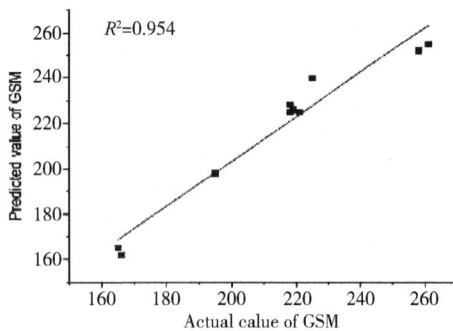

Fig. 3   Correlation between actual and fuzzy model predicted GSM

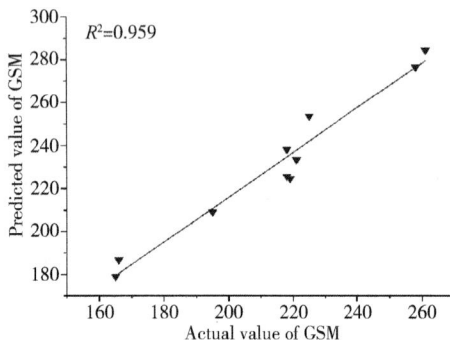

Fig. 4   Correlation between actual and mathematical model predicted GSM

4   Conclusions

The current research dealing with the forecasting problems of areal density in an industrial environment, mainly introduced a new factor called 'K_y' for 1×1 rib fabrics. The obtained value of this constant have potential application to predict areal density of finished knitted fabrics only using the basic knitting parameters; along with more accuracy, quick and easy approach than previously established K factors for a particular process route. Moreover, fuzzy model also exhibited excellent prediction performance for areal density of similar knit fabric. Both this models have effective benefits for the knit industry in terms of prediction and reproduction of 1×1 rib fabric.

References

[1] BLACK D H. Shrinkage control for cotton and cotton blend knitted fabrics[J]. Text Res J, 1974, 44(8): 606-611.

[2] MUNDEN D L. The geometry and dimensional properties of plain-knit fabrics[J]. J Text I, 1959, 50(7): 37-41.

[3] NUTTING T S, LEAF A V. A generalized geometry of weft-knitted fabrics[J]. J Text I, 1964, 55(1): 45-53.

[4] KUMAR T S, SAMPATH V R. Prediction of dimensional properties of weft knitted cardigan fabric by artificial neural network system[J]. J Ind Text, 2013, 42(4): 446-458.

[5] Cotton Incorporated. Engineered Cotton Knits Guideline[J/OL]. http: //www. cottoninc. com/product/Tech-Assistance-Training/Engineered-Cotton-Knits-Guidelines/.

[6] SOUZA A A U, CHEREM L F C, SOUZA SM A G. Prediction of dimensional changes in circular knitted cotton fabrics [J]. Text Res J, 2010, 80(3): 236-252.

[7] HEAP S A, GREENWOOD P F, LEAH R D, et al. Prediction of finished weight and shrinkage of cotton knits-the starfish project. part I: introduction and general overview[J]. Text Res J, 1983, 55(2): 109-119.

[8] RAY S C. An insight to the modeling of 1×1 rib loop formation process on circular weft knitting machine using computer [J]. Journal of the Institution of Engineers, 2015, 96(2): 99-106.

[9] HOSSAIN I, HOSSAIN A, CHOUDHURY I A. Color strength modeling of viscose/lycra blended fabrics using a fuzzy logic approach[J]. J Eng Fiber Fabr, 2015, 10(1): 158-168.

Morphological Study and Antibacterial Activity Investigation of Modified Wool Fibers with Enzyme

REZA Assefi Pour[1*], HE Jinxin[1, 2]

[1] *Department of Textile Chemistry and Dyeing & Finishing Engineering, College of Chemistry, Chemical Engineering & Biotechnology, Donghua University, Shanghai, 201620, China*

[2] *The Key Laboratory of Textile Science & Technology, Ministry of Education, College of Textiles, Donghua University, Shanghai, 201620, China*

* *Corresponding author's email: reza@ mail. dhu. edu. cn*

Abstract: Herein, the effect of microbial trans-glutaminases (m-TGases) on morphology and antibacterial behavior of wool fabric were investigated. It is well-known that due to non-toxic and eco-friendly characteristics of enzymes their use in textile industry is one of the most attractive field in industrial enzymology. In this work the effect of different concentrations of m-TGases on properties of the wool fibers was evaluated. The morphological changes of untreated and treated samples were examined using scanning electron microscope (SEM). The results showed that by more increasing in concentration of m-TGases, some surface damages were appeared which is indicated by damaged scales and less cuticle surface in SEM images. Besides, the antibacterial properties of wool samples were investigated using agar diffusion test method. Antimicrobial activity of untreated wool as well as treated wool with different concentration of m-TGases was investigated against Staphylococcus aureus, SA, as gram-positive bacteria and the results indicated that m-TGases shows anti-bacterial activity.

Keywords: Microbial trans-glutaminases (m-TGases); Wool; Antibacterial; Morphology

1 Introduction

Up to now, enzymes have been used in textile production and mainly used in preparatory finishing. The application of enzymes such as proteases, lipases, protein disulfide isomerase and trans-glutaminase on the modification of wool properties has been reported[1-10]. M-TGases as an enzyme can catalyze acyl transfer reaction between glutamine and lysine through introducing covalent cross-links. As wool fibers mainly consist of protein, therefore m-TGases can be used to modify the properties of wool keratin[11]. The effect of enzymatic treatment of wool fabric on some physico-chemical properties, and dyeability with an acid dye were investigated[12-13].

In this work we chose m-TGases to study its concentration effect on wool treatment process. The 5%, 10%, and 20% owf of m-TGases were used for treatment of wool and surface morphology and antibacterial activity were evaluated.

2 Experiments

Pre-treated (scoured) woolen fabric (195g/m², plain weave structure) was provided by Youngor Woolen Textile Co., Ltd., Ningbo, China. Microbial trans-glutaminases (m-TGases) were procured from Yiming Biological Products Co., Ltd., Jiangsu, China. Acetic acid was purchased from Merck, Germany. Standard washing soap and standard synthetic detergent were supplied by Shanghai BaiMao Chemicals Co. Ltd., China. Three different concentrations of m-TGases, such as 5%, 10%, and 20% w/w, were used to treat the wool fabric at a liquor to fabric ratio of 40 : 1. The pH and temperature of the liquor was maintained at 9-10, and 37℃, respectively. One of the important factors, which affects the mechanical properties of wool as well as energy consumptions, is the processing time which was set for one hour. To prevent the hydrolyzation of wool, the enzymes were inactivated in an acidic aqueous solution with pH = 5, adjusted by the using acetic acid, at 80℃ for 5 minutes and then the substrate was washed with cold water. After that the fabric with enzymes, the substrate was dyed with the madder (50% owf) and acetic acid (5% v/v) at a liquor ratio of 50 : 1. Water bath shakerDL-2003 (16), (Suzhou Sidale Printing and Dyeing Machinery Co., Ltd., China) was used for Dyeing. The Dyeing bath temperature of 40℃ was raised to 80℃ over 20min period and was further continued for 60min. The surface morphology of the untreated and treated dyed wool fabric was observed by using SEM, Hitachi TM-1000, Japan. The antibacterial properties of wool samples were investigated using agar diffusion test method. To do this, the described method in literature was followed[14].

3　Results and Discussions

3.1　Surface Morphology Investigation

SEM images of untreated and treated wool with enzyme were shown in Fig. 1. Besides, the 5%, 10%, and 20% owf of m-TGases were used for treatment of wool and the surface morphology analysis was studied. Our results showed that by adding more enzyme the surface of wool is damaged (Fig. 2). Therefore, it is very important to find an optimum concentration of m-TGases. By analyzing the data, it is found that m-TGases with the concentration of 10% owf lead to the best surface morphology. It means that with this amount although the surface morphology is changed but it doesn't cause to damage in the surface of wool. In fact, by adding proper amount of m-TGases surface morphology of wool was changed and rough surface is prepared. The high magnification SEM image (Fig. 3) of treated wool with 10% m-TGases as optimum condition was characterized and the obtained result presented in Fig. 3.

3.2　FTIR Analysis

FTIR spectra of untreated and treated wool textiles with m-TGases enzyme were examined in the 4000-500cm^{-1} wave number range and the obtained results are shown in Fig. 4.

In the both spectra, the main characteristic peaks of

Fig. 1　SEM images of untreated and treated wool

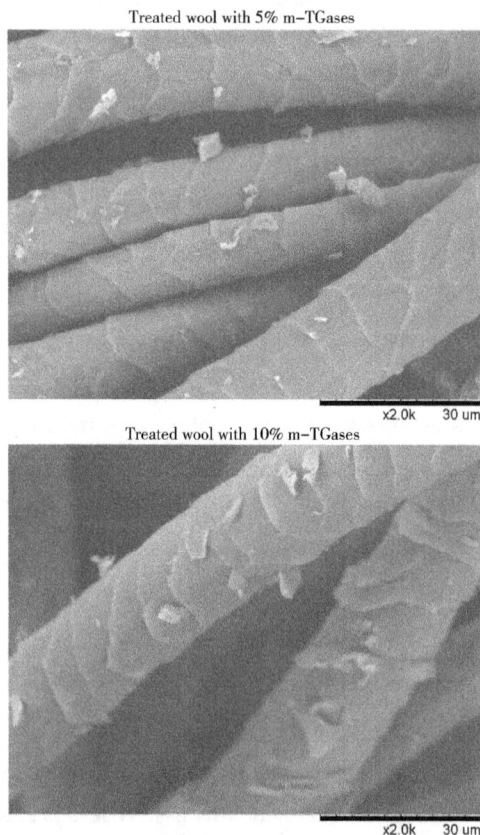

Fig. 2　SEM images of treated wool with 5%, 10%, and 20% owf. m-TGases

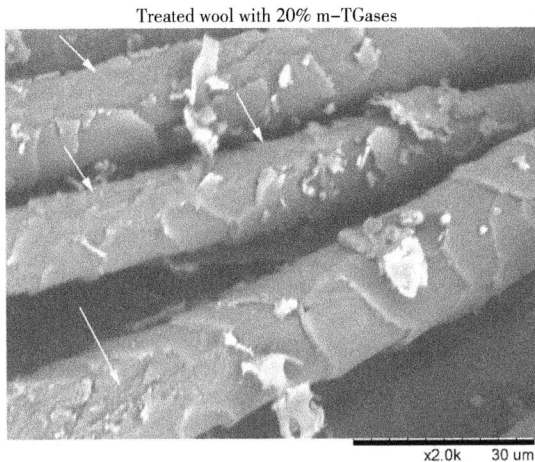

Treated wool with 20% m-TGases

x2.0k   30 um

Fig. 2   SEM images of treated wool with 5, 10, and 20% owf. m-TGases

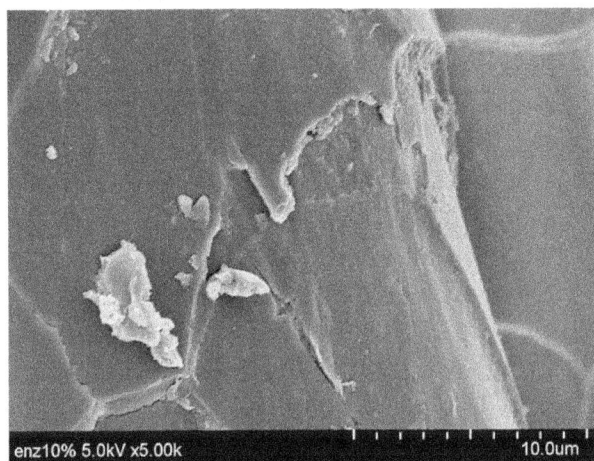

enz10% 5.0kV x5.00k   10.0um

Fig. 3   The high magnification SEM image of treated wool with 10% m-TGases as optimum condition

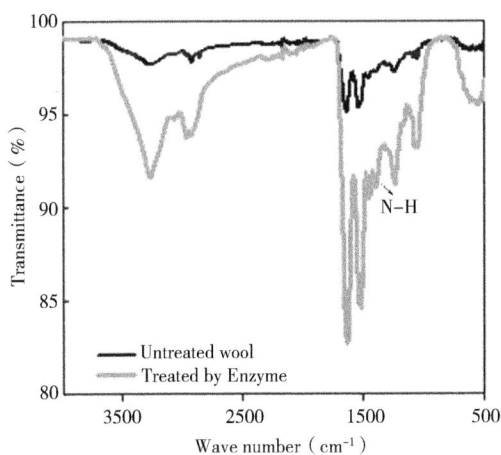

Fig. 4   FTIR spectrum of untreated and treated wool with m-TGases

wool with the functional groups such as —COOH— (carboxyl), —OH (hydroxyl), and—NH_2 (amino) groups were found. It can obviously be seen that the band intensity at ~ $1385cm^{-1}$ relating to N-H bonds for the treated wool with m-TGase is higher than untreated one due to the crosslinking of wool by enzyme.

3.2   Anti-Bacterial Activity

Antimicrobial activity of untreated wool as well as treated wool with different concentration of m-TGases was investigated against Staphylococcus aureus, SA, as gram-positive bacteria and the obtained results presented in Fig. 5. As can be seen m-TGases shows anti-bacterial activity.

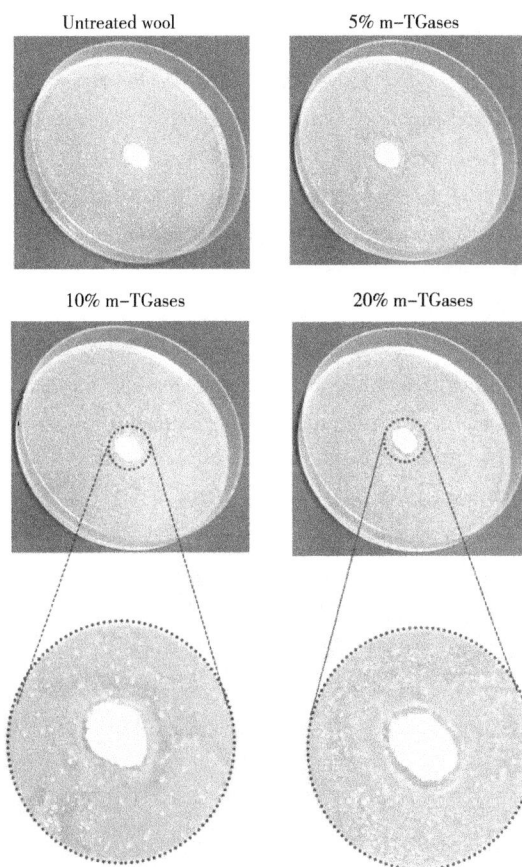

Fig. 5   Antibacterial assessment of untreated wool and treated wool with various concentrations of m-TGases against SA bacterium by agar dilution method

4   Conclusions

In this study, we studied surface morphology of wool during the treatment by various concentration of m-

TGases. To do this and by considering in the structure of wool which is full of various amino acids, m-TGases enzyme with the capability of cross-linking of two main amino acids (Glutamine and Lysine) was selected. The treatment of wool with different concentrations of m-TGases was performed and the results indicated that there is critical concentration for enzyme. In fact, by using extra concentration of m-TGases the surface of wool will be damaged. Also, anti-bacterial activity was investigated and the results indicated that by adding of m-TGases, wool fiber will show anti-bacterial activity which is useful to employ enzyme treatment as an important process to get the multi-objective wool.

References

[1]MADHU A, CHAKRABORTY J N. Developments in application of enzymes for textile processing[J]. Journal of Cleaner Production, 2017, 145: 114-133.

[2]MOJSOV K. Enzymatic treatment of wool fabrics-opportunity of the improvement on some physical and chemical properties of the fabrics[J]. The Journal of the Textile Institute, 2017, 108(7): 1136-1143.

[3]WANG P, CUI L, WANG Q, et al. Combined use of mild oxidation and cutinase/lipase pretreatments for enzymatic processing of wool fabrics[J]. Engineering in Life Sciences, 2010, 10(1): 19-25.

[4]MOHAMED S A, KHAN J A, Al-Bar O A M, et al. Immobilization of Trichoderma harzianum α-Amylase on Treated Wool: Optimization and Characterization [J]. Molecules, 2014, 19(6): 8027-8038.

[5]PRAJAPATI C D, SMITHE, KANE F, et al. Selective enzymatic modification of wool/polyester blended fabrics for surface patterning[J]. Journal of Cleaner Production, 2019, 211: 909-921.

[6]IGLESIAS M S, SEQERIOS C, GARCIA S, et al. Eco-friendly anti-felting treatment of wool top based on biosurfactant and enzymes[J]. Journal of Cleaner Production, 2019, 220: 846-852.

[7]KARANIKAS E K, KOSOLIA C H, ZARKOGIANNI M, et al. Effect of enzymatic treatment on the dyeing properties of protein wool fibers[J]. Fibers and Polymers, 2013, 14(2): 223-229.

[8]PARVINZADEH M. Effect of proteolytic enzyme on dyeing of wool with madder[J]. Enzyme and Microbial Technology, 2007, 40(7): 1719-1722.

[9]GASHTI M P, ASSEFIPOUR R, AMIR Kiumarsi, et al. Enzymatic surface hydrolysis of polyamide 6, 6 with mixtures of proteolytic and lipolytic enzymes[J]. Preparative Biochemistry and Biotechnology, 2013, 43(8): 798-814.

[10]PARVINZADEH M. A new approach to improve dyeability of nylon 6 fibre using a subtilisin enzyme [J]. Coloration Technology, 2009, 125(4): 228-233.

[11]TESFAW A, ASSEFA F. Applications of transglutaminase in textile, wool, and leather processing[J]. International Journal of Textile Science & Engineering, 2014, 3: 64-69.

[12]IBRAHIM N A, El-SHAFEI H A, ABDEL-AZIZMS, et al. The potential use of alkaline protease from Streptomyces albidoflavus as an eco-friendly wool modifier[J]. The Journal of the Textile Institute, 2012, 103(5): 490-498.

[13]MONTAZER M, PAJOOTAN E, LESSAN F. Microbial trans-glutaminase enhances the physical and mechanical properties of depigmented wool[J]. Engineering in Life Sciences, 2012, 12(2): 216-222.

[14]REHMAN F, SANBHAL N, NAVEED T, et al. Antibacterial performance of Tencel fabric dyed with pomegranate peel extracted via ultrasonic method[J]. Cellulose, 2018, 25(7): 4251-4260.

Macropixel Analysis for Instantaneous Quality Control of Neppy Mélange Yarn Production

HABIBA Halepoto[1,2]*, GONG Tao[1,2], KASHIF Kaleem[2]

[1] *Engineering Research Center of Digitized Textile and Fashion Technology, Ministry of Education, Shanghai, 201620, China*

[2] *College of Information Science and Technology, Donghua University, Shanghai, 201620, China*

Corresponding author's email: taogong@dhu.edu.cn

Abstract: This paper discusses a simple MATLAB based model to determine real-time homogeneity of neppy mélange yarn fabrics. Currently, the mélange yarn industry relies only on visual assessment and experience, however, this algorithm proposes the solution for the quality assessment of textile mélange yarn industry. Herein, the designed algorithm determine the real-time of nep detection from neppy mélange yarns, and calculated inhomogeneity of neps about 91%. This strategy may be helpful for textile mélange yarn industry and can be further used in other types of fashion yarns.

Keywords: Computer vision; Neppy yarn; Macropixel analysis; Real-Time

1 Introduction

Blending different fibers yield different types of fancy yarns[1]. There has remained strong market potential for fancy yarns and these fancy yarns have remained eye-catching compared to conventional yarns[2] and among others, the mélange yarns are one type of fancy yarns[3]. There are a wide variety of looks and colors of the mélange yarns[4]. This class of yarns is produced by either by mixing different colored fibers into the blow room or sometimes they are mixed or blended at the draw frames[5]. One of the major class of these mélange yarn is neppy mélange yarn, in which a certain amount of neps are introduced to get a unique aesthetics.

Textile image processing is gaining much attention recently. To date, several researchers have focused on various aspects of textile image processing including defect detection in woven fabrics[6-7], fabric weave pattern recognition and yarn color recognition[8-9]. However, to the best of our knowledge, none of the researchers have focused on textile image processing for mélange yarn industry quality assurance and textile testing are one of the central department of any yarn spinning industry. Some quality tests, including yarn count, even-ness, tenacity, elongation at break, shade matching, and variation, the visual appearance of finished goods are performed before the shipment, in order to avoid any cancelation of the order. A couple of decades ago, the shade matching and variation were one of the main reason for the cancelation of orders, therefore, in past decades, too much research have been done to for shade matching and minimizing the variation, and thus various technologies have been developed to avoid rejections of the order.

Despite numerous research in other quality parameters, less attention has been paid to assess the visual appearance of finished goods. Even at present, neppy yarn texture recognition relies on human skills and experience and thus performed manually by visual inspection. The method of visual inspection is, of course, incompetent, laborious, and time-consuming as well as involves problems of subjective human factors, monotonous and tiredness, physical and mental load, and low efficiency. However, in order to fully understand the aesthetic of mélange yarn, fully image feature extraction or image segmentation is necessary to understand the different spatial/lattice positions and range/colors domain of the single element in an image (only matching the shade of yarn is not enough). This might be understood easily by two related features i. e. tone and texture, in terms of gray scale in which each pixel in the image has its own intensity value[10]. Herein, the tone is defined as the variation in gray level of an image, and the texture is defined as the dimensional distribution of tone as a cluster of pixel intensities that repeat itself in a specific region of image[11]. To date, mélange yarn industry only relies on the spectrophotometry which despite being very expensive fails to determine the homogeneity or inhomogeneity of the yarn texture generated by neps into mélange yarn.

This dimensional distribution might be analyzed in terms of regularity in the histogram (statistically), in parallel lines (structurally), with empiric prototypical (model based) and after wavelet transformation (transform based)[12]. HARALICK et al proposed a gray-level co-occurrence matrix by generating matrix through clustering and correlating those clusters with their neighboring clusters[10]. In the gray-level co-occurrence matrix, the scale of scrutiny is a critical step to ensure all important information is present[13].

Herein, we have proposed a simple MATLAB based algorithm to determine the homogeneity of neppy mélange yarn, which might be fruitful for textile mélange yarn industry to determine the textural effect also along with shade matching and other quality parameters.

2 Experimental

2.1 Materials

The Xinjiang medium grade cotton available in the Wuxi No. 1 Cotton Spinning Mill for routine production was used for this study. The basic fiber and yarn properties are given in Tab. 1.

2.2 Methods

We collected a real-time manufacturing video with a digital camera (available in industry) of neppy mélange yarn fabric. The simulations of all the images and analysis of continuous-level moving block algorithm were done using MATLAB v2017b (The Mathworks, MA, USA). In this paper, we aimed to determine real-time monitoring for final neppy yarn. At first, we monitored

and studied real-time analysis of neppy mélange fabric during its manufacturing (Fig. 1).

Tab. 1　The basic properties of fiber and yarn

Name of property	Value
Fiber staple length	28. 7mm
Fiber fineness	4. 38μg/inch
Yarn count	20 Ne
Nep content	3%

For the first time, we have proposed a strategy for real-time controlling of neps and its homogeneity intoneppy yarn fabrics.

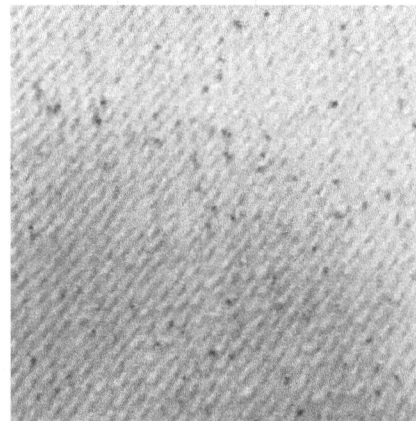

Fig. 1　The test image of neppy mélange yarn fabric

2.3 Kernel Density Function

Kernel density function is one of the most popular non-parametric density function. The multivariate kernel density function with the points x_i, i = 1, 2, 3, $\cdots$, n, characterize the population and unknown density functions $f(x)$[14-15], may be mathematically expressed generally as equation (1).

$$\widehat{f}(x) = \frac{1}{nh^d} \sum_{i=1}^{n} K \frac{x-x_i}{h} \qquad (1)$$

For image feature extraction, the kernel might be broken into the product of two different radially symmetric kernels since the image feature space is composed of two independent domains (in our case, spatial position and color) with different natures.

$$\widehat{f}(x) = \frac{c}{n(h_s)^p(h_r)^q} \sum_{i=1}^{n} k_s \left(\left\| \frac{x-x_i}{h_s} \right\|^2 \right) k_r \left(\left\| \frac{x-x_i}{h_r} \right\|^2 \right) \qquad (2)$$

Where × is a pixel, k_s and k_r are the profiles used in the two respective domains, h_s and h_r are employed bandwidths in spatial-range domains and c is the normalization constant. There are two main parameters that have to be defined by the user: the spatial bandwidth h_s and the range band width h_r.

2.4 Macropixel Analysis

Macropixel analysis scrutinizes the self-information contained in an image at different sublevel (macropixels) to generate homogeneity curve by the collective standard deviation of all sublevels[16]. Macropixel analysis works by collaborative scanning of discrete level tiling and continuous-level moving block that uses non-coinciding tiles and all possible sublevels of an image, respectively. In addition, it should be assumed that the elements conforming an image are indivisible and the images are binary only containing object values of either 0 or 1.

3 Results and Discussions

3.1 Neps Detection

At first, we have obtained results of applying an algorithm. This algorithm was applied to segmented images of the dataset of neppy mélange yarn fabric. The performance of the proposed method was tested. The Kernel density estimation plots of neppy yarn fabric are shown in Fig. 2. This kernel function helped to determine the neps in real time during the manufacturing of neppy mélange yarn fabric.

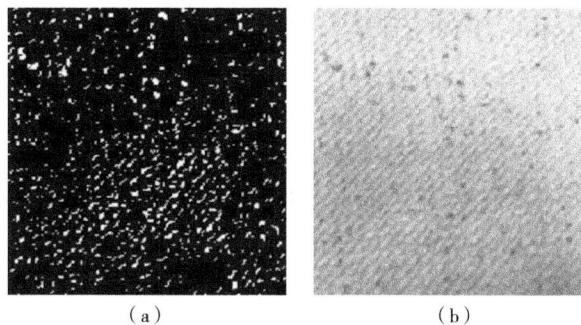

(a)   (b)

Fig. 2　The nep detection of neppy mélange yarn fabric (a) Neps detection using 388 frames; (b) Original frame from 388 frames

Herein, the total of 388 frames was analyzed for the neppy yarns, thus there corresponding colored images were transformed into binary images, as shown in Fig. 3. This binary conversion of images would result in the better analysis of the homogeneity, in order to avoid the surficial and textural effects of the neppy mélange fabric.

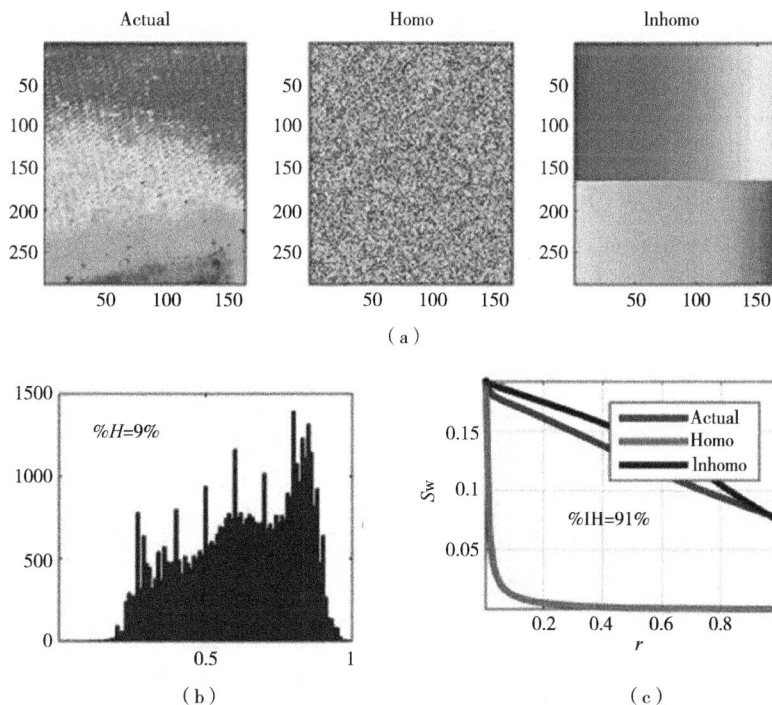

(a)

(b)   (c)

Fig. 3　Homogeneity Analysis of neppy mélange yarn fabric: (a) Homogeneity demonstration of actual as well as modeled homogenous and inhomogeneous neppy mélange yarn fabric; (b) Histogram of actual neppy mélange yarn fabric; (c) Homogeneity curve showing 9% of homogeneity

3.2 Homogeneity Analysis

Homogeneity analysis of neppy mélange yarn fabric is very beneficial for textile mélange yarn industry to also discuss the homogeneity parameter along with other parameters to fit the standard and to avoid lot cancelations. Homogeneity demonstration of actual as well as modeled homogenous and inhomogeneous neppy mélange yarn fabric can be seen from Fig. 4(a), the matching sample was less homogenous thus its demonstration resembles more with the demonstration of inhomogeneous demonstration. Moreover, it is also fruitful to see the distribution of homogeneity, which is shown in the histogram of actual neppy mélange yarn fabric (refer, Fig. 4(b). Furthermore, the homogeneity curve showing 9% of homogeneity of neps over the fabric is displayed in Fig. 4(c).

$$IH\% = 100 - H\% \tag{7}$$

Since the homogeneity was only 9%, therefore the curve of neppy fabric is close to the inhomogeneous curve. The inhomogeneity of the image can be calculated by equation 7. This represents that the fabric was more inhomogeneous i.e. 91%. This inhomogeneity is desired for aesthetic functionality and appeal the observer in the yarn design of neppy mélange yarn.

4 Conclusions

In this study, a simple MATLAB based model to determine real-time homogeneity of neppy mélange yarn fabrics was proposed which might be a helpful tool in the quality assessment of textile mélange yarn industry to replace the existing manual inconsistent visual assessment based on experience only. The neps from neppy mélange yarn fabric production were detected using kernel density algorithm. We determined that the inhomogeneity determined by the MATLAB code was as high as 91%, which is, of course, impossible to be determined just by bare eyes. Therefore, it is very helpful for the textile industry and thus, further can be used in other different types of fashion yarns.

References

[1] BEHERA B K, HARI P K, BANSAL S, et al. Effect of different blending methods and blending stages on properties of milange yarn[J]. 1997.

[2] GONG R H, WRIGHT R M. 6-Structures and formation of fancy yarns[M]. Fancy Yarns, 2002: 33-59.

[3] MOGHASSEM A R. Study of dyed cotton fibers with direct dye in spinning processes and its effect on the properties of cotton mélange yarn[J]. International Journal of Engineering-Transactions B: Applications, 2007, 20(2).

[4] KAN C W, WONG W Y. Color properties of cellulase-treated cotton denim fabric manufactured by torque-free ring spun yarn[J]. Textile Research Journal, 2011, 81(9): 875-882.

[5] GHAREHAGHAJI A A, TAVANAIE H, KARIM S K. Study on the Interactions between mélange yarn properties and fiber damage[J]. Arabian Journal of Geosciences, 2011, 4(7-8): 1117-1130.

[6] ZHANG K, YAN Y, LI P, et al. Fabric defect detection using salience metric for color dissimilarity and positional aggregation[J]. IEEE Access, 2018, 6: 49170-49181.

[7] LI Y, ZHAO W, PAN J. Deformable patterned fabric defect detection with fisher criterion-based deep learning[J]. IEEE Transactions on Automation Science & Engineering, 2017, 14(2): 1256-1264.

[8] KHAN B, WANG Z, HAN F, et al. Fabric weave pattern and yarn color recognition and classification using a deep ELM network[J]. Algorithms, 2017, 10(4): 117.

[9] KHAN B, FANG H, WANG Z, et al. Bio-inspired approach to invariant recognition and classification of fabric weave patterns and yarn color[J]. Assembly Automation, 2016, 36(2): 152-158.

[10] HARALICK R M, SHANMUGAM K, DINSTEIN I. Textural features for image classification[J]. IEEE Transactions on Systems, Man, and Cybernetics, 1973, 3(6): 610-621.

[11] BHARATI M H, MACGREGOR J F. Texture analysis of images using principal component analysis[C]. Proceedings of SPIE/Photonics Conference on Process Imaging for Automatic Control, Boston: The International Society for Optical Engineering, 2000, 27-37.

[12] BHARATI M H, LIU J J, MACGREGOR J F. Image texture analysis: methods and comparisons[J]. Chemometrics & Intelligent Laboratory Systems, 2004, 72(1): 57-71.

[13] MISSIAEN J M, THOMAS G. Homogeneity characterization of binary grain mixtures using a variance analysis of two-dimensional numerical fractions[J]. Journal of Physics Condensed Matter, 1995, 7(7): 2937.

[14] FUKUNAGA K, HOSTETLER L D. The estimation of the gradient of a density function, with applications in pattern recognition[J]. IEEE Transinftheory, 1975, 21(1): 32-40.

[15] COMANICIU D I. Nonparametric robust methods for com-

puter vision. 2000.

[16] HAMAD M L, ELLISON C D, KHAN M A, et al. Drug product characterization by macropixel analysis of chemical images[J]. Journal of Pharmaceutical Sciences, 2010, 96 (12): 3390-3401.

Anisotropic Mechanical Properties of Carbon Fiber Nonwoven Fabric Reinforced Thermoplastic with an Open Hole

SHAO Yuanyi[1], MATSUSHITA Masaya[2,3], OHTANI Akio[3], YANG Yuqiu[1]*

[1] *College of Textiles, Donghua University, Shanghai, 201620, China*

[2] *Yuho Co., Ltd., Osaka, 5300003, Japan*

[3] *Advanced Fibro-Science, Kyoto Institute of Technology, Kyoto, 6068585, Japan*

* *Corresponding author's email:* amy_yuqiu_yang@ dhu. edu. cn

Abstract: In this paper, carbon fiber/polypropylene fiber anisotropic nonwoven fabrics were produced by carding method and parallel laid-up process. The nonwoven fabrics were used to facture composite though pressed-molding. The anisotropic tensile properties of the specimens with and without open hole in machine direction (MD) and transverse direction (TD) were characterized. Furthermore, to investigate the relationship between anisotropy and the length of carbon fibers, the carbon fibers in length of 50mm and 70mm were respectively used to manufacture nonwoven fabrics. The fiber orientation was observed to clarify the anisotropic mechanical properties. The results showed that the nonwoven fabric anisotropic could be influenced by carding method. Specimens in MD showed superior static properties than which in TD.

Keywords: Non-woven fabric; Composites; Carding; Anisotropic; Notched

1 Introduction

In recent years, fiber reinforced plastic (FRP) with resin reinforced the advantages of high strength, light weight, flexibility and durability. Therefore, they have been widely used in various applications, such as airplane, automobile, sports goods[1-4]. Meanwhile, with the expansion of FRP utilization in the future, the reused fibers will be actively promoted. One of the methods of using reused fiber is to produce nonwoven fabric[5-6]. After press-molded, the nonwoven fabric became composite material. The possibility of the composite material using recycled carbon fiber nonwoven fabric was investigated.

However, the randomly oriented fiber reinforced materials such as isotropic materials cannot be said to give full play to the excellent mechanical properties of composite materials as basic anisotropic materials. In addition, in order to make more effective use of reused fibers with the same mechanical properties in expected direction as virgin materials, it is necessary to control the orientation angle through carding process to make it anisotropic. Therefore, it is expected that the use of nonwovens reinforced composites controlled by fiber orientation will become more frequently used in the future. However, the present situation is that the mechanical properties of nonwoven composites with anisotropic properties have not been discussed so far.

It is reported that mechanical connection is a very convenient and widely used assembly of structural components because they can transfer high load. Therefore, notched strength of composites is an important property widely used by designers. Many researchers focus on the effects of different factors on notched strength, including laminate size, lamination orientation and thickness, processing quality.

In this study, the mechanical properties of anisotropic CF/PP nonwovens reinforced composites in mechanical properties of machine direction (MD) and transverse direction (TD) were studied. Fiber orientation and length were carried out to clarify the influence of initial fiber length on the anisotropic mechanical properties.

The tensile properties of specimens with and without a hole were measured. The declining rate of notched specimens were used to investigate the sensitivity of the hole.

2 Materials and Methods

2.1 Materials

The raw materials of CF/PP nonwoven fabric were polypropylene fiber and carbon fiber with the weight ratio of 40 : 60. The length of PP fibers was 50mm. To investigate the influence of carbon fiber length on the anisotropy, the carbon fibers were cut into 50mm and 70mm, respectively. The carbon fiber is T700SC-12k, provided by Toray, and the polypropylene fiber was provided by Daiwabo Polytec Co, Ltd.

2.2 Manufacturing Methods

Thecarbon fiber non-woven fabrics were manufactured by carding method. The webs were outputted by a low speed rotated roller and layered by parallel laid-up, which resulted in the final direction was in accordance with the carding direction. After that, webs became non-woven fabrics by needle-punched process. The weight per unit area was controlled as $250g/m^2$. Each type of needle-punched non-woven fabric was cut into pieces in transverse direction and machine direction, respectively. The pieces were laid up in the same direction. To control the thickness of hot-pressed composite close to 2mm, eight layers of pieces were laminated for one piece of composite. The laminated nonwoven fabrics were hot-pressed by using heat press molding machine (SATOH Co., LCD, Japan) into CF/PP composites. The condition of hot-press molding was 3MPa pressure, 230℃, and 240 sec press time. The cooling systems with cold water was switch on the moment the hot-pressed molding was over.

The code of CF/PP with carbon fiber of 50mm and 70mm were marked as 50-CF and 70-CF, respectively.

2.3 Fiber Orientation

Thecross section of specimens was polished by sandpapers firstly and then by aluminum powder. The polished cross sections were observed and photos were taken by optical microscope with a digital camera. As Fig. 1, the length of long axis a and short axis b was measured by Image J and the fiber orientation angle θ (degree measure) can be calculated from Equation (1):

$$\theta = \cos^{-1}\left(\frac{b}{a}\right) \tag{1}$$

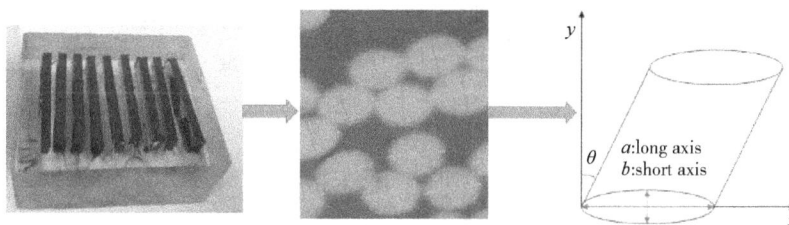

Fig. 1 The step of measure the degrees of carbon fibers

2.4 Fiber Length

The specimens were cut from CF/PP composites and heated in the oven at 400℃ for 2 hours to burn out PP. After burning, the left carbon fibers were picked up by tweezer and placed on white paper. The length of fibers was measured by tweezer. The number-average fiber length could be calculated as Equation (2):

$$\bar{l} = \frac{\sum N_i l_i}{N_i} \tag{2}$$

where, l_i is the length of carbon fiber, N_i is the number of fibers at the length of l_i.

2.5 Tensile Test

Tensile properties of samples were performed using a universal testing machine (55R4206, Instron, Japan). For tensile test, the notched and unnotched specimens with were prepared in both machine direction and transverse direction from the CF/PP composites. The unnotched specimens were cut into 200mm×20mm. As Fig. 2, each notched specimen in size of 200mm×30mm was dilled with a hole in diameter of 10mm in the center of the specimen. Clamping distance was 100mm and the tests were performed at a constant crosshead speed of 1mm/min. The notched strength can be calculated as Equation (3):

$$\sigma_N = \frac{F}{(W-D)T} \qquad (3)$$

where, σ_N is notched strength, F is the maximum load, D is the diameter of the hole, W and T is the width and thickness of the specimen.

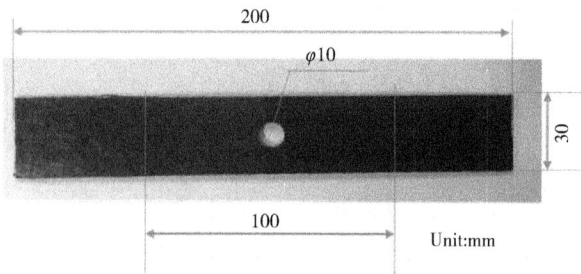

Fig. 2　Notched specimens

2.6　Failure Mode of Notched Specimen

To observe the failure mode of notched specimen, step by step observation was performed. The specimen was in the tensile test at a test speed of 1mm/min, after the cracks could be seen and gradually expanded, the load was quickly adjusted below 70% of average maximum load and slowly to 0. The specimen was taken down from the machine and the surface of the failure area was polished by sandpaper and aluminite powder.

2.7　SEM Observation

The fracture surfaces of the specimens were cut from tensile specimens and observed by scanning electron microscopy (SEM, S-3000N, Hitachi Japan). Before the SEM observation, the fracture surfaces were sputter-coated with gold.

3　Results and Discussions

3.1　Fiber Orientation

Fig. 3 shows the typical cross section of samples in MD and TD. It could be obviously seen that many fibers were perpendicular to the cross section in machine direction, which indicated the fibers were more oriented in machine direction and less oriented in transverse direction.

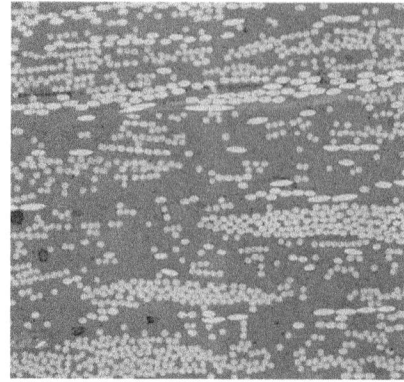

(a)

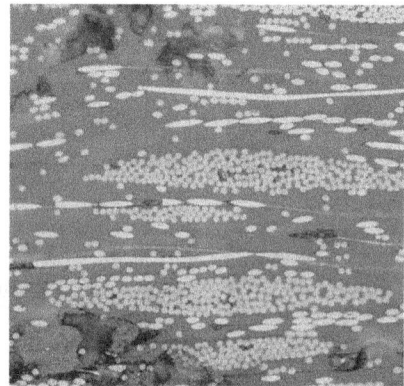

(b)

Fig. 3　The typical cross section of samples in (a)MD and (b)TD

The frequencies of carbon fibers in each direction was shown in Fig. 4. The machine direction was defined as 0. For 70-CF, the frequencies of carbon fibers in 0-10 degrees and 80-90 degrees were both above 50% and below 20%, respectively. For 50-CF, less carbon fibers were in 0 - 10 degrees compared with 70 - CF, which the frequencies were above 40%. However, for the carbon fibers in 80-90 degrees, the frequency was above 20%, which was higher than that of CF-70. The results showed the initial fiber length influenced the fiber orientation, which was that with the increasing of carbon fiber length, more fibers were aligned in the carding direction.

3.2　Fiber Length

As shown in Fig. 5, the residue average length and rate of length maintenance of carbon fibers. From the result of carbon fiber length, it could be seen the average length did not reached the initial length, which indicated the carbon fibers were damaged in carding process. It showed the carbon fibers were broken in carding

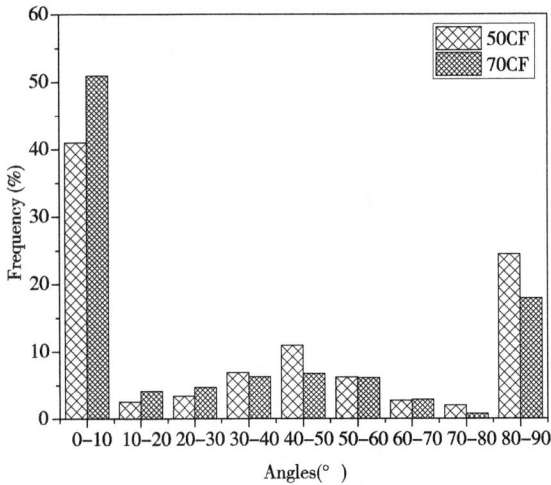

Fig. 4 The frequencies of carbon fibers in each angle

process because the residue length was shorter than initial length. From the rate of length maintenance, the carbon fibers with 70mm length were more easily broken.

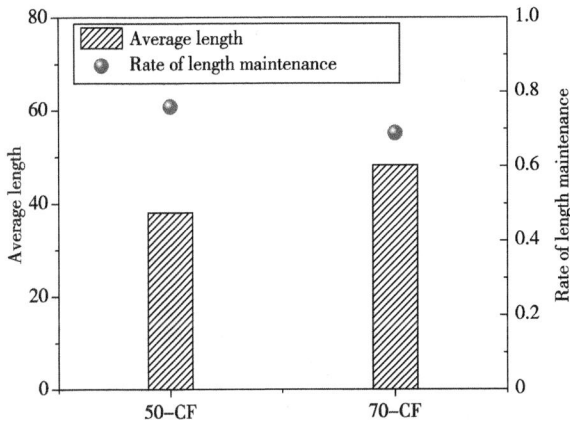

Fig. 5 Average length and rate of length maintenance

3.3 Tensile Strength

Fig. 6 shows the typical tensile stress-strain curves of notched and unnotched in MD and TD. Fig. 7 (a) and (b) show the tensile strength of notched and unnotched specimens. The ratio of MD/TD of unnotched tensile strength is 1.87 and 2.77 in 50-CF and 70-CF, respectively. It could be concluded that tensile strength in machine direction was higher than transverse direction in each sample, which confirmed the anisotropic tensile properties were obvious. Furthermore, the ratio of carbon fibers in length of 70mm was high than that of 50mm, which indicated the length of carbon fibers influenced the anisotropic. In addition, there was a marked drop of strength and aspect intensity ratio after dilled a hole in the

center of the specimen. The anisotropic mechanical properties were caused by fiber direction. The declining rate of notched specimens was lager in MD than that of TD, which showed more sensitive to the hole in MD.

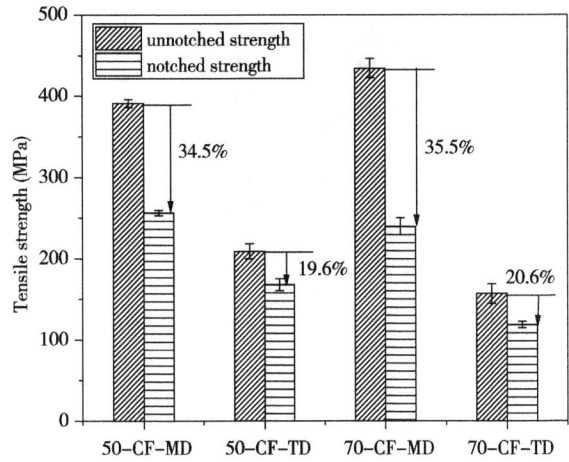

Fig. 6 Tensile strength of unnotched specimens and notched specimens

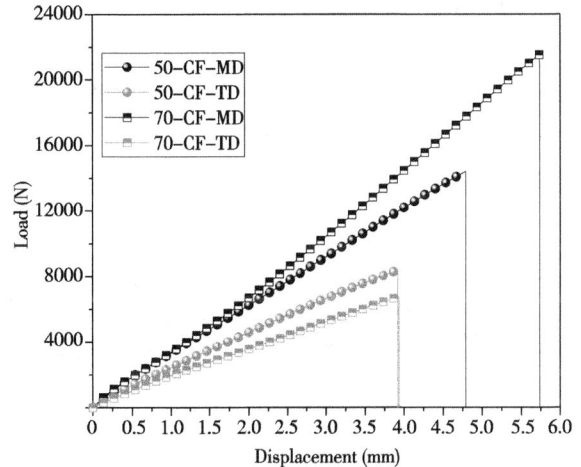

(a)

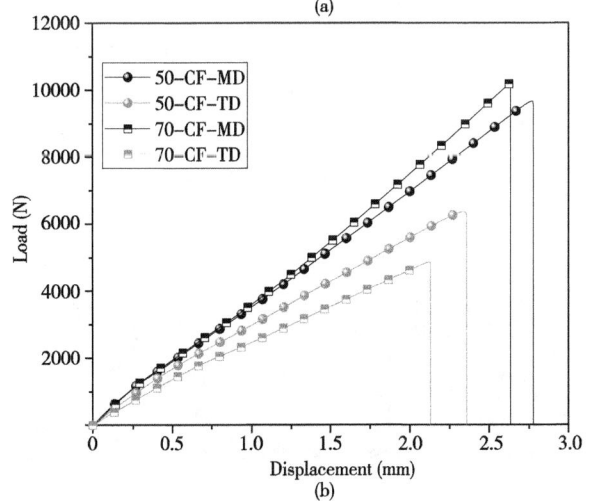

(b)

Fig. 7 Typical tensile curves of (a) unnotched specimens and (b) notched specimens

3.4 Failure Mode of Notched Specimen

The typical tensile fracture of notched specimen is shown as Fig. 8. It could be seen that the fibers were pulled out and broken and the matrix was broken.

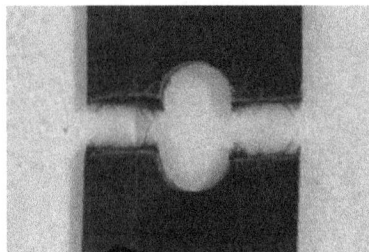

Fig. 8 Typical tensile fracture of notched specimen

From the photos taken before the breakage as shown in Fig. 9, it could be seen the cracks is along to the interface of fibers and matrix. If the interface between fiber and resin was not strong enough, the crack in specimens propagated along the interface[7]. The hole caused the stress concentration, so the break occurs around the hole. For the samples of TD, the fibers perpendicular to the tensile direction are more than that of MD, therefore, the cracks were easily to occur, which resulted in more sensitive to the hole.

Hole

Fig. 9 Cracks in the interface of fibers and matrix

3.5 SEM Observation

The fracture surfaces of tensile specimen were observed by SEM as Fig. 10. The carbon fibers were long and covered the fracture surface as Fig. 10(a). After the long carbon fibers were cut, the fracture could be seen

(a)　1mm　　　(b)　100μm

Fig. 10 SEM of fracture surfaces (a) magnification of 50 (b) magnification of 400

as Fig. 10(b). The carbon fibers were broken and bonded with matrix. In addition, the fibers were pulled and the interface between fibers and matix was broken.

4 Conclusions

The carding process has a great influence on the physical properties of anisotropic nonwoven fabric reinforced materials. Samples in MD showed superior properties than which in TD. The declining rate of notched specimens described the specimens in MD was more sensitive to the hole. The fiber orientation proved that more fibers were perpendicular to the machine direction. The anisotropic mechanical properties were caused by fiber direction.

Acknowledgements

The authors thank Yuho Co., Ltd., Japan for manufacturing the nonwoven fabrics. Also, the work was supported under the State Scholarship Fund of the China Scholarship Council (Award No: 201806630113).

References

[1] MA Y, YOKOZEKI T, UEDA M, et al. Effect of polyurethane dispersion as surface treatment for carbon fabrics on mechanical properties of carbon/nylon composites[J]. Composites Science and Technology, 2017, 151: 268-281.

[2] MA Y, ZHANG Y, SUGAHARA T, et al. Off-axis tensile fatigue assessment based on residual strength for the unidirectional 45 carbon fiber-reinforced composite at room temperature[J]. Composites Part A: Applied Science and Manufacturing, 2016, 90: 711-723.

[3] ZHANG Z, YANG Y, HAMADA H. The effects of open holes on the fracture behaviors and mechanical properties of glass fiber mat composites[J]. Science and Engineering of Composite Materials, 2015, 22(5): 555-564.

[4] MA Y, JIN S, ZHANG S. Effect of trigger on crashworthiness of unidirectional carbon fibre reinforced polyamide 6 composites[J]. Plastics, Rubber and Composites, 2018, 47(5): 208-220.

[5] WONG K, MOHAMMED D S, PICKERING S, et al. Effect of coupling agents on reinforcing potential of recycled carbon fibre for polypropylene composite[J]. Composites Science and Technology, 2012, 72(7): 835-844.

[6] PIMENTA S, PINHO S T. Recycling carbon fibre reinforced

polymers for structural applications: technology review and market outlook[J]. Waste Management, 2011, 31 (2): 378-392.

[7] MA Y, YANG Y, SUGAHARA T, et al. A study on the fail-

ure behavior and mechanical properties of unidirectional fiber reinforced thermosetting and thermoplastic composites [J]. Composites Part B: Engineering, 2016, 99: 162-172.

Development of Sisal Decorticating Machine and Evaluation of Its Performance at Various Settings

HAFIZ Muhammad Zahid Farooq[1], SHARJEEL Ahmed[2], MUHAMMAD Usman[2], FAHEEM Raza[2], ZHENG Lian-gang[1], MUHAMMAD Usman Ghani[1] *

[1] *Key Laboratory of Textile Science & Technology, Ministry of Education, College of Textiles, Donghua University, Shanghai, 201620, China*

[2] *State Key Laboratory for Modification of Chemical Fibers and Polymer Materials, International Joint Laboratory for Advanced Fiber and Low-dimension Materials, College of Materials Science and Engineering, Donghua University, Shanghai, 201620, China*

* *Corresponding Author's email*: Usmanmeo@ qq. com

Abstract: This paper represents a study on the "Development of Sisal Decorticating Machine and Evaluation of its Performance at Various Settings". This study consists of two stages, in the 1st stage lab-scale decorticator machine was developed with the collaboration of M/s Dawood Textile Engineering Works, Faisalabad. This machine was built on the concept of blades on the beater with the mote knife-edge at a specific gauge interval from the beater blades. During the 2nd stage, the performance was checked at different settings in the Department of Fibre & Textile Technology, UAF. The samples of sisal plant leaves of three species were collected. The extraction of sisal fibre was done for different species of sisal fibres at various speeds of the beater and different gauges between the stationary knife plate and rotating the knifed cylinder. The percentage of the weight of extracted sisal fibres obtained per leaf after washing was measured and tested against the strength, elongation, tenacity parameters by following the standard procedure proposed by ASTM committee.

Keywords: Sisal guage, Weight percentaqe; Five stages; Different species

1 Introduction

Sisal (Agavesisalana) is a monocotyledon, one of the 300 species of the Agave genus, which is one of the 21 kinds of the Agavaceae family. They are all tropical or sub-tropical plants. At present sisal and several other species are cultivated for their fibres in about 24 countries in Central and South America, East Africa, Madagascar and Asia. One key objective of this research is to develop a new design that can be accessed by small-hold farmers. Other factors considered were the safety of operation and overall efficiency. Other variables considered in this regard include material selection, weight and thinness of the material, gauging between the stationery knife and knifed cylinder and its speed. Electricity and diesel can be used as an energy source to run

mechanical decorticators. Sisal fibre is suitable for the manufacture of several products such as ropes, sacks, bags, carpets and mats, pulp for papermaking dartboards, buffing cloth, filters, wall covering, geotextiles, floor mattresses and handicrafts. During the past two decades, sisal fibres have also been used as reinforcement in cement agent in rubber and polymer-based composites[1]. The demand for sisal worldwide is consistently increasing because it is environment-friendly in comparison with synthetic fibres. The most precious aspect of the sisal plant is fiber extraction and therefore one of the most significant elements of sisal production is fiber extraction. The broken fibers and pulp (waste) that are also used as natural fertilizers or feed for animals[2].

Harvesting is done by hand. All the lower leaves are

cut off from the plant bole with a sharp flexible knife at an angle of more than 45 degrees to the vertical. Not only is the harvest labor requirement of 100 working hours per ton of fiber high, but also the work involves a great deal of stooping, lifting and carrying substantial weights and avoiding sharp spines at the end of the sisal leaves. Small scale sisal farming has inefficiently experienced in the growth of sisal fibre processing. A majority of the small scale farmers process their sisal manually[3]. Hand processing is a tedious, laborious and slow practice that results in low fiber productivity and low fiber quality. The acidic sap released during manual decoration also creates skin irritation and pain. So far, the attempts made to address this problem have not succeeded. Therefore there is a need to develop appropriate technology for decorticating sisal. The technology should be efficient and affordable. It will be served to support the revival of the industry and provide a sustainable livelihood for the small scale farmers and traders. This project will design to undertake and redesign the previously made decorticator by seeking of new innovation.

We will develop a design for prototype sisal decorticator for small-scale farmers, which can be locally manufactured. The decorticator should be portable so that it can be transported from one place to another. It should also be cheaper than the available decorticators because it could acquirable for small scale farmers, Who can't afford the large automatic decorators available. The device should provide acceptable quality fiber that can get a decent market price just like automatic decoration. Using the decorating device, sisal fiber is obtained from the leaf by scraping or mechanical means. The invention of the decorticator machine was the revolutionary step in the extraction of sisal fibres from the plants both in terms of safety and efficiency[4]. The sisal fibre leaves are beaten by a rotating the roller. Roller has the knives on its surface. The leaves are pressed through rollers and only the fibres remained, the obtained fibres are washed in water to get shiny, smooth, and clear fibres[5-6]. The short fibres and waste matter which are further used as natural fertilizers or animal feed. The sisal fibre consists of cellulose 65%, hemi-cellulose 12%, lignin 9.9%, moisture content 10 (%) and me-chanical properties are Density 1450(kg/m^3), Flexural-modulus 12.5-17.5GPa, microfibrillar angle 20^0, lumen-size 11mm, tensile-strength 68MPa, Young's modulus 3.774GPa[7-9].

2 Materials and Method

2.1 Material

The samples of sisal leaves of different species were collected. The samples were of the same age. The species were Haiti sisal, wild agave AmericanSisalana, wild long leaf sisal. According to the dimensions of the leaves, the gauge was 2mm, 3mm and 4mm between the stationary knife plate and rotating knife cylinder of decorticating machine.

2.2 Method

Sisal leaves are fed endwise and fibres are produced through the nibbling action ofthe machine. After the leaf or fiber is removed, it is then scrapped in the opposite direction. The leaves are fed into the machine by hand, the butt end is first presented because the thick end must be thrushed through the narrow gap between the breast plate and the downward rotating knives. After pushing the leaf for its length, it is then removed and exposed fibers are grasped so that the tip of the leaf can be decorated similarly. As a leaf is introduced, the knives gradually smash and chip off the leaf tissue at close intervals against the breast plate and only a few centimeters or even millimeters of the leaf is decorated at any moment. The crushed part continues to beat as long as the leaf is inside the machine and knives begin to behave as scrapers when the leaf is removed, separating the leaf pulp down the bundle length. Many of short fibres are whisked away out during the first stage before the leaf is reversed for the tip half to be treated. In addition, a few of the long fibres may be lost owing to grip on the slippery fibres being more tenuous than that on the leaf itself. Frequently a whole leaf may be lost as it may be pulled out of the operator's hand, particularly during the second stage. Fibres may be washed either in the decorticator in a tank soon after decortication.

The different steps of the operating machine are described as following.

Step 1: Insert the leaf without tips and edges pines inside the machine.

Step 2: Draw out the extracted fibres rapidly.

Step 3: Insert the other side of a leaf.

Step 4: Again withdraw the extracted fibres from the machine.

Step 5: Extracted Fibres.

2.3 Experiment

The experiment was performed on the decorticator which consists of a rotating wheelset with blunt knives that beats the leaves in entry so that only the fibres remain. Decorticated fibres have to be washed before involving the drying process which might be achieved by drying in the sun or blowing hot air into the fibres to facilitate faster and more efficient drying. Consideration of the beater-drum speed, quality of the raw sisal, the process was chosen for drying the fibres, clearance angle between the beater drum and the anvil ensures the best quality both in terms of process and product is achieved.

After conducting many tests and considerations more combinations were developed in geometry and kinematics of an open Belt Drives to acquire the proper speed for decortication of different species of sisal. Three speeds were used 1550r/min, 1650r/min, 1850r/min for the decortication purpose of these species sisal leaves which have a ratio (D_1 : D_2) 4. 5 : 4, 6 : 5, 6 : 4. 5 respectively. The speed varies via Belt Drive Combinations, V-the belt was chosen for the coupling of the power system and the beater drum.

Here, $D1$ is Motor Pulley Diameter in inches and $D2$ Drum Pulley Diameter in inches.

Experiments were conducted according to the following research plan as shown in Tab. 1.

Tab. 1　Research variables

Varieties of sisal leaf "A"	Speed of rotatiing knifed cylinder"S"	Gauge setting b/w rotating & stationary cylinder"G"
Wild Haiti sisal	1850r/min	2mm
Wild agave American Sisalana	1650r/min	3mm
Wild long leaf sisal	1550r/min	4mm

2.4　Geometry

After several attempts at increasing the attainable drum speed, while using the variable speed motor, it was decided to use different sets of pulleys with a fixed speed motor that run at 1400r/min. Details of the belt drive are given in Fig. 1 overleaf. Given the two pulley diameters, the speed ratio of the drive may be calculated as follows:

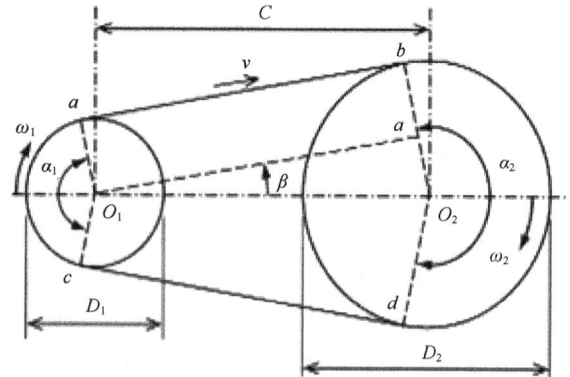

Fig. 1　Geometry of motor pulleys

$$G = \omega / \omega_m = \frac{D1}{D2}$$

$$L = 2C + \pi + (D_1 + D_2) + \left(\frac{D_2 + D_1}{2}\right)$$

Thus, if the length of the belt is given and the centre distance is unknown, then the appropriate centre distance may be determined as follows:

$$C = \frac{-a_1 \pm \sqrt{a_1^2 - 4a_0}}{2}$$

$$a_1 = \frac{\pi D_1 + \pi D_2 - 2L}{4}$$

$$a_2 = \frac{(D_2 - D_1)^2}{8}$$

3　Results and Discussions

After the manufacturing of the machine, the sisal fibre was graded on the behalf of leaf weight (g), fibre weight (g) and the waste percentage of the fibre extracted from the sisal leaves. The results have shown in the Tab. 3, Tab. 4 and Tab. 5 of the fibres of different species e. g. Wild Haiti, Wild agave American and Wild Long Leaf respectively against speed and gauge.

Tab. 2   Various belt drive combinations

Motor pulley diameter D1(inches)	Drum pulley diameter D2(inches)	Drive center distance C(inches)	Belt length L(inches)	Drum speed ω(r/min)
6.00	4.00	24.50	63.00	2100
6.00	4.50	24.50	63.80	1850
6.00	5.00	24.50	64.75	1650
5.00	4.50	24.50	61.7	1540
5.00	4.00	24.50	61.10	1740
4.50	4.00	24.50	59.20	1550

Tab. 3   Results of wild haiti decorticated fibres quality

Testing was done in Lab E-212 of Department of Fibre & Textile Technology, University of Agriculture, Faisalabad

GAP CLEARANCE:2mm				SPEED:1850r/min	
3mm				1650r/min	
4mm				1550r/min	

Wild Haiti plant (Sisal Leaves) V1		Decortication			Quality
		Remarks on Decortication Quality			
Variety	Speed	Gauge (mm)	leaf wt. (g)	fibre wt. (g)	Wt%age of fibre	Visual analysis
---	---	---	---	---	---	---
V1	1850	2	239	9	3.76	Good but with fibre cuts
V1	1850	3	224	15	6.69	Good
V1	1850	4	255	22	8.67	Good
V1	1650	2	229	13	5.67	Fair
V1	1650	3	250	20	8.00	Fair
V1	1650	4	255	27	10.58	Fair
V1	1550	2	232	16	6.89	Poor
V1	1550	3	239	22	9.20	Poor
V1	1550	4	242	28	11.57	Poor

Tab. 4   Results of wild agave american decorticated fibres quality

Testing was done in Lab E-212 of Department of Fibre & Technology, University of Agriculture, Faisalabad

GAP CLEARANCE:2mm				SPEED:1850r/min	
3mm				1650r/min	
4mm				1550r/min	

Wild agave American (Sisal Leaves) V2		Decortication			Quality
		Remarks on Decortication Quality			
Variety	Speed (r/min)	Gauge (mm)	Leaf wt. (g)	Fibre wt. (g)	Weight percentage of fiber (%)	Visual analysis
---	---	---	---	---	---	---
V2	1850	2	213	10	4.69	Good but with many short fibers
V2	1850	3	270	13	4.81	Good

Variety	Speed (r/min)	Gauge (mm)	Leaf wt. (g)	Fibre wt. (g)	Weight percentage of fiber (%)	Visual analysis
V2	1850	4	309	18	5.82	Fair
V2	1650	2	265	17	6.41	Poor
V2	1650	3	206	29	14.07	Poor
V1	1650	4	237	35	14.81	No significant
V1	1550	2	214	27	12.61	No significant
V1	1550	3	206	31	15.04	No significant
V1	1550	4	232	39	16.81	No significant

Tab. 5   Results of wild long leaf decorticated fibres quality

Testing was done in Lab E-212 of Department of Fibre & Textile Technology, University of Agriculture, Faisalabad

GAP CLEARANCE: 2mm	SPEED: 1850r/min
3mm	1650r/min
4mm	1550r/min

Wild long leaf plant (Sisal Leaves) V3	Decortication				Quality
	Remarks on Decortication Quality				
Variety	Speed	Gauge (mm)	leaf wt. (g)	fibre wt. (g)	Wt% of fibre	Visual analysis
V3	1850	2	530	32	6.04	Good but less no of fibre
V3	1850	3	517	29	5.72	Good
V3	1850	4	546	38	6.96	Good but with green particles
V3	1650	2	486	37	6.61	Fair but with green particles
V3	1650	3	497	39	7.85	Poor
V3	1650	4	328	41	12.5	Poor
V3	1550	2	384	56	14.58	No significant
V3	1550	3	365	61	16.71	No significant
V3	1550	4	428	68	15.89	No significant

The mean value of Weight percentage of useable fibres obtained for different speeds was 5.901%, 9.722% and 13.256% for $S1$ (1850r/min), $S2$ (1650)r/min and $S3$ (1550r/min) respectively.

The mean value of Weight percentage of useable fibres obtained for different variety or species were 7.887%, 10.563% and 10.429% for V1 (Wild Haiti sisal plant leaves), V2 (Wild agave American Sisalana plant leaves) and V3 (Wild long leaf sisal plant leaves) respectively.

The mean value of Weight percentage of useable fibres obtained for different gauge was 7.584%, 9.788% and 11.507% for $G1$ (2mm), $G2$ (3mm) and $G3$ (4mm) respectively.

These results of the extracted weight of fibre show that Weight percentage of Useable fibres increased by increasing gauge, leaf size but decreased by increasing the speed of the cylinder.

4 Conclusions

In this research paper, it is tried to minimize the cost of the machine through material selection. Most of the parts of the decorticator were made from mild steel which is readily available in the country and relatively cheap. This means that the offered price to farmers is affordable. The angle bars used in the frame construction are to be welded together to produce a rich structure and design. Due to this, it is possible to make mass production by prototype decorticator. As most small scale sisal farmers live in arid areas, not all of them have ready access to electricity. Hence an internal combustion engine of a rating of at least 3h is recommended to drive the machine, thereby mechanizing the decortication process.

References

[1] VERMA A, et al. Fabrication and characterization of chitosan-coated sisal fiber-phytagel modified soy protein-based green composite[J]. Journal of Composite Materials, 2019, 53(18): 2481-2504.

[2] MASCIA N, DODADON B, VILELA R. Glued laminated timber beams reinforced with sisal fibres[J]. 2018.

[3] CORBIERE-COLLIER T, et al. Life cycle assessment of biofibres replacing glass fibres as reinforcement in plastics[J]. Resources, Conservation and Recycling,2001,33(4): 267-287.

[4] CHIANELLI-JUNIOR R, et al. Mechanical characterization of sisal fiber-reinforced recycled HDPE composites [J]. 2013,16,1393-1397.

[5] DE SANTIS S, et al. Test methods for textile reinforced mortar systems [J]. Composites Part B: Engineering, 2017, 127: 121-132.

[6] MUTHANGAYA M, MSHANDETE A M,KIVAISI A K. Two-stage fungal pre-treatment for improved biogas production from sisal leaf decorticationresidues[J]. International journal of molecular sciences, 2009, 10(11): 4805-4815.

[7] CARVALHO D E, BELLO C B, et al. Experimental tests for the characterization of sisal fiber reinforced cementitious matrix for strengthening masonry structures [J]. Construction and Building Materials, 2019, 219: 44-55.

[8] NARAYANAN V, ELAYAPERUMAL A, SATHIYA G K. Prediction of tensile properties of hybrid-natural fiber composites[J]. 2012,43.

[9] SAMOUH Z, et al. Mechanical and thermal characterization of sisal fiber reinforced polylactic acid composites[J]. Polymers for Advanced Technologies, 2019, 30(3): 529-537.

Preparing Carbon Nanotube Film-Made Yarns by Acid Treatment

[1] XU Siyue, XU Fujun[1] *

[1] College of Textiles, Donghua University, Shanghai 201620, China

* Corresponding author's email: fjxu@ dhu. edu. cn

Abstract: Multifunctional applications of textiles draw a great amount of attention to design and produce yarns with great mechanical and electrical properties. Carbon Nanotube(CNT) yarn because of its excellent performance have already made a high impact on the intelligent textiles and aeronautical technologies. However, the scale of the traditional CNT yarns limited their long-term using. An effective method for preparing a novel CNT yarns through the use of acid treatment in this study. The yarns were twisted by the slim and long CNT films and then be treated in the HNO_3 solution in order to enhance the properties. After that, the tensile strength and modulus of treated CNT film-made yarns increased by 86% and the conductivity increased by 233%. Observations of scanning electronic microscopy (SEM) also showed that the treated CNT film had a more compact structure after functionalized by acid solution.

Keywords: Carbon nanotube; Acid treatment; Film; Yarn

1 Introduction

With the development of the electronics technoogy and intelligent textiles, there are high demand of quality Carbon Nanotube (CNT) yarns[1-3]. As one kind of nanomaterials, CNT yarns composed of CNT fibers, have the unique advantage of 1D structure to be applied in these rising fields. Inside the CNT fiber, CNTs connected each other to make up of bundles and bundles entangled to form the networks of CNT fiber[4]. Therefore, the orientation and density of CNTs and CNT bundles in the CNT structure have an important influence on the properities of CNT fibers and yarns. Regretly, so far up to now the theoretical properties of CNT yarns still much more excellent than that of CNT yarns when pratical using[5].

Besides, the nano scale of CNT yarns have the possibility to break down when manufacturing and cause problems, which limited their permanent application. In order to make full use of CNT yarns, CNT fibers are usually twisted into piled yarns as a traditional method[6].

However, when piled yarn is suffering load, the weakest fiber break down first, making it hard to suffer load in the same time for the total fibers[7]. In this study, we proposed an effective method for preparing a novel CNT yarn, which was named as film-made yarn. Compared with the piled yarns, it has higher breaking strength and better mechanical performance. In addition, the CNT film was more economical and easier to produce in a large scale and this method provides an access to continually treat CNT yarns in order to fufill different properties. Acid treatment, as a convinent way to improve the structure of CNT and enhance the conductivity[8]. The CNT film-made yarns were treated with HNO_3 in this work.

2 Experiments

2.1 Materials

The multi-walled CNTs with 25nm diameter and nearly 20 walls were fabricated into CNT film by floating chemical vapor deposition, supplied by Suzhou Institute of Nano-Tech and Nano-Bionics, Chinese Academy of Sciences. The thickness of CNT film was about 13.7μm. The CNT film will be cut into 1mm to make film-made yarns.

2.2 Film Treatment

The HNO_3(16 M) with 65%–68% purity used in the experiment was purchased to immerse the CNT films for 1–4 hours and dried under ambient conditions.

2.3 Preparation of Film-Made Yarns

The Fig. 1 showed that the process of twisting CNT film into yarn. A novel device was designed to prepare the film-made yarns. One tip of CNT film was fixed and another tip was rotated by the motor driving.

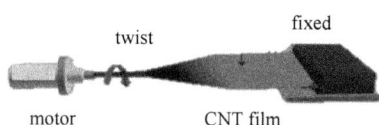

Fig. 1 The process to fabricate twisted CNT yarn

2.4 Property Testing of Film-Made Yarns

CNT films were cut out along the CNT preferential aligned direction with 1mm width. The specimens were mounted onto a rigid paper with a hole. The CNT films were tensile tested using an XQ – 2 tensile tester (Shanghai Xusai Instrument Co., China) at a crosshead speed of 0.5mm/min with a gauge length of 10mm (ASTM D882). The electrical resistence was recorded through a digital multi-meter (Agilent, 34410A, USA).

2.5 Characterization

The morphologies and microstructures of the films were observed using Field Emission Scanning Electron Microscopy (HITACHI S–4800), High-resolution Transmission Electron Microscopy (JEOL JEM–2100) and Raman spectroscopy analyses (in Via-Reflex).

3 Results and Discussions

3.1 SEM Measurement of CNT film

Fig. 2 showed that for the pristine film, there are many pores distributed unevenly between the CNT bundles. After acid treatment, first with the treated time increasing, the orientation of CNT bundles increased and being desitified in total, which made it possible for the enhancement of mechanical property. However, when being treated excessively under the acid, the structure of CNT film was destoryed.

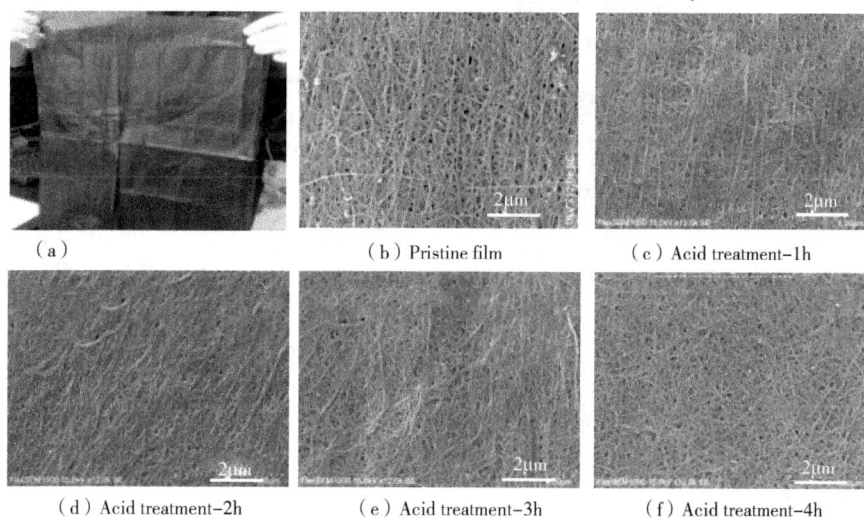

(a) (b) Pristine film (c) Acid treatment-1h

(d) Acid treatment-2h (e) Acid treatment-3h (f) Acid treatment-4h

Fig. 2 (a) Picture of pristine CNT film; (b)–(f) Mornology of CNT film after 1h/2h/3h/4h acid treatment

3.2 Mornology of CNT Film-Made Yarns

After being twisted into yarns, the diameter of yarns first decreased and then increased slightly with the longer acid treatment time(Fig. 3). It is because that acid make the CNT film being more flexible and easier to be twisted to a compact structure, enabling the diameter decreased first. Then the acid made some defects on the CNT, which hindered the fabrication of yarns.

The Fig. 4 verified this that acid treatment could affect the assembly structure of CNT. Compared with the pris-

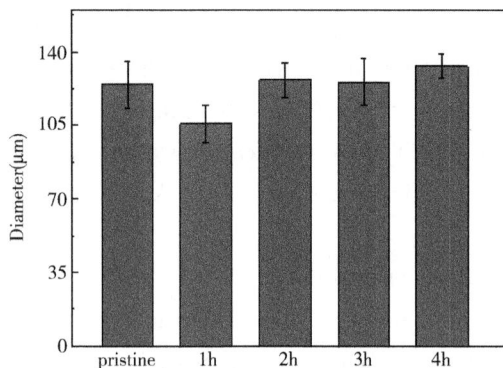

Fig. 3 Diameter of CNT film-made yarns before and after acid treatment

tine CNT yarn, the acid treated yarns were cleaner because acid was able to remove the impurities such as metal particles which left by the production. With the

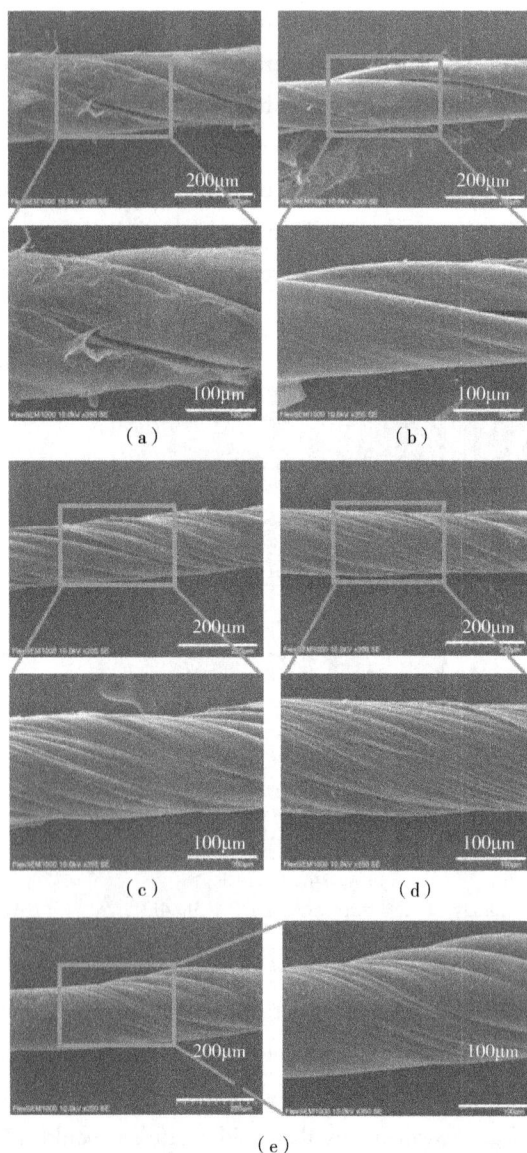

(a)　(b)

(c)　(d)

(e)

Fig. 4 SEM images of (a) pristine; (b) 1h; (c) 2h; (d) 3h; (e) 4h

increasing immersing time, the CNT films were twisted more compact with more obvious grooves on the surface of film-made yarns.

From the Fig. 5, it can be seen that with increasing acid treatment time, the vaule of ID/IG first increased and then decreased. It indicated that the acid treatment enhanced the graphe structure inside the CNT film-made yarns at first. But for too long treatment time, the graphe structure had been ruined and degree of defects increased. Meanwhile, the vaule of I2D/IG first decreased and then increased, which was affected by chemical doping. The use of acid changed the electrical networks of CNT.

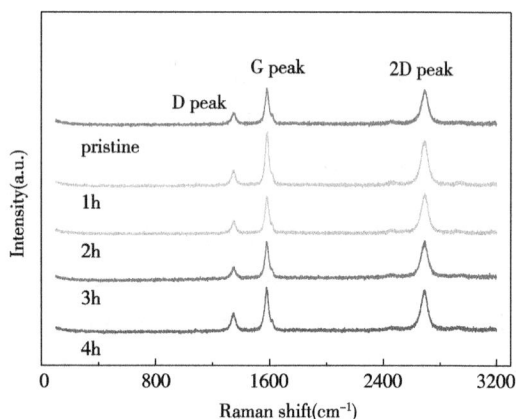

Fig. 5 Raman shift of CNT yarns before and after acid treatment

3.3 Mechanical Property of CNT Film-Made Yarns

Asshownin Tab. 1, the after acid treatment film-made yarns all showed better mechanical behavior compared with the pristine yarn. The tensile strength of acid treated for 2h treated yarn was increased from 130MPa to 240MPa (86%) due to the improvement structure of CNT yarn. The Modulus and strain were increased from aroud 1Gpa to 5Gpa and 37% to 30% respectively for the 2h treated yarn.

3. 4 Electrical Property of CNT Film-Made Yarns

The conductivity of all the acid treated CNT yarns were increased and for the most improved one, the vaule of conductivtiy increased 233%. It was resulted from the oxygen functional groups attached to the CNT yarns induced by the acid as well as the improvement structure of CNT tubes, which was in accordacne with the Fig. 6.

Tab. 1　Mechanical properties of CNT film-made yarns under different acid treatment time

Sample	Strength(MPa)	CV(%)	Modulus(GPa)	CV(%)	Strain(%)	CV(%)
pristine	129. 94	3. 12	1. 168	0. 08536	36. 786	1. 11012
1h-treated	218. 73	40. 76	5. 74902	0. 15113	27. 898	3. 6991
2h-treated	243. 56	40. 32	4. 9222	0. 5	30. 318	3. 897
3h-treated	194. 33	36. 96	5. 3464	0. 32	21. 478	2. 246
4h-treated	173. 14771	10. 89	5. 42178	0. 26	24. 2	2. 3654

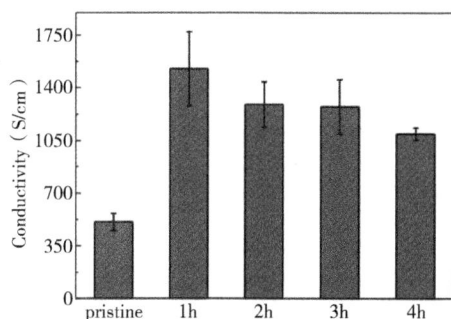

Fig. 6　Conductivity of CNT yarns before and after acid treatment

4　Conclusions

In this study, an effective method for preparing a novel CNT yarns through the use of acid treatment. The yarns were twisted by the slim and long CNT films and then be treated in the HNO_3 solution in order to enhance the properties. After that, the tensile strength and modulus of treated CNT film-made yarns increased by 86% and the conductivity increased by 233%. This method enables more possible applications of intelligent textiles.

References

[1] LU W, ZU M, BYUN J H, et al. State of the art of carbon nanotube fibers: opportunities and challenges[J]. Advanced Materials, 2012, 24(14): 1805-1833.

[2] KANG T J, CHOI A, KANG D H, et al. Electromechanical properties of CNT-coated cotton yarn for electronic textile applications[J]. Smart Materials & Structures, 2011, 20(1): 015004.

[3] KANG B J, HAN S H, PARK J S. Sheet resistance, transmittance, and chromatic property of CNTs coated with PEDOT: PSS films for transparent electrodes of touch screen panels[J]. Thin Solid Films, 2014, 572: 68-72.

[4] JUNG Y, CHO Y S, LEE J W, et al. How can we make carbon nanotube yarn stronger? [J]. Composites Science and Technology, 2018: S0266353817322066.

[5] BEESEM A M, WEI X, SARKAR S, et al. Key factors limiting carbon nanotube yarn strength: exploring processing structure property relationships [J]. Acs Nano, 2014, 8(11): 11454-11466.

[6] WANG K, MENG Q, ZHANG Y, et al. High-performance two-ply yarn supercapacitors based on carbon nanotubes and polyaniline nanowire arrays[J]. Advanced Materials, 2013, 25(10): 1494-1498.

[7] SABELKIN V, MISAK H E, MALL S, et al. Tensile loading behavior of carbon nanotube wires[J]. Carbon, 2012, 50(7): 2530-2538.

[8] MIASAK H E, ASMATULUS R, O'MALLEY M, et al. Functionalization of carbon nanotube yarn by acid treatment [J]. International Journal of Smart & Nano Materials, 2014, 5(1): 34-43.

Comparative Analysis of National Textile Standards Along the Belt and Road

FENG Hanxiao[1], XUE Wenliang[1], WEI Mengyuan[2], QIAN Jingfang[1], LIU Yunying[1], DING Yi[1]

[1] *Key Laboratory of Textile Science & Technology, Ministry of Education, College of Textiles, Donghua University, Shanghai, 201620, China*

[2] *Shanghai Customs, Technical Center for Industrial Product and Raw Material Inspection and Testing od SHCIQ, Shanghai, 200135, China*

* *Corresponding author's email: liuyy@ dhu. edu. cn*

Abstract: This paper makes a comparative analysis of the standards of the total number, product standard, method standard quantity and the bid mark rate of difference countries on the basis of sorting out the standardization and the relevant standards of textiles of the 65 countries along the belt and Road. According to the specific conditions and characteristics of various countries' standards, and based on the comparison of regional standards and international standards system, it is found that countries in Central and Eastern Europe rely on the European standards system, which has a higher level of standardization and internationalization. Especially, textile and garment technical regulations of standards have stricter provisions on children's safety and ecological environment protection. At the same time, because the level of standardization of developing countries along the Belt and Road is not uniform, there is a lack of product category specification, the level of standardization improvement is not high enough in these countries, and the relevant standards are mainly focused on product standards, and many of them are limited primarily to the characteristics, sizes and specifications of textiles.

Keywords: Belt and Road; Standardization; Textile; Analysis

1 Introduction

With the deepening of the "Belt and Road" Initiative initiative, China's links with the whole world have become increasingly close, which the trade has been frequent. When China's products "go out", whether China's technical standards can be recognized has been as a key.

The 65 countries along the "Belt and Road" are as follows[1] (Tab. 1):

Tab. 1 List of countries along the "Belt and Road"

Area	Quantity	Country name
ASEAN	10	Singapore, Malaysia, Indonesia, Myanmar, Thailand, Laos, Cambodia, Vietnam, Brunei Darussalam, Philippines
East Asia	1	Mongolia
South Asia	8	India, Pakistan, Bangladesh, Afghanistan, Sri Lanka, Maldives, Nepal, Bhutan
West Asia	18	Iran, Iraq, Turkey, Syria, Jordan, Lebanon, Israel, Palestine, Saudi Arabia, Yemen, Oman, United Arab Emirates, Qatar, Kuwait, Bahrain, Greece, Cyprus, Egypt, Sinai Peninsula

Area	Quantity	Country name
Central Asia	5	Kazakhstan, Uzbekistan, Turkmenistan, Tajikistan, Kyrgyzstan
Commonwealth of Independent States	7	Russia, Ukraine, Belarus, Georgia, Azerbaijan, Armenia, Moldova
Central and Eastern Europe	16	Poland, Lithuania, Estonia, Latvia, Czech Republic, Slovakia, Hungary, Slovenia, Croatia, Bosnia and Herzegovina, Montenegro, Serbia, Albania, Romania, Bulgaria, Macedonia

2　Regional Standards

2.1　European Standards

Albania, Montenegro, Serbia, Macedonia, Turkey and Bosnia and Herzegovina are candidates for the European Union, and the remaining Central and Eastern European countries are members of the European Union.

The nature of European standards is that national standards of member states must be consistent with European standards. The three major standardization bodies continue to formulate new harmonized standards in their own fields according to the needs of economic development. As of January 2019, there are nearly 20,000 European standards, more than 2,500 textile related standards, and the standard classification is classified according to the international standard classification ICS number. The product category is complete, of which the product standard accounts for about 15%, and the method standard accounts for about 62%, 36% of product standards and 87% of method standards directly adopt ISO standards[2-4].

2.2　CIS Standard

The Commonwealth of Independent States, referred to as CIS, is a cooperative consortium formed by the joint efforts of most former Soviet states, although the standard system framework for the continuous entry and withdrawal of countries since 1991 has not changed.

The GOST standard is a national standard established by the former Soviet Union. After the collapse of the Soviet Union, GOST was transformed into a regional standard, which was managed by the Standardization, Measurement and Accreditation Committee (EASC) of the Commonwealth of Independent States. As of January 2019, there were more than 42,000 GOST standards, about 1,154 related textile standards, 340 product standards, 6.5% from ISO, more than 560 method standards, and 28% from ISO. For 12%, in addition to the ISO standard, there are standards such as EN and IEC, and the CIS standard is gradually merging with international and European standards[5].

2.3　Gulf Standard

Members of the Gulf Cooperation Council for Arab States (GCC) include the United Arab Emirates, the Sultanate of Oman, the State of Bahrain, the State of Qatar, the Kingdom of Saudi Arabia and Yemen.

The standard name issued by the Gulf Standards Organization (GSO) is the Gulf Standard, code-named GSO. As of January 2019, GSO has 15 technical committees specializing in the development of Gulf standards, covering chemical textiles, mechanical specifications, food agriculture, energy and many other fields. More than 23,000 standard specifications and more than 1,500 items have been released. Technical regulations. There are 656 current standards in the textile industry and 55 technical lists, of which product standards account for about 30%, method standards account for about 69%, and ISO standards are used. The adoption rate is 90%. The Gulf standard focuses on basic textile products, and there are no good specifications for production equipment and some high-performance textiles[6-7].

3　Standardization of Official Member States of the ISO

3.1　Relevant Information of ASEAN and Mongolian Members

Vietnam, Thailand, Indonesia and Singapore focus on issues such as formaldehyde, azo, and heavy metals, focusing on ecology and consumerprotection[8]. In addition, Singapore is more concerned with the standards of security and national characteristics, focusing on the integration with international standards[9]. Generally speaking, the development of the textile industry in these countries is not as strong as China's, but the bilateral relationship is close. The Uniform Guidelines stipulate that ASEAN member countries should prioritize the adoption of appropriate international standards, eliminate unnecessary trade barriers, and classify standards[10] to promote the vitality of the ASEAN market and reduce trade barriers.

3.2 Relevant Situation in South Asian Countries

India's textile-related standard categories are divided into self-contained systems, product standards are mostly, and attention has been paid to coordination with international standards[11]; Pakistan's standardization is based on the principle of using international standards as much as possible[12]. In terms of number, the textile industry is in good development. , especially jute; Nepal's textile industry is relatively backward, and the degree of regulation is not high[13]; Sri Lanka's textile industry standardization activities are more active[14]; Afghanistan is one of the least developed countries in the world, and years of war has caused its economy to collapse. Standardization construction is relatively backward.

3.3 Relevant Situation in Countries in West Asia

The textile industry is the main industry in Egypt, but in recent years, Egypt has paid more attention to food safety, home appliances and building materials[15]. The number of product standards and method standards in textiles is almost the same; the textile industry is one of the major industries in Syria. There are textile spinning standards, textile standards account for about 11% of the national standard, and the development is relatively good; although the textile industry in Israel, Lebanon, Iraq, Jordan and other countries is also one of the major industries, the development level is general, and the relevant standards are also not sound.

4 National Standardization of Informal Member States of ISO

There are three categories of members of the International Organization for Standardization: full members,

correspondents, and subscriber members. Only formal members have the right to vote at the meeting. Therefore, it can be considered that the standardization work of correspondents, subscribing members and non-ISO organizations is not perfect. Of the countries along the route, only Yemen and the Maldives are not ISO members.

4.1 ASEAN Countries

The standardization authority in Cambodia is the Cambodian Industrial Standards Agency (ISC), which is code-named CS. Cambodia's standardization work is lagging behind, and the overall situation is at an early stage. At present, there are more than 900 national-standards[16].

The standardization and support department of Laos is the Laos Standard Measurement Department (DOSM). The level of economic development is not high, and the overall awareness of standardization is poor. At present, there are only 434 national standards, of which 402 use ISO and IEC standards, and the adoption rate is 92.6%[17].

The standard authority in Myanmar is the National Standard for Research and Innovation (DRI) code-named UBS. Myanmar's economic development is slow, and most industries are still unable to support Myanmar's standardization and testing. Currently, there are 65 UBS standards for 27 textile standards[18].

Brunei's national standards authority is the National Standards Center (PSK), the national standard code is PBD, and there are currently 82 national standards, and there are no textile-related standards[19].

4.2 South and West Asian Countries

Bhutan's standard authority is the Bhutan Standards Bureau (BSB). Bhutan's national standard code is BTS, a total of 253 items, there is no current textile-related current standards, the overall adoption rate is 87.4%, and more IEC, ISO standards.

The Palestinian Standards Authority is the Palestinian Standards Association (PSI). The national standard code of Palestine is PS. At present, there are more than 3,600 national standards[20], 408 textiles, 80 product standards, 61% from ISO, 182 method standards, 60% from ISO, and the overall adoption rate is about 60%.

5 Conclusions

In general, the three major regional standardization systems, the degree of standardization in Central and Eastern Europe is relatively high, and technical regulations also impose strict regulations on child safety and ecological protection. Due to the influence of the former Soviet Union, the CIS countries have the same system and few textiles, and they are concentrated on textile raw materials. The Gulf Organization has adopted international standards as regional standards, combining textiles and chemistry into one department, and the classification is not very detailed. Although 10 countries in Southeast Asia have formed ASEAN, the economic strength between countries is too great, and there is no unified system to regulate and guide. However, scholar Chen Fuzhi predicted that even if the textile industry technology of ASEAN countries generally lags behind China, it cannot ignore the trend of technical regulations to follow suit, and the constraints will become more and more demanding.

The rest of the countries along the "Belt and Road" are mostly developing countries, and the level of standardization in these countries is uneven. First of all, the overall national standard adoption rate is generally not high, that is, the degree of integration with the international level is not high, and the degree of standardization is not high, many categories of specifications are missing, the existing standards are concentrated on conventional fabrics, and the product standards are relatively high. More, made the characteristics and size requirements. Secondly, there are also many countries with various reasons such as war and chaos, the construction of the standardization system is sluggish, the project is scarce, and there is almost no binding ability. Moreover, the degree of standardization implementation is also reflected in the construction of the website, and the construction of some countries is low. It is difficult to display information such as the construction of the Afghanistan ANSA website.

References

[1] One Belt and One Road to build an information platform. http: //www. ydylstandards. org. cn/.

[2] ZHU M H, XU B. Overview of European standardization system[J]. Standard Science, 2018 (12): 6-10.

[3] LUO Z L. Analysis of China and Europe textile apparel standards and technical regulations [J]. Standard Science, 2013 (12): 84-87.

[4] HU Y H. Analysis of EU green textile ecolabel system[J]. Standard Science, 2011 (01): 83-86.

[5] International council. http: //easc. by/.

[6] Middle Eaststandardization organization. http: //www. tbtmap. cn/mbsc_106/zdsc/zdgk_3068/201802/t20180208_2117642. html.

[7] MA N, JI X F. Research on the status quo of Saudi standardization development [J]. Standard Science, 2017 (12): 8-13.

[8] CHEN F Z. Overview of technical trade measures for textiles in Southeast Asia[J]. Cooperative Economy and Technology, 2018(03): 106-107.

[9] LIAO X R, TANG J W. The status quo of Singapore standardization system and its enlightenment to China[J]. Standard Science, 2018 (06): 11-14.

[10] FENG H Y. ASEAN standardization policy strategy[J]. Standard Science, 2018 (06): 6-10.

[11] FANG L, ZHOU S H, YU J. Interpretation of the latest national standardization strategy in India[J]. Standard Science, 2018 (12): 64-69+73.

[12] ZHUANG Y Y, CUI Y J. A survey of the development of standardization in Pakistan [J]. Standard Science, 2018 (04): 10-14.

[13] ZHANG S M, ZHUANG Y Y. Nepal's standardization system and its characteristics [J]. Standard Science, 2018 (04): 19-23.

[14] YANG Q B, ZHUANG Y Y. Sri Lanka standardization system and its characteristics [J]. Standard Science, 2018 (04): 15-18.

[15] WANG J G, XUE P, WANG S H. Overview of the development of Egyptian standardization[J]. Standard Science, 2017 (12): 21-28.

[16] YU J M. The status quo of Cambodia's standardization management system and standardization[J]. Standard Science, 2018 (07): 11-14.

[17] WEI Y J. Laos standardization management system and standardization status[J]. Standard Science, 2018 (07): 19-22.

[18] ZENG Y Q, YU J M. The status quo of standardization management system and standardization in Myanmar[J]. Standard Science, 2018 (06): 23-26.

[19] MA T R, WEI Y J. The status quo and characteristics of

Brunei standardization[J]. Standard Science, 2018 (07): 23-27.

[20] MA N, WANG J G, WU Z H. Overview of Palestinian standardization development [J]. Standard Science, 2017 (12): 29-36.

The Location Choice of OFDI in China's Textile and Apparel Enterprises: Global Value Chain Perspective

ZHAO Junli[1]*, DING Jieli[1], WANG Min[1]

[1] *Glorious Sun School of Business & Management, Donghua University, Shanghai, 200051, China*

* *Corresponding author's email:* zjl@ dhu. edu. cn

Abstract: Based on the 949 Chinese textile and apparel firm-level data in the list of overseas investment enterprises from 2011 to 2015, the paper analyzes the whole distribution, value chains distribution and influence factors in location selection of outward foreign direct investment (OFDI) of Chinese textile and apparel (T&A) enterprises. The paper finds in overall data: Chinese T&A enterprises have market seeking motivation and efficiency seeking motivation, but no significant strategic resources seeking motivation in general. T&A enterprises tend to invest in countries with high economic system quality, but with low political system quality. The paper finds in T&A different value chain categories: The R&D and design organizations are not sensitive to the technical level of the host country, for them transportation convenience and service industry are more preferred. The manufacturing and processing organizations are greatly affected by the labor resources and labor costs of the host country. The operation and sales organizations are sensitive to the market size of the host country. The quality of economic system has a significant positive correlation with OFDI in the operation and sales segments and the manufacturing and processing organizations, but not significant in the R&D design process organizations. The quality of political system has little or negative impact on different value chain activities.

Keywords: Textile and apparel enterprises; OFDI; Location selection; Global value chain

1 Introduction

The textile and apparel (T&A) industry is the representative of China's traditional industries. The increase of domestic labor costs and trade frictions make the export of textiles and apparel difficult. However, outward foreign direct investment (OFDI) in Chinese textile and apparel enterprises increased rapidly since 2012. With the development of global value chain, the object of international direct investment of multinational corporations has also turned to various processes within the product. Under such a background, OFDI in today's textile and apparel enterprises has new characteristics. Based on the location selection theory and the global value chain theory, the influencing factors on OFDI location selection of China's textile and apparel enterprises were studied. We use the conditional logic model to analyze the relationship between the location selection of T&A enterprise and two factors: the investment motivation of and the host country system. The whole distribution and value chains distribution are tested separately. Although the academic research on the OFDI has been quite sufficient, there is a lack of OFDI research from global value chain. The textile and apparel industry has a long production chain whose different value chain activities are distributed in different countries. The contribution of the article is to study the foreign direct investment of enterprises through global value chain perspective based on the firm-level data of textile and apparel enterprises.

2 Literature Review and Hypothesis

The prior studies on foreign direct investment are mainly conducted in the context of developed countries. The location choice of OFDI from developing countries is under-researched[1]. This chapter mainly focuses on the investment motivation and host country system of outward FDI in Chinese textile and apparel enterprises. The hypotheses are put forward from above two aspects. The motivation of FDI can be divided into three types: market seeking, efficiency seeking and resource seeking[2-3]. Market size has been widely examined in the existing literature as a location selection factor affecting OFDI, which is positively correlated with FDI inflow[4-6]. Today's textile and apparel enterprises are actively seeking overseas markets in order to sell in the global market, so it is assumed that:

H1a: The market size and market potential of the host country have positive influence on OFDI location choice.

The efficiency-seeking motivation refers to that aim of OFDI enterprises is to reduce labor costs and improve the overall production efficiency of enterprises. Although some scholars thought that there is no efficiency-seeking in China's OFDI (Buckley, 2007)[4], Chinese textile and apparel enterprises are labor incentive. With the increase of domestic labor costs, many textile and apparel enterprises transfer the manufacturing activities to low labor cost places. Therefore, it is assumed that:

H1b: The more abundant the host country's labor resources and the lower the labor cost, the more possibility the textile and apparel enterprises invest in these countries.

With the long-term accumulation of technology and capital of T&A enterprises in China, there are many T&A enterprises aiming to the higher value added activities, such as R&D, fashion design, brand operation. For textile machinery manufacturing, high-quality fabrics production and fashion design, there is still a big gap with that in developed countries. In order to shorten the gap, there is motivation to pursue the strategic resources. Therefore, it is assumed that:

H1c: The abundance of strategic resources in the host country has positive effect on OFDI location choice of Chinese T&A enterprises.

A good political system environment will reduce the investment risk, and protect the private property of enterprises in the host country. The following assumption is then put forward:

H2a: The possibility for textile and apparel enterprises to set up investment branches in the host country is positively related to the quality of the country's political system.

It is more convenient to sell and export in higher quality economic system[7]. Therefore, the following hypothesis is put forward:

H2b: The possibility for textile and apparel enterprises to set up investment branches in the host country is positively related to the quality of the country's economic system.

3 Variables, Data and Results

3.1 Variables and Data

This paper uses conditional (fixed-effects) logistic model (MacFadden, 1973). In the logic model adopted in this paper, the value of dependent variable is 0−1. If an individual chooses a scheme, it is marked as 1 (choice=1); otherwise, it is marked as 0 (choice = 0). The original data come from Directory of Foreign Direct Investment Enterprises (Institutions) from 2011 to 2015.

The value chain activities of enterprises overseas can be classified into four different activities (Xu and Chen, 2008; Meng and Dong, 2015)[8-9]: research & development (R&D) and design, manufacturing and processing, sales and operation, and non-profit foreign agencies. From our statistic analysis, R&D and design activities are mostly distributed in developed countries such as the United States, Italy, Japan, South Korea and Britain. The manufacturing and processing organizations are mostly distributed in Asian countries such as Cambodia, Vietnam and Burma. The operation and sales organizations are distributed in both developed and developing countries. Tab. 1 shows definition and types of the main variables.

This paper selects the top 35 host countries where China's textile and garment enterprises invest. These 35 host countries include about 90% OFDI investment projects of domestic enterprises. The data of 887 Chinese T&A enterprises establish 949 overseas branches in the 35 host countries from 2011 to 2015. The choice of the host country is marked as 1, while for the rest of the 34 countries tag is 0, the overall observation is about

33215. Logarithms of some non-proportional variables were taken for subsequent analysis. Tab. 2 shows the overall results estimated by Stata15. 0.

Tab. 1　Definition and types of variables

Variable types	Variable name	Description	Proxy
Independent variable	Choice	Choice of host country	0-1
Dependent variables	lngdp	Market size of host country	Logarithmic value of GDP
	lnpgdp	Market potential of host country	Logarithmic value of GDP per capita
	labor	Labor endowment	Rural population/Total population
	lncost	Labor cost	Logarithmic value of per capita national income
	Tech	Endowment of strategic resources	The proportion of high-tech exports
	Inst	Quality of political system	Comprehensive indicators of global governance indicators
	Ief	Quality of economic system	Comprehensive score of economic freedom
Control variables	Service	Level of service industry development	Added value of services/GDP
	Internet	Communication level	Number of Internet security servers per 100 people
	lntraffic	Logistics and transportation level	Container throughput
	opentrade	Trade openness	Host country import and export /GDP
	lndist	Geographic distance	Spherical distances of major cities

3.2　Results

There are 114 R&D and design investment branches, 427 related manufacturing & processing branches and 775 operation & sales branches. Conditional logistic regression is conducted for the whole sample and three samples respectively.

Tab. 2 shows the results in whole T&A industry and in different value chain activities. The results show that the market size and market potential have a significant positive effect on China's textile and garment enterprises when they choose host countries. This verifies hypothesis H1a, indicating that China's textile and garment enterprises have strong market seeking motivation for their OFDI. Host country labor resources of enterprise location choice has significant positive effect, and the choice of host country labor costs for enterprises is obviously negative effect, assuming H1b verified, this

shows that China's textile and garment enterprises tend to go to cheap labor resources, low labor cost countries, reflects the efficiency of the strong seek motivation; Use high-tech products export to represent the strategic resources results negative correlation with the enterprise investment orientation, conflict with hypothesis H1c, shows that T&A industry of China has no strategic resources motivation.

The results of political system quality and economic system quality have strong significance, but the host country's political system quality is negatively correlated with the investment tendency of enterprises, which is inconsistent with hypothesis H2a. The results of economic system quality of the host country show a positive correlation with enterprise investment tendency, which is consistent with hypothesis H2b.

Tab. 2　Results of impact of factors on OFDI location selection in T&A enterprises

Variable	(1) Overall results	(2) Operation and sales	(3) R&D and design	(4) Manufacturing and processing
lngdp	0.448 ***	0.628 ***		
	(-4.89)	(-6.76)		

Variable	(1) Overall results	(2) Operation and sales	(3) R&D and design	(4) Manufacturing and processing
lnpgdp	2. 172 **	−0. 173 *		
	(3. 38)	(−2. 21)		
Tech	−0. 0478112 ***		−0. 0212	
	(−6. 03)		(−1. 10)	
Labor	6. 041966 ***			9. 436 ***
	(10. 47)			(−9. 22)
lncost	−1. 549381 *			1. 026 ***
	(−2. 32)			(−5. 78)
Inst	−0. 3937716 ***	−0. 295 ***	0. 0156	−0. 294 **
	(−6. 31)	(−5. 31)	(−0. 1)	(−3. 25)
Ief	0. 0879267 ***	0. 0585 ***	−0. 0195	0. 0406 **
	(8. 77)	(−6. 11)	(−0. 76)	−2. 73
lndist	−0. 394528 ***	0. 0886	−0. 307	−0. 425 ***
	(−4. 64)	(−1. 24)	(−1. 76)	(−3. 38)
lntraffic	0. 1444497	−0. 0451	0. 841 ***	−0. 0223
	(1. 79)	(−0. 52)	(−5. 52)	(−0. 37)
Service	0. 0172149 *	−0. 0235 **	0. 0564 **	0. 00794
	(2. 32)	(−3. 25)	(−2. 82)	(−0. 72)
Internet	0. 0003168 ***	0. 000432 ***	0. 000103	0. 000564 ***
	(4. 03)	(−5. 5)	(−0. 53)	(−4. 06)
Opentrade	0. 0064165 ***	0. 00310 *	−0. 00753 *	0. 00134
	(3. 61)	(−2)	(−2. 32)	(−0. 87)
N	33215	21450	3300	10980

Note Robust Z-values appear in parentheses. $*p < 0. 05$, $**p < 0. 01$, $***p < 0. 001$.

4　Conclusions

Based on OFDI location selection theory and global value chain theory and conditional logistic regression model, this paper uses the 949 samples of China's textile and apparel enterprises from 2011 to 2015 in the list of Overseas investment enterprises (Institutions) to study the influencing factors of location selection of OFDI in Chinese T&A enterprises.

Through statistic analysis, it is found that Chinese textile and apparel enterprises investing abroad not only in developing countries such as some countries in Southeast Asia and Africa, but also in developed countries such as Italy, America, Japan. The number of enterprises investing in either host countries is almost the same.

Further, it is found that the largest activities of value chain of Chinese textile and apparel enterprises abroad are operation and sales, followed by manufacturing and next are R&D and design. Among them, R&D and design branches are mainly distributed in developed countries, manufacturing and manufacturing branches are mainly distributed in developing countries, and operation and marketing branches are distributed in both developed and developing countries.

The conditional logic model is used to empirically analyze the relationship between the investment decision of enterprises and the location selection factors of the host country. The conclusions about influence from investment motivation and institutional factors are as follows:

(1) China's textile and apparel enterprises in general have market-seeking motivation and efficiency-seeking motivation. When choosing the location of the host country, they tend to go to countries and regions with large market scale and abundant cheap labor resources, but the strategic resource motivation of textile and apparel enterprises is not significant.

(2) On the influence of institutional factors, textile and apparel enterprises tend to invest in countries with high quality of economic system, but invest in countries with poor quality of political system. The quality of the political system of developing countries is generally lower than that of developed countries. The reason may be that resource-seeking enterprises prefer to invest in the countries with a less strict political and environmental system.

(3) Operation and sales institution are more sensitive to the market scale of the host country. The branches of R&D and design are not sensitive to the technology level of the host country, but prefer good transportation and service industry. The manufacturing and processing branches are greatly affected by the labor resources and labor cost of the host country.

(4) The quality of political system has little or negative correlation with the choice of operation and sales, manufacturing and processing, R&D and design. The quality of economic system has a significant positive relationship with the choice of operation and sales, manufacturing and processing. But the quality of economic system has no significant effect on R&D and design activities.

References

[1] LI M, LI D, MARJORIE L, LIU S H. Chinese MNEs' outward FDI and home country productivity: the moderating effect of technology gap[J]. Global Strategy Journal, 2016 (6): 289-308.

[2] GLAISTER K W, BUCKLEY P J. Strategic motives for international alliance formation [J]. Journal of Management Studies, 1996, 33: 301-332.

[3] JIANG G H, JIANG D C. Location selection of China's outbound investment: panel data test based on investment gravity model[J]. The Journal of World Economy, 2012(9): 21-40.

[4] BUCKLEYP J, CLEGG L J, CROSS A R, et al. Erratum: the determinants of chinese outward foreign direct investment [J]. Journal of International Business Studies, 2007, 38 (4): 499-518.

[5] CHENG L K, MA Z. China's outward FDI: past and future [C]. China's outward FDI, 2007: 545-578.

[6] RAMASAMY B, YEUNG M, LAFORET S. China's outward foreign direct investment: location choice and firm ownership [J]. Journal of World Business, 2010, 47(1): 17-25.

[7] YANG Y P, GAO Y. Investment site selection of "Belt and Road" countries—institutional distance and perspective of overseas Chinese network[J]. Economic Perspectives, 2017 (04): 41-5.

[8] XU K N, CHEN J. Location determinants of value chain of transnational corporations [J]. Economic Research Journal, 2008(03): 138-149.

[9] MENG X, DONG Y D. The distribution of value chain of China's OFDI and its influencing factors[J]. International Economics and Trade Research, 2015, 31(04): 40-51.

Effect of Stitch Structure on Reading Performance of Fabric-Based Embroidered UHF RFID Tags

CHEN Yingxue[1], **YANG Xudong[1]**, **WANG Tingting[1]**, **HU Jiyong[1,2]***, **YU Jinlin[2]**

[1] *Department of Technical Textiles, College of Textiles, Donghua University, Shanghai, 201620, China*

[2] *Jiangsu Danmao Textile Co., Ltd, Danyang, 212351, China*

* *Corresponding author's email*: hujy@ dhu. edu. cn

Abstract: As the demand for rapid preparation techniques for low-cost RFID fabric tags is increasing, the embroidered technology has been attempted to fabricate tag antennas. But the effects of stitch structures on the performance of tag antennas have rarely been studied. Since the structure of embroidered stitch is related to the antenna geometry, this study was prepared two sets of UHF RFID tag antennas by changing the main embroidered stitch structure parameters such as the embroidered thread structure and the stitch length, and tested and analyzed the electrical and gain property of these antennas. And again, the read performance of the corresponding tag was evaluated, and the effect of the change in stitch structure on the read performance of the tag was analyzed. The results showed that antennas embroidered with copper wire wrapped yarns have higher energy transfer efficiency than that with single copper wire yarns. When the stitch length is increased from 0. 9mm to 5mm, the reading distance of the embroidered tag is firstly increased and then decreased. And also, the optimal stitch length for reading distance is at 1. 7mm, and the reading distance is 12. 95m. When the stitch length is 5mm, the minimum distance is 9. 56m. In summary, this study founded that the embroidered thread structure and the stitch length is important to improve the performance of the fabric-based embroidery antenna for RFID tag and the read range.

Keywords: Embroidery; Stitch structure; RFID; Conductive yarn; Antenna

1 Introduction

Based on the endless application potential for wearable radio frequency identification (RFID) tags in identification, monitoring and sensing, there are more and more researches on the antenna structure and fabrication of RFID tags. Among them, the UHF RFID antenna of the T-matched structure is particularly widely used because of its miniaturization. So, it is a preferred structure of the antenna.

Some scholars[1] have simplified the topological structure of the T-matched antenna based on the concentrated distribution of the radiated current on the outer edge of the antenna conductor. That is, the boundary portion of the original antenna conductor is mainly retained. The RFID tag has a 10% reduction in read range compared to a fully printed tag, but ink consumption has been reduced by nearly 50%. At the same time, Nico-las[2] used conductive yarn to embroider a simplified topology antenna, which not only has low-cost and time-effective, but also find that the read range is equivalent to the embroidered full-topology antenna, reaching 8m. Embroidery with conductive yarn is one of the preferred techniques for meeting the low cost and rapid manufacturing of fabric antennas due to its processing compatibility with various textile substrates and technical maturity in the textile industry. The embroidery process parameters mainly include the stitch type, the stitch pitch and the stitch length[3-5]. From the foregoing analysis, the simplified T-matched antenna of this topology can be embroidered from a single conductive yarn, so the embroidery process parameters are mainly the stitch length and the embroidery yarn. Obviously, as shown in Fig. 1, according to the principle of embroidery and the topographic profile length of the actual embroidered antenna, it is difficult to control the position of the pin, so that each segment of the antenna conductor profile is regular and the topology size does not deviate from the design value.

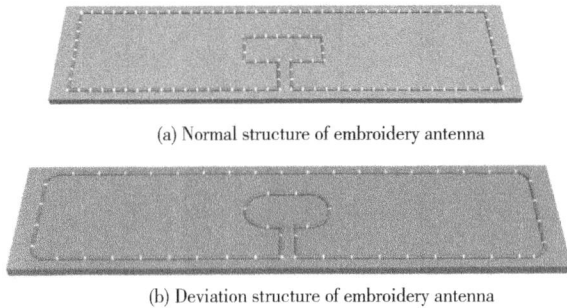

(a) Normal structure of embroidery antenna

(b) Deviation structure of embroidery antenna

Fig. 1　The structure of embroidered antenna

In summary, although the embroidery process has been widely used to fabricate RFID antennas and fabric-based flexible electrons, especially when the topology of the antenna is simplified. Little attention has been paid to the process of embedding an RFID antenna with a single conductive yarn[6] and the influence of corresponding process variations on the performance of the antenna. In view of this, this paper will focus on the stitch structure of the embroidery antennas, that is, the effect of the structure of the embroidery conductive yarn and stitch length on the topological size and reading performance of the tag antenna.

2　Experiments

Based on the above literature analysis, this experiment was based on the T-match antenna structure.

2.1　Materials

Thetags were fabricated on polyester non-woven fabric, with a weight of $79g/m^2$ and a thickness of 0.73mm. The relative dielectric constant measured at 900 MHz was 1.13±0.01, and the dielectric loss was 0.00118±0.02. The bottom line was made of conductive yarn, and the top line was made of polyester sewing thread(40S/2). The tag chip we used was higgs−4 series RFID IC with the wake-up power of −18 dBm. We attached the IC to the antenna with conductive silver epoxy.

2.2　Structure of Conductive Yarn

Copper wires of the same diameter were selected, and the antennas were made of conductive yarns of straight line (copper wire) and spiral structure (copper wire wrapped yarn). The test results show that the linear structure of the tag had a gain of 1.08 dBi and a read range of 12.78m. The tag of the spiral structure was 1.21 dBi and the reading range is 13.32m. When the chip was packaged with the antenna, a part of the distributed capacitor was usually introduced. And this spiral structure introduced an inductive reactance, thereby canceling the capacitive reactance in the equivalent circuit[7], the maximum energy transfer was achieved. So, the subsequent experiment selected the copper wire wrapped yarn to embroider the antenna.

2.3　Design of Stitch Length

The stitch length (Ls) was the distance between two stitch tips along the direction of the stitch movement. According to the actual embroidery situation, a set of antennas were embroidered with different stitch lengths. Their stitch length and regularity were listed in Tab. 1.

Tab. 1　Parameter design of embroidered tag antenna with different stitch lengths

Sample	Stitch length(mm)	Deviation angle
1#	0.9	—
2#	1.1	—
3#	1.3	—
4#	1.5	—
5#	1.7	—
6#	1.9	5°
7#	2.1	8°
8#	3	15°
9#	4	20°
10#	5	30°

3　Results and Discussions

3.1　Resistance of Embroidered Antenna Conductor

As shown in Fig. 2, the stitch length has a significant influence on the resistance of the UHF RFID embroidered antenna. And the resistance of the tag antenna gradually decreases in the range of the stitch length from 0.9mm to 1.7mm. When the stitch length exceeds

2mm, the line resistance of the antenna conductor approaches a smoothness. In order to deeply analyze the reason why the resistance exhibits this trend with the stitch length, the topological structure of the antenna at different stitch lengths is characterized and compared below.

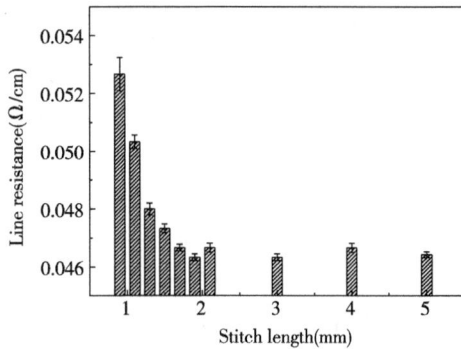

Fig. 2　Resistance values of embroidered tag antennas with different stitch lengths

As can be seen from Fig. 3, when the stitch length is between 0. 9 and 1. 5mm, the conductive yarn exhibits different degrees of buckling. And as the stitch length increases, the number of spirals becomes smaller in per unit length. So, the wire resistance of the antenna conductor is reduced. When the stitch length is 1. 7 – 5mm, the conductive yarn approaches straight, and there is no significant difference in resistance.

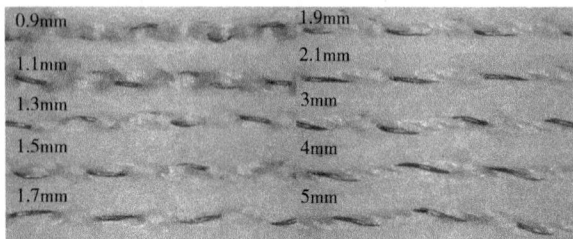

Fig. 3　Conductive yarn morphology at different stitch lengths

3. 2　Impedance of UHF RFID Embroidered Antenna

In Fig. 4, the impedance of the chip and the antenna varies with frequency, and the intersection of the two is the impedance matching frequency. When the stitch length is 1. 7mm, the matching frequency between the embroidered antenna and the chip impedance is around 920MHz. Moreover, in the frequency of 860~960MHz, when the stitch length is 5mm, there is almost no intersection between the embroidered antenna and the chip, that is, the impedance matching between the antenna

and the chip is poor, so the energy loss is increased.

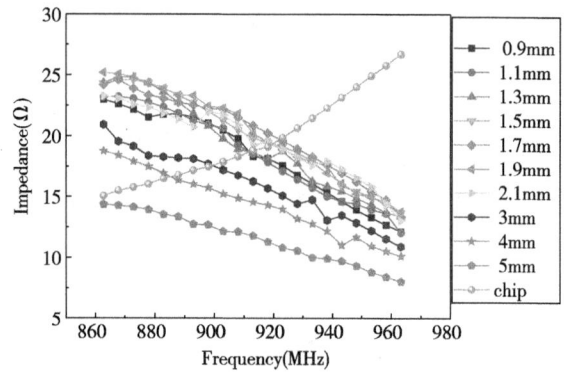

Fig. 4　Comparison of port impedance between UHF RFID tag antenna and chip with different stitch lengths

In order to further understand the variation of the real and imaginary parts of the impedance at different stitch lengths, we select two kinds of stitch length samples with better and poor impedance matching of the above antenna ports. And the real and imaginary parts of the impedance are analyzed in depth. Here, the two stitch lengths are 1. 7mm and 5mm, respectively. And their impedance components are shown in Fig. 5.

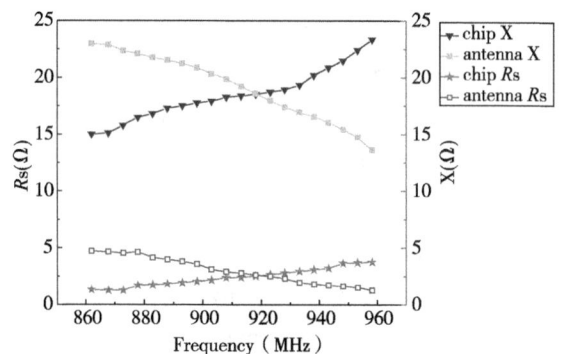

（a）Stitch length of 1.7mm

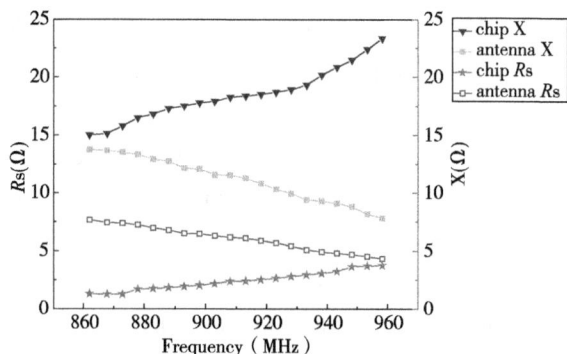

（b）Stitch length of 5mm

Fig. 5　Antenna and chip resistance and reactance

It can be seen from Fig. 5(a), The intersection of the antenna and the chip and the reactance are both around 920MHz, which is consistent with the results shown in Fig. 4. However, Fig. 5(b) shows that there is almost no intersection in resistance and reactance between the antenna and the chip in the 860-960MHz, which shows the antenna impedance and the chip impedance are poorly matched. And the energy loss is high.

The above results indicate that, due to the morphological buckling of conductive yarn and the embroidery process deviation of tag antenna structure when the stitch length is 0.9-1.5mm, the overall structure of the antenna is damaged to some extent, resulting in the changes of antenna resistance and impedance.

3.3　Gain of UHF RFID Embroidered Antenna

In Fig. 6, in the range of the stitch length of 0.9-5mm, the gain first increases and then decreases. When the stitch length is 1.7mm, the impedance matching between the antenna and the chip is good. The energy loss is the smallest and the gain reaches a maximum value of 0.81dBi.

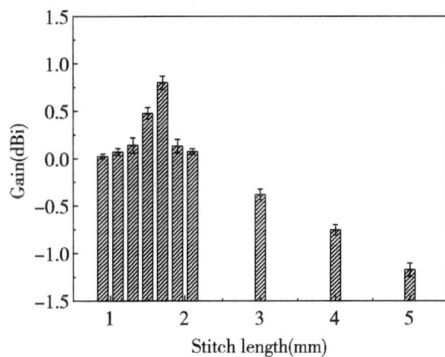

Fig. 6　Maximum gain of UHF RFID embroidered tag at 915MHz

3.4　Reading Performance of UHF RFID Embroidered Tag

The read range of the fabric-based UHF RFID tag is a basic indicator for determining the success of the antenna and package. The specific test results are shown in Fig. 8.

As can be seen from Fig. 7, the antenna tags embroidered with 9 stitch lengths have better reading effects. However, in the range of the stitch length of 0.9-5mm, the read range first increases and then decreases

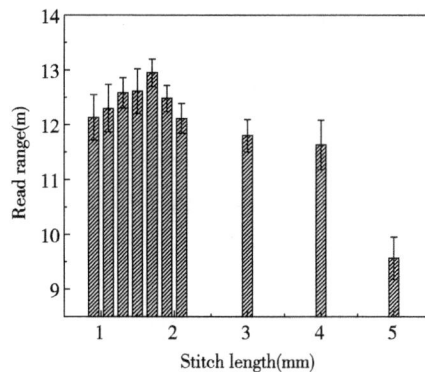

Fig. 7　Read range of the corresponding tags for the embroidered antenna of different stitch lengths

and the read range is the farthest when the stitch length is 1.7mm. The impedance matching between the antenna and the chip is good at this time and the energy loss is small. The gain of the antenna is large, so the reading distance is the largest, reaching 12.95m, which exceeds 50% of the earlier research results[2], that is, read range of 8m.

4　Conclusions

In this work, we studied the effect of the stitch structure on the read performance of fabric-based UHF RFID embroidered tags. The effect of stitch length on antenna performance and tag read range presented significant parabolic nonlinear changes. And the impedance matching and reading performance of the tag was optimal when the stitch length is 1.7mm and the maximum read range was 12.95m, which exceeds 50% of the earlier research results. Compared with copper wire as the embroidered thread, the copper wire wrapped yarn had better performance of the tag. This is because the wrapped yarn spiral structure was beneficial for achieving impedance matching between the antenna and the chip for maximum energy transfer.

References

[1]MARINDRA A, PONGPAIBOOL P, WALLADA W, et al. An optimized ink-reducing hollowed-out arm meander dipole antenna structure for printed RFID tags [J]. International Journal of Microwave and Wireless Technologies, 2017, 9 (2): 469-479.

[2]RECHET N, GINESTET G, TORRES J, et al. Cost-and

time-effective sewing patterns for embroidered passive UHF RFID tags[C]. International Workshop on Antenna Technology: Small Antennas, Innovative Structures, and Applications, IEEE, 2017.

[3] MORADI E, TONI B, UKKONEN L, et al. Characterization of embroidered dipole-type RFID tag antennas[C]. International Conference on RFID-technologies & Applications, IEEE, 2013.

[4] MORADIE, BJOMINEN T, UKKONEN L, et al. Effects of sewing pattern on the performance of embroidered dipole-type RFID tag antennas[J]. IEEE Antennas and Wireless Propagation Letters, 2012, 11: 1482-1485.

[5] WANG R. Effect of process parameters on DC resistance of fabric-based embroidery transmission line[J]. Industrial Textiles, 2016, 34(5): 6-11.

[6] IVSIC B, GALOIC A, BONEFACIC D. Durability of conductive yarn used for manufacturing textile antennas and microstrip lines[C]. International Symposium on Antennas and Propagation & USNC/URSI National Radio Science Meeting, IEEE, 2016.

[7] ZHANG W, GAN Q. Design, simulation and practice of UHF RFID tag antenna [M]. Beijing: Electronic Industry Press, 2012:36-45.

Construction of Literature Database on Textile and Apparel for Countries Along the Belt and Road

DONG Zheng-e[1]*, CHEN Hui-lan[2], FENG Qing[3]

[1] *Department of Sci-tech Novelty Retrieval and Reference Consultation, Library, Donghua University, Shanghai, 201620, China*

[2] *Library, Donghua University, Shanghai, 201620, China*

[3] *Department of Special Resources and Digital Engineering, Library, Donghua University, Shanghai, 201620, China*

* *Corresponding author's email*: dzee071107@ dhu. edu. cn

Abstract: As an important cultural carrier, textile & apparel contains a country's cultural traditions and values. From the ancient Silk Road to the Belt and Road, people in China and other countries along the Belt and Road have more cultural connections and emotional resonances in the field of textile and apparel, and these contents are lacking in today's communication process, and there is need to supplement. In addition, countries along the Belt and Road can make full use of the historical opportunity of the Belt and Road initiative, adhere to the combination of "going out" and "bringing in", deepen exchanges and cooperation in the field of textile and apparel culture, and revitalize countries along the Belt and Road. It is primary to collect, collate, research and share the literature on textile and apparel along the Belt and Road. A literature database on textile and apparel for countries along the Belt and Road was constructed from four levels. Firstly, the overall literature of eight regions in China, East Asia, ASEAN, West Asia, South Asia, Central Asia, CIS and Central and Eastern Europe was launched in the form of a map. All the resources of all countries in the region below will display by clicking on each region icon. Secondly, a list of all resources by default will be provided in home page, specifically related to the cover of the document, title, author, publisher and publication date. Thirdly, classified navigation will be provided for all resources, in which the geography, the document type, subject, publication year and Language will be supplied. Finally, in terms of the document details page, the books, journals, newspapers are displayed in the same way as the existing books. It will be valuable to inject fresh blood into the research and inheritance of cultural heritage of countries along the Belt and Road, also to break the border between countries.

Keywords: Literature; Database; Textile and Apparel; Belt and Road

1 Introduction

In 138 BC and 119 BC, more than 2,000 years ago, Zhang Qian of the Han Dynasty of China came to Central Asia twice, visited many countries in the Western Region, and opened the door to China's access to the world, which is the famous Silk Road[1]. In September 2013, the Silk Road Economic Belt and the 21st Century Maritime Silk Road (the Belt and Road), gave the Silk Road providing a golden opportunity for all walks of life to expand to the outside world with a new era of connotation. The Belt and Road is an initiative and concept of cooperative development. It is intended to rely on the joint symbiosis between China and other countries to create a community of interests, a community of interests and a community of responsibility for political mutual trust, economic integration, and cultural inclusion. The Belt and Road initiative has provided good conditions for cultural exchanges between China and the 65 countries along the Belt and Road. As a cultural carrier, textile & apparel contains a country's cultural traditions and values. In addition to making full use of the historical opportunity of the Belt and Road Initiative, China will vigorously promote the going out of Chinese textile and apparel culture and promote the characteristics of Chinese textile and apparel. In addition to the dissemination of culture in countries and regions along the Belt and Road, it is also necessary to bring in the textile and apparel cultures of countries along the route, and to revitalize the textile and apparel culture between the countries along the Belt and Road to make them related to each other. Complementing each other, and ultimately promoting more effective inheritance, exchange and cooperation between the international areas in the history, culture, education and communication of textiles and apparel.

After more than five years of development, the Belt and Road has achieved initial success. All walks of life have responded to the Belt and Road Initiative and carried out a lot of research. At the same time, they have also explored many development models of the Belt and Road worth learning from. In the textile and apparel industry, Sani embroidery will take this historical opportunity to more effectively protect and inherit China's national culture[2]. Initiating the training of talents in the higher vocational textile trade practice course was explored from four aspects such as cooperation with universities and colleges along the Belt and Road, talent orientation and enterprise talent demand, school-enterprise cooperation and the overall professional quality and ability of the faculty[3]. Italy, the first G7 economy to sign the Belt and Road memorandum of understanding, ushered in a new textile opportunity on the Belt and Road, which increased its exports to countries outside the EU by 2.9% due to its export growth to Chin[4]. The quantitative assessment of global multi-regional models provided shows that the Northern Line Strategy has the greatest potential for textile exports[5]. SGS helps textile companies understand the Belt and Road initiative[6]. It finds that Guangzhou has advantage in the clothing and textile industry under the B&R Initiative[7]. It's worth paying more attention to how to "go out" but lacking relevant research on "please come in". In the textile and apparel industry, although the relevant research on "going out" has begun to emerge, it still needs to form a cluster development; and there is a lack of related research on textile and apparel as a medium for the history, culture, education and dissemi nation of countries along the Belt and

Road. Therefore, textile and apparel needs to learn from the integrated symbiosis model of the National Museum along the Silk Road and the Silk Road International Library Alliance, and play a due role in promoting the exchange of mutual understanding of the world civilization, insisting on "please come in" Combining with "going out", jointly carrying out multi-channel and diverse cultural exchange activities, strengthening the research on textile and apparel history, culture, education and communication along the countries, it is expected to enhance exchanges and cooperation, realize cultural integration and symbiosis, and ultimately promote building a colorful spiritual home for the people of all countries in the world.

On the other hand, the countries along the Belt and Road belong to different cultural systems and have their own language, writing and customs. The Belt and Road construction period is long, covering a wide area and affecting many people. The national systems and territories of the countries along the line vary greatly. The ethnic and religious cultures are diverse. To achieve mutual trust, cross-cultural barriers, cross-cultural misunderstandings, cross-cultural conflict and cross-cultural shock need to be overcome[8]. Therefore, it is necessary to enhance the understanding between China and the countries along the Belt and Road. Deepening the exchange of humanities and knowledge is an important way to eliminate barriers and misunderstandings and promote mutual understanding. With the advancement of the Belt and Road construction, the increase in the exchange and dissemination of Chinese culture, coupled with the understanding of Chinese culture along the traditional Silk Road countries, the influence of Chinese culture on the countries along the Belt and Road gradually deepening, the influence of Chinese culture is gradually expanding. But overall, the comprehensive strength of Chinese cultural external communication is still relatively weak. Textile and clothing is an important cultural carrier and medium. From ancient times to the Qing Dynasty, the textile costumes and events worthy of writing on the Silk Road were numerous: the Han Dynasty's Zhang Qian twice went to Central Asia to visit many countries in the Western Regions with high-quality silk[9]; In an Eastern Han Dynasty tomb on the outskirts of Loulan, silk fragments and Greek colored fabric fragments were un-earthed. The introduction of cotton as a tribute from a-broad to China and the introduction of cotton varieties provide evidence for understanding the cultural exchange of textiles and costumes on the Silk Road of the Han Dynasty[10]. It can be seen that from the ancient Silk Road to the present the Belt and Road, people in China and other countries along the line have more cultural connections and emotional resonances in the textile and apparel industry, and these contents are lacking in the process of communication today. The first condition of this is the collection and sorting of the literature on textiles and apparel of the countries along the Belt and Road.

Therefore, this paper intends to build a literature database of textile and apparel in countries along the Belt and Road to provide a unified platform for collection, organization, research, sharing, communicating and mutual authentication.

2 Content and Structure of the Literature Database

The literature database on textile and apparel for coun-tries along the Belt and Road as was constructed from four levels, which Schematic frame was shown in Fig. 1. Firstly, the overallliterature of eight regions in China, East Asia, ASEAN, West Asia, South Asia, Central Asia, CIS and Central and Eastern Europe was launched in the form of a map. All the resources of all countries in the region below will display by clicking on each region icon. Secondly, a list of all resources by default will be provided in home page, specifically related to the cover of the document, title, author, publisher and publication date. Thirdly, classified navigation will be provided for all resources, in which the geography (the first level is 8 regions, the next level is targeted to specific countries), the document type (books, journals, newspapers, photos), subject, publication year, and Language will be supplied. Finally, in terms of the document details page, the books, journals, newspapers are displayed in the same way as the existing books. The photo details page needs to display thumbnails, title, language, year of shooting, introduction and link to view the original image.

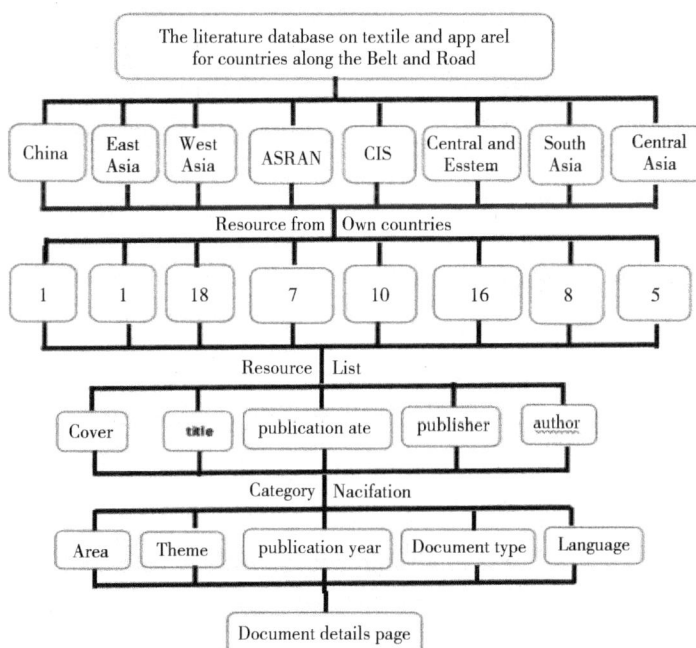

Fig. 1　Schematic frame of the literature database on textile and apparel for countries along the Belt and Road

3 Conclusions and Perspectives

The literature database on textile and apparel for coun-tries along the Beltand Road as a platform represents a comprehensive and expandable literature. To better serve the research community of the Belt and Road Initiative, we will continue to collect related data and update this database regularly in the future. Our next plan is to obtain more public data on textile and apparel for different countries along the Belt and Road. The database, including the complete list of references used for compilation, and the user Guide are freely available at its homepage and at its web page. It will hopefully be used to stimulate researchers to investigate multiculturalism and to understand the tradition and essence of textile and apparel culture in countries along the Belt and Road.

It is expected that the database will contribute to promote more effective inheritance, exchange and cooperation between international in history, culture, education and communication of textile and apparel. It is believed that the construction of the database will help to understand the tradition and essence of textile and apparel culture in the countries along the Belt and Road. While protecting and inheriting the rich and colorful textile and apparel cultures of various countries, we will give full play to the historical and cultural advantages of textile and apparel in various countries. The new historical period will be carried forward, prospering the modern textile and clothing culture, leading the people with the culture first, insisting on the combination of going out and introducing, deepening the exchanges and cooperation in the textile and garment field. It not only injects fresh blood into the research and inheritance of cultural heritage of countries along the Belt and Road, but also is the important link of world civilization, breaking the border among countries.

Acknowledgements

This research was financially supported by Donghua University 2019 Humanities and Social Sciences Major Project—Special project of the Belt and Road Fund (Grant No. 237 – 10 – 0108019) and Humanities and Social Sciences Base Cultivation Project (Grant No. 2232019H—02).

References

[1]CHEN Y. Historical review of the silk road and new development of the belt and road[J]. Journal of Changchun University, 2019, 29(5): 92-95.

[2]XIAO P, SU L L, SU F. Research on the inheritance and development of sani embroidery under the belt and Road initiative[J]. Sinogram Culture, 2019(10): 153-155.

[3]ZHAO S J. Analysis on talent cultivation of higher vocational textile trade practice course under the belt and Road initiative[J]. Progress in Textile Science & Technology, 2019 (5): 57-59.

[4]CUI S J. Embark on the belt and Road Italian textile industry [J]. Textile Science Research, 2019(5): 26-27.

[5]CUI L B, SONG M L, Economic evaluation of the belt and Road initiaive from an unimpeded rade ersective[J]. Inernational Journal of Logisics-Research and Applications. 2019, 22 (1), 25-46.

[6]ZHANG C. SGS helps textile businesses understand China's belt and road initiative[J]. Knitting International, 2019(1): 8-9.

[7]LUO X, HAN Y A, ZHONG S. Analysis on the trade structural competitiveness in manufacturing industry between guangzhou and the belt and Road participating countries based on lafay index[C]. 2018.

[8]CHEN J, OU X. Research on intercultural communication of foreign police training under the perspective of belt and road [J]. Journal of Liaoning Administrators College of Police and Justice, 2019 (2): 36-40.

[9]WANG Y P. Comment on professor yun yuntao's study of foreign civilization in the han dynasty[J]. International Sinology, 2018(3): 192-194.

[10]DONNER E J, ZHAO W. Early history of cotton[J]. World Agriculture, 1980(4): 41-45.

Finite Element Analysis of Compressibility of Warp-Knitted Spacer Fabrics: Effect of Geometric Variations of Spacer Monofilaments

ZHANG Yuan[1], LIU Yanping[1]*

[1] *Key Laboratory of Textile Science &Technology, Ministry of Education, College of Textiles Donghua University, Shanghai, 201620, China*

* *Corresponding author's email:* liuyp@ dhu. edu. cn

Abstract: Warp-knitted spacer fabrics have a three-dimensional construction consisting of two separate outer layers connected by spacer monofilaments. Nowadays, Warp-knitted spacer fabrics are widely used in cushion materials, human body protection and automotive interior for their excellent compression performance, air and moisture permeability. The compression deformation behavior of spacer fabric is very complicated due to the specific structure and non-linear mechanical behavior of monofilaments. In recent years, lots of finite element models have been established to understand compression mechanism of spacer fabrics. However, the real geometry of spacer monofilaments and the geometric variations of spacer monofilaments are always neglected. In this research, finite element (FE) analysis was conducted to study the compression property of warp-knitted spacer fabrics by considering geometric variations of spacer monofilaments. Eight unit cells with 64 spacer monofilaments in total were reproduced based on precise geometric information obtained from Micro-X-ray computed tomography (μCT) scanning. According to the geometric analysis, it was found that there are discrepancies in spatial shapes of spacer monofilaments in different unit cells, maybe owing to different wear condition of each needle and inhomogeneous mechanical property along the length direction of spacer monofilaments. Eight FE models were created from eight unit cells which fully considered the contact between spacer monofilaments and outer layers, between outer layers and compression platens, among spacer monofilaments. The simulation results showed that initial spatial shape of spacer monofilament has an obvious effect on the compression performance of the spacer fabric, the slighter the buckling and torsion of spacer monofilament, the greater the compression resistance of spacer fabric under the same compression displacement. This study is useful to improve the compression property of spacer fabrics in knitting and heat-setting process by optimizing geometry and property parameters.

Keywords: Warp-knitted spacer fabrics; Compression behavior; Finite element analysis

1 Introduction

Warp-knitted spacer fabric consists of two separate outer layers connected with spacer monofilaments as innerlayer[1]. The unique sandwich-like structure gives the fabric excellent cushion property, air permeability, moisture conductivity and thermoregulation[2-3]. The spacer monofilament can be vertical or inclined and the fabric thickness can be changed from 3mm to 65mm[4]. Therefore, the properties of spacer fabric can be designed due to the strong structural designability. In recent years, the spacer fabrics as cushion materials are widely used for car seats, bed mattresses, insoles, bra cups, human body protectors and medical materials for healing wounds

or preventing chronic wounds[5-9]. In addition, it can be used as reinforcement of composite materials, such as textile reinforced concrete[10].

In recent years, extensive experimental studies and finite element analysis have been conducted to investigate the compression behavior of spacer fabrics. Miao and Ge[11] studied the compression property of warp-knitted spacer fabrics found three typical deformation stages of compression stress-strain curve including linear elasticity stage, collapse plateau stage and densification stage. Liu[12] et al. also analyzed the effect of structure parameters on the compression performance spacer fabrics. Brisa[13] et al. studied the compressibility of a single vertical spacer monofilament of spacer fabric with finite element method. Liu[14] et al. reported a FE study on the compression behavior of a typical spacer fabric structure based on the precise geometry of a unit cell reconstructed from μCT scanning by fully considering the yarn interactions among all the fabric components and material's nonlinearity. However, only one unit cell of spacer fabric was selected for compression simulation which ignored geometrical variations of spacer monofilaments among different unit cells .

In order to go deep into the study on compression deformation behavior of spacer fabrics, the purpose of this paper was to analyze the effect of geometrical variations of spacer monofilaments on compression behavior by FE simulation which fully considered the yarn interactions and nonlinear material properties of spacer monofilaments. This study can be conductive to a better standing of how geometrical variations of spacer monofilaments influence the compression behavior of spacer fabric.

2 Geometrical Analysis of Spacer Fabrics

A typical warp-knitted spacer fabric knitted on a GE296 double-needle bar Raschel machine with six yarn guide bars was used for thisstudy[15]. The fabric has a thickness of 7. 52mm and a density of 134. 08kg/m³. Its two outer layers were separately knitted with four sets of 300D/96F polyester multifilaments and the spacer layer connecting two outer layers was knitted with another two sets of 0. 2mm diameter polyester monofilaments.

Fig. 1 shows structural features of the fabric examined by using a microscope (HITACHI TM3000) and aμCT system (Scanco/VivaCT 40, SCANCO Medical AG, Switzerland). The two separate outer layers are joined together with the spacer monofilaments[Fig. 1 (a) and (b)], and the monofilament overlaps are covered and wrapped by the fluffy multifilament overlaps and underlaps[Fig. 2 (c) and (d)]. It can be confirmed that the spacer fabric has a highly heterogeneous and discontinuous structure.

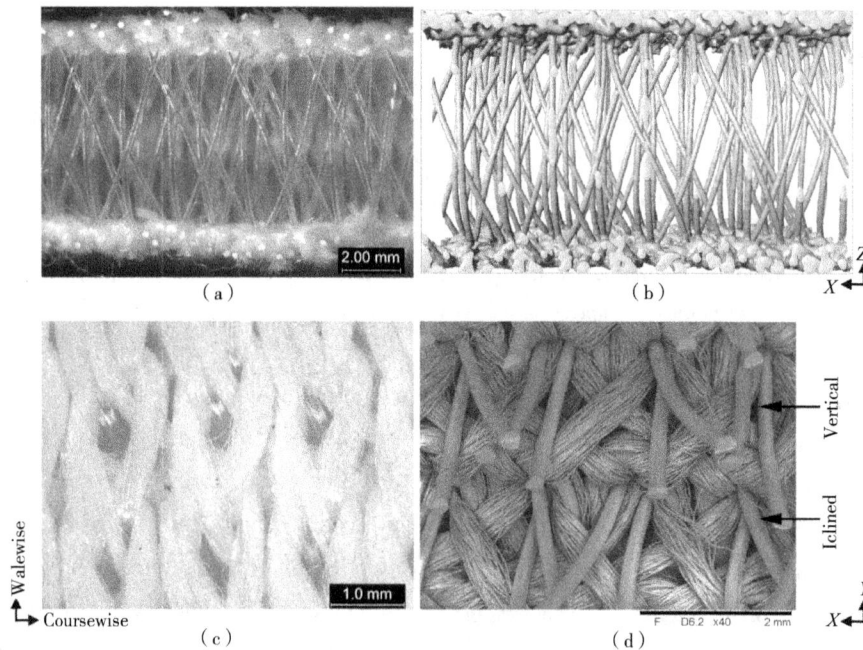

Fig. 1 Photographs of the spacer fabric: (a) Microscopic side view; (b) μCT reconstruction side view; (c) External side of outer layer; (d) Internal side of outer layer

The initial shape of spacer monofilaments in a spacer fabric are not identical maybe owing to inhomogeneous mechanical property along the lengthwise of the spacer monofilament, inconsistent yarn tensions during knitting and different wear condition of each needle. Because of these factors cannot be eliminated, geometric variations of spacer monofilaments are inevitable.

In order to obtain the exact coordinates of spacer monofilaments, the fabric was scanned through the thickness direction by using the μCT system. Fig. 2 presents one of binarized slices in which white dots represent the cross-sections of spacer monofilaments and eight complete unit cells totally containing 64 spacer monofilaments were selected in this study.

The trajectories in X—Y plane of eight spacer monofilaments in eight unit cells are presented in Fig. 3. It is found that the shape of spacer monofilaments at the same locations in different unit cells are basically similar, but there are obvious geometric variations among spacer monofilaments in different unit cells. The enclosed area of trajectory is used for expressing the buckling of monofilaments, as shown in Tab. 1. It can be found that the lager internal area, the greater buckling scale of monofilament.

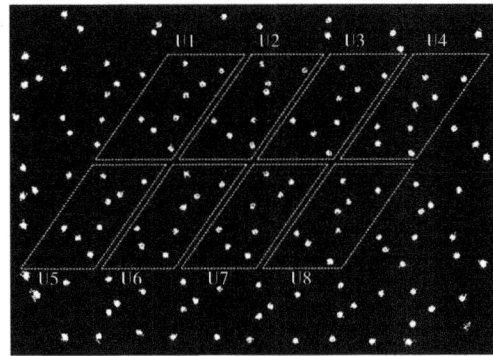

Fig. 2   A binarized slice from μCT scanning with 8 unit cells

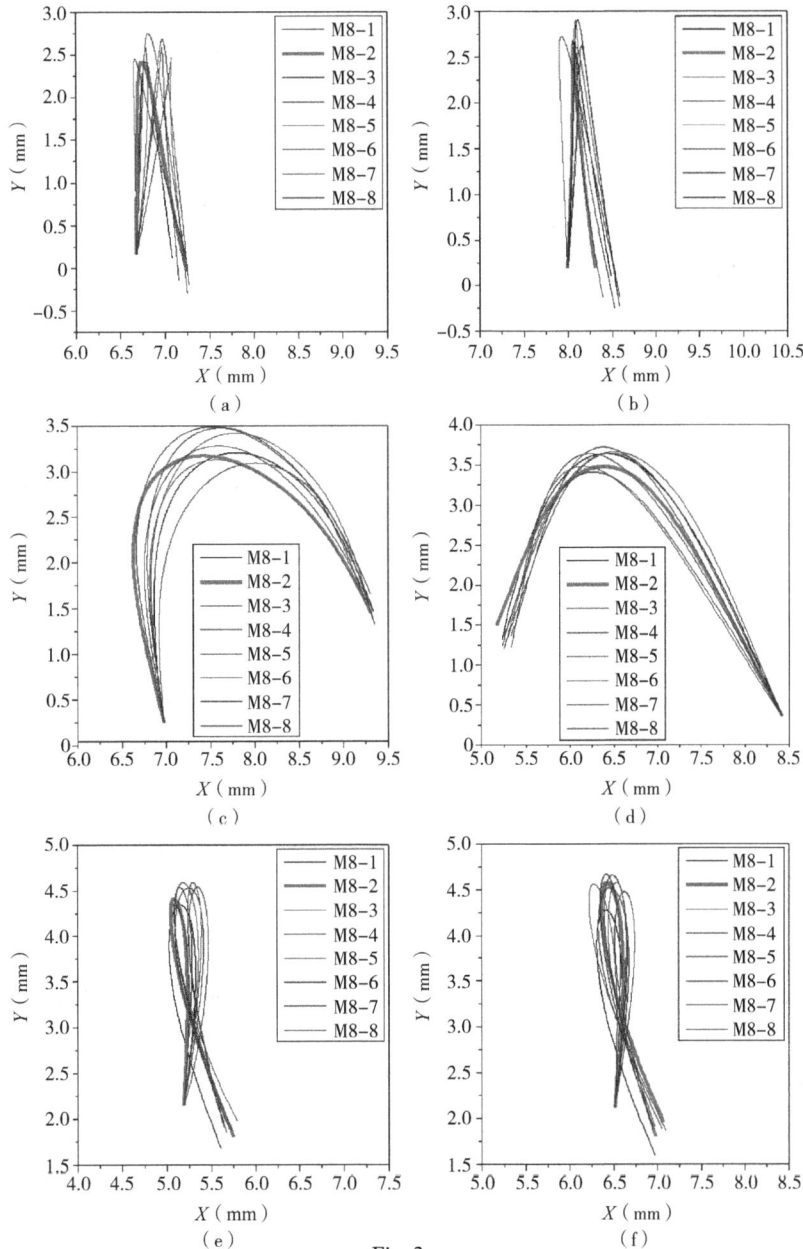

Fig. 3

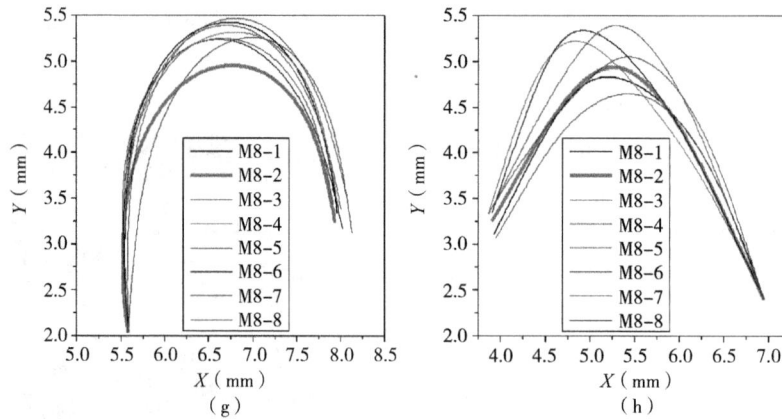

Fig. 3　Trajectories in X—Y plane of 8 spacer monofilaments in 8 unit cells: (a) S1; (b) S2; (c) S3; (d) S4; (e) S5; (f) S6; (g) S7; (h) S8

Tab. 1　The enclosed area of trajectoies in X—Y plane of eight spacer monofilaments in eight unit cells

Unit cell	Enclosed area (mm^2)								
	S1	S2	S3	S4	S5	S6	S7	S8	Sum
U1	0. 52	0. 61	4. 72	5. 69	0. 46	0. 43	5. 49	4. 09	21. 99
U2	0. 7	0. 32	4. 99	5. 05	0. 4	0. 48	4. 61	3. 9	20. 44
U3	0. 63	0. 66	4. 95	4. 91	0. 37	0. 58	5. 36	3. 79	21. 26
U4	0. 52	0. 76	4. 58	4. 99	0. 54	0. 5	5. 35	4. 28	21. 53
U5	0. 85	0. 36	5. 3	5. 64	0. 45	0. 42	5. 39	4. 29	22. 71
U6	0. 58	0. 49	5. 08	5. 52	0. 41	0. 45	5. 36	4. 47	22. 35
U7	0. 62	0. 87	4. 54	5. 31	0. 56	0. 48	5. 05	4. 54	21. 97
U8	0. 82	0. 85	5. 41	5. 21	0. 39	0. 45	5. 29	3. 88	22. 29

3　Finite Element Modeling

Finite element models were developed in Ansys 14. 5 to measure compression behavior of different fabric unit cells. In FE models, diameter and Poisson's ratio of monofilament, thickness and Young's modulus of outer layer were taken 0. 2mm, 0. 3mm, 0. 2mm and 12833MPa, respectively. The nonlinear material property of monofilament was considered. The internal multipoint constraint (MPC) approach was used to connect the eight beams to the two shells. It was also assumed that outer layers were made of shells and monofilaments were made of beam. It fully considered the contact between outer layers and monofilaments, outer layers and rigid platens and the contact among monofilaments in the unit cell. More details about the FE model refer to Liu'sresearch[14].

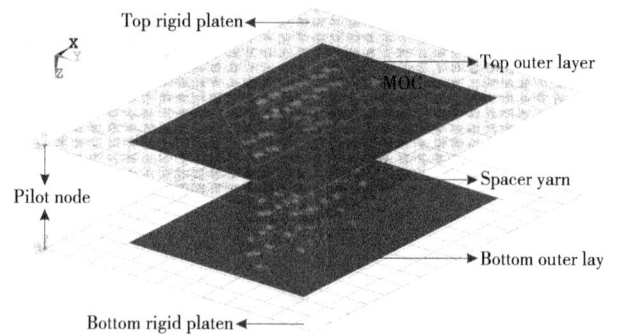

Fig. 4　FE model of the spacer fabric containing 8 unit cells

The load-displacement relationships of eight FE models are shown in Fig. 5. It is obvious from Fig. 5 that the geometrical variations among spacer monofilaments in different unit cells have a significant effect on the compression behavior of a unit cell. The spacer monofilaments in U1, U2, U3 and U4 present smaller buckling scale, and the corresponding FE models show higher compression force and longer plateau stage; however, the fabrics with larger buckling scale including U5, U6, U7 and U8 exhibit smaller compression force and shorter plateau stage. It indicates that the internal area can effectively reflect the buckling scale of monofilaments and it is consistent with the compression behavior of spacer fabric to a certain extent. The small buckling scale of monofilaments help to improve the compression resistance of fabric, including increasing the compression force and plateau stage length, so that the fabric can absorb more energy in the plateau stage and quickly reach a stable state after entering the densification stage.

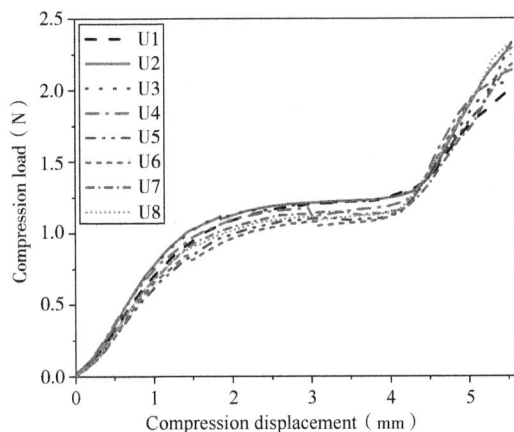

Fig. 5　Load-displacement relationships of eight FE models

4　Conclusions

The compression behavior of a warp-knitted spacer fabric was investigated with finite element method based on the precise geometry of fabric obtained from CT scanning. The simulation compression load-displacement relationship was agreement with the compression test result. The geometrical analysis of spacer fabrics found that the geometric variations of monofilaments in different unit cells have a significant effect on the compression behavior of a unit cell. This research help to go deep into the study on deformation behavior of spacer fabric and guide the study on other types of spacer fabric.

References

[1] SHEIKHZADEH M, GHANE M, ESLAMIAN Z, et al. A modeling study on the lateral compressive behavior of spacer fabrics[J]. The Journal of the Textile Institute, 2010, 101 (9):795-800.

[2] LIU Y P, HU H. Compression property and air permeability of weft-knitted spacer fabrics[J]. The Journal of the Textile Institute, 2011, 102(4):366-372.

[3] ARUMUGAM V, MISHRA R, MILITKY J. Investigation on the thermo-physiological and compression characteristics of weft-knitted spacer fabrics[J]. The Journal of the Textile Institute, 2017, 108(7):1095-1105.

[4] YE X H, HU H, FENG X W. Development of the warp knitted spacer fabrics for cushion applications[J]. Journal of Industrial Textiles, 2008, 37(3):213-223.

[5] YE X H, FANGUEIRO R, HU H, et al. Application of warp-knitted spacer fabrics in car seats[J]. The Journal of the Textile Institute, 2007, 98(4):337-343.

[6] RAJAN T P, SOUZA L D, RAMAKRISHNAN G, et al. Comfort properties of functional warp-knitted polyester spacer fabrics for shoe insole applications[J]. Journal of Industrial Textiles, 2016, 45(6):1239-1251.

[7] YIP J, NG S P. Study of three-dimensional spacer fabrics: molding properties for intimate apparel application[J]. Journal of Materials Processing Technology, 2009, 209:58-62.

[8] LIU Y P, HU H, LONG H R, at al. Impact compressive behavior of warp-knitted spacer fabrics for protective applications[J]. Textile Research Journal, 2012, 82(8):773-788.

[9] WOLLINA U, HEIDE M, LITZ W M, et al. Functional textiles in prevention of chronic wounds, wound healing and tissue engineering[J]. Current Problems in Dermatology, 2003, 31:82-97.

[10] ARMAKAN D M, ROYE A. A study on the compression behavior of spacer fabrics designed for concrete applications[J]. Fibers and Polymers, 2009, 10(1):116-123.

[11] MIAO X H, GE M Q. The compression behavior of warp knitted spacer fabric[J]. Fibres & Textiles in Eastern Europe, 2008, 16(1):90-92.

[12] LIU Y P, HU H, ZHAO L, et al. Compression behavior of warp-knitted spacer fabrics for cushioning applications[J]. Textile Research Journal, 2012, 82(1):11-20.

[13] BRISA V J D, HELBIG F, KROLL L. Numerical characterisation of the mechanical behaviour of a vertical spacer yarn in thick warp knitted spacer fabrics[J]. Journal of Industrial Textiles, 2015, 45(1):101-117.

[14] LIU Y P, HU H. finite element analysis of compression behavior of 3D spacer fabric structure[J]. International Journal of Mechanical Sciences, 2015, 94:244-259.

[15] LIU Y P, HU H. An experimental study of compression behavior of warp-knitted spacer fabric[J]. Journal of Engineered Fibers and Fabrics, 2014, 9(2):61-69.

Braided Rope Sensor Based on Carbon Nanotube Yarn

BAI Yunfei[1], XIA Qi[1], FENG Jianghan[1], LIU Han[1], ZHENG Jialin[1], XU Danyao[1], SALEEMI Sidra[1], QIU Yiping[1], XU Fujun[1]*

[1] *College of Textiles, Donghua University, Shanghai, 201620, China*

* *Corresponding authors email*: fjxu@ dhu. edu. cn

Abstract: Carbon nanotube (CNT) is exhibited outstanding electrical, mechanical, and structural properties. CNT yarn is widely used in textile structures as multifunctional yarn and is suitable as strain sensor. Here, use two methods for braiding CNT yarn into rope to make sensing ropes. The properties of CNT yarn and different ropes were tested, then according to the result the best method was chosen for the preparation of sensing rope. Results show the CNT yarn have enough strength to be used in braiding process, CNT embedded rope structure has more stable sensing property than CNT braided rope structure. The rope has approximately ≥7% resistance change ratio per 10% strain, so the embedded rope structure is the optimal structure for sensing rope. The sensing rope will help to improve the development of strain sensor in textile structure.

Keywords: Carbon nanotube; Strain sensor; Braided rope

1 Introduction

Carbon nanotube (CNT) is exhibited outstanding electrical, mechanical, and structural properties, and proved to be an extremely promising candidate for various applications in material science[1-5]. At present, there are three commonly used methods for the preparation of CNT yarns: direct spinning, solution spinning and carbon nanotube array spinning. Carbon nanotube array spinning is the better method to prepare CNT yarns currently[6].

Carbon nanotube yarns are widely used in textile structures as multifunctional yarns. They have piezo resistive effect and can be used as strain sensors[7-8], such as nondestructive testing, which are mainly used for crack propagation of composites. Carbon nanotube yarns can be combined with a variety of materials such as bandages, gloves, socks and so on to monitor and prevent. At the same time, carbon nanotube yarns have excellent mechanical and electrical properties, so they can be used in many fields, such as conductive materials, pressure sensing materials, microstrip antennas and so on.

However, CNT yarns have not been used in rope braiding. Ropes usually need to bear huge force, and their unexpected rupture would bring hidden dangers[9]. If CNT yarn strain sensors are used in ropes, the stress situation of the rope would be observed, and rupture caused by unbearable force would be prevented. But there are many limitations in current CNT yarn preparation methods. Single CNT yarns still have some weaknesses, such as minor diameter, poor abrasion resistance, easy to produce too much hairiness in preparation, so it is difficult to realize industrial application[10].

In order to obtain sensing rope, theCNT film was twisted into a yarn and embedded in the rope to achieve the preparation of the rope sensor. With this process, the CNT yarn could have enough diameter and mechanical properties to be braided in ropes. The optimal braiding structure for sensing rope was also discussed.

2 Experiments

2.1 Preparation of CNT Yarn

To make a large-diameter and high-strength CNT yarn,

twisting a CNT strip to form a composite yarn. The diameter, twist angle and CNT volume fraction of the yarn are controllable by adjusting the film strip's width and twisting process. In addition, the twisting process provides shear force, which improves the yarn's surface orientation.

Fig. 1 (a) shows the schematic diagram of twisting process. Here's the operation steps: Cut the CNT film into strips. Set the rotating speed of the twisting motor. Fix both ends of the strip to prevent untwisting. Then start the twisting machine for yarn preparation. Fig. 1 (b) shows the CNT yarn.

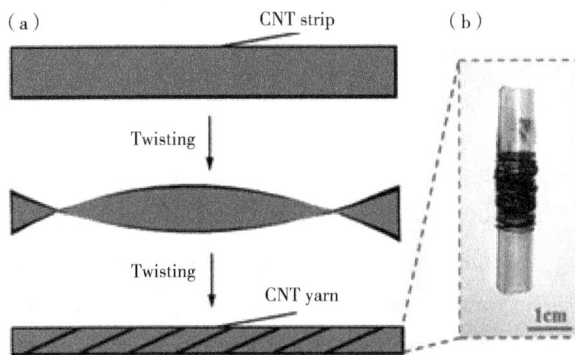

Fig. 1　Preparation of CNT yarn: (a) Twisting mechanism; (b) The CNT yarn

2.2　Braiding of the Sensing Rope

There are two main methods to achieve the braided rope with CNT yarn in it: CNT braided process and CNT embedded process.

For the CNT braided process, CNT yarn is interwound cyclically with other common yarns to be braided into the rope. Use a braiding machine[Fig. 2(a)] to prepare the rope. In the process, one of the braiding yarns is CNT yarn and the other are common yarns[Fig. 2(b)]. The position of braiding point should be controlled, or the rope would be inhomogeneous. Tension of the braiding yarns needs adjustment during the braiding process, in order to prevent the CNT yarn's elongation. To adjust the tension, pause the machine and rotate the carrier. Fig. 2 (c) shows the CNT braided rope.

For the CNT embedded process, 8 yarns are braided into a rope as the outer layerand the CNT yarn is embedded into the rope as a core yarn. In the process, put

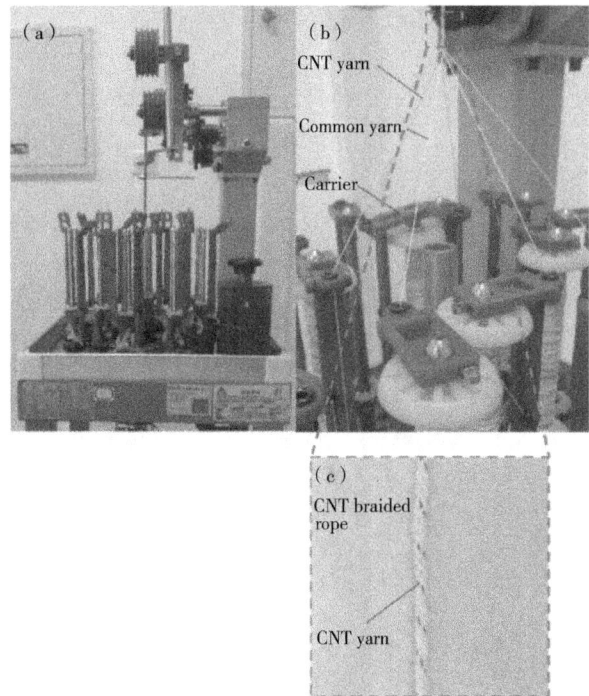

Fig. 2　Preparation of CNT braided rope: (a) The 16−carrier braiding machine; (b) Braiding machine with yarns, use 8 carriers of the machine in the preparation, one is CNT yarn; (c) CNT braided rope

common yarns on the carriers of the braiding machine and CNT yarn as the core[Fig. 3(a)]. A pre-tension on CNT yarn is necessary, in order to keep it straight. The CNT yarn would be embedded into the rope during the braiding process. To show the inner structure of the rope, use transparent nylon yarn as braiding yarn. Fig. 3 (b) shows the CNT embedded rope, it's clear that CNT core yarn is straight in the transparent rope.

3　Results and Discussions

3.1　Structure of the CNT Yarn

With the twist of 6 twists/cm, the CNT yarn is obtained by single untwisted CNT film, which the width is 5mm. As shown in Fig. 4 (a), the SEM image of the twisted CNT yarn, from which it can be seen obviously that twist and spiral of the CNT yarn. The diameter of the yarn is quite uniform at 220μm and the twist angle of the CNT yarn is about 15 °.

After rupture, stress relaxation occurred inside the yarn and fiber in the yarn slipped, thus the CNT yarn is untwisted and converted back into CNT film[Fig. 4(b)].

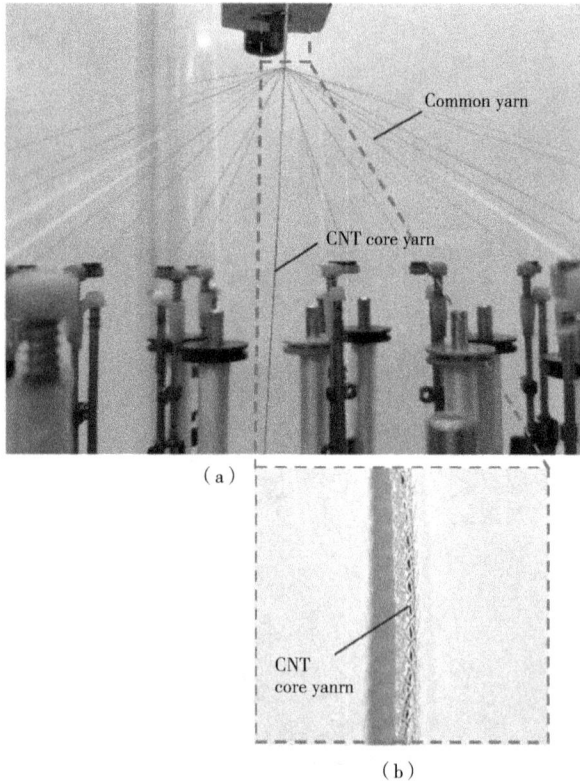

Fig. 3　Preparation of CNT embedded rope: (a) Braiding machine with yarns, which the CNT yarn as core yarn; (b) Transparent CNT embedded rope with core yarn inside

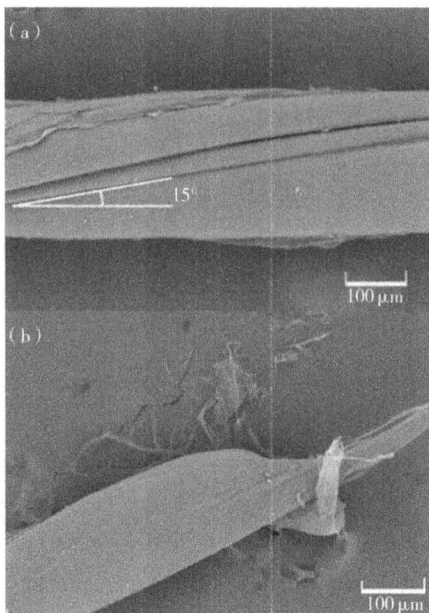

Fig. 4　SEM image of the CNT yarn: (a) Yarn with obvious twist and spiral figure; (b) Ruptured CNT yarn, which untwists into flat structure

3. 2　Mechanical Property of the CNT Yarn

As shown in Fig. 5, the maximum strain at fracture of the twisted CNT yarn is 20%, and the stress increases to 80MPa, these values of strength are higher than the values of traditional CNT yarns.

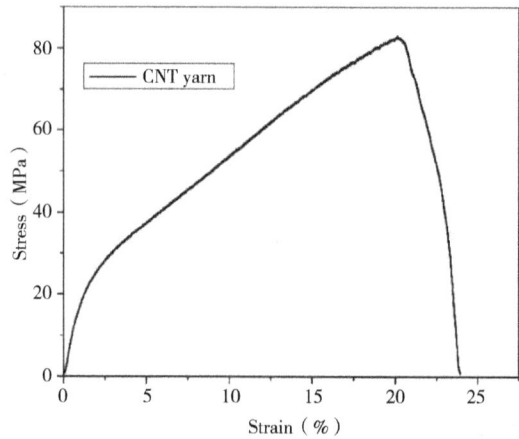

Fig. 5　Stress-strain curve of the CNT yarn

The good mechanical properties of the CNT yarns should be attributed to the action of twisting. Firstly, the twisting process fills the internal spaces inside yarn and increases volume content, so the compact structure achieved. Secondly, the shear force caused by twisting improves the orientation of carbon nanotube arrangement.

Because of the good mechanical properties, this CNT yarn can be used in rope braiding process.

3. 3　Sensing Performance of the CNT Yarn

The resistance change rate of the CNT yarn in the strain range of 35% is obtained by sensing performance test, in which the Y-axis is the resistance change rate and the X-axis is the strain (Fig. 6). The result shows that the curve is smooth, and there is a good correspondence between strain and resistance change ratio, which is about 12% resistance change per 10% strain.

3. 4　Optimization of the Braiding Processes

The sensing performance of the two different structure ropes was tested. Fig. 7(a) shows the sensing performance of the CNT braided rope: as the strain increases, the resistance change rate fluctuates significantly, and comparing to the CNT yarn, the linearity is affected to obvious extent. The main reason is that the carbon nanotube yarn generates buckling during the braiding process, and when the rope is stretched, the CNT yarn

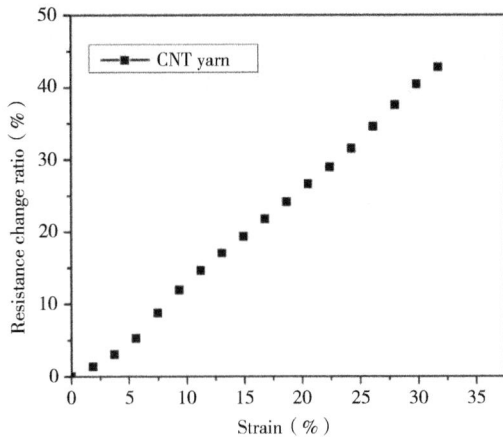

Fig. 6　Sensing performance of the CNT yarn

itself not only is elongated, but also suffers the pressing effect of the nearby yarns, so the fluctuation is significant. In addition, the sensing performance will be further affected due to the direct exposure of the sensing yarn to the complex application environment.

Fig. 7(b) shows the sensing performance of the CNT embedded rope: compared with the CNT braided rope, the rope with the CNT core yarn embedded in it has a moderate fluctuation in the resistance change ratio, the sensing performance is improved because the sensing yarn in the rope keeps straight and is not subjected to obvious buckling. The rope's resistance change ratio is approximately ≥7% per 10% strain, which is obviously lower than single CNT yarn, but it is enough to reflect the rope's elongation.

After comparison between the two braiding process, it's obvious that CNT embedded structure is the better structure for rope sensor based on CNT yarn.

4　Conclusions

In summary, prepared CNT yarn with good properties as strain sensor, then realized the combination of CNT yarn sensor and braiding rope. Compared different braiding process and chose the optimal one. Finally, prepared braided rope sensor based on CNT yarn Twisted CNTstrip into sensing yarn. Observed the yarn's structure, tested its mechanical properties and sensing performance. The yarn has 220μm diameter, 80MPa strength and good breaking elongation as 20%. As a result, this CNT yarn is suitable for rope braiding. The

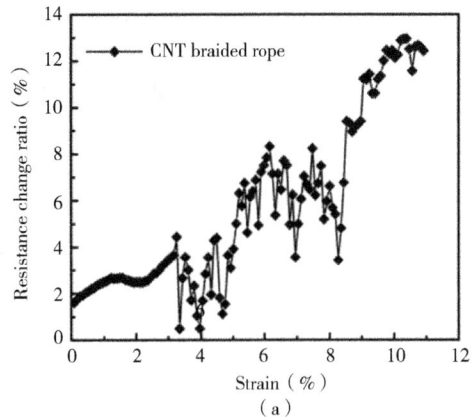

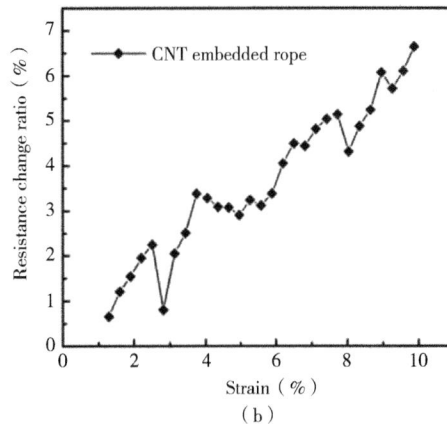

Fig. 7　Sensing performance of different structure ropes: (a) Sensing performance of CNT braided rope; (b) Sensing performance of CNT embedded rope

sensing performance test showed that there is a good correspondence between its strain and resistance change ratio, which is about 12% resistance change per 10% strain. So, it can be used as a strain sensor.

After that, used two different methods to braid rope sensor with CNT yarn and other common yarns, then compared their sensing performance in order to choose an optimal structure for rope sensor. Results showed that CNT embedded rope structure had more stable sensing property than CNT braided rope structure. The rope has approximately 7% resistance change ratio per 10% strain, which is enough to observe its elongation, so it's practical to use CNT yarn in braided rope. The sensing rope will help to improve the development of strain sensor in textile structure.

References

[1] YAKOBSON B I. In fullerenes—recent advances in the chemis-

try and physics of fullerenes and related materials[J]. Electrochemical Society,Pennington, NJ,1997,5 (97-42):549-560.

[2] YU1 M F,LOURIE O,et. al. Strength and breaking mechanism of multiwalled carbon nanotubes under tensile load[J].

[3] IIJIMA S, Helical microtubules of graphitic carbon[J]. Nature,1991(354):56-58.

[4] LIU W,XU F J,ZHU N H,et al. Mechanical and Electrical Properties of Carbon Nanotube/Polydimethylsiloxane Composites Yarn[J]. Journal of Engineered Fibers and Fabrics, 2016,4(11):36-42.

[5]]OLAND E,RUNE S,SHAUN F. Condition monitoring technologies for synthetic fiber ropes-a review[J]. International journal of prognostics and health management,2017, 8(2): 14-15.

[6] FRACKOWIAK E, BEGUIN F. Electrochemical storage of energy in carbon nanotubes and nanostructured carbons[J]. Carbon,2002,40(10):1775-1787.

[7] Skin-like pressure and strain sensors based on transparent elastic films of carbon nanotubes[J]. Natrual Nanotechnology 2011,6:788-792.

[8] BAUGHMAN R H,ZAKHIDOV A A,et. al. Carbon Nanotubes-the Route Toward Applications[J]. Science,2002,297 (5582):787-792.

[9] O'DONNELL H,HOFFMAN T J,BARKER F H. Rope tension monitoring assembly and method:U. S. Patent, 6123176 [P]. 2000-9-26.

[10] BAUGHMAN R H,CUI C,ZAKHIDOV A A, et al. Carbon nanotube actuators[J]. Science,1999,284(5418):1340-1344.

Carbon Nanotube/Polyaniline Coating on Fabric for Electromagnetic Interference Shielding

LAN Chuntao[1], QIU Yiping[1]*

[1] *Key Laboratory of Textile Science & Technology, Ministry of Education, College of Textiles, Donghua University, Shanghai, 201620, China*

Corresponding author's email: ypqiu@ dhu. edu. cn

Abstract: High performance EMI shielding materials are urgently needed to protect human beings as well as precision devices from EMI radiation. In this work, carbon nanotube (CNT) and polyaniline (PANI) were stepwise deposited on cotton fabric to fabricate textile-substrate EMI shielding material. After the introduction of PANI, gaps between CNTs were filled and the coated fabric possessed a continuous network of conductive materials in microscopic scale. The sheet resistance sharply declined from 2. 4kΩ/sq of pure CNT coated fabric to 48. 4Ω/sq of CNT/PANI coated fabric, demonstrating the important of the introduction of PANI in coating. As a result, the coated fabric exhibited a good EMI SE of 13. 41dB. This work presents a simple and convenient approach to obtain high performance EMI shielding fabrics.

Keywords: Electromagnetic interference; Textile-substrate material; Coating; Carbon nanotube; Polyaniline

1 Introduction

With the rapid development of electronic technologies, the ubiquity of electromagnetic wave has become an essential part on the earth[1-2]. At the same time, electromagnetic interference (EMI), which not only deteriorates the performance of precision devices nearby but also threatens the health of human beings, gradually become the fourth environmental pollution on the earth[3-4]. To protect human beings as well as precision devices from EMI, textile-substrate material is a super-excellent choice for EMI shielding[5-6]. Moreover, they have broad applications among civilian, commercial and military fields.

Two popular approaches are used to construct textile-substrate EMI shielding materials, including blending and coating. For blending method, conductive fibers, such asstainless steel fiber and carbon fiber, are blended with conventional filaments or short fibers[7]. Fabrics obtained by this method always possess low flexibility because of the stiff conductive fibers. As contrast, the shielding fabrics formed by coating approach exhibit better wearing comfort because the micron-sized thickness of coatings do not impede the flexibility of conductive fabrics[8-10]. Carbon nanotube (CNT) with extremely good electrical properties is an excellent building block for EMI shielding fabrics[11]. However, it is hard for CNTs to construct an efficiency conductive network which is essential for the consumption of electromagnetic energy only by themselves due to their one-dimensional structure. To enhance the connection of conductive network formed by CNTs, a promising approach is to introduce another type conductive material which is able to connect individual CNTs. Polyaniline (PANI) has become one of the most attractive polymers due to its high electric conductivity, lightness, environmental stability, and ease of synthesis[12].

In this work, CNTs and PANI were stepwise deposited on cotton fabric to fabricate textile-substrate EMI shielding material. After the introduction of PANI, the gaps between CNTs were filled and the sheet resistance of CNT/PANI coated fabric sharply declined to 48. 4Ω/ sq. As a result, the coated fabric exhibited a good EMI

SE of 13. 41dB. This work presents a simple and convenient approach to obtain high performance EMI shielding fabrics.

2 Experiments

2. 1 Materials

carbon nanotubes (CNTs) with10-20nm diameter were purchased from Tanfeng technology Company (soochow). Aniline was obtained from Aladdin (Shanghai). Sodium dodecyl benzene sulfonate (SDBS), ammonium persulphate, sodium chloride (NaCl) and sodium hydroxide (NaOH) were obtained from Sinopharm Chemical Reagent Co. Ltd.

2. 2 Preparation of CNT and PANI Suspension

0. 5mg CNT powder was dispersed in 10mL deionixed (DI) water with the assistance of SDBS. Then the mixture sonicated under 80℃ for 30min. 1. 0mg/mL and 1. 5mg/mL CNT suspension were also prepared.

The PANI suspension was obtained by the polymerization of aniline. Typically, ammonium persulphate was dropwise added in aniline. 0. 4mol/L, 0. 6mol/L and 0. 8mol/L PANI were prepared.

2. 3 Preparation of CNT/PANI Coated Fabric

The cotton fabric was first dipped in CNT suspension for 10min and then washed by DI water. After that, the wet fabric was putted in to aniline solution. Then, ammonium persulphate was dropwise added in aniline and fabric stored for 10min, followed by the washing of DI water. The processes was repeated to obtain coated fabric with different deposition cycle. The deposition cycle changed from 1 to 3 in this work. Finally, the fabric was dried under 80℃.

2. 4 Characterization

A Hitachi S-4800 field-emission scanning electron microscope (FE-SEM) was used to observe the surface morphologies of fabric. Photographs were captured by a camera (Canon PC1680). Standard two-probe method was employed to measure the surface resistance of the samples referring to AATCC 76—2005 by means of Fluke 15B multimeter. A Rohde & Schwarz ZVL6 type vector network analyzer (VNA) was used to measure EMI shielding effectiveness of coated cotton fabrics in the frequency range of 3. 9-6. 0 GHz (C-band).

3 Results and Discussions

3. 1 The Schematic of the Construction of CNT/PANI Coated Fabric

As illustrated in Fig. 1, the raw cotton fabric was first immersed in the suspension of CNT for 10 minutes to adsorb CNTs. Subsequently, the fabric contained CNTs was dipped into PANI suspension. The coating was further fixed by 60℃ thermal treatment. By repeating these immersion and drying steps, multilayered CNT/PANI coating was constructed. The obtained fabric was denoted as n-(CNT/PANI), where n is the deposition number.

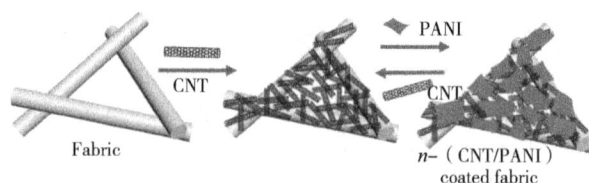

Fig. 1 Schematic of the construction of n-(CNT/PANI) coated fabric

3. 2 The Morphologies of n-(CNT/PANI) Coated Fabric

The obtained CNT/PANI coated fabrics werecharacterized by scanning electron microscopy (SEM), as shown in Fig. 2. In Fig. 2(a), the surface of raw fiber was clear with some small stripes. The original surface of fabric was covered and became rough after the deposition of CNT and PANI materials. With the increased concentration of CNT, the coating exhibited more compact structure, as shown in Fig. 2(b)-(d). When the concentration of CNT was 1. 5mg/mL, the areas between CNTs was still filled by PANI. The CNT and PANI in coating formed a continuous network. As shown in Fig. 2(e)-(f), PANI became the main part in coating with the increase of PANI concentration. The coating became thicker and more compact with the increase of deposition number[Fig. 2(g)-(h)].

3. 3 The Flexibility of n-(CNT/PANI) Coated Fabric

The obtained CNT/PANI coated fabric still exhibited a good flexibility despite the large deposition mass. As demonstrated in Fig. 3(a), the raw cellulosic fabric was

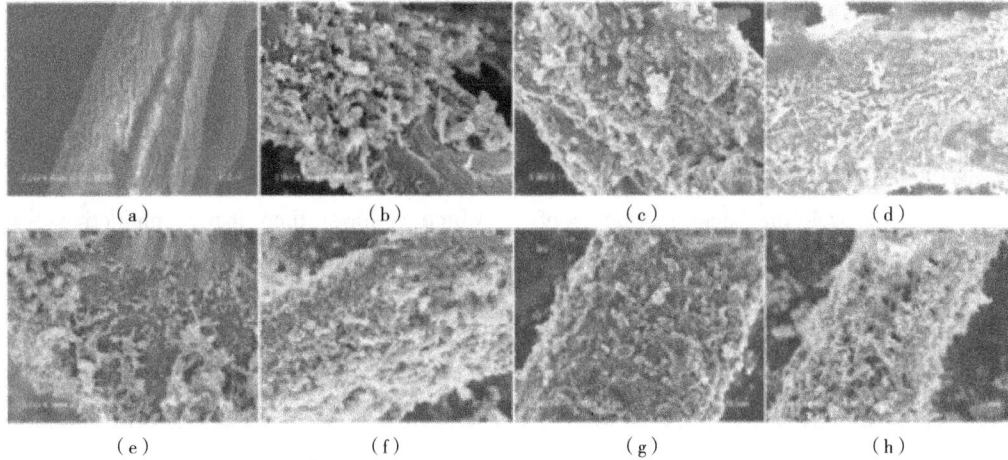

Fig. 2   SEM images of (a) raw fabric;(b)0.5mg/mL;(c)1.0mg/mL;(d)1.5mg/mL CNTs with 0.4mol/L PA-NI of 1-CNT/PANI coated fabric;(e)0.6mol/L;(f) 0.8mol/L with 1.5mg/mL of CNT/PANI of 1-CNT/PANI coated fabric;g) 2-CNT/PANI coated fabric;(h)3-CNT/PANI coated fabric

white and stood on one transparent tube. After depositing 3-layer CNT/PAH coating, the fabric became black because of the color of CNTs and showed a same bending trend of raw fabric. This same bending degree firmly indicated that the coating deposited on fabric changed the flexibility of raw fabric a little. Furthermore, the coated fabric was able to fold other shapes, such as a small fan, due to the great flexibility of fabric[Fig. 3(b)].

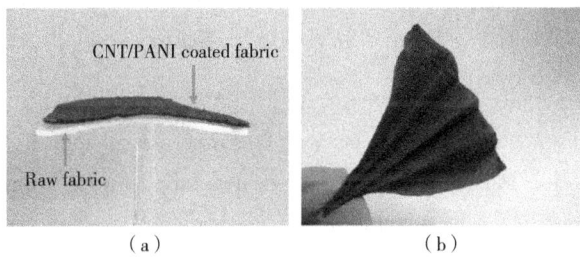

Fig. 3   Photographs of (a) raw fabric and 3-(CNT/PANI) coated fabric on a thin transparent tube and(b) 3-(CNT/PA-NI) coated fabric fold up into a small fan

3.4   The Deposition Mass and Thickness of n-(CNT/PANI) Coating

The deposition mass of CNT/PANI coating and the different thickness of fabric before and after coating were exhibited in Fig.4. As shown in Fig.4(a), the deposition mass was obtained by the mass difference of fabric before and after coating. As presented in the histogram, the deposition mass was increased with the increase of deposition cycle. Larger deposition mass of coating made conductive nanomaterials connect better. After three times of deposition, the CNT/PANI coated fabric reached a deposition mass of 0.24g. Moreover, the thickness of the fabric was also increased after the deposition of coating[Fig. 4(b)]. The thickness was increased by 0.27mm after three times deposition.

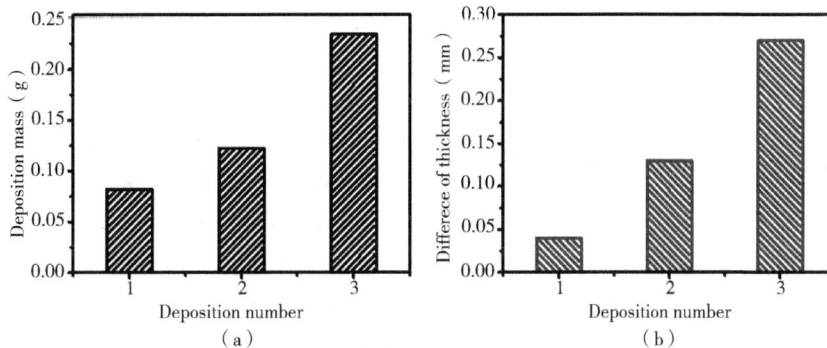

Fig4.   (a) Deposition mass of n-(CNT/PANI) coating on fabric as a function of deposition number;(b) Thickness's difference of fabric before and after deposition of n-(CNT/PAH) coating as a function of deposition number

3.5 The Sheet Resistance of Pure CNT Coated Fabric and n-(CNT/PANI) Coated Fabric

The conductive performance of material is a significant factor for EMI shielding. A low sheet resistance value indicates an excellent conductive performance. As shown in Fig 5(a), although the sheet resistance of pure CNT coated fabrics decreased with the increase of deposition number, the coated fabric still had a sheet resistance of 2.4kΩ/sq after three times of deposition. This large sheet resistance of CNT coated fabric is the result of the bad connection of CNT networks. In contrast, CNT/PANI coated fabrics showed relative low sheet resistance because of the introduction of PANI [Fig.5(b)]. Specifically, the sheet resistance of 3-(CNT/PANI) coated fabric was as low as 48.4Ω/sq which is lower than many conductive coated fabrics. The big different sheet resistance between pure CNT coated fabric and CNT/PANI coated fabric indicates the significance of the introduction of PANI.

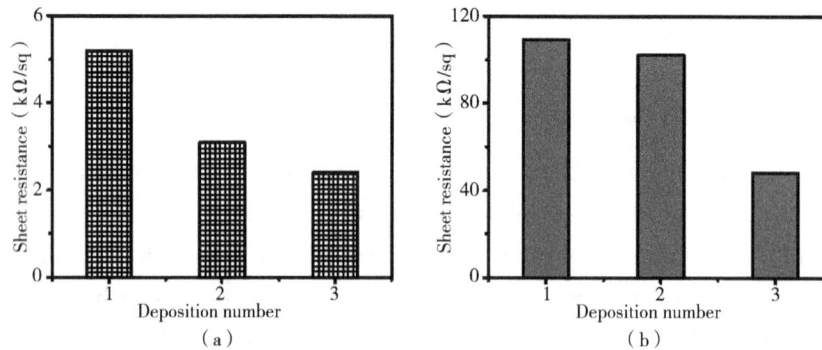

Fig.5 (a) Sheet resistance of CNT coated fabric as a function of deposition number; (b) Sheet resistance of n-(CNT/PANI) coated fabric as a function of deposition number.

3.6 The EMI Shielding Performances of n-(CNT/PANI) Coated Materials

The EMI SE refers to the reduction of electromagnetic interference and defined as the logarithmic ratio of incident to transmitted power. Mathematically, SE is expressed in decibels (dB) as following: $SE = -10\log\left(\dfrac{P_t}{P_i}\right)$, from which we can see that a higher SE value represents a better shielding performance. The EMI SE of n-(CNT/PANI) coated fabric was investigated in the frequency range of 3.9−6.0GHz (C band). As shown in Fig. 6(a), the EMI SE of n-(CNT/PANI) coated fabric was enhanced by the increasing deposition cycle of assembly. were 5.6, 8.2 and 13.4dB for the fabrics with $n = 1$, 2 and 3, respectively. The enhanced EMI shielding performance of n-(CNT/PANI) with the increase of deposition number is because of the more compact and thicker coating on fabric. The reflection loss (SE_R) and absorption loss (SE_A) are two part of the total SE value. They can be given as $SE_R(dB) = -10\log(1-R)$ and $SE_A(dB) = -10\log\left(\dfrac{T}{1-R}\right)$, respectively. The values of SE_A went up sharply and SE_R showed a slight increase with the increase of deposition cycle. Moreover, SE_A of all coated fabrics were higher than SE_R which suggests an absorption-dominant EMI shielding for coated fabrics.

The EMI SE characterization set-up used directly measures the transmitted power (T) and reflected power (R). The absorbed power (A) can be calculated given that constant incident power ($I = 1$mW) was used; i. e. $A = 1 - R - T$. Fig.6(b) shows the A, R, T value of n-(CNT/PANI) coated fabric as a function of deposition number. The reported power values are the average values in the C-band frequency range. It can be seen that the absorption powers of all coated fabrics were around 0.6mW, much higher than reflection power. The high absorption power indicates the incident power of electromagnetic energy was mainly absorbed by the coated fabric. The lower reflection power decreased the secondary damage caused by the coated fabric which is important for EMI shielding material.

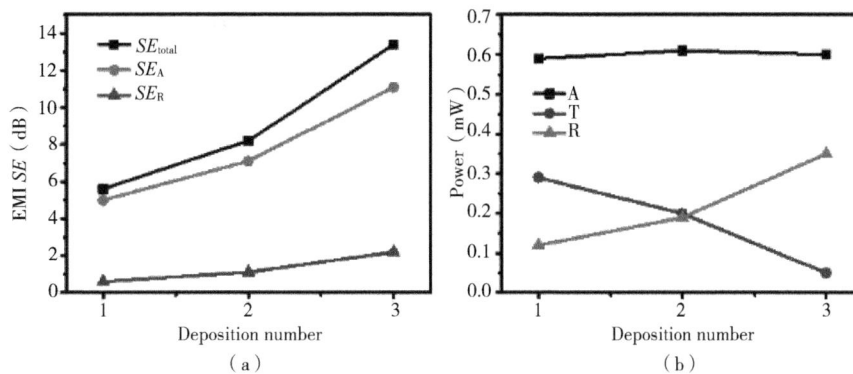

Fig6 (a) EMI shielding effectiveness of the n-(CNT/PANI) coated fabric, where $n = 1$, 2 and 3; (b) Power balance in the C-band frequency range for n-(CNT/PANI) coated fabric as a function of deposition number

4 Conclusions

In summary, textile-substrate EMI shielding material was obtained by the stepwise deposition of conductive CNTs and PANI. The coated fabric still retained the flexibility of raw material. After the introduction of PANI, the gaps between CNTs were filled. The sheet resistance sharply declined from 2.4kΩ/sq of pure CNT coated fabric to 48.4Ω/sq of CNT/PANI coated fabric. As a result, the coated fabric exhibited a good EMI SE of 13.41dB. This work presents a simple and convenient approach to obtain high performance EMI shielding fabrics.

References

[1] AMELI A, NOFAR M, WANG S, et al. Lightweight polypropylene/stainless-steel fiber composite foams with low percolation for efficient electromagnetic interference shielding [J]. ACS Applied Material Interfaces, 2014, 6 (14): 11091-11100.

[2] CAO M S, WANG X X, CAO W Q, et al, Ultrathin graphene: electrical properties and highly efficient electromagnetic interference shielding[J]. Journal of Materials Chemistry C, 2015, 3(26): 6589-6599.

[3] ZOU L H, ZHANG S L, LI X P, et al, Step-by-step strategy for constructing multilayer structured coatings toward high-efficiency electromagnetic interference shielding [J]. Advanced Materials Interfaces, 2016, 3(5): 1500476.

[4] ZHANG L Q, YANG S G, LI L, et al. , Ultralight cellulose porous composites with manipulated porous structure and carbon nanotube distribution for promising electromagnetic interference Shielding [J]. ACS Applied Material Interfaces,

2018, 10(46): 40156-40167.

[5] WANG Q W, ZHANG H B, LIU J, et al. Multifunctional and water-resistant mXene-decorated polyester textiles with outstanding electromagnetic interference shielding and joule heating performances [J]. Advanced Functional Materials, 2019, 29(7): 1806819.

[6] WANG Q L, XIAO S L, SHI S Q, et al. Self-bonded natural fiber product with high hydrophobic and EMI shielding performance via magnetron sputtering Cu film[J]. Applied Surface Science, 2019, 475: 947-952.

[7] ÇEKEN F, KAYACAN O, OZKURT A, et al. The electromagnetic shielding properties of some conductive knitted fabrics produced on single or double needle bed of a flat knitting machine[J]. Journal of the Textile Institute, 2012, 103(9): 968-979.

[8] CHEN Z, YI D, SHEN B, et al. Semi-transparent biomass derived macro-carbon grids for efficient and tunable electromagnetic shielding [J]. Carbon, 2018, 139: 271-278.

[9] ZHAO H. HOU L, BI S Y, et al. Enhanced X-band electromagnetic-interference shielding performance of layer-structured fabric-supported polyaniline/cobalt-nickel coatings[J]. ACS Appl Mater Interfaces, 2017, 9 (38): 33059-33070.

[10] JIA Y, LI K Z, XUE L Z, et al. , Mechanical and electromagnetic shielding performance of carbon fiber reinforced multilayered (PyC-SiC) n matrix composites[J]. Carbon, 2017, 111: 299-308.

[11] ZENG Z, JIN H, CHEN, M J, et al, Lightweight and anisotropic porous MWCNT/WPU composites for ultrahigh performance electromagnetic interference shielding [J]. Advanced Functional Materials, 2016, 26 (2): 303-310.

[12]LI P, JIN Z Y, PENG L L, et al. Stretchable all-gel-state fiber-shaped supercapacitors enabled by macromolecularly interconnected 3D graphene/nanostructured conductive polymer hydrogels [J]. Advanced Materials, 2018, 30 (18): 1800124.

Development of Ancient Spinning Tools and Its Technological Exchange Between China and West Through Maritime Silk Road

CHEN Sisi[1], QIU Yiping[1, 2]*

[1] *College of Textiles, Donghua University, Shanghai, 201620, China*

[2] *College of Textiles and Apparel, Quanzhou Normal University, Quanzhou, 362000, China*

* *Corresponding author's email*: ypqiu@ dhu. edu. cn

Abstract: China has started the Road and the Belt Initiative since 2013 in order to help the social and economic development of the countries along the ancient Silk Road and Maritime Silk Road. Studying the cultural and technical exchange between ancient China and the West is important for understanding the history of the people and the textile industry development on both sides. As one of the most important tools in textile industry, the yarn spinning tools in ancient China included the drop spindle, hand-operated spinning wheel and the pedal spinning wheel, while Europe did not use the spinning wheels till they were brought from China in about 13th century through the Maritime Silk Road. This study focuses on the development of spinning tools in ancient China and the corresponding technical exchange between China and the West most likely through Maritime Silk Road. It analyzes the impacts of the spinning wheels from China on the development of textile industry in the West.

Keywords: Spinning; Textile technology; Technology exchange; Maritime Silk Road

1　Introduction

In the 18th century, the inventions and applications of machine spinning, Jenny and steam engine, triggered the first Industrial Revolution, making Europe quickly become the center of the world textile industry. As a result, the European textile industry greatly surpassed the Chinese textile industry both in quality and quantity. However, before the first Industrial Revolution, China's ancient textile and dyeing technology were always at the leading level in the world. The development of textile technology in the world could be divided into three stages. The first stage was the primitive textile stage in which fiber processing mainly relied on simple tools and manual operations. The second stage was the comprehensive invention and improvement of manual textile machinery, which started in China in about 500 BC and gradually transferred to the rest of the world in the next 10 centuries. The third stage was the industrial production, which was formed after the invention of perfect textile institutions and the formation of modern factory system. It took place in Europe in the 18th century and spread to the rest of the world in a century[1]. This article puts emphasis on the second stage when the spinning wheels were introduced from Ancient China to the West.

2　The Development of Spinning Tools in Ancient China

Spinning is the process of twisting fibers together into a continuous thread. In the world textile history, the spindle (Fig. 1) was the earliest spinning tool, which could be traced back to the Neolithic age. Its structure was extremely simple, consisting of a whorl and a shaft. However, spinning drop with low working efficiency was completely controlled by the strength of human hands, and the speed of rotation could vary from person to person or from time to time, which affected the evenness of the yarn. With the requirement of fabric quality and the shortage of yarn that spun by the spinning drop, Chinese craftsmen created the spinning wheel. According to the literature and archaeology research, the hand-operated spinning wheel (Fig. 2) appeared earliest, although there was no specific evidence whether it appeared in the Warring States period or before. However, the spinning wheel in silk paintings in ancient tombs unearthed in the Western Han dynasty proved that the hand-operated spinning wheel was fully utilized in the Han dynasty[2].

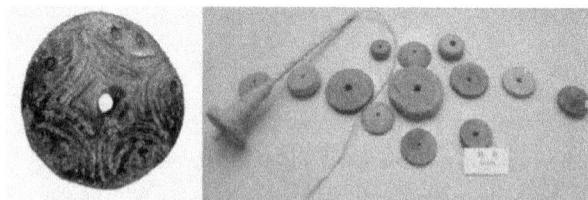

Fig. 1 The spindle consists of a whorl and a shaft, which can be traced back to the Neolithic age

Fig. 2 The hand-operated spinning wheel

Although the spinning wheels were mainly used for twisting, doubling, weft winding and drafting, the function of the ancient spinning machine experienced a long process of improvement. But the spinning wheels had different functions due to their different structures. When the spindle was at a low position in the spinning wheel, its main function was to draft and pull short fibers such as silk flocculent or cotton to form uniform yarn. This kind of hand spinning wheel was still used for spinning cotton after the Yuan Dynasty, while the pedal looms were used for spinning silk flocculent at that time. When the spindle was parallel to the spinning shaft, a single strand of yarn was doubled or twisted into a double or multiple strand of yarn. And when the

spindle of the hand flat knitting machine was installed above the spinning shaft, two people worked together. One of them rolled the hand shank which had the spindle rotated, while the other in front of the spindle slowly pulled back the yarn. If the person who pulled the yarn was far from the spindle, the drafted and twisted yarn was longer, the yarn was of better twist and high drafting quality, which was especially suitable for the strong twisting yarn with high quality[3].

Compared with the spindle, the manual spinning wheel had much higher production efficiency and could produce yarns of different thickness, strength and twist with high quality according to the feature of the yarns. Furthermore, the structure of the hand spinning machine was simple and easy to operate. However, the requirement of two people working together on one machine, namely one person doing spinning and the other rotating, was waste of labor. Besides it was very difficult to grasp the short fibers like the silk flocculent and the cotton staple. In addition, kinking often occurred and uneven yarns were caused when they spun. This led to the advent of the pedal lift heald loom (Fig. 3), which changed the operation of the two hands from the previous manual operation to the spinning operation. Later, people added pedals to the spinning machine, the pedal loom, which was widely used in the Western Han Dynasty. The earliest image of the pedal spinning wheel could date from the Eastern Han dynasty in stone statue of Cao Zhuang unearthed in Jiangsu province.

Fig. 3 The pedal lift heald loom

3 Spinning Tools Development in Early Europe

For Europe, the spinning wheels were introduced to Europe in the late Middle Ages. Before that time, the spindles were the main spinning tools which used to spin all the threads for fabrics and clothing from Egyptian mummy wrappings to tapestries, and even the ropes and sails for ships, which had a long history of 9000 years[4]. As one part of the spindle, the whorls were made of clay and stone, like sandstone or limestone, but later the materials from bone, porcelain, glass to precious metals and semi-precious stones carved and decorated the whorls in all kinds of sizes and shapes. But the spindle shaft was thought to be made of wood, which was easy to be disintegrated as time gone. And the shaft was used for spinning, twisting fibers such as flax, hemp, cotton into yarns. In different place and different period, there were different types of the spindles, like supported spindles, bottom whorl drop spindles and top whorl drop spindles.

The supported spindles (Fig. 4) gave the users more control of the weight of the yarn and varied from different styles of spinning and yarn weight[5]. Some spun yarns were wound on the top of the whorl with a long shafts from the ground to the thigh like Navajo[6]. Some had a whorl on the top with a hook on the top and the spun yarns were wrapped around the lower end of the spindle like the high whorl lap spindle in Icelandic Viking times. Soft yarn would be produced due to less strained yarn and the separation between the drafting and spinning[7].

The bottom whorl spindle (Fig. 5) was always used in plying yarn that was above the whorl, such as Turkish drop spindles whose low whorl spindle had two arms that intersect to make a cross. When it turned much more slowly than winding onto a regular spindle it created a center pull ball of yarn. [7]

As for the top whorl drop spindles, there was a disc on the top of the shaft and a hook at the top. It was pretty easy to wrap the yarn on and usually used in finer weight yarns like lace because it was lighter with quick revolution[8].

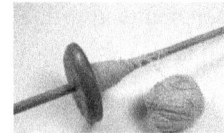

(a)

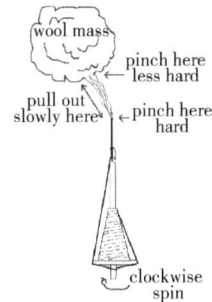

(b)

Fig. 4 The supported spindles

Fig. 5 The bottom whorl spindle

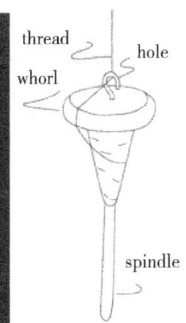

(a)   (b)

Fig. 6 The top whorl drop spindles

4 Chinese Spinning Wheel in Europe

Even though the spindles occupied an important position in European history, there were numerous shortcomings of the spindle. When spinning with a hand spindle, the strength of the twisting was difficult to be controlled by the hand, leading to the irregular speed of the rotation of the spindle. As a result, it influenced the evenness of the spun yarn. Furthermore, rubbing the spindle shaft once only spun a short yarn. This was a slow process and severely limited the subsequent production of fabrics. The invention and implementation of the spinning wheel in the later Middle Ages increased the amount of yarns available for the production of textiles. This had an important social and economic impact on Europe. [9]

With regards to the question how the more advanced spinning tools or machines were transferred to Europe, it keeps unsolved. Actually during the 13th century, Chinese marine technology had great development. The biggest seaport in the world was located in Quanzhou, a coastal city in Fujian Province in east coast of China. It attracted many foreigners including the merchants, sailors and travelers came to China for doing business through the Maritime Silk Road. It might transfers the spinning wheels to the west. According to some literature, the occasional encounter such as that resulting from the journey of Marco Polo in 1271-95 alerted the West to the superiority of Chinese technology and stimulated a vigorous westward transfer of techniques, though the connection between China and the West remained tenuous in ancient times. Western knowledge of silk technology, the magnetic compass, paper making, and porcelain were all derived from China[10]. The spindle wheel could also be introduced at that time. But the spread of the spindle wheel in Europe went through several centuries. Although there were no surviving examples of early medieval spinning wheels that can prove the existence of the spinning wheels in the 13th century, some researchers like Patricia Baines wrote in her book about spinning wheels, spinners and spinning, which reported the existence of spinning wheels in Persia in 1257, and the earliest known artwork depicted the spinning wheel with long bamboo spokes were from China about 1270. All of these demonstrated the spinning wheel were applied prior to that time[11]. The spinning wheel was famous as charkha wheel in China,

with which the spinner operated the hand crank with one hand and spun off the yarn from the end of the spindle with the other hand, thus creating the term "spindle wheel".

5 The Impact of the Spinning Wheel on Europe

After spindle wheels were introduced into Europe in the Middle Ages, it aroused the revolution of the production of yarns, which did improve the productivity and gave rise to the medieval textile industry flourishing. The process of cloth manufacture had been partially mechanized upon the introduction of spinning wheels and fulling mills[12]. Whereas, it provided a refined environment for the beginning of the Renaissance. In the end, the economic and social standing of medieval woman were elevated because of the spinning wheel[13]. Besides, the textiles were so important in Europe that encouraged the formation of textile guilds or industry associations, which regulated the price and quality of this valuable product. The members of the organization could enjoy the crucial political, social, and economic power. Trade fairs that specialized in textiles spurred the big cities to emerge, which moved the centers of Europe from a traditional agricultural economy to a new one based on commerce. The large scale trade of large quantities of valuable goods encouraged the international banks to be established. Great financial success could be achieved by concentrating solely on the movement of textiles. A revitalized shipping industry created a class of middlemen whose wealth was based upon the movement of textiles along the great water routes of Western Europe.

As a new class of professionals emerged within the textile industry and the fortune accumulated, new legal concepts centered on long-term contracts and international trade required the development of new statutes to regulate and protect the individuals taking part in this trade. Meanwhile, the legal scholars came into contact with the writings of Roman lawyers, scholars, philosophers, scientists and their commentaries on the intellectual leaders of Greece and Rome. This was the beginning of early modern Europe's love affair with the classical world, which today was known as the Renaissance. As well as, the spinning wheel did benefit the establishment of the textile industry which could be the first to successfully apply the technology of the Industrial Revolution[13].

6 Conclusions

Despite both China and the West had unique developments of spinning tools in their own initiative because of the few connections between China and the West in ancient times due to the far distance and the lack of the technology, Chinese textile technologies were obviously superior to that in Europe before 13th century. After the 13th century, numerous advanced textile technologies had been transferred to Europe through the Maritime Silk Road, which had a huge impact on European textile development, economy, female status improvement. Furthermore, those paved the way for the Renaissance and made great contribution to the Industrial Revolution.

References

[1]ZHAO H S, XING S Y. History of mass textile technology [M]. Jinan: Shandong Science and Technology Press, 2015.

[2] CHEN W J. Chinese textile scinence and technology (Ancient part)[M]. Bejing: Science Press, 1984.

[3]ZHAO C Z. Chinese science and technology (Textile volume)[M]. Beijing: Science press, 2002.

[4]ELIZABETH, BARBER. Hand spinning, Women's work: The first 20000 years[J]. Women, Cloth and Society in Early Times, Norton and Company, 1994.

[5]AYRE, KATIEL. All in a whorl-a selective annotated bibliography of resources for hand-spindle spinners[M]. 2017.

[6]KROLL, CAROL. The whole craft of spinning from the raw material to the finished yarn[J]. Courier Corporation, 1981.

[7]HOCHBERG, BETTE H. Handspindles[J]. Santa Cruz: Bette and Bernard Hochberg, 1980.

[8]LEMON H. The development of hand spinning wheels[M]. Textile History, 1968: 83-91.

[9]WALTON P. The story of textiles: a bird's eye view of the history of the beginning and the growth of the industry by which mankind is clothed[J]. J S Laurence, 1912.

[10]ROBERT, NEEDHAM J. The genius of China: 3000 years of science, discovery and invention[J]. New York: Simon and Schuster<Based on the works of Joseph Needham>,2007.

[11]ELEANOR R. Spinning yarns: The archaeological evidence for hand spinning and its social implications, c ad 1200-1500[M]. Medieval Archaeology,2016,2(60): 266-299.

[12]ROBERT A B, History of technology[J]. Encyclopedia Britannica, 2018.

[13]WHITE L. Technology assessment from the stance of a medieval historian [J]. The American Historical Review, 1974,1(79): 1-13.

Fabrication and Acoustic Characterization of Natural Cellulose Fabric/Epoxy Composites for Percussion Musical Instruments

GAO Qiang[1], LIU Fanxizi[1], QIU Yiping[1, 2]*

[1] Department of Technical Textiles, College of Textiles, Donghua University, Shanghai, 201620, China

[2] Department of Technical Textiles, College of Textiles, Quanzhou Normal University, Quanzhou, 362000, China

* Corresponding author's email: ypqiu@ dhu. edu. cn

Abstract: In this study, hemp, flax, ramie, and jute fabrics are adopted to reinforce epoxy matrix composites in order to explore the feasibility for replacing wood in musical percussion instruments. The fabrics are treated with alkaline solutions to improve interfacial adhesion between the fibers and epoxy. The composites are fabricated using hand-lay and vacuum assisted resin infusion process. The mechanical properties and acoustic dynamic modulus, acoustic radiation damping coefficient, acoustic impedance of the composite are tested and compared with the wood regularly used to make the musical percussion instruments. It is found that the mechanical and acoustic properties of the composites are within the range of those of the wood. It implies that it could be feasible to replace the wood with the natural cellulose fiber reinforced composites in percussion musical instrument production.

Keywords: Natural cellulose fiber; Composite; National percussion instrument; Acoustic properties; Alkali treatment

1 Introduction

Wood is the material of choice for musical instrument production due to its unique mechanical and acoustic properties. However, the requirements for wood selection of musical instruments are very strict, not only require the integrity of the wood, but also the specific requirements of the microstructure. Therefore, only a few woods and some parts of them are suitable for making musical instruments. And wood is affected by temperature and humidity, it is easy to deform and mold, and the resources that can be used as wood for specific instruments are becoming scarce[1-2]. Therefore, it is imperative to find substitutes for wood.

Natural fibers have relatively low specific density and high specific strength and modulus which are comparable to those of glass fibers. In addition, natural cellulose fibers are abundant in source, inexpensive, renewable, and biodegradable. Therefore, the range of raw materials for musical instruments has gradually shifted from wood to natural fibers. In order to replace the traditional material mahogany used in guitars, Qiu et al[3] prepared laminated flax/hemp fiber reinforced polylactic acid composites with different fiber volume fractions and different fiber surface treatment methods were prepared. The flexural modulus, density, damping characteristics and sound transmission speed show that the alkali-treated high fiber volume fraction of plant fiber reinforced polylactic acid composite has excellent mechanical properties, and its sound propagation speed is similar to that of mahogany. It indicates that the flax/hemp enhanced polylactic acid green composite was a reasonable alternative to mahogany for guitars. Duraisamy[4] et al used composites of flax and bamboo fiber and epoxy resin to simulate alternative guitar fingerboards, exploring the effects of modulus, thickness and density, and temperature and humidity on the natural frequency and damping of the composite. The results show that the flexural modulus, thickness and density played an important role on the acoustic performance of the composite material, while humidity has a greater influence on the natural frequency of the material than temperature. Hemp fiber reinforced composites are more suitable as an alternative to guitar fingerboards than bamboo fibers. Phillips[5] et al. developed a flax fiber composite sandwich structure for stringed instruments with the same mechanical properties as wood. Certain manmade fiber reinforced composites have also been adopted as potential alternative materials for musical instruments. Ono[6-7] et al. used carbon fiber, glass fiber, and polyurethane foam to prepare sandwich composites with similar acoustic performance to the US West Plus Spruce. However, the production of folk percussion instruments with plant fibers reinforced composites could be more attractive due to the above mentioned advantages and thus is worth for further studies. In this paper, four kinds of hemp plain weave fabrics of hemp, flax, ramie and jute are selected as reinforcing components, and epoxy is used as the matrix to prepare natural fiber fabric/epoxy composites. The mechanical and acoustic properties of the composites were tested and compared with those of the wood used in the percussion instrument, in order to explore the feasibility of using the composite as a substitute for wood for percussion musical instruments.

2 Experiments

2.1 Material Preparation

Hemp, flax, ramie and jute fabrics were selected as the reinforcement and a high temperature and low viscosity epoxy resin, ML5417 was supplied by Wells Advanced Materials (Shanghai) Co., Ltd. The cellulose fibers have hydrophilic and relatively weak surfaces which may create a weak interface with matrices, resulting in low mechanical properties of the composite. In response to this, surface alkali treatments[8] was applied to the fabrics before impregnation into the resin. The fabrics were cut into 46cm × 36cm pieces which were subsequently infiltrated in a solution of 5% NaOH for 45min, and then dried at 80℃. Four pieces of the fabrics were

stacked on a glass plate and impregnated using vacuum assisted resin infusion molding (VARIM) as shown in Fig. 1.

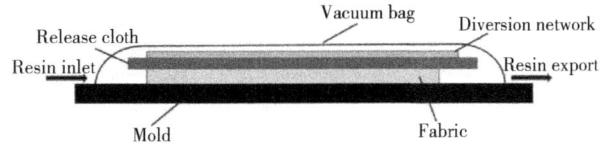

Fig. 1　Schematic diagram of VARIM molding process

2.2 Acoustic Test

In the transverse vibration, the direction in which the vibration element is displaced and the induced stress direction are perpendicular to each other. The resonant frequency of the transverse vibration is mainly affected by the size of the specimen and the method of controlling the motion. The distance between the support point on the specimen and the edge of the specimen is $0.224L$ (L is the length of the specimen), which coincides with the node of the fundamental frequency vibration, and the fundamental resonant frequency f_r is expressed as:

$$f_r = \frac{w_n}{2\pi} = \frac{k_n^2}{2\pi}\sqrt{\frac{EI}{\rho A}} \qquad (1)$$

where w_n is the angular frequency, k_n is determined by vibration characteristic equation, E is the specimen dynamic elastic modulus in GPa, I is the bending moment of inertia, A is the specimen cross-section area (mm^2), ρ is the density (kg/m^3), n is determined by vibration characteristic equation.

The resonant frequency f_n of the wood specimen under transverse free vibration was tested. The dynamic elastic modulus and three important parameters for characterizing the vibration performance of the material were calculated by the relationship between the frequency and the dynamic elastic modulus as follows:

$$E = \frac{48n^2f_n^2L^4}{h^4\beta_n^2} \qquad (2)$$

The specific dynamic elastic modulus E/ρ, sound radiation damping coefficient R, and acoustic impedance coefficient Z were calculated as follows:

$$\frac{E}{\rho} = \frac{48n^2f_n^2L^4}{h^4\beta_n^2} \qquad (3)$$

$$R = \sqrt{E/\rho^3} \qquad (4)$$

$$Z = \rho v = \sqrt{\rho E} \qquad (5)$$

where L is specimen length (m), h is specimen thickness (cm), β_n is constant related to the boundary conditions of the specimen. The fundamental frequency β_1 should be 4.73, and the β values of 2, 3 times up to n times of harmonics are represented by $\beta_2, \cdots, \beta_n$ respectively: $\beta_2 = 7.853$, $\beta_3 = 10.996$, when $n > 3$, $\beta_n = (n+1/2)\pi$.

2.2 Acoustic Test

In this study, the acoustic vibration characteristics of the composites were tested using a lateral free vibration test method with double-end free boundary conditions[9]. A diagram of the test setup is illustrated in Fig. 2. The geometric size of the composite specimens was 160mm×15mm×(2-3)mm. A nylon thread was used to suspend the sample parallel to the wooden stick fixed by the metal frame, and the contact point of the nylon thread and the sample was located at the node to ensure the distance between the two nodes was 88mm. A steel ball of about 0.11g in mass and the distance between the ball and the specimen was 150mm.

During the experiment, one end of thespecimen was struck at 18mm from the node with the steel ball, and a sound signal was collected by a microphone located at the other end of the specimen. The microphone converted the sound signal into an electric signal, which was transmitted to a signal amplifier and a low-pass filter system.

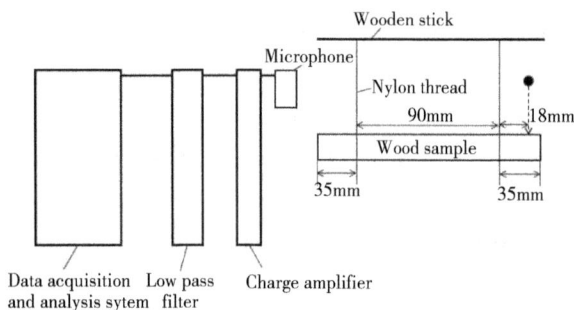

Fig. 2 Schematic diagram of lateral free vibration test

The sampling frequency was 10kHz/s, and the acquired data was processed by the Fast Fourier Transform (FFT) method to obtain a spectrum of the sound, and the natural vibration frequency of the specimen was determined according to the recorded spectrum (frequency response function).

3 Results and Discussions

3.1 Effect of Alkali Treatment on Acoustic Properties of Composites

From Tab. 1, it can be seen that after alkali treatment, the specific dynamic moduli (E/ρ) of the hemp/epoxy and flax/epoxy composites decreased somewhat in both warp and weft directions because elastic moduli of the composite decreased after alkali treatment due to increased yarn crimp in both warp and weft directions[10-11]. The specific dynamic moduli of ramie/epoxy and jute/epoxy composites significantly increased because alkali treatment increases their tensile moduli of ramie composites and jute composites. It should be pointed out that the two types of fabrics also developed increased crimp after the alkali treatment. However, the alkali treatment seemed to be able to increase the interfacial bonding between the ramie and jute fabric and epoxy and therefore could compensate the negative effect of increased crimp by alkali treatment. For the hemp and flax fabrics, the alkali treatment did not show significant effect on interfacial bonding improvement.

The alkali treatment lowered acoustic radiation damping coefficient of hemp/epoxy composite and flax/epoxy composites decreased, but promoted the those of ramie/epoxy resin and jute/epoxy composites, indicating that alkali treatment could improve the acoustic vibration efficiency of the ramie and jute composites.

The acoustic impedance of the hemp and flax composites did not change significantly, although alkali seemed the lower the value a little, due to a decrease in the specific dynamic modulus. Similarly, acoustic impedance of ramie and jute composites did not change significantly but tended to increase somewhat, due to an increase in the specific dynamic modulus.

Tab. 1 Average value of acoustic vibration performance parameters

Sample			Dynamic elastic modulus (GPa)	Specific dynamic elastic modulus (GPa · cm³/g)	Acoustic radiation damping coefficient [m³/Pa · s³]	Acoustic impedance (Pa · s/m)
Hemp	Warp	Control	5.20	4.15	1.63	2.55
		Alkali treated	4.78	3.82	1.56	2.45
	weft	Control	10.41	8.32	2.31	3.61
		Alkali treated	8.77	7.02	2.12	3.31
Flax	Warp	Control	5.00	4.17	1.71	2.45
		Alkali treated	4.28	3.58	1.58	2.26
	weft	Control	8.89	7.43	2.28	3.26
		Alkali treated	7.39	6.17	2.08	2.97
Jute	Warp	Control	5.07	4.13	1.66	2.49
		Alkali treated	5.69	4.64	1.76	2.64
	weft	Control	6.09	4.96	1.82	2.73
		Alkali treated	6.94	5.65	1.94	2.92
Ramie	Warp	Control	3.34	3.00	1.55	1.93
		Alkali treated	4.45	3.76	1.64	2.30
	weft	Control	4.44	3.98	1.79	2.23
		Alkali treated	5.42	4.58	1.81	2.53
Wood	Vertical		8.54	12.75	5.33	2.39
	Horizontal		1.36	2.03	2.13	0.96

3.3 Comparison of Acoustic Properties of Hemp Fabric/Epoxy Resin Composites with Those of Wood

It can be seen from Fig. 3 that the frequencies of the composites and those of the eucalyptus were both within the range of 0-5 kHz. Among them, the first to fourth order natural frequencies of the eucalyptus were the highest, indicating that the sound of the striated stroke was crisp and loud, and the eucalyptus specimen was tested along parallel to the grain direction. When the wood specimen was cut along perpendicular to the grain direction and tested, the natural frequencies of the first to fourth orders had small peaks, although the frequencies had similar values, which makes the sound of the horizontal stroke of the perpendicularly cut eucalyptus specimen appeared to be relatively low. This indicated that the acoustic characteristics of the eucalyptus wood were highly anisotropic.

Comparing the natural frequencies of the composite materials with those of eucalyptus, it was found that all four natural frequencies of the composite material were between the first to the fourth order of natural frequencies of the eucalyptus, and the shapes of the spectral curve were similar, indicating that the composites can be tailored to have the same natural frequencies as the eucalyptus by change fiber orientation and volume fractions in preferred directions in the composites. The sound could be evenly amplified and radiated into the air, and the tone of the composite material prepared in this experiment could be in between those of the samples cut along parallel and perpendicular to the grain of the wood. In other words, all the natural cellulose fabric reinforced composites should have the potential to be used to replace eucalyptus wood in manufacturing percussion musical instrument.

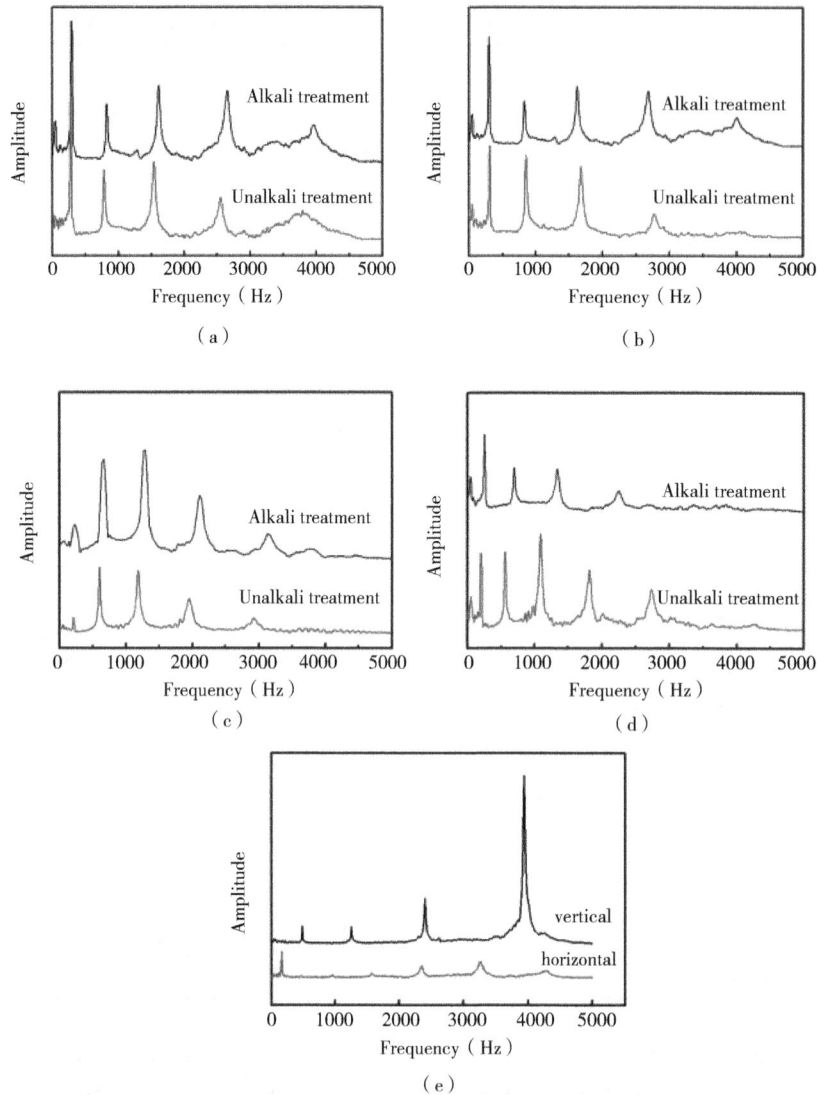

Fig. 3　Composite material and eucalyptus frequency response function map: (a) Hemp fabric/epoxy composite; (b) Linen fabric/epoxy composite; (c) Ramie fabric/epoxy composite; (d) Jute fabric/epoxy composite; (e) Beech

4　Conclusions

In this paper, four different hemp fiber reinforced epoxy resin composites were prepared by vacuum assisted resin infusion molding (VARIM) for four different natural cellulose fabrics before and after alkali treatment. The acoustic properties of the composites were systematically studied and analyzed. Alkali treatment could lower the specific dynamic moduli, acoustic radiation damping coefficient, and acoustic impedance of the hemp and flax/epoxy composites while the opposite was true for the ramie and jute/epoxy composites. The alkali treatment could increase the crimp of the yarns in the fabrics which could have a negative effect on these properties while the improved interfacial bonding by alkali treatment could have a positive impact. The net outcome of the treatment varied depending on which factor was more dominant. The natural frequencies of the composites were well in the range of those for the eucalyptus wood, indicating that it could be possible to use the composites to replace wood in making percussion musical instruments, since composite properties could be adjusted by altering the orientation and volume fractions of fibers in desirable directions.

References

[1]ZHOU H. The applications of carbon fiber in Musical Instruments[J]. Textile Report,2015,(11):62-66.

[2] DAMODARAN A,LESSARD L,BABU A S. An overview of fibre-reinforced composites for musical instrument soundboards[J]. Acoustics Australia,2015,43(1):117-122.

[3]QIU X. Development of green composites to be used in acoustic musical instrument industry[D]. Shanghai:Donghua University,2014.

[4] DURAISAMY A. Understanding the acoustic behaviour of natural fiber composites and the effects of temperature and humidity[D]. Montreal:McGill University,2017.

[5] PHILLIPS S,LESSARD L. Application of natural fiber composites to musical instrument top plates[J]. J. Composite Mater. ,2011,46(2):145-154.

[6] ONO T,ISOMURA D. Acoustic characteristics of carbon fiber-reinforced synthetic wood for musical instrument soundboards[J]. Acoustical Sci. Technology,2004,25(6):475-477.

[7] ONO T,OKUDA A. Acoustic characteristics of guitars with a top board of carbon fiber-reinforced composites[J]. Acoustical Sc. Technol. ,2007,28(6):442-443.

[8]RAY D. The mechanical properties of vinylester resin matrix composites reinforced with alkali-treated jute fibres[J]. Composites Part A Appl. Sci. Manufact. ,2001,32:119-127.

[9] MA L. Study on Relationships between wood structures and acoustic vibration properties[D]. Hefei:Anhui Agricultural University,2005.

[10]HE L. Effect of fiber content on mechanical properties and vibration damping characteristics of bast fiber reinforced composites[J]. J. Hunan Univ. ,2018,45(12):66-72.

[11] MIN R. YANG G. Effect of surface modification on the properties of flax fiber reinforced pla stereocomplex composites[J]. China Plastics Industry,2014,42(09):71-75.

Analysis of Innovation Capabilities Within the World Textile University Alliance (WTUA) Under the Belt and Road Initiative

VASILIJE Petrovic[1]*, NIKOLA Zivlak[2], MARIJA Pesic[1], DANKA Joksimovic[1], ANITA Milosavljevic[1]

[1] *University of Novi Sad-Technical faculty, Mihajlo Pupin, Zrenjanin, 23000, Serbia*
[2] *Emlyon business school Asia, Shanghai, 200241, China*

* *Corresponding author's email*: vlp@ eunet. rs

Abstract: This paper considers some of the possibilities for networking of scientific, technological and creative knowledge of member Universities of World Textile University Alliance (WTUA) within Belt and Road Initiative. In order to increase the visibility of the WTUA, it is proposed to create an infrastructure that will enable long-term support for the integration of design of the fashion products within the geographical area of all members of the WTUA. Besides of these activities, paper also considers the cooperation of WTUA members with the economy in precisely defined areas, for example, development of working clothes, technical textiles, etc. Also, the activities of WTUA members´ cooperation in the unused potentials for the development of the textile sector in certain regions of the world are also considered.

Keywords: Belt and Road Initiative; World Textile University Alliance; Fashion design; Work clothes; Hemp

1 Introduction

World Textile University Alliance(WTUA) was founded in 2018 at Donghua University in Shanghai, within the Belt and Road Initiative. WTUA was founded by 32 internationally recognized universites in the field of textile and fashion engineering, design, technology and innovation.

There's a wide range of possibilities of cooperation within the WTUA. We can talk about at least three regions with different potentials. Those are the experiences of East Asian economy, East African countries and Central European countries. Cooperation can be based for example between Donghua University from China, MOI University from Kenya and the University of Novi Sad from Serbia. This cooperation in the textile and clothing sector has the potential to significantly contribute to the development of the economies of all three countries.

Cooperation can be based on the experiences from China, as the world's strongest developing economy and securing jobs for the fast-growing young population in Kenya.

2 Potentials of the Serbian Textile Industry for Cooperation

The textile and clothing industry represents significant production branches in Serbia, import dependent, export oriented, with tradition in the European and world market.

The textile industry plays an important role in the economy of the Republic of Serbia by number of enterprises, number of employees, and 10% participation in foreign trade. It is recognizable on foreign markets, first of all, on the market of the countries of the European Community.

For potential business partners, investors, the Serbian textile industry can offer as follows[1-2]:

❖ Production of finished clothing products in the full export;

❖ Good conditions for investors in the finishing operations;

❖ Joint investment in existing production capacities;

❖ Textile and footwear factories can work effectively in joint high-quality jobs for European traders. There is the ability to quickly react and create small orders with fast processing time;

❖ Great opportunities can be found in making clothes, i. e. in making ready-made clothes.

❖ The trained workforce for the textile industry is distinguished as a great advantage for foreign investors, as well as duty-free exports to Russia, Belarus, Kazakhstan, Turkey, CEFTA, EFTA, EU.

Undoubted advantage that Serbia has is reflected in the many years of experience. Serbia is a country of long history and tradition in the production of textile and clothing. Textile industry was the leading export branch in the past, and today this industry produces mostly for well-known world brands, with whose companies it has successful cooperation that has been going on for years[3].

Key chances for the development of the Region are as following[4]:

❖ Good geo-strategic position of Serbia——road, rail and air traffic network and proximity to the border with the European Union enables the development of the region and the placement of products and services on the markets of neighboring countries;

❖ International free trade agreements signed by the Republic of Serbia enable easier business conditions in the foreign market, while state and donor programs and projects provide greater chances for the improvement of entrepreneurs operating in this industry;

❖ Revitalization of production in large textile companies that are bankrupt or in the process of privatization by finding adequate investors who are able to comply with the agreed terms, for a long time;

❖ Branding the products from the Region.

3 Potentials of the Serbian Textile Industry for Cooperation with China

Serbia is one of the countries included in the BRI and China + CEEC platform. It has a growing collaboration with China and presents a potential hub for CBEC in the Balkan region. In their 2019 E- Commerce report concerning Serbia, Statista (Statista, 2019), indicates that revenue in the E-commerce market amounts to 354 million USD, with expected annual growth rate (CAGR 2019—2023) of 9. 6% and a market volume of 510 million USD by 2023.

The Fashion segment revenue in 2019 amounts to 68 million USD with expected an annual growth rate (CAGR 2019—2023) of 9. 4%, resulting in a market volume of 98 million USD by 2023. The market's largest segment is apparel with a market volume of 52 million USD. User penetration is expected to hit 50. 7% by 2023. The average revenue per user (ARPU) currently amounts to 87. 18 USD, according to Statista (ibidem).

According to the Development Agency of Serbia, textile industry is quite relevant in Serbia, employing more than 250,000 workers and exporting more than 5 billion USD, with 1,800 active companies.

4 Development of Infrastructure to Increase Visibility of WTUA

We consider that the WTUA at its initial stage of development, must be visible throughout the entire geographical area of the Belt and RoadInitiative. For the initial activities in order to increase visibility of WTUA, the creation of infrastructure that will provide long-term support for the integration of design fashion products within the geographical area of all members WTUA is proposed. This can be achieved by connecting all members of the WTUA i. e. scientific research institutions and using the economy of knowledge. Achieving of this goal requires research into the design of new products in the fashion industry based on the authentic cultural heritage of people living in the entire geographical area of the Belt and Road Initiative. In order to achieve this, we should work on the following activities: establishing a center for research and development of the fashion industry of WTUA, Research and identification of authentic motifs from the national culture and tradition of the people from the WTUA, round tables, Creating a database of authentic symbols and elements of fashion design, an exhibition of collected authentic symbols that can be used in fashion design, public competition for creating models with authentic symbols, education of SMEs and students, exchange of lecturers in the field of design and production technology, realization of a pilot project for the production of new clothes, organizing scientific meetings, organizing fashion shows of new products to as many universities from WTUA[2,6-7].

The developed infrastructure will enable new forms of cooperation of WTUA members with the economy in specific areas, for example, development of working clothes, technical textiles, etc. Similar forms of cooperation can be undertaken in these forms of cooperation.

Also, the developed infrastructure can enable realization of the activities of cooperation of the WTUA members and in the unused potentials for the development of the textile sector in certain world regions. For example, Serbia was a leading producer of hemp. This production was extinguished 50 years ago. However, there is now an open market for a huge number of hemp products. WTUA members can undertake activities, along with investors, to restore hemp production in Serbia.

5　Internationalization of the Serbian Textile Industry

In the framework of the project "One belt, One Road", one and a half billion dollars of Chinese investments have been allocated for Serbia. A large Chinese company has the attempts to invest in the construction of a strategic port on the Danube, not far from the bridge "Mihailo Pupin" which was built by the Chinese company China Road and Bridge Corporation (CRBC).

The attractiveness of the region of Southeast Europe, in which Serbia is located, for investors from China lies in the closeness of the single market of the European Union. Serbia is on the "ancient Silk Road". Reviving the direction of the "Silk Road" that would go from Western China, via Central Asia, Iran, Turkey, via Bosphorus, Piraeus and deeper to the Balkans through Serbia to Central Europe is very important for Serbia.

According to some information, using this direction would shorten the time of transportation of Chinese goods to the countries of Western Europe three times.

One more project announced by Chinese investors is also a large industrial park that they would make. A part of Chinese industrial production, probably from textile sector, would be organized here and the products would be placed on the Central European market.

6　Conclusions

This paper considers some of the possibilities for networking of scientific, technological and creative knowledge of member Universities of World Textile University Alliance (WTUA) within Belt and Road Initiative. In order to increase the visibility of the WTUA, it is proposed to create an infrastructure that will enable long-term support for the integration of design of the fashion products within the geographical area of all members of the WTUA. Besides of these activities, paper also considers the cooperation of WTUA members with the economy in precisely defined areas, for example, development of working clothes, technical textiles, etc. Also, the activities of WTUA members' cooperation in the unused potentials for the development of the textile sector in certain regions of the world are also considered.

For example, hemp production in Serbia can be restored.

For its potential business partners, investors, the Serbian textile industry can offer a variety of cooperation agreements in the mutual works.

References

[1] https://www. pks. rs/accessed on July 1, 2019.

[2] http://www. banat-fashion. rs/accessed on July 3, 20219.

[3] PETROVIC V, GASOVIC M, MODNA kolekcija, et al. Mihajlo Pupin[M]. Zrenjanin, 2016.

[4] PETROVIC V. European textile platform for the future of clothing and textile, regional textile conference[J]. Sustainable Development of the Textile Industry in Republic of Macedonia, 2012, 10:04-05.

[5] https://ras. gov. rs/accessed on July 5, 2019.

[6] STOJANOVIC N, PAVLOVIC M, JOKSIMOVIC D, et al. Teamworking on a fashion collection inspired by the Serbian

culture in Hungary[C]. 9th International Scientific - Professional Symposium Textile Science and Economy, Technical Faculty, Zrenjanin,2018,10: 55-67.

[7]JELENA Djukic, PETROVIC V,JOKSIMOVIC D,et al. National costumes of Uzice Region[C]. 10th International Scientific-Professional Symposium Textile Science and Economy, Technical Faculty Zrenjanin,2019,3:177-185.

Numerical Analysis of the Filter Membrane Fouling Process via the Dynamic Growth of Particles on 3D Virtual Membranes in a CFD-DEM Coupled Process

OBED Akampumuza[1], XU Huilin[1], QUAN Zhenzhen[1, 2], ZHANG Hongnan[1],
QIN Xiaohong[1*], WANG Rongwu[1], YU Jianyong[2]

[1] *Key Laboratory of Textile Science & Technology, Ministry of Education, College of Textiles, Donghua University, Shanghai, 201620, China*

[2] *Innovation Center for Textile Science and Technology, Donghua University, Shanghai, 201620, China*

Corresponding author: xhqin@ dhu. edu. cn

Abstract: In this work, a 3D virtual nanofiber membrane bearing precisely controlled porosity and fiber alignment closely matching what we have in real non-woven membranes was generated via a Matlab code. Computational fluid dynamics (CFD) was then used to solve the governing equations for the flow of fluid coupled with the discrete element model (DEM) to track the flow of particles, their deposition and adhesion properties on the fiber surface. Particle interactions resulted in dendrites and their effect on the membrane efficiency and pressure drop was analyzed. The findings show that, as the particles dynamically piled on the fibers, the membrane's pressure drop and capture efficiency progressively increased.

Keywords: 3D virtual membranes; CFD-DEM; Dynamic growth of particles

1 Introduction

Non-woven fiber membranes are used in various fields to perform different functionalities. In filtration, they help in air and water purification whereas in medical arena, nanofibrous scaffolds act as extra cellular matrices fortissue regeneration.

Simulation of virtual membrane performance helps in the optimization of membrane properties before the actual fabrication effort is undertaken, saving on both the financial resources and time requirements needed to accomplish the actual procedure. Numerous authors have employed computational fluid dynamics to model the filter performance as well as formulate filtration theories[1-2]. On the other hand, in the biomedical field, porous scaffolds enable the proliferation of nutrients and oxygen to cells embedded within their microstructure[3]. Using 3D virtual fibrous scaffolds, Woo et al[4] showed that their pore architecture influenced the effective diffusivity of air within their structure and by using

the diffusion application module of a commercial FEA software, they determined the spatial oxygen concentration gradient in the created medium to propose means by which this diffusivity could be optimized. Furthermore, the ease with which air percolates through filters during usage goes hand in hand with the comfort of use. Discrete element Methods (DEM) simulations are capable of accurately predicting the motion of individual particles in systems even accounting for all the interactions taking place in form of particle-particle and particle filter contact and sticking process. This is done by considering all the forces in play and additionally, solving the corresponding equations numerically. In this work, CFD-DEM coupling process is exclusively applied in air filtration to investigate the membrane fouling process. It should be noted that during air filtration, two distinct stages are encountered whereby in the initial stage, only fibers will be responsible for capturing majority of the particles while in the later stage, the earlier deposited particles will act as deposition surfaces resulting in the formation of particle clusters on the filter over the course of time. This second stage is what is responsible for membrane fouling[5]. One aspect of membrane fouling is that the deposited particles progressively block the pores resulting in a decrease in permeability this too hikes the pressure drop. In this research, three different inter-connected steps were worked on that included the fabrication of the virtual nanofiber membranes, computational fluid dynamics (CFD) based analysis of the fluid flow through them and a study of particle interactions and their loading process onto these membranes.

2 Design of the Physical Model

2.1 Geometry Fabrication, Domain Setup and the Meshing Process

The virtual non-woven membrane was fabricated using Matlab software. Cylinders representing nanofibers were deposited randomly along the *XY* axis while the filter thickness was let to grow along the *Z*-axis to occupy a 3D space forming a membrane of uniform nanofibers (1μm with different lengths) with overall dimensions of 50μm×50μm×8μm and a solid volume fraction (SVF) of 0.1379 ($\varepsilon = 0.8621$). The membrane thickness was built from five layers of nanofibers and the sequence of this growth is given in Fig. 1. This mode of membrane fabrication enabled accurate representation of the volume occupied by each individual fiber element which in turn allowed for the convenient calculation of total fiber volume fraction from the expression.

$$V_m = \frac{\pi d_f^4}{4}(L_{f1} + L_{f2} + L_{f3} + \ldots + L_{fn}) \quad (1)$$

4 layers of fibers

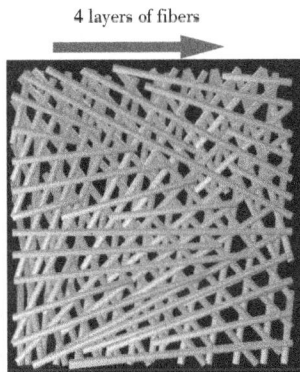

Fig. 1　Membrane formation process

5 layers of fibers

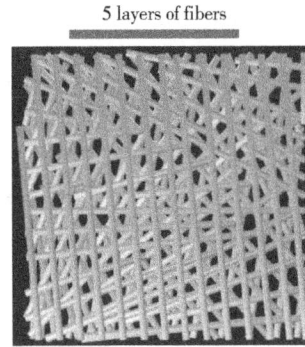

Fig. 1　Membrane formation process

This model was processed in STAR CCM+™, a commercial computational fluid dynamics software. Here, appropriate boundary conditions were applied for the simulation process given by Tab. 1 and Fig. 2(a). Accordingly, the fluid entered into the simulation domain through a velocity-inlet to generate a pressure-outlet boundary. The general computational domain width was 30μm, with a filter domain approximately 8μm in thickness positioned in its middle so that the inlet and outlet boundaries were a distance of 12μm from either sides of the filter domain. Then prior to the simulation process, polyhedral mesh was administered to the domain as a whole, Fig. 2(b). Polyhedral mesh creates conformal mesh interfaces between different domain regions aptly controlling the distribution of grid points.

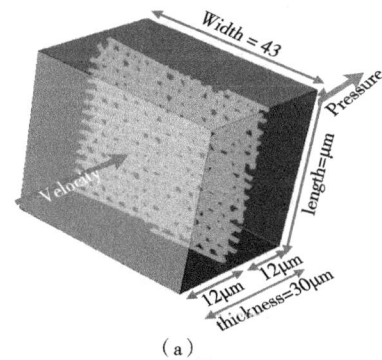

(a)

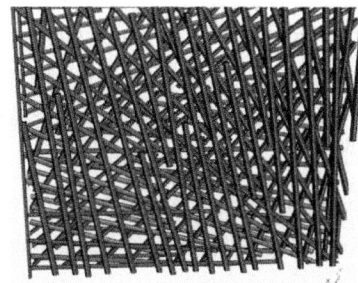

(b)

Fig. 2　The computational domain and the mesh

Tab. 1　Boundary conditions applied to the computational domain

Boundary	Boundary condition
Inlet	Velocity inlet
Outlet	Pressureoutlet
Domain sides	Symmetry sides
Fibers	Solidwalls

2.2　Numerical Models Applied

The flow through a fiber membrane where the Reynolds number is less than unity has been shown to be characteristically laminar in which the inertial effects are negligible and the relationship between theflow velocity and pressure drop linear[6]. Accordingly, a laminar, implicit unsteady flow in the void spaces between the fibers was solved numerically using the star CCM+ CFD code. By solving the Navier-Stokes equations, CFD helps in resolving the velocity field profiles over the fibers.

The governing equations are given by:

$$\nabla \cdot U_o = 0 \tag{2}$$

$$\frac{\partial U_0}{\partial t} + u_0 \cdot \nabla U_0 = \nabla\left(\frac{P}{\rho}\right) + v \nabla \cdot \nabla U_0 \tag{3}$$

Likewise, for the particle flow model, the particle flight path was tracked using the Lagrangian model where thevelocity change of each particle (of mass m_p) during its free motion in the system

was individually tracked by integrating the Newton's second law of motion. This considers the effect of both fluid forces on the particles (external forces- $\vec{f}_{ext}$) and particle-particle forces (contact forces- $\vec{f}_{con}$):

$$m_p \frac{\mathrm{d}^2 x}{\mathrm{d}t^2} = \vec{f}_{con} + \vec{f}_{ext} \tag{4}$$

The dilute nature of the particle flows meant that very few or no particle collisions took place during flight whereby most of the interaction took place at the fiber surface. The ensuing particle-fiber and particle-particleinteractions were modeled using the soft sphere Discrete Element Model formulation under the Hertz-Mindlin model, which resolves the contact forces (f_{con}) into normal and tangential collision forces, Equation (5) & (6).

$$\vec{f}_{ij}^n = \vec{f}_{el}^n + \vec{f}_{diss}^n = (-K_n \delta_{nij}^{3/2} - \eta_n v_{rn} \vec{n}_{ij}) \vec{n}_{ij} \tag{5}$$

$$\vec{f}_{ij}^t = \vec{f}_{el}^t + \vec{f}_{diss}^t = (-K_t \delta_{tij}^{3/2} - \eta_t v_{rn} \vec{n}_{ij}) \tag{6}$$

In the event of a collision, the amount of kinetic energy lost was determined by thecoefficient of restitution (e).

$$Coefficient\ of\ restitution(3) = \frac{Relative\ velocity\ after\ collision}{Relative\ velocity\ before\ collision} \tag{7}$$

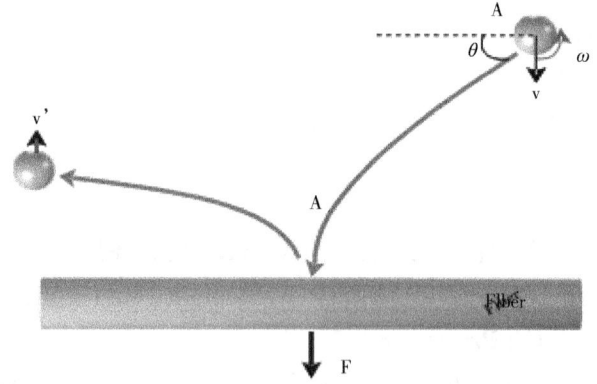

Fig. 3　An illustration of the particle-fiber impact process and the mechanics involved

On the other hand, the ensuing sustained particle contact or cohesion of particles into agglomerates was facilitated by intermolecular forces. The intermolecular attraction (Van der Waals) forces between particle surfaces during this agglomeration stage was given by the Johnson-Kendall-Roberts (JKR) model which enables the inclusion of surface energy during contact.

$$F_{cohesion} = R_{min} W \pi F \tag{8}$$

R_{min} is the minimal radius of surfaces in contact, W is the work of cohesion (J/m^2), and F is a multiplication model blending factor with a value of 2 for the JKR model used in this case.

3　Results and Discussions

3.1　Surface Particle Deposit Morphology Visualization

As the particle laden air was continuously passed through the membrane, particles were removed and observed to dynamically accumulate on the membrane surface giving dendritic particle morphologies (Fig. 4).

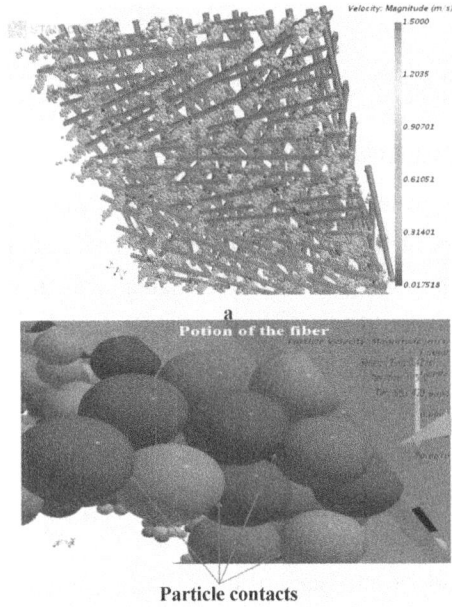

a
Potion of the fiber

Particle contacts

Fig. 4　Contacts between particles spurred by soft sphere physics in JKR approach to facilitate agglomeration

3.2　The Response of the Filter's Pressure Drop and Filtration Efficiency with Dynamic Particle Accumulation

To establish the deposition efficiency of the filter medium, firstly, the average number of particles exiting the computational domain over a number of consecutive time-steps (N) were averaged (averaging was meant to reduce on the errors). Then, a ratio of these particles (N) to the total injected number (N_0) within the same period span was calculated to give the penetration (K).

$$K = \left(\frac{N}{N_0}\right) \qquad (9)$$

From the above, efficiency of the filter (E) could be got using the relationship below:

$$E = 100 - K \qquad (10)$$

To ensure consistency in the results, face velocities of 0.5m/s, 0.75m/s and 1m/s were used. In each of these cases, a correlation can be observed in the trend displayed by the respective plots. The plots of the increment in deposition efficiency and pressure drop with the growth of particle deposits on the filter surface are given in Fig. 5—Fig. 7 below. In all, the clusters of particles on the filter surface spurred an increase in its filtration efficiency. The explanation for this is that, the deposited particles protruded above the fiber surfaces to provide new surface areas for particle deposition greater than that prevailing on the fiber. On the other hand, pressure drop can also be observed to rise steadily. The presence of secondary structures (dendrites) results in an extra drag experienced by air as it comes into contact with the filter. Due to this, as the fiber surface gets increasingly loaded with particles, a gradual rise in pressure drop will be experienced. In Fig. 3, it is evident that increasing the face velocity led to a significant increase in the pressure drop of the medium. An increase in the values of particle deposition efficiency can be observed too. The increase in face velocity can be explained by Darcy's theory in which pressure drop of a filter medium is directly proportional to the inlet velocity.

$$\langle u \rangle = \frac{k}{\mu} \nabla P \qquad (11)$$

On the other hand, the increase in efficiency with the increasing velocity can be attributed to the interception range within which the 0.6μm particles used in thus study fall. Particles within the interception regime possess an appreciable amount of inertia in that an increase of their flow speed will increase their chances of bumping into the obstacles (fibers). To optimize the membrane quality, a balance has to be maintained between the efficiency and pressure drop. This is done by using the Figwre of merit (FOM) or quality factor (QF) (Fig. 8).

$$FOM = \frac{\ln(P)}{\Delta P} \qquad (12)$$

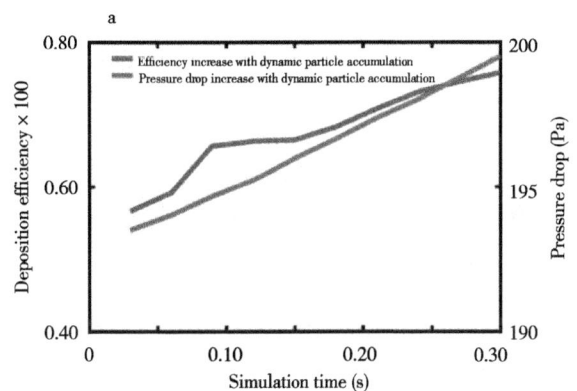

Fig. 5　Efficiency and pressure drop at 0.5m/s

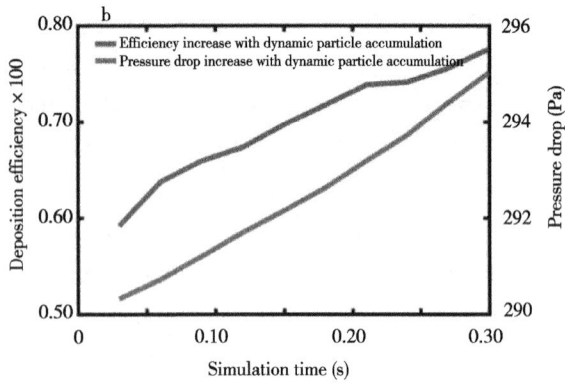

Fig. 6 Efficiency and pressure drop at 0.75m/s

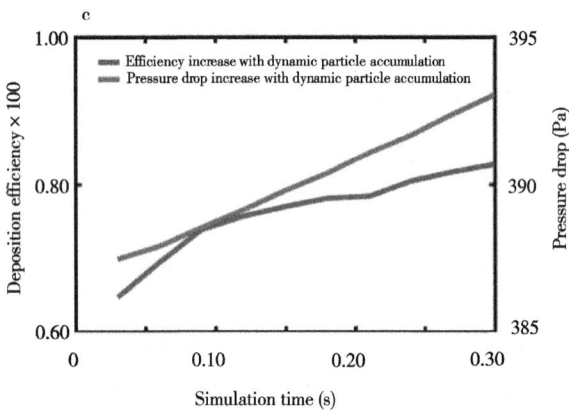

Fig. 7 Efficiency and pressure drop at 1m/s

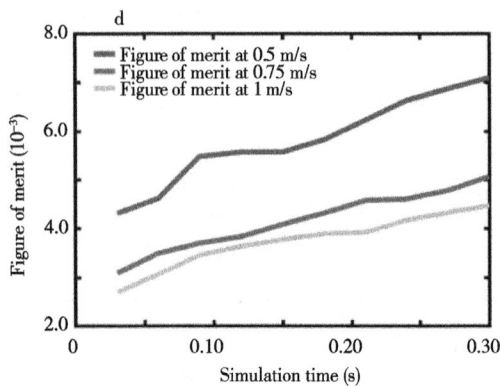

Fig. 8 The respective values for the Figwre of merit (FOM) at 0.5m/s, 0.75m/s and 1m/s

Whereas an increase in both pressure drop and filtration efficiency was achieved with increasing velocity, the Fig. of merit (FOM) shows that as the face velocity was increased, the quality of the filter went down. This is can be attributed to the fact that the rate of rise in the pressure drop far outpaced the increased in filtration efficiency.

4 Conclusions

It can be concluded that force displacement models in the discrete element methods can be successfully used in analyzing the dynamic accumulation of particles on a filter medium during the filtration process. The dynamic growth of particles on the filter progressively increased both the membrane's particle capture efficiency and pressure drop. Whereas increasing the face velocity slightly boosted the filtration efficiency, the results show that this negatively affected the overall filter quality. This could be attributed to the rise in pressure that was not quite commensurate with the increase in the filter efficiency. In the event of an appreciable increase in filtration efficiency, it would have kept the quality factor pretty high.

Acknowledgements

This work was partly supported by the Chang Jiang Youth Scholars Program of China and grants (51773037 and 51973027) from the National Natural Science Foundation of China to Prof. Xiaohong Qin as well as the Innovation Program of Shanghai Municipal Education Commission, Fundamental Research Funds for the Central Universities and DHU Distinguished Young Professor Program to her. This work has also been supported by grant (51803023, 61771123) from the National Natural Science Foundation of China to Dr. ZHANG Hongnan and Prof. WANG Rongwu and the Shanghai Sailing Program (18YF 1400400), the Project funded by China Postdoctoral Science Foundation (2018M640317) and the Fundamental Research Funds for the Central Universities (2232018A3-11) to Dr. QUAN Zhenzhen.

Nomenclature

Symbol	Description
3D	three-dimensional geometry
CFD	Computational Fluid Dynamics
DEM	Discrete Element Methods

FEA	Finite Element Analysis
JKR	Johnson-Kendall-Roberts model
SVF	membrane's Solid Volume Fraction
V_m	membrane volume
ε	membrane porosity
∇P	pressure gradient
δ_n	normal overlap
δ_{tij}	tangential overlap
η_t	tangential damping coefficient
η_n	normal damping coefficient
d_f	fiber diameter
e	coefficient of restitution
F	model blending factor for the JKR model
$F_{cohesion}$	cohesion force
f_{con}	contact forces
$\overrightarrow{f_{diss}^n}$	tangential normal forces
$\overrightarrow{f_{el}^n}$	normal elastic force
$\overrightarrow{f_{el}^t}t$	angential elastic force
f_{extf}	orces exerted by the fluid on the particles
$\overrightarrow{f_{ij}^n}$	normal collision force
$\overrightarrow{f_{ij}^t}$	tangential collision force
k	membrane permeability
K_n	normal spring stiffness
K_t	tangential spring stiffness
L_f	fiber length
m_p	particle mass

$\overrightarrow{n_{ij}}$	is the unit vector pointing from particle i to particle j
R_{min}	minimum radius of the surface in contact
$\overrightarrow{t_{ij}}$	t is the tangential unit vector at the contact point that lies on the
v_{rn}	the relative velocity of the particles in the normal direction
W	work of cohesion

References

[1] HOSSEINI, S A,TAFRESHI H V. 3-D simulation of particle filtration in electrospun nanofibrous filters[J]. Powder Technol,2010, 201(2):153-160.

[2] SAMBAER W M,ZATLOUKAL, KIMMER D. 3D air filtration modeling for nanofiber based filters in the ultrafine particle size range[J]. Chem Eng Sci, 2012, 82: 299-311.

[3] ALEGRET N,DOMINGUEZ-ALFARO A,MECERREYES D. 3D scaffolds based on conductive polymers for biomedical applications[J]. Biomacromolecules, 2019, 20(1):73-89.

[4] WOO JUNG J, et al. Evaluation of the effective diffusivity of a freeform fabricated scaffold using computational simulation [J]. J Biomech Eng-T ASME, 2013, 135(8).

[5] WANG J. Effects of particle size and morphology on filtration of airborne nanoparticles[J]. KONA Powder Part J, 2013, 30:256-266.

[6] WANG Q, et al., Simulating through-plane permeability of fibrous materials with different fiber lengths [J]. Modell Simul Mater Sci Eng,2007, 15(8):855-868.